First International Conference on Self-Adaptive and Self-Organizing Systems

SASO 2007

Proceedings

First International Conference on Self-Adaptive and Self-Organizing Systems

SASO 2007

9-11 July 2007
Cambridge, Massachussets

Edited by

Giovanna Di Marzo Serugendo
Jean-Philippe Martin-Flatin
Márk Jelasity
Franco Zambonelli

CPS Conference Publishing Services

Los Alamitos, California
Washington • Tokyo

IEEE computer society

IEEE Computer Society Order Number P2906
ISBN 0-7695-2906-2
ISBN 978-0-7695-2906-6
Library of Congress 2007926504

Additional copies may be ordered from:

IEEE Computer Society
Customer Service Center
10662 Los Vaqueros Circle
P.O. Box 3014
Los Alamitos, CA 90720-1314
Tel: + 1 800 272 6657
Fax: + 1 714 821 4641
http://computer.org/cspress
csbooks@computer.org

IEEE Service Center
445 Hoes Lane
P.O. Box 1331
Piscataway, NJ 08855-1331
Tel: + 1 732 981 0060
Fax: + 1 732 981 9667
http://shop.ieee.org/store/
customer-service@ieee.org

IEEE Computer Society
Asia/Pacific Office
Watanabe Bldg., 1-4-2
Minami-Aoyama
Minato-ku, Tokyo 107-0062
JAPAN
Tel: + 81 3 3408 3118
Fax: + 81 3 3408 3553
tokyo.ofc@computer.org

Individual paper REPRINTS may be ordered at: <reprints@computer.org>

Editorial production by Silvia Ceballos
Cover art production by Joe Daigle/Studio Productions
Printed in the United States of America by The Printing House

IEEE Computer Society
Conference Publishing Services (CPS)
http://www.computer.org/cps

First International Conference on Self-Adaptive and Self-Organizing Systems

SASO 2007

Keynotes

Research Track, Session 4: P2P Systems

Research Track, Session 5: Data Collection and Aggregation

Research Track, Session 6: Combinatorial Optimization

Research Track, Session 7: Management and Control

Research Track, Session 8: Security

Applications Track

Work-in-Progress Track, Session 1: Software Engineering and Multiagent Systems

Work-in-Progress Track, Session 2: Self-Adaptation

Work-in-Progress Track, Session 3: Self-Organization

Foreword from the General Co-Chairs

We would like to welcome you to Boston and to the inaugural meeting of SASO: The IEEE International Conference on Self-Adaptive and Self-Organizing Systems.

The complexity of current computer systems and their astonishing lack of robustness and manageability has led the software engineering, distributed systems and management communities to look for inspiration in diverse fields to find new ways of designing and managing networks, systems and services. In this endeavor, self-organization and self-adaptation have emerged as two promising facets of a paradigm shift.

Self-adaptive systems work in a top-down manner. They evaluate their own global behavior and change it when the evaluation indicates that they are not accomplishing what they were intended to do, or when better functionality or performance is possible. Self-organizing systems work bottom-up. They are composed of a large number of components that interact according to simple and local rules. The global behavior of the system emerges from these local interactions. Although it is sometimes difficult to deduce properties of the global system by studying only the local properties of its parts, such systems have been shown to frequently exhibit remarkable degrees of robustness.

Despite their surface differences, these two approaches have begun to merge into a common framework. Common principles of self repair, redundancy, and variability are already evident, but perhaps there are many more common principles that we can learn by studying both self-organizing and self-adaptive systems. Is there a common underlying analytical framework that can allow us to make predictions about such systems or that can inform and guide our design methodologies?

The aim of SASO is to form a new intellectual community by providing a forum where we can, as a community, develop the foundations of a new principled approach to engineering systems, networks and services based on self-adaptation and self-organization. Achieving this objective requires the development of theories, frameworks, methodologies, tools, middleware infrastructures, testbeds, best practices, etc. In doing so, SASO seeks to foster cross-pollination between diverse research fields and encourage technology transfers.

SASO was born from the merger of several existing communities and their representative meetings:

- SelfMan (International Workshop on Self-Managed Networks, Systems & Services), from the integrated management community;
- ESOA (International Workshop on Engineering Self-Organising Applications), from the agent community;
- SELF-STAR (International Workshop on Self-* Properties in Complex Information Systems), from the distributed systems and P2P communities;
- IWSAS (International Workshop on Self-Adaptive Software), from the embedded systems and software engineering communities.

Each of these communities had begun to feel that they were looking at part of a larger picture and that there was much to be gained by working in the larger context that SASO can provide.

Organizing a conference is a demanding task. Creating a new conference is a monumental task. We are grateful to have worked with an outstanding Technical Meeting Committee and Program Committee Chairs who have assembled an excellent technical program. Our particular thanks go to the Steering Committee Chair, Jean-Philippe Martin-Flatin, for his inexhaustible enthusiasm for the project, to Paul Robertson, for undertaking the thankless task of Finance Chair and to Roy Sterritt and Michael Hinchey, for ably guiding us through the IEEE labyrinth. We also thank our industrial sponsors for their generous financial support of SASO.

We look forward to many future SASO meetings and hope that they can serve as a catalyst for increased maturity and depth of research in this exciting, new discipline.

Ozalp Babaoglu, University of Bologna, Italy
Howard E. Shrobe, Massachusetts Institute of Technology, USA

Editorial by the Program Committee Co-chairs

It is our pleasure to welcome you to the First IEEE International Conference on Self-Adaptive and Self-Organizing Systems (SASO 2007).

This new conference is articulated around three tracks: the Research Track (10-page papers), the Work-in-Progress Track (4-page papers), and the Applications Track (4-page papers).

A total of 120 full papers and 28 short papers were submitted to this conference. We accepted 25 full papers for the Research Track (acceptance ratio: 20.8%), 20 short papers for the Work-in-Progress Track, and 6 short papers for the Applications Track. Among the 26 short papers, 18 were initially submitted as full papers.

The high number of submissions for the first edition of a conference series, together with the variety of topics covered by these papers, indicates that there is currently a large and interdisciplinary community interested in self-adaptive and self-organizing systems. We hope that SASO will continue to offer a natural home to this community, previously fragmented in a number of workshops in rather isolated disciplines.

Research papers are organized into eight sessions: Design Methodology, Foundations; Provocative Ideas; Synchronization/Desynchronization; P2P Systems; Data Collection and Aggregation; Combinatorial Optimization; Management and Control; and Security. Work-in-Progress papers are grouped into three sessions: Software Engineering and Multiagent Systems; Self-Adaptation; and Self-Organization. Applications papers make up one session.

We are very grateful to our international Program Committee and the additional reviewers that have provided high quality reviews for the submitted papers. This has greatly served to shape the current program.

We would like to thank our sponsor, the IEEE Computer Society's Task Force on Autonomous and Autonomic Systems (TF-AAS). We are also grateful to our technical co-sponsors: ACM SIG on Operating Systems (SIGOPS); ACM SIG on Artificial Intelligence (SIGART); and IEEE Systems, Man, and Cybernetics Society (SMCS). Finally, this event would not have been possible without generous donations from our patrons: Cisco Systems, Microsoft, BAE Systems, BBN Technologies, BT, and Telcordia. We thank them too.

We hope that you will learn and benefit from this conference, and that you will enjoy your stay in Boston.

Giovanna Di Marzo Serugendo, Birkbeck College, University of London, UK
Jean-Philippe Martin-Flatin, NetExpert, Switzerland
Márk Jelasity, Hungarian Academy of Sciences and University of Szeged, Hungary
Franco Zambonelli, Università di Modena e Reggio Emilia, Italy

Steering Committee

Steering Committee Chair

Jean-Philippe Martin-Flatin, NetExpert, Switzerland

Steering Committee Members

Ozalp Babaoglu, University of Bologna, Italy
Giovanna Di Marzo Serugendo, Birkbeck, University of London, UK
David Hales, University of Bologna, Italy
Márk Jelasity, Hungarian Academy of Sciences and University of Szeged, Hungary
Robert Laddaga, BBN Technologies, USA
Paul Robertson, Massachusetts Institute of Technology, USA
Howard E. Shrobe, Massachusetts Institute of Technology, USA
Franco Zambonelli, Università di Modena e Reggio Emilia, Italy

Technical Meeting Committee

General Co-chairs
Ozalp Babaoglu, *University of Bologna, Italy*
Howard E. Shrobe, *Massachusetts Institute of Technology, USA*

Program Committee Co-chairs
Giovanna Di Marzo Serugendo, *Birkbeck, University of London, UK*
Jean-Philippe Martin-Flatin, *NetExpert, Switzerland*
Márk Jelasity, *Hungarian Academy of Sciences and University of Szeged, Hungary*

Work-in-Progress Track Chair
Franco Zambonelli, *Università di Modena e Reggio Emilia, Italy*

Applications Track Chair
Franco Zambonelli, *Università di Modena e Reggio Emilia, Italy*

Industry Chair
Fabrice Saffre, *BT, UK*

Tutorial Chair
David Hales, *University of Bologna, Italy*

Finance Chair
Paul Robertson, *Massachusetts Institute of Technology, USA*

Panel Chair
Robert Laddaga, *BBN Technologies, USA*

Publicity Chair
Hermann De Meer, *University of Passau, Germany*

Sponsor Chair
Jean-Philippe Martin-Flatin, *NetExpert, Switzerland*

Publication Chair
Giovanna Di Marzo Serugendo, *Birkbeck, University of London, UK*

Local Arrangements Chair
Thomas J. Greene, *Massachusetts Institute of Technology, USA*

Program Committee

Karl Aberer, EPFL, Switzerland
Gul Agha, University of Illinois at Urbana-Champaign, USA
Leonard Barolli, Fukuoka Institute of Technology, Japan
Yaneer Bar-Yam, New England Complex Systems Institute, USA
Umesh Bellur, I.I.T. Bombay, India
Ernst Biersack, Institut Eurécom, France
Raouf Boutaba, University of Waterloo, Canada
Sven A. Brueckner, NewVectors, USA
Fabián E. Bustamante, Northwestern University, USA
Vinny Cahill, Trinity College Dublin, Ireland
Geoffrey Canright, Telenor R&D, Norway
Alexander Clemm, Cisco, USA
Geoff Coulson, Lancaster University, UK
Jim Crutchfield, University of California, Davis, USA
Hermann De Meer, University of Passau, Germany
Marco Dorigo, Université Libre de Bruxelles, Belgium
Bruce Edmonds, Manchester Metropolitan University, UK
Olivier Festor, INRIA, France
Christof Fetzer, Technical University of Dresden, Germany
Noria Foukia, University of Otago, New Zealand
Pierre Fraigniaud, University Paris Sud, France
Luca Maria Gambardella, IDSIA, Switzerland
David Garlan, Carnegie Mellon University, USA
Kurt Geihs, University of Kassel, Germany
Nigel Gilbert, University of Surrey, UK
Maria Gini, University of Minnesota, USA
Marie-Pierre Gleizes, IRIT Toulouse, France
Indranil Gupta, University of Illinois at Urbana-Champaign, USA
David Hales, University of Bologna, Italy
Salima Hassas, University Claude Bernard, Lyon, France
Manfred Hauswirth, DERI, Ireland
Michael Hinchey, NASA, USA
James Won-Ki Hong, POSTECH, Korea
David Hutchison, Lancaster University, UK
Christian Igel, Ruhr-Universität Bochum, Germany
Hai Jin, Huazhong University of Science and Technology, China
Gail E. Kaiser, Columbia University, USA
Anthony Karageorgos, University of Thessaly, Greece
Randy H. Katz, University of California, Berkeley, USA
Alexander Keller, IBM T.J. Watson Research Center, USA
Anne-Marie Kermarrec, INRIA, France
Scott Kirkpatrick, Hebrew University of Jerusalem, Israel
Mark Klein, Massachusetts Institute of Technology, USA
Robert Laddaga, BBN Technologies, USA
Stefano Leonardi, University of Rome La Sapienza, Italy
Emil Lupu, Imperial College London, UK
Clémence Magnien, CNRS and Université Pierre et Marie Curie, France
Paul Marrow, BT, UK

Additional Reviewers

Iqbal Ahamed, Marquette University, USA
Varsha Apte, I.I.T. Bombay, India
Paolo Bellavista, Università degli Studi di Bologna, Italy
Nicola Bicocchi, Università di Modena e Reggio Emilia, Italy
Steffen Bleul, University of Kassel, Germany
Manfred Bortenschlager, Salzburg Research, Austria
Mélanie Bouroche, Trinity College Dublin, Ireland
Davy Capera, IRIT Toulouse, France
Matteo Casadei, Alma Mater Studiorum - University of Bologna, Italy
Pohao Chang, Riverglass, Inc., USA
Anis Charfi, SAP Research, Germany
Philippe Cudre-Mauroux, EPFL, Switzerland
Vasilis Darlagiannis, EPFL, Switzerland
Xavier Defago, JAIST, Japan
Francesco De Mola, Università di Modena e Reggio Emilia, Italy
Bill Donkervoet, University of Illinois at Urbana-Champaign, USA
Jim Dowling, Swedish Institute of Computer Science, Sweden
Alessandro Duminuco, Eurecom, France
Taoufik En-Najjary, Institut Eurecom, France
Luca Foschini, DEIS - University of Bologna, Italy
Wojtek Galuba, EPFL, Switzerland
Daniela Gavidia, Vrije Universiteit Amsterdam, The Netherlands
Jean-Pierre Georgé, IRIT Toulouse, France
Philip Gross, Columbia University, USA
Parisa Haghani, EPFL, Switzerland
MyungJoo Ham, University of Illinois at Urbana-Champaign, USA
Anthony Harrington, Trinity College Dublin, Ireland
John Hopprich, Cisco, USA
Le Hung Vu, EPFL, Switzerland
Brent Ishibashi, University of Waterloo, Canada
Gabriel Jakobson, Altusys Corp., USA
Rajesh Karmani, University of Illinois at Urbana-Champaign, USA
Anh Le, University of Waterloo, Canada
Zhen Li, Rutgers University, USA
Marco Mamei, Università di Modena e Reggio Emilia, Italy
Jean-Pierre Mano, IRIT Toulouse, France
Kirill Mechitov, University of Illinois at Urbana-Champaign, USA
Rene Meier, Trinity College Dublin, Ireland
Pietro Michiardi, Eurecom, France
Marco Montes de Oca, Université Libre de Bruxelles, Belgium
Akihiro Nakao, The University of Tokyo, Japan
Rammohan Narendula, EPFL, Switzerland
Andrea Omicini, Alma Mater Studiorum, Universita di Bologna, Italy
Benno Overeinder, Vrije University, The Netherlands
Julian Padget, University of Bath, Great Britain
Dimitrios Pezaros, Lancaster University, Great Britain
Fabio Pianese, Institut Eurecom, France
Carlo Pinciroli, Université Libre de Bruxelles, Belgium

Vahe Poladian, Carnegie Mellon University, USA
Barry Porter, Lancaster University, Great Britain
Andrea Prati, Università di Modena e Reggio Emilia, Italy
Roland Reichle, University of Kassel, Germany
Rudolf Roth, Fraunhofer FOKUS, Germany
Aline Senart, Trinity College Dublin, Ireland
Steven Simpson, Lancaster University, Great Britain
Paul Smith, Lancaster University, Great Britain
Riky Subrata, University of Sydney, Australia
Richard Tateson, BT, UK
Elio Tuci, Université Libre de Bruxelles, Belgium
Matteo Vasirani, Universidad Rey Juan Carlos Madrid, Spain
Mirko Viroli, Alma Mater Studiorum - University of Bologna, Italy
Michael Wagner, University of Kassel, Germany
Sonia Waharte, University of Waterloo, Canada
Thomas Weise, University of Kassel, Germany
Danny Weyns, Katholieke Universiteit Leuven, Belgium
Ralf Wolter, Cisco Systems, Germany
Jin Xiao, University of Waterloo, Canada
Michael Zapf, University of Kassel, Germany

Keynotes

Plenary Keynote 1

Michael G. Hinchey: Biological Inspiration.

Abstract: Greater understanding of biology in modern times has enabled significant breakthroughs in improving healthcare, quality of life, and eliminating many diseases and congenital illnesses. Simultaneously there is a move towards emulating nature and copying many of the wonders uncovered in biology, resulting in "biologically inspired" systems. Significant results have been reported in a wide range of areas, with systems inspired by nature enabling exploration, communication, and advances that were never dreamed possible just a few years ago. We warn, that as in many other fields of endeavor, we should be inspired by nature and biology, not engage in mimicry. We describe some results of biological inspiration that augur promise in terms of improving the safety and security of systems, and in developing self-managing systems that we hope will ultimately lead to self-governing systems. We concentrate on the concept of swarm-based exploration missions that will enable NASA to explore space more efficiently and collect data never before available to scientists. We discuss several new self-x properties that will make such missions possible and that will also have application in other areas.

Biography: Michael G. Hinchey is Professor of Computer Science and Director of the Graduate Program at Loyola College, Baltimore, MD, USA. Until January 2007, he was Director of the NASA Software Engineering Laboratory, located at NASA Goddard Space Flight Center in Greenbelt, MD. He now serves as a NASA expert consultant. Prior to joining the US government, at various times he held positions at the level of full professor in the US, Australia, Sweden, Ireland and the UK. This summer he is Visiting Professor at Pontifícia Universidade Católica do Rio de Janeiro. He received a B.Sc. in Computer Science from University of Limerick, Ireland, an M.Sc. in Computation from University of Oxford, UK, and a Ph.D. in Computer Science from University of Cambridge, UK. He is Chair of the IEEE Technical Committee on Complexity in Computing, Vice Chair of the IEEE Technical Committee on Autonomous and Autonomic Systems, and is the IEEE Computer Society's representative to IFIP Technical Committee 1 (Foundations of Computer Science), which he currently chairs.

Plenary Keynote 2

Gerald Jay Sussman: Designing for Applications Unanticipated by the Designer

It is hard to build robust systems: systems that have acceptable behavior over a larger class of situations than was anticipated by their designers. The most robust systems are evolvable: they can be easily adapted to new situations with only minor modification. How can we design systems that are flexible in this way?

Observations of biological systems tell us a great deal about how to make robust and evolvable systems. Techniques originally developed in support of symbolic Artificial Intelligence can be viewed as ways of enhancing robustness and evolvability in programs and other engineered systems. By contrast, common practice of computer science actively discourages the construction of robust systems.

Research Track, Session 1: Design Methodology, Foundations

Novel Mathematics-Inspired Algorithms for Self-Adaptive Peer-to-Peer Computing *

Steven Y. Ko and Indranil Gupta
Dept. of Computer Science
University of Illinois at Urbana-Champaign
Urbana IL 61801
{sko, indy}@cs.uiuc.edu

Yookyung Jo
Dept. of Computer Science
Cornell University
Ithaca, NY 14853
ykjo@cs.cornell.edu

Abstract

This paper describes, and evaluates benefits of, a design methodology to translate certain mathematical models into the design of novel, self-adaptive, peer-to-peer (p2p) distributed computing algorithms ("protocols"). This methodology is potentially a good vehicle for translating natural phenomena, representable via mathematical models, into practical p2p protocols. Concretely, our first contribution is a set of techniques to translate certain discrete "sequence equations" rigorously into new p2p protocols called "sequence protocols". Sequence protocols are self-adaptive, scalable, and fault-tolerant, with applicability in p2p settings like Grids. A sequence protocol is a set of probabilistic local and message-passing actions for each process. These actions are translated from terms in a set of source sequence equations. Without having each process simulate the source sequence equations, the emergent behavior of a sequence protocol in a p2p system is equivalent to, and predicted by, its source sequence equations. This paper's second contribution is a new self-adaptive Grid computing protocol called "HoneyAdapt". HoneyAdapt is derived from sequence equations modeling adaptive bee foraging behavior in nature. HoneyAdapt is intended for Grid applications that allow Grid clients, at run-time, a choice of algorithms for executing chunks of the application's dataset. HoneyAdapt tells each Grid client how to adaptively select at run-time, for each chunk it receives, a "good" algorithm for computing the chunk - this selection is based on continuous feedback from other clients. We present analysis, large-scale simulation results, and deployment results.

1. Introduction

The last few years have seen an increased interest in nature-inspired design of self-adaptive algorithms (i.e., "protocols") for distributed peer-to-peer (p2p) systems, e.g., [3, 5, 26]. This paper adopts an alternative approach, that is both rigorous and practical, for translating natural phenomena into novel p2p protocols. Non-Computer scientists have, since the inception of their respective fields, used *mathematical models* to represent their ideas, results, and natural phenomena, e.g., see [21, 22]. Our approach is then to create *design methodologies* [11] that translate these mathematical models into *equivalent* p2p protocols.

Abstractly, a design methodology is targeted at a particular class of mathematical models (e.g., discrete sequence equations in a particular format and structure), and defines a set of techniques that takes as input any instance of the targeted class of models, e.g., a specific set of equations satisfying the specified format and structure. In turn, the methodology generates an output that is a p2p protocol, in the sense that it is an algorithm run completely locally by each process in a decentralized p2p system.

Most importantly, the p2p system-wide behavior of this generated protocol is *equivalent* to that of the set of equations input to the methodology. The protocol running at each process does *not* simulate the sequence equations themselves. Instead, the protocol involves simple local and message-passing actions, so that the *emergent system-wide behavior* is equivalent to the mathematical behavior of the input sequence equations[1].

The concrete contributions of this paper are two-fold:

I. We describe a novel design methodology for translating sequence equations into a class of novel p2p protocols called *sequence protocols*. The techniques in this methodology ensure that the emergent system-wide behavior of a sequence protocol is provably equivalent to, and can be predicted by, the source set of sequence equations from which it is translated. Sequence protocols are completely decentralized, involve low and scalable per-process communication overheads and memory, and are highly fault-

*This work was supported in part by NSF CAREER grant CNS-0448246 and in part by NSF ITR Grant CMS-0427089.

[1]Equivalence will be defined more precisely soon, in Section 2.

tolerant. Most importantly, they are self-adaptive because their emergent behavior in a p2p system inherits the equilibrium points from the sequence equations.

II. In order to demonstrate the utility and properties of nature-based sequence protocols, we design and evaluate a new self-adaptive Grid computing protocol called *HoneyAdapt*. HoneyAdapt is a p2p protocol and is derived from sequence equations modeling adaptive bee foraging behavior in nature. HoneyAdapt is intended for Grid applications that allow Grid clients, at run-time, a choice of algorithms for executing chunks of the application's dataset. HoneyAdapt tells each Grid client how to adaptively select at run-time, for each chunk it receives, a "good" algorithm for computing the chunk - this selection is based on continuous feedback from other clients. We present analysis of the protocol, as well as experimental results from both large-scale simulations involving 1000's of clients, and a smaller-scale 30-node PC cluster deployment.

In general, sequence protocols are intended for large-scale p2p applications that contain hundreds to thousands of processes (e.g., Grid applications, distributed storage, and p2p applications), and that seek to incorporate self-adaptivity by utilizing emergent probabilistic properties of the system. For instance, HoneyAdapt is a generic Grid protocol with applications to parallel sorting, graphics-rendering, astronomy data-processing, etc. For concreteness in this paper, we evaluate HoneyAdapt only in the parallel sorting problem setting (Section 5.2). Further, we briefly present a different sequence protocol called the *Multiplicative protocol* (Section 3).

Related Work: The class of sequence protocols we discuss are a superset of Markov chain algorithms because the latter considers only immediate history of states, while the former considers arbitrarily long histories. Our consideration of sequence protocols is different from the simulation of sequence protocols, as in [23].

Previously in [11], we presented a design methodology to translate *continuous differential* equations into distributed protocols. Unfortunately, those techniques are inapplicable for translating sequence equations as the latter are *discrete*. Further, sequence equations have relatively more pronounced and interesting phase change behavior.

Population protocols [1, 18] also involve large process groups, but are different from ours. Differences in protocol performance for infinite versus finite-but-large group sizes were studied in [15]. Methodologies in general have been used to systematize the design process in many fields, e.g., [4], but in distributed computing, they have begun to emerge only recently, e.g., [16]. Sequence protocols are quite different from checkpointing and virtual synchrony protocols; the latter two are less scalable. Like our basic sequence protocols, many classical distributed algorithms also operate in rounds, e.g., [20]; however, to our knowledge, none are generated from sequence equations.

System Model: For simplicity of analysis, we assume a closed group of N processes, which are non-faulty. The processes communicate by reliable message-passing over a network. N is assumed to be very large. In practice, reliable communication can be provided by TCP channels. The non-faulty process assumption largely holds for Grid settings (e.g., for HoneyAdapt). This assumption can be relaxed in practice for other sequence protocols, e.g., the one in Section 3 works even under massive process failures.

Sequence protocols operate in "rounds" of time, thus we assume all processes know exactly when each round begins. This assumption can be satisfied via one of NTP, TIME, or DAYTIME services (e.g., via NIST servers), that provides coarse granularity synchronization. (Our HoneyAdapt deployment in Section 5.2 does not use the notion of rounds, and is thus asynchronous.) Finally, we assume that each process can sample other processes uniformly at random - this can be implemented via membership protocols such as CYCLON [24] or via a peer-sampling service [14].

Section 2 describes the new design methodology. A case study of a simple sequence protocol is presented in Section 3. Section 4 details the HoneyAdapt protocol, and Section 5 presents experimental results for HoneyAdapt. We conclude in Section 6.

2. Translating Sequence Equations into Sequence Protocols

We present an innovative design methodology that translates certain types of sequence equations into new p2p protocols which we call *sequence protocols*. The canonical single-variable sequence equation is of the form $x_{m+1} = f(x_m, x_{m-1}, \ldots, x_{m-k})$, where k is a constant non-negative integer, f is a function with a finite number of terms, m takes on integer values $\geq k$, and all x_i's take real values $\in [0, 1]$. We also extend our methodology to multi-variable sequence equations with a finite number of variables (say, l variables). This equation system would contain one equation, in the above format, for each of the variables $x1, x2, \ldots xl$, with the right-hand side function for xj denoted as fj. To avoid notational confusion, we will use a subscripted index (e.g., x_i) to represent the time index i for a given variable. We use a side-index (e.g., xj) to denote the jth variable in a multi-variable equation [2]. Thus, xj_i denotes the value of variable xj at time i. Time, in these equations, thus takes discrete positive integer values.

The sequence protocol derived from a system of sequence equations is an algorithm that runs locally at each

[2]We avoid using x^j because superscripts are used in Section 2 to denote power terms. We also avoid $x[j]$ or $xj(i)$ and such expressions, in order to keep our variables uncluttered.

process in the p2p system. Like the original sequence equations, a sequence protocol operates in system-wide *rounds*, where each process knows the exact time at which each round starts. A round corresponds to a discrete time in the sequence equations, i.e., the subscript i in xj_i. At any given time (i.e., at the start or in the middle of a round), state at a process p is maintained locally as an $l-bit$ tuple consisting of l *state variables*. This is denoted as $< x1(p), x2(p), \ldots, xl(p) >$, where the value of the jth bit $xj(p)$ represents whether the process is in (sub-) state xj (if state variable $xj(p)$ is 1) or not. Finally, we use the term xj_i to denote the *system-wide fraction* of processes in (sub-) state xj at time i (for $1 \leq j \leq l, i \in N$). Thus, $xj_i(p)$ is a binary variable ("state variable xj at process p" at time i), while "xj_i" is a system-wide real number $\in [0, 1]$.

Equivalence between the sequence equations and the sequence protocols is defined as follows: for any (i, j), the *value* of xj_i predicted by the sequence equations, is the same as the *fraction* of processes in state xj at time i in the p2p system. Thus, a sequence protocol has the same time-based trajectories and equilibrium points as the source sequence equations. Notice that processes themselves are not simulating the equation, but instead run actions that make the *emergent* behavior in the distributed system the same as the sequence equations.

2.1. Basic Translation Methodology

For the sake of exposition simplicity, let us start with single-variable sequence equations only[3]:

$$x_{m+1} = f(x_m, x_{m-1}, \ldots x_{m-k}) \quad (1)$$

Here, k is a constant non-negative integer, and all $x_i \in [0, 1]$. m is a notation standing for a positive integer representing time. An example sequence equation would be the multiplicative equation $x_{m+1} = r \cdot x_m$.

Suppose f is written as a sum of a finite number of elementary *terms* (positive or negative). Section 2.2 shows that our translation works for multi-variable terms that are either polynomial or non-polynomial. We convert: (i) the equation variable into a state variable for the protocol, and (ii) each term in the function f into a set of protocol actions. For the variable x, a local state variable is defined at each process - this takes on boolean values, indicating whether the process is in that state or not. For process p, we call this as the "state variable x at p". When the state variable at process p is 1, we say that "p is in state x"; when the state variable is 0, we say that "p is out of state x".

The core techniques in the methodology lie in translating the terms from function f into protocol actions. Recall that the protocol actions must ensure that if the *fraction* of processes in state x, at the start of a given round, is the value x_m, and the values of these fractions at the starts of the immediately previous $k-1$ rounds were $x_{m-1}, \ldots x_{m-k+1}$ respectively, then the fraction of processes in state x at the start of the immediately following round will be equal to: $x_{m+1} = f(x_m, x_{m-1}, \ldots x_{m-k})$.

Overview of Generated Sequence Protocol: First, each process p maintains the following state variables at any time: (i) $x(p)$, the state of process p in the current round, (ii) $x_{-1}(p), x_{-2}(p), \ldots, x_{-k}(p)$, the states of p in the immediately previous k rounds, and (iii) $x_{next}(p)$, a running variable for the state of p for the immediately next round. $x_{next}(p)$ is continuously updated during the current round (based on actions and messages described below). For multi-variable sequence equations, (i)-(iii) is maintained for each of the variables.

Second, at the start of each round at process p, the following initializing actions are taken: (1) for each $i = -k$ to -2, $x_{-i}(p)$ is replaced by $x_{-(i-1)}(p)$, (ii) $x_{-1}(p)$ is set to $x(p)$, (iii) $x(p)$ is set to $x_{next}(p)$, and (iv) $x_{next}(p)$ is initialized to a value of zero. In other words, the oldest remembered state for the process is forgotten and the rest shifted by one, the last round's state is remembered as the most recent state, the current state is updated from the running state variable, which in turn is initialized for the current round.

Once this initialization is complete, process p can respond to messages for this round as well as execute actions for this round. All messages are tagged with the round number in which they are generated, and messages from rounds older than the current one are dropped[4].

In each round, process p executes two types of actions – *Token Generation*, followed by *Token Relay and Apply*. Token generation creates a number of *token* messages, based on the terms in the sequence equations. Token messages are then *relayed* to other processes through random walks. In turn, when p receives tokens, it *applies* these tokens to $x_{next}(p)$. We elaborate below:

1. Token Generation: Each generated token can be either *positive* or *negative*. Positive (resp. negative) tokens are generated for each positive (resp. negative) term in f. The goal of the token generation procedure is to have the N processes create, in a decentralized manner, per round, an expected number of $T \times N$ positive (resp. negative) tokens for each positive (resp. negative) term T, where the value of T is computed by substituting variables within it with fractions of processes in respective states.

2. Token Relay and Apply: When process p, with $x_{next}(p) = 0$, receives a positive token, it *consumes* the token by setting $x_{next}(p)$ to 1. When a process with $x_{next}(p) = 1$ receives a negative token, it consumes the token by setting $x_{next}(p)$ to 0. If none of these two con-

[3]Later (in Section 2.2), we extend our techniques to equations with multiple variables.

[4]This is only a round-based protocol and does *not* require strong underlying mechanisms like virtual synchrony.

ditions apply, the process forwards the received token to a random non-faulty target process. Thus, each token takes a random walk until it is consumed. The following theorem shows the equivalence of the sequence protocol and sequence equations:

Theorem 1: Consider a multi-variable sequence equation system in l variables $\{x1, x2, \ldots, xl\}$ ($xi \in [0,1]$), and a sequence protocol so that: (i) for each term T appearing in the sequence equation, per round, $T \times N$ tokens are generated and applied as described above (where the value of T in expression $T \times N$ is computed by substituting variables within it with fractions of processes in respective states), with all tokens positive if T is positive and negative otherwise; and (ii) these tokens are relayed and applied appropriately. Then, the sequence equations can be used to predict, at any time (i.e., at the start of any round), the expected fractions of processes that will be in states $\{x1, x2, \ldots, xl\}$, at the start of the next round.

Proof: For each variable index $j \in \{1, 2, \ldots l\}$, the proof follows by induction on (discrete) time. The base induction step is: in the current round m, for each j, let the fraction of processes in state xj be xj_m, and in the immediately preceding k rounds, fractions of processes in state xj were $xj_{m-1}, \ldots xj_{m-k}$ respectively. The induction step is: during the mth round, adding all positive and negative tokens for state xj, the total expected number of tokens for xj is $= N \times fj(\{xh_i\}_{i=m,h=l}^{i=m-k,h=1})$. Due to the relaying, the *probability* of a process having $xj_{next}(p) = 1$ at the end of the mth round, is this number divided by N, or $fj(\{xh_i\}_{i=m,h=l}^{i=m-k,h=1})$, as desired. □

Although a process has to execute token generation at the start of each round, the relay and apply operations are completely asynchronous across processes in the system. Thus, no synchrony is required within the round. Further, in our analysis of the sequence protocols, we will assume that the round duration is long enough for the token relaying to quiesce, i.e., for the system to reach a state where none of the remaining tokens may be consumed anymore by any of the processes. In practice though, this restriction does not violate our scalability goals. Each token would typically transit through a logarithmic number of processes until it is consumed. Thus, in a given round, if each process generates a constant number of tokens, the message overhead per process will be logarithmic in group size. Finally, our protocol implementations limit the length of a round - thus extra tokens can be lost if the round expires - yet, our experiments in Sections 3 and 5 show this does not affect convergence behavior.

2.2. Token Generation

At the start of the round, each process p generates a series of tokens *for each term in each source sequence equation*, based on the following rules. For Theorem 1 to hold, we desire that for each term T in the sequence equations, an expected $T \times N$ tokens are generated system-wide per round. We describe below how polynomial, multi-variable, and non-polynomial terms, all fall under Theorem 1.

2.2.1 Polynomial Terms:

Constant term of form $T = r$, where r is a constant: Process p (regardless of its current state) *generates an average of $|r|$ tokens*. This is achieved by generating $\lfloor |r| \rfloor$ tokens, and then generating an extra token with probability $(|r| - \lfloor |r| \rfloor)$. If $r > 0$, all these tokens are positive, otherwise they are all negative. Since each processes creates an expected r tokens, the expected number of tokens created system-wide is $r \times N$. Notice that this token generation action requires no message exchange.

Linear terms of form $T = r \cdot x_{m-j}$, where $j \leq k$: Process p first checks if j rounds ago, it was in state x. If indeed $x_{-j}(p) = 1$, then p generates an average of r tokens, in a similar manner to the constant term translation in the last paragraph. If $x_{-j}(p) = 0$, then p generates no tokens. If the current round is m, then a fraction x_{m-j} processes satisfy $x_{-j}(p) = 1$, thus the expected number of tokens generated is $x_{m-j} \times N \times r = T \times N$. Notice that this token generation action requires no message exchange.

Multiplicative terms of form $T = r \cdot \Pi_{i=m}^{i=m-k} x_i^{(j_i)}$ (each j_i a non-negative integer, some j_i positive): Let i' be the highest value of i in the term T such that exponent $j_i > 0$. Process p first checks if $(m - i')$ rounds ago it was in state x, i.e., if $x_{-(m-i')}(p) = 1$ (where $x_0(p) = x(p)$). If not, it takes no action. If yes, it sends out $(\sum_{i=m}^{i=m-k} j_i) - 1$ sampling messages, each to one target process, chosen uniformly at random. Target processes acknowledge the sampling message - for each sampling message, random targets are retried (after a time-out) until an acknowledgement is received. Non-faulty target processes reply immediately with the list of states they were in for the last k rounds. Process p then checks whether for all $b = 1$ to $(\sum_{i=m}^{i=m-k} j_i) - 1$, the bth process that sent a reply was in the state indicated by the bth variable occurring in the product $T/r \cdot x_{i'} = x_{i'}^{(j_{i'}-1)} \cdot \Pi_{i=i'-1}^{i=m-k} x_i^{(j_i)}$, when the individual variables of the product are arranged arbitrarily. If this condition is true, process p generates an average of r tokens, otherwise it generates none. Since the probability of this condition being true at a process is $T/r \cdot x_{i'}$, and the fraction of processes with $x_{-(m-i')}(p) = 1$ is $x_{i'}$, the expected number of tokens generated system-wide is $x_{i'} \times T/r \cdot x_{i'} \times N = T \times N$.

2.2.2 Translating Sequence Equations with Multiple Variables: The presented methodology (with techniques from both Sections 2.2.1 and 2.2.3) can be generalized to translate a system of sequence equations. A system of sequence equations with $l > 1$ variables $\{x1, x2, \ldots, xl\}$ specifies a sequence equation for each $xj(1 \leq j \leq l)$: $xj_{m+1} = fj(xh_b, 1 \leq h \leq l, m-k \leq b \leq m)$. Here, fj has a finite number of terms, k is a constant non-negative integer, and $\forall h, b : xh_b \in [0,1]$. In the derived sequence protocol, for each j $(1 \leq j \leq l)$, each process maintains one state variable xj, along with a memory of the last k values of it. Separate token generation actions are created from each fj and executed at each round. The tokens generated from fj are tagged with j so that they are applied only to state variables xj. Note that if fj contains terms with xh_* $(h \neq j)$, then the token generation actions related to state variable xj easily generalize may involve sampling values of state variables other than xj.

2.2.3 Non-Polynomial Terms: Translation of a non-polynomial term requires each round to be split into a known number of *subrounds*, and the use of *subtoken* messages. Just like for rounds, each process knows when each subround starts. Subtokens do not affect state variables directly, but instead contribute towards generation of tokens. The actions for individual terms are tied together by calculating the maximum number of subrounds across all terms, and using this as the number of subrounds per round in the overall sequence protocol. We ignore such tying issues below, focusing only on individual terms.

Division terms $T = r/x_{m-i}$ $(0 \leq i \leq k$, with $x_0 \equiv x)$: Split each round into two subrounds. In the first subround, process p (regardless of its state at the round start) iteratively selects one target process uniformly at random (which acknowledges with the value of its local $x_{-i}(p)$), until a reply is received from a target process that satisfies $x_{-i}(p) = 1$. A count of the number of acknowledging targets is kept. If their total is z, p generates an average $r \cdot z$ tokens. In the second subround, the tokens are relayed and applied as usual. Since $E[z] = 1/x_m$, the expected number of system-wide tokens is $N \times r \cdot 1/x_m$, as desired.

Fractional Terms: In a sequence equation with l distinct variables $x1, x2, \ldots, xl$, consider a canonical term $T = r \cdot \frac{\sum_{j=1}^{j=l} b_j . a_j . xj}{\sum_{j=1}^{j=l} a_j . xj}$, where a_j's are all positive real numbers, and each b_j is a boolean with value either 0 or 1.

To translate this term, two subrounds are required per round. In the first subround at process p, for each j such that $xj(p) = 1$, p generates an average a_j subtokens. Each subtoken is tagged with the value of j that generated it. Then, p multicasts these subtokens to *all* other processes in the group. In the second subround, p selects one subtoken at random from those received. Suppose the tagged value is j' - if $b_{j'}$ (in term T) is 1, process p generates an average r tokens; if $b_{j'}$ is 0, p generates no tokens[5].

[5]If a process receives no subtokens after the first subround, it needs to sample other processes to "copy over" their received subtokens.

Each process receives, via the multicast, for each j, $N \times a_j \cdot xj$ subtokens carrying j. The above sampling then means that it generates r tokens only with probability T/r. Thus the expected number of tokens generated system-wide is $N \times T/r \times r = T \times N$.

Recursive Translation: Define a term T as *translatable* if any of the above techniques (including this one) can be applied to it, so that the derived protocol generates an expected $T \times N$ tokens per round. Now, given a term T', suppose it can (1) be rewritten into one of the above forms (polynomial, division, or fractional) by substituting with dummy variables a finite set of *sub-terms* occurring in it, so that: (2) each of the sub-terms itself is translatable. Then T itself is translatable. This recursive translation can be achieved by designing actions for term T' as follows: split the round into two sub-rounds, and translate each substituted sub-term (say g) in the first sub-round by generating subtokens and relaying these subtokens until each process has either 0 or 1 subtokens for each substituted sub-term. The second sub-round uses the translated action from T, except that the actions relating to the substituted sub-term sample whether or not a process received a g subtoken.

3. Case Study: Detecting Global Triggers

In order to demonstrate that even the simplest sequence equation can lead to useful sequence protocols, we present a case study of the *Multiplicative protocol*. This is derived from a one-variable sequence equation containing only one term, yet can be used to detect a threshold-based global property. The reader will find sequence protocols for detecting other global properties in [12].

In a self-adaptive p2p system, we are interested in a global *threshold trigger* for a metric of interest, denoted as R. Concretely, suppose each process p proposes its value R_p for R. Then we wish to detect whether the system-wide average value of R_p is above or below a specified threshold $thresh$. A threshold trigger can be used to detect, for instance, possible partitioning of a p2p overlay, by setting R_p = number of neighbors of process p, and $thresh$ to a value based on the overlay structure (e.g., for a random overlay, $thresh = O(\log(N))$). This problem is solved by the Multiplicative protocol, described below.

The Multiplicative Protocol: The Multiplicative protocol is derived from the multiplicative equation $x_{m+1} = r \cdot x_m$ $(r > 0$ and $x_* \in [0,1])$. The sequence protocol is derived using the polynomial linear translation (Section 2.2.1). The resulting sequence protocol has only one action per round per process.

The emergent behavior of the protocol can be analyzed via the sequence equation itself. Equilibrium occurs when $x_{m+1} = x_m$, i.e., $x = r \cdot x$, or $x \cdot (1-r) = 0$. For all $r \neq 1$, the only equilibrium point is $x = 0$. For stability of equilibria, we use a well-known result from Lorenz [22]:

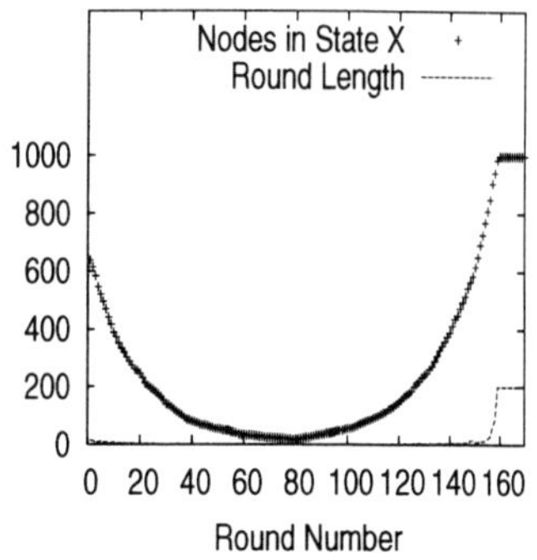

(a)

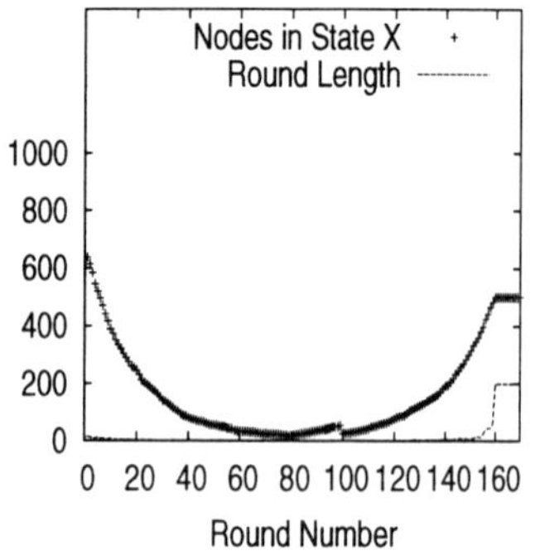

(b)

Figure 1. Multiplicative Protocol: Basic Phase change and Massive Failure. (a) The value of r_{avg} changes from 0.95 to 1.05 at t=80. $N = 1000$. (b) Same as (a), except that 50% of the processes fail at t=100. Convergence occurs at t=206. $N = 1000$.

Lorenz's Stability Condition: For a sequence equation $x_{m+1} = f(x_m)$, an equilibrium point $x = x_\infty$ is stable if and only if $|f'(x)|_{x=x_\infty} < 1$.

For the multiplicative map, $f'(x) = r$ at all x. If $r < 1$, the system converges towards the sole stable point $x = 0$. However, if $r > 1$, $x = 1$ is the sole stable point while $x = 0$ becomes an unstable point.

Convergence Times: We are interested in X, the number of processes in state x. For $r < 1$, with $X = N$ initially, $E[X]$ after t rounds is $= (N \cdot r^t)$. The expected convergence time towards $X = 0$ is $\log_{1/r}(N)$ rounds. For $r > 1$, $X = 1$ initially implies that after t rounds $E[X] = r^t$, giving an expected convergence time of $\log_r(N)$, towards $X = N$.

Average Threshold Trigger Detection: To implement a threshold trigger $thresh$ for metric R, we use the Multiplicative protocol where each process p uses a value of $r = \frac{R_p}{thres}$ for the sequence protocol. In the multiplicative equation, replacing r with $r_{avg} = \sum_p (r_p)/N$, does not change the behavior of the equation. Thus, when $r_{avg} < 1$, the systems stabilizes with all processes out of state x; when $r_{avg} > 1$, the system converges and stabilizes with all processes in state x. Thus, detection can be achieved at an initiating process by querying, after enough time for convergence, the current states of the a small *control group* of processes selected randomly. If a majority of processes in the control group are found to be in state x, then the initiator concludes that the system-wide average of R_p is $> thresh$, otherwise it concludes that this average is $< thresh$.

Experimental Results: We give simulation data from a synchronous simulation done on a PC with 1.7 Ghz Intel Celeron CPU, 256 MB RAM, WinXP Pro. The Mersenne Twister pseudorandom generator was used. There are $N = 1000$ non-faulty processes. Round length is limited to 200 periods, each process receives and sends tokens once per period, and the overlay is a complete graph. Figure 1 plots both the number of processes in state x, as well as the time until the last token is consumed in each round. Figure 1(a) shows that when r_{avg} is changed from 0.95 to 1.05 at t=80 onwards, the system dramatically changes from a convergence on $x = 0$ to a convergence on $x = 1$. Also, when $r_{avg} > 1$, not all tokens are consumed since each round becomes the maximum 200 periods, but this does not affect convergence. Figures 1(b) shows that massive failure of 50% of processes (at time $t = 100$) does not affect convergence.

4. HoneyAdapt: Adaptive Grid Computing

We present HoneyAdapt, a self-adaptive protocol for Grid computing. HoneyAdapt is generically applicable in several highly parallelizable Grid applications that use the master-worker paradigm, e.g., SETI@Home, physics and meteorological applications, etc. In the master-worker paradigm, a *master host* initially contains the (large) data set that has to be processed. The master then hands out data chunks to other *clients* (workers), connected amongst each other through a p2p overlay. All chunks are assumed to be the same size. Each client gets one chunk at a time.

The problem we address is the following. The clients are free to use any one of several alternative algorithms $1, 2, \ldots, A$ for each chunk. However, neither master nor the clients can guess which algorithm is the "best" for any chunk in any given data set. This is especially true of data sets with mixed types of chunks, where individual chunks may have a different "best" algorithms. This goal is similar to that of AI algorithms for evaluation and tracking of "experts" [13]. However, those are exhaustive and potentially expensive if applied to a p2p distributed system.

Our solution to this problem is called *HoneyAdapt*. HoneyAdapt is a sequence protocol derived from sequence equations that model the foraging behavior of honeybees as they attempt to select, in a decentralized manner, the "best" nectar source(s) from among multiple available sources [9, 21]. HoneyAdapt allows clients to adapt among A component algorithms *on the fly*, i.e., at run time. The most attractive aspect of HoneyAdapt is its *black-box* nature; HoneyAdapt requires no knowledge of the internal characteristics of the application or input data, instead using active feedback from the clients at *run time*. However, as our experiments indicate, HoneyAdapt works best when long sequences of chunks in the data-set are "similar" in nature.

We describe the protocol in Section 4.1 and its analysis in Section 4.2. HoneyAdapt is applicable to parallel sorting, graphics rendering, and other data processing applications. We show in Section 5.2 that when applied to parallel sorting, HoneyAdapt (called *HoneySort*) *outperforms traditional sorting algorithms such as Quicksort and Insertion sort.* HoneyAdapt and HoneySort are proof of concept systems, and are not (yet) meant to compete with state of the art sorting systems [2]. HoneyAdapt can also be easily optimized for specific applications, e.g., by combining it with machine-learning techniques; however, these are beyond the scope of this paper.

4.1. The HoneyAdapt Sequence Protocol

We describe the HoneyAdapt sequence protocol below. This sequence protocol runs synchronously in rounds. During each round, each client processes only one chunk. For clarity, the initial description also refers to the sequence equation and the honeybee behavior. Consider a group of clients (honeybees) trying to select the best from among A multiple algorithms (nectar sources) based on measured individual running times for the chunks at the clients (measured quality of nectar sources). At any point of time, a given client (honeybee) is said to be in state i if it is using algorithm i on the current chunk (if honeybee has just foraged, i.e., visited, nectar source i), where $i \in \{1, 2, \ldots A\}$. Let the fraction of clients (honeybees) in state i at start of round t be $a_i(t)$. We use a variant of the equations in [9] that model the actual honeybee behavior:

$$a_i(t) = a_i(t-1)\cdot(1-pf_i) + \left(\frac{sq_i \cdot pd_i \cdot a_i(t-1)}{\sum_{j=1}^{A} sq_j \cdot pd_j \cdot a_j(t-1)}\right)\cdot \sum_{j=1}^{A} pf_j \cdot a_j(t-1) \quad (2)$$

This is an $A-$variable system of sequence equations, and HoneyAdapt is derived from it using techniques for fractional, polynomial, and recursive translation from Section 2. Although the sequence protocol would have each state maintain an $A-$tuple of states (one for each variable), we have the restriction that each client can be using exactly one algorithm at any given point of time, i.e., at any client, exactly one of the A state variables is 1. This means that at any time t, $\sum_{i=1}^{A} a_i(t) = 1$. In addition, our initial conditions are that for each i, at least one client uses algorithm i, i.e., for each i, some client p has $a_i(0)(p) = 1$ initially.

In the above equation, for each i, sq_i is the *quality* of algorithm i (nectar source i), calculated on the fly depending on the algorithm and the chunks currently being processed. Also, pf_i is the *following probability*, and pd_i is *dancing probability* - both $\in (0, 1]$ and are fixed.

When a client uses algorithm $i \in \{1, 2, \ldots A\}$, on a data chunk, it calculates a "quality" for i, denoted as $sq_{i,p}$. $sq_{i,p}$ is inversely related to the running time for that chunk; a shorter execution time translates to a higher quality. sq_i in equation (2) is thus the average of $sq_{i,p}$ across all clients p using algorithm i in that round. At the round's end, p decides to *dance* with dancing probability pd_i (similar to a bee dance to advertise the nectar source it just foraged). Dancing means generation of a number of *advertisement messages supporting algorithm* i. The number of advertisements generated at client p is proportional to quality $sq_{i,p}$ in the round. These are then multicast to *all* other clients.

Then, with following probability pf_i, client p decides to *follow*. This means p *samples a random advertisement* from those received; the value of j supported therein will be used as next round's algorithm (this accounts for the second term on the right hand side of equation (2)). On the other hand, if p decides not to follow (with prob. $1 - pf_i$), it continues to use old algorithm i (this accounts for the first term on the right hand side of equation (2)).

4.2. Analysis of the HoneyAdapt Protocol

Theorem 1 tells us that HoneyAdapt's emergent behavior is equivalent to the equation (2). If for all $i = 1$ to A, the fraction of processes using algorithm i in round $(t-1)$ is $a_i(t-1)$, then the fraction of processes using algorithm i (for any i) in round t is that specified by the equation (2). We analyze below the convergence behavior of HoneyAdapt.

Lemma 1: If all sq_i's are unique and non-zero, all pd_i's are equal to each other, and all pf_i's are equal to each other, then HoneyAdapt has exactly A equilibrium points, each corresponding to a unique i with $a_i(t) = 1$.

Proof: $\forall i$, let $pd_i = pd$ and $pf_i = pf$. Equilibrium points occur when $\forall i : a_i(t) = a_i(t-1)$, i.e., from equation (2), when $\forall i$: either $a_i(t) = a_i(t-1) = 0$, or $\frac{pf}{sq_i \cdot pd} = \frac{\sum_{j=1}^{A} pf \cdot a_j(t-1)}{\sum_{j=1}^{A} sq_j \cdot pd \cdot a_j(t-1)}$. Notice that the right hand side of the second equation is independent of i. There cannot be any equilibrium point with stable values $a_i \neq 0, a_j \neq 0, i \neq j$, since then $sq_i = sq_j$, a contradiction. Hence proved. □

Theorem 2: If all sq_i's are unique and non-zero, all pd_i's are equal to each other, and all pf_i's are equal to each other, then HoneyAdapt has only one *stable* equilibrium point, at which $a_{i_{max}} = 1$, where $\forall j \neq i_{max} : sq_{i_{max}} > sq_j$.

Proof: An equilibrium is stable iff all eigenvalues of the Jacobian matrix have absolute values < 1. Without loss of generality, let $i_{max} = A$. Since $a_A = 1 - \sum_{i=1}^{A-1} a_i$, we need to consider only the $(m-1) \times (m-1)$ Jacobian matrix H. This turns out to be:

$$H_{ij} = 0\,(i \neq j)\,, H_{ii} = 1 - pf + \frac{sq_i}{sq_A}\cdot pf$$

Here, $1 \leq i, j \leq m-1$. Now, we use an easy extension of Lorenz's stability condition to multi-variable sequence equations (for a proof of this extension, see [12]): in a sequence equation with multiple variables, the stability condition at an equilibrium point is that all eigenvalues of the Jacobian at that point should have absolute values < 1.

The eigenvalues of the above matrix are its diagonal elements. Since $pf \in (0, 1]$, we have $H_{ii} \geq \frac{sq_i}{sq_A} \cdot pf > 0$. Recall that $\forall i : 1 \leq i < A$, we have $sq_i < sq_A$. Thus, all eigenvalues $H_{ii} = 1 - pf \cdot (1 - \frac{sq_i}{sq_A}) < 1$. Hence, absolute values of all eigenvalues are < 1. □

Convergence Times: Consider a small perturbation from the equilibrium point $a_A = 1$. From Theorem 2, we have that $\forall i \neq A$: $a_i(t) = \left(1 - pf\left(1 - \frac{sq_i}{sq_A}\right)\right)^t a_i(0)$. The convergence speed time is thus logarithmic in N. Notice that the message traffic depends on parameter pd, but pd does not affect equilibria or convergence speed.

5. Experiments with HoneyAdapt

Section 5.1 presents simulations of HoneyAdapt, and Section 5.2 its behavior for the parallel sorting problem.

5.1. HoneyAdapt Simulation Results

We experimentally study HoneyAdapt and several variants of it, via our implementation in a custom C simulator. Our implementation relaxes many of our previously stated assumptions. Firstly, each client (node) at the end of a chunk execution, does not create tokens as in Section 4.1. Instead it creates a *single advertisement message* carrying a weight that is set to the quality of the used algorithm on the latest chunk. Secondly, HoneyAdapt as described so far, had each client choose its current chunk's algorithm either by sampling advertisements ("sample") or by retaining its recently-used algorithm ("memory"). However, we evaluate an additional three strategies defined by {memory vs. memoryless} × {greedy vs. sampled}.

We use a network topology generated via BRITE's [17] flat router Waxman model, with 1000 routers. Each client is assigned to one random stub in the network topology. The Grid computing overlay topology is a random graph, with each client selecting $M = 6$ random neighbors[6].

Table 1 summarizes our experimental parameters. We consider a master-client Grid application, where the master data is split into chunks that are handed out sequentially to requesting clients. Each client has a choice of a fixed set of algorithms to process each fetched chunk, and uses HoneyAdapt to make this run-time choice. HoneyAdapt's success depends on series of chunks being "similar" in nature - we study this by assigning each chunk one of several discrete but finite *types*. Types differ in that each has a different set of average execution times for each of the component algorithms, given a chunk of that type. For each type, we first randomly rank all algorithms, i.e., from the fastest to slowest. Next, we assign a per-chunk average execution time for each algorithm, according to its $rank$, as $(min\_duration + rank \cdot distance)$ seconds. At runtime, the execution time of each chunk of a particular type is chosen independently, and as a random number in an interval $[-range, +range]$ around the above average. Finally, types are assigned to chunks using a parameter *cluster size*, where a cluster is a sequence of consecutive chunks of the same type. Each cluster's type is selected randomly.

[6]Higher values of M gave similar results, hence are not shown.

Table 1. Default Parameters for Simulations.

# of total chunks	100,000
Cluster size	10,000
# of types	10
# of algorithm	10
min_duration	10 seconds
distance	10 seconds
range	1 second
dancing probability	1.0
following probability	0.9
propagation	randomwalk with 10 hops
# of nodes	1,000

Our main metrics are: (1) % chunks that end up being executed with their individual fastest component algorithms, and (2) running time for the entire data set, calculated as sum of execution times for all chunks across all clients.

Algorithm Variations: We evaluate four variants of HoneyAdapt, as defined by {memory vs. memoryless} × {greedy vs. sampled}. Recall that the original algorithm in Section 4.1 uses {memory, sampling}. In comparison, *memoryless* means that a client, that decides not to follow, chooses a next-algorithm *at random* from among all choices. *Greedy* means that a client, that decides to follow, selects as the next-algorithm *greedily*, by choosing an algorithm with the highest quality among all received advertisement messages within the last round only.

Figure 2(a) shows the percentage of choosing the best algorithm for a set of chunks. When *memoryless* strategy is used, there is a significant difference between *greedy* and *sampled*, while using the *memory* strategy shows no difference between *greedy* and *sampled*. Since {*memoryless, greedy*} strategy gives the best performance, we use it as a default in the rest of our experiments.

Propagation Methods: Figure 2(b) shows a comparison of two techniques to spread advertisement messages in the overlay - random walk (with a TTL=time-to-live) and a broadcast (with a TTL). Different plot points correspond to different values of TTL. The two algorithms define similar boundaries, hence we use a random walk from now on.

Cluster Size: Figure 3 varies the number of consecutive chunks of same type (cluster size) and plots the percentage difference between the actual running time and the optimal running time for the data set. The optimal running time is a lower bound on the runtime, since it is the total execution time assuming *each chunk* is executed with the best (i.e.,

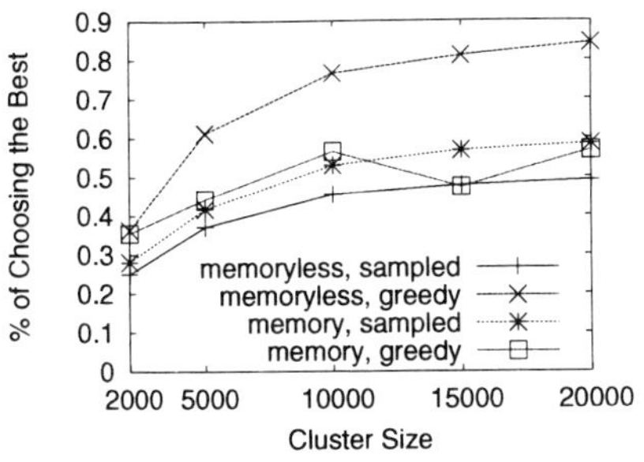

(a)

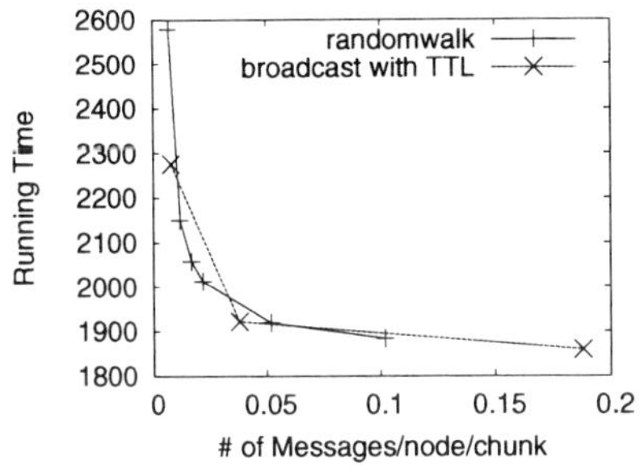

(b)

Figure 2. HoneyAdapt Variants. (a) Algorithm selection: {memory vs. memoryless} × {greedy vs. sampled}. (b) Message propagation: randomwalk vs. broadcast with TTL

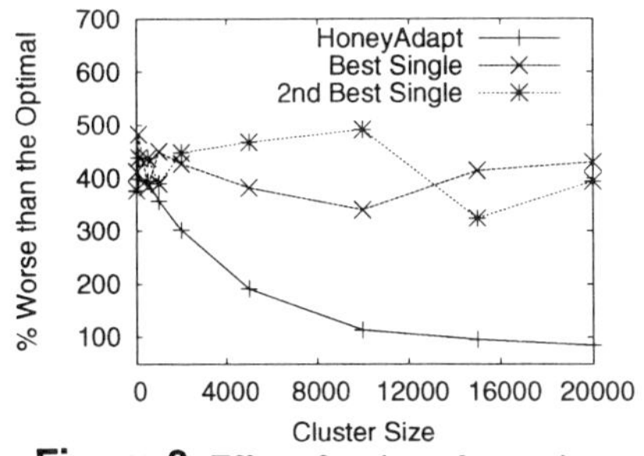

Figure 3. Effect of various cluster sizes.

fastest) algorithm for it[7]. For 1000 nodes in the system, notice that (1) HoneyAdapt does far better than using only one algorithm for all the chunks in the data set (we plot the best two algorithms for the data set), and (2) the performance of HoneyAdapt levels out after a cluster size. This indicates that with 1000 nodes, for cluster sizes over 10,000, HoneyAdapt is only about twice as worse as the optimal.

Scalability: Figure 4 shows the effect of varying the number of nodes from N =200 to 4,000. Cluster size is set as $10 \cdot N$, in order to allow nodes to adapt sufficiently well. In order to maintain a constant per-node bandwidth due to advertisements, these are spread using a random walk with TTL scaled up with N as $TTL = \frac{N}{500}$. The plot shows that the bandwidth and relative running time of HoneyAdapt both improve with N. Notice that the bandwidth is high for

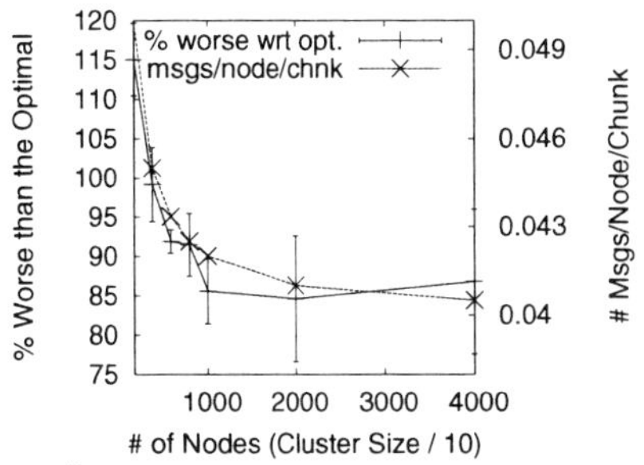

Figure 4. HoneyAdapt with various numbers of nodes.

low values of N because of the non-scalable cost at each node, of fetching each chunk from the master.

5.2. HoneySort Protocol and Experiments

We present HoneySort, HoneyAdapt's variant for the parallel sorting problem[8]. In this problem, the master initially partitions the input array into approximately equal sized chunks by using multiple pivots, so that it can concatenate the final results from all clients to produce the output. Each client has a choice of several sorting algorithms for each chunk. HoneySort differs from HoneyAdapt in three aspects: (1) It is *completely asynchronous and does not use the concept of rounds at all.* Thus, when a client p sorts a chunk, it fetches the next chunk immediately. (2) It uses an additional probabilistic parameter called randomization probability, denoted as pr. While picking an algorithm for the next chunk, a client chooses a random algorithm with probability pr, otherwise it uses the default following algorithm with pf ({memory, sampled}). (3) Advertisements are forwarded only to immediate overlay neighbors, and only the latest advertisement from each neighbor is used.

We deployed HoneySort on a Linux PC cluster with a TCP-based overlay, which is a complete graph by default (see Figure 7 for random overlays). Component algorithms are classical Quicksort and classical Insertion sort [7]; randomized quicksort and mergesort yield similar results. Datasets consist of 8 B integer element input arrays created via SortGen [10].

Figures 5(a) and (b) show running times respectively for completely random and pre-sorted input arrays. In each case, HoneySort is as fast as the best algorithm - Quicksort and Insertion sort respectively. Figure 6(a) shows data for heterogeneous arrays, where groups of *dynamic change unit* chunks are selected within the input array, and groups are alternately random and sorted. Thus, an x-axis value of 20 means the first 20 chunks are sorted, next 20 randomized, next 20 sorted, and so on. *The plot shows that HoneySort outperformed both Insertion sort and Quicksort for heterogeneous arrays.* Finally, Figure 7 shows that making the overlay random does not affect running time.

[7]Note that this optimal variant is difficult to implement in a blackbox manner, i.e., without knowing the nature of chunks.

[8]HoneyAdapt and HoneySort are *not* equivalent; the latter is a practical adaptation of the former.

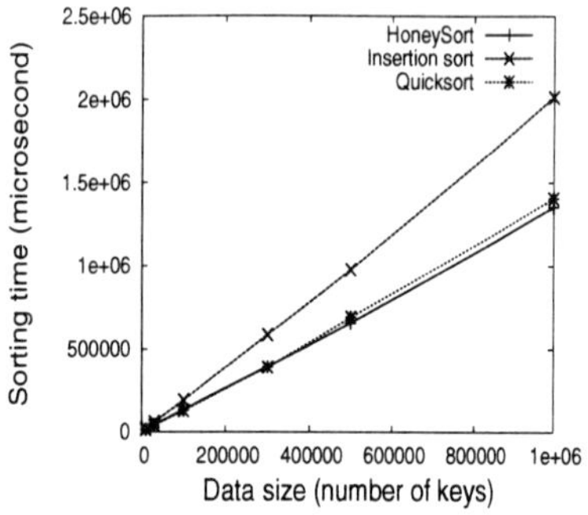

(a)

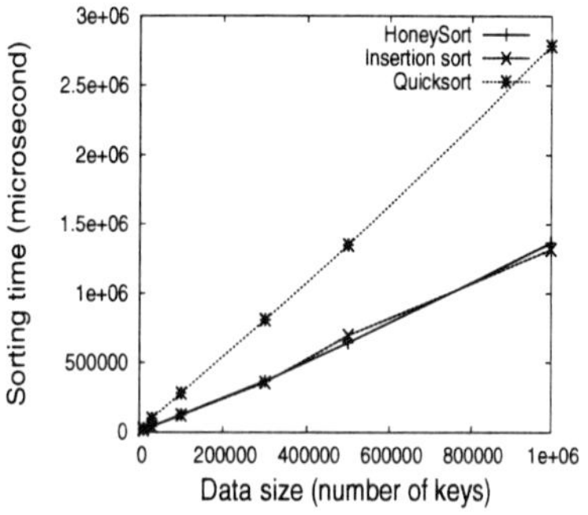

(b)

Figure 5. **HoneySort:** (a) On Random input. With chunk size approx. 1000 and with 6 client machines; (b) On Pre-sorted input. With chunk size approx. 1000 and with 6 client machines.

6. Summary

A new class of p2p algorithms (protocols) called "sequence protocols" can be derived systematically from multi-variable sequence equations, that are perhaps originally based on natural phenomena. Sequence protocols are self-adaptive, scalable, and fault-tolerant. They can be used to detect global triggers (Multiplicative Protocol) or enable clients in a large-scale Grid application to adapt at run-time to execute large data-sets more efficiently. HoneySort, an adaptive parallel sorting protocol, outperformed well-known algorithms Insertion Sort and Quicksort.

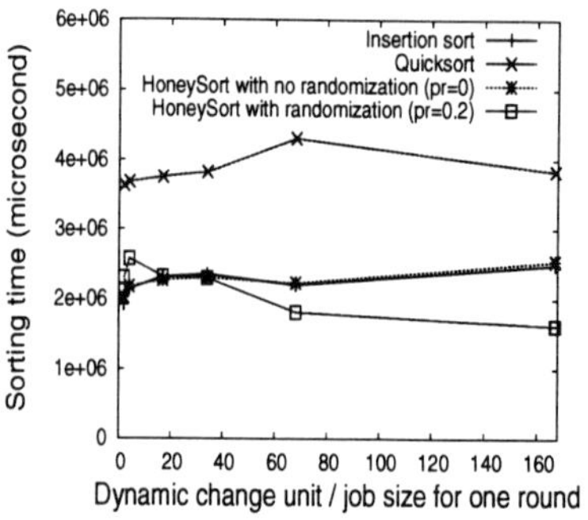

Figure 6. **HoneySort on heterogeneous arrays.** Input array has 1 million entries, chunk size approx. 3000 elements, 333 chunks total. With 6 client machines. Randomization prob. $pr = 0.2$. Groups of dynamic change unit (x-axis) chunks are alternately random and sorted.

Node Degree in Overlay	HoneySortRunning Time (ms)
2	945183
15	1086741
29	882870

Figure 7. **Effect of Client Overlay topology on HoneySort.** With 30 clients. Input array has 1 million entries, chunk size approx. 5000 elements, thus a total of 200 chunks.

References

[1] D. Angluin, J. Aspnes, et al, "Computation in networks of passively mobile finite-state sensors", *Proc. ACM PODC*, 2004, pp. 290-299.

[2] R. Arpaci-Dusseau, A. Arpaci-Dusseau, D. E. Culler et al, "Searching for the sorting record: experience with NOW-Sort", *Proc. SIGMETRICS Symp. Par. and Distbd. Tools*, 1998.

[3] O. Babaoglu et al, "Design patterns from biology for distributed computing", *Proc. Eur. Conf. Complex Sys.*, Nov. 2005.

[4] Arvind, "Bluespec: A language for hardware design, simulation, synthesis and verification", *Proc. MEMOCODE*, page 249, 2003.

[5] G. di Caro, M. Dorigo, "AntNet: Distributed Stigmergic Control for Communications Networks", *Journ. AI Res.*, 9, 1998, 317-365.

[6] R. Bhagwan et al, "Total Recall: System Support for Automated Availability Management", *Proc. Usenix NSDI*, 2004.

[7] T.H. Cormen, C.E. Leiserson, R.L. Rivest, C, Stein, *Introduction to Algorithms*, MIT Press, 2nd Ed., 2001.

[8] D. Kempe, A. Dobra, J Gehrke, "Gossip-based computation of aggregate information", *Proc. IEEE FOCS*, 2003, pp. 482-491.

[9] S. D'Silva, "Collective decision making in honeybees", Unpublished, http://www.msu.edu/user/dsilva/beepp2.ps

[10] J. Gray, Sorting Benchmark, http://research.microsoft.com/barc/SortBenchmark.

[11] I. Gupta, "On the design of distributed protocols from differential equations", *Proc. ACM PODC*, 2004, pp. 216-225.

[12] I. Gupta and Y. Jo, "On the Use of Sequences, Phase Changes, and HoneyBees For Designing Adaptive Distributed Systems", Technical Report UIUCDCS-R-2005-2523, UIUC, Feb. 2005.

[13] M. Herbster and M. K. Warmuth, "Tracking the Best Expert", *Proc. ICML*, 1995, pp. 286-294.

[14] M. Jelasity, R. Guerraoui, A.-M. Kermarrec and M. van Steen, "The Peer Sampling Service: Experimental Evaluation of Unstructured Gossip-Based Implementations", *Proc. Middleware*, 2004.

[15] T.G. Kurtz, *Approximation of population processes*, Reg. Conf. Series in Appl. Math., SIAM, 1981, ISBN 0-89871-169-X.

[16] B. T. Loo et al, "Implementing Declarative Overlays " *Proc. SOSP*, 2005, pp. 75-90.

[17] A. Medina et al, "BRITE: An Approach to Universal Topology Generation", *MASCOTS*, 2001, page 346.

[18] M. Merritt, G. Taubenfeld, "Computing with infinitely many processes", *Proc. DISC*, Springer LNCS 1914, 2000, 164-178.

[19] M. Mitzenmacher, "The power of two choices in randomized load balancing", *IEEE TPDS*, 12:10, Oct. 2001, 1094-1104.

[20] M. O. Rabin, "Randomized Byzantine generals", *Proc. FOCS*, 1983, pp. 403-409.

[21] T. Seeley, *The Wisdom of the Hive*, Harvard Univ. Press, Hardcover Ed., 1996.

[22] S. H. Strogatz, *Nonlinear Dynamics and Chaos: With Applications to Physics, Biology, Chemistry and Engineering*, Perseus Book Group, First Ed., 2001.

[23] A. Uresin and M. Dubois, "Parallel asynchronous algorithms for discrete data", *JACM*, 37:3, July 1990, 588 - 606.

[24] S. Voulgaris, D. Gavidia and M. van Steen, "CYCLON: Inexpensive membership management for unstructured P2P overlays", *JNSM*, 13:2, June 2005, 197-217.

[25] Closed forms for the logistic map, http://www.mathpages.com/home/kmath188.htm.

[26] Mute: Simple Anonymous File Sharing, http://mute-net.sourceforge.net.

Self-Organizing Replica Placement – A Case Study on Emergence

Klaus Herrmann
University of Stuttgart
Institute of Parallel and Distributed Systems (IPVS)
Universitätstr. 38, D-70569 Stuttgart
klaus.herrmann@acm.org

Abstract

The concept of self-organization is rapidly gaining importance in the area of distributed computing systems. However, we still lack the necessary means for engineering such system in a standardized way since their common properties are rather abstract, and the mechanisms from which self-organization emerges are too diverse. Therefore, it has become common practice to engineer computing systems by taking inspirations from well-known case studies of biological systems. However, the concepts found in such systems are in many cases only partially transferable to the domain of distributed computing systems since biological systems are subject to vastly different constraints compared to those in a computing system. Our contributions in this paper are the following: (i) *We present a case study of a self-organizing software system that originates from the domain of distributed computing systems. Therefore, its concepts can be exploited in other distributed computing systems much more directly.* (ii) *We give a detailed analysis of the emergent properties of the system and the mechanisms by which they arise.* (iii) *We generalize the mechanisms by which self-organization emerges in this system and present a catalog of design questions that may help engineers in creating arbitrary self-organizing systems.*

1 Introduction

In recent years, the research area revolving around *self-organization* and *emergence* in computer science has grown up from a niche discipline to a major topic. This is especially true in the area of distributed systems where the following factors contribute to this development:

1. Emerging technologies like wireless sensor networks [1] and mobile ad hoc networks [12] result in highly dynamic distributed systems that do not provide any clear-cut management interfaces. Such systems tend to collate spontaneously such that no single administrative authority can assume responsibility for their organization or management.

2. Large-scale distributed information systems like Content Delivery Networks [34], Peer-to-Peer systems [2], and Publish/Subscribe infrastructures [9] escape classical management attempts due to their sheer size. Dynamic usage patterns of clients lead to the inherent need for timely adaptation. However, centralized management is prohibitive as this would reduce scalability drastically.

3. The growing dynamics of a large variety of distributed computing systems raises the need for more autonomous systems that may adapt to changing working conditions with minimal manual intervention. In an industrial context, this leads to a reduction of management costs and to a more timely adaptation of the respective systems.

Case studies of self-organizing systems outside the computer science domain (e.g. from biology) show that a self-organizing system commonly consists of a group of relatively simple entities (e.g. ants, bees, or fish) that interact to achieve complex adaptive group behavior. From a technical viewpoint, lower-level components that are simple and homogeneous are easy to manufacture and maintain. Moreover, the redundancy inherent to such a system implies robustness as well as scalability. But how can the lower-level components of a system and their interactions be designed to produce the desired behavior of the overall technical system? Despite several years of intense research, the field of *self-organizing software systems* is still in its infancy, and we lack the necessary general means for developing self-organizing software systems in a reliable and dependable way.

Studies of individual biological systems have enabled technical solutions for specific problems. The most successful mechanism that has been transferred in this way is that

0-7695-2906-2/07 $25.00 © 2007 IEEE

of trail-laying ants which has been employed, in a number of technical applications [4, 3, 27, 23, 6, 5, 20, 29]

From such case studies, we may understand how specific natural systems work. However, transferring these mechanisms to distributed computing systems proves difficult. Biological systems solve very specific problems and their components are situated and interact in the physical world using air temperature, light signals, chemicals, etc. The difference in abstractions between the biological world and the domain of computing systems is rather large. Therefore, many biological case studies have only limited value for the engineering of concrete software systems.

In this paper, we present the first case study of a self-organizing software system that is not based on biological models. This system, called *Ad hoc Service Grid* (ASG) [14, 15, 16], originates from the domain of distributed computing systems and is situated in the area of Ambient Intelligence. It provides mechanisms for the self-organized replication and placement of services in such an environment. Our emphasis in this study lies on the analysis of the emergent effects perceivable in the ASG. We show how a small set of local rules, executed by service replicas, results in cost-efficient and adaptive global replica placement patterns. It turns out that these simple rules lead to qualitatively different interaction schemes at a higher level of abstraction. Based on the description of the low-level algorithm, we will derive and investigate the mechanisms that lead to these higher-level emergent effects. Furthermore, we generalize the mechanisms that contribute to the emergence in our system, and we propose a catalog of general design questions that can help engineers in dividing the complex problem of creating a self-organizing software system into different aspects.

The rest of this paper is structured as follows: In the next section, we discuss some related work. In Section 3, we introduce the ASG model, including a discussion of the algorithm for self-organized replica placement. Subsequently, we analyze the high-level behavior that can be observed in the overall system. In Section 4, we investigate the relation between the lower-level actions taken by replicas and the emergent higher-level behavior of the overall system. We reveal hidden interactions between replicas and give a detailed discussion of the mechanisms that take effect in the emergence of the higher-level behavior. In Section 5, we generalize these qualitatively new concepts and present the resulting catalog of design questions. We present our conclusions in Section 6.

2 Related Work

The case studies that are at the basis of self-organizing software systems research are conducted by biologists, physicists, and mathematicians. They reveal the mechanisms by which certain natural systems achieve self-organized behavior. This includes, for example, pattern formation in ant colonies [30], swarm flocking behavior [33], thermo regulation in honey bee nests [22], the synchronized flashing of fireflies [31], and the aggregation behavior of slime molds [25], just to name a few. These studies investigate the inherent feedback mechanisms and diverse communication patterns based on light emission, air temperature fluctuation, pheromones, and the like, establishing abstract models of the respective natural systems.

These models inspire computer scientists to apply similar mechanisms, for example, to radio frequency allocation [32], computer security [10], network routing [4], document clustering [28], and optimization problems [5]. Most of these solutions remain rather isolated, representing approaches to very specific problems in computer science.

Attempts to categorize the plethora of nature-inspired mechanisms and to make them accessible as a kind of self-organization tool box have been made by Parunak [21] and, more recently, by Mamei et al. [24]. They try to create a taxonomy that allows an assessment of arbitrary computer science problems such that the most fitting method may be picked to solve them. This is a qualitatively new step as it proposes a more general attempt to engineering self-organizing software systems. Albeit, it is still a bottom-up approach that relies on existing systems as example cases.

Top-down approaches are rare. For example, Gershenson proposes a general methodology for designing and controlling self-organizing systems that introduces mechanisms for "reducing friction" and "promoting synergy" between a system's elements [11]. Such concepts are valuable since they further our general understanding of self-organization. However, it is quite hard to translate them into more tangible ones related to a concrete problem. Wright et al. present a measure of self-organization and propose to use this measure in order to let a genetic algorithm evolve a given system towards self-organization [35]. However, the validity of this modeling approach has only been shown for abstract scenarios. Again, this approach provides additional insight, but it is hard to apply it in practice.

The work presented in this paper is a part of the bottom-up strand. However, the system we investigate originates from the domain of computing systems. Therefore, the concepts do not need to be transformed in any way and are much more easily applicable to other computing systems. Moreover, we do not simply present yet another design pattern. Instead, we attempt to generalize a number of important aspects found in the design of the presented system. These aspects are meant to support a top-down engineering methodology by separating the monolithic view into sub-views that may greatly facilitate the engineering process. Thus, our hope is to close the gap between bottom-up and top-down approaches a little bit from both ends.

3 Ad hoc Service Grid

In recent years, the vision of *Ambient Intelligence* (AmI) [7] has produced considerable research efforts. The main idea of AmI is that mobile users may wirelessly access services (anywhere and anytime) that support them in their daily activities without putting any administrative burden on them. One essential building block of AmI are infrastructures that allow local access to local, facility-specific services. To enable services that enhance the user's interaction with his current environment, the Ad hoc Service Grid enriches the physical surrounding of the user (e.g. at shopping malls, construction sites, and trade fares) with dedicated computing resources that enable service provisioning. One example scenario is a shopping mall that offers *ambient services* to customers, enabling them to navigate through the mall, find certain products quickly, and optimize the contents of their shopping cart, for example, according to the overall price or quality. Such services pertain to the local environment of the user and are provided by the local ASG resources that have been distributed over the shopping mall.

The Ad hoc Service Grid infrastructure [16] is easy to setup, flexibly scalable, and requires minimal administrative effort. The easy setup and the flexibility at the networking layer is achieved by adopting *Mobile Ad hoc Networking* (MANET) technology. To minimize the administration overhead, we have created a software layer that we call *ASG Serviceware*. This software has the task of providing basic support for running services within an ASG in a self-organized fashion. That is, all aspects of executing services and adapting to changing user demands shall be managed autonomously by this software.

In the following sections, we briefly describe the relevant aspects of the existing ASG system in preparation of our analysis of its emergent properties. A very detailed description of the ASG including the full experimental setup and many quantitative evaluations can be found in [15].

3.1 System Model

The ASG is based on the concept of *Service Cubes* (also called *Cubes* or *nodes* hereafter). A Service Cube is a PC-class computer dedicated to service provisioning that provides ad hoc networking capabilities and computing power. It has no peripheral devices (display or input devices), relies on a permanent power supply, and is equipped with a wireless network interface. In order to cover a given location with Ambient Services, a number of these Service Cubes is distributed over the location such that they can spontaneously set up a wireless multi-hop network connecting all Cubes. Thanks to the concept of self-contained Service Cubes, an ASG network has a highly modular structure: New modules (Cubes) can be added and existing ones can be removed or repositioned to re-shape the network in an ad hoc fashion. This provides a flexible way of scaling an ASG to an appropriate size and allows for a quick and easy setup. No extensive planning and no construction work is necessary to cover a location in this way. Clients that wish to use ASG services, enter the facility and automatically become a part of the ad hoc network since their mobile device connects to any of the Cubes in an ad hoc fashion. We assume the existence of some technology that allows for a seamless hand-over such that clients may move freely through the ASG network and always stay connected to at least one Cube.

3.2 Self-Organized Replica Placement

An ASG network may take an arbitrary shape and may consist of different numbers of Cubes. Furthermore, the network shape and the number of Cubes as well as the volume of clients, their location, and their demand may vary over time. Temporary network partitions may occur regularly and have profound influence on service availability. In addition to these dynamics, the transmission capacity of the wireless medium is the most scarce resource in such a system. In order to cope with the dynamics and to relieve the network from unnecessary traffic, the ASG Serviceware employs a mechanism for the dynamic replication and placement of services inside an ASG network.

To implement this mechanism, we have developed a purely decentralized service replication and placement algorithm [16, 15]. A service may consist of one or more replicas, and each of these replicas runs the algorithm locally in regular intervals to find a better position within the ASG network. A group of replicas that repeatedly executes the algorithm, distributes itself within an ASG network such that the global communication costs are minimized.

In this case study, we analyze this emergence of global, cost-efficient placement patterns from the local actions of the individual replicas. Despite the fact that there is no global process or knowledge in the system, and even though replicas do not communicate in order to coordinate their placement decisions, global coordination is achieved. The whole system of replicas converges to a stable, low-cost placement that covers the entire network. Moreover, if significant changes occur due to the afore-mentioned dynamics, the distributed algorithm adapts the global placement accordingly to re-establish a cost-efficient placement.

However, as we will see in the following description of the algorithm, the lower-level actions taken by replicas do not directly imply this higher-level behavior of the overall system. How does an adaptive global placement emerge? What are the hidden mechanisms that lead to these patterns?

3.3 Distributed Placement Algorithm

The placement algorithm allows a replica to *migrate* from one node to another, to *replicate* (clone itself and subsequently migrate both clones), or to *dissolve* (remove itself from the system). The immediate goals of every individual replica are to:

1. Maintain a balance between the flows of requests coming in via the set of neighbor nodes. This is achieved using migrations.
2. Avoid that requests have to travel large distances between their sender (client) and the receiving service replica. This is done by creating new replicas.
3. Avoid idle replicas. This is done by dissolving idle replicas.

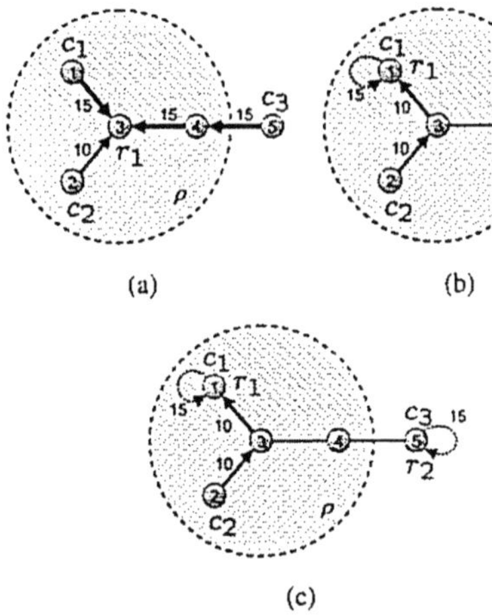

Figure 1. Using the replication radius to reduce the distance spanned by requests.

Let us assume that the ASG network is a graph $G = (N, E)$ and that a replica r_1 is running on node $v \in N$. v has a set of neighbor nodes N_v that contains all nodes in N that are direct neighbors of v. All requests received by r_1 are routed to v via some node in N_v. A series of requests coming in via a neighbor is also called a *message flow*. Such a message flow is called *dominant* iff its volume (number of messages per time unit) is greater than the accumulated volume of all remaining message flows entering v. A flow is called *significant* if there is no single incoming flow with a greater volume. We also call the respective neighbor nodes *dominant* or *significant* respectively. Each instance of the algorithm constantly inspects the volumes of the incoming message flows of its replica and periodically takes a local adaptation decision based on this observation. The algorithm has three rules for the possible adaptations:

1. **Idle Rule:** A replica dissolves (is removed) if it receives less then α requests in a time interval m.
2. **Replication Rule:** A replica replicates to neighbor nodes u and w, if it receives a significant message flow via u that consists of requests with an average path length of more than ρ hops. An example is depicted in Figure 1(a) where v is node 3, u is node 4, and $\rho = 1$. w is either set to the dominant node among the remaining neighbors (node 1 in Figure 1(a)), or the second replica stays at its current node if such a dominant node does not exist. ρ is called the *replication radius*.
3. **Migration Rule:** A replica migrates to a neighbor node u, if the message flow that is coming in via u is dominant. Figure 2(a) shows an example where r_1 is running on node 3, and node 4 is the dominant node.

The placement algorithm invokes these rules in the order in which they are listed above. In each run, the first rule whose condition triggers is executed, and the remaining ones are skipped. When a new service is installed on an ASG, it starts with a single, initial replica that is put on an arbitrary node.

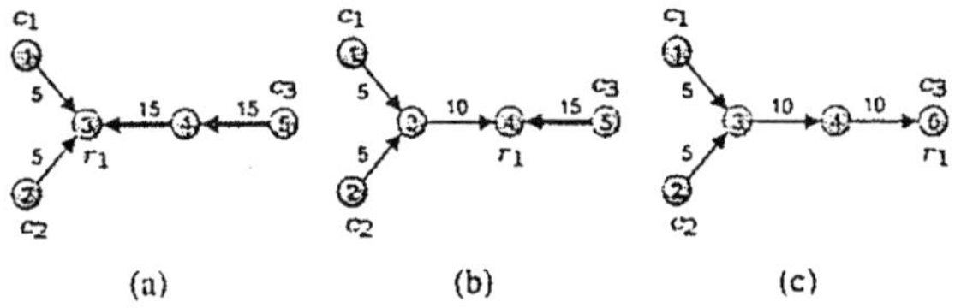

Figure 2. Exploiting dominating flows for incremental cost optimization.

Of course, the success of the above adaptations is heavily depending on the clients' choice of replicas. Our basic assumption is that clients always choose the replica that is closest to them in terms of network hops. This is enforced by the distributed ASG lookup service [17]. The instances of this service are distributed in the ASG network such that each client has at least one instance in its one-hop neighborhood. A query to this instance yields the service replica that is closest to the client's current position.

3.4 Higher-Level Behavior

Our main goal is to use as little wireless bandwidth as possible since this is regarded as being the most critical resource in the ASG. Therefore, we evaluate the ASG system based on the communication costs. These costs are defined as the *number of message transmissions per time unit* that is necessary to serve all client requests. If a client sends a request to a service that is n network hops away, this results in n transmissions of the request message.

The first global observation that can be made when the system is running is that the overall communication costs are successively reduced. Figure 3 shows how the overall costs produced in the system per simulation tick decreases over time to less than 50% of the initial value. The algorithm is run every 10.000 ticks, and with each run, there is a notable drop in costs. Additionally, every 50.000 ticks, the client request patterns are changed. This is done by recomputing the probabilities with which a client that is connected to a node w sends a request for the service. Due to the continuous attempt to maintain a good placement, the initial increase in cost that is caused by such perturbations is countered, and the cost reduction continues.

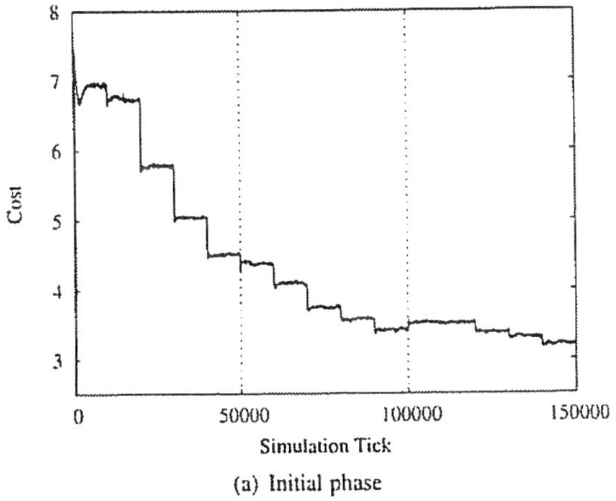

Figure 3. Communication cost optimization.

Figure 4 depicts an example of an ASG network that runs a service (nodes that host replicas are black). The figure shows how the replicas spread out to cover the network. Changes in client request patterns are indicated by marks in the upper left corner of the snapshots. Note how the replicas adapt quickly (within 3 iterations of the placement algorithm) to changes and retain a stable placement until the next perturbation occurs. After the third perturbation, stability is maintained until perturbation number eight is applied to the system.

4 Emergence of a Global Replica Placement

The quick reduction of the costs and the adaptiveness displayed by the higher-level behavior of our system are, of course, the result of the actions collectively taken by the replicas. However, the transition from the replicas' actions at the lower level to the global behavior at the higher level (Figure 5) is not obvious at first glance. How are replicas connected to each other? How do they interact to achieve global coordination? After all, the actions taken by replicas appear to be rather self-centered and isolated from each other. Why do migrations towards dominant neighbors and replications towards long request paths actually generate a stable, cost-efficient, adaptive, global replica placement?

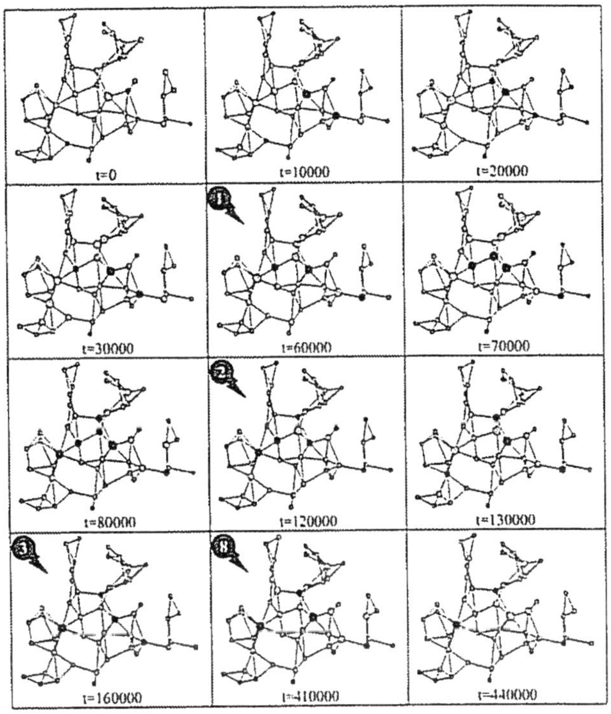

Figure 4. Placement snapshots.

To fully understand how this transition occurs, we have to consider concepts that are rather different from those used to describe the placement algorithm and that fill the gap between the two levels depicted in Figure 5. In this section, we will investigate what happens *behind the scenes* through the interactions taking place in the system. We will show that feedback plays a vital role in the emergence of the global behavior and how a certain form of competition among replicas controls their global distribution.

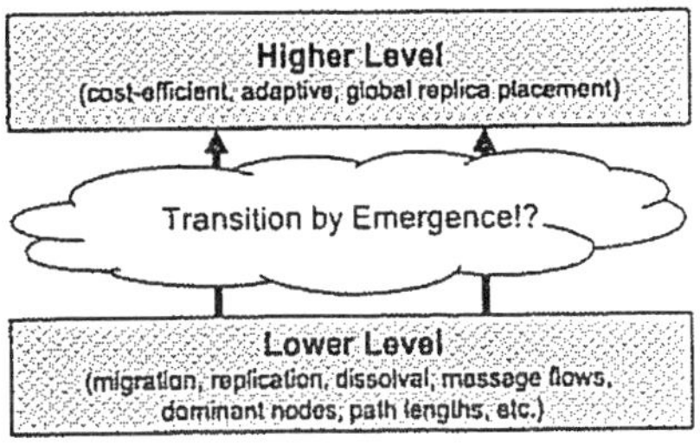

Figure 5. Emergence: The big picture.

4.1 Migration – Basic Feedback Process

It is intuitively clear that the algorithm's migration rule pushes a replica towards the bulk of clients that send requests to it. In combination with the fact that the ASG lookup service always tries to assign the closest replica to any client, this creates a feedback loop. This whole feedback process has three phases that are depicted in Figure 6: Let us assume that a given ASG network (denoted by the oval) is served by two replicas r_1 and r_2. Initially, r_1 is in a state of imbalance since it receives client requests (indicated by the arrows) from a single direction (Figure 6(a)). The migration rule will force r_1 to migrate towards this direction. By this movement, r_1 suddenly becomes the closest replica for a set of clients that sent their requests to r_2 before (Figure 6(b)). Thus, by moving towards its clients, r_1 attracts more clients which, in turn, pulls r_1 even more towards the direction of client requests. This is a positive feedback effect which takes place in the attraction phase and drives the system towards a new configuration quickly. After a while, r_1 enters the region where its clients are positioned and the requests start coming in via more than one neighbor node. This decreases the attraction until the dominant message flow depletes and the motion of r_1 stops. This *depletion phase* (Figure 6(b)) introduces a negative feedback process that has a strong stabilizing effect as it slows down r_1 quickly. In Figure 6(c), the system has reached an equilibrium state where no distinct *force* is applied to either of the replicas. Moreover, the average length of the request paths, and therefore the costs, are minimal when our example system is in this state. In the *fluctuation phase*, the system stays in this state until notable changes or fluctuations occur in the request patterns of clients that lead to an imbalance again and restart the adaptation process.

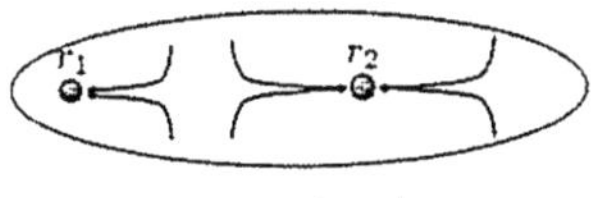

(a) Attraction phase

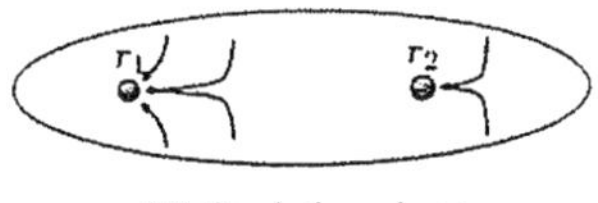

(b) Depletion phase

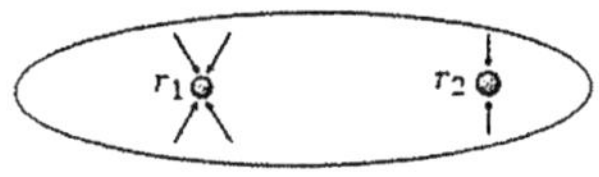

(c) Fluctuation phase

Figure 6. The three feedback phases.

Figure 6 clearly shows how replicas are coupled and interact indirectly via message flows. Each message flow is consumed by some replica, and each time a flow is redirected to a different replica (due to changes in the distance to clients), another replica potentially enters a state of imbalance since it looses this very message flow. In our example, r_2 is thrown out of its equilibrium state as r_1 attracts a portion of its clients 6(a). Therefore, r_2 is also forced to migrate in order to regain its equilibrium (Figure 6(c)).

In general, the migration rule applies a force to the system that leads to an automatic adaptation each time a deviation from the equilibrium state occurs.

4.2 Replication and Removal – Adapting to the Network

The replication rule applies a different kind of force to the system of replicas: The replication radius ρ leads to the creation of replicas until each replica covers a portion of the network with a radius of about ρ. Therefore, this rule leads to an adaptation of the number of running replicas to the size of the network. If the network grows and clients start sending requests from the new regions, the system automatically creates new replicas to cover them. This ensures that client requests travel at most ρ hops on average, which, in turn, controls the overall communication costs.

The idle rule is the counterpart of the replication rule in the overall mechanism for the control of the number of running replicas. If the number of clients diminishes, then less requests are issued throughout the network. Therefore, less replicas have to be maintained in order to serve these requests. Some replicas, for which the number of requests falls below the threshold of α, will then be automatically removed, and their clients start using other replicas. Due to the indirect coupling between the replicas, this may lead to migrations among the remaining replicas in order to compensate the possible imbalance caused by this change. The idle rule may also be viewed as a sort of *garbage collection* as it constantly removes unused replicas.

4.3 Adaptive Cell Structuring

Due to the the fact that clients always use the closest replica, the collective adaptation process of all replicas creates a global pattern consisting of the cells of a Voronoi decomposition. In each cell, a replica serves all requests being issued inside the cell. The replica placement algorithm replicates and migrates the set of replicas such that a stable configuration of Voronoi cells is created.

Figure 7 depicts how the cell structure changes if the replica configuration is changed. For this simplified example, we assume that the plane is densely populated with nodes and that client requests are issued uniformly from all nodes. Figure 7(a) shows a stable Voronoi cell pattern with three replicas: Each replica is placed at about the center of its cell and, thus, the forces applied by client requests are

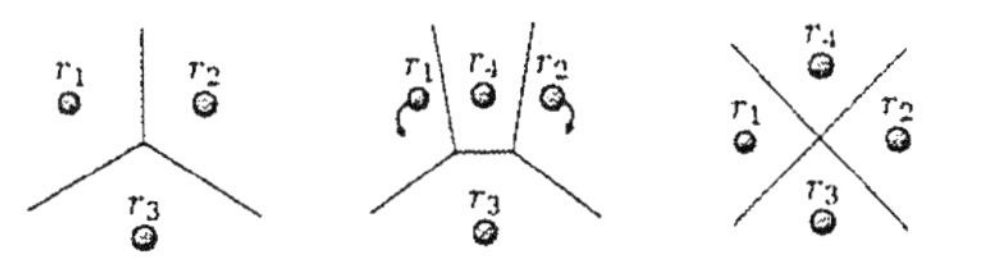

(a) Stable (b) Disturbance (c) Re-stabilized

Figure 7. Adaptation of the cell structure.

about the same in all directions. Let us assume that, due to some disturbance in the request patterns, a new replica r_4 is created between r_1 and r_2. The resulting Voronoi diagram is shown in Figure 7(b). This disturbance changes the cells of r_1 and r_2 such that they are close to the borders of their cells. Since the requests coming from the upper part of the plane are now redirected to r_4, they start receiving an unbalanced flow of requests. According to the migration rule, r_1 and r_2 are forced to move to a position where the flows are in balance again. The resulting four-cell setup is depicted in Figure 7(c). Thus, a reconfiguration on a global scale is caused by a local disturbance without any direct communication taking place between the replicas.

4.4 Adaptation Cycle and Attractors

As we have seen in the qualitative analysis of the hidden effects of our simple replica placement algorithm, it introduces an *adaptation cycle*. It implicitly defines the notion of a stable state as follows:

Definition 1 (Stability Condition) *The state of the overall replica system is stable iff*

1. *the incoming message flows of all replicas are balanced (i.e. there is no dominant node),*
2. *no replica serves requests that average a path length of more than p hops, and*
3. *each replica receives a sufficient amount of requests per time unit.*

In such a state, non of the adaptation rules is triggered and, thus, the current replica placement is retained.

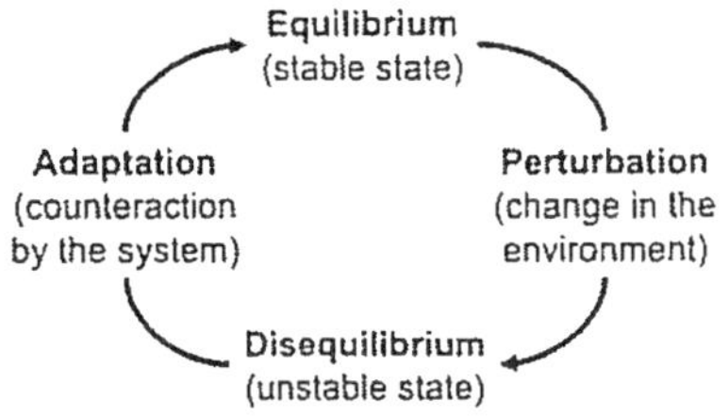

Figure 8. Adaptation cycle.

Perturbations due to changes in client behavior or network topology can push the system into an unstable state in which the stability condition is violated. This automatically leads to adaptations through the respective rules of the distributed placement algorithm until a new stable state is reached (cf. Figure 8). This resembles a classical *control loop* that counters every deviation from the prescribed *set point*. However, in our case, the set point is no particular placement or any geometrical characteristics thereof, as one may expect. Instead, the set point is *stability*. In complex systems terminology, this set point is also called an *attractor* [26]: Let α be a replica placement and let β a state of the environment that the replica system has to adapt to (client request pattern, network topology etc.). Among the set S of all possible system states (α, β), there is a subset $S_{stab} \subseteq S$ that satisfies the stability conditions:

$$S_{stab} = \{(\alpha, \beta) \in S \mid \alpha \text{ fulfills Def. 1 under } \beta\}$$

Through the adaptation cycle, the replica system is constantly attracted to some placement α^i such that $(\alpha^i, \beta^j) \in S_{stab}$ for the current environment state β^j. If, through some sort of dynamic change, the environment enters a different state β^k such that $(\alpha^i, \beta^k) \notin S_{stab}$, then this instability automatically triggers an adaptation and pushes the replica system into a new state α^l such that $(\alpha^l, \beta^k) \in S_{stab}$ holds again until the next environmental change.

But how is stability related to our original goal of reducing the communication cost in the overall system? For each individual replica, a stable state implies that the local costs cannot be immediately reduced by an adaptation. As indicated in Figure 2, a migration towards a dominant node has a potential for reducing the local costs since the sum of request flows received from the remaining nodes ($\mathcal{F}_{rest}$) may have to travel one hop further while the hop count of the dominant flow ($\mathcal{F}_{dom}$) is reduced by one. Due to the definition of dominance, we have $\mathcal{F}_{rest} < \mathcal{F}_{dom}$, and the number of transmissions per time unit required to transport the client requests to the migrated replica is reduced by $\mathcal{F}_{dom} - \mathcal{F}_{rest} > 0$. In a stable state, a replica does not have this immediate possibility of reducing the local costs. Thus, the costs are the lowest that are currently achievable by the replica. There may well be possible migrations that eventually lead to a reduction. However, the replica may only speculate about them. Therefore, the stable state represents a local cost minimum for this particular replica. The communication cost in the overall system is the sum of all local costs. Thus, the overall costs are at a local minimum if all replicas are in a stable state. In other words, the system is constantly forced into some cost-efficient attractor. This attractor state may not represent the overall global cost minimum, but this is the best we can achieve with a purely distributed heuristic approach in a dynamic environment.

5 Generalization of the Results

In the preceding qualitative analysis of our simple replica placement system, we have shown that its complex high-level behavior is a consequence of the interactions among the individual replicas. Replicas are coupled and interact indirectly through the message flows that are an attribute of their environment (network topology and client behavior). This interaction is much more complex than is indicated by the rather simple placement algorithm. It can be explained using concepts like feedback, adaptive cells, adaptation cycles, and attractors that fill the *semantic gap* (depicted in Figure 5) between the lower-level actions and the higher-level behavior.

This case study has its own value in the same sense as studies of biological systems do: It may inspire new technological solutions that solve related problems with similar self-organization approaches. However, the concepts and technologies employed here are much closer to those of systems that may potentially exploit them in different information technology contexts.

Beyond being a blueprint, our system can be valuable with respect to another important question: *Can this study give some indications as to how such a self-organizing system may be purposefully engineered in general?*

We cannot derive a complete engineering process. However, the self-organized replica placement system has some characteristics and features that may be applicable in a more general context. In the following, we analyze these general features and pose some questions that should be answered by engineers in order to create similar characteristics in other systems. The aim is to divide the immensely complex task of creating self-organization into a number of interrelated subtasks that a software engineer may tackle individually. This reduces the required effort and may lead to a faster decision about the applicable mechanisms, or it may also lead to the early recognition of the fact that a given problem does not lend itself for a self-organizing solution at all. Moreover, the concepts that should be applied in the design and the vocabulary that is necessary to argue about them differ dramatically from those used in conventional software engineering. The following *catalog of design questions* and the concrete example of the ASG system should help in adjusting to this new language.

- **Self-organization and adaptation:** The self-organization process described in this paper has the inherent goal of adapting the system to changing external conditions in order to preserve its cost-efficiency. There may be other self-organization processes that do not necessarily aim at adaptation. However, we think that in the area of self-organizing software systems, adaptation is always an inherent requirement.
  - *What is the subject of adaptation in the system?*
- **Adaptation and optimization:** Adaptation may be defined as a continuous optimization process. An adaptive system recognizes any shift towards suboptimal states (usually caused by a changing environment) and counters this shift by optimizing the system's state to fit the new environment. This form of optimization is an online task. It has to be repeated constantly, and it has to lead to some solution in a timely fashion in order for the system to stay operational. In this sense, it is beneficial to think of the nature of this adaptation process at the beginning of any design phase.
  - *What is the optimization criterion?*
  - *Which mechanisms can be applied in order to adapt (optimize) the system?*
  - *Is the optimization task very complex?*
- **Optimization vs. acceptability:** The nature of the systems that we regard is such that an optimal solution will be achievable only in rare cases. This is due to the fact that we deal with decentralized online optimization. Realistically, the best we can hope for is an *acceptable* solution. This may represent a problem for some systems whose survival depends on their optimal configuration.
  - *Is an acceptable solution good enough for a given system?*
- **Local and global optimization:** One of the beneficial features that is commonly assigned to self-organizing systems is their decentralization [19, 18]: The actors in a self-organizing system act locally, and their view is restricted to their immediate neighborhood. In terms of optimization, this imposes a constraint upon the system: A acceptable (low-cost) global configuration must be achievable through a combination of locally acceptable solutions. Or, more generally, a mapping of the local to the global acceptability criterion must exist. In our system, every replica tries to reach an equilibrium state with respect to the incoming message flows. As we have shown in Section 4.4, the combination of local equilibriums maps to a low-cost global state.
  - *Is there a mapping of the local to the global acceptability criterion in the given system?*
- **Coupling (interaction) via the subject of work:** A key to the global coordination of any decentralized adaptation process can be a local coupling of the actors via the very subject of the adaptation. In the ASG, there is no global coordination involved. Replicas indirectly coordinate their respective locations with their

local neighbors (closest fellow replicas) by influencing each other's message flows (cf. Sections 4.1 and 4.3). At the same time, these message flows are subject to the optimization task. This general principle is called *Stigmergy* [13]. In the same way as termites coordinate their nest-building actions via the structures they build, replicas coordinate their placement activities via the message flows that they try to balance. Discovering and exploiting such a coupling can greatly simplify the design of a concrete self-organization mechanism. It should be noted, that some form of indirect interaction exists in most cases, and it is important to understand its character in any case.

  - *Is stigmergic coordination possible in the given system?*
  - *What is the subject of optimization, and are the actors coupled by it?*

- **Feedback process:** The simple feedback process in the system evolves from *(i)* replicas moving towards the clients that send requests and *(ii)* the clients always choosing the closest replica. This process involves positive feedback that leads to a fast convergence to a cost-efficient state as well as negative feedback that stabilizes the system when such a state is approached. This mechanism is the driving force behind the concept of self-organized replica placement. Similar processes are common in natural self-organizing systems. Thus, it can be beneficial to look at a problem that requires self-organization from the feedback perspective.

  - *Is there some feedback mechanism inherent to the problem, or*
  - *can one be designed for the given system?*

- **Stable attractors:** The system must have attractor states that are approached by virtue of the self-organization algorithm. Moreover, these attractors must be cost-efficient with respect to the cost function of the system, and they must be stable in the sense that the attractiveness of such a state must not disappear as a consequence of the system entering it. This would result in a system that constantly approaches good states without ever reaching one. Metaphorically speaking, the resulting system should behave like a ball that is constantly rolling down-slope towards low-cost states by itself with respect to the acceptability criterion. The answers to the following questions are not obvious in most cases. Moreover, they heavily depend on the definition of the system as well as on the criterion for optimality or acceptability.

  - *Does the given system have stable attractors?*
  - *How can these be approached locally through the adaptations of the actors within the system?*

6 Conclusions

The current approach to engineering self-organizing software systems is heavily relying on copying mechanisms found in biological systems. While this can be fruitful, we argue that computer science should start developing its own core concepts for this task. In this paper, we have presented the first case study of an original self-organizing distributed software system that employs concepts originating from the distributed system domain.

We have investigated the mechanisms and concepts that lead to the emergence of a globally coordinated replica placement from simple and local actions executed by individual service replicas. These concepts fill the gap that exists between the lower-level actions of the components in the system and the higher-level complex behavior of the overall system. Like any existing case study, this one can be used as a blueprint for the design of similar concepts in comparable systems. Subsequently, we have generalized the concepts leading to the emergence in the ASG system in an attempt to present more general guidelines for engineering self-organizing software systems. Our catalog of design questions helps in structuring the design process and supports the engineer in dealing with the central problems involved with achieving self-organization. It serves as a conceptual framework rather than a formal engineering process. However, it divides the complex task of engineering a self-organizing software systems into subtasks that are much more easily handleable. Moreover, it helps in deciding if a given problem can be solved by a self-organizing software system.

References

[1] I. F. Akyildiz, W. Su, Y. Sankarasubramaniam, and E. Cayirci. Wireless Sensor Networks: A Survey. *Computer Networks*, 38(4):393–422, 2002.

[2] S. Androutsellis-Theotokis and D. Spinellis. A Survey of Peer-to-Peer Content Distribution Technologies. *ACM Comput. Surv.*, 36(4):335–371, 2004.

[3] L. Carrillo, J. L. Marzo, P. Vilà, and C. A. Mantilla. MAntS-Hoc: A Multi-Agent Ant-Based System for Routing in Mobile Ad Hoc Networks. In *Proceedings of Setè Congrés Català d'Intelligència Artificial (CCIA'2004)*, pages 285–292, 2004.

[4] G. Di Caro and M. Dorigo. Ant Colonies for Adaptive Routing in Packet-Switched Communications Networks. In Eiben et al. [8], pages 673–682.

[5] M. Dorigo, G. D. Caro, and L. M. Gambardella. The Ant Colony Optimization Meta-Heuristic. *Artificial Life*, 5(2):137–172, 1999.

[6] M. Dorigo, G. D. Caro, and M. Sampels, editors. *Ant Algorithms, Third International Workshop, ANTS 2002, Brussels, Belgium, September 12-14, 2002. Proceedings*, volume 2463 of *Lecture Notes in Computer Science*. Springer-Verlag, 2002.

[7] K. Ducatel, M. Bogdanowicz, F. Scapolo, J. Leijten, and J.-C. Burgelman. Scenarios for Ambient Intelligence in 2010. Technical Report, The IST Advisory Group (ISTAG), 2001.

[8] A. E. Eiben, T. Bäck, M. Schoenauer, and H.-P. Schwefel, editors. *Parallel Problem Solving from Nature – PPSN V, 5th International Conference, Amsterdam, The Netherlands, September 27-30, 1998, Proceedings*, volume 1498 of *Lecture Notes in Computer Science*. Springer-Verlag, 1998.

[9] P. T. Eugster, P. A. Felber, R. Guerraoui, and A.-M. Kermarrec. The Many Faces of Publish/Subscribe. *ACM Comput. Surv.*, 35(2):114–131, 2003.

[10] S. Forrest, S. A. Hofmeyr, and A. Somayaji. Computer Immunology. *Communications of the ACM*, 40(10):88–96, Oct. 1997.

[11] C. Gershenson. A General Methodology for Designing Self-Organizing Systems. Technical Report 2005-05, ECCO, May 2005.

[12] S. Giordano. *Mobile Ad hoc Networks*, pages 325–346. John Wiley & Sons, Inc., New York, NY, USA, 2002.

[13] P. P. Grassé. La reconstruction du nid et les coordinations inter-individuelles chez *Bellicositermes natalensis* et *Cubitermes sp.* La théorie de la stigmergie: Essai d'interpretation des termites constructeurs. *Insectes Sociaux*, 6:41–83, 1959.

[14] K. Herrmann. Ad hoc Service Grid – Self-Organizing Distribution of Ambient Services. Report PTB-IT-13, Physikalische Technische Bundesanstalt, Wirtschaftsverlag NW, Verlag für neue Wissenschaft GmbH, Mar. 2006. (ISBN 3-86509-509-7).

[15] K. Herrmann. *Self-Organizing Infrastructures for Ambient Services*. Phd thesis, Berlin University of Technology, July 2006.

[16] K. Herrmann, K. Geihs, and G. Mühl. Ad hoc Service Grid – A Self-Organizing Infrastructure for Mobile Commerce. In *Proceedings of the IFIP TC8 Working Conference on Mobile Information Systems (MOBIS 2004)*. IFIP – International Federation for Information Processing, Springer-Verlag, Sept. 2004.

[17] K. Herrmann, G. Mühl, and M. A. Jaeger. A Self-Organizing Lookup Service for Dynamic Ambient Services. In *25th International Conference on Distributed Computing Systems (ICDCS 2005)*, pages 707–716, Piscataway, NJ, USA, June 2005. IEEE Computer Society Press.

[18] K. Herrmann, M. Werner, and G. Mühl. A Methodology for Classifying Self-Organizing Software Systems. *International Transactions on Systems Science and Applications*, 2(1):41–50, Sept. 2006.

[19] F. Heylighen and C. Gershenson. The Meaning of Self-organization in Computing. *IEEE Intelligent Systems*, 18(4):72–75, July – Aug. 2003.

[20] K. M. Hoe, W. K. Lai, and T. S. Tai. Homogeneous Ants for Web Document Similarity Modeling and Categorization. In *Proceedings of the Third International Workshop on Ant Algorithms (ANTS 2002)*, Sept. 2002.

[21] H.V.D.Parunak. Go to the Ant: Engineering Principles from Natural Multi-Agent Systems. *Annals of Operations Research*, 75:69–101, 1997.

[22] J. Jones, M. Myerscough, S. Graham, and B. Oldroyd. Honey Bee Nest Thermoregulation: Diversity Promotes Stability. *Science*, 305:402–404, 2004.

[23] I. Kassabalidis, M.A.El-Sharkawi, R. II, P. Arabshahi, and A.A.Gray. Swarm Intelligence for Routing in Communication Networks. In *Proceedings of the IEEE Globecom 2001*, Nov. 2001.

[24] M. Mamei, R. Menezes, R. Tolksdorf, and F. Zambonelli. Case Studies for Self-organization in Computer Science. *Journal of Systems Architecture*, 2006.

[25] A. F. M. Marée and P. Hogeweg. Modelling Dictyostelium Discoideum Morphogenesis: The Culmination. *Bulletin of Mathematical Biology*, 64(2):327–353, Mar. 2002.

[26] J. Milnor. On the Concept of Attractor. *Communications in Mathematical Physics*, 99(2):177–195, 1985.

[27] Y. Ohtaki, N. Wakamiya, M. Murata, and M. Imase. Scalable Ant-based Routing Algorithm for Ad-hoc Networks. In *Proceedings of the 3rd IASTED International Conference on Communications, Internet, and Information Technology (CIIT 2004)*, 2004.

[28] V. Ramos and J. J. Merelo. Self-Organized Stigmergic Document Maps: Environment as a Mechanism for Context Learning. In *AEB'2002 – 1st Spanish Conference on Evolutionary and Bio-Inspired Algorithms*, pages 284–293, Feb. 2002.

[29] R. Schoonderwoerd, O. Holland, and J. Bruten. Ant-like Agents for Load Balancing in Telecommunications networks. In *Agents '97, Proceedings of the First International Conference on Autonomous Agents*, pages 209–216, New York, NY, USA, 1997. ACM Press.

[30] R. V. Sole, E. Bonabeau, J. Delgado, F. P., and J. Marin. Pattern Formation and Optimization in Army Ant Raids. *Artificial Life*, 6(3):219–226, 2000.

[31] S. H. Strogatz and I. Stewart. Coupled Oscillators and Biological Synchronization. *Scientific American*, 269(6):102–110, Dec. 1993.

[32] R. Tateson. Self-organising Pattern Formation: Fruit Flies and Cell Phones. In Eiben et al. [8].

[33] J. Toner and Y. Tu. Flocks, Herds, and Schools: A Quantitative Theory of Flocking. *Physical Review E*, 58(4), 1998.

[34] A. Vakali and G. Pallis. Content Delivery Networks: Status and Trends. *IEEE Internet Computing*, 7(6):68–74, Nov. 2003.

[35] W. A. Wright, R. E. Smith, M. Danek, and P. Greenway. A Generalisable Measure of Self-Organisation and Emergence. In *Proceedings of the International Conference on Artificial Neural Networks – ICANN 2001*, volume 2130 of *Lecture Notes in Computer Science*, pages 857–864. Springer-Verlag, Aug. 2001.

A Space- and Time-Continuous Model of Self-Organizing Robot Swarms for Design Support

Heiko Hamann and Heinz Wörn
Institute for Process Control and Robotics
Universität Karlsruhe
76128 Karlsruhe, Germany
Email: {hamann, woern}@ira.uka.de

Abstract

Designing and implementing artificial self-organizing systems is a challenging task since they typically behave non-intuitive and only little theoretical foundations exist. Predicting a system of many components with a huge amount of interactions is beyond human skills. The currently common use of simulations for design support is not satisfying, as it is time-consuming and the results are most likely sub-optimal.

In this work, we present the derivation of an analytical, time-, and space-continuous model for a swarm of autonomous robots based on the Fokker-Planck equation. While the motion model is in most parts physically motivated, the communication model is based on a heuristic approach. A showcase application to a recently proposed scenario of collective perception in a huge swarm of robots with very limited abilities is given and the simulation results are compared to the model. Despite the high level of abstraction, the prediction discrepancies are small and the parameters can be mapped one-to-one from the model to the control algorithm. Finally, we give an outlook on the capabilities of the proposed model, discuss its limitations, and suggest an improvement that could reduce the number of empirically determined parameters.

1 Introduction

The ongoing advances in electronics and robotics have made it possible to build small sensor nodes as well as small robots at low cost [2, 4, 17]. By this evolution it became feasible to implement large sensor networks and groups of 50 or more robots, so-called artificial robot swarms [1, 5]. While the hardware is available, the development of the control software is still a challenge. To minimize the complexity of the entire system and due to the limited capabilities of an individual robot, the development targets simple rules and, in an allusion to nature, one hopes for emergent behavior of the robot group that leads to the solution of the predefined task.

In the following, we assume that the hardware is given and not part of the design decision. The problem is to find an appropriate control algorithm for the robot swarm to execute a given task. However, the design of self-organizing and emergent behavior is very difficult. There are no general methods available that support the engineer in designing and optimizing the control algorithm. First steps to establish such a theory of self-organizing behavior in robotics have been proposed recently [12, 9, 11]. The fundamental substance of these approaches is a model that approximately predicts the behavior of the swarm. At least the exact prediction of emergence is considered a contradiction in terms by some researchers as they define emergent behavior by its unpredictability [6]. Alternatively to the new field of emergence consider the three body problem, as it is already hard to find the exact motions of three defined bodies by Newtonian mechanics [3]. Naturally predicting emergent behavior is a tough task but whether it is feasible or not is unanswered presently. A similar question can be asked for the task of approximately predicting emergence. This is just a re-setting of the previous question since we then restate: How accurate could such a prediction possibly be?

In this work we expand the set of available models by an analytical approach that describes space continously and explicitly rather than approximating it discretely. In many self-organized swarms the effectivity of the behavior depends primarily on spatial inhomogeneities that are hard to approximate by a discrete approach. Thus, it can be

0-7695-2906-2/07 $25.00 © 2007 IEEE

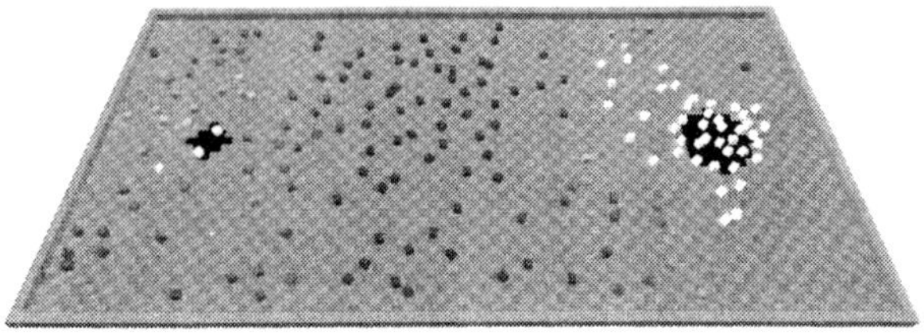

Figure 1. Screen-shot of the simulation showing two circular target areas of different size and cubic robots with their value of the potential field indicated by their brightness (the brighter the higher the value).

inferred that an explicit and exact representation of space is useful in these cases.

In the next section we describe the showcase scenario to which we apply our model in section 3. In section 4 we give numerical results and finally we discuss the capabilities and limitations of the proposed model in section 5.

2 A Scenario of Collective Perception and the Trophallaxis Strategy

As an example we choose the scenario of collective perception in a swarm of robots as described and analyzed by Schmickl et al. [15]. In this scenario a big group of up to 1000 robots moves within a rectangular area bounded by walls. Initially, the robots are uniformly distributed. Their task is to discriminate collectively between two target areas, to choose the bigger one, and to aggregate there, for example, to do some work. See Fig. 1 for a screen-shot of a typical situation in the simulation (using the simulation platform *LaRoSim* by Schmickl et al. [14]). The strategy that solves this problem is inspired by trophallaxis, a frequently observed behavior in social insects, as reported [15].

It is assumed that the robots can communicate by infra-red devices using a simple protocol allowing them to exchange data like floating point values. Additionally, they can tell whether they are within one of the target areas by sensing a not further defined special characteristic of these. This task needs to be solved collectively, since a single robot cannot measure the size of an area. Thus, without programming the measuring procedure explicitly the designer has to find a control strategy that develops an emergent behavior solving this task. Such a strategy, in the following called *trophallaxis strategy*, inspired by natural organisms was proposed by Schmickl et al. [15]. The term trophallaxis denotes the regurgitation (the controlled flow of stomach contents back into the mouth) of food by one animal for another. While the main purpose of this behavior is the food transfer, at least in bees and ants it serves also as a means of communication. The trophallaxis strategy uses it in terms of communication only.

The fundamental idea of the trophallaxis strategy is to build up a virtual potential field $P(\mathbf{r}, t)$ that assigns a value to each point in space $\mathbf{r}$ at each time t. It should develop a smooth gradient that leads a robot to the global maximum of the potential field at the bigger target area. However, as the field is stored in the internal memory of the robots the values are only defined at positions where a robot resides. Say $\mathbf{R}_\mathbf{i}(t)$ denotes the position of a robot, then the update rule for its potential field value $P(\mathbf{R}_\mathbf{i}, t)$ is defined by

$$P(\mathbf{R}_\mathbf{i}, t+\Delta t) = P(\mathbf{R}_\mathbf{i}, t)+A(\mathbf{R}_\mathbf{i}, t)+T(\mathbf{R}_\mathbf{i}, t)-C(\mathbf{R}_\mathbf{i}, t), \quad (1)$$

where A, T, and C are defined as follows. A is the addition amount

$$A(\mathbf{R}_\mathbf{i}, t+\Delta t) = \begin{cases} r_{\text{add}} & \text{if } \mathbf{R}_\mathbf{i}(t) \text{ is within a target area} \\ 0 & \text{else} \end{cases}, \quad (2)$$

for addition rate r_{add}. See table 1 for the standard values used, if not explicitly given. The values are given in robot diameters, whereas the rates depending on time are given for $\Delta t = 1$. T is the transfer amount

$$T(\mathbf{R}_\mathbf{i}, t+\Delta t) = (P(\mathbf{R}_\mathbf{i}, t) - P(\mathbf{R}_\mathbf{j}, t)) r_{\text{transfer}}, \quad (3)$$

for the position of a neighbor $\mathbf{R}_\mathbf{j}$ that is in communication distance d_{comDist} and transfer rate r_{transfer}. This transfer is performed in a negotiation between neighboring robots via the infra-red communication devices that additionally allow the robots to determine the direction of their neighbors [18]. C is the consumption amount

$$C(\mathbf{R}_\mathbf{i}, t+\Delta t) = P(\mathbf{R}_\mathbf{i}, t) r_{\text{consmpt}}, \quad (4)$$

with consumption rate r_{consmpt}.

It is intuitive and substantiated by simulation runs that in the average the maximum of the potential field is at the bigger target area. Hence, a robot should in general turn to its neighbor with the highest potential field value and try to approach it. But the movement of a robot is only partially determined by the gradient of the potential field as the movement is randomized. Depending on the actual value of P a defined ratio of the robot's movements is random. This movement ratio is given by

$$m(\mathbf{R}_\mathbf{i}, t) = \max(\min\left(\frac{P(\mathbf{R}_\mathbf{i}, t) - \delta_{\text{aggr}}}{1000}, 0.75\right), 0), \quad (5)$$

Table 1. Standard parameters.

Parameter	Value
average density $\overline{\rho}$	0.117188
number of robots	375
arena gages	80×40
communication distance d_{comDist}	3.5
avoiding distance $d_{\text{avoidDist}}$	0.75
robot radius	0.5
target area radii	1 and 5
addition rate r_{add}	50
consumption rate r_{consmpt}	0.01
transfer rate r_{transfer}	0.5
aggregation threshold δ_{aggr}	0

for an aggregation threshold δ_{aggr}. For $P(\mathbf{R}_\text{i}, t) < \delta_{\text{aggr}}$ we have $m(\mathbf{R}_\text{i}, t) = 0$ that defines all the robot movements to be random. For $P(\mathbf{R}_\text{i}, t) \geq 750 + \delta_{\text{aggr}}$ we have the maximal ratio $m(\mathbf{R}_\text{i}, t) = 0.75$ which means that in three out of four times the robot moves to its neighbor with the highest potential.

This strategy turns out to be effective in discriminating between the differently sized target areas [15]. Now a human designer of this control algorithm would have to find optimal parameter settings. This is a difficult task, since predicting the dynamics of such a complex system with an immense number of interactions is not part of the human skills. The traditional way to solve this problem is to start with an educated guess, test this parameter setting using a simulation, change one parameter by a little, test it again, and so on. As the parameters are not mutually independent, since the simulation of hundreds of robots is usually slow and hard to parallelize, and as the decisions of a careless designer might be made based on statistically insignificant data, this procedure is inefficient, time-consuming, and sometimes even ineffective. In the following we propose a tool that supports a designer in his decision which parameter setting to take.

3 Model

In this section we present our system of partial differential equations (PDE) that serves as a model for swarm robotics. The given derivation of the model is oriented at the trophallaxis strategy of the above scenario but the model is not bounded to this particular scenario. Similar PDE systems were applied to a variety of applications. See for example the framework of so-called Brownian agents by Schweitzer [16] or the science of synergetics founded by Haken that describes self-organization of patterns (chapter six in [8]).

3.1 PDE of the Robot Density

The behavior of a single robot basically consists of two distinct parts: navigation and communication. First we derive the model describing the navigation part. Since the effects of acceleration (inertia, friction, and slip) are of minor importance in small robots, we assume that the driving direction and the velocity can be changed in jumps. The change of an agent's position R_i over time is given by the following Langevin equation:

$$\frac{dR_i}{dt} = -m(\mathbf{R}_\text{i}, t) \left. \frac{\nabla P(\mathbf{r}, t)}{\|\nabla P(\mathbf{r}, t)\|} \right|_{R_i} v + (1 - m(\mathbf{R}_\text{i}, t))\xi(t)v. \tag{6}$$

v is the constant nominal velocity. $\xi(t)$ is a normalized noise term $\|\xi(t)\| = 1$, with mean $\langle \xi(t) \rangle = 0$, and uncorrelated in time $\langle \xi(t)\xi(t') \rangle = \delta(t - t')$ (see [13] for details). This equation is interpreted that the robots move with velocity v either towards the maximum of P with a probability of $m(\mathbf{R}_\text{i}, t)$ or otherwise to a random direction.

From this microscopic model we derive a macroscopic model that describes the probability density function of the robot's positions (Fokker-Planck equation). This is, however, longish and unfortunately the mathematical interpretation of the above Langevin equation is unclear. Since ξ exhibits jumps there are jumps in R_i, too. But then it is unclear which value to take for $m(\mathbf{R}_\text{i}, t)$. While this necessitates an additional clarifying definition in the mathematical and physical context, here, it is clearly defined by the underlying control algorithm that the value of $\mathbf{R}_\text{i}$ before the jump has to be used. We omit the derivation of the Fokker-Planck equation here and refer to [7, 19] for further details. The related equation for the robot density $\rho(\mathbf{r}, t)$ is:

$$\begin{aligned}\frac{\partial}{\partial t}\rho(\mathbf{r}, t) = &- \nabla \left[m(\mathbf{r}, t) \frac{\nabla P(\mathbf{r}, t)}{\|\nabla P(\mathbf{r}, t)\|} v\rho(\mathbf{r}, t) \right] \\ &+ \frac{1}{2}\nabla^2 \left[(1 - m(\mathbf{r}, t))^2 v\rho(\mathbf{r}, t) \right].\end{aligned} \tag{7}$$

To simplify the formalism we interpret ρ as a particle density instead of a probability density. This is achieved by defining

$$\forall t : \int_\mathbf{r} \rho(\mathbf{r}, t) d\mathbf{r} = N, \tag{8}$$

where N denotes the number of robots in the swarm.

Equation 7 is a first approximation but additionally we have to take into account that the robots cannot aggregate in arbitrarily high densities. This is, on one hand, due to physical constraints but, on the other hand, due to the implemented collision avoidance behavior. The robots are programmed

0-7695-2906-2/07 $25.00 © 2007 IEEE

to keep a distance of at least $d_{\text{avoidDist}} = 0.75$ robot diameters to each other. Since this avoiding procedure is not always successful in a crowded area the upper bound is defined by the size of the robot (radius of 0.5). We expect for the maximal density ρ_{max}:

$$\frac{1}{\pi d^2_{\text{avoidDist}}} \leq \rho_{\text{max}} \leq \frac{1}{\pi 0.5^2}. \tag{9}$$

Obviously already for densities below but close to the maximal density the goal-oriented movements of a robot become more difficult to be performed successfully in a saturation-like process. This is caused by an effect as it is described in collision theory by the increasing effective collision frequency for increasing density. A robot being permanently forced to the collision avoiding state cannot move purposefully. We have empirically determined a function that gives the probability of a goal-oriented movement being successful depending on the density: $m_{\text{sat}}(\rho) = e^{-9\rho}$. The model is sensitive to the root ρ_{root} of this function but not to the characteristics of it on the interval $[0, \rho_{\text{root}}]$. The root corresponds directly to the maximal effective density and can be determined in a single simulation run. For a better estimation the average time a robot spends in the collision avoiding state depending on the density can be measured. Including this function in equation 7 we get the final PDE for the robot movement

$$\begin{aligned}\frac{\partial}{\partial t}\rho(\mathbf{r},t) = &- \nabla\left[m(\mathbf{r},t)m_{\text{sat}}(\rho(\mathbf{r},t))\frac{\nabla P(\mathbf{r},t)}{\|\nabla P(\mathbf{r},t)\|}v\rho(\mathbf{r},t)\right] \\ &+ \frac{1}{2}\nabla^2\left[\left(1-m(\mathbf{r},t)\right)^2 v\rho(\mathbf{r},t)\right]. \end{aligned} \tag{10}$$

Using this equation the effect of robots slowing down in areas of high density as some or all of their goal-oriented movements cannot be executed is modeled. The function m_{sat} does not appear in the second summand because the random movements are not relevantly influenced by high densities.

3.2 PDE of the Potential Field

In the following, we model the communication of the robots, i.e. the dynamics of the potential field. Unfortunately, there is no exactly defined and physically motivated way of deriving a partial differential equation for the communication as it exists for the robots' motion. However, the characteristics of the scenario addressed here allow an intuitive derivation.

At first consider the transferring process. A robot determines the difference between its own potential field value and the value of a neighbor that is within communication range. Then a part of this difference defined by r_{transfer} is transfered to the robot with the smaller value. This exactly corresponds to the implementation of the Laplace operator using the finite difference method with a coefficient. However, this coefficient is hard to determine as it is strictly depending on the distance, i.e. the effective coefficient c_e for a distance d is given by $c_e = c^d$; but in the simulation the distance between transferring robots has no effect to the amount that is transferred as long as they are in communication range. Additionally, robots can transfer their amount of the potential field just by moving around which is also a diffusion process describable by the Laplace operator. The selected definition of the transfer coefficient is motivated by the above reasoning and was empirically approved:

$$c_{\text{transfer}} = r_{\text{transfer}}^{1/d_{\text{comDist}}}. \tag{11}$$

By this definition, we ensure that the effective coefficient for distance d_{comDist} is the transfer rate r_{transfer}. The underlying assumption of total connectivity is discussed in section 5.

Modeling the consumption process is straight forward. Since a single robot consumes $r_{\text{consmpt}}P(\mathbf{R},t)$, the consumption at a position $\mathbf{r}$ is defined by $r_{\text{consmpt}}P(\mathbf{r},t)\rho(\mathbf{r},t)$ because ρ gives the expected number of robots as defined above. With the same reasoning the addition process is modeled. Hence, the PDE for the potential field is given by

$$\begin{aligned}\frac{\partial}{\partial t}P(\mathbf{r},t) = \quad & r_{\text{transfer}}\nabla^2 P(\mathbf{r},t) \\ &- r_{\text{consmpt}}P(\mathbf{r},t)\rho(\mathbf{r},t) \\ &+ \delta_{\text{onTarget}}(\mathbf{r},t)r_{\text{add}}\rho(\mathbf{r},t), \end{aligned} \tag{12}$$

with

$$\delta_{\text{onTarget}}(\mathbf{r},t) = \begin{cases} 1 & \text{if } \mathbf{r} \text{ is within a target area at time } t \\ 0 & \text{else} \end{cases}. \tag{13}$$

The prediction of this model is only qualitatively correct because we assume that the limited amount added to the system is dispersed over the whole area. But in the microscopic simulation it is distributed in singularities leading to higher values than in our model. However, it turns out that at least for sufficiently high densities (about $\rho > 0.07$) there is a constant relationship between the potential field in the model and in the simulation. We get a quantitative model by multiplying the potential field values of the model with an empirically determined scaling factor of seven. This factor is determined by drawing samples of the potential field from the simulation and dividing them by the prediction of the un-scaled model. The need of such a free parameter is, in general, dissatisfying. However, here it needs to be measured just once for the scenario. In section 5 we suggest an improvement that might help to reduce the number of empirical parameters although this is a tradeoff between the complexity of the model and the need for empirical parameters. On the other hand the accuracy of the model, as presented in the next section, without an intensive optimization of the empirical parameters shows the insensitivity of the model to these values.

4 Numerical Results

In this section we compare the predictions of the proposed model to the simulation results by Schmickl et al. [15] and give a short overview of the capabilities.

At first the number of robots aggregating in a circle of radius ten around each target area are observed while varying the target radii between one and five. See Fig. 2 for the predictions of the model compared to the simulation results of Fig. 5(b) in [15]. The performance of the model is good except for equally sized target areas. In this situation robots in the area between the targets are attracted alternately by one or the other target due to variance in the potential field. Since P in our model represents the mean only, a correct gradient is defined at all time leading to an overestimation of the aggregation process.

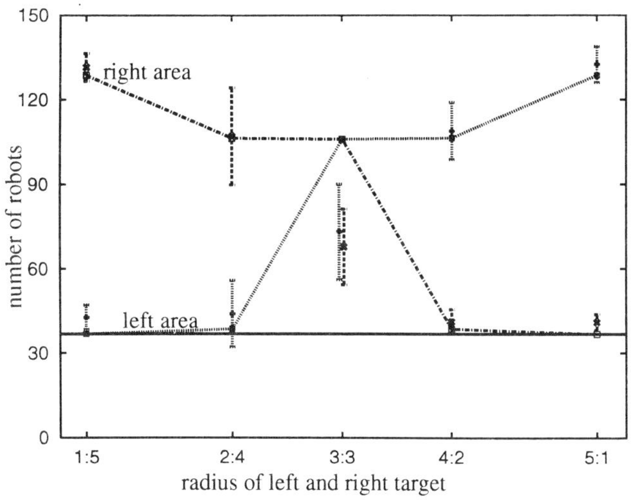

Figure 2. Number of aggregating robots with varied target area radii, comparing the model (lines) to the simulation (confidence intervals). The horizontal line gives the expected number of robots if there is no aggregation.

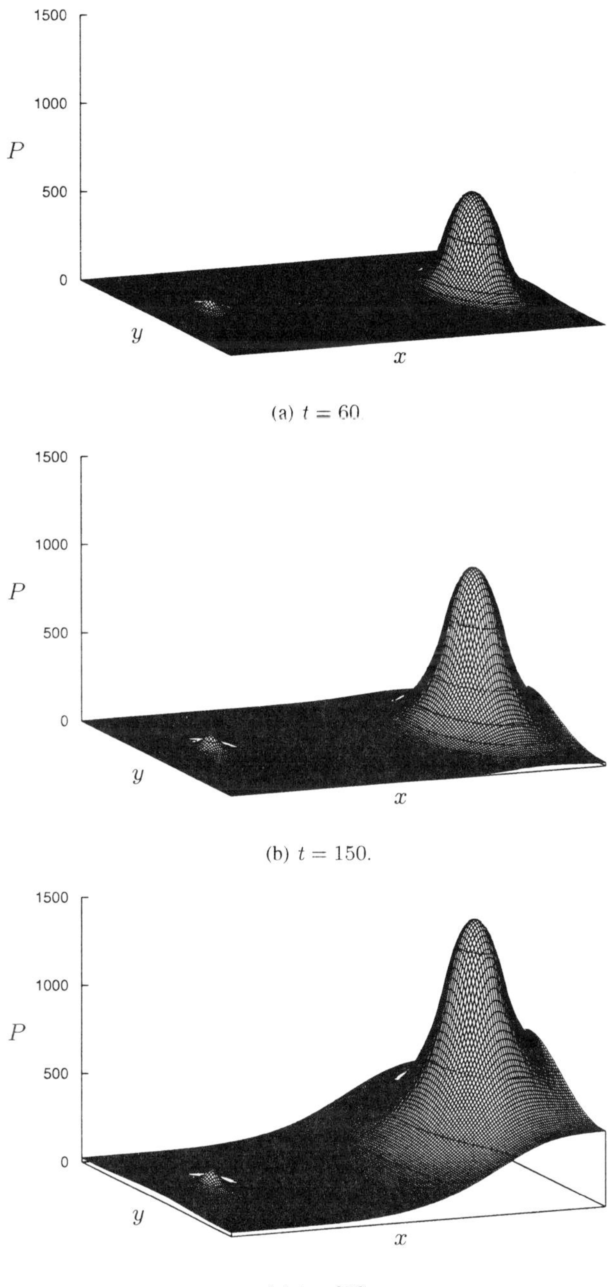

(a) $t = 60$.

(b) $t = 150$.

(c) $t = 250$.

Figure 3. Dynamics of the potential field as predicted by the model. Target area at the right peak is 25 times bigger than the left one.

In Fig. 3 we show the typical dynamics of the potential field with one target area being 25 times bigger than the other one (compare to Fig. 6(a-c) in [15]). The values at the bigger target increase until a steady state is reached, i.e. the efflux due to transferring and consumption is equal to the afflux.

In the following, we investigate the effect of a varied density. While changing the density, we observe the number of robots aggregating in the circular area with radius ten

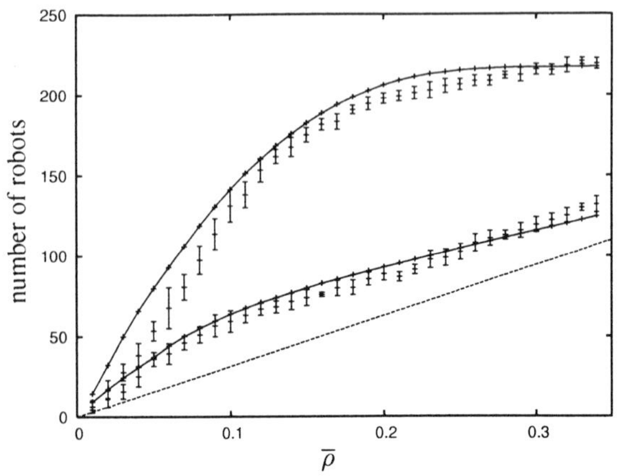

Figure 4. Number of aggregating robots with varied average density $\overline{\rho}$, comparing the model (solid line) to the simulation (confidence intervals). The dashed line gives the expected number of robots if there is no aggregation.

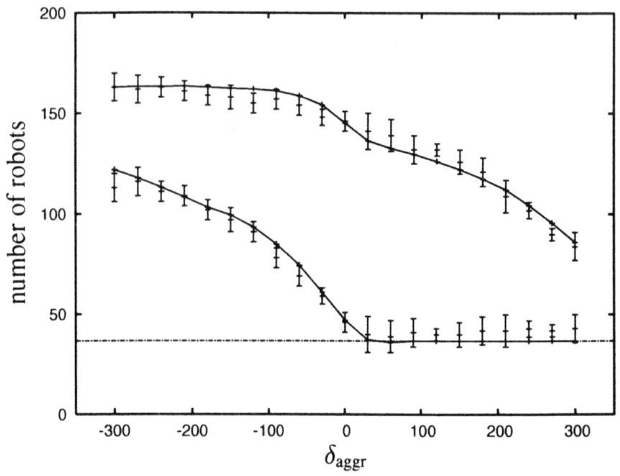

Figure 5. Number of aggregating robots with aggregation threshold δ_{aggr}, comparing the model (solid line) to the simulation (confidence intervals). The dashed line gives the expected number of robots if there is no aggregation.

around the target areas. The aggregation threshold is set to $\delta_{aggr} = -50$. See Fig. 4 for the results (corresponds to Fig. 7 in [15]). The dashed line shows the expected number of robots in the target area under the assumption of uniform distribution. For low densities our model overestimates the aggregation which is again a problem of variance. For such low densities the probability of encounter is low. Therefore the variance in the potential field is high and our model working on means is too optimistic.

Now we vary δ_{aggr} and observe again the aggregation process around the two target areas, see Fig. 5 (corresponds to Fig. 9 in [15]). The dashed line shows again the expected number of robots in the target area under the assumption of uniform distribution. The prediction of the model is good although it is ambiguous whether the wave-like behavior around $\delta_{aggr} = 0$ for the bigger target is the correct representation of the underlying process. Again our model does not predict the slight aggregation process at the smaller target for $\delta_{aggr} < 0$ due to the effect of variance. The mean values of the potential field there lead to totally random movements ($m(\mathbf{R}_i, t) = 0$).

To show the possibilities of parameter optimization that are provided by the proposed model we present two-dimensional parameter scans. For such scans the complexity increases quadratically in the resolution. In Fig. 6 the prediction of aggregated robots at the two target areas are given with varied average density $\overline{\rho}$ and aggregation threshold δ_{aggr}. Fig. 6(a) shows the number of aggregated robots at the smaller target area and Fig. 6(b) gives the number for the bigger area. The lower plain gives the expected number of robots in case of a uniform distribution. Fig. 4 and Fig. 5 are slices of these surfaces. At the bigger target area we have a low sensitivity to δ_{aggr} and a saturation effect for high densities. At the smaller target area we have no aggregation for $\delta_{aggr} < 0$ independent of the density and almost a linear dependency on the aggregation threshold for $\delta_{aggr} > 0$ and $\overline{\rho} > 0.15$.

In Fig. 7 we vary the aggregation threshold and the radii of the target areas between one and seven. Interestingly the number of aggregated robots in total increases intensely if both radii are above four as it can be seen in Fig. 7(b) and the size of the smaller target area affects the aggregation at the bigger one as more robots aggregate at the bigger target for radii 4:5 than for 3:5 to 1:5 and the same for 5:6 and 6:7.

There is a clear benefit for a human optimizer to have such a visualization of the parameter landscape. Both qualitative and quantitative dependencies are discovered immediately. 700 evaluations were needed for Fig. 6. Using a simulation about ten runs per scan point would be needed for statistical significance which would make a standard personal computer run for weeks compared to less than 24 hours for the 700 evaluations by a numerical solver of the model.

5 Discussion and Future Work

In this work we have shown that the presented simple model of communication already yields a good accuracy in the prediction. To become an off-the-shelf design support for software engineers in swarm robotics the application

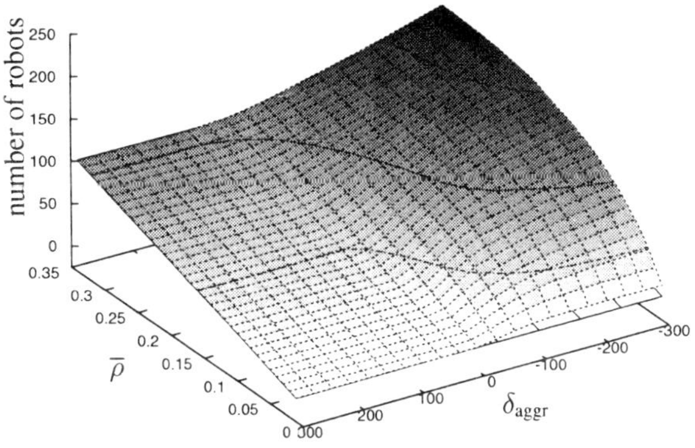

(a) Small target area (radius of 1).

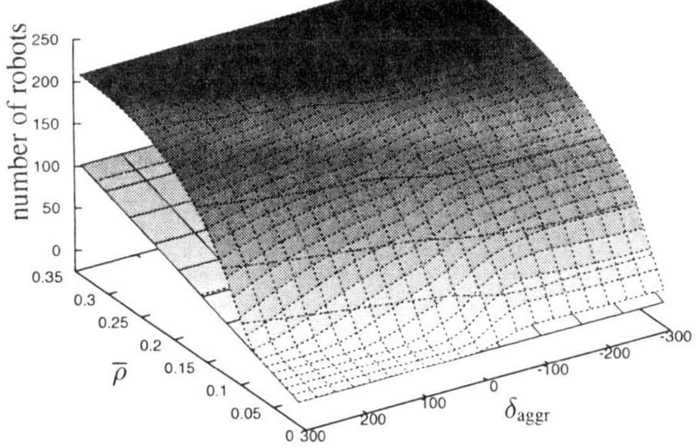

(b) Big target area (radius of 5).

Figure 6. Scan over two parameter intervals: aggregation threshold δ_{aggr} and average density $\overline{\rho}$. Shown is the number of aggregated robots at both target areas. The lower plain gives the expected number of robots in case of a uniform distribution.

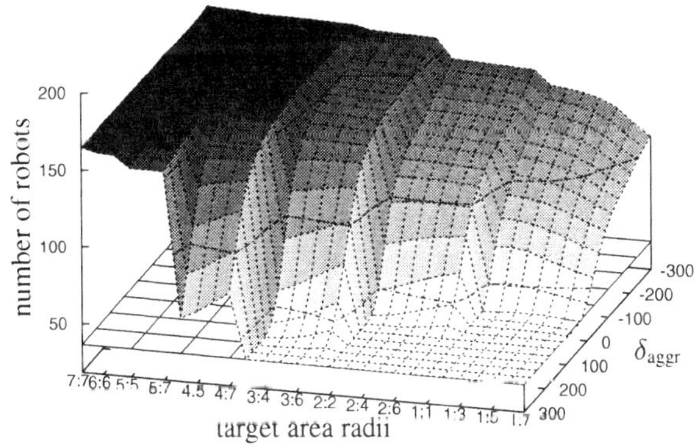

(a) Aggregation at the left target area, ordered by radius of the left area, increasing from right to left.

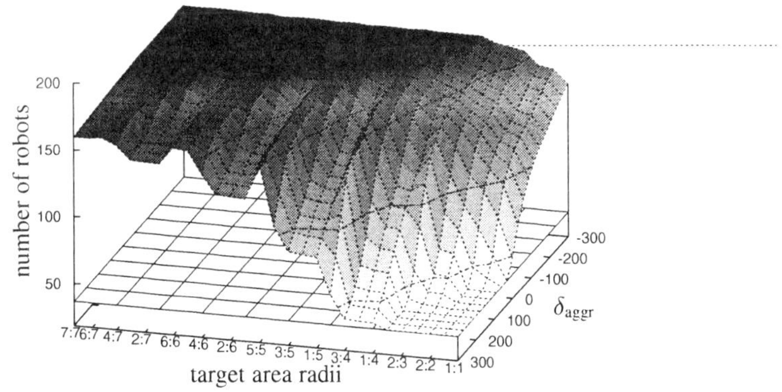

(b) Aggregation at the right target area, ordered by radius of the right area, increasing from right to left.

Figure 7. Scan over two parameter intervals: aggregation threshold δ_{aggr} and the target area radii. Shown is the number of aggregated robots at the target areas.

to different scenarios has to be shown, a higher accuracy is needed, a validation against experiments in hardware is inevitable, and the number of empirically determined parameters needs to be reduced. In the following we discuss the limitations and possible improvements of the proposed model.

By modeling the transferring process with a diffusion term in equation 12, we assume total connectivity in the network of robots. This seems overly optimistic. However, the required small local densities that break the connectivity are only reached with even smaller average densities as the robots abandon certain areas and aggregate in this scenario. The change from total connectivity to several clusters with decreasing density is not a smooth but a phase transition [10]. Therefore, the proposed model is only inaccurate concerning connectivity for the small interval below the critical density. Additionally, just the mean of the potential field is modeled. This mean is only slightly, if at all, changed by a temporarily broken connectivity since the amount of the stopped flux in the potential field is retained in the other cluster and after the reconnection values increase temporarily to above the mean. Thus, a temporarily decomposition into several clusters increases the variance and leaves the mean of the potential field almost unchanged.

The main issue of the presented model is that we are using mean values only. Especially for values close to thresholds defining a qualitative change in the behavior the variance has a huge effect. For example, even if the gradient of the potential field is in average well defined and leading the robots to the target, it could still be misleading in arbitrarily close to 50 percent of the time. This would effect the robots to move in average arbitrarily slow towards the target.

We plan to extend the proposed model by an explicit representation of communication yielding the variance by modeling the connectivity in the underlying network. This can be done by considering the probabilities of different sized clusters depending on the local particle density or by iteratively modeling the multi-hop propagation of a message from source to drain. This will help to reduce the number of empirically determined parameters. This research will be accompanied by experiments of stepwise increasing complexity using our swarm robot Jasmine [1] and we plan to compare this work to other available models.

Acknowledgments

The authors thank Thomas Schmickl and Christoph Möslinger for providing the data of their simulation runs and the simulation.
Hamann is supported by the German Research Foundation (DFG) within the Research Training Group GRK 1194 Self-organizing Sensor-Actuator Networks.

References

[1] Jasmine robot - project website, 2007. http://www.swarmrobot.org/.

[2] I. F. Akyildiz, W. Su, Y. Sankarasubramaniam, and E. Cayirci. A survey on sensor networks. *IEEE Communications Magazine*, 40(8):102–114, August 2002.

[3] J. Barrow-Green. *Poincaré and the three body problem.* American Mathematical Society; London : London Mathematical Society, 1997.

[4] G. Caprari, P. Balmer, R. Piguet, and R. Siegwart. The autonomous microbot alice: a platform for scientific and commercial applications. In *Proc. of the Ninth Int. Symp. on Micromechatronics and Human Science*, pages 231–235, Nagoya, Japan, 1998.

[5] N. Correll, C. Cianci, X. Raemy, and A. Martinoli. Self-organized embedded sensor/actuator networks for "smart" turbines. In *IEEE/RSJ International Conference on Intelligent Robots and Systems Workshop on Network Robot System: Toward intelligent robotic systems integrated with environments*, 2006.

[6] V. Darley. Emergent phenomena and complexity. In R. Brooks and P. Maes, editors, *Artificial Life 4*, pages 411–416, 1994.

[7] J. L. Doob. *Stochastic Processes.* Wiley, New York, 1953.

[8] H. Haken. *Synergetics – an introduction.* Springer, 1978.

[9] S. Kornienko, O. Kornienko, and P. Levi. Swarm embodiment – a new way for deriving emergent behavior in artificial swarms. In P. Levi, M. Schanz, R. Lafrenz, and V. Avrutin, editors, *Autonome Mobile Systeme*, pages 25–32, 2005.

[10] B. Krishnamachari, S. Wicker, R. Bejar, and M. Pearlman. Critical density thresholds in distributed wireless networks. In *Communications, Information and Network Security*, pages 1–15, 2002.

[11] K. Lerman, C. Jones, A. Galstyan, and M. Mataric. Analysis of dynamic task allocation in multi-robot systems. *Int. J. of Robotics Research*, 25(3):225 – 241, 2006.

[12] A. Martinoli, K. Easton, and W. Agassounon. Modeling swarm robotic systems: A case study in collaborative distributed manipulation. *Int. Journal of Robotics Research*, 23:415–436, 2004.

[13] H. Risken. *The Fokker-Planck Equation*. Springer, 1984.

[14] T. Schmickl and K. Crailsheim. Trophallaxis among swarm-robots: A biologically inspired strategy for swarm robotics. In *Proceedings of the 1st IEE/RAS-EMBS International Conference on Biomedical Robotics and Biomechanotronics*, 2006.

[15] T. Schmickl, C. Möslinger, and K. Crailsheim. Collective perception in a robot swarm. In E. Sahin, W. M. Spears, and A. F. T. Winfield, editors, *Proceedings of the Second Swarm Robotics Workshop*, volume 4433 of *LNCS*, 2007.

[16] F. Schweitzer. *Brownian Agents and Active Particles. On the Emergence of Complex Behavior in the Natural and Social Sciences*. Springer-Verlag, Berlin Heidelberg New York, 2003.

[17] J. Seyfried, M. Szymanski, N. Bender, R. Estana, M. Thiel, and H. Wörn. The I-SWARM project: Intelligent small world autonomous robots for micro-manipulation. In E. Sahin and W. Spears, editors, *Swarm Robotics Workshop: State-of-the-art Survey*, pages 70–83, Berlin Heidelberg New York, 2005. Springer-Verlag.

[18] M. Szymanski, T. Breitling, J. Seyfried, and H. Wörn. Distributed shortest-path finding by a micro-robot swarm. In *Ant Colony Optimization and Swarm Intelligence*, LNCS, pages 404–411. Springer, 2006.

[19] N. G. van Kampen. *Stochastic processes in physics and chemistry*. North-Holland, Amsterdam, 1981.

0-7695-2906-2/07 $25.00 © 2007 IEEE

A Nonlinear Multi-agent System designed for Swarm Intelligence: the Logistic MAS

Rodolphe Charrier
LORIA - Nancy University
Nancy, France
Rodolphe.Charrier@loria.fr

Christine Bourjot
LORIA - Nancy University
Nancy, France
Christine.Bourjot@loria.fr

Francois Charpillet
LORIA - INRIA Lorraine
Nancy, France
Francois.Charpillet@loria.fr

Abstract

Ant algorithms and flocking algorithms are the two main programming paradigms in swarm intelligence. They are built on stochastic models, widely used in optimization problems. However, though this modeling leads to high-performance algorithms, some mechanisms, like the symmetry break in ant decision, are still not well understood at the local ant level. Moreover, there is currently no modeling approach which joins the two paradigms. This paper proposes an entirely novel approach to the mathematical foundations of swarm algorithms: contrary to the current stochastic approaches, we show that an alternative deterministic model exists, which has its origin in deterministic chaos theory. We establish a reactive multi-agent system, based on logistic nonlinear decision maps, and designed according to the influence-reaction scheme. The rewriting of the decision functions leads to a new way of understanding the swarm phenomena in terms of state synchronization, and enables the analysis of their convergence behavior through bifurcation diagrams. We apply our approach on two concrete examples of each algorithm class, in order to demonstrate its general applicability.

1 Introduction

Bio-inspired algorithms are increasingly important in distributed AI, giving rise to new paradigms and questioning conventional artificial intelligence approaches. Intelligence is no more considered as an individual characteristic only, but also as a swarm emergent phenomenon. This is the rooting principle of the so-called swarm intelligence. The challenge is to understand its mechanisms so as to build algorithms which will artificially reproduce this massively distributed intelligence and control its emergence to a certain extent. This field of research is quite recent, but specially active and prolific [3].

One of the major challenges of this kind of algorithms is to produce self-organization within the system, that is to find a transition from an uncoordinated state to a stable or metastable one. The question is therefore how to correlate individual entity behavior to give rise to a collective coordination without any global controller, and under the constraint of individual limited perceptions.

Swarm algorithms have many applications especially in optimization problems : notably, Ant Colony Optimization (ACO) [6] and Particle Swarm Optimization (PSO) [11], two major examples. The former takes inspiration from real ant colonies, and the latter from flocking birds and particle physics models. One can point out the similarity of the scientific genesis in both cases: at the beginning, biological observations lead to mathematical formulations based either on stochastic processes and statistical measures [5] for the ants behavior, or on deterministic rules for the flocking behavior [17]. In the latter case, birds are replaced by particles in the PSO developments, and deterministic rules are mixed with stochastic variables. However, these two models are quite different, and no work to our knowledge tends to make them join together. Our assumption in this paper is that an abstract and generic model exists that unifies these two approaches.

Contrary to previous approaches, our approach is a theoretical one, due to the origin of the model. We start with an abstract model, namely the nonlinear Coupled Map Lattice (CML), which has its origin in deterministic chaos theory. Questioning this field leads us to propose a derived model which is a reactive situated Multi-Agent System (MAS) called Logistic Multi-Agent System (LMAS). In this paper, the LMAS will prove to be able to implement the two main classes of swarm intelligence phenomena in a unified theoretical formulation. Compared to the previous approaches, it radically changes the way of interpreting the involved mechanisms by connecting them to state synchronization processes, namely a universal concept in nonlinear sciences [16]. The LMAS changes also the way of visualizing the dynamics using bifurcation diagrams.

0-7695-2906-2/07 $25.00 © 2007 IEEE

To begin with, we explain the LMAS in section 2; we then implement it on a basic flocking problem in section 3 which is an example of a self-organized system, and -in a deeper way- on the ant binary bridge experiment in section 4, which is the origin of ant algorithms and an example of self-adaptive system. These concrete problems demonstrate the main aspects of our model.

2 Logistic MAS Conception

2.1 Rooting principles

The logistic MAS (LMAS) takes its inspiration from the coupled map lattice (CML) models used by physicists for studying spatiotemporal chaos phenomena, in particular in the field of hydrodynamics (simulation of turbulent flows) or condensed matter physics. Currently these computational models are of great interest in theoretical physics. We are especially interested in CML using nonlinear quadratic maps, namely logistic maps. The physicist Kaneko have widely explored these types of CML since 80's [10]. He has also intended to extend its use to the general study of complex systems. The next three subsections introduce the CML, the logistic map features, and finally how and why the logistic MAS derives from the CML.

2.1.1 Definition of a logistic CML

A CML is a discrete time and space computation model in which states take their values in a continuous domain. It is sometimes considered as a cellular automaton with continuous states. A minimal CML based on the local map f and a nearest-neighbors diffusive coupling is expressed in the usual form given by :

$$x_i(n+1) = (1-\epsilon)f(x_i(n)) + \frac{\epsilon}{N(V_i)} \sum_{j \in V_i} f(x_j(n)) \quad (1)$$

where $x_i(n)$ is the state variable in site i at time n, ϵ is the diffusive coupling coefficient, V_i is the fixed neighborhood of site i which includes $N(V_i)$ other sites. When f is the classical nonlinear parametric logistic map, it is defined on the interval $[0,1]$ by the recursive relation :

$$x(n+1) = f(x(n)) = 4a\, x(n)(1-x(n)) = f^{n+1}(x(0)) \quad (2)$$

If the parameter $a \in [0,1]$, then $[0,1]$ is invariant through f. This nonlinear map is completely described by its bifurcation diagram, which is shortly explained in the next section. Nevertheless, after many iterations (about thousands) the resulting CML generates a wide range of behaviors from a full synchronization of cell states to a full chaotic and desynchronized behavior of cell states according to the ϵ and a parameters values. We let the interested reader refer to the bibliography for further information about this subject.

2.1.2 Some features on the logistic map

The logistic map is a well known polynomial mapping, very easy to compute, but with very complex outcomes. It comes from a demographic model created by Pierre François Verhulst, and was popularized in 1976 by the biologist Robert May. The logistic map has been widely studied in its standard form (2), where a is the control parameter. This form is derived from the population equation which is a macroscopic formulation. Nevertheless, this map, as well as its conjugated forms (deduced from the original one by a variable transformation), are widely studied and used nowadays for their intrinsic mathematical properties, independently of their population aspect, notably in the CML studies. The figure 1 shows the bifurcation diagrams of two conjugated logistic maps. They have been calculated for 500 iterations with 500 samples in the interval $[0,1]$. Although the bifurcation diagram differs from one form to another, the global qualitative behavior is the same. The quantitative behavior follows some universal laws (like for example the definition of Feigenbaum constants) [19]. Bifurcation diagrams show $x(\infty) = f^{\infty}(x(0))$ according to the control parameter: as a decreases from 1 to 0, the map evolves respectively from a completely chaotic behavior (densely dark bands) to a very precise one, associated to a single fixed point. This specific behavior from complete randomness to complete order under the influence of a single parameter is very useful, and semantically rich. We will exploit these mathematical properties as a generator of agent behavior, with the first map for the flocking modeling, and the second one for the ant algorithm.

2.1.3 Genesis of the logistic MAS

We have to point out some characteristics of the CML approach, which differs from an agent-based approach designed for swarm intelligence. On the one hand, the CML is a field approach where cells are fixed in a given topology, as artificial neural networks are, whereas the agent-based approach is similar to a particle approach, where entities may be mobile in a independent space called the environment. Consequently, the neighborhood of agents depends on time and space. On the other hand, the CML model is designed as a closed system, whereas a multi-agent system is often an open system which has to adapt to external influences mediated by the environment. The induced changes are listed below:

- the transformation of the CML cells into reactive agents which can move in space implies the encapsulation of the coupling and control parameters inside the agent. These parameters become therefore local internal variables, in contrary to their global aspect in CML. A logistic map governs as well agent decision making.

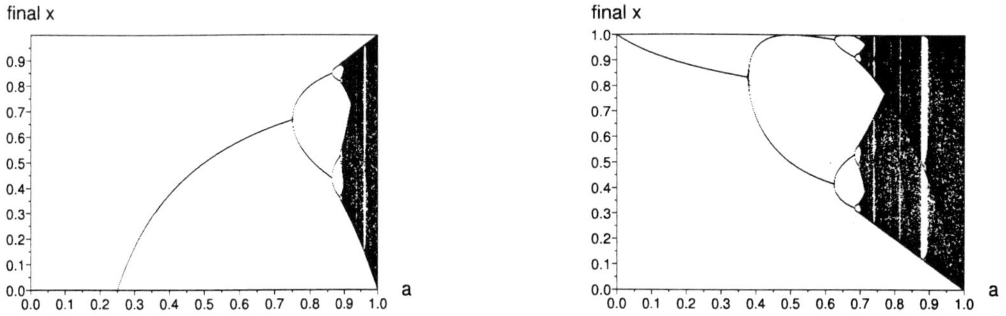

(a) Map 1 : $x_{n+1} = 4ax_n(1 - x_n)$

(b) Map 2 : $x_{n+1} = 1 - a(1 - 2x_n^2)$

Figure 1. Bifurcation diagrams over $[0, 1]$ after 500 iterations

- the open aspect of the system produces a distinction between entities and their environment, and increases the importance of the adaptation processes and the flows of exchanged data. This implies the dependence of agent state variables on environment perceptions.

Although these differences, many variations on the CML model are close to our case studies, notably the globally randomly coupled map lattice [12], which can be considered as an approximate situation of moving cells. This assumption is not the current issue of this paper, but this specific CML provides theoretical and numerical useful results we think available for LMAS. In addition, numerical simulations are quite a common procedure in CML studies, since mathematical proofs are hard to do in most cases. So are LMAS studies, as the two concrete swarm applications will show it in this paper. To conclude, the LMAS model has a lot to share with the CML one, and can take advantage of existing results on CML.
However, contrary to CML, the concepts of MAS hold an appropriate semantics and structure for handling swarm intelligence. This paper is devoted to present the LMAS and to show its potential.

2.2 Mathematical formalism

The logistic multi-agent system (LMAS) belongs to the reactive MAS class of systems. We take inspiration from the influence-reaction scheme of Ferber-Müller [8] to describe the LMAS.

2.2.1 Global system design

The LMAS is composed of a set A of N_a agents situated in a discrete space called the environment, denoted Env, which is the medium of all the interactions between agents. Our interaction model is indeed an entirely indirect one. We denote by $t \in \mathbb{N}$ the time step variable. Let us identify some usual definitions: $s_i(t)$ is the state of agent i, and $\sigma(t)$ the state of the environment at time t. The state transition equation of the complete system is resumed by the following equation system:

$$\begin{cases} s_i(t+1) & = F(s_i(t), \sigma(t)) \; \forall i \in \{1, \cdots, N_a\} \\ \sigma(t+1) & = G(\sigma(t), s_1(t+1), \cdots, s_N(t+1)) \end{cases} \tag{3}$$

The first equation expresses the fact that agents perceive their environment before changing their internal state; the second one expresses the change of the environment state through the combined influences of agents derived from their updated states. The explicit coupling between these two parts of the system makes a natural distinction between the local and the global level and makes clear the computation schedule.

2.2.2 The logistic agent model

The logistic agent is a reactive agent whose internal behavior is governed by a logistic map (fig.1). So as to simplify the description of the involved mechanisms, and because we do not need more for the present, we consider only scalar quantities. But it is obvious that the same design principles apply in a vector space. The agent internal state s is a tuple of the following variables: $s = \langle x, a, \epsilon \rangle$.
Let D denote the interval $[0, 1] \subset \mathbb{R}$.

- $x \in D$ is the decision variable for the agent to perform some actions
- $a \in D$ is the internal control variable, because it operates as the control parameter in the agent logistic map
- $\epsilon \in D$ is a coupling variable for an agent with other agents in its neighborhood; it is similar to the diffusing coupling parameter in CML modeling

The internal state thus takes its values in a continuous domain. D stays invariant through the used map. The agent state transition is expressed in the equation system:

$$\begin{cases} a(t+1) &= F_a(\sigma(t)) \\ \epsilon(t+1) &= F_\epsilon(\sigma(t)) \\ x(t+1) &= F_x(x(t), \sigma(t), a(t+1), \epsilon(t+1)) \end{cases} \quad (4)$$

This system makes clear how state variables are interwoven and shows the computation steps. $\sigma(t)$ appears explicitly in the equations because it is the source of the agent perceptions. One can notice that a and ϵ transitions arise only from agent perceptions on the environment expressed by the σ dependency.
Let us expand the transition function F_x for the x variable, which is a compound of several operators: one form of the $a(t+1)$-parameter logistic map f_a, an $\epsilon(t+1)$-coupling operator I_ϵ, and a perception function p. This is summarized in the formula:

$$\begin{array}{l} F_x(x, \sigma, a, \epsilon) = f_a(I_\epsilon(x, p(\sigma))) \\ \text{where } \forall (y, z) \in D^2, I_\epsilon(y, z) = (1-\epsilon)y + \epsilon z \end{array} \quad (5)$$

If we write down $u(t) = I_\epsilon(x(t), p(\sigma(t)))$ and choose the logistic map defined in equation (2), the transition equation for the internal x variable becomes:

$$\begin{cases} u(t) = (1 - F_\epsilon(\sigma(t)))x(t) + F_\epsilon(\sigma(t))\, p(\sigma(t)) \\ x(t+1) = 4F_a(\sigma(t))\; u(t)(1-u(t)) \end{cases} \quad (6)$$

This latter transition equation makes explicit the agent decision making based on environment perceptions. The action step then is the process in which the decision variable x is interpreted and used to effect an action. In the next section, we propose a basic structure for the environment which allows the agents to perceive it.

2.2.3 The environment and its fields structure

Our environment concept is close to the multi-layered one described in [1], where computational fields play an important part. One then defines fields on the environment Env. A field is a mapping from the environment to a numerical domain D_{field}. With regard to our model, this domain is often the interval $D = [0,1] \subset \mathbb{R}$. As the environment is a discrete space, it can be defined as a set of sites (let K be the number of sites): $Env = \{site_k | 0 \leq k \leq K\}$.
A field maps therefore a site k of Env to D_{field} :

$$\begin{array}{rll} field: & Env & \rightarrow D_{field} \\ & site_k & \rightarrow field(site_k) \end{array}$$

The state σ of the environment is defined as the tuple of all existing fields at time t. We are now able to define the agent perception processes.

2.2.4 Agent perception and action principles

In our model, agents perceive some fields of the environment. An agent perception function thus concerns a particular field and achieves a mapping of this field to the agent's state definition domain, namely D. An agent perception applies to a local neighborhood because of its limited capabilities. Perception functions depend on the handled problem and have to be specified after the environment structure has been completely defined.
The environment update concerns the second equation of the global system (3) and occurs after the update of each agent internal state. In particular, agent actions generate some modifications in the environment. They are of two main types. The first one consists in environment fields modifications: an agent can change values of a field at its current location. The second one is the agent location modification: an agent moves relatively to its current location. This latter information is stored as well in a dedicated environment field.
The model structure we have just described is abstract and generic. In the next sections, we will show how it is implemented to a basic flocking instance, and afterward to an ant algorithm problem, with two different ways for analyzing it. This enables to make clear the involved mechanisms in each case.

3 Flocks modeling with LMAS

3.1 Introduction on flocking algorithms

Reynolds proposed in [17] an algorithm to simulate the phenomenon of flocking birds which is considered as an emergent phenomenon example in complex systems. The algorithm principles are based on three deterministic behavioral rules: maintain a minimum distance from others, match velocities with others in its neighborhood, and move toward the perceived center of mass in its neighborhood. Since that time, many other algorithms have been devised to improve its performances, and stochastic versions arose so as to perform optimization problems. This led to the field of particle swarm optimization [11].
A particular interesting instance is the simulation of moving human crowds presented in [18]. The x and y spatial coordinates are computed by means of separate logistic maps. This allows to control the whole crowd with the single control parameter of the map. This parameter is used as a global one, and the resulting behavior can thus not be self-organized. Moreover, there is no coupling factor between agents. The aim of the authors was to achieve a credible virtual simulation, but this specific way of using logistic maps has to our knowledge not been more explored nor theorized. This however is precisely our goal as the following

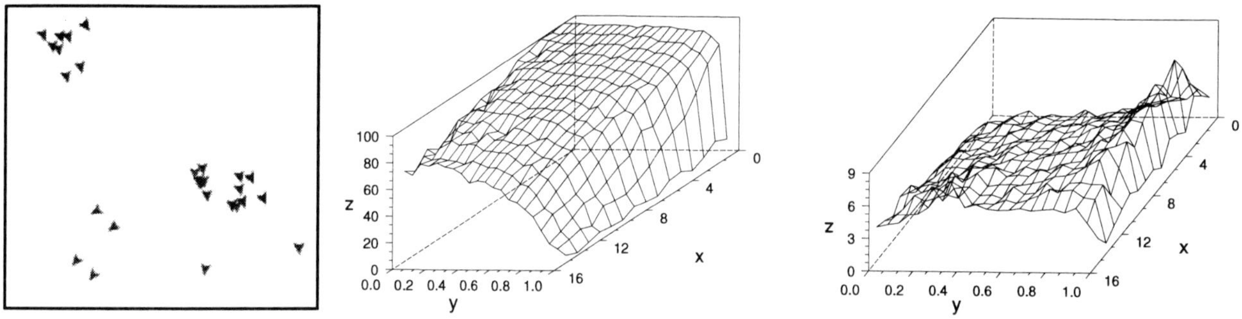

(a) Example of flocks forming (b) Mean of cluster number on z-axis, radius of neighborhood on x-axis, ϵ_0 on y-axis (c) Standard deviation on z-axis, radius of neighborhood on x-axis, ϵ_0 on y-axis

Figure 2. Cluster number anlysis according to the coupling coefficient and to the neighborhood radius with $N = 100$ agents

will demonstrate it.

3.2 A basic flocking model with LMAS

In our context, flocking means the way an agent population gets self-organized into clusters of similar agent behaviors. We will not yet study the stability of such clusters but their distribution according to time and agent perception capacities. We present here the most simple implementation of the LMAS for flocking. Let us list its specifications:

- Agent state: the state of the agent i at time t is expressed in the following tuple: $s(t) = \langle x_i(t), a_i, \epsilon \rangle$. The x variable depends on the considered agent and on time. The a variable is determined randomly as a constant value in $[0, 1]$ according to a uniform distribution; it depends on the considered agent. The ϵ variable remains here a constant factor independent of the considered agent. This case proceeds from a perception of a constant field. Finally, the logistic map is the one which corresponds to the first bifurcation diagram 1(a).

- Environment and fields : the environment is a 2D discrete torus with three fields denoted X, N, and E storing respectively the cumulated x variables of each agent on a given site k at time t, the cumulated number of agents on site k at time t, and the ϵ-field. Let us notice that several agents can be located in the same site at the same time, and that the environment has no memory; this means that these fields equal zero before the environment update occurs at time t. Their definitions are expressed in the following formula on a site k at time t (an agent is indexed by i):

$$N_k(t) = \sum_{i \text{ on } k} 1 \tag{7}$$

$$X_k(t) = \sum_{i \text{ on } k} x_i(t) \tag{8}$$

$$E_k(t) = \epsilon_0 \tag{9}$$

ϵ_0 is given as a constant in the interval $[0, 1]$.

- The perception function p_i^x of an agent i corresponds to the mean of the X field over a neighborhood denoted $V(i)$ centered on the site where the agent i is located. The perception function p_i^ϵ is associated to the ϵ-field. This is expressed by the formula:

$$p_i^x(t) = \frac{\sum_{k \in V_i} X_k(t)}{\sum_{k \in V_i} N_k(t)} \tag{10}$$

$$p_i^\epsilon(t) = E_{k(i)}(t) = \epsilon_0 \tag{11}$$

It is easy to verify that $p_i(t)$ always belongs to $[0, 1]$ since it operates as a weighted mean on variables belonging to the same interval.

- The internal state update is described in (6)

- Moving action: since velocity is defined as a 2D vector, the speed or the magnitude of velocity remains here a constant whereas we modify its direction according to the updated $x(t+1)$; if α denotes this direction, then we write down $\alpha = 360 \times x$ to get α in degrees for example. We denote by k' the agent new site location.

- Updating action: at first, the environment fields are reset. All agents then update them: an agent i modifies the fields on its new site location k' according to the following equations:

$$\begin{aligned} N_{k'}(t+1) &= N_{k'}(t+1)+1 \\ X_{k'}(t+1) &= X_{k'}(t+1)+x_i(t+1) \end{aligned}$$

3.3 Results and discussion

A computer simulation with $N = 100$ agents in a 30×30 torus environment shows in fig.2(a) that groups of agents arise to form flocks (a small part of the whole is shown). This flocking phenomenon increases as ϵ tends to 1. This latter issue is made clear in the chart in fig.2(b). Let us explain first how it is build: the measure used here consists in counting the number of agent clusters formed at each time step. Two agents belong to the same cluster if and only if their internal x differ from a given threshold and they belong to the same neighborhood. The threshold is set here to 0.01 which corresponds to one percent of the maximum value of x. Let $N_c(t)$ denote this number of clusters. The measure average out this on 1000 consecutive time steps from 1000 to 2000 after the transient period, expressed by:

$$\bar{N}_c = \frac{1}{1000}\sum_{t=1001}^{t=2000} N_c(t) \qquad (12)$$

The chart on fig.2(b) shows the variations of $\bar{N}_c$ according to $\epsilon \in [0,1]$ and according to the neighborhood radius belonging to $[1,15]$. The maximum neighborhood radius is the half of the environment size. The diagram on fig.2(c) shows the standard deviation on the same series of numbers. Let us now consider the issues of those two diagrams. The flock forming is non-existent, that is $\bar{N}_c \approx 100$, ϵ and the neighborhood radius get closer respectively to 0 and 1; it means that each agent belongs to a cluster formed by itself. As asserted before, The flock forming is more and more important, that is $\bar{N}_c$ is small, as ϵ and the radius get closer respectively to 1 and 15. Let us notice the shape of the chart : a very sharp decreasing arises when ϵ is close to 1 and the neighborhood radius small. It gets smoother as the radius gets bigger. It is reinforced by the fact that the corresponding standard deviation on fig.2(c) is high in this area; that reveals some perturbations in stability for the bigger formed clusters. The initial uniform distribution of the control variable inside the agents is partly the reason of this instability: the bifurcation diagram on fig.1(a) shows that about 10 per cent of the agents has got a chaotic behavior, which implies instability.
These results confirm an intuitive feeling on the flocking phenomenon, "Birds of a feather flock": flocking emerges easier as the radius of interaction and the level of similarities between agents increase. The fundamental change in this mechanism with respect to the classical algorithm, is that the flocking occurs because of agent state synchronization and not because of appropriate rules. This is indeed a more universal concept.

4 Ant binary bridge modelling with LMAS

4.1 A short ant algorithms survey

The paradigm of ant colony is currently studied and applied a lot in swarm intelligence as well as in other scientific fields [7]. However, dynamical and convergence analysis of ant algorithms [20, 9] are very recent and appear after many years of experimental issues. The stochastic approach succeeds in simulating the global phenomenon but is not sufficient to really explain specific features of ant colony mechanisms, like the symmetry break which occurs in the binary bridge experiment for example, or like the specific involved dynamics of the colony. Merkle's recent work [13] has been a step forward in this regard, but with a deterministic model of ant dynamics.
To analyze these phenomena in a simple way, we resume the modelling of the binary bridge experiment, since this experiment shows the basis of the collective choice mechanism of ant colonies without any optimization aspects. It is also the simplest instance of a graph-based ant algorithm from which all other instances derive. In addition, we will handle the problem with the LMAS model described in section 2.2 and demonstrate this new modeling approach for simulating the binary bridge experiment and providing a new visualization of its dynamics.

4.2 The original binary bridge model

Deneubourg and al. published an experiment together with a mathematical model in [5], explaining the trail following behavior of ants when foraging. They use the argentine ant species which collectively selects a path to a food source. They particularly studied the self-organization process that achieves this goal. More precisely, the experimental protocol consists of a binary bridge A and B, connecting the ant-nest to the food source. Branches have the same distance, so the problem is not to select the shortest path; ants have only to choose one of the branches to get to the food source. Along the way to the food source, and while returning back to the nest, they lay down pheromones. We would like to point out the underlying assumptions : the bridge has got two equal long branches, the pheromone does not evaporate, and the amount of pheromone on a bridge is proportional to the number of ants crossing the bridge. The experiments are of short duration so that the amount of pheromone evaporation is negligible. Finally, ants are supposed to cross the bridge one by one. This leads to the following model [5]:

- A_i (respectively B_i) is the number of ants choosing the branch A (respectively B) after the ith ant crosses the bridge : i acts as the global time step of the algorithm. An amount of pheromone of value 1 is laid down by each ant on the chosen branch.

- P_A (respectively P_B) is the probability the $i+1$th ant chooses A (respectively B) :

$$P_A = 1 - P_B = \frac{(K + A_i)^n}{(K + A_i)^n + (K + B_i)^n} \quad (13)$$

  This formula has been obtained by a statistical analysis on the experimental protocol. The best fit to the experimental data is given with parameter values $K = 20$ and $n = 2$.

This stochastic model produces the expected results: all the ants end up choosing the same branch after a while, even if neither branch is favored *a priori*. This branch is called the winning branch. Moreover it is not a problem of distance optimization since the branches are equally long, but a pheromone optimization.
After this short recall, a question remains unsolved : *what is the cause of the global symmetry break at the local ant level?* And if this question cannot be answered completely, can we model it differently to obtain a better understanding of the phenomena? This question has indeed already been attempted in [15, 2], where the authors study it from a global point of view by using coupled differential population equations. Using such techniques, one succeeds in explaining the symmetry break in ants behavior, while providing a global visualization of the phenomenon. However, this approach is an analytical one, not a constructive one. Our aim is therefore to pursue this approach on the local level of ants and to provide a link between local and global description levels. In short, the major issue for us consists in determining in which way local deterministic mechanisms could produce such a global phenomenon? We will show that our abstract model of logistic MAS is appropriate to achieve this objective with some adapted specifications. This is the topic of the next section.

4.3 Algorithm design

4.3.1 Environment definition

The environment $Env = (V, Ed)$ is a small graph, where V is the set of nodes and Ed the set of edges, composed of only three nodes and two edges. One of the nodes is the nest, and the others correspond to the binary bridge destinations A and B (fig. 3). We define two main fields in the environment: a pheromone field τ [14], and an agent state field X. We will distinguish in our model two types of agent influences on the environment, which are indirect interactions, each relating to one of these fields: a pheromone

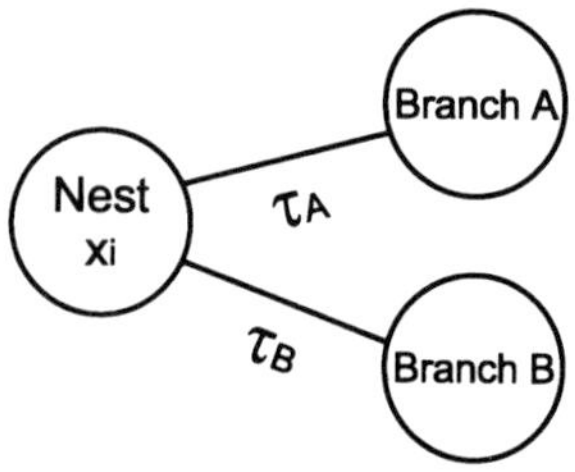

Figure 3. Scheme of the binary bridge

deposit on edges of the graph has a long range interaction effect stored by the field τ, and an internal state deposit on the current node has a short range interaction effect stored by the field X. These fields are defined in the specific case of a finite graph topology by:

$$\begin{aligned} X: \quad & V && \to D = [0,1] \\ & v_k && \to X_k && (14) \\ \tau: \quad & Ed && \to \mathbb{R}^+ \\ & e_{kl} && \to \tau_{kl} && (15) \end{aligned}$$

Each node is indexed by an integer and so is X. We denote by X_0 the nest. Each edge is indexed by two integers, and so is τ. Moreover, these fields evolve with time since ants change their value. On the contrary, a third field $Ek = \epsilon_0$ is involved but remains constant like in the flocking case. Agent perception functions depend on these fields.

4.3.2 Agent perception-decision-action loop

We now describe the perception-decision-action scheme of the agent's internal mechanism. In this case, the time step of the algorithm corresponds to the event of one agent crossing the binary bridge.

- Perception : at time t a new agent i, leaving the nest, perceives the environment fields. The perception functions are expressed in the following way for each state variable:

$$\begin{cases} p_x(t) = X_0(t) = x_{i-1}(t) \\ p_a(t) = max\{\tau_a, \tau_b\} \\ p_\epsilon(t) = \epsilon_0 \end{cases} \quad (16)$$

  An agent perceives the internal x-value of the preceding agent on the current node (the nest). It perceives the amounts of pheromone by reading the field τ, and by capturing the maximum amount of this field. It selects the edge where the field is maximum as the base edge for its moving decision. Finally, it perceives as well the constant ϵ-field. ϵ_0 may represent the individual communication characteristics of the given ant species.

- Decision making: the transition of the internal state variables (4) is given by the following equations:

$$x_i(t+1) = f_a^k((1-\epsilon_0)x_i(t) + \epsilon_0 x_{i-1}(t)) \quad (17)$$
$$a_i(t+1) = \frac{\alpha}{\alpha + p_a(t)} \quad (18)$$

The formula (17) describes the individual communication level between agents : if $\epsilon_0 = 0$, no local contact between agents occurs. We are then in a mass recruitment situation as described in [3]: only the pheromone trail can influence the agent. Usual ant algorithms are based on this assumption. However if $\epsilon_0 \neq 0$, individual information exchange occurring in the agent neighborhood is taken into account: $x_{i-1}(t)$, laid down by the preceding agent, is involved in the computation.
We use the second form of the logistic map $f_a(x) = 1-a(1-2x^2)$ (fig.1) with k iterations to get the behavior described in the bifurcation diagram. The a variable depends on time according to the formula (18) in a decreasing way: a varies from 1 to 0 as the amount of pheromone varies from 0 to $+\infty$. The α parameter governs the analytic function form. Finally a threshold enables to make the decision:
if $x_i(t+1) > threshold$ choose the branch with τ_{max} else choose the other.
As we are in a simple case with only two edges connected to the nest node, it is convenient to choose a threshold set to $\frac{1}{2}$. This rule is relative to the branch where the pheromone amount is maximal, since the agents perform here a pheromone amount optimization. The deviation with the highest amount expresses the agent autonomy.

- Action: this corresponds to the update of the environment, that is the update of its two fields according to the following equations:

$$\begin{cases} X_0(t+1) = x_i(t+1) \\ \tau_{chosenedge}(t+1) = \tau_{chosenedge}(t) + x_i(t+1) \end{cases} \quad (19)$$

The pheromone updating is a cumulative process without evaporation. Indeed, the original model for simulating this experiment did not implement any evaporation process because of the short experimental time scale which did not allow evaporation to proceed.

Initial conditions correspond to the experimental ones: the initial amount of pheromone is zero and the initial control parameter is close to 1, it means that randomness is high at first.

4.4 Implementation and results

The resulting algorithm is **Algorithm 1**. The simulation results can be viewed in figure 4. On the same graph, the ratio of ants traversing the branch, averaged over ten runs, is plotted for both the winning and the loosing branch. The mean of the control variable over ten runs is plotted as well. To understand those charts and their associated variations, we must bear the bifurcation diagram of fig.1(b) in mind.

In the three cases, we identify the symmetry break at the point where the winning and loosing curves begin to converge respectively to 1 and 0. In each case, the symmetry break occurs exactly when the control variable a reaches the value 0.5. This result is not very surprising regarding the logistic bifurcation diagram in figure 1(b): before this point, in the area $a > 0.5$, both branches are explored: this implies that the agent system oscillates quite identically between x-values below and above 0.5. After this point, in the area $a < 0.5$, x still oscillates for a while but always above 0.5. In this area, the decision remains invariant and the symmetry break is complete. The ant ratio curves in the graph 4(a) fits well with the experimental data curves[5]. But this comparison remains a qualitative one because of the lack of experimental data. The k-value is currently not significant enough.
The two graphs 4(b) and 4(c) with $\epsilon_0 = 0.5$ are surprising because they only differ in the iteration number of f. One can notice that the graph 4(b) is quite the same as 4(a) with an odd logistic map iteration number, whereas graph 4(c) shows a long term symmetry break with an even iteration number k. The following section demonstrates the impor-

Algorithm 1 Binary bridge with LMAS

```
Initialization
τ_A, τ_B ← 0
N_A, N_B ← 0
for ant i = 1 to N do
  init : x_0 ← random(0,1)
  Perception
  read τ_max ← max{τ_A, τ_B}
  index_max ← argmax_{A,B} {τ_A, τ_B}
  index_min ← argmin_{A,B} {τ_A, τ_B}
  Decision
  threshold ← 1/2
  a ← α/(α + τ_max)
  x_i ← f_a^k(x_0, x_{i-1}, ε_0)
  if x_i < threshold then
    Action 1
    N_{index_max} ← N_{index_max} + 1
    τ_{index_max} ← τ_{index_max} + x_i
  else
    Action 2
    N_{index_min} ← N_{index_min} + 1
    τ_{index_min} ← τ_{index_min} + x_i
  end if
end for
```

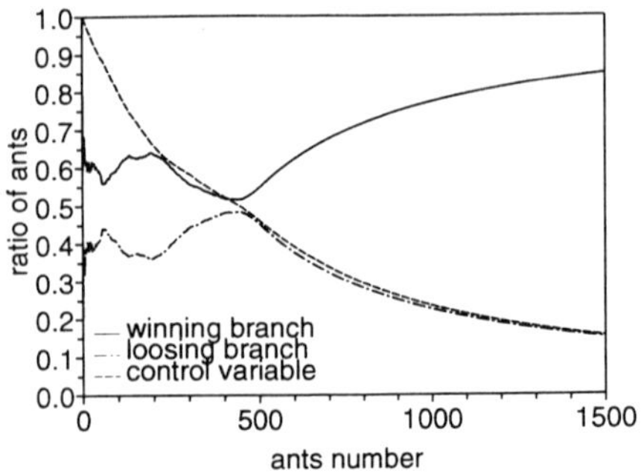

(a) Case with $\epsilon_0 = 0$ and $k = 500$

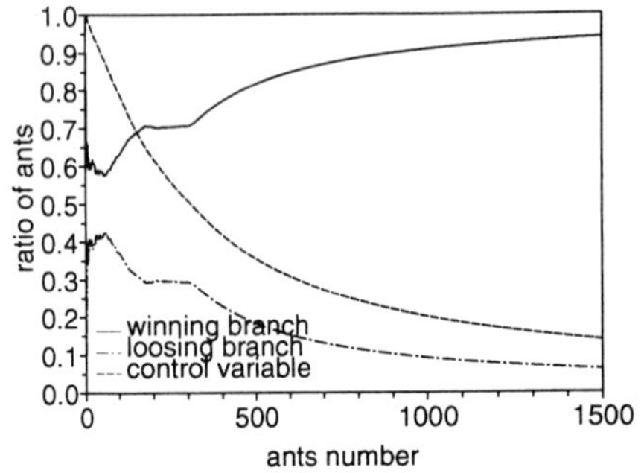

(b) Case with $\epsilon_0 = 0.5$ and $k = 499$

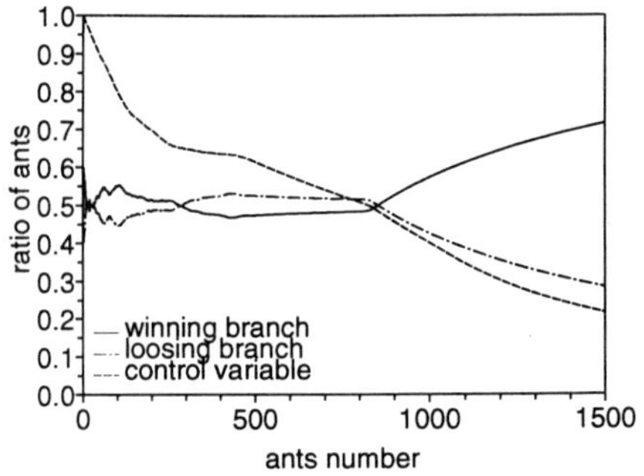

(c) Case with $\epsilon_0 = 0.5$ and $k = 500$

Figure 4. Simulation results of the binary bridge : mean curves over 10 runs with 1500 ants

tance of a collective bifurcation diagram building to explain this, and to provide some qualitative convergence analysis.

4.5 Qualitative convergence analysis and discussion

An explanation of the case 4(c) can be given by considering the bifurcation diagram in fig.5. To start with, let us consider how it is made. The graph is not an individual one as it was for the logistic agent, but a collective one: we have plotted every (x, a) pair of values for each agent crossing the bridge at time t. The graph is to read from right to left because a is decreasing in time. If we apply this process on the case 4(b), we obtain a diagram very similar to the individual bifurcation diagram 1(b). In the case 4(c), the achieved diagram fig.5 can be analyzed as follows: when the number of iterations k of each individual logistic map is even, the system only selects the lower branch of the diagram, because of the even oscillation period. But this is not the single cause of the long term symmetry break. One observes that the control variable levels off (fig.4(c)) at the bifurcation cascade points, which delays the symmetry break.

This collective diagram thus provides a very useful tool to follow the whole dynamics, since it gives a qualitative analysis of the global algorithm convergence. As a matter of fact, it shows that the ant algorithm become stabilized as the colony converges to a global state. This global state corresponds to single fixed points, belonging to the left branch of the collective bifurcation diagram. It means therefore that a global agent state synchronization occurs on those fixed points. Contrary to the flocking case, this synchronization proceeds from the pheromone field, which is collectively build by the agents: we are faced with a self-adaptive system. The binary bridge experiment is an appropriate experiment to display this synchronization, and the collective bifurcation diagram is an appropriate tool to point this phenomenon out. This global visualization is made possible

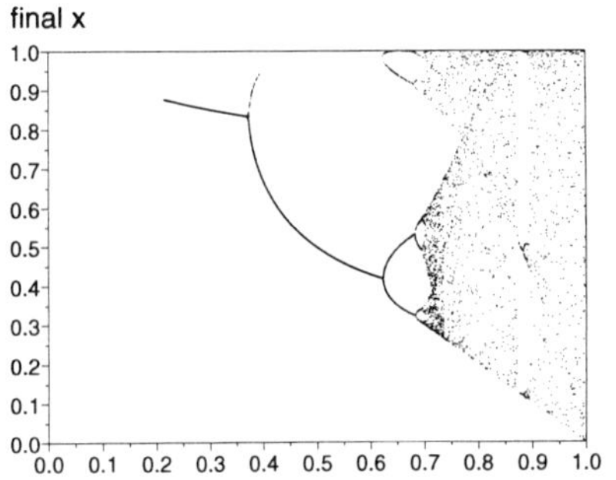

Figure 5. Bifurcation diagram with $N = 1500$ ants, $\epsilon_0 = 0.5$ and $k = 500$

because of the same map distributed to each agent. One can as well get information about the system, given by the distribution of the a variable at time t. For instance, one can determine whether the collective behavior is focused near a particular a value or widely distributed, how dispersed the agent behaviors are, and how far the system is away from ending fixed points.

5 Final discussion and conclusion

Results showed that the logistic MAS applies itself to both flocking simulation and binary bridge experiment. The LMAS approach is an elegant and relevant way to demonstrate the synchronization process in these two main primordial swarm phenomena, by state coupling in the flocking case, and by a strong decentralized influence on the environment in the ant case. Expressing them in such a common modelling framework, enabled us to make clear the main difference between the two processes, which has never been done to our knowledge. State synchronization argues for the generality of our model. The choice of the logistic map may nevertheless appear as a limitation of the scope of LMAS. Firstly, some previous developments in CML studies lead us to confirm this choice: cluster synchronization, and thus the flocking phenomenon, would not occur with every nonlinear map. A conjecture in CML studies [4] actually postulates that the map used has to exhibit some periodic windows in the chaotic area of its bifurcation diagram, so as to let cluster synchronization emerge. The logistic map is consistent with this conjecture contrary to the tent map for example. Secondly, the population equation aspect of the logistic map fits well with the swarm phenomena, since these phenomena may be considered as instances of population problems. Consequently, the fact that a piece of this global population effect may be found again as a cause at the local level of entities and within entities, seems totally coherent.

To conclude, this paper presented the logistic agent, which uses a deterministic nonlinear map, namely the logistic map, to govern its own internal state. This agent is part of a logistic multi-agent system supposed to be a generic modeling for swarm intelligence. The local control variable and coupling variable inside the agent are novel features. These variables decentralize control and govern the chaotic level of agent decisions by means of perceptions. The behavior profile according to the control variable is known *a priori* through a bifurcation diagram and it is the same for each agent. This approach provides theoretical tools and visualization tools from the modern dynamical system theory, so as to follow and analyze the dynamics of the whole multi-agent system.

The interpretation of both flocking phenomenon and ant colony behavior in terms of synchronization processes is the most salient contribution of this paper. This approach has to go deeper, theoretically speaking, about cluster stability, global convergence, and nonlinear map choices. The presented LMAS has also to be matched with more applied problems. In this way, we intend to match it with optimization problems like other swarm-based algorithms. We have tested it on some small instances of the symmetric TSP with promising results. LMAS is a promising modeling tool for swarm intelligence.

References

[1] S. Bandini, S. Manzoni, and C. Simone. Dealing with space in multi–agent systems: a model for situated mas. In *AAMAS '02: Proceedings of the first international joint conference on Autonomous agents and multiagent systems*, pages 1183–1190, New York, NY, USA, 2002. ACM Press.

[2] R. Beckers, J. Deneubourg, S. Goss, and J. Pasteels. Collective decision making through food recruitment. *Insectes sociaux*, 37(3):258–267, 1990.

[3] E. Bonabeau, M. Dorigo, and G. Theraulaz. *Swarm Intelligence. From Natural to Artificial Systems*. Studies in the Sciences of Complexity. Oxford University Press, New York Oxford, 1999.

[4] M. G. Cosenza and J. Gonzalez. Synchronization and collective behavior in globally coupled logarithmic maps. *Progress of Theoretical Physics*, 100(1):21–38, 1998.

[5] J. Deneubourg, S. Aron, S. Goss, and J. Pasteels. The self-organizing exploratory pattern of the argentine ant. *Insect Behavior*, 3:159–168, 1990.

[6] M. Dorigo, V. Maniezzo, and A. Colorni. The ant system: optimization by a colony of cooperating agents. *IEEE Transactions on Systems, Man, and Cybernetics*, 26(1):1–13, 1996.

[7] M. Dorigo and T. Stützle. *Ant Colony Optimization*. The MIT Press, 2004.

[8] J. Ferber and J. Müller. Influences and reactions : A model of situated multiagent systems. In *Proceedings of ICMAS96*, 1996.

[9] W. J. Gutjahr. A graph-based ant system and its convergence. *Future Gener. Comput. Syst.*, 16(9):873–888, 2000.

[10] K. Kaneko. *Theory and applications of coupled map lattices*. John Wiley & Sons, 1993.

[11] J. Kennedy and R. C. Eberhart. Particle swarm optimization. In *Proc. of the IEEE Int. Conf. on Neural Networks*, pages 1942–1948, Piscataway, NJ, 1995. IEEE Service Center.

[12] S. C. Manrubia and A. S. Mikhailov. Mutual synchronization and clustering in randomly coupled chaotic dynamical networks. *Phys. Rev. E*, 60(2):1579–1589, Aug 1999.

[13] D. Merkle and M. Middendorf. Modeling the dynamics of ant colony optimization. *Evolutionary Computation*, 10(3):235–262, 2002.

[14] H. Parunak. Go to the ant: Engineering principles from natural multi-agent systems. *Annals of Operations Research*, 75:69–101, 1997.

[15] J. M. Pasteels, J. L. Deneubourg, and S. Goss. Self-organization mechanisms in ant societies. i: Trail recruitment to newly discovered food sources. *Experientia, Suppl.*, 45:155–175, 1987.

[16] A. Pikovsky, M. Rosenblum, and J. Kurths. *Synchronisation, a universal concept in nonlinear sciences*, volume 12 of *Cambridge Nonlinear Science Series*. Cambridge University Press, 2003.

[17] C. W. Reynolds. Flocks, herds, and schools: A distributed behavioral model. *Computer Graphics*, 21(4):25–34, 1987.

[18] N. Saiwaki, T. Komatsu, T. Yoshida, and S. Nishida. Automatic generation of moving crowd using chaos model. *IEEE Int. Conference on System, Man and Cybernetics*, 4:3715–3721, 1997.

[19] H. G. Schuster and W. Just. *Deterministic Chaos : An Introduction*. WILEY-VCH Verlag GmbH and Co. KGaA, Weinheim, 2005.

[20] T. Stützle and M. Dorigo. A short convergence proof for a class of ant colony optimization algorithms. *IEEE Trans. Evolutionary Computation*, 6(4):358–365, 2002.

Research Track, Session 2: Provocative Ideas

Text Display and Graphics Control on a Paintable Computer

William Butera
Digital Enterprise Group, Intel Corporation
william.j.butera@intel.com

Abstract

Consider a display architecture where every pixel has its own dedicated graphics engine. Toward this end, we recast the rendering and graphics control of text for use on a paintable computer. Work on paintable computing is reviewed with a focus on the programming model based on autonomous, mobile code fragments (pfrags) which self-assemble into larger virtual structures. A device simulator is used to demonstrate pfrags interacting to form 2D coordinate scaffolds. Text characters, embodied as pfrag "seeds", use the scaffold to direct their migration and distribute models of the text and associated graphics code to the paint nodes. Affine transformations are demonstrated as an example of finely distributed graphics control.

1. Introduction

Consider the scaling limitation for large area, real time display systems. For systems based on the generic architecture of fig. 1, data from a variety of external image sources (both natural and synthetic) must first pass through a graphics engine for rendering and formatting. The rendered output is then channeled to a display component for distribution to individually addressable display elements (pixels). Efforts to scale up the number of pixels ultimately confront a number of obstacles, both quantifiable engineering hurdles and subtler impediments to acceptance by the end users.

Engineering limitations are typically caused by shared resources that bottleneck; *e.g.* graphics engines with finite aggregate compute capacity, and data buses with bounded transmission bandwidth. Manufacturing processes for the displays likewise have difficulty maintaining adequate yield as the number of pixels per display increases. For the end customer, ultra high resolution wide area displays must be treated as fixed objects that are mechanically and electrically sensitive, require substantial infrastructure, are often bulky, are always complex, and are difficult to reconfigure opportunistically.

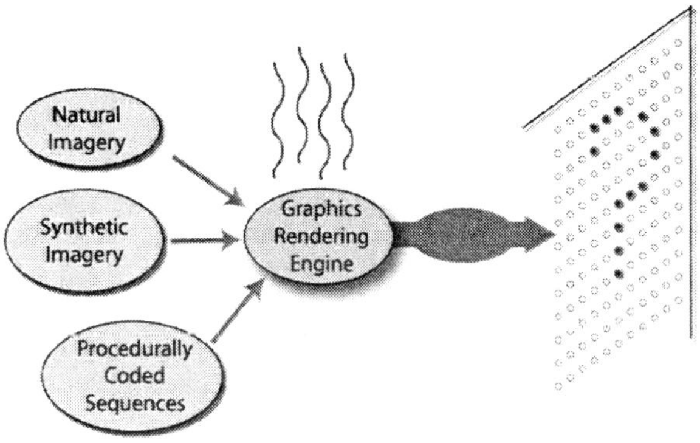

Figure 1 Process and data flow in display systems. Image data from multiple sources converges on a single graphics engine for decompression, color space conversion, rendering, formatting and scaling. The graphics engine passes rasterized data through high bandwidth channel to the display.

The last decade has seen dramatic headway made on a portion of this problem space – namely that of the display component. Emblematic of this is the work on electrophoretic ink (e-ink) where advances in the production and handling of microcapsules have yielded bi-stable, printable displays with the viewing affordances of paper and refresh rates nearing those of early CRT's [3] [7].

Nevertheless, progress on the display component has only underscored the unmet challenges at the system's level. Design of backend systems with sufficient rendering power and transmission capacity to feed a 10^9 pixel display in real time still outpaces today's best engineering practice. Contemporary solutions adopt the approach of tiling the active display area among autonomous display systems operating in synchrony, much in the spirit of early systems that rack mounted multiple TV's into a rectangular grid. This paper looks at carrying this simple approach to a novel extreme. Specifically, we propose assigning a full-featured graphics system to every pixel.

Core to this approach is the architectural work on "paintable computing" and its associated programming methodology based on informational self-assembly [2]. Architecturally, paintable computers are defined as *agglomeratse of numerous, finely dispersed, ultra-miniaturized computing particles; each positioned randomly, running asynchronously and communicating locally.* Individual computing nodes are vanishingly cheap, freely expendable, and consequently are handled as bulk.

We present initial work on applying the architecture and programming model of *paint*[1] to the design of display systems. In doing so, we motivate the question "can the display systems themselves become paintable?". The goal is to create display systems with the same characteristics we target for *paint*; scalability, ability to reconfigure, resilience to fault, and self-repair. As a first step, this paper describes a proof-of-concept software demonstration of rendering and simple graphics control for anti-aliased text.

Section 2 summarizes the work on paintable computing, with a focus on the programming model for self-assembly of mobile code. Section 3 lays out the mechanics of text rendering. Self-replicating process fragments ("pfrags") interact to construct a 2D coordinate system. Individual text characters, encoded as single pfrag "seeds", then use the 2D scaffold to migrate to a predetermined position. Section 4 extends basic pfrag rendering behaviour to support simple graphics control functions such as translation and scaling. Section 5 samples related work. Section 6 states the conclusions, previews future work and expands on important system-design questions that this work portends.

2. Background – Paintable Computing

Work on paintable computing pursues the vision of a machine consisting of thousands of sand-grain sized processing nodes, each fitted with modest amounts of processing and memory, positioned randomly and communicating locally. Individually, the nodes are resource poor, vanishingly cheap and regarded as freely expendable. Yet, when mixed together they cooperate to form a machine whose aggregate compute capacity grows with the addition of more nodes. The ultimate goal is to recast computing as a particulate additive to ordinary materials such as cloth, furniture, building materials or paint.

2.1. Hardware Architecture

The atomic element of a *paintable* is the particle. Characteristic specs include a '486 class micro, an internal clock running at ~ 200 MHz, and 250K-1M of RAM for code and data storage. All the I/O to the micro is gated through a wireless transceiver supporting a full duplex rate in the range of 1-20 Mb/s. Communication is via asynchronous links to the nearest neighbors. A power subsystem harvests power from the immediate environment with minimal constraints on the particle's placement. Once exposed to power, each particle builds an enumerated list of the neighbors with which it can communicate.

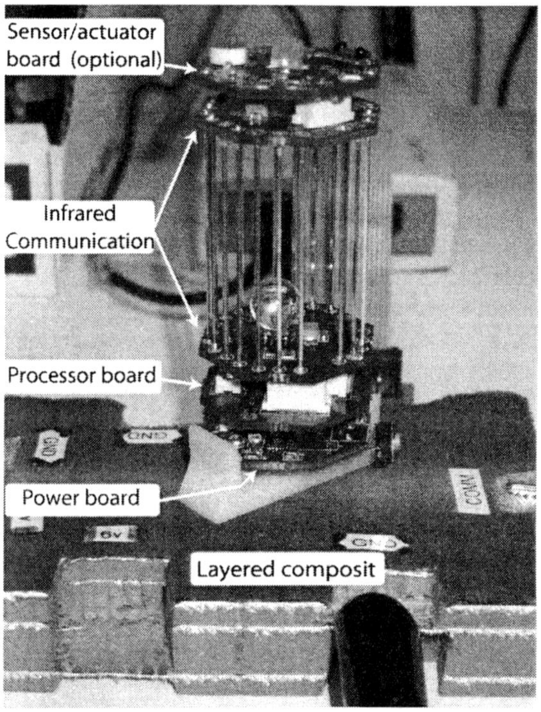

Figure 2 Pushpin Computer

First pass COTS version of a paint particle. Arranged in a 5-board stack, the 1.25" x 3" form factor is comparable to that of a salt shaker. Base board (power board) fitted with catheterized nails that thumb-tack into a layered composite consisting of three conducting planes separated by non-conducting foam. System specs: 32-bit RISC processor, 66 MHz clock, 256 KB SRAM and 2 MB FLASH. Communication via 4 Mbs infrared link to neighbors within a 4.5" radius.

[1] Throughout this report, the terms *paint* and *paintable* (when italicized) are used interchangeably to denote a paintable computer

Work on the actual hardware was originally subordinated in favor of progress on the programming model and simulated embodiments of representative applications. The characteristic specs were enshrined into both a hardware reference model and a device simulator. In the interim, an initial COTS[2] version of the hardware is complete in small quantities for SW development (fig. 2). Manufacture of initial ensemble of 1000 performed under contract to DARPA [12].

2.2. Programming Model

The programming model is based on the concept of process self-assembly -- *the unsupervised re-assembly of a running process from fragments of code that are mobile in a virtual environment.* Process self-assembly is loosely modeled on the metaphor of reversible self-assembly in the material world, In material self-assembly, local chaotic interactions between autonomous physical elements (biological cells, gas molecules, Wall street traders) produce global behavior that is well ordered [13] [14]. In process self-assembly, the atomic elements are virtual – autonomous, mobile fragments of code with state. These process fragments (pfrags) use local messaging to emulate the forces that direct material self-assembly. Pfrags then use these simulated forces to direct their further migration, ultimately arriving at a predetermined spatial ordering.

Fig. 3 illustrates the two cornerstones of this programming model; pfrags that are self-contained, and memory that is locally shared and probabilistic. The shared memory model is patterned after bulletin board systems that communicate via lossy update channels. Every particle contains a local entry to the bulletin board (the HomePage) where resident executables can read and write tagged data (posts). An additional segment of memory (the I/O space) is reserved for mirrored instances of the HomePages from the neighboring particles. Posts to a local HomePage appear – with an unbounded latency and non-zero probability of failure – at the mirror sites on all the particles within the network neighborhood. For an executable running in a given particle, the HomePage is read-write and the I/O space is read-only.

All software executed in *paint* is represented as process fragments. Pfrags are self contained and sized to fit entirely in the RAM space of a single particle[3] Inter-pfrag messaging is coded as posts (variable length key-value pairs) and gated through the I/O space. All writes must be to the HomePage. Reads can come from anywhere in the I/O space. In response to periodic interrupts from the particle's OS, a pfrag will scan the I/O space and, depending on what it finds there, will execute one of several predefined behaviors – post more data on the HomePage, request a transfer to a neighboring particle, self-delete, or simply idle.

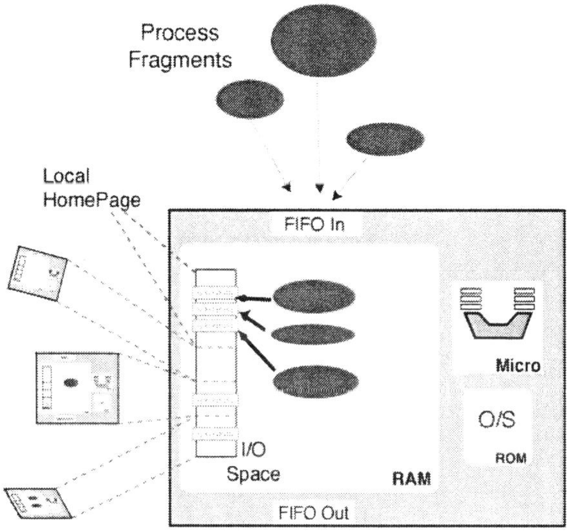

Figure 3 Programming Model
Distributed processes are embodied as ensembles of autonomous migratory process fragments ("pfrags"). Inter-pfrag communication via tagged messages (posts) that are posted on local bulletin board memory segment (HomePages). Copies of the HomePages from neighboring particles assembled into read-only I/O space.

The pfrag's continual, free running evaluation of its environment (as encoded in the I/O space) is the key driver for adaptation on *paint*. For example, if a pfrag read from the I/O space the value of the variables **y** and **z** and bound their sum to an internal variable **x**, then the pfrag would constantly be re-adding **y** and **z** to keep the value of **x** current. Section 3 reflects on the utility of this approach.

2.3. Tools

The work reported here predates the availability of the pushpin hardware, and was consequently developed and tested on the device simulator. Written in Java 1.1, this simulator models each particle functionally as an instance of a template Java object. An associated viewer supports visualization, and generation of image sequences. A GUI supports execution control (Run/Step/Stop), and selection of salient system parameters such as communication radius, number of

[2] Commercial Off-The-Shelf – a designer's term of endearment to denote systems constructed exclusively from commercially available components (i.e. no custom parts).

[3] none the pfrags of this report are larger than 600 bytes in size.

particles, degree of randomness in particle placement, and positioning of I/O portals for insertion of pfrags into ensemble.

3. Text Display

The method for positioning and display of a text character builds on the metaphor of a "directed seed". Seeds are single pfrags containing a character modeled as a sequence of geometric primitives, and a rendering algorithm capable of interpreting the model to compute an RGB pixel value.

As a precursor to "seeding the text", two reference points are externally declared and serve as insertion points for a sequence of pfrags that interact to build a 2D coordinate system. With this scaffold in place, the text pfrag is then inserted. It migrates to its pre-assigned position, and covers a bounded neighborhood with lightweight copies of itself. These copies act as portable rendering programs that are customized for the rendering of the one single character.

The remainder of this section describes this method in detail, with special attention to the adaptation strategies embodied in the pfrags. Sample results illustrate how individual pfrag adaptation, together with local messaging, enable groups of pfrags to cooperatively form robust virtual structures.

3.1 Anchors and Gradients

Creation of a 2D coordinate system begins with the selection of two externally defined reference points[4] and the establishment of a gradient field centered about each of these points.

Gradient fields as a natural phenomena (thermal, chemical, electro-magnetic) have become a common abstraction for messaging in physically distributed systems, with individual communities developing their own domain-specific variation. In the *paintable* PM, the generic gradient is realized as a lightweight pfrag that enters the particle ensemble through a single point and propagates virally, ultimately inserting a single copy of itself into every particle. Once a region is blanketed, the gradient pfrags message locally to generate a fractional estimate of the shortest path distance back to the source. These distance estimates are normalized to the communication radius of the particles.

Messaging between spatially proximal Gradients is mediated by posts to the HomePage (fig. 5). Each Gradient continually scans the I/O space for posts from neighboring Gradients. In response to what it finds, a Gradient will either update its own post, delete itself, or simply do nothing. Fig. 4 specifies this adaptation procedure.

```
1. if HC < HCmin + 1,
     then self-delete1
2. else if a page in the I/O space has
   no post from a Gradient,
     then propagate a copy of the
     Gradient to the neighboring
     particle.
3. else if HC > HCmin + 1,
     then update post to set
     HC = HCmin + 1
4. else,
     do nothing
```

Figure 4 Gradient - Adaptation procedure

The adaptation procedure is based on two values:

`HC`	the Gradient's own posted hop count
`HCmin`	the minimum hop count found in the I/O space (i.e. The hop counts from the neighboring Gradients)

3.2. 2D Coordinates

The arrival at one anchor point of the Gradient from the other anchor triggers the insertion of a Coordinate pfrag. Coordinate virally deposits a single copy of itself into every particle. Coordinate triangulates off the two Gradient distance estimates to synthesize a 2D coordinate that it then includes in its HomePage post (fig. 7a). These coordinates are normalized to the radius of the network link that defines a particle's neighborhood. The error bound on the coordinate depends directly on the accuracy of the Gradient distance estimate. This error performance has been treated both analytically and experimentally in the context of amorphous computing [10].

As with the Gradient pfrag, adaptation in the Coordinate pfrag is a by-product of the free running generative process (fig. 6). Fig. 7b shows the response of this process to an areal failure. The particles within an irregularly shaped patch were disabled. The 2D distortion in the immediate vicinity of the failure is due to the fact that the Gradient's shortest path distance estimates to the corresponding anchor point no longer map to Euclidean distance. However, the normalized amplitude of this distortion falls off with increasing distance from the failure zone. Self-repair follows if the area is repopulated with new particles.

[4] Placement of the reference points along a boundary of the particle ensemble eliminates the need for a symmetry-breaking third point

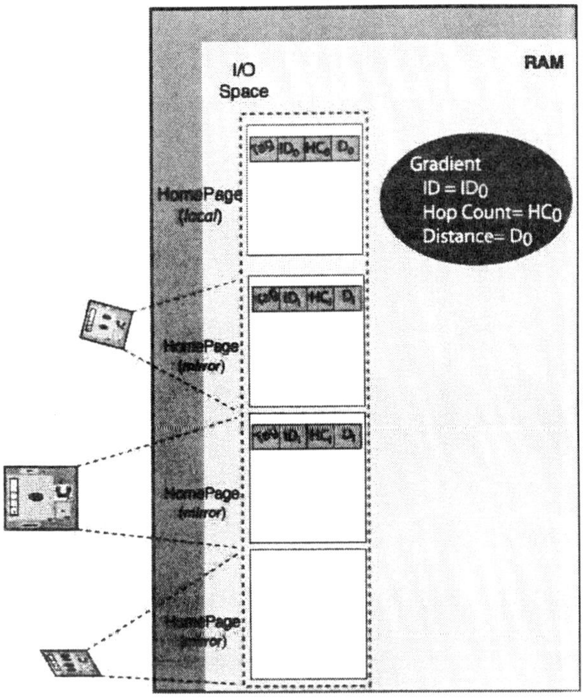

Figure 5 Gradient - Run Time

Run time environment as viewed through the I/O space of a single particle. This particle contains only one pfrag - the Gradient. I/O space consists of local HomePage plus mirrored copies of HomePages from three neighboring particles. Gradient sees its own post in local HomePage, and posts from other Gradients in two of the three neighbors. Entries in Gradient post:

Tag = key unique to Gradient pfrags
ID = identifier used to group Gradients.
HC = integer hop count
D = fractional distance

```
1. if either Gradient is missing,
    then self-delete.
2. else if an uninfected neighbor is
   found,
    then propagate a copy to that
    neighbor.
3. else,
    read the Gradient posts, re-
    triangulate and update the local
    Coordinate post as necessary.
```

Figure 6 Adaptation rules for Coordinate pfrag

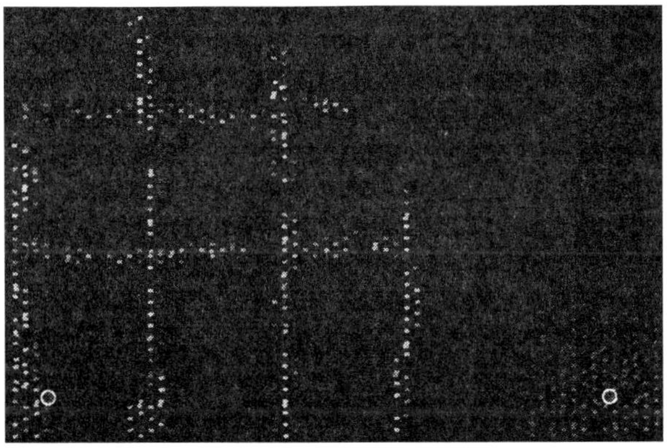

(a)

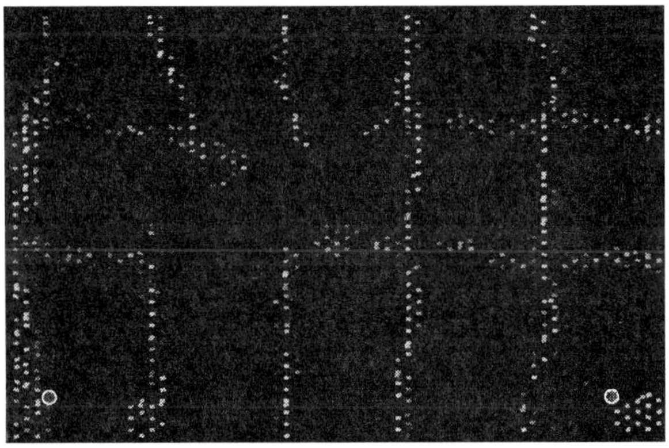

(b)

Figure 7 Coordinate System: Construction & Adaptation

Initial state is 3000-particle ensemble devoid of pfrags. In the construction phase (a), two anchor points are externally positioned (bottom) and assigned a 2D position. Gradient fields, emanating from each anchor, append the assigned 2D position to their HomePage posts. The arrival of a Gradient from one anchor at the other anchor triggers the insertion of a Coordinate pfrag that triangulates off of the posted Gradient distances to estimate a 2D position. Estimation procedure is free running, and automatically adapts to subsequent particle failure. Distortion caused by an areal failure (darkened area near center) is localized (b).

3.3 Text Rendering

Individual text characters are embodied as single pfrags. A Text pfrag contains three elements in its state vector:

1. a model of the character expressed as geometric primitives such as lines, arcs and splines.
2. a preferred position on the 2D coordinate system (relative to the 2D coordinate system).
3. a bounding box (likewise relative to the 2D coordinate system)

A text pfrag enters the particle ensemble at a random point, migrates to its preferred 2D location (fig. 8a), and then spawns lightweight copied of itself. The spawned copies limit their propagation to the spatial patch defined by the bounding box. The copies then compare the local 2D coordinate to the character model, compute the corresponding RGB pixel value, and post this value in the HomePage[5].

Fig. 8b illustrates this approach applied to a single character; an upper case '**A**'. The '**A**' is encoded as three straight lines, each defined by two endpoints. The rendering procedure calls for:

- reading the local 2D coordinate,
- calculating the shortest path distance to the nearest geometric primitive (a stroke)
- computing a monochrome pixel value by inversely weighting a maximum intensity, by the distance from the nearest stroke.

Note how this use of intermediary gray levels computed as a function of distance from a stroke, produces the antialiasing known to be important for legibility [4].

Two crucial components of this approach are adaptation, and inter-pfrag messaging between the Text seed and its copies.

In order to message to its spawned copies, the Text pfrag employs a broadcast technique similar to that of the Gradient. Posts from the Text pfrags contain an integer hop count and a variable length payload appended to the end of the post (table 1). The seed Text pfrag assumes a hop count that is fixed to zero. Text copies adopt a hop count that reflects the number of network hops back to the seed (fig 9). The Text seed signals to its copies by posting an new payload containing an incremented revision number. Copies look at posts from a neighbor with a smaller hop count for a payload update. They then read this payload update and append it to their own post – effectively propagating the change. Beyond a revision number, payloads can contain any amount of data in any prearranged format. However in this work, the payloads always contain new state vector data.

The second pillar of this approach is asynchronous, free running adaptation. The Text pfrag's behavior is defined by its adaptation procedure operating on the static state vector and the dynamic environment. The dynamic environment is defined by posts in the I/O space. The procedure described in fig 10 supports basic operations such as erasure of the character, in addition to the graphics transformations of the next section.

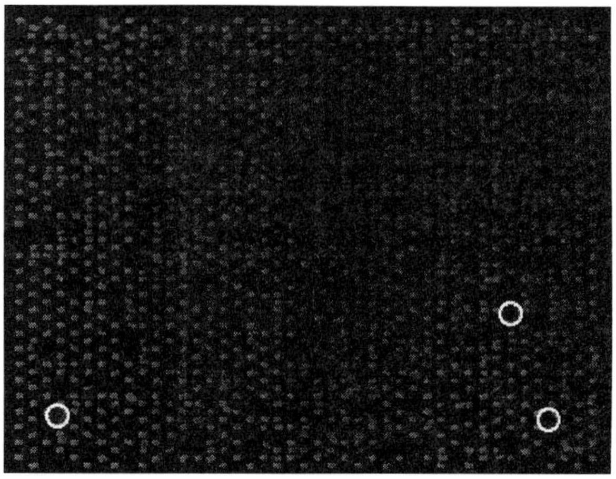

(a)

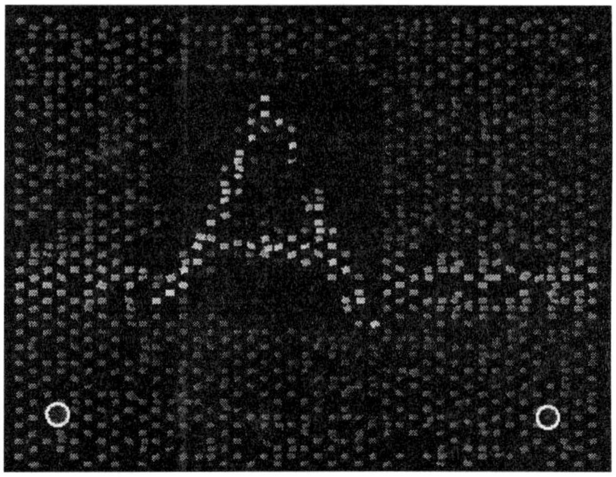

(b)

Figure 8 Text Seed: Positioning and rendering
(a) An ensemble of 1000 particles is initially configured with a coordinate system (not shown) relative to two anchor points (I/O ports along bottom edge). A single Text seed (red) enters through a third I/O port and migrates toward a coordinate that has been pre-stored in its internal state vector.
(b) Once in position, the original seed (red) spawns lightweight copies of itself. The copies limit their propagation to the area defined by their internally specified bounding box. For each particle within the bounding box, the seed's copy compares the local coordinate against the geometric model of the character to arrive at an anti-aliased pixel value.

[5] In this paper, we do not explicitly specify the agency by which the RGB post gets translated into a visible pixel intensity. However in the pushpins of fig. 2, a free running internal display routine scans the HomePage and maps posted RGB values to signals which directly drive a tri-color LED on the sensor/actuator board.

Table 1 Text Pfrag: Post definition

Entry:	Description:
TAG	Pfrag ID unique to the Text pfrag
CID	ID unique to instance of this character
HC	Integer hop count
PLD len	Length of payload
PLD rev	Revision ID for payload
PLD body	Variable length payload

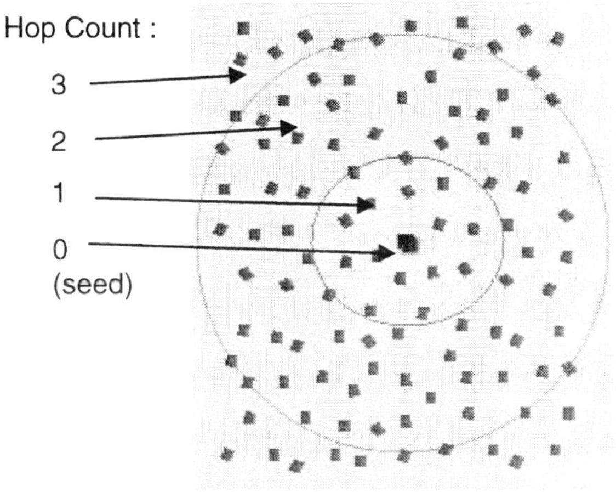

Figure 9 Text Pfrag: Messaging topology

4. Graphic Control

Simple graphics control is recast as message passing and manipulation of the adaptation rules. With changes in the state vector automatically reflected in the rendered character, graphics manipulation can be effected by signalling changes of the state vector. In our sample embodiment, an external agency broadcasts a coded graphics command[6] to the Text seeds. Each seed then parses the message, encodes the state changes into a payload, and updates its posts to include the new payload. The updated payload eventually arrives at the copies, which in turn internalize the new state data. The adaptation rules do the rest.

Fig. 11 illustrates this process for translation and scaling. Translation is expressed as a 2D offset to a Text pfrag's preferred position. The seed moves, and messages the new center position to its copies. Those copies that find themselves outside the new bounding box self-delete. Other copies suddenly find unpopulated neighboring particles that are within the new bounding box, and respond by propagating new

[6] eg. parameters for an affine transformation

```
1. if no Coordinates posts are found on
   the local HomePage,
    then self-delete.
2. else if a neighboring particle is
   inside the bounding box but does not
   contain a post from a copy pfrag,
    then propagate a copy to the
    uninfected neighbor.
3. else if a neighbor with a posted hop
   count smaller than the local hop
   count has a higher payload index,
    then copy the new payload and
    update post.
4. else if the updated payload changes
   the bounding box and the pfrag is
   outside the new bounding box,
    then self-delete.
5. else
    re-compute the RGB value and
    update post
```

Figure 10 Text Pfrag:
Adaptation rules for spawned copies

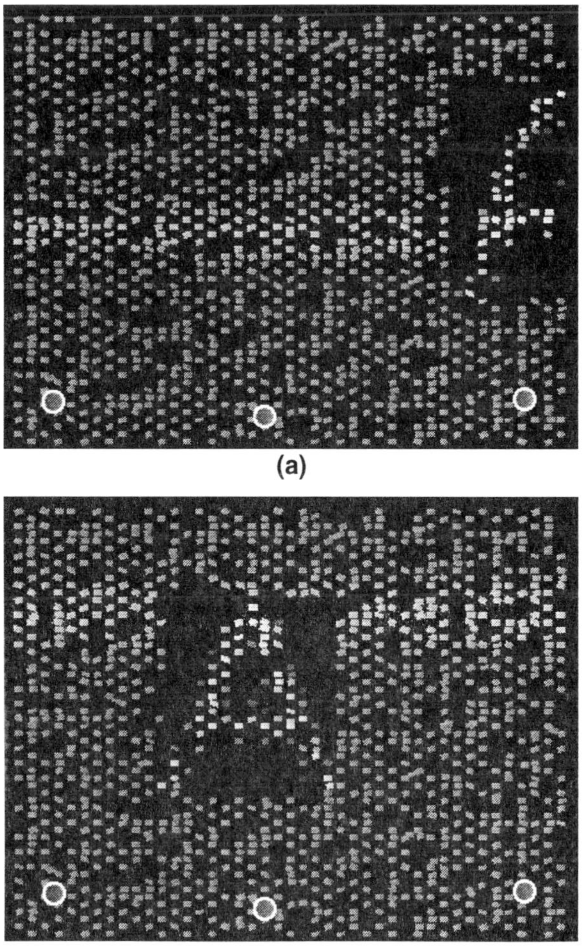

(a)

(b)

Figure 11 Translation (a) and Scaling (b)

0-7695-2906-2/07 $25.00 © 2007 IEEE

copies to the unpopulated neighbors. All copies recomputed the local pixel color. Translational offsets above some threshold have the effect of sliding the rendered character out of view (fig. 11a). However even in cases where the copies are completely absent, the seed remains waiting to restore the character should further translation again bring the character into view.

Scaling can likewise be effected by a change in the bounding box. Fig. 11b illustrates the effect of scaling the bounding box by a factor of 0.95 (compare with fig. 8b). The simple vehicle of resizing the bounding box suffices only within a bounded range of scale factors. As the scale factor continues to shrink, the copies will be able to apply rendering schemes of near arbitrary sophistication to maintain legibility.

5. Related Work

The vision of deeply embedded, finely grained, freely configurable computing is one that is shared among multiple communities. One such community proceeds from the assumption that relentless cost drivers in the established silicon IC sector will deliver much of the desired hardware functionality in the near term. In addition to paint, this guild includes groups working on wireless sensor networks [6], and those working on denser 'amorphous' computing meshes programmed around biological metaphors

At the level of node architecture, paint has the strongest commonality with the ever-shrinking sensornet nodes [8]. However the two camps diverge in their approach to software – largely due to the difference in target inter-node spacing (meters vs. millimeters) and the attendant application domains. This difference is most apparent when considering the ratio of energy dissipation for computing relative to that of communications. In mainstream sensornet designs, communications dominate the power budget. By contrast, the *paint* PM targets node densities where energy consumption is skewed heavily toward the computing elements.. At the extreme of this domain are systems of regular meshes that are being prototyped for next generation Tera-scale computing [16] [17]

The distributed software architecture based on process self-assembly is but one sample of a broader trend toward modeling distributed software systems on the metaphor of self-assembly as it occurs in the material world. A closely related effort in amorphous computing drew inspiration from biology to develop a programming model based on programmed self-assembly [1] and demonstrated its utility over a wide range of pattern formation; both 2D and 3D.

At a larger length scale, neighborhood programming has been shown to be a useful coding abstraction for sensornets and robotic swarms. In [15], tests on object tracking applications demonstrate the capacity for reducing algorithm complexity and increasing code density.

6. Coda

6.1. Discussion

Much work remains. And the results to date are little more than suggestive. Yet, to the degree that the challenges of *paintable* computing yield to continuing research, the current scaling limitations on conventional display systems lose their relevance. Revisiting fig. 1, the fine grain spatial distribution of the graphics function removes the two bandwidth bottlenecks associated with channeling all input into a single point for serial processing followed by a redistribution to the pixel raster for display.

Paint systems where the nodes are truly autonomous, where there are no shared resources and where the inter-node messaging is strictly local, all scale freely – at least until more subtle system bounds take hold[7]. Self-repair and the ability to freely reconfigure likewise follow from modularized software built around the requirements of spatial locality and ongoing adaptation.

However all this comes at a price. If the only purpose were to build a display, the approach as described here would never pass engineering muster. A minimum transmission bandwidth of a 500-byte pfrag per text character is impractically wasteful. Noise variance in the coordinate estimates yields characters with intolerable spatial distortion. And the shear manufacturing cost of dedicating a full featured graphics engine to every pixel1 make the economics unworkable.

However none of these problems are fundamental. As an alternate to sending the entire pfrag, one could send only a 16-bit character code and 2D center point, and then deed the generation of the associated pfrag to the processing element at the point of reception (similar to token passing described in [1]). Likewise, there exist a variety of alternate techniques employing global stimuli[8] for estimating 2D position on *paint*-like ensembles [9, 5, 11]. And even for the approach of this paper, the distortion in the 2D positional estimate is tied to the inter-particle spacing. Shrinks in the device

[7] power, environmental capacity to dissipate heat, available surface to paint over

[8] Techniques include acoustic ranging, RF time-of-flight, and strength of received signals.

geometry of the particles, and the attendant reduction of inter-particle spacing, will reduce the variance as perceived by a viewer.

The most sobering engineering reality check relates to the proposed 1-to-1 ratio of computing elements to pixels. As a stopgap, one could the ease the cost by assigning multiple pixel elements to each processing element. But in the context of a display-only, the cost savings realized by this strategy will never suffice.

A compliment to lowering the system cost is to justify the system cost. This suggests a strategy of broadening the application domain by driving the development of a "paintable display" toward subsumption of additional components from the standard computing architecture. The pixel display that already annexed the graphics controller should also incorporate the processing, the memory, the external networking, and the remaining I/O modalities into a single distributed machine.

What can this distributed machine do? Work to date has demonstrated its capacity for storage, communication and signal processing in the context of plausible applications [2]. Ongoing work is building on these basics to realize distributed estimation and control. In those applications where the underlying paintable is performing some useful, compute-intensive task, addition of display becomes an incremental cost.

6.2 Conclusions

An alternate architecture for display systems has been advanced based on extensions to ongoing work on paintable computing. We showed how this approach has the potential for overcoming the key scaling limitations of conventional display systems (I/O bandwidth, rendering capacity, defect tolerance). The operation of a display was mapped to the *paint* programming model. A proof-of-principle implementation of distributed rendering and graphics control for text characters was presented. *Paint*, when used exclusively as a display system, is prohibitively expensive. We discussed alternatives for cost reduction with a focus on displays as an incremental add-on to a *paint* ensemble already operating as a stand-alone distributed computer.

6.3. Future Work

The most demanding open points relating to display on *paint* involve the use of increasingly sophisticated image models for both decoding and encoding, and the need to revisit basic hardware assumptions as the particle ensemble scales up to 10^4 pebbles arranged in a 3D topology.

Paint's architecture naturally favors compute load over transfer bandwidth[9]. At least initially, this biases the paintable toward display of model-based coded imagery. The nuance in this case being that the models should themselves be amenable to a distributed representation.

The text characters of this report were coded using a pen stroke as an image model. The quest for ever richer display output will drive the creation of distributed versions of ever more complex models:

- distributed postscript for imagery coded procedurally as a sequence of pen strokes,
- motion-compensated frequency transformations for natural imagery coded a'la MPEG-1 and MPEG-2,
- a distributed variant of openGL for synthetic imagery,
- and ultimately, a distributed hybrid in the vain of MPEG-4 and MPEG-7

The dual to model-based decoding is model-based encoding[10]. As a massive nonlinear search through a collection of heterogeneous models, model-based encoding is an interesting problem in its own right. The relevance to the paintable display problem is that the *coded imagery is only as rich and/or efficient as the models that the images are coded against*. The models employed for display on *paint* necessarily lend themselves to distributed representations -- representations whose power naturally scale with increasing particle count.

Finally, while software will remain the focus of continued development, it must proceed against the backdrop of evolving hardware. Both the simulator and the pushpin environments were characterized by ~ 10^3 particles, a 2D topology, a tri-color LED bound to each particle, and a communication radius that incorporated 10-20 neighbors. The progression to 10^4 pebbles will challenge all of these assumptions, raising questions about; the need to dynamically alter the pixel/processor ratio, methods for self-configuring a 2D display surface on a 3D particle ensemble, and the utility of halftoning with small reflective display elements as an alternative to power-hungry tri-color emitters.

Should be fun.

---

[9] Anathema to this architecture are unencoded RGB pixel data that is streamed through a single entry point for fanout to the entire ensemble.

[10] e.g. the dual text rendering would be to project a text character on to *paint* fitted with a dense array of photo sensors, and have the paint produce a single Text pfrag that encodes the character.

Acknowledgements

The research of this report was performed at the Physics & Media Group at MIT's Media Laboratory. It was supported by the NSF (CCR-0122419 Center for Bits and Atoms) and DARPA (DAAD16-00-R-0012 Microsystems Technology Office). Special thanks to Prof. Neil Gershenfeld, Prof. Joe Jacobson and Robert Tulis for enthusiastic support and insightful feedback.

References

[1] H. Abelson, D. Allen, D. Coore, C. Hanson, G. Homsy, T. Knight, R. Nagpal, E. Rauch, G. J. Sussman, and R. Weiss *Amorphous Computing* Communications of the ACM, vol. 43, pp. 74-82, 2000.

[2] W.J. Butera, *Programming a Paintable Computer*, Ph.D. in Media Arts and Sciences. Cambridge, MA: Massachusetts Institute of Technology, 2002, pp. 1-176.

[3] B. Comiskey, J. D. Albert, H. Yoshizawa, and J. Jacobson, *An electrophoretic ink for all-printed reflective displays*, Nature, vol. 394, pp. 253-255, 1998.

[4] J. Foley, A. van Dam, S. Feiner, and J. Hughes, *Computer Graphics: Principles and Practice*, Reading, Massachusetts: Addison-Wesley, 1991. pp.132-142

[5] L. Girod, V. Bychkobskiy, J. Elson, and D. Estrin. *Locating tiny sensors in time and space: A case study.* In Proceedings of the International Conference of Computer Design (ICCD) 2002.

[6] G. T. Huang, "Casting the Wireless Sensor Net," in *Technology Review*, July/August 2003, pp. 50 – 56.

[7] J. Jacobson, B. Comiskey, B. Turner, J. Albert, and P. Tsao, *The last book*, IBM Sytems Journal, vol. 36, pp. 457-463, 1997.

[8] J. L. Hill, *System Architecture for Wireless Sensor Networks*, Ph.D. in Computer Science. Berkeley CA: University of Californmia, Berkeley, 2003, pp. 1-186.

[9] K. Langendoen and N. Reijers. *Distributed localization in wireless sensor networks: a quantitative comparison.* The International Journal of Computer and Telecommunication Networking, 43(4):499–518, November 2003.

[10] R. Nagpal, *Organizing a Global Coordinate System from Local Information on an Amorphous Computer*, Massachusetts Institute of Technology, Cambridge, Massachusetts, A.I. MEMO 1666, August 12, 1999.

[11] K. Pahlavan, L. Xinrong, and J. Makela. *Indoor geolocation science and technology.* IEEE Communications Magazine, 40(2):112–118, February 2002.

[12] DARPA Technical Report *Technology Evaluation for Paintable Computing and Paintable Displays: RF Nixel* Seedling Massachusetts Institute of Technology, April 2006

[13] N. B. Bowden, *Order and Disorder: Mesoscale SelfAssembly and Waves*, Ph.D. in Department of Chemistry. Cambridge, Massachusetts: Harvard University, 1999, pp. 307.

[14] George Whitesides and Bartosz Grzybowski *Self-Assembly at All Scales* Science vol 295 March 29, 2002

[15] Kamin Whitehouse, Cory Sharp, Eric Brewer, David Culler *Hood: A Neighborhood Abstraction for Sensor Networks* ACM MobiSYS'04, June 6-9 2004 Boston MA

[16] S. Vangal, J.Howard, et. al. *An 80-Tile 1.28 TFLOP Network-on-chip in 65nm CMOS* IEEE International Solid-state Circuits Conference, February 11-15 2007, San Francisco, CA

[17] ISSCC 2007: Intel's TeraFlops Design http://www.realworldtech.com/page.cfm?ArticleID=RWT040307000414

Neural Network of a Cognitive Crow: An interacting map based architecture[‡]

Vishwanathan Mohan[†], Pietro Morasso[*]
[†]*Doctoral School on Humanoid Technologies, Italian Institute of Technology, Genova, Italy.*
[*] *Neurolab, DIST, University of Genova, Via Opera Pia 13, Genova 16145 Italy.*
e-mail:vishwanathan.mohan@unige.it

Abstract

Studies on animal reasoning can serve as a very relevant guide in building artificial systems that autonomously evolve their cognition and develop new skills in structural/functional coupling with their environments. New Caledonian crows display sophisticated abilities in fashioning tools and using them to acquire otherwise unobtainable food rewards. We may consider this an act of creativity, during which a cognitive agent reasons about things that do not yet exist but could exist as a result of his actions. However, the computational basis of such cognitive processes have remained elusive. Taking the example of tool manufacture by Caledonian crows, we explore an interacting self organizing map based architecture for virtually manipulating neural activity so as to achieve ones goals in novel situations. Simulation results demonstrate how interactions between sensori-motor space, action space and work space can be exploited in new situations to find action/action sequences that result in known intermediate states (sub goals) that in turn lead to the overall goal.

1. Introduction

Everyone can think about things and effortlessly carry out "what if" tasks, i.e. perform virtual actions to simulate what happens to them in 'virtual worlds'. Studies from animal reasoning reveal many interesting behaviors, demonstrated by animals that have all the hallmarks of similar brain processing in humans. Seeing a squirrel accessing the possibility of obtaining nuts from a nut dispenser placed inaccessibly high above the ground, or observing a chimp using a small stick to reach an otherwise unreachable larger stick and then using the larger stick to obtain a banana, or even corvids fashioning wires into hooks, fall short of astonishing us unless we question their computational basis or try to make robots do similar tasks, that we often take as granted for humans.

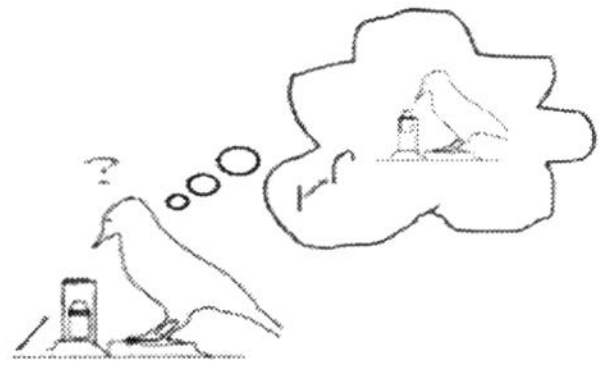

Figure.1. Giving a mental look: Tool making Caledonian Crows.

An interesting case of novelty in behavior was demonstrated by Betty, the Caledonian crow, who lived in Oxford [13, 14,15], when she faced the task of extracting a food basket kept at the bottom of a transparent vertical tube and her usual tool was not available to her. Instead, she found a straight piece of wire lying nearby. Betty had already had experience of successfully using a bent twig to extract the food from the vertical tube and, about one year before, the experience of playing and bending flexible pipe cleaners. Then she is faced with the new and non-trivial task of determining how to retrieve the food from the tube using the only tool available: a straight wire. As reported in the above mentioned study, after a short hesitation she pushed one end of the wire into the tape holding the tube and moved the other round with her beak, making a hook, using which she successfully extracted the food. She repeated this performance 90 percent of the time she faced the same situation. It is not uncommon to encounter similar situations in our daily lives when we have to reason about things that do not yet exist but could exist as a result of our actions. What sort of computational architecture could account for the creative process demonstrated by Betty? What sort of search space is involved? How is it constrained? What are the representations? How are they acquired? How are they invoked? What are the planning mechanisms? Using an interacting self organizing map based architecture, we explore some the above questions, seeking to eventually find answers to some of them.

[‡] This research was partly supported by EU FP6 Project GNOSYS

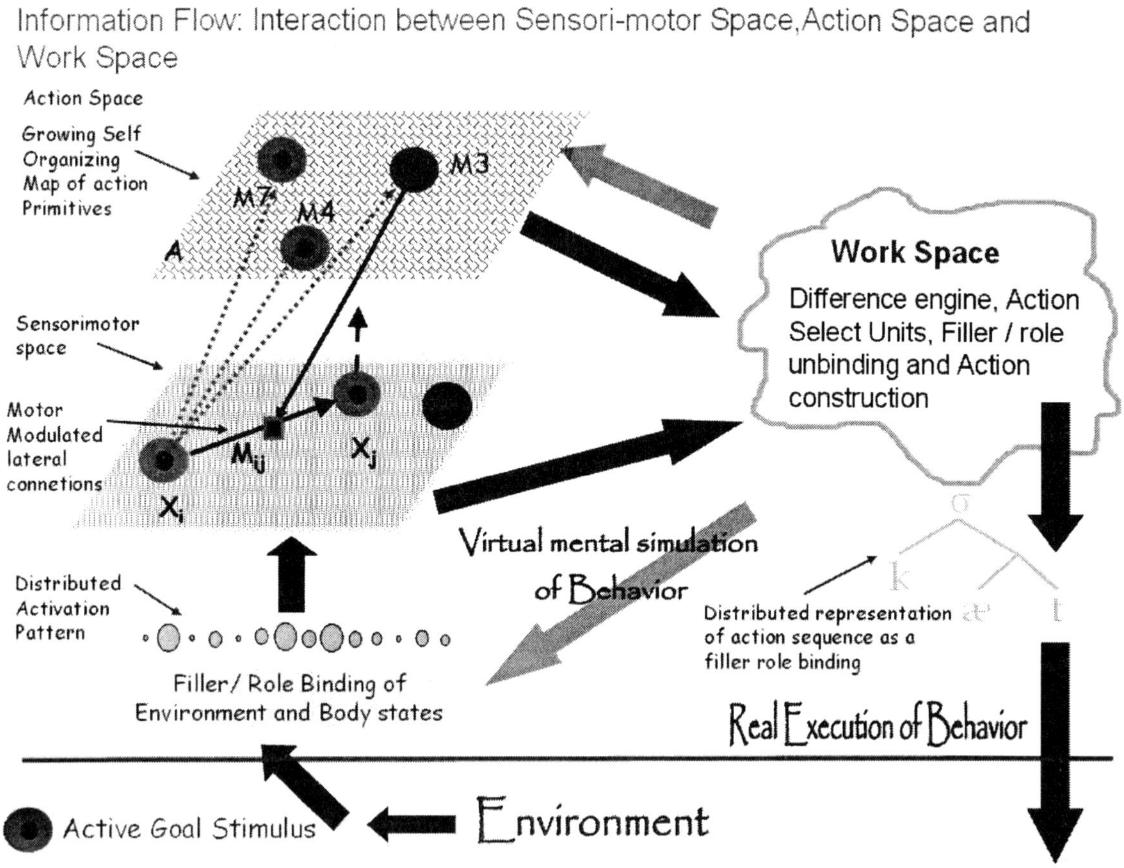

Figure 2. The Global Picture: Activations in the action space modulate the lateral connection strengths and thereby induce anticipatory shifts of the activity peak in the sensorimotor map, thus eliciting perceptual activity which is *similar to that which would have occurred* if the action was performed in reality. Activity in the sensorimotor space projects back into the action space via intermap connectivity, to solve the inverse problem of finding action sets which map the transformation from initial condition to active goal. Both maps pass active information into the workspace which keeps track of the overall actions and consequences encountered in reaching the goal stimulus. New inputs, if detected, are accounted for by recruiting new neurons with suitably tuned receptive fields; new solutions and sequences, if found, are accounted for by forming new lateral and intermap connectivity.

2. Global Picture of the Architecture

2.1. Filler/Role bindings of Activity Vectors

The sensorimotor space and action space are self organized using standard techniques to learn sensory state representations S_j and primitive motor actions M_i, created by filler/role bindings of different environmental stimuli. A distributed sensory/action representation S_j is defined by a collection of structural roles $\{r_i\}$ each occupied by a filler $\{f_i\}$. The connectionist realization of S_j is an activity vector

$$s_j = \sum_i f_i \otimes r_i \qquad (1)$$

which is the sum of vectors realizing the filler/role bindings, because in these tensor product representations, the additivity property holds, i.e. the pattern realizing the structure as a whole is the superposition of patterns realizing all of its constituents; moreover, the pattern realizing a constituent is the tensor product of a pattern realizing the filler and a pattern realizing the structural role it occupies. In higher cognitive domains such as language and reasoning, mental representations can be recursive: the fillers or roles of S_j have themselves the same type of internal structure as S. And these structured fillers $\boldsymbol{f}$ or roles $\boldsymbol{r}$ in turn have the same type of tensor product realization as S_i. Such filler/role bindings have been extensively used in many fields: linguistics [2], spatial transformations [10,11], judgments of analogical similarity [12], among others. In our case, they provide an organized way of representing groups of salient objects present in sensory situations and primitive action building blocks (and action sequences) in a distributed manner. Example Sensory Situations: hunger + food, stick + food + reach error, food + curved wire; Example Action Sequences; Temporal roles; Contextual roles; Positional roles etc are bound with Action Primitives like Grasp, Reach etc (which in turn may be bound with fillers which contain information like coordinates of locations, constraints etc). We also additionally use the 'Cons' and 'Ex' operators [2] for the construction of combined parent tensor product representations of different child representations and the inverse operation of extracting relevant component information from the parent representation. The Cons(p,q) operator constructs a combined representation S_{sm} of two different trees 'p' and 'q'. The connectionist realization of Cons operator is given by equation 2:

$$s_{sm} = Cons(p,q) = p \otimes r_{env} + q \otimes r_{body} = W_{consP} \cdot p + W_{consQ} \cdot q \quad (2)$$

W_{ConsP} and W_{ConsQ} are the corresponding weight matrices and are given by:

$$W_{consP} = \mathrm{I} \otimes r_{env}\,;\ W_{consQ} = \mathrm{I} \otimes r_{body} \quad (3)$$

'I' is a feedforward recursion matrix, i.e. a matrix of Identity function for the entire representational space, as defined by Slomensky et al [2].

$$\mathrm{I} = \sum_{k=0}^{\infty} 1^{\otimes k} \quad (4)$$

If we consider 4-d roles and 2-d fillers, S_{sm} is a 16-d vector. Similarly, inverse operator Ex (S_{sm}, n) extracts the child representation of depth n from the parent. 'Ex' operator may be of more importance for the lower level action execution blocks which have to unbind each motor goal, and the corresponding fillers (Coordinates of the point to be reached, constraints etc in case of a reach goal). The sensorimotor space and action space in figure 1 are trained to represent the percepts and primitive actions (like reach, grasp etc) using the vectors realized by filler role bindings given by eqn 2. These primitive actions are sufficient to virtually reason and produce behaviors of relative amount of complexity like obtaining food by reaching with a stick or using a small stick to reach an otherwise unreachable larger stick and then using the larger stick to obtain the food (classical two stick paradigm solved by chimps) to mention a few.

In an earlier work we proposed forward inverse motor control architecture coupled with a recurrent neural network to generate some of these behaviors with simple robotic embodiment [3]. In this work we concentrate on architectures that account for more difficult problems like those solved by the Caledonian crows [15]. Both maps are self organized using standard methods; such that the input weight vectors π_i of a unit i converges on an average to the stimulus for which i is the best matching unit. The winner in the sensorimotor space and the corresponding 16-d representational vector for the case of the stimulus 'food+tool+hunger' is shown in figure 3.

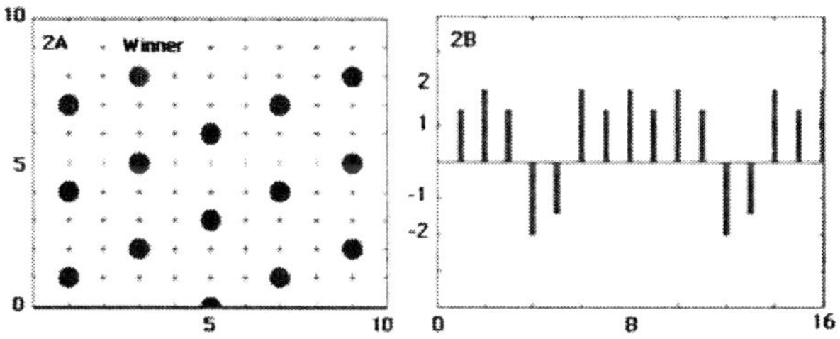

Figure 3. a: Shifts in activity in the Sensorimotor space; b: Filler Role bindings of activity vector corresponding to the wining neuron.

We detect novelty when the difference between the current stimulus s and the best matching weight vector π_i exceeds a vigilance threshold $\vartheta \in [0,1]$. Whenever the threshold is exceeded, we reset the error measures and generate a new unit 'j' that has its receptive field centered at the new representation. This new unit as of now does not have connections, either lateral or intermap: such connectivity will grow during future explorations, whenever goal oriented actions and consequences emerging out of the new situations will be discovered. We get back to this issue later in the article when we consider the case of Betty the Caledonian Crow.

2.2. Dynamics and Connectivity

2.2.1. Situation-Action-Consequence loop

Let x_i be the activation of unit i in the sensorimotor space. The activation dynamics of each unit in this space is as follows:

$$\tau_{sm}\dot{x}_i = -x_i + U_i(s) + \kappa \sum_j M_{ij} \Theta(x_j) \quad (5)$$

Analogous to neural fields, the first term $-x_i$ introduces an exponential relaxation to the dynamics and Θ a sigmoid activation function. The second term U_i is a feedforward input to unit i, which can either come from the environment (sensory input) or from the work space in the form of a constructed virtual representation of a stimulus 's'. In particular, we choose U_i to be a softmax function with nice computational properties [1], defined as follows:

$$U_i(s) = \frac{S_i(s)}{\sum_j S_j(s)} \quad (6)$$

$$S_i(s) = \exp \frac{-(\pi_i - s)^2}{2\sigma_s^2} \quad (7)$$

Where π_i is the codebook vector of unit '*i*' and '*s*' the stimulus in the form of a filler/role binding. The third term in eqn. 5 describes the contribution made by lateral connectivity between units in the sensorimotor space to the activation of unit *i*. However, the crucial difference from standard models is that we use the lateral connectivity as a means to allow the activity in the action space to couple with the dynamics of the sensorimotor space (hereafter SM space). In other words, the lateral connections M_{ij} of equation 5 learn which motor signals contribute, on average, to a transition from the stimulus s_i to a stimulus s_j. This is done by defining M_{ij} as the scalar product of the weight vector w_{ij} and the current motor activation in the action space 'm' as in equation 8.

$$M_{ij} = < w_{ij}, m_i > \quad (8)$$

More precisely, if an action m_i results in a transition from stimulus s_i to s_j, then the lateral connectivity is $M_{ij} = w_{ij}.m_i$, where the weight vector w_{ij}, associated with every lateral connection (*i j*), could be thought of as the codebook vector of that connection [7]. The training of these lateral connections is relatively straightforward. During training, the agent carries out pseudo-random exploratory actions from known initial conditions in SM space. The sensory consequences are provided by the environment and the lateral connections between the initial and final receptive populations in the SM map are trained to map the action which led to the ensuing consequence.

In this way, activations in the action space modulate the lateral connection strengths and thereby induce anticipatory shifts of the activity peak on the sensorimotor map. Interaction between action space and sensorimotor space by virtue of motor modulated lateral connectivity thus embeds *'Situation-Action-Consequence' loops or Forward Models* into the architecture and offers a way of eliciting perceptual activity in the sensorimotor space, *similar to that which would have occurred* if the action was performed in reality.

2.2.2 Situation-Goal-Action loop

This is the inverse problem of generating goal oriented behavior, i.e. finding actions/action sequences possible from the initial state in SM space that eventually lead to the desired active goal stimulus. We account for the inverse problem by projecting back the activity in sensorimotor space into the action space to find a set Y_m of motor actions that may eventually be useful in reaching the goal. Hence, signals flow between the sensorimotor map and the motor system in both directions. In the anticipation process, motor signals from the action space modulate corresponding lateral connections and cause predictive excitations. In the action selection process, the signals are emitted from the sensorimotor map back to the motor layer to induce the motor excitations that should turn predictions into reality. The activation dynamics of the action space is given by equation 9:

$$\tau_m \dot{m}_j = -m_j + A_j + \eta \left(\frac{\sum_i C_{ij} S_i(s)}{\sum_j \sum_i C_{ij} S_i(s)} \right) \quad (9)$$

where 'm_j' is the activation of unit *j* in the action space. Inputs A_j and η come from the workspace and define interactions between workspace and action space. Units in the workspace can selectively activate units in the action space using these inputs, which further cause shifts in activity in the SM space through motor modulated lateral connectivity as defined in equation 8. We will get back to this issue more precisely in later parts of this article.

The third term in eqn. 9 models the forward projection of activity in SM space into the action space. We define C_{ij} as an elementary connection between i^{th} neuron in the SM space to the jth neuron in the action space. The intermap connections model a kind of heteroassociation between the activities in sensorimotor and action spaces. These connections, usually trained in a Hebbian way ($\Delta C_{ij} \propto \varsigma U_i M_j$) have been used efficiently in several computational architectures; for example, bidirectional coordinate transformation from proximal to distal spaces for targeting reaching movements based on force fields [1]. However, the problem is slightly more complex when we consider behaviors like the 'two stick paradigm' and especially the case of 'Betty', as compared to problems of spatial navigation, which are also goal directed, but in which the link between initial and final sensory states is mathematically well defined (by Euclidian distance measures, forward kinematics etc). In contrast, the *Aha moment* in which Betty discovers that the action of bending the straight wire into a hook shape is the trick for fetching the food, cannot be expressed mathematically in a straightforward way. Further, we still need to explain the case when *there is no action / action sequence available* from the initial situation to reach the goal (as in Betty's case) and the further problem of making new hetero-associative connections between the two spaces, which might enable Betty to solve the same problem in future. So when do we form inter map connectivity? The proposed solution can be formulated as follows: we connect the ith element in the SM space to the jth element in the action space if executing action M_j is rewarding under the presence of stimulus s_i. However, it is not trivial to anticipate that executing action M_j is rewarding in order to achieve a particular goal: in fact, an initial sensory condition s_i may have hetero-associations with many actions in the action space but not all of them may be useful for the current goal (they may be rewarding for some other goals). Here comes the problem of selecting the action M_j , which is best for solving the current goal, out of a set of actions Y_m which are possible from a given sensory stimulus s_i (The inverse may also be true: i.e. a goal state may hetero-associate with many actions, but not all of them may be possible for the agent, from the initial condition in the sensorimotor space. In fact, this was one of the problems faced by Betty.) To solve this crucial problem, we propose the notion of *Workspace*, composed of a collection of supportive subsystems: 1) the difference engine, 2) the action select unit, 3) the representation unbinder and temporal binder for final action sequence construction. We explicate the nature of utility of these subsystems and the modality of interactions of the workspace with other parts of the architecture in the next section.

3. Reasoning in State Space

To clearly elucidate the complete sequence of interactions between the action space, SM space and workspace, we break up the complete process into three distinct phases: Preparatory Phase, Reflective Phase and Revelation Phase [5]. Before we come to the case of the Caledonian crow, we analyse each phase separately.

3.1. Preparatory Phase

As the name indicates, in this phase resources needed to deal with a particular kind of problem are activated in the workspace, in order to facilitate the process of delineating a plan of action in the next phase. Let x_i be the initial active state in the sensorimotor space. We begin by storing the codebook vectors of this unit x_i in a temporary location in the workspace for use during the reflection phase. Then, we present the *SM* space with a goal *G*, equivalent to reaching a state that perceives stimulus s_G. Let us also consider that, by simulating eqn. 5, the $x_G{}^{th}$ unit in the *SM* space is now the best match to the applied goal stimulus s_G. Then, the problem at hand is to find an action / action sequence $\{m_i, m_j...\}$ from the action space that enables us to reach via motor modulated lateral connections, the state x_G from x_i in the sensorimotor space.

After presentation of goal stimulus s_G and finding the active unit x_G in the SM space for that stimulus, the preparatory phase involves two more additional steps. The first step is to ensure a way to identify if the sensory goal has been reached during the reflective phase as a consequence of virtual execution of actions in the action space. For this purpose we invoke the notion of a difference engine (DE), which simply eliminates differences between the initial (and intermediate) states and the active goal state. Of course, because of the flexibility of filler/role bindings we can also use difference engines to find out what exactly is the difference between the present and goal states (by unbinding the representations into constituents, useful for making analogies), but for the current discussion we keep the functionality very simple. So, at present the difference engine in the workspace has two inputs, s_G and s_i which are the codebook elements of the active goal *G* and the initial /subsequent states x_i. The output of the DE is 1 if the state reached in SM space is same as the Goal state. In case the goal state is successfully reached, the complete sequence of action is outputted by the temporal binder, which has the function of binding every action primitive active in the Action space during the transition from x_i to x_G with an appropriate temporal role (so that the lower level execution units have information of *what to do when*). This kind of representation of action trees, whose nodes form motor goals, is analogous to the metaphor of "motor vocabulary" and "motor ontology" [5].

Secondly in the preparatory phase, after presenting the goal stimulus, we project the goal activation in the SM space to the Action space and identify the set of actions Y_G that are linked to the goal (through inter map connections). This set of actions Y_G linked to an active goal form the first input to the action select unit in the workspace. These are further used in the reflective phase to decide weather executing an arbitrary action m_k from set Y_k associated to any arbitrary sensory stimulus s_k is actually rewarding to reach the current active goal. This is extremely critical because, an initial sensory condition may hetero-associate to many actions in the action space that may not be useful for a particular goal (they may be rewarding for some other goals). Here comes the problem of selecting that action m_k which is useful for solving the current goal from a set of actions Y_k which are possible from a given sensory stimulus s_k. It is also interesting to note that also the inverse may occur: a goal state may hetero-associate with many actions, but not all of them may be possible from the initial condition in the sensorimotor space. We are not assuming that by *mere training* there always exist actions available in the action space, which are linked to the goal, but only that there are a few primitive actions which may be linked to the goal by previous experience and exploration. For example, in the case of Betty there was an action of using the curved wire to pull the food which she had already learnt, which was associated with the food reward/goal due to previous experience. The real problem is the fact that even though she had this action linked to the goal, the initial situation she was in, did not support that action, which eventually led to the tool manufacture and novelty in behaviour. And we are not assuming here that this action is also present in the training set. So our assumption of linking some primitive actions to goals and initial conditions does not imply that solutions to all problems lie in the training set. We get back to this issue in the revelation phase.

3.2. Reflective Phase

In the preparatory phase, the sensory-motor map of the agent receives a goal G, i.e. it reaches a state that perceives stimulus s_G; then the agent found the active unit in the SM space x_G, passed its codebook vector to the DE, projected the activity in SM space into the action space to find the set Y_G of active actions corresponding to the goal state and transferred the set of active actions for that goal as the first input of the action select unit. The "reflective phase", as the name indicates, is a phase of continuous reflections between the SM and Action spaces with an aim to find a potential solution that eventually leads to the goal.

The reflective phase consists of the following steps:

a) Projection of the activity corresponding to the initial sensory situation x_i to the action space using eqn. 9 (A=0) and finding the set of actions Y_i that is linked to the initial condition;-

b) Finding the action m_s which is possible from the initial condition and which is also useful in moving towards the active goal, i.e. finding element m_s which belongs to the set Z defined by $Y_G \cap Y_i$.

   There many be more than one action present in set Z, which implies there are different ways to reach the same goal, in these cases one may imagine using either one of them or having a higher level selection process, however for animal reasoning paradigms it is reasonable to consider that there are not unlimited amount of actions which overlap in the two sets at any one particular sensory state. We consider the other extreme possibility of Z being a null set in the revelation phase.

c) Activating the unit corresponding to 'm_s' in the action space by making A_s=1, and thereby introducing motor induced lateral excitations in the SM space that cause a peak shift from the initial sensory state x_i to a new state x_j equivalent to perceiving the situation that is the consequence of executing action m_s from x_i. Is x_j the goal to be reached? This can be found out by passing the code- book vector of x_j as second input to the difference engine. If x_j is not equal to x_G, then we once again look for actions which are now possible from x_j, by projecting it into the action space and repeating step b.

By this process of continuous reflections, we are moving in a well defined manner to different locations in the sensory and action spaces, on the way to eventually reach the final active goal as shown in figure 4.

The reflective phase will always converge to a reasonable sequence of actions to be performed to approach the goal, in different circumstances, under the condition that Z is not a null set. We come to the case of Z being a null set in the next section. Use of interactions between the sensorimotor and action spaces to virtually simulate goal oriented behaviour

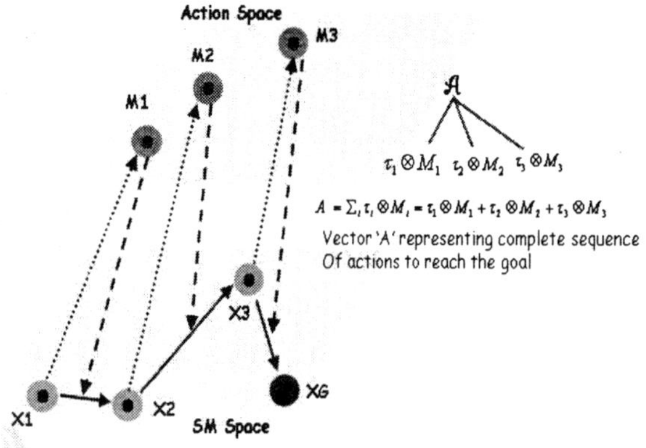

Figure 4: Computational processes in the reflective phase.

resonates very well with emerging biological evidence in support of the simulation hypothesis towards generation of cognitive behaviour mainly (a) Simulation of Action [5,8], (b) Simulation of perception [6,8], and (c) Anticipation [6].

3.3. Revelation Phase

The preparatory and reflective phases are sufficient to mentally rehearse a plan of action for directly achieving a goal using learnt single chunks of sequences of object/action. In this section, we use the interacting map based architecture to find a possible way to deal with novel situations when there is no solution embodied in the training set, i.e. there are no built in / pre trained inter map connections and lateral connections to solve the problem by just exploiting the dynamics of SM and Action space. Before attempting to offer an explanation to the case of novel behavior demonstrated by Betty, using the architecture based on interacting maps, it is worthwhile to precisely define the following.

a) *Novel Problem*: In our terminology, a novel problem is a situation in which Z is a null set; i.e. either the initial state (and knowledge gained through training) is not suited for executing actions which are needed to reach final state or when the representation of the situation in the SM space is detected to be novel (i.e. crosses the threshold of vigilance).

b) *Solution to a Novel Problem*: Finding a solution to a novel problem is in one way equivalent to finding a further sensory state s_n in the SM space that projects to an action set Y_n in the action space, such that $Y_G \cap Y_n$ is not null. If the representation of the situation is detected to be new (in the sense of crossing a threshold of vigilance), finding a solution also involves unbinding the parent representation into component roles, and then a further processes of reflections using the component representations coupled with interactions with the workspace. We will further elaborate on this issue in discussion on Caledonian crows later in this section.

c) *Sub goal*: In our terminology, a sub goal is a state vector s_{SG} in the SM Space that associates with an action set Y_{SG} in action space, which contains elements that form an intersection with both action sets Y_I (associated with the initial condition s_i) and Y_G (associated with the active goal).

We shall now consider how the coupled interaction between SM space, action space and workspace explains the behavior demonstrated by Betty. For the sake of clarity we use a pictorial representation of the situation along with a brief explanation of what happens in actual computational terms.

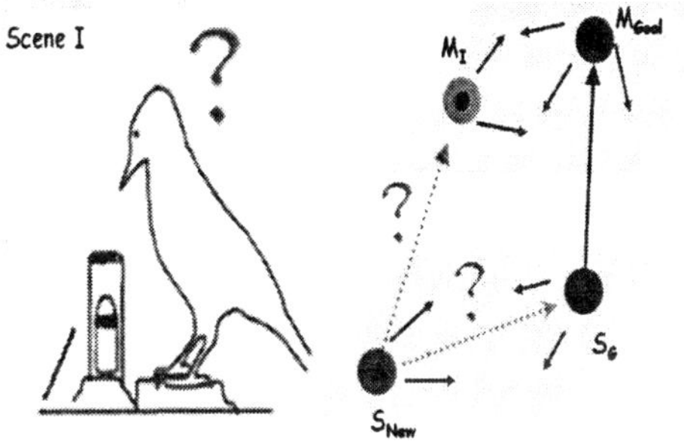

Figure 5. Scene I.

Figure 5 depicts the initial situation faced by Betty and the corresponding situation in the SM and Action spaces. Betty is hungry, she finds the food basket kept inside the tube, but there is no curved wire available (her usual tool), to get the food. However there is a straight wire in the scene. According to the experimenters, Betty had previous experience of playing with and bending straight wires. Betty also knew to use a curved wire to extract the food basket from the tube. So it is reasonable to consider that she had a representation of a straight stick and also had an inter map connection associating the straight wire in SM Space to the action of 'bending' in the action space. We are not assuming that Betty also had a prior representation of the new situation itself. The situation (Straight wire + food + tube + hunger) will be detected as a novel representation when ever it is presented to the SM Space and a new neural unit will be formed with receptive field tuned to this representation. Also this new unit will initially not have any lateral or intermap connectivity to associate with. So initially there is no action / action sequence which directly leads to the goal of obtaining food from the new situation.

We considered the following component roles in the sensorimotor and action space for the simulations.

Body Roles: Hunger, Reach Error, Resign/Bored, Occupancy Constraints

Environment Roles: Food, Tube, Curved wire and Straight wire.

Action Primitives: Grasp, Reach, Bend, Use of Curved wire, Search

All roles were taken to be 4-d and fillers 2-d for simplicity, indicating the presence or absence of that role in the current representation. So, in scene I the situation in the sensorimotor, action and work space is as follows: A novel representation s_{new} (Hunger + Food + Tube + Straight wire) is detected and a new unit is formed to decode this representation. There are no actions associated with s_{new} and so the sets Y_{new} and Z are both null. All representations of situations using components are constructed using equations 1, 2 and 3, as illustrated in 10.

$$s_{new} = Cons(S_{Body}, S_{Env})$$

$$s_{Env} = \sum_e f_e \otimes r_e = f_f \otimes r_f + f_t \otimes r_t + f_c \otimes r_c + f_s \otimes r_s \quad 10$$

$$s_{body} = \sum_i f_i \otimes r_i = f_h \otimes r_h + f_e \otimes r_e + f_b \otimes r_b + f_r \otimes r_r$$

We begin to tackle the novel situation starting from the preparatory phase. The goal is to obtain the food and reach a state of no hunger. The codebook vectors of the goal state s_G form the first input of DE. Then the goal stimulus is projected onto the action space to find action set Y_G linked to the goal. Let us consider that the complete set of actions from the action space associated to the goal of reaching a state of no hunger is {Reach, Grasp, Search, and Use of curved wire}. It is reasonable to consider all the above four actions have value in obtaining food in one situation or the other. For example, if Betty was hungry, she would have searched for food; if food was available then she would have reached for and grasped it and so on.

Even though Betty has a set of actions Y_G associated with the task of obtaining food, the initial situation she perceives does not permit her to execute any of them. Moreover, as the representation of the situation is novel, we cannot directly proceed to the reflective phase from the preparatory phase since there are no lateral and intermap connections to project activity between the two spaces. Here we invoke the utility of the third subsystem in the work space: the filler role unbinding unit. Whenever a novel situation is detected, this system unbinds the representation into its components and finds the collective set of actions Y_{new} that are linked to each active component role present in the situation. This unbinding involves extracting the child representations using the Ex operator and examining the fillers of the child representations to detect if a particular role is active or not. The extraction process is analogous to the Construction process and is summarised in equations 11:

$$s_{env} = Ex(s_{new}, U_{env}) = s_{sm} \otimes U_{env} = W_{Exenv} s_{new} \qquad (11)$$

where s_{env} is the child at depth 1 of the representation s_{new}, and the roles Food, Tube, Wire etc are the children of s_{env} (or at depth 2 w.r.t. the parent s_{new}) and can be extracted in similar ways. The vector U_{env} is the unbinding vector of the child and W_{exNew} is the weight matrix corresponding U_{env}, constructed in similar ways as mentioned in eqns 2 and 3. By this process of unbinding, or decomposition, we get a new set C whose components are the roles that are active in the new situation. In the case of Betty, decomposing the situation into components gives a set C containing the roles R_{food}, R_{tube} *and* $R_{straight\ wire}$. Once the active roles for a new situation are detected, the next task is to find the set of actions Y_{new} that are separately linked to each active component role present in the situation. This can be easily done by presenting each component role separately to the SM space, projecting its activity to the action space and finding the consequences of the action using lateral connections or, in other words, by a process of reflection operated separately on each active child. One question which arises here is that how do we know if a particular action linked to a child component is actually useful for the parent new representation and moreover useful in obtaining present active goal itself?

Since we already have the set Y_G of actions associated to the goal, in the action select unit, the utility of an action associated to a child representation (and those associated to consequences ensuing out of performing those actions in further cycles of reflections) can be determined if the intersection of those sets of actions with Y_G is not null. Figure 6 gives a pictorial representation of this situation in the case of Betty: on detection of the new representation s_{new}, the codebook elements are transferred to the unbinding system in the workspace which outputs a set C $\{R_{food}, R_{tube}, R_{straight\ wire}\}$, that is a set of roles whose fillers are active in the new representation.

Figure 6: scene II.

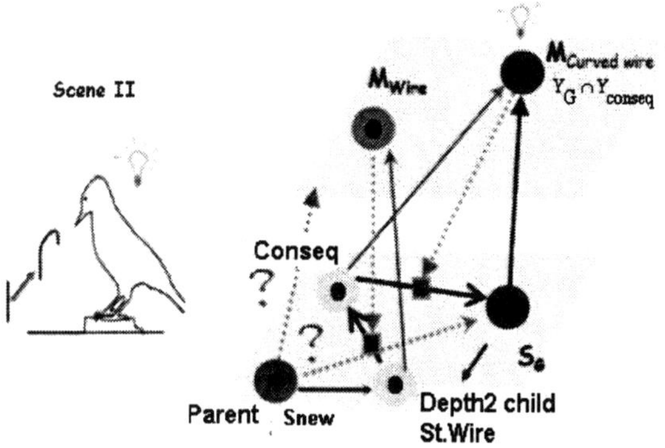

Then, in the phase of reflections during which individual components are applied separately, Betty discovers the fact that projecting the straight wire onto the action space gives the action 'bend' novel consequences: in particular, an activity shift in the SM Space, equivalent to that of perceiving the representation of the curved wire. Projecting the curved wire once again to the action space gives the action '*use of curved wire*' which forms an intersection with set Y_G of actions associated with the active goal. This is surely a progress in moving towards the goal, in other words, by unbinding the representation of the novel situation into components and reflecting on the components separately, Betty managed to reach a further sensory state s_{conseq} in the SM space that projects to an action set Y_{conseq} in the action space, such that the set Z is not null. In other words she now knows the fact that the action of bending could be useful in moving from s_{new} to s_G in the SM Space. But the problem is not solved yet, as there are no lateral connections trained for s_{new}. Hence, we are left with one final task of determining the representation $S_{ConsNew}$ of the situation that is equivalent to perceiving the consequence of performing the action '*Bend*' now on s_{new} itself. This constructed representation is the result of transformation of s_{new} as a result of virtually executing the action '*bend*' on one of its active child role '*St.Wire*'. This can be constructed by using simple ideas from set theory, as we already have the set C of active roles in s_{new}, the set C_{ini} which is child representation $R_{st.wire}$ under consideration and the set C_{fin} which is the ensuing consequence of performing the action '*bend*' on '*St.Wire*' i.e $R_{Curved\ Wire}$. The construction is illustrated below:

$$S_{ConseqNew} = Cons(\overline{\overline{C \cap C_{ini}} \cap C_{Fin}}) \qquad (12)$$

The '*Aha moment*' of Betty comes when this constructed representation $S_{ConseqNew}$ is applied to the SM Space, because even though the representation s_{new}

was detected to be novel initially, the reconstructed representation $S_{ConseqNew}$ i.e. the consequence of executing the action '*bend*' on s_{new}, will not be detected as novel, as Betty already had previous experience of this situation (hunger+ food+ tube + curved wire), and she also has lateral and intermap connections from here that directly lead to the goal. In our terminology, the Aha moment comes when the agent reaches a state like $S_{ConseqNew}$ in the SM Space that is both reachable from the initial situation and from where there are well defined actions that lead to the goal (or projection of a state that gives rise to a set Z which is not null). Figure 8 shows the matlab simulation of the task dynamics for the case of Betty.

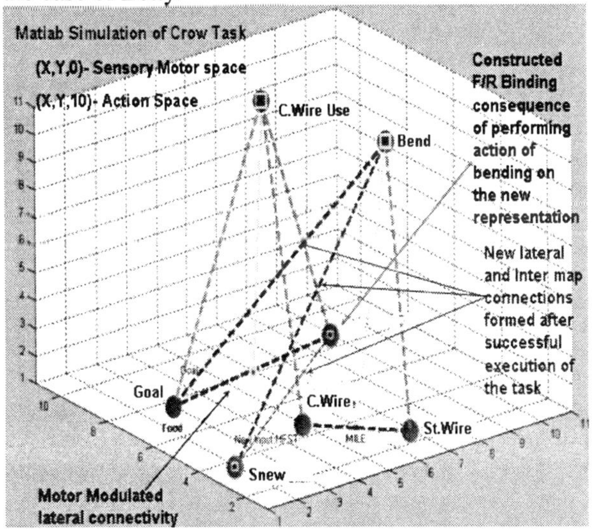

Figure 7. Simulation of the Crow Paradigm.

We are still left with one final task, that of forming new lateral and intermap connections for the representation s_{new} such that in case the same situation is encountered in future, the problem will be solved directly in the Preparatory and Reflective phases. After solving the task in a new situation for the first time, a lateral connection (dotted red line) is formed form the representation s_{new} to the representation $S_{Conseqnew}$ that is tuned to the action '*Bend*' in the action space. There are two intermap connections (blue lines), one each connecting s_{new} and *Goal* to the action '*bend*' in the action space. The consequence of forming these connections is that, the next time Betty encounters the same situation, by mere reflection she will find an action '*bend*' that forms an intersection with set Y_G of useful actions linked to the goal. Simulating motor modulated lateral connectivity will lead her from s_{new} to $s_{Conseqnew}$; this is equivalent to perceiving the situation in which she has her regular tool (curved wire), projecting which results in the action '*Curved wire use*' that once again forms an intersection with set Y_G and executing which directly leads her to the goal in SM Space. Figure 8 (scene III) presents a pictorial view of the plan of action in future solutions for the same problem.

Figure 8: scene III.

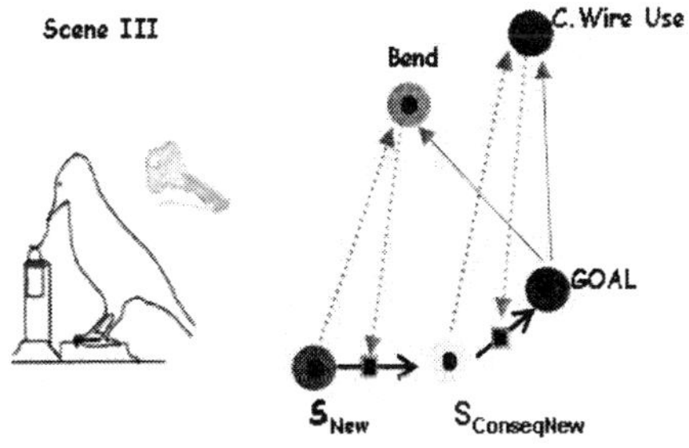

Figure 8: Task dynamics incase the same situation is encountered in future.

4. Concluding Remarks

One of the central aspects of higher level cognitive behavior is the ability to build and manipulate internal models that enable behaviors to be decoupled from direct control of the environment, thereby eliciting perceptual activity similar to that which would have occurred if the behavior was performed in reality. Studies from animal reasoning reveal many interesting behaviors demonstrated by animals that have all the hallmarks of similar brain processing in humans.

Taking an example of novelty in behavior demonstrated by Caledonian crows, we show how process relevant task decomposition coupled with interactions between sensorimotor space, action space and work space account for the generation of new learnt sequences of object/action, which can be used in getting to sub-goals, that in turn lead to the overall goal.We propose a scheme to represent abstract groups of objects and action primitives, using a collection of linear operators in vector space that involve tensor product based variable bindings. This is analogous to their use in linguistics to embed discrete symbolic structures that describe linguistic objects into a well defined connectionist system. Fillers are bound to roles via tensor product to form constituents that are combined by superposition to form trees, which can themselves act as fillers to further parent representations. Growing sensorimotor and action spaces have receptive fields tuned to map above representations, thereby forming internal models of tasks that can be used in future to virtually perform predictive motor control, imagery, inference and planning. The process of reaching an active goal state from the initial situation is split into three phases, the preparatory phase during which resources needed to tackle the problem are activated, the reflective phase during which potential solutions are generated and finally the revelation phase that deals with novelty. In the phase of reflection, while motor signals from the action space modulate corresponding lateral connections and cause activity shifts in the sensory motor space, activity in the sensorimotor space project back to the motor layer to induce the motor excitations that should turn predictions into reality. The preparatory and reflective phases are sufficient to mentally rehearse a plan of action for directly achieving a goal using learnt single chunks of sequences of object/action in different circumstances. The revelation phase as the name indicates, attempts to find the promising one, in situations when either the initial state (and knowledge gained through training) is not suited for executing actions that are needed to reach final state or when the representation of the situation in the SM space crosses the threshold of vigilance. The mode of operation in the revelation phase involves a combination of analogy and constrained search, during which knowledge about possible *(from initial situation)* and useful *(for the active goal)* object action pairs and their ensuing consequences are considered, by a process of unbinding the child representations and a running a further process of reflection on them. We illustrate how the 'Aha moment' for Betty comes in the phase of revelation, when she reaches a reconstructed known intermediate state like $S_{ConseqNew}$ in the SM Space that is both reachable from the initial new situation and from where there are well defined actions that lead to the goal. One may also imagine moving backwards from the goal in novel situations, by taking an action linked to the goal, associating it backwards to the SM space, then taking the active state in SM space, projecting it back to the action space and thereby finding if any intermediate State exists in SM space which has actions that are common to both that state and the initial situation. The proposed architecture is quite general and the example of Betty is considered merely for the sake of discussion and clarity. We must also note here that the proposed architecture is only one of the many ways people seem to work out novel solutions and the plan of action often goes beyond mere generalization, usually involving methods of directed search, analogy, verbal reformulation, simplification, divide and conquer, seeking help and finally resignation to mention a few.

5. Acknowledgements

This work was partly supported by the EU FP6 project GNOSYS and a doctoral fellowship to V.Mohan from the Italian Institute of Technology. The work also benefits from all our partners of GNOSYS project. Thanks to all of them.

6. References

[1] Morasso, P., Sanguineti, V., Self-organization, Cortical Maps and Motor Control. (North Holland, 1997).

[2] Smolensky, Paul & Legendre, Géraldine. *The Harmonic Mind:* From Neural Computation to Optimality-Theoretic Grammar Vol. 1 and II. MIT Press (2006).

[3] Mohan V, Morasso P. A Forward / Inverse Motor Controller for Cognitive Robotics. "Artificial Neural Networks - ICANN 2006", Lecture Notes in Computer Science, vol 4131/2006, p. 602-611, Springer, Berlin/Heidelberg, (2006).

[4] M.Minsky. The Emotion Machine, Simon & Schuster Adult Publishing Group, (2006).

[5] V.Gallese, T.Metzinger. Motor Ontology: The representational reality of Goals, actions and selves, Philosophical Psychology,Vol 16.(2003).

[6] G,Hesslow. Conscious thought as a simulation of Behavior and Perception, Trends in Cognitive Sciences, Vol6.(2002).

[7] Marc Toussaint. A sensorimotor map: Modulating Lateral connections for Anticipation and Planning, Neural Computation 18,1132-1155.(2006)

[8] Grush, Rick, Emulation and Cognition. Doctoral Dissertation, University of California, San Diego, (1995).

[9] A.Sloman. What the Minds Eye tells the Minds Brain, Draft copy, www.cs.bham.ac.uk/ research/projects / cosy /papers/cosy-dp-0503.

[10] Abbot.L,T.J.Sejnowski, Neural Codes and Distributed representations.MIT Press.(1999).

[11] Pouget.A, T.J.Sejnowski, Spatial Transformations in parietal cortex using basis functions, J.Cognitive Neuroscience,9,222-237.(1997).

[12] T.A.Plate. Distributed representations and nested compositional structure.PhD .diss, U.Toronto.

[13] Chappell J & Kacelnik J. Selection of tool diameter by New Caledonian crows Corvus moneduloides Animal Cognition 7:121-127, (2002).

[14] Weir AAS, Chappell J& Kacelnik A. Shaping of Hooks in New Caledonian Crows. Science 297:981-3, (2002).

[15] Emery NJ & Clayton NS, The Mentality of Crows: Convergent Evolution of Intelligence in Corvids and Apes. (Science 306: 1903-1907, (2004))

[16] GNOSYS project documentation: www.ics.forth.gr/gnosys

Evolution of Cooperative Information Gathering in Self-Replicating Digital Organisms *

Benjamin E. Beckmann, Philip K. McKinley, David B. Knoester, and Charles Ofria

Department of Computer Science and Engineering
Michigan State University
East Lansing, Michigan 48824
E-mail: {beckma24,mckinley,dk,ofria}@cse.msu.edu

Abstract

We describe a study in the application of digital evolution *to the problem of cooperative information gathering. In digital evolution, self-replicating computer programs evolve to perform tasks and optimize resource usage in order to survive within a user defined computational environment. Instruction-level mutations during replication and CPU-cycle rewards for desired behavior produce natural selection within the population. The evolution is open-ended and not limited by human preconceptions. The contributions of this work are (1) to demonstrate that cooperative information gathering can evolve in digital organisms and (2) to provide insight into the fundamental processes governing evolution of such behavior.*

Keywords: *digital evolution, cooperative behavior, natural selection, data collection, sensor network.*

1. Introduction

As computing systems increasingly interact with the physical world, for example through wireless sensor networks and embedded systems, they are often required to operate in extreme situations. To remain effective, these systems must adapt to dynamic network conditions, conserve energy, compensate for hardware and software failures, fend off attacks, and optimize performance, all with minimal human intervention [1, 2]. Moreover, achieving these goals typically requires interaction and cooperation among multiple nodes, some of which may be malfunctioning or physically compromised. The complexity of designing robust computational systems has led many researchers to investigate *biologically-inspired* approaches. Natural organisms have an amazing ability to adapt to unforeseen circumstances. This adaptability can be codified in computational systems either through biomimetics [3], which mimics behaviors found in natural organisms, or through evolutionary computation [4–6], which models the natural processes that produce those behaviors. Both approaches have shown considerable promise in supporting the design of robust distributed systems [7–19].

Our work investigates the role *digital evolution* [20] might play in designing robust distributed systems. Digital evolution is a form of evolutionary computation in which populations of self-replicating computer programs, referred to as *digital organisms*, evolve to perform tasks within a user defined computational environment. The "genome" of a program is its sequence of instructions, typically drawn from an instruction set exhibiting certain robustness properties (see Section 2). When they replicate, digital organisms are exposed to instruction-level mutations. The resulting variation in genomes, combined with differential fitness to their environment (in the system we use here, organisms are rewarded with additional CPU cycles for exhibiting desired behaviors), produces natural selection within the population. Tracing the evolution of the digital organisms can provide insight into the evolutionary process, often revealing unexpected and strikingly clever solutions [21].

We are conducting a set of studies that explore how evolution can be "harnessed" to aid in the design of robust communication services. In an earlier study [22], we demonstrated that populations of digital organisms can evolve the ability to perform leader election. In this paper we report on a set of experiments that address the evolution of cooperative information gathering. The main contributions of this work are (1) to demonstrate that such behavior can evolve in digital organisms and (2) to provide insight into the fundamental processes governing evolution of this be-

* This work was supported in part by the U.S. Department of the Navy, Office of Naval Research under Grant No. N00014-01-1-0744, National Science Foundation grants EIA-0130724, ITR-0313142, and CCF 0523449, and a Quality Fund Concept grant from Michigan State University.

havior. Combined, these studies help to identify which local behaviors enable complex global behaviors to *emerge* in the population. Effectively, this approach provides researchers with a "digital Petri dish" in which solutions to complex problems can evolve. In the case of communication operations, algorithms produced through digital evolution can be codified and evaluated using both traditional simulation techniques as well as experimentation on sensor hardware. These activities constitute our ongoing work, discussed later.

The remainder of this paper is organized as follows. Section 2 provides background on AVIDA [23], the digital evolution platform used in this study. Section 3 describes how, during the evolutionary process, rewards are given to individuals for performing a set of basic tasks, which lead to self-organizing information gathering behavior. Experimental results are presented in Section 4, followed by concluding remarks in Section 5.

2. Background

Evolutionary computation (EC) is a broad field focused on applying the basic principles of Darwinian evolution to solving optimization problems. The most well-known EC method is the genetic algorithm (GA) [4], an iterative search technique in which the individuals in the population are encodings of candidate solutions to an optimization problem. In each generation, the fitness of every individual is calculated, and a subset of individuals are selected, recombined and/or mutated, and moved to the next generation. Genetic programming (GP) [5, 6] is a related method where the individuals are actual computer programs. Both approaches have been successfully used to solve complex problems, even producing patentable designs [24].

Digital Evolution. While evolutionary computation has been studied since the 1960's, the specific field of digital evolution is much younger. The first experiments with populations of self-replicating computer programs were performed in 1990 in a system called Coreworld [25], and later improved upon in Tierra [26]. In 1993, Ofria and colleagues began development of AVIDA [20, 23], currently the most widely used digital evolution platform and the one used in this study. AVIDA was developed primarily to provide a better understanding of evolution in nature. Observing evolution in digital organisms enables scientists to address questions that are impossible to study with organic life forms, for example, by explicitly disabling whole categories of mutations and seeing how that constraint affects the population. However, unlike mere numerical simulations and other evolutionary computation techniques, digital organisms possess the ability to evolve in an open-ended fashion: whether a given organism self-replicates and moves into the next generation depends on its environment and its interaction with other organisms.

Over the past several years, AVIDA has been used to conduct pioneering research in the evolution of biocomplexity, with an emphasis on understanding the evolutionary design process [21, 27–29]. However, the search power of AVIDA can also be used to address complex problems in science and engineering [22, 30–32]. In this paper we demonstrate that a self-organizing, information gathering system can evolve in an environment where individuals die and are replaced continuously. In a later phase of this study we will port evolved algorithms for this and other operations to an experimental sensor testbed for evaluation. While evolved solutions may share the inherent imperfections of natural organisms, they might also be resilient to unexpected conditions, where human-designed algorithms are limited and/or brittle.

AVIDA Operation. Figure 1 depicts the structure of an AVIDA population and an individual digital organism (Avidian). Each Avidian comprises a circular list of assembly-like instructions (its genome) and a virtual CPU, and each occupies a *cell* within a virtual environment. AVIDA instructions enable an organism to perform simple mathematical operations, such as addition, increment, and bit-shifts, as well as interact with the organism's environment, for example, by sending a message to a neighboring organism, or outputting a number to the environment. The execution of instructions by an Avidian's CPU controls the behavior of the organism, including replication of its offspring. The architecture used in the study described here contains three general-puropse 32-bit registers (AX, BX, CX), two general-purpose stacks, and four special-purpose *heads* (READ-HEAD, WRITE-HEAD, FLOW-CONTROL-HEAD, and INSTRUCTION-HEAD). The READ-HEAD and WRITE-HEAD are used solely for self-replication, while the other two are used to allow non-sequential execution flow and as an instruction pointer.

Self-replication is a critical aspect of digital evolution, and distinguishes it from other forms of evolutionary computation. To avoid extinction, an organism must be able to produce offspring. This means that the instructions comprising the organism's genome must contain a sequence that will create a copy of the genome and split it off. In AVIDA, doing so requires the organism to copy its own instructions one-by-one to a newly allocated space and then issue an H-DIVIDE instruction. Each copy operation is subject to random mutations that can change the instruction, insert an extra instruction, or delete the instruction. A key property of AVIDA's instruction set that differs from traditional computer languages, is that it is not possible to construct a *syntactically incorrect* genome [30]. Hence, while random mutations will produce many genomes that do not

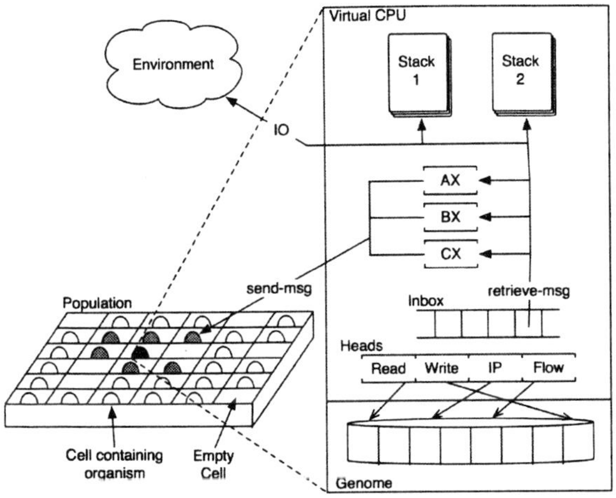

Figure 1. An AVIDA population (left) and the structure of an Avidian (right)

perform any meaningful computation, their instruction sequences will still be valid. After replication, the offspring is placed in another cell, terminating any organism already residing there. Each AVIDA run begins with a single default organism capable of only replication; this organism is an ancestor to every organism present in the run.

AVIDA Environment. In AVIDA, digital organisms compete against each other for survival. Specifically, they compete for space within a fixed population that is confined to a planar grid of cells, shown bottom left of Figure 1. Avidians can gain a competitive advantage through mutations and outcompete other Avidians by producing offspring faster. Therefore, it is likely that more copies of a highly fit Avidian's genes are present in the population relative to less fit Avidians, pushing the latter toward extinction. To gain a competitive advantage, Avidians either (1) become more efficient replicators through code optimization, or (2) perform user defined tasks. A *task* in AVIDA is a mechanism to reward or punish the offspring of an Avidian that has successfully performed a specific function during its lifetime. Tasks are defined in terms of an organism's observable behavior, or *phenotype*, which manifests itself in two ways: IO between an Avidian and the environment, and messages sent between two Avidians. Upon replication, the offspring of an organism that has completed a task receives a bonus in terms of CPU cycles, increasing its own chance of replicating successfully.

Avidians exchange information by sending messages to neighbors. Table 1 describes messaging instructions. The SEND-MSG instruction sends a message to a neighboring cell. Each Avidian has a *facing*, a pointer to one of its neighbors, used to determine the recipient of a message. An Avidian can change its facing by executing the ROTATE-TEMPLATE instruction, which rotates an organism to the direction specified by a *template* (a sequence of no-operation instructions [30] following the instruction). When a message arrives, it is placed into the recipient's inbox, shown in Figure 1, for later retrieval. An Avidian can read a message from its inbox into its virtual CPU with the RETRIEVE-MSG-ZERO instruction. If no message is available, zeros are written to the designated registers.

Table 1. Communication-related instructions

Instruction Name	Default behavior
SEND-MSG	$Send(BX, CX)$.
RETRIEVE-MSG-ZERO	If $\exists\, msg$ **then** $BX \leftarrow msg_{label}$, $CX \leftarrow msg_{data}$ **else** $BX \leftarrow 0$, $CX \leftarrow 0$
GET-ID	$BX \leftarrow$ Cell ID.
ROTATE-TEMPLATE	Rotate the facing of the organism to direction specified by template.

3. Problem Description

The abundance of self-organizing behaviors in natural systems leads to questions as to how these behaviors evolved. Ants, bees, and birds all exhibit behaviors that are both self-organizing and cooperative [3]. Many classical distributed algorithms such as leader election, data gathering, consensus, and load balancing, also require system level behaviors similar to those found in nature. For this reason, researchers have investigated biologically-inspired approaches to designing computational systems. Examples include mimicking the social behavior of insect colonies in robotic foraging [3, 33, 34], using chemotaxis to facilitate robust network routing [9], modeling colony behaviors in consructing highly-available services [7] and applying the concept of emergent behavior to the design of robust protocols and distributed systems design [8, 10, 35–38].

However, while such biomimetic approaches have achieved considerable success, they are limited to codifying behaviors observed in nature today. In fact, those behaviors were produced through millions of years of evolution. In other words, biomimetic approaches seek to imitate the *results* of evolution, but do not exploit the power of natural selection to produce solutions that best fit the environment. For example, we might design the control software on a micro-robot so that it mimics behaviors found in ants. However, while the robot may possess some physical characteristics reminiscent of an ant, *it is not an ant*. On the other hand, if we had the ability to *evolve* the control software, taking into account the capabilities of the robot and the characteristics of its environment, we might discover behaviors that are more effective in controlling the robot and completing tasks, than imitated ant behavior. Indeed, the evolved behaviors might not exist in *any* living creature. Digital evolution gives us this power.

Our research uses AVIDA to study the evolution of cooperative behavior. We have previously demonstrated the ability of Avidians to perform leader election [22] and adapt to the environment in order to conserve energy [39]. Solutions evolved *off-line* can be deployed in simulators and on actual hardware (the programs do to not continue to evolve once deployed). We are currently developing a tool to translate AVIDA genomes to code that can execute directly on motes. In this paper we focus on a particular type of cooperation needed in sensor networks and other distributed systems, namely, gathering information from multiple locations and delivering the data to a collection point ("sink" node). Figure 2 depicts the desired behavior in the context of AVIDA. Here, we define sensed data as a unique 32-bit random ID that is statically assigned to each cell. To gain access to a cell's ID, the occupying Avidian must execute the GET-ID instruction. An Avidian reading its cell ID is analogous to the sensing of an external stimulus local to a sensor. Next, the cell ID must be delivered to the collection point by the population of Avidians. A successful journey depends on the level of cooperation within the population. The solution must be highly robust, overcoming continuous turnover in the population that results in lost messages and terminated organisms.

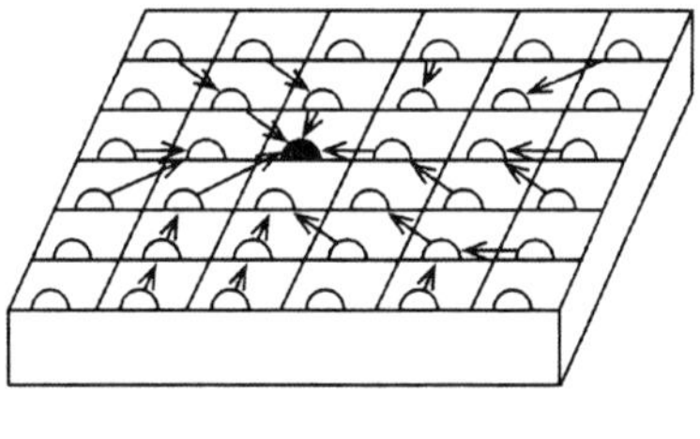

Figure 2. Desired information gathering behavior with black semicircle denoting the collection point.

AVIDA enables the user to define a set of (often simple) tasks and observe how evolution combines them to produce more complex behaviors. In this study, we extended AVIDA's task library to include several communication-oriented tasks listed in Table 2. The tasks in Table 2 are divided into two sections; tasks that reward organisms for sending cell IDs (upper), and tasks that reward organisms for efficient directional message sending (lower). The "linear" tasks reward the sending of IDs not sent previously by the organism; these will be discussed later. The tasks in the lower set place a selective pressure on the population to send messages toward the collection point, by rewarding organisms for sending messages that make progress toward the collection point, and punishing those that send messages away from the collection point. Progress is determined using minimum hop count between nodes. Hop count was chosen because the total amount of energy used to send a message to the collection point is proportional to the number of hops the message traverses on its way to the collection point. Section 4 describes the global information gathering behavior evolved as a result of integrating these tasks into AVIDA.

Table 2. Tasks to promote information gathering behavior.

Task Name	Rewarded Sending Behavior
SENT-SELF	own cell ID
SENT-ID-NOT-SELF	cell IDs other than own
SENT-ID-LINEAR	unique cell ID
SENT-ID-NOT-SELF -LINEAR	unique cell ID other than own
SENT-TOWARD	message toward collection point
SENT-NOT-TOWARD	message not toward collection point (negative reward)
SENT-ID-TOWARD	cell ID toward collection point

To better illustrate how AVIDA uses tasks, let us consider the SENT-SELF task, which rewards an organism for sending its cell ID as the data field of a message. Table 3 shows an example of AVIDA code that completes the SENT-SELF task. The organism executing this code obtains its cell ID, which it sends to a neighbor as the data field of a message. The code in Table 3 is handwritten, however as will be shown in Section 4.2, the evolved code produced by AVIDA is comparable. Algorithm 1 gives pseudo-code for the AVIDA function that checks for completion of the SENT-SELF task. This code is executed whenever an organism sends a message. If the function returns 1.0, the calling organism will be credited. If the organism replicates in the future, its offspring will receive a bonus in the form of virtual CPU cycles.

Throughout an experiment only limited global information about the AVIDA environment is available to the population directly. For example, the location of a collection point within the population must be discovered through the evolutionary process. The only environmental knowledge an organism has access to is its position in a Cartesian co-

Table 3. Sample AVIDA code that reads an organisms cell ID into its virtual CPU's CX register and then sends the contents of the CX register as the data field of a message to the northwest.

#	Instruction	Description
1	GET-ID	$CX \leftarrow$ Cell ID
2	NOP-C	
3	ROTATE-TEMPLATE	face northwest
4	NOP-B	
5	SEND-MSG	$Send(BX, CX)$

Algorithm 1 Task-SentSelf(TaskContext ctx): This task rewards an organism for sending a message where the data field of the message contains the sender's ID.

```
msg ← ctx.GetMessage()
if msg = NULL then
  return 0.0
end if
if msg.GetData() = msg.GetSender().GetCellID() then
  return 1.0
end if
return 0.0
```

ordinate space, which is obtained through the use of the GET-POS instruction. It should be noted that the evolutionary process is also solely responsible for finding and coordinating instruction usage. We do not provide any prior knowledge regarding an instruction's usage or operand(s). We seed the population with an organism capable of only self-replication. The usage of an instruction and its combination with other instructions to achieve a task must be evolved.

4. Experimental Results

Evolving a information gathering application in AVIDA using the instructions and tasks described previously is very much an experimental process. The task configurations described here represent only a small sampling of the experiments conducted. We describe three sets of experiments: 1) initial evolution of information gathering behavior; 2) elimination of undesirable individual behavior; and 3) using a mobile collection point. In each experiment a population of 625 organisms was organized in a 25×25 grid and allowed to evolve for 200,000 updates. An *update* is a measure of time within AVIDA. In this study, an average organism executes 30 instructions per update. After update 200,000, mutations were turned off, and the populations were allowed to stabilize over another 20,000 updates.

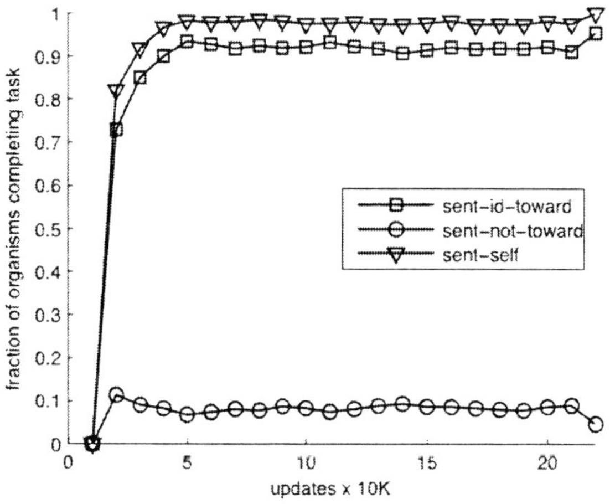

(a) initial results

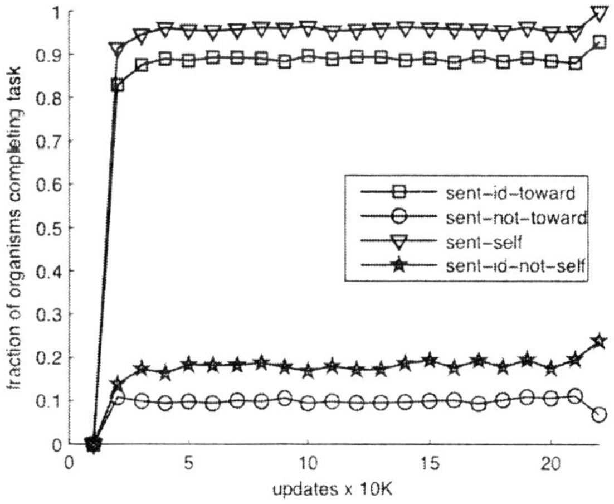

(b) addition of SENT-ID-NOT-SELF task

Figure 3. Task completion in initial tests.

4.1. Initial Runs

The goal of our initial experiment is to evolve Avidians that send their cell IDs through the network of organisms to the collection point. Configuring AVIDA and initiating runs using the tasks with static rewards, described in Table 2, we observed the beginnings of information gathering behavior. Figure 3 shows the results of two separate experiments formulated as a proof-of-concept. In the runs that correspond to Figure 3(a), we rewarded organisms for sending their own cell ID in the direction of the collection point, through the use of the SENT-ID-TOWARD and SENT-SELF tasks. We also discouraged sending messages that did not make progress toward the collection point by punishing individuals who completed the SENT-NOT-TOWARD task. In the runs that correspond to Figure 3(b), we added the SENT-ID-NOT-SELF task to reward organisms for forwarding received IDs. This task is highly dependent on neighboring

Avidians sending valid cell IDs because Avidians have no way of determining whether an ID is valid. The results in both Figure 3(a) and 3(b) plot the fraction of organisms that have achieved each task, averaged over ten runs. Figure 3(a) clearly shows that the SENT-ID-TOWARD and SENT-SELF tasks are performed by a large majority of the population. Further, once mutations were turned off at update 200,000, 100% of the organisms in the population were sending their own cell ID, while approximately 95% were sending messages toward the collection point.

Although Figure 3(b) is similar to Figure 3(a), the underlying behaviors in these sets of runs differ in an important way. Both sets of runs produced messages containing cell IDs that were destined for the collection point. For Figure 3(a) the collection point received 37.2 unique cell IDs, on average, with a standard deviation of approximately 3.74. However, with the addition of the SENT-ID-NOT-SELF task, in Figure 3(b), this number increased to 132.8, on average, with a standard deviation of approximately 12.59. The nearly four-fold increase in ID collection was caused solely by the SENT-ID-NOT-SELF task, which promoted ID forwarding.

Along with the cooperative behavior needed to deliver cell IDs to the collection point, we also observed selfish behavior within the population. One example of this behavior arose in multiple runs represented in Figure 3(a). Not rewarding the forwarding of received IDs allowed Avidians to repeatedly send their own cell ID without checking for a received message, effectively eliminating ID forwarding. Even with the addition of the SENT-ID-NOT-SELF task, selfish behavior evolved in some runs. Specifically, Avidians evolved to store, on their stack, a subset of the messages they received, repeatedly forwarding only the stored subset. This strategy was successful because they were likely to store and forward another Avidian's cell ID, while many other messages, possibly containing valid IDs, remained in their inbox and were never forwarded.

4.2. Linearly Increasing Rewards

To reduce the selfish behavior described above, we introduced ID-sending tasks whose rewards increase linearly with the number of uniquely forwarded cell IDs. Replacing the SENT-ID-NOT-SELF task with the SENT-ID-NOT-SELF-LINEAR task offers an incentive for individuals to continually check their inbox. Figure 4 shows the results of this change with respect to task completion. Comparing Figure 3(b) and Figure 4 reveals no significant difference, so an expectation of similar performance in collecting cell IDs is expected. Indeed, the average number of IDs collected in the Figure 4 runs is 113.2 with standard deviation of approximately 6, which is a small decline in the collection totals. The number of messages sent within the population, however, is significantly reduced, as shown in Figure 5. Specifically, the replacement of the SENT-ID-NOT-SELF task with the SENT-ID-NOT-SELF-LINEAR task reduced the total number of messages by approximately 25%. In a sensor network, this decrease in network traffic would represent a large energy savings. We also combined the SENT-SELF and SENT-ID-NOT-SELF-LINEAR into the SENT-ID-LINEAR task and obtained similar results.

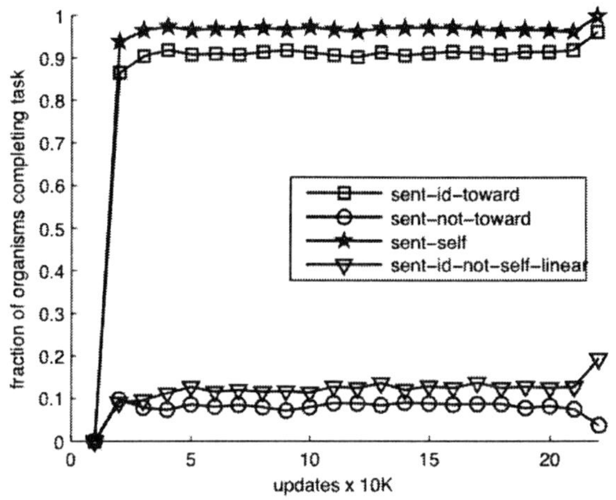

Figure 4. Runs replacing SENT-ID-NOT-SELF **task with** SENT-ID-NOT-SELF-LINEAR **task.**

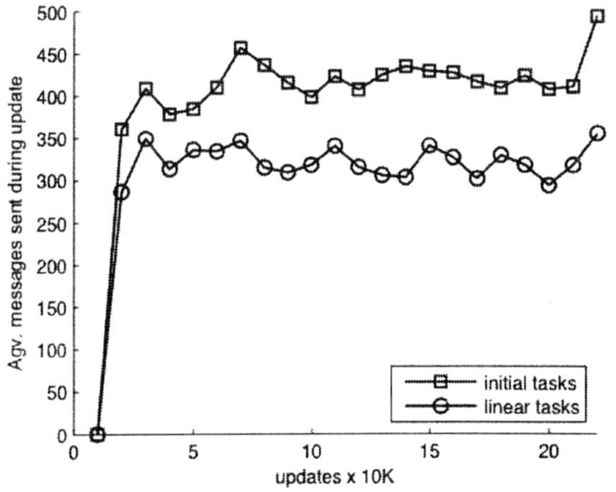

Figure 5. Average number of messages sent in runs from Figures 3(b) and 4

Table 4 shows a sample of a genome evolved in one of the runs from Figure 4. Three sections of the genome are shown, each corresponding to a critical behavior produced through evolution. Lines 2 – 7 show the evolved instruction sequence used to read the organism's cell ID, rotate to face the collection point, and send its cell ID. As shown in Table 3, a handwritten solution that performs equivalent behavior can be written in only one less line. Lines $9-13$ show the evolved instruction sequence used to forward a received message. If a message is present in the Avidian's inbox it is retrieved and then forwarded, possibly switching the order of the message's contents. Finally, lines $15-23$ show the organism's evolved copy loop. By including multiple H-COPY instructions in the copy loop, the organism replicates with fewer executed instructions. Most of the code in Table 4 could be mapped onto the virtual machine of a sensor node with little modification. We plan to extend this work by encoding an evolved genome on a set of wireless sensor devices and empirically testing the system's effectiveness under real-world conditions.

Table 4. Portion of evolved genome.

#	Instruction	Description
1	...	
2	GET-ID	$CX \leftarrow$ Cell ID
3	NOP-C	
4	SUB	$BX \leftarrow BX - CX$
5	ROTATE-TEMPLATE	face northwest
6	NOP-B	
7	SEND-MSG	$Send(BX, CX)$
8	...	
9	RETRIEVE-MSG-ZERO	$BX \leftarrow inbox.front().label$ $CX \leftarrow inbox.front().data$
10	IF-LABEL	If NOP-A was last copied
11	NOP-A	execute next inst., else skip
12	SWAP	$BX \leftrightarrow CX$
13	SEND-MSG	$Send(BX, CX)$
14	...	
15	H-SEARCH	FLOW-HEAD $\leftarrow$ inst. 16
16	H-COPY	copy instruction
17	H-COPY	from READ-HEAD
18	H-COPY	to WRITE-HEAD
19	IF-LABEL	If NOP-C was last copied
20	NOP-C	execute next inst., else skip
21	H-DIVIDE	split organism into two
22	H-COPY	
23	MOV-HEAD	INSTR.-HEAD $\leftarrow$ inst. 16
24	...	

Figure 6 depicts the behavior of the population in one of the runs from Figure 4. Each subfigure shows the state of a small area (11×11) of the population (25×25), centered on the collection point (labeled 'B') at varying times during evolution. (The evolution of the full population can be viewed at http://www.cse.msu.edu/~mckinley/avida.) A solid gray square represents the existence of an Avidian that has not sent a message prior to the end of the update, whereas, a solid black square represents an Avidian that has done so. A line emanating from a solid black square represents a sent message that made progress toward the collection point. A solid black square with no line emanating from it represents an organism that has sent a message that did not make progress toward the collection point. A hollow square represents an Avidian that has sent a message to a cell which was not occupied when the message was sent.

Figure 6(a) shows a subsection of the population a short time after the run started. The grid has filled up with organisms, denoted by the presence of squares, and a subset of Avidians, located on the bottom of the grid, has begun to send messages toward the collection point. Figure 6(b) shows this trend continuing and, for the first time, cells whose IDs have been communicated to the collection point: A hollow circle denotes a cell whose ID has been received at the collection point for the first time during this update, and a solid circle represents a cell whose ID was previously received by the collection point. Figure 6(c) shows the population of Avidians after 2,000,000 updates. At this time point 337 out of 625, or $\approx 54\%$, of the cell IDs have been collected. The rather low percentage of cell IDs collected is due to the high turnover rate, roughly 5% per update, within the population, which causes the loss of messages containing valid IDs when an Avidian holding these messages is overwritten. Even with a high turnover rate, however, more than half of the cell IDs were collected. It should be noted that with continued evolution the number of random IDs reaching the collection point continues to increase.

4.3. Moving the Collection Point

In the next set of experiments, we modified the runs described above by relocating the collection point periodically to determine if Avidians could adapt to the change. As shown in Figure 7, the collection point initially starts in the center of the population, position $(12, 12)$. After 50,000 updates the collection point is relocated to position $(0, 0)$, where it remains until update 100,000. At update 100,000 the collection point is again relocated, this time to position $(24, 24)$, where it remains for the next 50,000 updates. The collection point is moved to it final position $(12, 12)$ at update 150,000.

Analyzing the data from these runs reveals evidence of a self-modifying network within the AVIDA population. Figure 8 plots the task completion fraction, which is similar to that in Figures 3(b) and 4. The spikes present in Figure 8 correspond to the fraction of organisms completing the SENT-ID-TOWARD and SENT-NOT-TOWARD tasks just after the collection point is moved. The center spike is much larger than the outer spikes because that data point occurs just after the collection point is moved from the northwest corner of the population to the southeast corner. When this

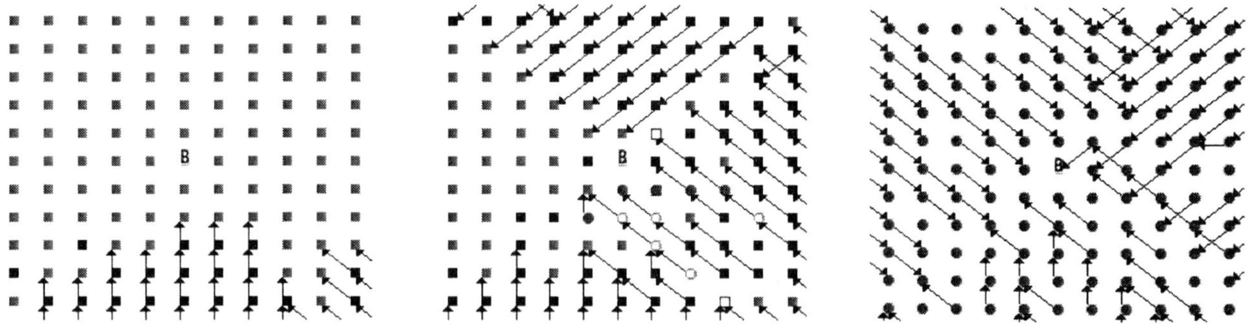

(a) update 500 (b) update 2,000 (c) update 2,000,000

Figure 6. Subsection (11×11) of the population (25×25) showing evolution of information gathering.

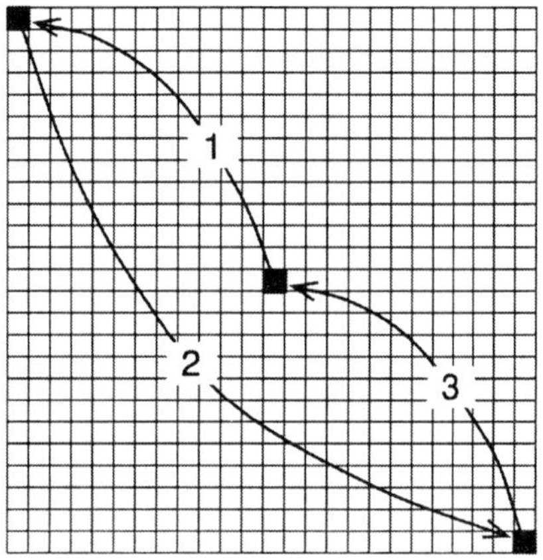

Figure 7. Movement of collection point

move occurs the entire population must adapt to send messages southeast, where as just prior to the move the majority of the messages in the population were being sent northwest. We also observed that the quantity of messages sent within the population does not increase substantially compared to the runs from Section 4.2, indicating the organisms adapted fairly quickly to the new environment.

It should be noted that natural selection drives the population's ability to adapt and find the new location of the collection point. Prior to the initial relocation of the collection point, organisms have already built up the functionality within their genome to send and forward ID carrying messages. The left side of Figure 9 shows a sequence of instructions that will send an organism's cell ID to the northwest. A mutation of line 4, shown in right side of Figure 9, causes the organisms to rotate to face southeast. Therefore, the rediscovery of the collection point is quicker than its initial discovery, because only the template following an instance of the ROTATE-LABEL instruction needs to be mutated for the data collection behavior to reappear.

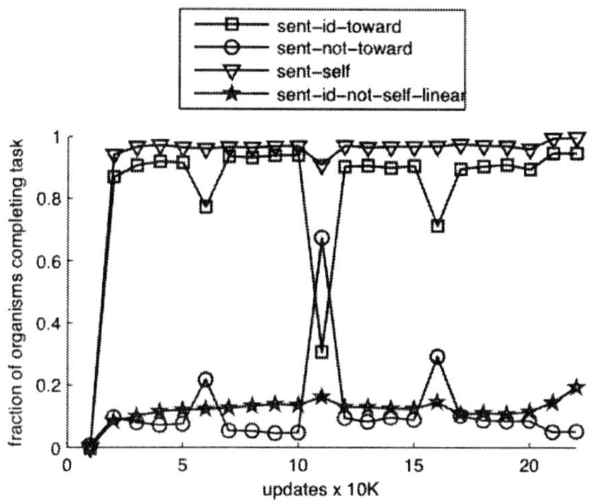

Figure 8. Results of moving collection point.

```
1 ...
2 GET-ID
3 ROTATE-TEMPLATE
4 NOP-B
5 SEND-MSG
6 ...
```

```
1 ...
2 GET-ID
3 ROTATE-TEMPLATE
4 NOP-C
5 SEND-MSG
6 ...
```

Figure 9. Mutation of template causing message to be send in a different direction.

5. Conclusions and Future Directions

We have used the AVIDA digital evolution platform to show that it is possible for a population of digital organisms to evolve self-organizing, information gathering behavior. Observing the evolutionary process provides insight into how to design new protocols and algorithms for highly dynamic environments. Evolved protocols may be resilient to adverse conditions, due to the population turnover rate and the environment's unpredictability.

Using digital evolution to design software is not without its limitations. Even though the language used in AVIDA is Turing complete, it is very low-level, and the virtual CPU used here is very simple: a single organism can store only 23 numbers, either in registers or on stacks. More complex architectures and instruction sets are under development. However, even with these limitations, AVIDA produced solutions to the problem of self-organizing information gathering.

We intend to extend this work into simulation and real-world sensor devices. We are beginning work on extending the AVRORA [40] simulator to handle AVIDA-evolved output. Using AVRORA, we plan to assess the effectiveness of AVIDA-evolved solutions to reliably gather information in real world situations. We are also studying the addition of mobility, using a system called THINKTANK. Specifically, we have recently developed an instruction set that includes simple motor control primitives and sensors. We expect to use this platform to evolve individuals that use these new features in order to traverse obstacle courses, elude predators, and catch moving targets.

The true benefit of evolving software in an artificial life system like AVIDA is the high-level of abstraction that it provides. Stating and implementing tasks that model behaviors of a system is an improvement over hand-coded implementation in a high-level programming language. Using this technique, a developer can work at the application level, focusing on high-level behaviors rather than lower-level concerns. If this technique proves to be successful in deployed networks, as technology allows, it will be applied to medium and large scale computing systems. Our early results are promising and indicate that evolving application level behaviors through artificial life is worthy of further investigation.

Further Information. Papers on digital evolution and the AVIDA software are available at `http://devolab.cse.msu.edu`. Information on evolving cooperative behavior can be found at `http://www.cse.msu.edu/~mckinley/avida`.

Acknowledgments. The authors gratefully acknowledge the contributions of the following individuals to this work: Jeffrey Clune, Sherri Goings, David Bryson, Richard Lenski, Heather Goldsby, and Betty Cheng.

References

[1] J. O. Kephart and D. M. Chess, "The vision of autonomic computing," *Computer*, vol. 36, no. 1, pp. 41–50, 2003.

[2] P. K. McKinley, S. M. Sadjadi, E. P. Kasten, and B. H. C. Cheng, "Composing adaptive software," *IEEE Computer*, vol. 37, no. 7, pp. 56–64, 2004.

[3] S. Johnson, *Emergence: The Connected Lives of Ants, Brains, Cities, and Software*. Scribner, 2002.

[4] J. H. Holland, *Adaptation in natural and artificial systems: An introductory analysis with applications to biology, control, and artificial intelligence*. University of Michigan Press, 1975.

[5] D. Goldberg, *Genetic Algorithms in Search, Optimization and Machine Learning*. Boston, MA, USA: Addison-Wesley, 1st ed., 1989.

[6] J. R. Koza, M. A. Keane, M. J. Streeter, W. Mydlowec, J. Yu, and G. Lanza, *Genetic Programming IV: Routine Human-Competitive Machine Intelligence*. Genetic Programming, Springer, 1st ed., 2005.

[7] J. Suzuki and T. Suda, "A middleware platform for a biologically-inspired network architecture supporting autonomous and adaptive applications," in *IEEE Journal on Selected Areas in Communications (JSAC), Special Issue on Intelligent Services and Applications in Next Generation Networks*, February 2005.

[8] R. J. Anthony, "Emergence: a paradigm for robust and scalable distributed applications," in *1st International Conference on Autonomic Computing (ICAC 2004), 17-19 May 2004, New York, NY, USA*, IEEE, 2004.

[9] O. Babaoglu, G. Canright, A. Deutsch, G. A. D. Caro, F. Ducatelle, L. M. Gambardella, N. Ganguly, M. Jelasity, R. Montemanni, A. Montresor, and T. Urnes, "Design patterns from biology for distributed computing," *ACM Transactions on Autonomous and Adaptive Systems*, vol. 1, no. 1, pp. 26–66, 2006.

[10] M. Jelasity and O. Babaoglu, "T-Man: Gossip-based overlay topology management," in *Proceedings of the 3rd International Workshop on Engineering Self-Organising Applications (ESOA 2005)*, (Utrecht), July 2005.

[11] S. Pleisch, M. Balakrishnan, K. Birman, and R. van Renesse, "Mistral: Efficient flooding in mobile ad-hoc networks," in *Proceedings of the Seventh ACM International Symposium on Mobile Ad Hoc Networking and Computing (ACM MobiHoc 2006)*, (Florence, Italy), May 2006.

[12] M. Mamei and F. Zambonelli, "Programming stigmergic coordination with the TOTA middleware.," in *4rd International Joint Conference on Autonomous Agents and Multiagent Systems (AAMAS 2005)*, pp. 415–422, 2005.

[13] G. Di Caro, F. Ducatelle, and L. Gambardella, "Swarm intelligence for routing in mobile ad hoc networks," in *Proceedings of the IEEE Swarm Intelligence Symposium*, (Pasadena, California, USA), November 2005.

[14] M. Guimarães and L. Rodrigues, "A genetic algorithm for multicast mapping in publish-subscribe systems," in *NCA '03: Proceedings of the Second IEEE International Symposium on Network Computing and Applications*, (Washington, DC, USA), IEEE Computer Society, 2003.

[15] A. Abraham and C. Grosan, "Evolving intrusion detection systems," in *Genetic Systems Programming: Theory and Experiences* (N. Nedjah, A. Abraham, and L. de Macedo

Mourelle, eds.), vol. 13 of *Studies in Computational Intelligence*, pp. 57–80, Germany: Springer, 2006.

[16] M. Maheswaran, S. Ali, H. J. Siegel, D. Hensgen, and R. F. Freund, "Dynamic mapping of a class of independent tasks onto heterogeneous computing systems," *Journal of Parallel and Distributed Computing*, vol. 59, no. 2, pp. 107–131, 1999.

[17] S. Pierre and G. Legault, "A genetic algorithm for designing distributed computer network topologies," *IEEE Transactions on Systems, Man and Cybernetics, Part B*, vol. 28, pp. 249–258, Apr 1998.

[18] A. Koyama, T. Nishie, J. Arai, and L. Barolli, "A new quality of service multicast routing protocol based on genetic algorithm," in *ICPADS '05: Proceedings of the 11th International Conference on Parallel and Distributed Systems (ICPADS'05)*, (Washington, DC, USA), pp. 655–660, IEEE Computer Society, 2005.

[19] P. Dasgupta, "Intelligent agent enabled genetic ant algorithm for P2P resource discovery.," in *Proceedings of the Third International Workshop on Agents and Peer-to-Peer Computing*, pp. 213–220, 2004.

[20] C. Ofria and C. O. Wilke, "Avida: Evolution experiments with self-replicating computer programs," in *Artificial Life Models in Software* (A. Adamatzky and M. Komosinski, eds.), pp. 3–35, Springer Verlag, London, 2005.

[21] R. E. Lenski, C. Ofria, R. T. Pennock, and C. Adami, "The evolutionary origin of complex features," *Nature*, vol. 423, pp. 139–144, 2003.

[22] D. B. Knoester, P. K. McKinley, and C. A. Ofria, "Using group selection to evolve leadership in populations of self-replicating digital organisms," in *Proceedings of the Genetic and Evolutionary Computation Conference*, July 2007. to appear.

[23] C. Ofria and C. O. Wilke, "Avida: A software platform for research in computational evolutionary biology," *Journal of Artificial Life*, vol. 10, pp. 191–229, 2004.

[24] J. R. Koza, M. A. Keane, M. J. Streeter, M. Mydlowec, J. Yu, and G. Lanza, *Genetic Programming IV: Routine Human-Competitive Machine Intelligence*. Springer, 2003.

[25] S. Rasmussen, C. Knudson, P. Feldberg, and M. Hindsholm, "The coreworld: Emergence and evolution of cooperative structures in a computational chemistry," *Physica D*, vol. 42, no. 1-3, pp. 111–134, 1990.

[26] T. S. Ray, "An approach to the synthesis of life," in *Artificial Life II* (C. G. Langton, C. Taylor, J. D. Farmer, and S. Rasmussen, eds.), pp. 371–408, Reading, MA, USA: Addison-Wesley, 1992.

[27] R. E. Lenski, C. Ofria, T. C. Collier, and C. Adami, "Genome complexity, robustness and genetic interactions in digital organisms," *Nature*, vol. 400, pp. 661–664, 1999.

[28] C. Adami, C. Ofria, and T. C. Collier, "Evolution of biological complexity," *Proc. Natl. Acad. Sci. USA*, vol. 97, pp. 4463–4468, 2000.

[29] C. O. Wilke, J. Wang, C. Ofria, C. Adami, and R. E. Lenski, "Evolution of digital organisms at high mutation rate leads to survival of the flattest," *Nature*, vol. 412, pp. 331–333, 2001.

[30] C. Ofria, C. Adami, and T. C. Collier, "Design of evolvable computer languages," *IEEE Transactions in Evolutionary Computation*, vol. 17, pp. 528–532, 2002.

[31] S. Chow, C. O. Wilke, C. Ofria, R. E. Lenski, and C. Adami, "Adaptive radiation from resource competition in digital organisms," *Science*, vol. 305, pp. 84–86, 2004.

[32] H. J. Goldsby, D. B. Knoester, B. H. Cheng, P. K. McKinley, and C. A. Ofria, "Digitally evolving models for dynamically adaptive systems," in *Proceedings of the ICSE Workshop on Software Engineering for Adaptive and Self-Managing Systems*, May 2007. to appear.

[33] M. Dorigo, V. Trianni, E. Şahin, R. Groß, T. H. Labella, G. Baldassarre, S. Nolfi, J.-L. Deneubourg, F. Mondada, D. Floreano, and L. M. Gambardella, "Evolving self-organizing behaviors for a swarm-bot," *Autonomous Robots*, vol. 17, no. 2–3, pp. 223–245, 2004.

[34] R. Schoonderwoerd, J. L. Bruten, O. E. Holland, and L. J. M. Rothkrantz, "Pheromone robotics," *Autonomous Robots*, vol. 11, no. 3, pp. 319–324, 2004.

[35] J. Debenham, "A multiagent system manages collaboration in emergent processes," in *Proceedings of the 4th International Joint Conference on Autonomous Agents and Multiagent Systems*, (New York, NY, USA), pp. 175–182, ACM Press, 2005.

[36] J. Cao, "Self-organizing agents for grid load balancing," in *5th International Workshop on Grid Computing (GRID 2004)*, (Pittsburgh, Pennsylvania, USA), pp. 388–395, IEEE/ACM, November 2004.

[37] M. Kubo, C. Dan, H. Sato, and T. Matubara, "An adaptive behavior of mobile ad hoc network agents," in *Proceedings of the 9th International Conference on Intelligent Autonomous Systems*, pp. 243–252, 2006.

[38] J. Rao and S. Biswas, "Controlled mobility: A mechanism for energy load distribution in sensor networks," in *Proceedings of GLOBECOM 2006*, November 2006.

[39] B. Beckmann, P. K. McKinley, and C. Ofria, "Evolution of an adaptive sleep response in digital organisms," Tech. Rep. MSU-CSE-07-19, Computer Science and Engineering, Michigan State University, East Lansing, Michigan, April 2007.

[40] B. L. Titzer, D. K. Lee, and J. Palsberg, "Avrora: Scalable sensor network simulation with precise timing," in *IPSN '05: Proceedings of the 4th International Symposium on Information Processing in Sensor Networks*, (Piscataway, NJ, USA), IEEE Press, 2005.

Research Track, Session 3: Synchronization/Desynchronization

Firefly-inspired Heartbeat Synchronization in Overlay Networks*

Ozalp Babaoglu
Univ. Bologna, Italy
babaoglu@cs.unibo.it

Toni Binci
Univ. Bologna, Italy
bincit@cs.unibo.it

Márk Jelasity
HAS & Univ. Szeged, Hungary
jelasity@inf.u-szeged.hu

Alberto Montresor
Univ. Trento, Italy
montresor@dit.unitn.it

Abstract

Heartbeat synchronization strives to have nodes in a distributed system generate periodic, local "heartbeat" events approximately at the same time. Many useful distributed protocols rely on the existence of such heartbeats for driving their cycle-based execution. Yet, solving the problem in environments where nodes are unreliable and messages are subject to delays and failures is non-trivial. We present a heartbeat synchronization protocol for overlay networks inspired by mathematical models of flash synchronization in certain species of fireflies. In our protocol, nodes send flash messages to their neighbors when a local heartbeat triggers. They adjust the phase of their next heartbeat based on incoming flash messages using an algorithm inspired by mathematical models of firefly synchronization. We report simulation results of the protocol in various realistic failure scenarios typical in overlay networks and show that synchronization emerges even when messages can have significant delay subject to large jitter.

1. Introduction

In cycle- or round-based distributed protocols (such as gossip protocols), it is often necessary that all nodes agree on when a new cycle starts. In other words, the local perceptions at nodes as to when cycles begin and end need to be synchronized so that we can talk about "cycles" of the system as a whole. For example, if the protocol requires periodic restarts (that is, all nodes need to be re-initialized), it is important that this event be synchronized [7, 9].

Heartbeat synchronization strives to have nodes in a distributed system generate periodic, local "heartbeat" events approximately at the same time. It differs from classical clock synchronization in that nodes are not interested in counting cycles and agreeing on the ID of the current cycle. Furthermore, there is no requirement regarding the length of a cycle with respect to real time as long as the length is bounded and all nodes agree on it eventually. What we are interested in guaranteeing is that all nodes start and end their cycles at the same time, with an error that is at least one, but preferably more, orders of magnitude smaller than the chosen cycle length.

This problem is rather difficult to solve in peer-to-peer overlay networks due to dynamism, failures and scale. In overlay networks, message delay can vary over a wide range [10] and churn can be significant with nodes leaving and joining the network continuously. In addition, overlay networks can be extremely large, containing millions of nodes. This implies that any proposed solution must be highly scalable. And finally, the solution needs to be decentralized for it to be usable in overlay networks where nodes have only partial information regarding the system as a whole.

Our approach to achieving robust, scalable and decentralized heartbeat synchronization is based on biological inspiration drawn from the flashing of fireflies. It is well know that in certain firefly species, male mem-

*Authors are listed in alphabetical order. Partial support for this work was provided by the European Union within the 6th Framework Programme under contracts 001907 (DELIS) and 27748 (BIONETS).

bers gather in large numbers at dusk and are able to synchronize their flashes such that eventually the entire swarm flashes in unison. What is surprising is that global synchronization emerges despite the fact that each member can observe only some small neighborhood of the swarm and can modifies its own flashing behavior based on this limited local information. Several mathematical models have been proposed to explain this phenomenon (see for example [13] and references therein). Decentralized synchronization protocols based on such models have been suggested before in the context of wireless sensor networks [16]. To our knowledge, mathematical models of firefly synchronization have not been applied to solve problems in large scale overlay networks.

The main contribution of the paper is twofold. First, in Section 3 we introduce a novel protocol for heartbeat synchronization in overlay networks that is based on an adaptive mathematical model of emergent synchronization of firefly flashing [3]. Second, in Section 4 we present extensive large-scale event-based simulation studies of the protocol in realistic scenarios involving message loss and delay, and demonstrate that the protocol can indeed achieve synchronization to a sufficient degree.

2. System Model

We assume that nodes are connected through an existing routed network, such as the Internet, where every node can potentially communicate with every other node. To actually communicate, a node has to know the address of another node. This is achieved by maintaining a *partial view* (*view* for short) at each node that contains a set of node descriptors. Views can be interpreted as sets of edges between nodes, naturally defining a directed graph over the nodes that determines the topology of an *overlay network*.

The network is highly dynamic; new nodes may join at any time, and existing nodes may leave, either voluntarily or by *crashing*. Our approach does not require any mechanism specific to leaves: spontaneous crashes and voluntary leaves are treated uniformly. Thus, in the following, we limit our discussion to node crashes. Byzantine failures, with nodes behaving arbitrarily, are excluded from the present discussion.

Communication incurs unpredictable delays and is subject to failures. Single messages may be lost, links between pairs of nodes may break. Nodes have access to local clocks that can measure the passage of real time with reasonable accuracy, that is, with small short-term drift.

```
loop
    wait until φ = 1
    P ← selectPeerList()
    send flash to all peers in P
end loop
```

(a) active thread

```
loop
    receive flash
    processFlash()
end loop
```

(b) passive thread

Figure 1. The skeleton of the heartbeat synchronization protocol.

3. The Synchronization Protocol

In this section we present an abstract protocol skeleton for firefly-inspired heartbeat synchronization and overview some of its possible instantiations based on different mathematical models of firefly flashing behavior. We briefly discuss the behavior of each model and argue that the most promising one is the adaptive model described in [3]. This model will be analyzed experimentally in Section 4.

3.1. The Protocol Skeleton

The protocol skeleton is shown in Figure 1. We assume that each node is an oscillator that can be characterized by its phase, ϕ, and the cycle length, Δ. The phase is a variable in the interval $[0, 1]$ and its dynamics are defined by a sawtooth function of time t, where we have $\partial\phi/\partial t = 1/\Delta$, such that the phase increases linearly from 0 to 1 in Δ time units. When the phase reaches 1, the node emits a "flash", which results in a ping message being sent to a set of peer nodes. Subsequently, the phase is reset to 0. The cycle length Δ can be initially different (or identical) at all nodes, depending on the implementation of PROCESSFLASH under consideration.

When the node receives a flash, method PROCESSFLASH is executed. This method is the heart of the synchronization algorithm. It is responsible for updating ϕ and possibly also Δ. That is, it can delay or advance the phase (and thereby the next flash), possibly as a function of the current phase, and it can adjust the cycle length as well. We will examine different implementations later in the section.

Method SELECTPEERLIST relies on an underlying overlay network which is used to return a list of neighbors. In our experimental analyses, we will assume that this overlay network is random and dynamic with a small, constant number of neighbors for each node. As such, SELECTPEERLIST returns a small, random set of peer nodes. More details on the practical implementation of this random overlay will be given in Section 4.

We now move on to describe three possible implementations of method PROCESSFLASH.

3.2. Phase-Advance and Phase-Delay

The simplest possible implementation of PROCESSFLASH sets $\phi = 0$ (phase-delay model) or $\phi = 1$ (phase-advance model). If we assume instant message delivery without failures, both choices result in the pairwise synchronization of the peers that sent and received the flash message. The only difference between the two choices is that in the case of phase-advance, a flash message is also emitted alongside the pairwise synchronization step.

This model assumes that all nodes have exactly the same fixed cycle length Δ. Obviously, since the model does not involve the adjustment of the cycle length, if we start with heterogeneous values at the nodes, or if the skew of the clocks is significant, the model is not guaranteed to converge.

Furthermore, the phase-advance model is highly impractical because of the cascading flash messages that are generated in the initial phase of the synchronization: advanced flash messages trigger more and more advanced flashes which quickly overloads the network.

We note that if one can guarantee that the cycle lengths are indeed identical at all nodes, then the phase delay model performs rather well according to our preliminary experiments. However, due to lack of space, we do not pursue this model further in this paper, in order to be able to fully focus on the Ermentrout model described in Section 3.4.

3.3. The Mirollo-Strogatz Model

The model of Mirollo and Strogatz [13] generalizes the simplistic phase-advance model in the following way. It introduces a third variable x, that we will call "voltage" to illustrate the intuition behind it. Voltage is defined by a non-linear function $f : [0,1] \to [0,1]$ as $x = f(\phi)$, where f is smooth, monotone increasing, and concave down (in other words, the first two derivatives of f are continuous and satisfy $f' > 0$ and $f'' < 0$). The model also requires $f(0) = 0$ and $f(1) = 1$.

The reason for introducing this nonlinearity through the new voltage variable is that it offers us an easy way to adjust the sensitivity of the phase adjustment depending on the actual phase. We advance the voltage by a fixed amount: $x' = \min(x+\varepsilon, 1)$ and set the phase to reflect the new voltage: $\phi' = f^{-1}(x')$, where x' and ϕ' is the new state after the update.

If the phase is close to zero, then this update rule will change the phase relatively little, while towards the end of the cycle the node will become more and more sensitive to incoming flash messages. Note that if $\varepsilon \geq 1$ then the model becomes identical to the phase-advance model.

Theoretical results in [13] indicate that if the underlying overlay network is a clique (all nodes are connected to all other nodes), and messages are delivered instantly and without failures, then the model guarantees convergence. Recently, the assumption about full connectivity has been relaxed in [11].

Our preliminary experimental results confirm that, apart from flooding problems similar to the phase-advance approach, the model is very sensitive to message delay and message loss.

3.4. The Adaptive Ermentrout Model

In the model of Ermentrout, the nodes have a variable cycle length [3]. This model was motivated by the fact that fireflies indeed cannot have identical cycle lengths initially.

In this model, the actual cycle length of node i becomes a variable δ_i which is bounded above and below: $\Delta_l < \delta_i < \Delta_u$. In addition to the new global parameters Δ_l and Δ_u, each node has a parameter Δ ($\Delta_l < \Delta < \Delta_u$) as well: its natural cycle length. A node will flash once in each Δ time units in the lack of interaction with other nodes. The model is expressed in terms of the frequencies $\Omega_l = 1/\Delta_u$, $\Omega_u = 1/\Delta_l$, $\Omega = 1/\Delta$ and $\omega_i = 1/\delta_i$.

Previous implementations of PROCESSFLASH updated the phase variable ϕ thereby adjusting the time of the next flash. The interesting feature of the model of Ermentrout is that PROCESSFLASH updates the variable ω instead of variable ϕ. If a flash arrives "too late" (that is, when $\phi < 1/2$), then the frequency is decreased (that is, cycle length is lengthened) while the phase remains unchanged. This increases the time until the next flash, so that it is more likely to be aligned with the next flash from the source of the received flash. Similarly, if the flash is "too early" ($\phi > 1/2$), then the frequency is increased towards Ω_u.

According to [3], the update formula applied by PROCESSFLASH becomes

$$\omega' = \omega + \varepsilon(\Omega - \omega) + g^{+}(\phi)(\Omega_l - \omega) + g^{-}(\phi)(\Omega_u - \omega) \quad (1)$$

where ω' is the new frequency, and the phase ϕ remains unchanged. The coefficients of the terms are ε, a parameter that controls the tendency of the frequency to move towards the common natural frequency Ω, and two functions g^{+} and g^{-} defined as

$$g^{+}(\phi) = \max(\frac{\sin 2\pi\phi}{2\pi}, 0) \quad (2)$$

$$g^{-}(\phi) = -\min(\frac{\sin 2\pi\phi}{2\pi}, 0). \quad (3)$$

Function g^{+} is positive when $\phi < 1/2$, otherwise 0, while g^{-} is positive when $\phi > 1/2$, otherwise 0. This way, (1) formally captures the frequency adjustments that belong to "late" and "early" received flashes, as explained in the intuitive discussion above, by moving the frequency towards the upper or lower bound, respectively.

The model has fewer assumptions (most importantly, it does not assume identical cycle lengths) which leads us to believe that it might be more appropriate in the typical overlay network scenarios we are interested in. Thus, from now on, we focus on this model only.

4. Experimental Results

The goal of this section is to evaluate the adaptive Ermentrout model in large overlay networks. Each node is running our heartbeat synchronization protocol on top of a *peer sampling service* which provides functionality for implementing the SELECTPEERLIST() method.

Peer sampling layer. The peer sampling service provides each node with a continously up-to-date random sample from the entire network. In this paper, we consider an instantiation of the peer sampling service based on the NEWSCAST protocol [8], which is attractive for its low cost, extreme robustness and minimal assumptions. The basic idea of NEWSCAST is that each node maintains a local set of random node addresses: the (partial) *view*. Periodically, each node sends its view to a random member of the view itself. When receiving such a message, a node keeps a fixed number of freshest addresses (based on timestamps), selected from those locally available in the view and those contained in the message. The protocol provides high quality (i.e., sufficiently random) samples not only during normal operation (with relatively low churn), but also during massive churn and even after catastrophic failures (up to 70% nodes may fail), quickly removing failed nodes from the local views of correct nodes.

In the following experiments, each node starts a NEWSCAST exchange every 10 seconds and messages contain 30 entries composed of IP address, port, and timestamp. Such a large number of entries avoids problems of disconnections [8]. A rough estimation of the overhead gives 16 bytes per entry $\times$ 30 entries, which means that a traffic of less than 50 bytes is generated at each node.

Synchronization layer. The heartbeat flash messages are simulated as simple UDP pings. The default cycle length Δ is equal to 1 second; the choice of such a small value is motivated by our desire to test the protocol in a difficult scenario where the cycle length is comparable to message latency. As supported by our simulations, synchronization can be obtained even in this case.

We use f to denote the *fan-out* of a node which determines the number of messages sent at each cycle. In our simulations, the fan-out is equal to the size of the NEWSCAST view, which is 30. We show, however, that a smaller fan-out (as low as 10 neighbors) is sufficient to correctly synchronize nodes.

Apart from Δ and f, the only other free parameter of the protocol is ε. Unless stated otherwise, in all our simulations ε will be equal to 0.01, a value which has proven to deliver good results.

Simulation environment. All of our experiments are event-based simulations performed using PEERSIM, an open-source simulator designed for large-scale peer-to-peer systems. It is publicly available on SourceForge [14]. Unless otherwise stated, our graphs show the averages over 50 experiments. When graphically feasible, individual results are displayed as distinct dots; a small random translation may be added to separate dots that are too close to be distinguishable.

All our experiments apply a transport layer that emulates some model of random latencies. To allow for scalability of simulations, if not otherwise stated, we adopt a simple transport layer that emulates random latencies, uniformly distributed between 1 and 200 ms. This is consistent with several measurements of all-pairs latencies of a group of nodes such as the King and Meridian data sets [4, 17]. Furthermore, it introduces the additional difficulty of a totally unpredictable latency. Further simulations with a publicly available data set will also be discussed.

Initial settings. At the beginning, a network containing between 2^{10} and 2^{16} nodes is created. Nodes emit their first flash in the first three seconds of their life and set their period randomly selected uniformly between 0.85s and 1.15 seconds, which also corresponds to the minimum and maximum cycle lengths Δ_l and Δ_u, respectively. In other words, nodes start completely unsynchronized, and their internal periods are subject to large skew. In simulations where churn is present, nodes joining the network are also initialized in this manner.

Measures of synchronization quality. Our main measure of the quality of synchronization is the *emission window* length, which measures the time between the first and the last flashes of a coherent emission (as described below). An *emission* is a collection of flash events, potentially occurring at different nodes. Informally, an emission is *coherent* if it is preceeded and followed by long "silent" intervals without flashes. For example, in most of our experiments, the protocol alternates short periods of time with flashes (few tens of milliseconds), with long intervals of silence (approximately one second, or longer depending on Δ). In our simulations, emissions are coherent when they are preceeded and followed by at least 200ms of silence. This value is used only for presentation purposes and has no effect on the protocol execution.

When experimenting with different cycle lengths, we will consider additional measures: the *relative emission window length*, expressed as percentage over the cycle length, and the *overhead*, measured as the average number of bytes transmitted, per node and per second. To estimate the latter, we assume that a ping message requires 32 bytes (IP header + UDP header + 4 bytes of message identification).

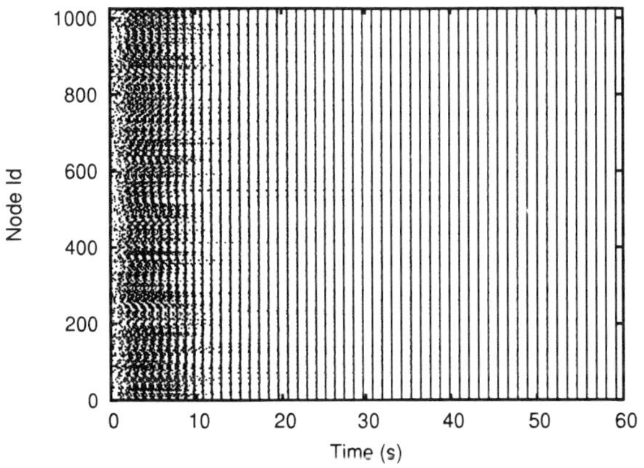

Figure 2. Flashes emitted by a network of 2^{10} nodes over an interval of 60 seconds.

Graphical intuition of the behavior of the protocol. We begin with three figures that graphically depict the behavior of the protocol as a function of time. To be graphically appealing, they are obtained from a single experiment.

In Figure 2, 1024 nodes are synchronized using our protocol. The time evolves along the x-axis, while individual nodes are shown on the y-axis. A dot with coordinate (x, y) represents a flash event executed by node y at time x. In the first seconds of simulation, flashes look like random noise, and no coherent emission can be identified. This is the effect of the initialization described above. After about 10 seconds, however, nodes starts to emit coherent emissions, represented by vertical lines, that become more and more defined as time passes.

Figure 3 zooms in on a single coherent emission (the last one of Figure 2). The x-axis is now relative to the beginning of the emission window, which lasts approximately 30ms. Each dot, again, represents an individual flash. The figure shows that nodes are even more synchronized than the 30ms value could suggest: many of the flashes are between 15ms and 27ms, with very few flashes outside this range.

While a short emission window is a good indicator of good synchronization, it does not tell the whole story: we need to examine the length of time between two coherent emissions. Figure 4 illustrates the time occurring

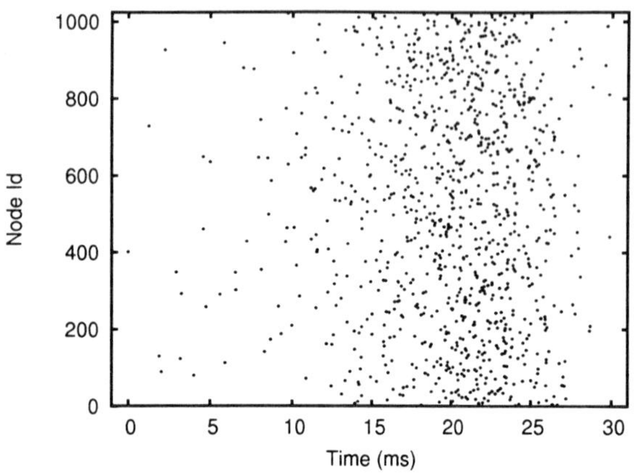

Figure 3. Flashes emitted by 2^{10} nodes during a single coherent emission.

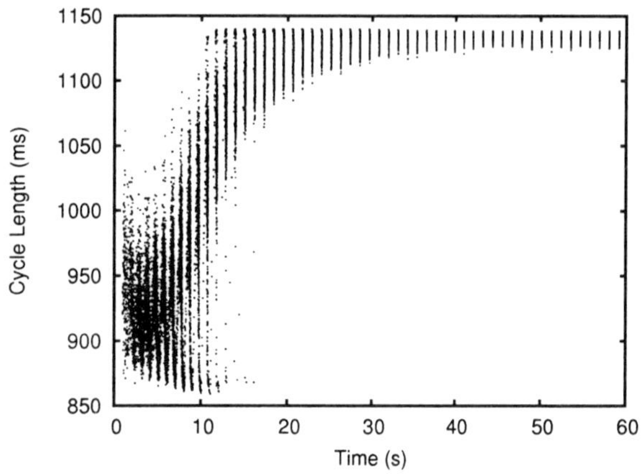

Figure 4. Individual periods for a network of 2^{10} nodes over an interval of 60 seconds.

between two consecutive flashes at each node. After the initial period, where synchrony is missing, nodes tend to adopt a uniform value that tends toward the maximum initial delay.

Scalability. For the sake of graphical presentation, the previous figures have been obtained by simulating a relatively small network (2^{10} nodes). Figures 5 and 6 show that our model is highly scalable by plotting the length of the emission window for network sizes ranging from 2^{10} to 2^{16} nodes. Figure 5 depicts seven individual experiments, one for each of the different sizes. The figure illustrates that fluctuations are possible, but are relatively small with respect to both the cycle length and the emission window. Figure 6 shows the average of

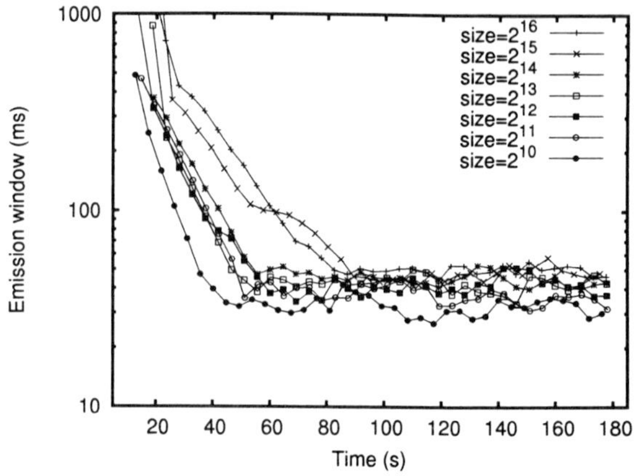

Figure 5. Length of the emission window as a function of time for different network sizes ranging from 2^{10} to 2^{16}. Each line represents a single experiment.

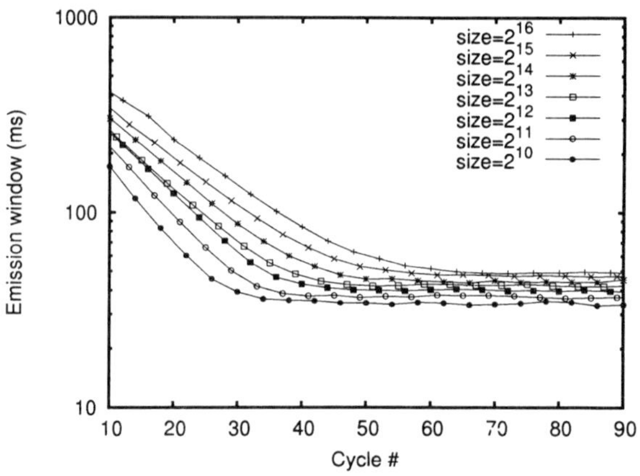

Figure 6. Length of the emission window as a function of cycle number, averaged over 50 experiments. Network sizes ranging from 2^{10} to 2^{16}.

50 experiments; here, each flash is tagged by an incremental counter maintained at each of the nodes, and experiments are aggregated based on this counter, rather than time. The reason is that coherent emissions occur at different time instants in distinct experiments, so aggregating them over time is meaningless.

Experimenting with parameters. So far, each flash event has been transmitted to all 30 neighbor nodes returned by NEWSCAST through the selectPeerList() method. We wondered whether this is strictly neces-

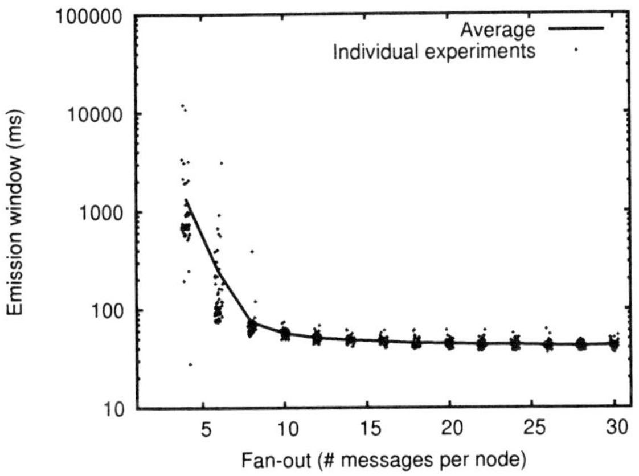

Figure 7. Length of the emission window as a function of fan-out.

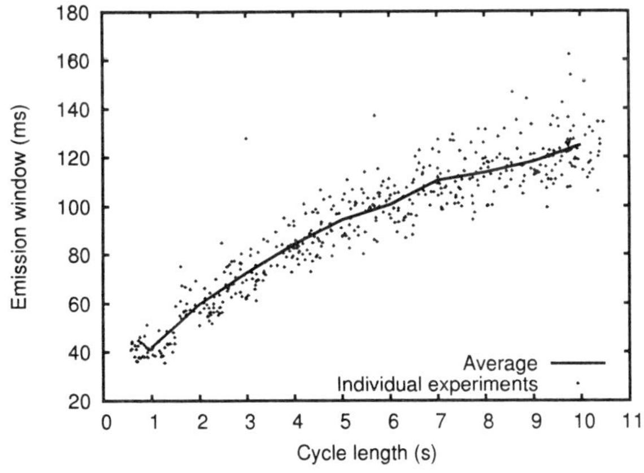

Figure 8. Length of the emission window as a function of cycle length.

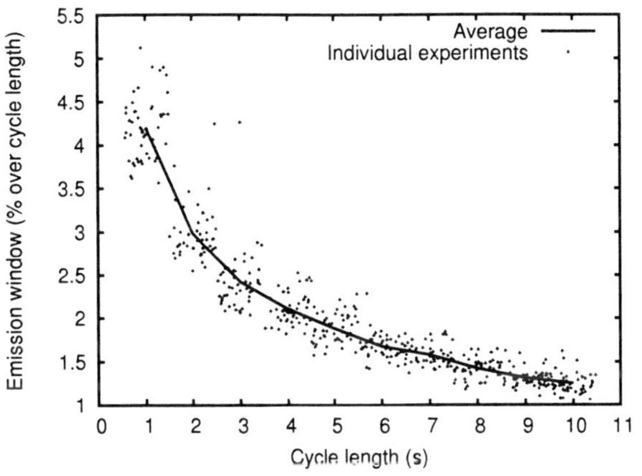

Figure 9. Relative emission window as a function of cycle length Δ.

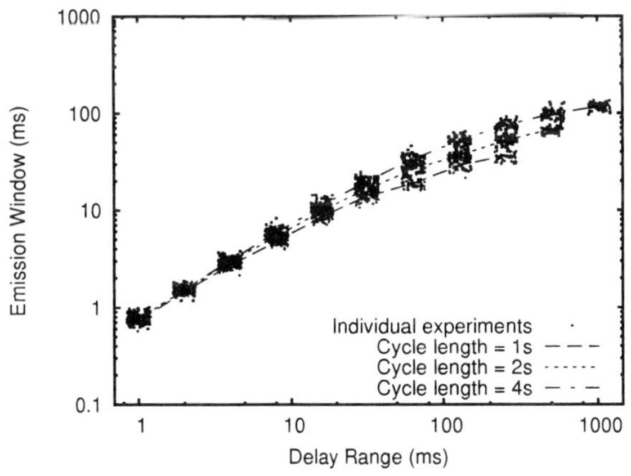

Figure 10. Length of the emission window as a function of maximum message latency.

sary to obtain convergence, and found that this is not the case. Figure 7 shows the length of the emission window as a function of the fan-out in a network of 2^{13} nodes. When fan-out is k, a flash is transmitted to only k nodes, selected randomly from the NEWSCAST view. It is interesting to discover that with as few as 10 messages, convergence to small emission window is still possible. With fewer nodes, however, it is possible to observe emission windows longer than Δ (i.e. larger than 1 second), meaning that no coherent emission is emitted for long periods of time.

Choosing the cycle length involves a trade-off between the speed of convergence and communication overhead. So far, we have demonstrated that 1 second is a feasible choice that allows for fast convergence (requiring only about 10 seconds); but the resulting overhead is quite large ($32 \times 30 = 960$ bytes per second). Figures 8 and 9 show that enlarging the cycle length not only reduces the overhead, but also improves the relative emission window length. Once again, the size of these networks is 2^{13}. In fact, with a cycle length of 10 seconds, the relative emission window is around 1.5% of the cycle length, compared to 4% with a cycle length of 1 second; and overhead is reduced by a factor of 10, requiring only 96 bytes per second. The only drawback is the slowing down of the protocol, which now requires up to 100 seconds before achieving the first coherent emission. But once nodes are synchronized, this problem will not be relevant any more.

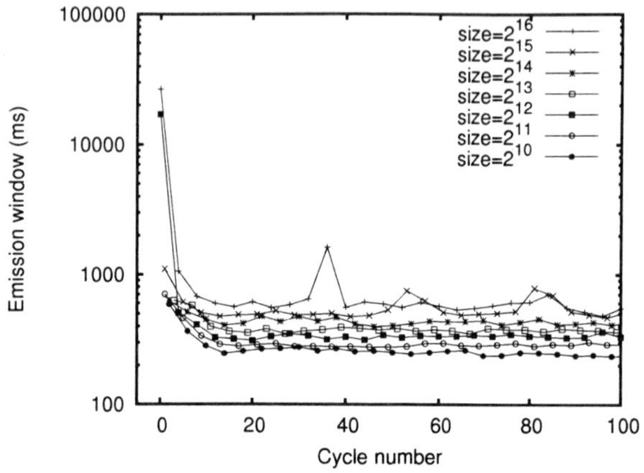

Figure 11. Length of the emission window at different cycles for the Harvard data trace.

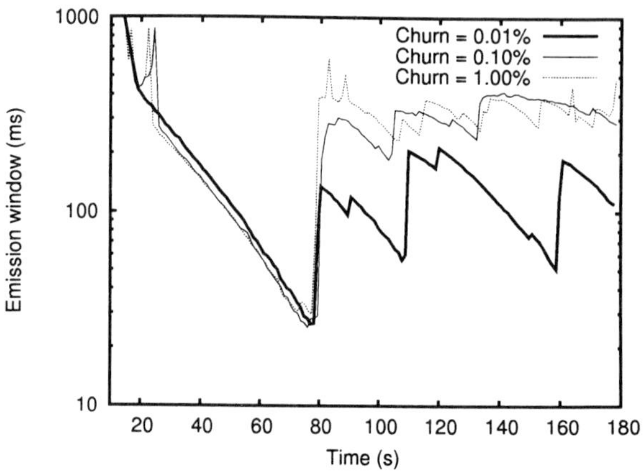

Figure 12. Three experiments with churn levels of 0.01%, 0.1%, 1%. The listening period is equal to 16 flashes.

Message latency. All experiments discussed so far were based on a simplified transport layer that delivers messages with random delays in the interval 1ms-200ms. This maximum value is obtained from the King data set [4], which reports the average pairwise latency between more than 1500 nodes. Both the King and the Meridian data sets [17] consider only the average latency without reporting the variance of the measurements. Raw data, when available, only show few measurements per pair of nodes.

To understand how our protocol behaves in other delay scenarios, we tried two alternative approaches. First, we studied the effect of the maximum delay on the emission window length as illustrated in Figure 10. There is a clear correlation between the maximum delay and the emission window length.

Next, we decided to use the Harvard data set [10], where the pairwise latency distance between 226 nodes in PlanetLab has been measured. An average of 100 measurements have been performed for each pair of nodes. Figure 11 is the corresponding of Figure 6 under this data set. This is a demanding data set: several measurements are larger than 1 second (the cycle length), and the maximum possible latency is equal to 41 seconds. Despite this wide variability, our algorithm is still able to synchronize large collections of nodes.

Churn. We conclude the experimental section showing the robustness of our protocol by testing it under two failure scenarios: churn and message losses.

A network is subject to *churn* if its membership is

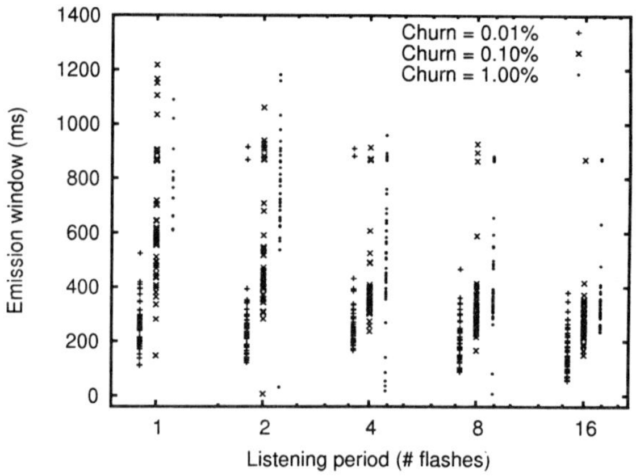

Figure 13. Emission windows as function of the listening period for churn levels of 0.01%, 0.1%, 1%.

continously evolving due to nodes joining and leaving the network. We simulated churn by "killing" a given percentage of nodes at each cycle, and substituting them with new ones. In other words, the size of the network remains constant, while its composition changes.

When analyzing the problem of churn, a small modification to the algorithm is required. If new nodes were allowed to emit flashes as soon as they join, identifying coherent emissions would be difficult, if not even impossible: not only their flashes could be outside the emission window of pre-existing nodes, but also they could perturb or even destroy the current synchronism.

For this reason, when a node joins the network, it initially behaves only as a listener: it receives flashes and modifies its period accordingly, but it does not emit flashes. In our protocol, this "listening" period is bounded by a predefined number of flashes, after which the node acts normally.

Figure 12 shows the temporal behavior of the protocol under three different churn scenarios: after the initial 60 seconds, 0.1%, 0.5% and 1.0% of the nodes are killed and substituted with new ones at each second. These scenarios are extremely harsh when compared to typical churn rates of 0.01% nodes per second that are observable in file sharing environments [1, 15]. The delay between when churn starts (60 seconds) and the time when the first "tooth" is observed is due to the listening period, which is fixed at 16 cycles. Cycle length, as illustrated in Figure 4, is equal to 1.13 seconds; so, 16 cycles corresponds approximately to 18 seconds. The "sawtooth" aspect of the Figure can be easily explained as follows. After its listening period, a recently added node may still not be in perfect sync, flashing a few hundred milliseconds before or after the others. A single outlier node may greatly enlarge the emission window; visually, this appears as a tooth. After its first flash, the outlier node is progressively brought in sync by the protocol, until the next outlier starts to emit flashes.

Our churn analysis is completed by Figure 13, where the behavior of the algorithm for different levels of churn and different lengths of the listening period are shown. Here, the size of the network is 2^{13} nodes. Each dot corresponds to one of 50 experiments, represented by the length of the emission window at the end of the simulation. It is possible to observe that, for short listening periods and large churn rates, the emission window can be located anywhere between 0 and 1 second. Furthermore, few dots are very close to 0 (isolated flashes with more than 200ms of silence before and after) and some dots are larger than 1 second (no periods of silence), suggesting a complete loss of synchrony. On the other hand, for longer listening periods and smaller churn rates, our algorithm works perfectly fine and maintains nodes in good synchrony.

Message losses. We do not include graphical results for our message loss studies, because there is a direct relationship between fan-out and message loss. A system that sends only 10 messages to random neighbors (out of 30 possible neighbors) can be compared to a system that sends 30 messages, 20 of which are lost at each cycle. Experimental results confirm that the emission window length remains acceptable for up to 66% of messages being lost. Beyond this threshold, quality of results rapidly degrades and becomes unusable.

5. Related Work

Synchrony has long received a lot of attention in many disciplines including mathematics, physics, biology and many others. In this section we focus on protocols that are responsible for creating and maintaining synchrony in networks.

In computer networks, *clock synchronization* has received the most attention, where each node in the network is required to align its own clock with a reference clock. The nature of the network on which a protocol is deployed largely determines the approach to be followed.

On the Internet, and similar networks, where the reference clock can be accessed in relatively few hops, and where the reference clock is reliable, the major issues in designing a protocol are to deal with the skew of the local clock and to approximate, predict and neutralize the probabilistic delays resulting from message transmission delays while communicating with the reference clock (for example, [2, 12]).

In dynamic overlay networks, time synchronization remains relatively unexplored. An interesting example is [6]. However, as with all time synchronization protocols, a robust and accurate reference clock is assumed to exist.

In wireless sensor networks the topology is geographic in nature and the reference clock can be many hops away which motivates different approaches to time synchronization (see [5] for an overview).

Heartbeat synchronization, where the nodes have to align with each other and not with a reference clock, has received little attention. This problem is interesting both as a primitive to achieve clock synchronization and also as a service in its own right. One example is [16], where the target environment is a sensor network. We have no knowledge of heartbeat synchronization approaches for peer-to-peer overlay networks, that are different from both sensor networks and static wired networks in that the network diameter is typically low, while at the same time unreliability and dynamism is very high.

6. Conclusions

In this paper we tackled the heartbeat synchronization problem in the context of overlay networks. Peer-to-peer overlay networks represent a special environment: nodes can communicate with each other directly using a routing service, involving relatively few hops in the physical network, unlike in the case of sensor networks, that have a geographic topology with a large diameter. However, the major challenge is represented by the dynamic character of overlay networks, the unreliable communication channels and the lack of reliable and robust components.

We proposed the application of the adaptive Ermentrout model [3] of firefly flashing synchronization to deal with the requirements of overlay networks. We have demonstrated that under various scenarios and parameter settings, the nodes synchronize their heartbeats to fall in an interval of 1%-10% of the cycle length of the periodic heartbeats.

Finally, we would like to stress that the scenarios, and especially the performance metrics were intentionally pessimistic, in order to represent a worst case analysis. For example, the emission window is defined to include all the flashes of all nodes, so a single outlier can have an arbitrarily large effect.

References

[1] Miguel Castro, Manuel Costa, and Antony Rowstron. Performance and dependability of structured peer-to-peer overlays. In *Proceedings of the 2004 International Conference on Dependable Systems and Networks (DSN'04)*. IEEE Computer Society, 2004.

[2] Flaviu Cristian. Probabilistic clock synchronization. *Distributed Computing*, 3(3):146–158, September 1989.

[3] Bard Ermentrout. An adaptive model for synchrony in the firefly pteroptyx malaccae. *Journal of Mathematical Biology*, 29(6):571–585, June 1991.

[4] Krishna P. Gummadi, Stefan Saroiu, and Steven D. Gribble. King: estimating latency between arbitrary internet end hosts. *Proceedings of the 2nd ACM SIGCOMM Workshop on Internet Measurment*, pages 5–18, 2002.

[5] An-Swol Hu and Sergio D. Servetto. On the scalability of cooperative time synchronization in pulse-connected networks. *IEEE Transactions on Information Theory*, 52(6):2725–2748, June 2006.

[6] Konrad Iwanicki, Maarten van Steen, and Spyros Voulgaris. Gossip-based clock synchronization for large decentralized systems. In Alexander Keller and Jean-Philippe Martin-Flatin, editors, *Self-Managed Networks, Systems and Services*, volume 3996 of *Lecture Notes in Computer Science*, Dublin, Ireland, June 2006.

[7] Márk Jelasity and Ozalp Babaoglu. T-Man: Gossip-based overlay topology management. In Sven A. Brueckner, Giovanna Di Marzo Serugendo, David Hales, and Franco Zambonelli, editors, *Engineering Self-Organising Systems: Third International Workshop (ESOA 2005), Revised Selected Papers*, volume 3910 of *Lecture Notes in Computer Science*, pages 1–15. Springer-Verlag, 2006.

[8] Márk Jelasity, Rachid Guerraoui, Anne-Marie Kermarrec, and Maarten van Steen. The peer sampling service: Experimental evaluation of unstructured gossip-based implementations. In Hans-Arno Jacobsen, editor, *Middleware 2004*, volume 3231 of *Lecture Notes in Computer Science*, pages 79–98. Springer-Verlag, 2004.

[9] Márk Jelasity, Alberto Montresor, and Ozalp Babaoglu. Gossip-based aggregation in large dynamic networks. *ACM Transactions on Computer Systems*, 23(3):219–252, August 2005.

[10] Jonathan Ledlie, Peter Pietzuch, and Margo Seltzer. Stable and accurate network coordinates. In *Proceedings of the IEEE ICDCS 2006*.

[11] Dennis Lucarelli and I-Jeng Wang. Decentralized synchronization protocols with nearest neighbor communication. In *Proceedings of the 2nd international conference on Embedded networked sensor systems (SenSys '04)*, pages 62–68, New York, NY, USA, 2004. ACM Press.

[12] David L. Mills. Improved algorithms for synchronizing computer network clocks. *IEEEACM Transactions on networking (TON)*, 3(3):245–254, 1995.

[13] Renato E. Mirollo and Steven H. Strogatz. Synchronization of pulse-coupled biological oscillators. *SIAM Journal on Applied Mathematics*, 50(6):1645–1662, 1990.

[14] PeerSim. http://peersim.sourceforge.net/.

[15] Stefan Saroiu, P. Krishna Gummadi, and Steven D. Gribble. A measurement study of peer-to-peer file sharing systems. In *Proceedings of Multimedia Computing and Networking 2002 (MMCN '02)*, San Jose, CA, USA, January 2002.

[16] Geoffrey Werner-Allen, Geetika Tewari, Ankit Patel, Matt Welsh, and Radhika Nagpal. Firefly-inspired sensor network synchronicity with realistic radio effects. In *Proceedings of the 3rd international conference on Embedded networked sensor systems (SenSys '05)*, pages 142–153, New York, NY, USA, 2005. ACM Press.

[17] Bernard Wong, Aleksandrs Slivkins, and Emin Gun Sirer. Meridian: a lightweight network location service without virtual coordinates. *Proceedings of SIGCOMM 2005*, pages 85–96.

Desynchronization:
The Theory of Self-Organizing Algorithms for Round-Robin Scheduling

Ankit Patel, Julius Degesys, Radhika Nagpal
Harvard University, Division of Engineering and Applied Sciences, Cambridge, MA 02139
{abpatel,degesys,rad}@eecs.harvard.edu

Abstract

The study of synchronization has received much attention in a variety of applications, ranging from coordinating sensors in wireless networks to models of fireflies flashing in unison in biology. The inverse problem of desynchronization, *however, has received little notice. Desynchronization is a powerful primitive: given a set of identical oscillators, applying a desynchronization primitive spreads them throughout the period, resulting in a round-robin schedule. This can be useful in several applications: medium access control in wireless sensor networks, designing fast analog-to-digital converters, and achieving high-throughput traffic intersections. Here we present two biologically-inspired algorithms for achieving desynchronization:* DESYNC *and* INVERSE-MS. *Both algorithms are simple and decentralized and are able to self-adjust to the addition and removal of agents. Furthermore, neither requires a global clock or explicit fault detection. We prove convergence, compute bounds for the running time, and assess the various trade-offs. To our knowledge, the theory of self-organizing desynchronization algorithms is presented here for the first time.*

1 Introduction

Fireflies have fascinated scientists and mathematicians alike with the phenomenon of *mutual synchronization*. In Southeast Asia, thousands of fireflies synchronize their flashing despite being spread over many miles. Mathematical models of this peculiar phenomenon remained elusive until the seminal works of Peskin [7] and Mirollo and Strogatz [6]. They were able to define a general class of local "flashing" algorithms that lead to global synchrony. Due to their simplicity and implicit fault-tolerance, these models have been easily extended to applied domains that require robust and accurate synchronization, such as wireless sensor networks [4, 5, 10].

Despite the popularity of synchronization, the "inverse" problem of spreading identical oscillators into a round-robin schedule has received surprisingly little attention. Here we define a new primitive, *desynchronization*, that addresses this inverse problem. Our motivation stems from biology: cells, acting as oscillators, control animal gaits and regulate heart valves through desynchronization. Many problems in multi-agent systems also require desynchronization. For example, in a wireless sensor network, nodes can avoid collisions and message loss by desynchronizing their transmission times. Similarly, sensor nodes can desynchronize their sampling times to distribute the energy cost while still providing efficient coverage.

In this paper we present two self-organizing, self-maintaining desynchronization algorithms: DESYNC and INVERSE-MS. DESYNC is inspired by particle diffusion and uses a simple local "spreading" rule to establish a global desynchronization. In contrast, INVERSE-MS is adapted from classic models of firefly synchronization [6]. INVERSE-MS is very fast but also brittle: it requires specialized assumptions that strongly limit its applicability. On the other hand, DESYNC is slower but more robust to message loss, message delay, and node birth and death.

Both algorithms require no centralized control, no global clock, and only a small, constant amount of state per agent. For both algorithms, we prove convergence, and analytically compute and compare convergence rates as a function of the number of nodes. Both algorithms are self-maintaining: when the number of nodes changes, they automatically adapt to reestablish a perfect round-robin schedule without any explicit fault detection. The simplicity of the self-organizing desynchronization algorithms allows them to work in a wide variety of settings. We describe several potential applications and explore the constraints involved. We also briefly discuss an implementation of DESYNC on TinyOS Telos motes and its application to TDMA, the full details of which are available elsewhere [1].

The main contribution of this paper is the design and analysis of two new self-organizing desynchronization algorithms. To the best of our knowledge, the detailed the-

0-7695-2906-2/07 $25.00

ory of self-organizing desynchronization algorithms is presented here for the first time.

The paper is organized as follows. Section 2 motivates the need for a desynchronization primitive, examines potential applications, and discusses previous work. Section 3 defines the general desynchronization framework and sections 4 and 5 present the DESYNC and INVERSE-MS algorithms. Section 6 compares the performance of the algorithms with respect to several metrics, and helps guide the application-dependent choice of an algorithm. A real implementation of the DESYNC algorithm in a sensor network testbed is presented in Section 7. Conclusions and future work are in Section 8.

2 Motivation and Background

Resource scheduling is defined as the ability to organize a schedule amongst competing agents that provides fair, responsive, and exclusive access to a shared resource. The resource scheduling problem rears its head in many settings, some of which are discussed below. The simplest solution is to use a *round-robin schedule*: it guarantees every contending agent access to the resource before any other agent gets access again. If each agent's slot (uncontested access to the resource for a period of time) is equally long, then a round-robin schedule provides an equitable solution.

Round-robin scheduling requires agents to agree on (1) the access order and (2) the time of the accesses. Most systems today come to this agreement by allowing all agents access to a global clock and computing a static access order ahead of time. But a centralized mechanism can be costly and error-prone in a dynamic distributed setting. We discuss some real applications where a decentralized mechanism is desirable.

TDMA in Wireless Networks. In a wireless network, neighboring nodes share a resource: the communication channel. Two nodes transmitting at the same time causes a collision and leads to message loss. Time Division Multiple Access (TDMA) is a protocol where nodes agree upon a round-robin schedule and take turns sending data. This approach provides collision-free message transmission and fully utilizes the bandwidth under high-load conditions. However, traditional implementations suffer from two problems: (1) they require that nodes have access to a common notion of global time, and (2) the schedule is fixed and therefore bandwidth is wasted if only a fraction of the nodes need to transmit. Access to a global clock and renegotiating schedules to recover bandwidth are both costly, especially when message loads are unpredictable. As a result, most systems use simpler contention-based protocols (e.g. 802.11) despite their poor performance under high load [9].

Analog-to-Digital Converters. In signal processing, an analog-to-digital converter (ADC) creates a digital representation of an analog signal by sampling the signal at a uniform rate. One method to design a fast ADC is to take n identical ADC units and interleave their sampling, thus creating a single sampler that is n times faster. Thus, fast sampling is achieved by desynchronizing the ADC units. Typical implementations have a single global clock that produces the base frequency and each ADC unit can be staggered by adding increasing numbers of delay elements. However such a circuit must be extremely precisely designed to achieve uniform sampling - any errors in design time can not be corrected in real-time [2].

Traffic Intersections. Here the agents are cars and the resource is the intersection. Signal lights act as locks on the intersection to prevent collisions. An autonomous intersection management system that allows the cars to desynchronize their use of the intersection could eliminate the need for traffic lights. Thus, desynchronization could allow for more efficient interleaving of the traffic streams, thereby increasing throughput and reducing the wait time at intersections [3].

At present, each of these applications invokes a global leader, in the form of a clock or a lock. But a centralized mechanism has many disadvantages: high implementation complexity, lack of robustness, and bottlenecks under high loads. Thus, the potential benefits of a decentralized desynchronization algorithm are significant.

3 Desynchronization Framework

In this section we present a general framework for exploring decentralized algorithms for desynchronization. The framework models nodes as *pulse-coupled oscillators*, an idea introduced by Peskin [7] and later developed by Mirollo and Strogatz in the context of cardiac/firefly synchronization [6].

Suppose there are n nodes that can communicate with each other. Each node is an oscillator with the same fundamental frequency ω and period $T = 1/\omega$. Let the nodes be labeled in clockwise order (e.g. Figure 1(a)). Throughout the paper, node labels are always 1-based and taken modulo n. Let $\phi_i \in \mathbb{S} = [0, 1]$ denote the phase of node i, where $1 \leq i \leq n$. For example, if $\phi_2 = 0.75$, then node 2 is 75% of the way through its cycle. The *phase neighbors* of node i are the nodes $i \pm 1$. The *system state* is a column vector $\vec{\phi} = [\phi_i] \in \mathbb{S}^n$, representing the phases of all n oscillators.

The *desynchronized state*, or *desynchrony*, is any system state $\vec{\phi}^*$ in which all n oscillators are evenly spread out in phase, oscillating at the same frequency, as shown in Fig-

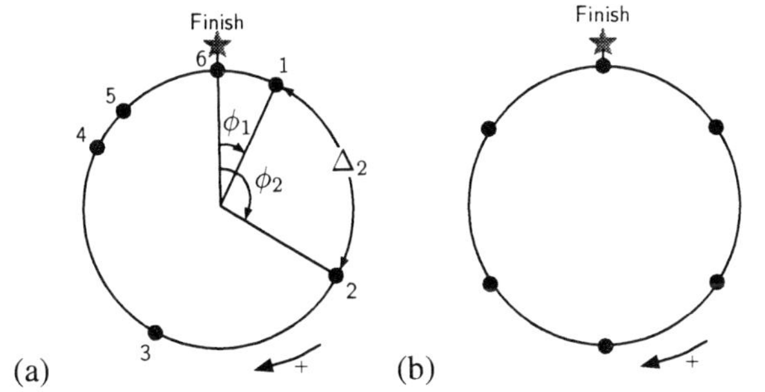

Figure 1. Desynchronization Framework. (a) Nodes move clockwise on the circle at frequency $1/T$, where T is the period. Nodes fire when they reach the finish line (red star). ϕ_i denotes the phase of node i and Δ_i represents the phase difference between consecutive oscillators. (b) The state of perfect desynchrony, where all nodes are evenly spaced in phase, shown here for $n = 6$ nodes.

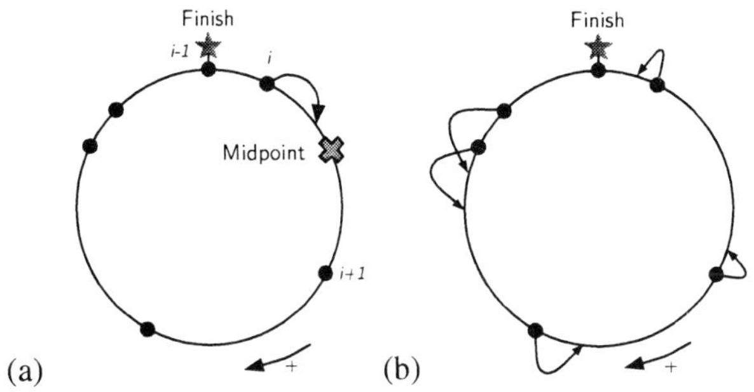

Figure 2. Desynchronization Algorithms. (a) DESYNC. After hearing a back neighbor $i-1$ fire, node i jumps towards the midpoint of its phase neighbors (open circle). (b) INVERSE-MS. After hearing any node fire, all nodes jump backwards. Nodes closer to reaching the finish line jump further back, while nodes earlier in their cycles take smaller jumps.

ure 1(b). Formally, we define desynchrony in terms of the phase differences between neighboring oscillators by introducing a new set of *delta-phase* variables: $\Delta_i \equiv \phi_i - \phi_{i-1} \pmod 1$, as shown in Figure 1(a). Let d be the mapping from $\vec{\phi}$ to $\vec{\Delta}$; that is, $\vec{\Delta} = d(\vec{\phi})$. In these variables, the desynchronized state is simply expressed as $\Delta_i^* = \frac{1}{n}$ for all i. Or, in vector form,

$$\vec{\Delta}^* = \frac{\mathbf{1}_n}{n} = \begin{pmatrix} \frac{1}{n} & \frac{1}{n} & \cdots & \frac{1}{n} \end{pmatrix}^T. \quad (1)$$

We can imagine nodes as beads moving clockwise on a ring with constant velocity, as shown in Figure 1(a). When a node crosses the finish line ($\phi = 1$), it *fires*, and resets ($\phi = 0$). Firing is a node's way of communicating its phase to other nodes. Upon hearing the firings of other nodes, a node may respond by "jumping" forwards or backwards in phase. From node i's perspective, the general algorithm reads

$$\phi_i' = f_i(\Phi; \alpha). \quad (2)$$

Or in vector form,

$$\vec{\phi}' = f(\Phi; \alpha), \quad (3)$$

where $f : \mathbb{S}^n \to \mathbb{S}^n$ is the *jump function*, ϕ_i' is the phase of node i after the jump, and Φ is the *total phase history* of all oscillators. The jump function f proceeds as follows: (1) examine Φ to determine which node i is next to fire, (2) move all nodes forward in phase until node i reaches the finish line, and (3) execute jumps f_j for all nodes $j \neq i$. In summary, f represents exactly one move-fire-jump event, with node i firing and all nodes $j \neq i$ jumping. Applying f a total of n times would execute exactly one round of n firings.

Equation (3) is the most general form of a desynchronization algorithm: each node jumps as a function of the histories of some (or all) of the nodes. The parameter $\alpha \in \mathbb{R}$ is a *jump size parameter* that controls how far a node jumps. When $\alpha = 0$ there is no jumping, and when $\alpha > 0$, a node jumps a nonzero amount. Since α is fixed ahead of time, we may sometimes suppress writing it for convenience.

Our main question is: *How should an individual node jump so that the whole system of identical nodes (all executing the same program) is driven to desynchrony?* Or, mathematically speaking: *What constraints on f are sufficient to guarantee that a system of nodes can achieve desynchrony?* In the following sections, we will introduce two algorithms, DESYNC and INVERSE-MS, that help to answer these questions.

4 DESYNC Algorithms

The DESYNC algorithm proceeds as follows. When node i reaches the end of its cycle ($\phi_i = 1$), it fires, thus notifying all other nodes that it is beginning a new cycle. After node i fires, it waits for node $i-1$ to fire. When node $i-1$ fires ($\phi_{i-1} = 1$), node i jumps to a new phase ϕ_i' according to jump function f, as shown in Figure 2(a).

All DESYNC algorithms have the following three characteristics: (1) nodes only use firing information from their two phase neighbors, (2) nodes jump only once per period, and (3) nodes stop jumping when the system reaches desynchrony.

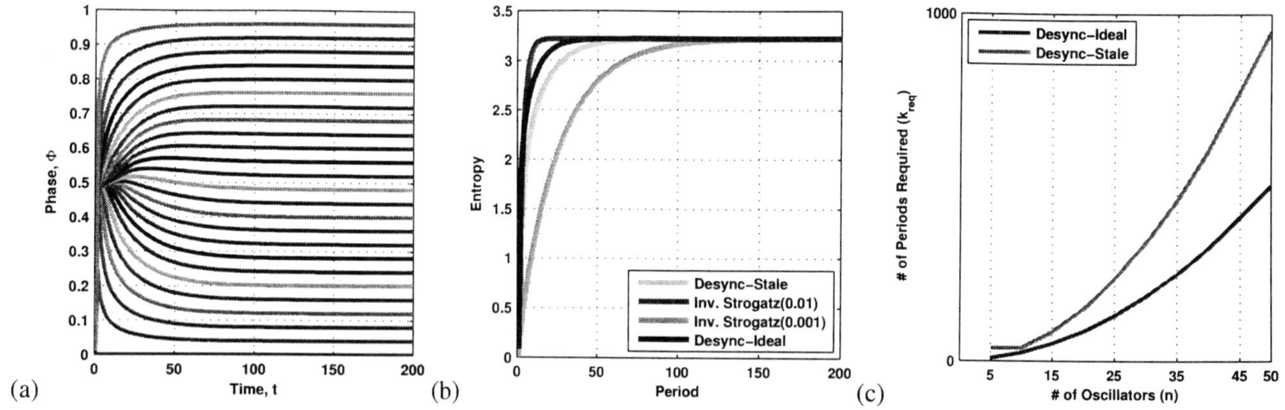

(a) (b) (c)

Figure 3. Phase vs. Time and convergence rates for several DESYNC variants ($n = 25$ nodes, 200 rounds, near-synchronized initial condition randomly chosen within $T/100$ fraction of phase, $\alpha = 0.95$). (a) Phase vs. Time (periods) for DESYNC-IDEAL . (b) Convergence rates as measured by entropy of phase configurations. DESYNC-IDEAL is the fastest DESYNC variant, followed by DESYNC-STALE. Stale information slows down convergence, as expected. INVERSE-MS is very fast for $\alpha = 0.01$ since all n nodes can jump at once, at the cost of steady state period lengthening. For $\alpha = 0.001$, DESYNC variants are much faster than INVERSE-MS. (c) Number of periods required to achieve ϵ-desynchrony for $\epsilon = 10^{-3}$. Both DESYNC-IDEAL and DESYNC-STALE require $O(n^2)$ periods.

4.1 Preliminaries

First, we note that the state of desynchrony is invariant to an overall shift in phase: for all constants C, $d(\vec{\phi}^* + C) = d(\vec{\phi}^*) = \vec{\Delta}^*$. Thus, it is natural to follow a system's desynchronization dynamics in the delta-phase variables, $\vec{\Delta} = d(\vec{\phi})$. It is important to note that a vector $\vec{\Delta}$ specifies only the relative distances between nodes and gives no information about the absolute phase of any node. It will be useful to interpret $\vec{\Delta}$ as a probability distribution. This is possible because $\Delta_i \geq 0$ for all i and $\sum_i \Delta_i = 1$. Thus, $\vec{\Delta} \in \mathcal{P}_n$, where $\mathcal{P}_n$ is the set of all probability distributions on n states.

In the next subsection, we will introduce the DESYNC algorithms. The inspiration for the DESYNC algorithms comes from the natural process of chemical diffusion. Given an initially non-uniform concentration gradient, the diffusion process smooths out sharp peaks and local disparities, until the gradient becomes completely flat. For our purposes, the vector $\vec{\Delta}$ plays the role of the concentration gradient and the desynchronization algorithm plays the role of diffusion. Eventually, the local smoothing of $\vec{\Delta}$ yields the uniform distribution, corresponding to perfect desynchrony.

Given this intuition, we will now introduce the DESYNC algorithms. An important design consideration is how quickly phase information is propagated to other nodes. Firings serve as messages to other nodes and if they are not received in time, a node may make a jump with "stale" information. Hence, we have designed two variants of the DESYNC algorithm: DESYNC-IDEAL and DESYNC-STALE. DESYNC-IDEAL works under idealized conditions where phase information is propagated instantaneously. On the other hand, DESYNC-STALE can handle stale information about the phases of other oscillators. For each variant, we present the algorithm, prove convergence, and compute rates of convergence.

4.2 DESYNC-IDEAL

The first DESYNC algorithm assumes that nodes can always access the exact positions of their phase neighbors. In this algorithm, node i fires and then waits for node $i-1$ to fire (when $\phi_{i-1} = 0$). At this point, node i takes a "global snapshot" of the system, acquiring the *exact* phases of nodes $i \pm 1$. Node i then computes the midpoint of its phase neighbors, $\text{mid}(\phi_{i-1}, \phi_{i+1}) = (\phi_{i-1} + \phi_{i+1})/2 = \phi_{i+1}/2$ (since $\phi_{i-1} = 0$). It then jumps a fraction α of the way towards that midpoint, as shown in Figure 2(a). All together, the algorithm, called DESYNC-IDEAL, reads

$$\begin{aligned} \phi_i' &= f_{\text{IDEAL},i}(\vec{\phi}; \alpha) \\ &= (1-\alpha) \cdot \phi_i + \alpha \cdot \text{mid}(\phi_{i-1}, \phi_{i+1}) \end{aligned} \quad (4)$$

Note that here a firing's only purpose is to trigger a node to take a snapshot and make a jump. We will make more substantial use of firings in the next section when we define a desynchronization algorithm that works in more realistic settings. But for now, we prove that the DESYNC-IDEAL algorithm achieves desynchrony.

Theorem 1 (DESYNC-IDEAL Convergence) *For all initial conditions and $\alpha \in (0,2)$, n oscillators whose dynamics are governed by* DESYNC-IDEAL *will be driven to desynchrony.*

Proof To prove convergence, we will cast the DESYNC-IDEAL algorithm as a linear dynamical system and show that desynchrony is the unique globally stable fixed point of the dynamics. We compute the dynamics in the delta-phase variables Δ_i because this leads to simpler proofs. By equation (4), we know that node $i-1$'s firing equalizes the phase distances between node i and its neighbors $i \pm 1$ so that

$$\Delta_i' = (1-\alpha)\Delta_i + \alpha\frac{\Delta_i + \Delta_{i+1}}{2} \qquad (5)$$

In matrix form, this can be written

$$\vec{\Delta}' = A_{\text{IDEAL}}\vec{\Delta} = PJ_{\text{IDEAL}}\vec{\Delta}, \qquad (6)$$

where P is the permutation matrix that accounts for the relabeling of nodes (i.e. node 1 becomes node 2, node 2 becomes node 3, and so on). The matrix J_{IDEAL} represents the jump in equation (5):

$$J_{\text{IDEAL}} = \begin{pmatrix} 1-\frac{\alpha}{2} & \frac{\alpha}{2} & & & \\ \frac{\alpha}{2} & 1-\frac{\alpha}{2} & & & \\ & & 1 & & \\ & & & \ddots & \\ & & & & 1 \end{pmatrix} \qquad (7)$$

It is easy to see that $A_{\text{IDEAL}}\vec{\Delta}^* = \vec{\Delta}^*$ and so the state of desynchrony is a fixed point, or equivalently, $\vec{\Delta}^*$ is an eigenvector of A_{IDEAL} with trivial eigenvalue $\lambda_1 = 1$. To prove global convergence to this fixed point, we must show that the non-trivial eigenvalues of A_{IDEAL} lie within the unit circle in the complex plane. It is straightforward to show that the characteristic polynomial of A_{IDEAL} is

$$\rho_n(\lambda;\alpha) = \lambda^n - \frac{\alpha}{2}\lambda^{n-1} - \frac{\alpha}{2}\lambda - (1-\alpha). \qquad (8)$$

Since ρ_n is a *stable polynomial* (see Appendix Definition A), we are guaranteed by Theorem 5 in the Appendix that all of its nontrivial eigenvalues lie inside the unit circle. Thus, DESYNC-IDEAL converges to desynchrony, irrespective of initial conditions. □

4.3 DESYNC-STALE

The DESYNC-IDEAL algorithm is an idealization because in most realistic settings a node cannot take global snapshots to get information about its phase neighbors. This is especially true in settings where message delays or unreliable links make it difficult to acquire the most recent updates on neighboring phases. Instead, nodes must use their firings to communicate phase information. Since nodes may jump in response to other nodes' firings, information from the last firings may not always be accurate. However, we show that if a node's jump size α is restricted, nodes can still use this "stale" information to desynchronize.

Here we introduce DESYNC-STALE, a DESYNC variant that relaxes the assumption of perfect phase information. We proceed by slightly modifying the DESYNC-IDEAL algorithm in (4) to use a midpoint estimate rather than the actual midpoint.

In general, node i uses its memory to estimate the midpoint between its phase neighbors $i \pm 1$, before making a jump towards that midpoint. From node i's perspective, the DESYNC-STALE algorithm reads

$$\begin{aligned} \phi_i' &= f_{\text{STALE},i}(\Phi;\alpha) \\ &= (1-\alpha)\cdot\phi_i + \alpha\cdot\text{mid}(\phi_{i-1},\tilde{\phi}_{i+1}), \end{aligned} \qquad (9)$$

where $\tilde{\phi}_{i+1}$ is a stale estimate of the true ϕ_{i+1}. Remember that node i executes a jump according to (9) only after it hears node $i-1$ fire. This means that node i always has accurate information about ϕ_{i-1}. But, it may have stale information about ϕ_{i+1}, since node $i+1$ may have jumped when node i fired.

To illustrate DESYNC-STALE and clarify the origin of "stale" information, we begin with a simple detailed example. Consider a network of three nodes—A, B, and C—initialized with phases $\phi_A = 0.6$, $\phi_B = 0.7$, and $\phi_C = 0.9$. Each node begins with no knowledge of the other nodes' phases. Node C fires first. Node B hears this firing and observes that its own phase $\phi_B = 0.8$. It uses this information to record that node C is 0.2 ahead of it. Node B then fires, and nodes A and C record B's relative position accordingly. Finally, when node A fires ($\phi_A = 0$), node B knows that it is 0.1 ahead of node A and 0.2 behind node C. Node B uses these two pieces of information to make its jump towards the midpoint, $\text{mid}(\phi_A, \phi_C) = (0+0.3)/2 = 0.15$.

The key point is that *Nodes A and C are not aware of this jump*, since node B has no means of communicating its new location until its next firing. Thus, nodes A and C are left with "stale" knowledge, $\tilde{\phi}_B$, of node B's true position, ϕ_B. Later on, when it is node A's turn to jump, it can only use this "stale" estimate of node B's phase to compute a midpoint. This is in contrast to DESYNC-IDEAL, where node A could simply see the exact phases of both its neighbors. Despite this "stale" information, we shall now prove that DESYNC-STALE will still achieve desynchrony.

Theorem 2 (DESYNC-STALE Convergence) *For all initial conditions and $\alpha \in (0,1)$, n nodes whose dynamics are governed by* DESYNC-STALE *will be driven to desynchrony.*

Proof The strategy is analogous to that of Theorem 1, except that we must augment the state of our system to keep track of the estimate $M = \tilde{\Delta}_{i+1}$. Thus we redefine the state of the system as the length $n+1$ vector $\vec{x} = (\Delta_1, \ldots, \Delta_n, M)^T$. We compute the dynamics in the delta-phase variables $\Delta'_i = \phi'_{i-1} - \phi'_i$ by taking the discrete difference of (9). In matrix form, the dynamical system is

$$\vec{x}' = A_{\text{STALE}}\vec{x} = P_{\text{STALE}} J_{\text{STALE}}\vec{x}, \tag{10}$$

where P_{STALE} is the permutation matrix that cyclically relabels nodes 1 through n and leaves M alone. The matrix J_{STALE} represents the jump in equation (9):

$$J_{\text{STALE}} = \begin{pmatrix} 1-\frac{\alpha}{2} & & \cdots & & \frac{\alpha}{2} \\ \frac{\alpha}{2} & 1 & \cdots & & -\frac{\alpha}{2} \\ & & \ddots & & \\ & & & 1 & \\ 1 & & & & 0 \end{pmatrix} \tag{11}$$

Here all blank entries are zero. The structure of this matrix represents both the jump and the storage of $Delta_1$ into the memory M for use in the next jump. It is easy to see that the length $n+1$ vector $\vec{x}^* = (\Delta_1^*, \ldots, \Delta_n^*, M^*) = (1/n, \ldots, 1/n)$ is a fixed point of A_{STALE} and we need only show global convergence. Computing the characteristic polynomial of A_{STALE} yields

$$\sigma_n(\lambda; \alpha) = \lambda^{n+1} - \frac{\alpha}{2}\lambda^2 - (1-\alpha)\lambda - \frac{\alpha}{2} \tag{12}$$

This is a stable polynomial and so by Theorem 5 in the Appendix we have that all the non-trivial eigenvalues lie inside the unit circle. Hence, DESYNC-STALE converges to desynchrony, irrespective of initial conditions. □

4.4 Convergence Rates to Desynchrony

For real applications, how quickly a desynchronization algorithm converges is important. Both DESYNC-IDEAL and DESYNC-STALE are linear algorithms and so can be represented as multiplications by some matrix A. Since the largest eigenvalue of A is always 1, it is the second largest eigenvalue, $\lambda_*(A)$, that tells us how quickly the system is driven to desynchrony [8]. From λ_*, we can compute how many rounds the algorithm requires to become desynchronized, as a function of n and α.

Definition Let $|\vec{\Delta}|$ denote the *desynchronization accuracy* of state $\vec{\Delta} \in \mathcal{P}_n$, defined as the sum of the absolute deviations from perfect desynchrony. Mathematically, $|\vec{\Delta}| = |\vec{\Delta} - \vec{\Delta}^*|_{L^1} = \sum_{i=1}^n |\Delta_i - \frac{1}{n}|$. We say that a system of nodes is *ϵ-desynchronized* if $|\vec{\Delta}| < \epsilon$.

Using techniques from linear algebra and Markov Chain theory, we can prove the convergence rates of both algorithms.

Theorem 3 (DESYNC Rates of Convergence) *A system of n nodes whose dynamics are governed by* DESYNC-IDEAL *will achieve ϵ-desynchrony in $O(n^2 \ln(\frac{1}{\epsilon})/\alpha)$ rounds for $n > 2$ and $\alpha \in (0,2)$. Furthermore, we conjecture that a system of n nodes whose dynamics are governed by* DESYNC-STALE *will achieve ϵ-desynchrony in $O(n^2 \ln(\frac{1}{\epsilon})/\alpha)$ rounds for $n > 2$ and $\alpha \in (0,2)$.*

Proof See Appendix. □

Figure 3 shows results from simulations, confirming Theorems 1-3. In each run, all nodes start out with randomized phases, tightly clustered in a $T/100$ size region, simulating a near-synchronous (worst-case) initial condition. Figure 3(a) shows that, despite both DESYNC algorithms desynchronizing in $O(n^2)$ rounds, DESYNC-STALE converges slower than DESYNC-IDEAL by a constant factor. Thus, for practical purposes, DESYNC-IDEAL can be significantly faster. This is expected since DESYNC-STALE uses stale information, which can lead to overshoot and oscillatory behavior, thus slowing down convergence. Figure 3(b) shows that the system entropy converges to $\mathcal{H}_{\max}$ at an exponential rate. Figure 3(c) shows the number of periods, $k_{\text{req}}(n)$, required to reach accuracy $\epsilon = 10^{-3}$ as a function of n, for $\alpha = 0.95$. The resulting convergence times confirm Theorem 3.

5 Inverse-MS Algorithm

There exists another class of desynchronization algorithms that are fundamentally different from the DESYNC family. In this framework — inspired by the firefly synchronization work of Mirollo and Strogatz [6] — when a node fires, *all* of the other nodes jump instead of just one. This implies that a node is affected by all other nodes, not just its phase neighbors. Within this class, we examine the INVERSE-MS algorithm, adapted and specialized from a bio-synchronization algorithm proposed in [6].

Inverse-MS Algorithm. Assume that node n is the next node to fire. After node n fires, *all* other nodes $i \neq n$ jump from phase ϕ_i to ϕ'_i where

$$\phi'_i = f_{\text{INVMS},i}(\vec{\phi}; \alpha) = \begin{cases} 1 & i = n \\ (1-\alpha)\phi_i & i \neq n \end{cases} \tag{13}$$

where $\alpha \in (0,1)$ is a jumpsize parameter (see Figure 2(b)). Note that all nodes (except the firing node n) jump at each firing. After jumping, nodes are relabeled according to the rule $i \to i+1$. In particular, node $n-1$ becomes node n and node n becomes node 1.

This algorithm does not produce the same type of desynchrony as DESYNC. Instead, we will have to adopt a less constraining definition of desynchronization in our analysis.

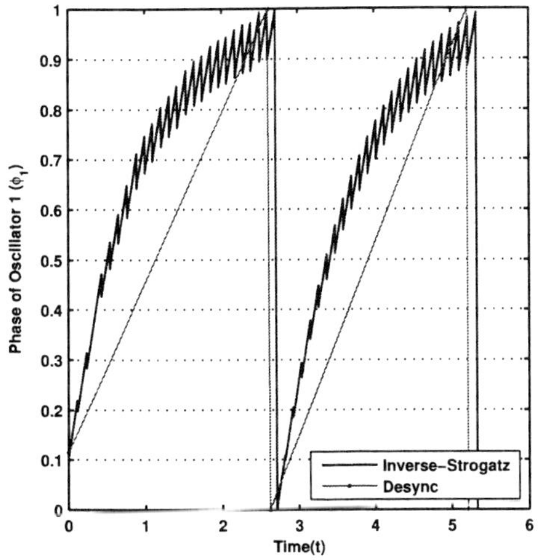

Figure 4. Comparison of steady states for DESYNC and INVERSE-MS algorithms. DESYNC is strongly desynchronized and has a static equilibrium with no jumping (red), while INVERSE-MS is weakly desynchronized and has a dynamic equilibrium, where each node is always jumping backwards (blue). Nonetheless, both algorithms achieve a steady period.

Definition A set of nodes is *weakly desynchronized* if the *time between consecutive nodes' firings are equal.*

Weak desynchronization allows oscillators to accelerate arbitrarily during their cycle, so long as the time between consecutive node firings is identical for all nodes, say some constant $S \in (0, 1)$. Of course, *strong desynchronization* — when $S = T/n$ — is a special case of weak desynchronization. Figure 4 highlights the difference between strong and weak desynchronization by showing the phase trajectory of a single oscillator under both the DESYNC and INVERSE-MS algorithms.

Theorem 4 (INVERSE-MS Convergence) *For all initial conditions and for $\alpha \in (0, 1)$, n nodes whose dynamics are governed by* INVERSE-MS *will be driven to (weak) desynchrony in $O(\frac{1}{n\alpha}\ln(\frac{n}{\epsilon}))$ rounds. However, the steady state period is lengthened to*

$$T^*(n, \alpha) = \frac{n\alpha T}{1-(1-\alpha)^n} \approx n\alpha T,$$

where the last approximation is for large n. Furthermore, the time between consecutive firings is $S \approx \alpha T$ for large n.

Proof We will show that INVERSE-MS can be expressed as a linear dynamical system and we will solve for the fixed point. We will also show that the fixed point is weakly desynchronous, and that for small α, it approaches strong desynchrony.

As with the DESYNC algorithms, it will be more convenient to do the analysis in the delta-phase variables, Δ_i. As before, assume that node n fires. Using equation (13) and accounting for the relabeling $i \rightarrow i + 1$, we have that

$$\Delta_i' = \begin{cases} \alpha T + (1-\alpha)\Delta_n & i = 1 \\ (1-\alpha)\Delta_{i-1} & i \neq 1 \end{cases} \tag{14}$$

To solve for the fixed point $\vec{\Delta}^*$, we use repeated substitution: $\Delta_n^* = (1 - \alpha)\Delta_{n-1}^* = \ldots = (1-\alpha)^{n-1}\Delta_1^* = (1-\alpha)^{n-1}[(1-\alpha)\Delta_n^* + \alpha]$. Solving, we get

$$\Delta_i^* = \frac{(1-\alpha)^{i-1}\alpha T}{1-(1-\alpha)^n}, \tag{15}$$

which approaches T/n as $\alpha \rightarrow 0$, by L'Hospital's Rule. Thus, the fixed point of INVERSE-MS deviates from strong desynchrony ($\Delta_i^* = T/n$) as a function of n, α, and i. But the time between consecutive firings, $S = \Delta_1^*$, is equal for all nodes, and so Δ^* is *weakly desynchronized.* In fact, $T^* = T^*(n, \alpha) = nS = n\Delta_1^*$, corresponding to n identically sized slots. Substituting the expression for Δ_1^* from equation (15), we have the desired result for $T^*(n, \alpha)$. The proof of convergence rate is given in the Appendix. □

Comparison to DESYNC. The INVERSE-MS algorithm's convergence is much faster than DESYNC for certain values of α, since all n nodes jump after any single node's firing (Figure 3(b)). However, INVERSE-MS's fast convergence comes at a price: (1) the steady-state period T^* is greater than the intrinsic oscillation period T (period lengthening), (2) every node must listen to every other node's firings, and (3) every node is always jumping backwards, even in steady-state (dynamic equilibrium). Note that DESYNC does not suffer from any of these problems, since each node's firing only affects its two phase neighbors and the steady state is a static equilibrium. Figure 4 compares the steady-state trajectory of a DESYNC node and an INVERSE-MS node over two periods.

Some applications may require an accurate and precise end-state period (e.g., time-interleaved analog-to-digital converters). For large n, the period lengthening ratio $L(n, \alpha) = T^*/T \approx n\alpha$ is linear in the number of nodes, n, and the jump-size parameter, α. A compensation strategy by setting $\alpha = 1/n$ is undesirable since it depends on the number of nodes, which maybe difficult to estimate accurately in settings where nodes come and go frequently. Nevertheless, if n is known and fixed ahead of time, α-compensation yields a fast desynchronization algorithm.

Properties	INVERSE-MS	DESYNC-IDEAL	DESYNC-STALE
Convergence Rate	$O(\log n/n)$	$O(n^2)$	$O(n^2)$
Period Distortion	$O(n\alpha)$	None	None
Robust to Message Loss	X	✓	✓
Add/Remove Nodes	✓	✓✓	✓✓
Converges on Multi-hop Topology[a]	X	✓	✓

Application	INVERSE-MS	DESYNC-IDEAL	DESYNC-STALE
ADC	X	✓	✓
Multi-core Processor	✓	✓	✓
Wireless TDMA	X[b]	X	✓
Intersection Traffic	X	✓	✓

Table 1. Overview of tradeoffs involved in DESYNC and INVERSE-MS algorithm. X=Inappropriate/Bad, ✓=Good, ✓✓=Excellent. (a) Preliminary results for multi-hop networks are based on simulations of a simple extension of the DESYNC algorithm. We are currently unable to find a way to extend INVERSE-MS to multi-hop. Full discussion is left for future work. (b) We are not yet able to extend INVERSE-MS to work in a TDMA setting.

6 Choosing the Right Algorithm for your Application

Self-organizing desynchronization is a powerful primitive that has many potential applications. The choice of desynchronization algorithm depends greatly on the constraints posed by the application environment. For example, message loss in wireless networks makes it impossible for nodes to observe all firings. Therefore, using an algorithm that is robust to missed firings is important. In other settings, the need to establish a precise period may outweigh all other concerns. To help guide the choice of a desynchronization algorithm, we present a brief overview of the tradeoffs (summarized in Table 1).

Convergence Rates. The rate of convergence is at odds with period distortion and robustness to message loss. A fast convergence rate means a quick response time to node membership changes, but it can drastically affect the periodicity of nodes' firings (INVERSE-MS only, see Section 5). A slow convergence rate means slower system response time to nodes entering and leaving, but allows for better periodicity and robustness to message loss. In simulations, INVERSE-MS is the fastest of all algorithms (see Figure 3) with the extra speed coming at the cost of a large period distortion.

Message Loss. In many settings, including wireless networks, message loss is an unavoidable reality. Therefore, robustness to missed firings is important. Here, the best option is to use a DESYNC variant, where missed firings affect only immediate neighbors and the jumpsize parameter α can be set to a low value in order to protect against lost messages. In contrast, INVERSE-MS is ill-suited for handling message loss. A missed firing in INVERSE-MS means that many nodes fail to jump, thereby altering several nodes' periods. Furthermore, achieving good desynchronization in networks with lossy links depends strongly on the algorithm's ability to generalize to a multi-hop topology. Preliminary results suggest that INVERSE-MS does not converge in multi-hop networks.

Adding and Removing Nodes. In settings where nodes enter and leave frequently (e.g. to conserve energy, returning when triggered by an asynchronous event), the system needs to respond quickly and reliably. Here INVERSE-MS suffers a major drawback: its period is a function of the number of nodes and so predicting it is difficult. In extreme situations, where nodes enter and leave incessantly, the period may become completely inaccurate. In DESYNC variants, on the other hand, a node's arrival or departure takes longer to propagate to the rest of the network, and so nodes are able to maintain a stable period throughout the process, at the cost of a slower convergence

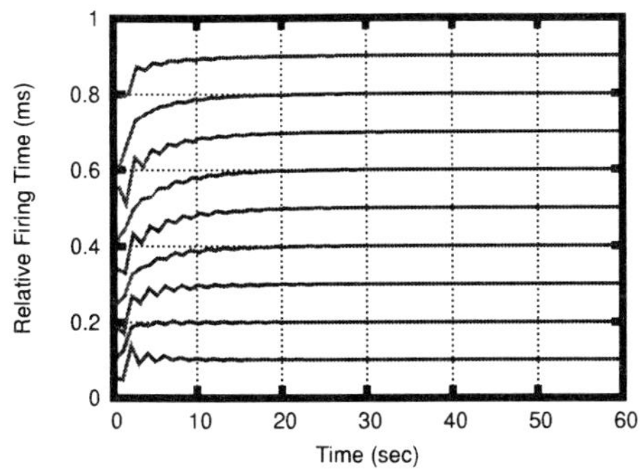

Figure 5. Relative Firing Times: 10 Telos motes placed within communication range of one another running a simple implementation of the DESYNC algorithm. Each node had a firing timer that had a default frequency of 1 second. Upon expiration of the timer, each node broadcasted a message to all other nodes. Shown here is the firing times of each node relative to an arbitrarily selected node whose firing was clamped to the horizontal axis. Note that the nodes achieve desynchronization within 15 periods.

rate.

7 Implementation

To further highlight the simplicity of the algorithm, we implemented the DESYNC algorithm along with a TDMA variation. The full details and results of these implementations can be found in [1]. The algorithms were implemented on several Telos wireless sensor motes running the TinyOS operating system. In the tests, 4-20 nodes were all placed within communication distance of one another on a table. Each node was initialized with a common timer period of 1 second. Whenever a node's timer expired, it broadcasted a message to the rest of the nodes indicating its firing. Nodes recorded the times of the nodes that fired immediately before it and after it relative to their own clocks. Once both firings were heard, the nodes calculated the midpoint and set their timer to fire a period later. The spacings of the firings of a typical run with 10 nodes are shown in Figure 5. Qualitatively, desynchronization is achieved quite quickly. For the ad-hoc TDMA protocol, we added code that had nodes send as much data as they could during their time slots. Table 2 shows abbreviated results of the performance of this algorithm. Of particular interest is the ability of the DESYNC-TDMA algorithm to share the bandwidth fairly and fully amongst the nodes. Furthermore, there is a graceful linear degradation with increasing numbers of nodes. In short, the DESYNC algorithm's simplicity and efficacy is a great advantage for any application that requires the desynchronization of fully-connected devices.

Nodes:	4	10	20
Total Throughput (Kbps):	**60.8**	**57.9**	**53.0**
(normalized, %)	(96.8)	(92.2)	(84.3)
Max Individual (Kbps):	15.2	5.8	2.8
Min Individual (Kbps):	15.2	5.6	2.4
Message Loss (%):	**0.2**	**0.3**	**0.5**

Table 2. DESYNC-TDMA's performance for varying numbers of nodes over 60-second runs. A comparison to other protocols can be found in [1]. In our experiments, the maximum rate at which a single node could transmit was 62.8 Kbps.

8 Conclusions and Future Work

As ad-hoc networks become more popular, algorithms for achieving desynchronization in a decentralized, self-organized manner will be increasingly important. In this paper we have designed, analyzed, and implemented two such algorithms: DESYNC and INVERSE-MS. The choice of algorithm depends on particular constraints posed by the application setting. INVERSE-MS is a good choice when the number of nodes is constant, all connections are reliable, the topology is fully-connected, and message delays/losses are negligible. In short, INVERSE-MS is fast but not robust. On the other hand, DESYNC is slower, but much more robust. It can handle an arbitrary number of nodes, unpredictable node arrivals and departures, and some message loss (reliability is only needed for the links between phase neighbors). The simplicity of both algorithms allows for wide applicability and we presented a successful implementation of DESYNC on a real sensor network testbed [1].

The desynchronization algorithms presented in this paper all rely on a single-hop, all-to-all topology. Thus, an important problem for future work is assessing performance on multi-hop networks. Computing an ideal desynchronization schedule that maximizes the sum of the slot sizes of all nodes seems hard, since the problem seems closely related to graph coloring and task scheduling. However, computing reasonable desynchronization schedules may be tractable. Our preliminary results suggest that: (a) DESYNC converges in multi-hop networks (though multiple steady states are possible), and (b) the optimal schedule is related to minimal graph coloring, and so is likely to be NP-hard. In contrast, INVERSE-MS fails to converge after the removal of just one edge from the topology, highlighting its strong dependence on regular topologies.

References

[1] J. Degesys, I. Rose, A. Patel, and R. Nagpal. Desync: Self-organizing desynchronization and tdma in wireless sensor networks. In *Proc. Conference on Information Processing in Sensor Networks*, Jan 2007.

[2] V. Divi. Scalable blind calibration of timing skew in high-resolution time-interleaved adcs. In *IEEE International Symposium on Circuits and Systems*, 2006.

[3] K. Dresner and P. Stone. Sharing the road: Autonomous vehicles meet human drivers. In *Proceedings of the Twentieth International Joint Conference on Artificial Intelligence, Hyderabad, India, January 2007.*, 2004.

[4] Y. Hong and A. Scaglione. Time synchronization and reach-back communications with pulse-coupled oscillators for uwb wireless ad hoc networks. In *"Proc. IEEE Conference on Ultra Wideband Systems and Technologies"*, Nov 2003.

[5] D. Lucarelli and I. Wang. Decentralized synchronization protocols with nearest neighbor communication. In *Proc. Conference on Embedded Networked Sensor Systems (SenSys)*, Nov 2004.

[6] R. Mirollo and S. Strogatz. Synchronization of pulse-coupled biological oscillators. *SIAM Journal of Applied Math*, 50(6):1645–62, Dec 1990.

[7] C. S. Peskin. *Mathematical Aspects of Heart Physiology*. Courant Institute of Mathematical Sciences, New York University, New York, 1975.

[8] J. S. Rosenthal. Convergence rates for markov chains. *SIAM Review*, 37(3):387–405, 1995.

[9] A. Tanenbaum. *Computer Networks*. Prentice Hall, 2002.

[10] G. Werner-Allen, G. Tewari, A. Patel, R. Nagpal, and M. Welsh. Firefly-inspired sensor network synchronicity with realistic radio effects. In *Proc. Conference on Embedded Networked Sensor Systems (SenSys)*, Nov 2005.

A Appendix

Here we present theory regarding convex polynomials and the proofs of the convergence rates of all analyzed algorithms.

Definition A: Stable polynomials A polynomial $\rho(\lambda) = \lambda^n - a_{n-1}\lambda^{n-1} - \cdots - a_0$ is **stable** if: (1) $\lambda = 1$ is a single ("trivial") root of $\rho(\lambda)$ and (2) the trailing coefficients $\{a_{n-1}, \ldots, a_0\}$ are nonnegative and less than 1.

Theorem 5 (Nontrivial Eigenvalues of Convex Polynomials) *The nontrivial roots of a stable polynomial lie inside the unit circle in the complex plane.*

Proof Let $\rho(\lambda)$ be a stable polynomial. Since $\rho(1) = 0$, we have that the sum of the trailing coefficients must be one, a fact that we will use later on. Consider any nontrivial root λ of ρ. We will show by contradiction that $|\lambda| < 1$. Suppose $|\lambda| > 1$. Then by rearranging ρ and applying the Triangle Inequality we have that $|\lambda|^n \leq a_{n-1}|\lambda|^{n-1} + \cdots + a_1|\lambda| + a_0 < \left(\sum_{i=0}^{n-1} a_i\right)|\lambda|^{n-1} = |\lambda|^{n-1}$, a contradiction since $|\lambda| > 1$. Hence $|\lambda| \leq 1$. Now suppose that $|\lambda| = 1$, i.e., $\lambda = e^{i\theta}$ with $0 < \theta < 2\pi$. (Note that $\theta = 0$ corresponds to the trivial root $\lambda = 1$.) Rearranging ρ as before gives us that $\lambda^n = a_{n-1}\lambda^{n-1} + \cdots + a_0$. Since the trailing coefficients are nonnegative, less than one, and sum to one, the right hand side is a convex combination of the points $\{1, \lambda, \ldots, \lambda^{n-1}\}$, all of which are on the boundary of the unit circle. Since the unit circle is a convex set, any convex combination of at least two distinct boundary points lies in the interior of the circle. But this contradicts the fact that the left hand side λ^n is on the unit circle, and hence it must be that $|\lambda| < 1$ for all nontrivial roots $\lambda \neq 1$.

Proof of Theorem 3:DESYNC-IDEAL Convergence Rate Note that the matrix A_{IDEAL} is stochastic (i.e. its entries are nonnegative and its columns sum to one). Hence we can associate a Markov Chain $\mathcal{X}_t$ with state space $\Omega = \{1, 2, \ldots, n\}$ with transition matrix A_{IDEAL}^T, thus linking the convergence rate of DESYNC-IDEAL with the mixing time of the chain. This chain takes $O(n)$ time to complete one "circuit" from state 1 back to state 1. Using the Central Limit Theorem and the symmetry of the ring, we can show that it takes $O(n^2 \ln(1/\epsilon)/\alpha)$ circuits multiplied by $O(n)$ time per circuit to mix. This implies that the number of periods require for DESYNC-IDEAL to reach ϵ-desynchrony is $O(n^2 \ln(1/\epsilon)/\alpha)$. □

Conjecture in Theorem 3:DESYNC-STALE Convergence Rate The nth power of A_{STALE} is very similar to the transition matrix of a symmetric random walk on a ring of n nodes, modulo a few edges. This suggests that $O(n^2 \ln(\frac{1}{\epsilon})/\alpha)$ periods are required to reach ϵ-desynchrony. MATLAB computations of eigenvalues in conjunction with simulations confirm these bounds. □

Proof of Theorem 4:INVERSE-MS Convergence Rate Equation 13 can be written in matrix form as $\vec{\Delta}' = C\vec{\Delta}$, where C represents the jump-and-permute steps of the INVERSE-MSalgorithm. The matrix J has non-trivial eigenvalues of magnitude $1 - \alpha$ and thus solving the equation $(1-\alpha)^F < \epsilon$ for the number of firings F yields $F > \frac{1}{\alpha}\ln(\frac{n}{\epsilon})$. Since there are n firings per round, the number of rounds require to reach accuracy ϵ is F/n, which is $O(\frac{1}{n\alpha}\ln(\frac{n}{\epsilon}))$, as desired. □

Clustering Distributed Energy Resources for Large-Scale Demand Management

Elth Ogston
Vrije Universiteit Amsterdam
elth@cs.vu.nl

Astrid Zeman, Mikhail Prokopenko and Geoff James
CSIRO ICT Centre
{astrid.zeman, mikhail.prokopenko, geoff.james}@csiro.au

Abstract

Managing demand for electrical energy allows generation facilities to be run more efficiently. Current systems allow for management between large industrial consumers. There is, however, an increasing trend to decentralize energy resource management and push it to the level of individual households, or even appliances. In this work we investigate the suitability of using adaptive clustering to improve the scalability of decentralized energy resource management systems by appropriately partitioning resources. We review the area of distributed energy resource management and propose a simple yet realistic model to study the problem. Simulations using this model show that straightforward clustering and distributed planning methods allow systems to scale, but may be limited to only a few hundred-thousand appliances. Results indicate that there is an opportunity to apply adaptive clustering techniques in order to discover more advanced grouping criteria that would enable groups to change as appliances' behavior changes. The simulations further suggest that even an extremely limited exchange of information between clusters can greatly improve management solutions.

1 Introduction

The electricity industry in many countries is facing a number of pressures due to increasing demand, the increasing "peakiness" of demand, and the prospect of carbon accountability. Managing demand for power is an alternative to the traditional solution of investing in expanding centralized generation capacity and the associated infrastructure. Controlling distributed energy resources, customer loads and small generators located close to load centers, in response to price signals and network constraints can give relief from the volatility of wholesale electricity prices and can assist constrained distribution networks during summer and winter demand peaks. Such responses also provide a mechanism to reward customers who choose to manage their energy use thoughtfully.

The inherently distributed nature of energy resource management, and the large savings to be made by even a small gain in efficiency, make it a compelling application in which to apply decentralized planning and control algorithms. Software resource agents running on customer premises or embedded in appliances, can be used to plan future energy consumption and to shift loads according to constraints placed on the system. Australia's Commonwealth Scientific and Industrial Research Organisation (CSIRO) currently has a live multi-agent test-bed for monitoring and controlling industrial loads and generators in electricity distribution networks [6]. The physical deployment of the GridAgents Platform is located in the CSIRO Energy Center in Newcastle, New South Wales, Australia.

To demonstrate the feasibility of using such platforms in the domestic household area, it is necessary to address system scalability. Current agent-based energy resource management systems employ central auctioneers or aggregating agents to combine information on energy consumption from resource management agents and feed this information back to the agents. The use of central components, and more significantly their communications infrastructures, is undesirable in systems that contain hundreds of thousands or millions of devices. We therefore investigate the possibility of clustering devices into more manageable, relatively independent, groups. In particular, in this paper we address two questions: (1) *to what extent is the quality of global solutions reduced by partitioning agents into groups,* and (2) *is it sufficient to choose these groups at random or can agents be classified so as to create more effective groups?*

To avoid demand peaks, resource management agents must be coordinated. One alternative is to cluster agents into separately coordinated groups. Even more interesting is the possibility of creating dynamic adaptive clusters which instead of using fixed criteria can group agents according to unforeseen behaviors and current demand characteristics. Before developing such complex algorithms, however, it is necessary to assess the problem area to determine if they are likely to improve on simpler methods. In this paper we make the following contributions to the study of using cooperating agents to reduce short term peaks in

0-7695-2906-2/07 $25.00 © 2007 IEEE

electricity demand:

- We define a simple yet realistic scenario in which to study the problem and propose and test a minimal demand planning/coordination algorithm which can be used as baseline when developing more advanced planing and control mechanisms.
- We study decentralizing the coordination and planning problem by dividing agents into independent clusters. We show that for small numbers of clusters the quality of global plans is not significantly reduced by partitioning the problem in this manner.
- We show that the choice of clustering criteria can make a difference to the system's ability to stabilize demand.
- We demonstrate that for larger numbers of clusters an extremely limited exchange of information between clusters can greatly improve global plans.

The work presented in this paper considers an abstract model of the energy requirements of simple refrigeration devices, verified by additional experiments using measurements of the behavior of a real appliance. The results listed above justify further research into the area of adaptive decentralized coordination and clustering algorithms for distributed energy resource applications, involving larger scale test-beds and the collection of more varied measurement data.

2 Background and Related Work

This section provides background on electricity generation and distribution, in particular in the Australian market, and describes current work on using agents for distributed energy resource management. Adaptive decentralized clustering methods will be described in Section 5 in relation to our experimental results.

2.1 Demand Management

The management of energy resources can take place on a variety of time-scales. Seasonal peaks in demand, for instance caused by widespread use of air conditioning in hot weather, can place considerable strain on the power grid. When demand exceeds capacity in a grid sector, brownouts can occur, making power temporarily unavailable to customers in the area. Additionally, power draining from neighboring sectors can cause relays to malfunction, resulting in costly blackouts. Measures for managing seasonal demand peaks include intelligent load shedding, in which certain areas are strategically blacked out, or contract agreements are made with larger consumers for supply to be reduced when necessary, in return for lower prices.

On a weekly and daily time scale, energy demand also follows regular highs and lows, corresponding to business hours and common daily routines such as meal times. Many energy retailers employ a dual pricing system with peak and off-peak hours to encourage households to shift flexible tasks, such as washing, to times when there is spare capacity.

While seasonal, weekly, and daily trends are the most visible to energy consumers, changes in demand on a much shorter time scale are likely to profit most from control by agent technology. In Australia, energy retailers purchase capacity, in the form of hedge contracts, many months in advance, according to forecasts of future needs. Since this energy use is planned, it is relatively cheap, with a price near the average expected price, typically around $40 (AUD) per megawatt hour. However, if customer demand exceeds the pre-purchased quota, additional energy must be bought on a spot market. In this market, prices are set per five minute interval. In January 2007 spot market prices in New South Wales ranged between $10.80/MWh and $5091.95/MWh [10]. Managing resources so as to reduce short term peaks in demand can thus result in significant savings. Micro-managing a device by shifting its energy consumption by a few minutes can have very little impact on the functioning of some appliances, but requires constant monitoring and communication, making it an appropriate task for computer agents.

2.2 Energy Generation and Distribution Infrastructure

Large energy producers and consumers (including retailers) in eastern Australia participate in a single wholesale market, the National Electricity Market (NEM) [10]. Within this market energy production is centrally managed so as to meet demand, set fair prices, and ensure reliability of supply. Producers submit bids stating the amount of energy they can generate at what cost and consumers submit predictions for consumption. These are matched, the lowest cost producers are instructed to supply energy, and a single price is set for all participants. This planning process is based on short-term forecasts of the volume of energy required over the next 24 hour period. Generators are scheduled in 5 minute dispatch intervals. Prices are set for each dispatch interval and provide a signal by which consumers can manage their individual demand. These dispatch and prediction intervals influence the time-scale at which electricity management agents can operate. The large volumes of electricity used in the NEM make it impossible to store energy for future use. This means that the NEM is unable to respond quickly to significant unpredicted changes in demand. On the whole, the less oscillation there is in demand, the better.

The NEM covers an area 4000 miles long, and serves eight-million end-use customers. Though it is possible for electricity to be traded over a distance of 4000 miles [13], transport of electricity between regions is limited by the capacity of the high-voltage transmission lines that interconnect them. Thus, in theory the whole of the NEM can be seen as a single very large-scale computational system in which tradeoffs in power use can be made between agents, regardless of location. In practice some restrictions apply and agent location may place some constraints on which agents may interact with each other. Currently, information on electricity demand is only exchanged between major players in the market. However, the installation of "smart-meters", and the ability to use transmission lines to carry data, means that in the future, even small consumers such as households could participate in energy management systems [2, 7].

2.3 Agents for Distributed Energy Resource Management

Previous research on multi-agent systems for electricity management has mainly focused on agent-based simulations of electronic market mechanisms [20, 18]. A couple recent efforts described below are building deployed agent systems.

The European CRISP project [17] carried out field studies in Sweden to assess the advantages of using intelligent agent and electronic market technologies. In the project's system model the electricity grid is divided into local areas, called cells. Coordination between agents and cells takes place through the Powermatcher electronic market [9]. In Powermatcher, agents within a cell submit bids for electricity production or use to a designated aggregator, called an SD-matcher, which manages the cell. Aggregated bid information is passed up a hierarchical tree of aggregators. The market equilibrium prices is calculated at the root node, and distributed back down the tree. This network configuration remains fixed over the duration of system operation.

Market mechanisms coordinate current power consumption and production based on a single price. Energy needs of devices at a particular time are, however, often dependent upon device behavior at other time intervals. Multi-commodity combinatorial markets can be used to coordinate prices over a number of time intervals, but quickly become overly complex as the number of intervals grows [4].

The GridAgents framework, developed for the Australian CSIRO testbed, explores a variety of alternatives to market-based control [6]. In particular, a method that uses genetic optimization to coordinate agent plans has been studied. A cap on energy use for a given period is set for a group of agents, which accordingly rearrange plans to minimize cost whilst considering local objectives [5].

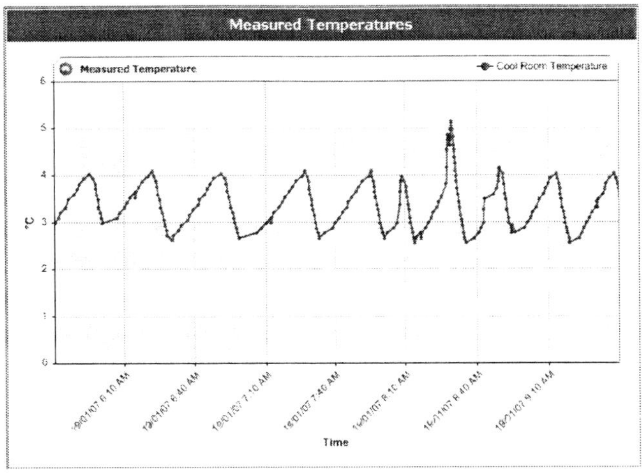

Figure 1. CSIRO cool-room agent operation.

Both the CRISP and GridAgents projects propose dividing agents into groups in order to meet system scalability objectives. In the CRISP project these groups take the form of cells, whose composition is based on the physical locations of devices. The project report, however, notes that group configurations which differ with the seasons are likely to improve on the system's ability to match supply to demand [17]. The GridAgents method of genetic optimization is also based on coordination within groups, of a size of around 500 agents. The project aims to further explore clustering methods by which these groups are defined [6]. In this paper we provide a detailed investigation of the factors involved in successfully creating improved clusterings for such systems.

3 Methodology and Scenario

The experiments presented in Section 4 evaluate the effectiveness of clustering distributed energy resources for the purposes of coordinating planned energy demand. Coordinating energy use locally within clusters of resources in place of centrally coordinating all resources has several advantages. First, it removes a dependance on a single central point of failure, improving system robustness. Second, it reduces the communication delay between resource agents and the coordinator, allowing planning to be done on a shorter time scale, or for additional planning/coordination rounds to take place. Third, it reduces the complexity of the coordination problem, allowing coordination to be done by a simpler, cheaper, controller. Fourth, it creates a system which is more scalable as adding new resource agents only requires creating additional clusters, rather than expanding the capacity of a central coordinator.

There are, however, a number of questions involved with the relative quality of centralized coordination of plans versus distributed cluster-based coordination. Clusters only have partial information on the total energy use of the system, implying that distributed coordination should produce a global plan that is worse than found with a central coordinator. We would like to know exactly how much worse in order to be able to weigh the relative costs and benefits of clustering resources. Additionally, there are questions about how to create clusters: what size should clusters be, what composition function should be used to choose cluster members, should cluster membership be fixed or dynamic? Creating a fixed set of fixed size clusters with random membership would greatly simplify the coordination problem. We thus, in particular, would like to know how much of an advantage more advanced clustering methods would have over simpler settings.

The experiments in Section 4 are designed to examine the difference between joint plans coordinated only within clusters and those produced using centralized coordination, and to compare the quality of joint plans produced using random versus carefully selected clusterings. In this section we first present out experimental methodology, and in particular the energy resources, coordination algorithm, and clustering criteria we consider.

3.1 Scenario

We consider a scenario where the power consumption of individual refrigerators in a city must be coordinated so as to keep their total energy use as constant as possible for a given short period. Exact data on the preferable scale of this problem, the precise range of energy requirements of household refrigerators, or the possible planning behaviors of agents controlling refrigerators is unavailable. In the following sections we describe the existing data and the estimations we use to set parameters for our experiments.

Refrigerators and freezers typically make up over 20% of total residential electricity consumption in Australia [1]. We thus focus on modeling refrigerators as our resource agents, being the largest single end-use offender of household energy consumption. Nearly all households in Australia have at least one refrigerator and about 30% own two. Nearly 60% of households own a separate freezer [1]. While it may possibly be desirable to coordinate the behavior of all devices within the NEM, initial systems are likely to be more modest. We consider the case of coordinating refrigerators in the city of Newcastle NSW which has a single 600MW coal-fired power plant, serving approximately 200,000 households. We would thus like to ensure system scalability to around 400,000 resource agents.

Our model of energy resources and their consumption requirements focuses on representing variable flexibility of resource agents in adjusting initial plans. During a typical planning cycle in the multi-agent systems on which we base this work, resource agents send initial plans to a coordinator, which computes aggregate energy use then sends suggestions for changes to the agents. In general, this planning and coordination occurs in multiple cycles in which agents make readjustments, send their new plans to the coordinator, and receive additional suggestions. Plans are also readjusted and re-coordinated as predictions of future energy use changes. In this study we consider relatively simple agents. For this reason we simplify the planning process to a single round in which agents each send multiple possible plans for the coordinator to select among. We assume that once set, and agent is free to follow its chosen plan. By varying the number plans an agent submits we can model resources that are more or less flexible in their energy consumption profiles.

3.2 Energy Resources

In this study we consider a single type of energy resource, an abstract cool-room, of which refrigerators are an example. Cool-rooms consist of an insulated chamber which must be kept within a given temperature range, and a compressor that can be turned on to lower the temperature. Their basic behavior is straightforward, when the compressor is off the room's temperature slowly rises towards the outside temperature, until the maximum of the temperature range is reached. The compressor is then turned on until the chamber cools to the minimum value of the temperature range.

The simple cool-room agents studied in this paper are modeled after the basic operation of the more advanced CSIRO cool-room agent currently being used to control industrial cool-rooms as well as domestic-sized refrigerators in the Newcastle Energy Centre. Figure 1 shows the monitoring interface of the agent controlling the canteen cool-room[1]. The agent is given the goal of keeping the temperature of the cool-room within a certain range by turning on and off either the compressor or a fan. The agent receives data on current electricity prices and attempts to avoid using energy when prices spike. Predictions for future plans are made based on the current temperatures inside and outside the cool-room, and a model of heat-loss properties based on a history of temperature behavior.

Realistic models of cool-rooms show that their short-term power consumption follows a periodic square wave [20], as illustrated in Figure 2. In this study we model refrigerators with three parameters, a compressor cycle length (C) that states the length of one period of this square wave, an on-time (T), which states the amount of time in which the compressor is on during that period, and a power value (P) that gives the amount of power used by the compressor when on.

[1] Available online at http://demc.com.au/DEMC/Canteen/Canteen.aspx.

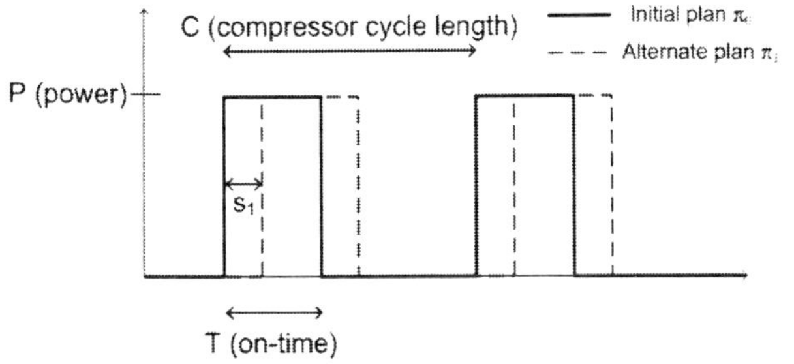

Figure 2. Plan Representation

We base the experimental values of the cool-room parameters on data giving the typical energy consumption per year of refrigerators and freezers currently sold in Australia [1]. The values of C and T for a refrigerator vary depending on use. From observations of refrigerators we estimate that cycle lengths vary between 20 and 60 minutes. Whirlpool's customer service website states that compressors in typical refrigerators are on for between 40% and 80% percent of the time. Based on these estimates we create a set of random refrigerator profiles for our experiments by choosing the yearly power consumption of an appliance at random from the list of Australian refrigerators, and choosing values of C and T uniformly at random from the ranges given above. The power used by the compressor, P, is calculated from the yearly power consumption, assuming that C and T are averages for the year. Plans are divided into one minute intervals in which the power consumption is either P when the compressor is on or 0 when the compressor is off. Each refrigerator agent is given an initial plans starting at a random point in its compressor cycle.

In these experiments we will consider planning based on expected energy use of a refrigerator for a term of two hours, to cover behavior over several compressor cycles. Because refrigerators only need to maintain a given temperature range, planning agents can be very flexible in choosing exactly when to turn compressors on or off. They thus have the option of creating a wide variety of plans for a given 120 minute interval. Since we are only interested in the effect of flexibility, we do not model exactly how agents can choose to change these plans. Instead we make the simplifying assumption that any plan that involves a time shift of the periodic power consumption square wave is acceptable to maximally flexible refrigerators. A refrigerator thus has a finite set of alternative energy-use plans it can follow, $\Pi = \{\pi_0, \ldots, \pi_{k-1}\}$. Given a refrigerator's initial plan, π_0, each alternative plan π_i is defined by a time shift s_i such that the power consumption at time t in π_i is that of plan π_0 at time $t - s_i$. In our experiments we consider time shifts s that are multiples of one minute intervals. Thus a refrigerator with a compressor cycle length of C minutes has C possible plans. Less flexible refrigerators are modeled as accepting only smaller subsets of plans.

3.3 The Desync Coordination Algorithm

We study a simple heuristic coordination algorithm that, given a fixed set of possible plans for each resource agent, attempts to choose the combination of plans that results in the best aggregate plan. This could be done with straightforward brute-force search of all the possible combinations. However, such a search quickly becomes prohibitively expensive as the number of resources considered grows. Instead we use a simplifying heuristic in which the resources are chosen sequentially, and their plans are selected according to a metric, without attempting to find the exact optimal combination. Plan coordination thus follows the sequence:

1. Each energy resource x_i sends to the coordinator its set Π_i of possible acceptable plans.
2. The coordinator goes through the resources sequentially, according to a certain order, and for each resource selects the plan that would best fit in the current aggregate. The selected plan is added to the current aggregate. The metric used to determine the "best fit" is described in Section 3.4.
3. The coordinator notifies each agent which of its possible plans was selected and is to be carried out.

The Desync coordination algorithm has the advantage that it is simple, requires minimal communication between the resource agents and the coordinator, and requires minimal computation by the coordinator. It has the disadvantage that there is no feedback to the agents which might have been able to be more flexible in their plans. A further disadvantage is that a complete search is not made to find the optimal combination of plans. For the purposes of analyzing the possible benefits of clustering, however, this simple algorithm is sufficient and provides a clear picture of the effects of clustering. The case for more complex algorithms is discussed in Section 5.

3.4 Plan Selection

The coordinator in our experiments aims to minimize the peak power usage in the aggregate plan. Aggregation of two plans, say π_j and π_k, denoted as $\pi_j + \pi_k$, simply involves adding the planned powers for each time interval. We denote by $f(\pi)$ the maximum (peak) power used in the plan π over its entire duration, in our case the time interval $[0, 120]$. For a given current aggregate plan, π_α, and a given set of possible plans for a resource agent, Π, the coordinator chooses the agent plan π_i for which $f(\pi_\alpha + \pi_i)$ is minimized. The full Dysnc algorithm is summarized in Algorithm 1.

Energy prices paid by energy distributors in Australia have two components, a price for a fixed amount of capacity, set in advance, and a spot price for energy use that exceeds that capacity. In this paper we do not consider the more complex planning problem of matching energy use to current costs, or a changing "cap" on energy demand [5]. We leave this problem to future work, discussed in section 5. Our main goal is to show that the underlying power consumption of agents can be coordinated so as to reduce variability in the "fixed" part of the energy use.

Algorithm 1: Desync algorithm.

Set the current aggregate plan π_α to zero usage
for *each resource agent* $x_i \in X$ **do**
  retrieve set of plans Π_i
  set the chosen plan for x_i as $\pi_i = \pi_{i,0}$
  set temporary maximum as $\mu = f(\pi_\alpha + \pi_i)$
  for *each subsequent plan* $\pi_{i,j} \in \Pi_i$ **do**
    if $f(\pi_\alpha + \pi_{i,j})$ *is less than* μ **then**
      set $\pi_i = \pi_{i,j}$
      set $\mu = f(\pi_\alpha + \pi_i)$
    end
  end
  update current aggregate as $\pi_\alpha = \pi_\alpha + \pi_i$
  send chosen plan π_i to the agent x_i
end

4 Experiments

In this section we present experiments to examine the following questions:

- How effective is Desync coordination? (Section 4.1)
- To what extent does reducing the flexibility of resources reduce the Desync algorithm's ability to coordinate energy use? (Section 4.2)
- In respect to planning, is actual cool-room behavior well represented by our abstract cool-room model? (Section 4.3)
- To what extent does dividing resources into clusters reduce the Desync algorithm's ability to discover improved global plans? (Section 4.4)
- Does clustering similar resources together differ from random clustering? (Section 4.5)
- How does system behavior change as the number of agents is increased? (Section 4.6)
- Does adding communication between clusters improve on non-interacting clusters? (Section 4.7)

4.1 Basic Desync Coordination Ability

Figure 3 compares two example aggregates of the plans of 640 maximally flexible refrigerators. The figure shows the aggregate power used at each minute interval when the refrigerators are left to choose their own plans, and the aggregate for the same refrigerators after Desync coordination. The figure shows that Desync coordination is able to effectively shift individual behaviors so as to flatten peaks in the overall power use.

In general the alternative plans for a resource agent can have different total power consumptions over the total time

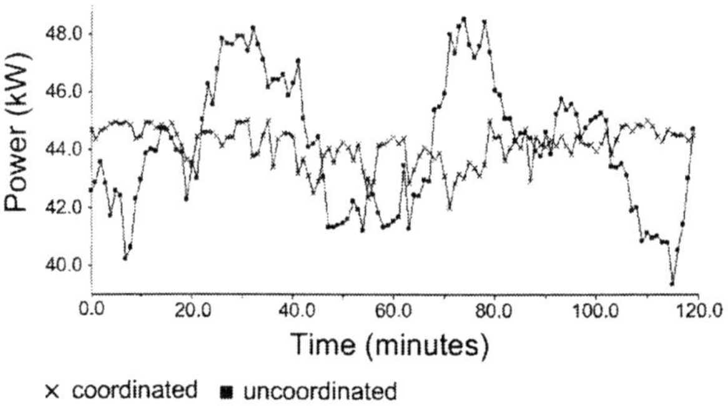

Figure 3. Aggregate power use, with and without coordination.

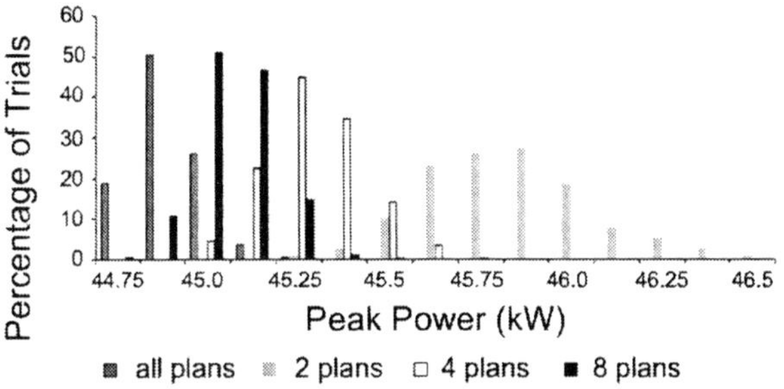

Figure 4. Distribution of peak power, less flexible agents.

interval. In order to keep the power consumption of all plans equal, and thus aggregate plans using different possible plans comparable, we artificially raise or lower the compressor power slightly when a shifted plan results in a refrigerator being on for a different period of time than in its initial plan. Thus a lower maximum power for a plan indicates a more constant plan. Without planning the maximum power used is 48.55 kW (out of a maximum possible 71.90 kW) while planning reduces this value to 45.01 kW.

The aggregate plans of refrigerators can vary, both with and without planning, because in the simulations each refrigerator chooses its initial plan at random for each trial and because agents can be aggregated in a different order in each trial. Without planning, the distribution for 1000 trials of the peak aggregate power varied between 46.00 kW and 51.51 kW. With planning, peak power consistently improves on these values, and is more predictable, varying from 44.70 kW to 45.27 kW.

4.2 Reducing Agent Flexibility

We next examine the effects of reducing the flexibility of resource agents in changing their consumption plans. We repeat the experiment from Section 4.1, but instead of allowing the coordinator to choose out of any possible plan for each refrigerator, each refrigerator submits only a small number of randomly chosen plans. Fully flexible refrigerators have between 20 and 60 possible plans. Figure 4

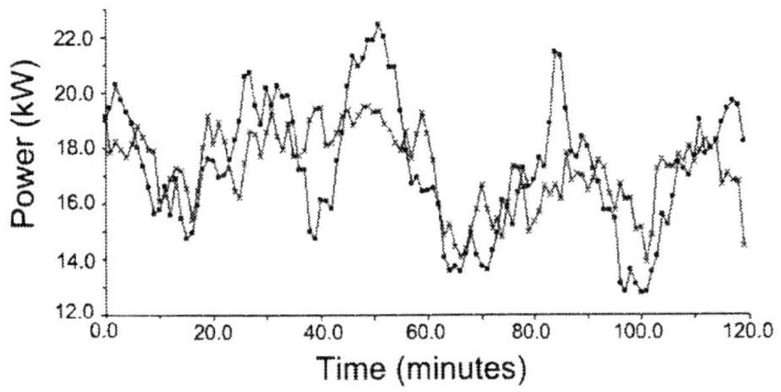

Figure 5. Aggregate power use, measured refrigerator data.

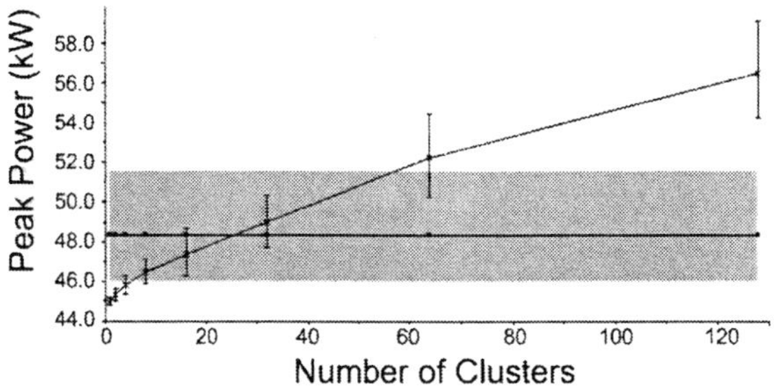

Figure 6. Peak power: random clusters.

shows the distribution of peak power for coordinated aggregate plans when refrigerators submit only 2, 4 or 8 possible plans. Even with very few plans to choose from, the Desync algorithm is able to find almost as good an aggregate plan as it does when given fully flexible agents.

4.3 Comparison to an Actual Refrigerator

Actual refrigerators have more complex behavior than the idealized cool-room model. We measured the behavior of a standard refrigerator over a period of several days. Without user intervention power usage of the appliance followed a regular square wave, in which the compressor was on for about 20 minutes then off for about 15 minutes. With user intervention however, spikes in power occurred when the door was opened, turning the light on. Opening the door also caused the compressor to stay on for longer. Every 24 hours a very high spike in power use occurred followed by a long cooling period, due to the operation of the automatic defroster.

The irregularity of behavior of actual appliances makes the coordination problem more difficult than for the model cool-rooms. Figure 5 shows example aggregates, with and without coordination, for 94 virtual measured refrigerators, created by breaking several days worth of measurements into two hour segments. Each virtual refrigerator is given 8 plans, made by shifting its initial plan by successive one minute intervals. Figure 5 shows that while Desync coordination becomes less effective in the non-ideal case, it still has a noticeable effect on lowering peaks in aggregate power. We will discuss possible effects of the behavior of real appliances further in Section 5.

4.4 Effect of Clustering

Figure 6 plots the peak power found in the global aggregate when dividing agents into 1, 2, 4, 8, 16, 32, 64, an 128 clusters, chosen at random for 640 agents. Values for the aggregate before and after coordination are plotted, marked at the average peak power found over 100 trials. Error bars, for the coordinated aggregate, and the shaded region, for the uncoordinated aggregate, indicate the minimum and maximum values seen. The graph shows that as agents are separated into more clusters, the aggregate plan formed by running the Desync algorithm independently in each cluster deteriorates. Interestingly, with more than 32 clusters the coordinated aggregate tends to be worse than the average aggregate obtained when no coordination was done at all and each refrigerator was simply left to follow its original randomly chosen plan. For less than 32 clusters however, clustering is an effective manner of distributing the coordination problem. With 128 clusters, coordination has a markedly detrimental effect on the systems. In the following experiments we shall investigate why distributed coordination performs so poorly with larger numbers of clusters.

4.5 Non-Random Clusters

The behavior seen in Section 4.4 should improve if the aggregate plans created in the individual clusters improve. The Desync algorithm's ability to coordinate plans should thus be enhanced by better clusterings in which refrigerators that have more compatible behaviors are grouped together. In Figure 7 clusters are created not at random, but so that clusters contain refrigerators with similar values of P, the power used by their compressor. This should make it easier for the Desync algorithm to make use of pairs of refrigerators whose plans can be shifted so that they complement each other. In fact, the figure shows that this *power-based clustering* criterion yields clusters with about the same behavior as random clusters.

In Figure 8 clusters are created in which refrigerators with similar compressor cycle times, C, are grouped together. Such *frequency-based clustering* does improve the aggregate plans. From this we conclude that clustering criteria used when dividing up agents does have an impact on the overall system behavior. The optimal criteria is likely to depend strongly on the actual behavior of the individual agents. We thus leave a further exploration into clustering methods for future work, discussed in Section 5.

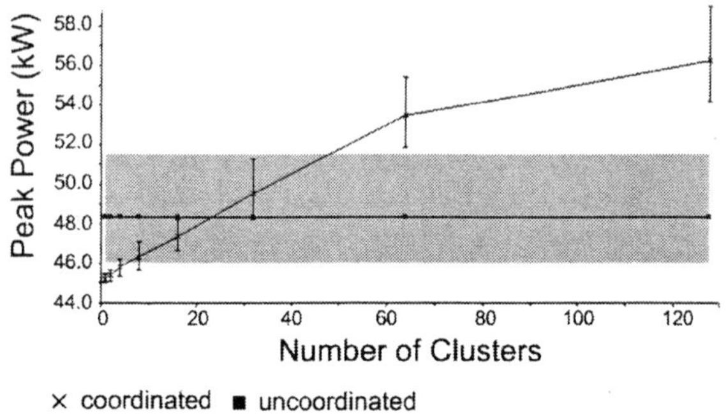

Figure 7. Peak power: P-based clusters.

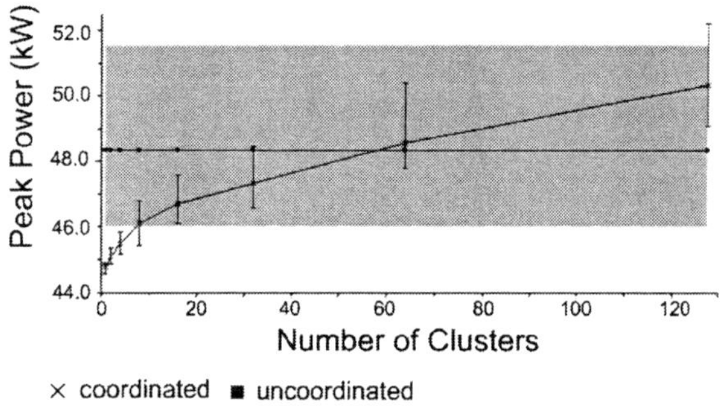

Figure 8. Peak power: C-based clusters.

4.6 Clustering and Scalability

A possible explanation for the poor coordination ability when agents are divided into more than 32 clusters is the small size of these clusters. Dividing 640 agents between 32 clusters produces clusters with only 20 agents each. It is possible that the Desync algorithm simply requires more agents to be able to produce acceptable aggregate plans.

We repeat the frequency-based clustering experiment from Section 4.5 using twice as many agents. We find, however, almost no difference in the influence of the number of clusters on coordination ability, in spite of the fact that the clusters in this experiment are twice as large. This indicates that there exists a limitation on the degree to which the energy resource coordination problem can be decentralized by dividing it into separate more manageable problems, independent of the overall size of the system.

Intuitively, this limitation can come from the nature of coordination itself. Looking back at the example aggregates in Figure 3 it can be seen that while coordination lowers the peak power in an aggregate, in doing so it increases the amount of time during which the aggregate is relatively high. When combining a two random aggregates, the chance of two high points overlapping thus increases after coordination. As the number of clusters increases the chance of undesired overlaps also increases. Hence, independent coordination in large numbers of clusters can result in worsening the global aggregate. Table 1 illustrates this. It compares coordinated and uncoordinated aggregates for 16 randomly chosen clusters, in an instance when the uncoordinated aggregate is slightly better than the coordinated one. The left side of the table shows the peak power in the individual plans of each of the clusters. It shows that within clusters coordination consistently improves over uncoordinated behavior, by between 8.5 and 21.5 percent. The right side of the table shows the result of aggregating the plans from the given clusters and those in the preceding lines. It shows that as more clusters are added to the aggregate, the global improvement made by coordination within clusters decreases, in spite of the local improvements made.

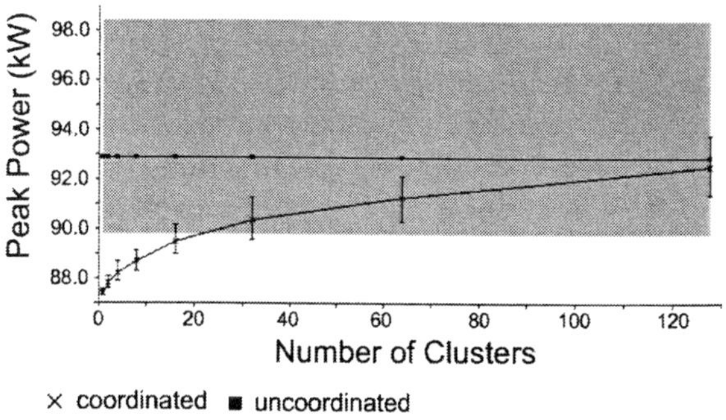

Figure 9. Frequency-based hierarchical clustering.

4.7 Hierarchical Desync Coordination

The experiment in Section 4.2 shows even a relatively small amount of flexibility on the part of individual resources allows Desync coordination to improve overall aggregates. This property may provide a solution to the limitations encountered when dividing the system into separate clusters. It indicates that by exchanging only a small amount of information, clusters may be able to sufficiently coordinate their plans. We test this by creating a simple hierarchical version of the Desync coordination algorithm. Resources are divided into separate clusters in which the Desync coordination algorithm is run twice, to produce two possible aggregate plans. These plans are then aggregated by a single higher level aggregator, again using Desync coordination. Figure 9 shows the result, when using frequency based clustering for 1280 agents. Compared to the results of frequency based clustering without the second level of coordination, this very low degree of synchronization between clusters does indeed significantly improve the overall aggregate plans. Better chosen information sharing between clusters could possibly have an even greater effect, and is a topic for future research, as discussed in Section 5.

5 Discussion and Future Work

The scenario in Section 3 set a goal of building a clustered energy planning system that can scale to at least

peak power of individual clusters				peak power in aggregate of current and preceding clusters			
	coordinated (kW)	uncoordinated (kW)	improvement		aggregate, coordinated (kW)	aggregate, uncoordinated (kW)	improvement
cluster 1	3.01	3.63	17.26%	cluster 1	3.01	3.63	17.26%
cluster 2	3.07	3.40	9.51%	clusters 1-2	5.94	6.57	9.70%
cluster 3	2.93	3.61	18.88%	clusters 1-3	8.71	9.24	5.65%
cluster 4	3.22	3.77	14.49%	clusters 1-4	11.58	12.51	7.45%
cluster 5	3.31	3.62	8.66%	clusters 1-5	14.80	15.47	4.38%
cluster 6	3.16	3.65	13.36%	clusters 1-6	17.72	18.93	6.39%
cluster 7	2.79	3.25	14.18%	clusters 1-7	20.31	21.27	4.50%
cluster 8	3.08	3.92	21.51%	clusters 1-8	23.08	24.64	6.32%
cluster 9	2.93	3.41	14.03%	clusters 1-9	25.88	27.70	6.56%
cluster 10	3.28	4.04	18.84%	clusters 1-10	29.04	30.93	6.11%
cluster 11	3.70	4.45	16.92%	clusters 1-11	32.58	33.56	2.92%
cluster 12	3.37	3.86	12.79%	clusters 1-12	35.92	37.38	3.91%
cluster 13	2.93	3.46	15.33%	clusters 1-13	38.57	40.42	4.58%
cluster 14	3.51	4.35	19.29%	clusters 1-14	41.64	42.62	2.30%
cluster 15	3.00	3.28	8.59%	clusters 1-15	44.57	44.76	0.41%
cluster 16	3.14	3.59	12.56%	clusters 1-16	47.59	47.46	-0.27%

Table 1. Effect of aggregating plans from random clusters with 40 agents each.

400,000 resource agents. Section 4 shows that using straightforward algorithms a system can easily be broken into 16 clusters in which coordinated energy use consistently improves on uncoordinated use, or up to 64 clusters in which coordinated use usually improves on uncoordinated. This gives clusters of between 25,000 and 6,250 agents. Given the simplicity of the Desync coordination algorithm, clusters of a few thousand agents are probably acceptable. However, there is a justifiable need to explore more sophisticated methods to both improve the number of clusters into which the system can be divided, and to increase the degree of improvement in power use created by coordination.

The experiments in Section 4 demonstrate three factors affecting global behavior of the system: the flexibility of individual agents in shifting power-use, the composition of clusters within which plans are coordinated between agents, and the degree of communication to coordinate plans between clusters. Each of these areas deserves further study.

Coordinating Resource Agents: This paper examined one difficulty in coordinating planned energy use: a lack of flexibility on the part of resource agents. Another main stumbling block is the unpredictability of the devices controlled by the agents. For this reason plans need to be constantly re-coordinated as predicted power-use changes. Refrigerators are amenable to planning because they can in effect store energy using the thermal mass of their contents. Other appliances, like pool pumps can be flexible because the exact time at which they operate is unimportant. There are, however, many devices, like light-bulbs that must act on demand. Given a fixed set of devices there is, thus, a limit on the degree to which the variability of their energy use can be controlled. On the other hand, the increasing prevalence of household devices with significant battery capacities, such as electric vehicles, is likely to make the planning and coordination problem easier, as their reserves can be called upon to make up for a lack of flexibility or predictability elsewhere.

Clustering: The presented experiments show that choosing more appropriate criteria for dividing agents into clusters can make coordination easier by matching up devices whose power consumption is complementary. The main problem that remains is how to discover the best clustering criteria. In addition, since device behavior can change over time, using the best criteria requires that clusters also change. A number of algorithms have shown that decentralized dynamic clustering is possible given predefined criteria [12, 16]. Clustering algorithms that discover the correct criteria based on current application requirements are still in early stages of research [11, 15, 19]. To study these further, more detailed models, test-beds and measurements are required.

Cluster Coordination: The experiments further indicate that some degree of coordination between clusters is needed. In current distributed energy resource systems this coordination is achieved through central auctioneers or aggregators. Inter-cluster coordination can also be imposed by means of energy caps: fixed limits on the amount of energy that should be used in a given period. A cap is usually expressed as a directive from an energy utility company to reduce electricity consumption for peak demand periods. Our experiments indicate that low quality information can also serve to coordinate clusters, suggesting that less structured aggregation algorithms may be also applicable [8].

Self-organization: The presented solution is hybrid — it combines distributed cluster-based coordination with a centralized method of determining clusters and hierarchical coordination between clusters. Ideally, all of these functions would be achieved in a completely self-organized way. Self-organization is typically defined as "a process in which pattern at the global level of a system emerges solely from numerous interactions among the lower-level components of the system. Moreover, the rules specifying interactions among the systems components are executed using only local information, without reference to the global pattern" [3]. There are, however, a few reasons why a hybrid solution is more suitable at this stage. First, the "numerous interactions among the lower-level components" that are essential for self-organization are often costly in terms of communication overhead. For example, many peer-to-peer approaches for distributed energy resource management are not feasible if the resource agents are limited to power-line communications. Second, self-organization results in non-deterministic outcomes. Often, this is one of its strengths, and one should not avoid far-from-equilibrium dynamics and symmetry-breaking behavior but rather exploit the opportunities for creating stable patterns out of fluctuations [14]. However, in order to be adopted by industry, the non-determinism of self-organizing patterns requires an appropriate verification process, and the search for most suitable verification methodology is still open. Finally, a complete self-organizing system for distributed energy resource management would depart too strongly from incremental advancements typically accepted by the industry. A more realistic approach suggests, instead, to deploy hybrid systems such as the one described in this work as an intermediate step on the path towards a completely self-organizing solution.

6 Conclusions

This paper examined two questions about the use of clustering in order to improve scalability of distributed energy management systems: (1) to what extent is the quality of global solutions reduced by partitioning resources into groups, and (2) is it sufficient to choose these groups at random or can resources be classified so as to create more effective groups? We have presented a simple model of energy management, and a simple coordination algorithm to study these questions. Experiments have shown that dividing resources into independently coordinated clusters improves the system's scalability, but the reduced quality of aggregate plans limits the number of potential clusters. We demonstrated that three aspects affect this limit: the flexibility of energy-use plans for individual resources, the criteria used to divide resources into clusters, and the information exchanged to coordinate plans between clusters.

References

[1] Australian Government, Department of the Environment and Heritage. www.energyrating.gov.au, January 2007.

[2] S. Borenstein, M. Jaske, and A. Rosenfeld. Dynamic pricing, advanced metering, and demand response in electricity markets. Technical Report CSEMWP-105, Center for the Study of Energy Markets, October 2002.

[3] S. Camazine, J.-L. Deneubourg, N. R. Franks, J. Sneyd, G. Theraulaz, and E. Bonabeau. *Self-Organization in Biological Systems*. Princeton University Press, 2001.

[4] P. Carlsson and A. Andersson. A flexible model for tree-structured multi-commodity markets. *Electronic Commerce Research*, 7(1):69–88, 2007.

[5] Y. Guo, J. Li, and G. James. Evolutionary optimisation of distributed energy resources. In *AI 2005: Advances in Artificial Intelligence, 18th Australian Joint Conference on Artificial Intelligence*, volume 3809 of *Springer - LNCS*, pages 1086–1091, December 2005.

[6] G. James, D. Cohen, R. Dodier, G. Platt, and D. Palmer. A deployed multi-agent framework for distributed energy applications. In *AAMAS 2006: Proceedings of the 5th International Joint Conference on Autonomous Agents and Multiagent Systems*, pages 676–678, 2006.

[7] I. G. Kamphuis, P. Carlsson, C. J. Warmer, J. C. P. Kester, and J. K. Kok. Distributed intelligence for supply/demand matching to improve embedding of distributed renewable energy sources. In *CRIS 2004: Proceedings of the 2nd International Conference on Critical Infrastructures*, October 2004.

[8] D. Kempe, A. Dobra, and J. Gehrke. Gossip-based computation of aggregate information. In *FOCS 2003: Proceedings of the 44th Annual IEEE Symposium on Foundations of Computer Science*, page 482, 2003.

[9] J. K. Kok, C. J. Warmer, and I. G. Kamphuis. Powermatcher: multiagent control in the electricity infrastructure. In *AAMAS 2005: Proceedings of the 4th International Joint Conference on Autonomous Agents and Multiagent Systems*, pages 75–82, 2005.

[10] NEMMCO, National Electricity Market Management Company Ltd. An introduction to australia's national electricity market, June 2005.

[11] E. Ogston, B. Overeinder, v. Steen, M., and F. Brazier. Group formation among peer-to-peer agents: Learning group characteristics. In *AP2PC 2003: Proceedings of the 2nd International Workshop on Agents and Peer-to-Peer Computing*, volume 2872 of *Springer - LNCS*, pages 59–70, 2004.

[12] E. Ogston, M. van Steen, and F. Brazier. Group formation among decentralized autonomous agents. *Applied Artificial Intelligence*, pages 953–970, October-December 2004.

[13] L. Paris, G. Zini, M. Valtorta, G. Manzoni, and N. D. Franco. Present limits of very long distance transmission systems. In *CIGRE: International Conference on Large High-Voltage Electric Systems*, 1984.

[14] M. Prokopenko. Design versus self-organization. In M. Prokopenko, editor, *Advances in Applied Self-organizing Systems*, page to appear. Springer-Verlag London, 2007.

[15] M. Prokopenko, P. M. rajah, and P. Wang. On convergence of dynamic cluster formation in multi-agent networks. In *ECAL 2005: Proceedings of the 8th European Conference on Artificial Life*, pages 884–894, 2005.

[16] L. Ramaswamy, B. Gedik, and L. Liu. A distributed approach to node clustering in decentralized peer-to-peer networks. *IEEE Transactions on Parallel Distributed Systems*, 16(9):814–829, 2005.

[17] G. J. Schaeffer and H. Akkermans. CRISP: Distributed intelligence in critical infrastructures for sustainable power. Technical Report ECN-FSP-WP53-002, Energy Research Center of the Netherlands, July 2006.

[18] L. Z. Varga, N. R. Jennings, and D. Cockburn. Integrating intelligent systems into a cooperating community for electricity distribution management. *International Journal of Expert Systems with Applications*, 7(4):563–579, 1994.

[19] R. Virrankoski and A. Savvides. TASC: topology adaptive spatial clustering for sensor networks. In *MASS 2005: Proceedings of the 2nd IEEE International Conference on Mobile Adhoc and Sensor Systems*, 2005.

[20] F. Ygge and H. Akkermans. Power load management as a computational market. In *ICMAS 1995: Proceedings of the 1st International Conference on Multiagent Systems*, 1995.

We kindly thank Alec Ogston for collecting the data used in Section 4.3.

Research Track, Session 4: P2P Systems

Merging Intra-Planetary Index Structures: Decentralized Bootstrapping of Overlays*

Anwitaman Datta
E-mail: anwitaman@ntu.edu.sg
School of Computer Engineering, NTU Singapore.

Abstract

Peer-to-Peer index structures distributed and managed over the planet, commonly known as structured overlays (e.g., Distributed Hash Tables), are posed to play the role of a fundamental building block for internet-scale distributed applications and information systems. One of the biggest impediment in realizing index distributed at intra-planetary scales is to be able to merge distinct indices that might have been constructed independently and separately, or have resulted from network partitions. By facilitating merger of such isolated index-structures, decentralized bootstrapping of structured overlays is made possible. We argue that such a self-organizational attribute of decentralized bootstrapping is of paramount importance for large scale systems. In this paper we provide algorithms and simulation based evaluation of merger of two tree-structured overlay networks. The experiments validate some intuitions, particularly we see how the merger operation can be carried out transparently from the end users in the sense that all keys that are accessible to any peer prior to the merger process continue to be accessible during and after the merger. Surprising at a first glance, we also observe that the overhead of data movement during merger of two overlays which originally partition the key-spaces arbitrarily is higher if there is more common content stored in the two networks. This counterintuitive behavior is on account of the fact that the assignment of partitions to peers change during the merger process, which in turn leads to movement of data. Since peers act based on local knowledge, the data already present in the other network is still unnecessarily moved, adding to the data transfer overhead.

Keywords: *Peer-to-Peer, Structured Overlay, Decentralized Bootstrapping, Overlay Merger, Scalability.*

*This work is partially supported by NTU's start up grant.

1 Introduction

The recent years have witnessed increased use of resources at the edge of the network - typically desktop computers interconnected across the internet provide services and run applications in a peer-to-peer manner, as an alternative to the traditional paradigm of using dedicated infrastructure and centralized coordination and control. Such overlay network technologies have found diverse applications spanning networking, information systems and distributed systems domains. Overlays are used for supporting various communication primitives like multicast, QoS and more reliable routing which are not readily supported by the internet infrastructure. From information systems perspective, the internet along with its end users is transmogrifying into a planetary scale file system and repository for information and content. P2P data management and information systems need index-structures. Structured overlays - distributed hash tables [13, 14] as well as range partitioned [1, 5] are such distributed index structures.

The operational phase of such structured overlays is often decentralized (including self-maintenance). Construction or bootstrapping of overlays has traditionally assumed a quasi-sequential approach, in which new peers would join by contacting some existing members of the network [5, 13, 14]. More recently, parallelized structured overlay construction mechanisms have been developed [1, 11], again assuming participating peers already know and can contact each other, e.g., using an unstructured connected network. All these structured overlay bootstrapping strategies thus implicitly assume logical centralization - even if distributed, e.g., a set of globally known rendezvous "seed" peers - which facilitates new peers to join and form one single network.

Imagine that any or several of these existing techniques are used to construct individual overlays based on distinct (disjoint) set of *seed* peers. These overlays will operate as isolated islands. If at a later time, some peers from one overlay network meets peers from another network (by whichsoever mechanism), existing overlay maintenance and construction mechanisms will fail to deal with it [4]. Facilitating merger of such originally isolated but evolved overlays into a single overlay network paves the way for decentralized bootstrapping of overlay networks. People can set up their own bootstrap seed peers to build smaller but functional overlay networks, and when they meet and wish to merge their network with others, the isolated overlays can coalesce to grow organically into a single larger overlay. Generally speaking, decentralized bootstrapping is a desirable self-organizational property for large-scale systems. Merger and thus decentralized bootstrapping occurs trivially in unstructured P2P systems, while current structured overlays lack it altogether.

In this paper we provide mechanisms for merger of structured overlays which is necessary for decentralized bootstrapping, for one major class of overlay networks which use prefix based routing and have tree topology, and evaluate the merger process based on simulations. Note that for multiple overlays to be able to coalesce, they should all be using the same protocol to start with. Inter-operability of multiple overlays, either based on same or different protocols is a related but distinct problem currently being researched in the networking community, and we will discuss and distinguish it from our objective in Section 2 on related works. We point out why such approaches diverge from some of the original goals of structured overlays and particularly are inadequate to address the need of data-oriented applications. For the sake of context and self-containment, a brief overview on structured overlays is provided in Section 3. In [4] we identified the distinct challenges faced by major classes of overlay topologies - tree and ring. In Section 4 we look at the challenges of merging overlays in general, and the algorithmic details and subtleties of merging tree structured overlays. Evaluation of our merger algorithms for a specific system - P-Grid [1] - is presented in Section 5. From the experiments we see that it is indeed possible to perform the merger process in a manner transparent to the end users, i.e., for any peer keys which were accessible to it prior to the commencement of the merger process continue to be always accessible to that peer. The experiments also reveal some apparently surprising behaviors, particularly pertaining to the volume of data transfer. In a typical setting the original networks are expected to have different key-space partitioning to begin with, and in this case, more common data in the networks at the beginning incurs more data movement overhead than if there were less data common in both networks. We conclude in Section 6. As noted in [4], merger of ring based overlays like Chord [14] is structurally a different problem. It is beyond the scope of this paper, and will be addressed separately. Furthermore, depending on application requirements, one may actually want to keep two distinct indices (and not merge them). When to merge or not merge, and how to expressly initiate such a merger is thus something to be decided by the application logic, and is not addressed here. The meeting of two peers from the originally distinct networks may happen by chance or design, and is again not an issue we deal with here. We concern ourselves with only a mechanism to merge two such distinct overlays when necessary, given that at least one peer from one network gets to contact another peer from the other network.

2 Related work

The networking community has recently looked into similar problem of dealing with multiple overlays based on potentially diverse topologies and protocols. Since the objective has typically been of end-to-end communication of hosts, these approaches have borrowed ideas from the networking domain - managing individual overlays as ASs/domains, and routing traffic from one overlay to another using BGP like mechanisms based on certain peers specifically designated as gateways [9, 2]. In the discussion of [9] the authors themselves point out the limitation of their approach in dealing with application layer functionalities, e.g., storage. There are several other efforts which try to integrate multiple overlays based on the idea of domains [6, 7], and have the same limitations when it comes to support application layer functionalities.

In a flat (domainless) overlay, one needs to know only the name of the resource to be sought, and locate it. Such a data-structure can thus readily be used as an index. However if it is necessary to already know specific domain (which is okay for end-to-end communication), then it can not be used as an universal index as has been the case with flat domainless overlays. Such domainless flat data-structures was also one of the original appeals of universal applicability of first generation structured overlays like distributed hash tables (DHTs).

Association of content with peers can potentially change with merger of overlays. Communication oriented applications do not need to deal with management of the stored content, which is however a critical issue for any data-oriented application, particularly if full recall (=1) is desired or needed. This issue has been overlooked in previous works [2, 6] which otherwise propose ring merger. A gossip based bootstrapping service [8] has been proposed as a generic mechanism for constructing an overlay in a parallelized manner [11] from scratch. We speculate that similar gossip based approach can also be used to merge multiple overlays. If such an approach is however indeed used, again, in itself it will not deal with the key-to-peer associations, and thus will not be directly useful.

Merger of overlays shares some resemblance with another essentially different issue - churn (membership dynamics). Merger of two overlays, seen from the perspective of individual peers (which is how these decentralized systems operate) can look very similar to new peers joining the network.

However, churn is a gradual process, and the system needs to continuously perform repair operations to rectify local view of peers in order to deal with the continuous membership changes. When two isolated networks need to merge, the magnitude of the population change with respect to their original population size is very high.

The problem we address in this paper, that of merger of two distinct overlays but using the same protocols is somewhat different from how peers across different overlay networks can establish end-to-end communication among themselves. For end-to-end communication, one can devise other strategies [9]. Merger of overlays and management of stored keys in such a merged network becomes necessary particularly when the overlay is used as a distributed index-structure and provide application layer functionalities, e.g. data storage [3, 10], which was one of the original purposes of such structured overlays.

3 Background: An overview on overlays

In recent years the concept of structured overlays has attracted a lot of attention because of its potential to become a generic substrate for internet scale applications.

Structured overlay networks comprise of the following three principal ingredients:

(i) Partitioning of the key-space (say an interval or circle representing the real number between the range $[0, 1]$) among peers, so that each peer is responsible for a specific key space partition. A peer responsible for a particular key-space partition should have all the objects[1] which are mapped into keys belonging to the corresponding key-space partition.

(ii) A graph embedding/topology among these partitions (or peers) which ensures full connectivity of the partitions, desirably even under churn (peer membership dynamics), so that any partition can be reached from any other partition - reliably and preferably, efficiently.

(iii) A routing algorithm which enables the traversal of messages (query forwarding), in order to complete specific search requests for keys, and hence the values associated with the keys.

Various applications can use transparently the (dynamic) binding between peers and their corresponding key-space partitions as provided by the overlay for resource discovery and communication purposes in a wide area network.

[1] In this paper we use the words object, data or key-value pairs interchangeably. Additionally, when context allows, we refer to querying or accessing the key to mean the key-value pair. How an object is associated with a key is an orthogonal issue determined by application needs and does not directly concern the indexing layer.

In storage and data-oriented applications, keys are generated using suitable (hashing) functions corresponding to the objects (values) to be stored or data to be indexed. The key-value pairs are then managed by the specific peers responsible for particular keys. Anyone who needs to access or manipulate the data thus needs to locate one of these responsible peers first. This is one of the principal functionality that structured overlays are designed to meet.

3.1 Redundancy and resilience

A structured overlay network needs to meet two goals to be functionally correct in locating stored key-value pairs:

(i) *Correctness of routing*: Starting from any peer, it should be possible to reach the correct peer(s) which are responsible for a specific resource (key).

(ii) *Correctness and completeness of keys-to-peers binding*: Any and all peers responsible for a particular key-space partition should have all the corresponding keys (and ideally, none other).

We use the information retrieval metric of *recall* to quantify the overlay's functional correctness. It can be interpreted as the probability that a key-value pair can be located if the key-value pair is actually present in the network, by querying for the corresponding key at any peer in the network.

Redundancy is a time tested approach to provide fault tolerance and is widely used in structured overlays as well. Multiple routes from any peer to any target key-space partition provides static resilience as well as flexibility to choose alternative routes in order to deal with load-imbalance and congestion. Replication of each key at multiple peers guarantees availability of the keys despite the fact that individual peers may be unreliable, and is also useful to deal with higher load. Correctness of routing in a dynamic environment is achieved by maintaining the peers' routing tables correctly over time and using a proper routing algorithm. Correctness and completeness of binding is achieved by moving the corresponding keys (content) as and when the key space partition a particular peer is responsible for changes, and synchronizing the content among replica peers.

3.2 Prefix-routing topology with structural replication (P-Grid)

In this paper we provide algorithms specifically designed to merge P-Grid [1] networks, which uses prefix based routing [12]. P-Grid abstracts a tree structure (Figure 1), and the algorithms we propose can be readily modified to merge other tree structured overlays.

P-Grid divides the key-space in mutually exclusive partitions so that the partitions may be represented as a prefix-free set $\Pi \subseteq \{0,1\}^*$. Stored data items are identified by keys in $\mathcal{K} \subseteq \{0,1\}^*$. We assume that all keys have length that is at least the maximal length of the elements in Π, i.e.,

$$\min_{k \in \mathcal{K}} |k| \geq \max_{\pi \in \Pi} |\pi| = \pi_{max}$$

Each key belongs uniquely to one partition because of the fact that the partitions are mutually exclusive, that is, different elements in Π are not in a prefix relationship, and thus define a radix-exchange trie.

$$\pi, \pi' \in \Pi \Rightarrow \pi \nsubseteq \pi' \wedge \pi' \nsubseteq \pi$$

where $\pi \subseteq \pi'$ denotes the prefix relationship. These partitions also exhaust the key-space, so to say, the key-space is completely covered by these partitions so that each key belongs to one and only one (because of exclusivity) partition.

In P-Grid each peer $p \in P$ is associated with a leaf of the binary tree, and each leaf has at-least one peer associated to itself. Each leaf corresponds to a binary string $\pi \in \Pi$, also called the *key-space partition*. Thus each peer p is associated with a path $\pi(p)$. For search, the peer stores for each prefix $\pi(p, l)$ of $\pi(p)$ of length l a set of references $\rho(p, l)$ to peers q with property $\overline{\pi(p, l)} = \pi(q, l)$, where $\overline{\pi}$ is the binary string π with the last bit inverted. This means that at each level of the tree the peer has references to some other peers that do not pertain to the peer's subtree at that level which enables the implementation of prefix routing for efficient search. The whole routing table at peer p is then represented as $\rho(p)$. Moreover, the actual instance of the P-Grid is determined by the randomized choices made at each peer for each level out of a much larger combination of choices. The cost for storing the references and the associated maintenance cost scale as they are bounded by the depth of the underlying binary tree. This also bounds the search time and communication cost. Figure 1(a) shows instances of P-Grid network (peer's path and routing table). e.g., in $\mathcal{N}_1$, peers A and F are mutual replicas and are responsible for the key-space with prefix 00. Peer A's routing table comprise of peers C and D from the partition with prefix 1 and peer B from the partition with prefix 01. Note that while P-Grid abstracts a tree-structure, there is actually no hierarchy.

Each peer stores a set of data items $\delta(p)$. For $d \in \delta(p)$ the binary key $\kappa(d)$ is calculated using an order-preserving hash function. $\langle \kappa(d), d \rangle$ is the key-value pair stored in the overlay.[2] $\kappa(d)$ has $\pi(p)$ as prefix but it is not excluded that temporarily also other data items are stored at a peer, that is, the set $\delta(p, \pi(p))$ of data items whose key matches $\pi(p)$ can be a proper subset of $\delta(p)$. Moreover, for fault-tolerance, query load-balancing and hot-spot handling, multiple peers are associated with the same key-space partition (*structural replication*). $\Re(\kappa)$ represents the set of peers replicating the object corresponding to key κ. Peers additionally also maintain references to peers with the same path, i.e., their replicas $\Re(\pi(p))$, and use epidemic algorithms to maintain replica consistency. Routing in P-Grid is based on greedy prefix matching [12]. So a query at A for any key with prefix 11 will be forwarded to one of peers C or D, and then this peer would forward the query to E. Peer F would however have forwarded it directly to E. E is responsible for all keys with prefix 11, and should thus answer the query.

[2]Depending on implementation, d may actually be a (set of) pointer(s) to the actual content.

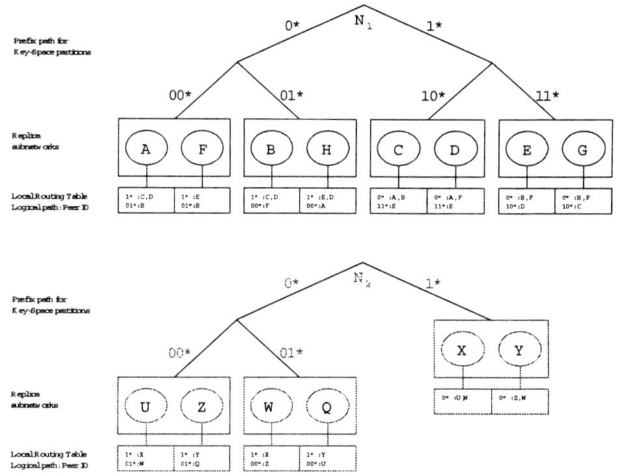

(a) Instances of P-Grid networks

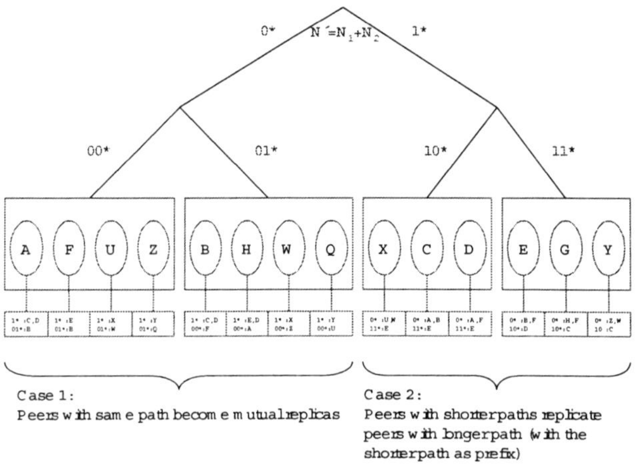

(b) A possible ideal P-Grid network when peers from both N_1 and N_2 networks meet. Cases 1 & 2 are discussed in Sections 4.1.1 & 4.1.2 respectively.

Figure 1. Merger of structurally replicated P-Grid networks

4 Merger operations

We denote peer p from network $\mathcal{N}_i$ as $p^{\mathcal{N}_i}$. Furthermore, we consider only two originally isolated networks $\mathcal{N}_1$ and $\mathcal{N}_2$. Extending our algorithms for merger of multiple networks is relatively straightforward subject to the ability to distinguish networks (based on some network identifier). Management of such network identifiers in a decentralized fashion can however be a sufficiently involved problem in its own right.

4.1 Meeting of peers from originally different networks $\mathcal{N}_i$ and $\mathcal{N}_j$

We consider the different actions necessary to merge two networks, once peers from two different networks meet. How the first such meeting occurs does not concern us. However in order to continue and complete the merger process, we induce further meeting of peers following this first (chance) interaction.

4.1.1 Interaction of peers $p^{\mathcal{N}_i}$ and $q^{\mathcal{N}_j}$ s.t. $\pi(p^{\mathcal{N}_i}) = \pi(q^{\mathcal{N}_j})$

Managing replica subnetwork (content synchronization): If peers from the two different networks meet, so that their paths are exactly the same (for example peers A and U from networks $\mathcal{N}_1$ and $\mathcal{N}_2$ respectively in Figure 1(a)), then they will execute anti-entropy algorithm to reconcile their content and become mutual structural replicas.

Such anti-entropy algorithm is already used among replica peers to keep the content updated among themselves. So in our example, originally A and U upon interaction will synchronize their mutual content. Later, A may run anti-entropy with F (which it does regularly anyway), so that F will then obtain the data items which originated in network $\mathcal{N}_2$.

We need to ascertain that despite the network merger process, whichever keys were originally accessible will continue to be accessible. It is easily achieved. E.g., peer D will always be able to access all the keys/content available at A before the merger process. The keys from the same key-space which were present in the other network would however be available only after the background replication synchronization has completed. So if D communicates with F after interaction between A and U but before an anti-entropy operation between A and F, then D may miss the keys which were originally available only in network $\mathcal{N}_2$. That is to say, a resource available originally only in $\mathcal{N}_2$ at U and Z (but with the same prefix 00 as A) will be definitely visible to D only when both A and F have synchronized their content, adding the key value pairs originally available only at U and Z.

Peers also update their view of the replica subnetwork for future runs of anti-entropy.

Network rewiring (routing table updates): One of the objectives of the merger process is also to update the routing tables at peers so that new routes among peers which belonged to the two originally different networks are established. The intuitive way to do it is to merge the peers' routing tables. So A can add an additional route to W (learnt from U) for the prefix 01. If this is done, then routing a query from D for the prefix 01 may end up in either of B, H or W since the actual route is chosen randomly at each hop out of all possible choices. This will however mean that keys which were originally deterministically accessible at D may not be anymore, and will depend on chance, until peers responsible for that portion of the key-space also complete the merger and synchronization process. Such effect is undesirable for most applications. The merger process should be transparent to end users, so that keys that were originally available should always continue to be accessible even during the merger process. Keys originating from the other network may then become available incrementally. It may be achieved variously. One possibility is to use all routing entries to forward queries at each level. This however leads to unnecessary traffic in the network. Furthermore, it will be difficult to change routing policy based on whether there is an ongoing merger process or not. So if this routing strategy is used, then there will be unnecessary traffic during the whole lifetime of the network, most of which is possibly when there are no ongoing merging process. An alternate strategy is to discriminate peers from originally different networks in the routing table references. So to say, for each level of the routing table, each peer may distinguish the peers which were originally in its network from the entries from the originally alien network that have been added during the merger process. Thus upon receiving a query, the peer forwards it to one appropriate peer which belonged originally to its own network, and one appropriate peer that it has learnt from the merging process. Moreover, this needs to be done for one query only once during the route forwarding process. Once the query is forwarded to a peer from the other network, it is in-fact desirable that it is circulated only among peers originally from that network in order to avoid redundancy and cycles.

In the long run, when the whole merger process is completed, i.e., when replicas have already run the anti-entropy algorithm among each other so that all peers from each subpartition have the same content, then the need to distinguish peers from different networks will cease to exist. However identifying completion of the merger process across the network in not tenable. A heuristic solution is to use a timeout $\mathcal{T}_{out}$. Thus, each peer locally decides to stop to distinguish peers from different networks after $\mathcal{T}_{out}$ time since it last encountered a new peer from the other network executing the merger algorithm.

4.1.2 Interaction of peers $p^{\mathcal{N}_i}$ and $q^{\mathcal{N}_j}$ s.t. $\pi(p^{\mathcal{N}_i}) \subset \pi(q^{\mathcal{N}_j})$

When two peers from $\mathcal{N}_1$ and $\mathcal{N}_2$ meet so that one's path is strictly a prefix of the other peer's path ($\pi(p^{\mathcal{N}_i}) \subset \pi(q^{\mathcal{N}_j})$), then the peer $\pi(p^{\mathcal{N}_i})$ with shorter path can execute a normal network joining algorithm - extending its path to replicate either the peer it met, or a peer this peer refers it to based on other considerations like load-balancing. To keep things simple, here we chose the option where the peer $p^{\mathcal{N}_i}$ simply decides to extend its path to replicate that of $q^{\mathcal{N}_j}$.

For example, Y may extend its path from 1 to 11 upon an interaction with either of E or G.

Once the peer extends its path, some of the keys stored at the peer ceases to be associated with the refined partition. For example, when Y extends its path from 1 to 11, as per the overlay's key-space partitioning principles, it is no more responsible for keys with prefix 10. These keys need to be shipped to other peers which are responsible for the corresponding prefixes. Pointers to suitable peers for these complementary subspaces where the key-value pairs need to be transferred can however be readily found from the routing table of the peer with originally longer path, i.e., $q^{\mathcal{N}_j}$. In fact these entries are also used by the peer as its own routing table entries for the new extended path, since it has no preexisting pointers/routing table entries for the path extension. For example, since Y did not know any peer with prefix 10 originally, it uses the information obtained from G, and thus adds C in its routing table for resolving queries with prefix 10. Since there were no preexisting such routes locally, there is also no need to distinguish these newly acquired routing entries.

Anti-entropy based synchronization of content belonging to the partition (represented by $\pi(q^{\mathcal{N}_j})$ and now also $\pi(p^{\mathcal{N}_i})$) also needs to be done among the structural replicas. Similarly the view of the replica subnetwork needs to be updated. In contrast to the meeting of peers with same path, where the new replica subnetwork includes all peers from the two original subnetworks, in this case, original replicas of $\pi(q^{\mathcal{N}_j})$ may decide to replicate a different part of the key-space, e.g., X eventually replicates the partition with prefix 10.

The replica subnetwork view can be updated either proactively or lazily. We use a mixed strategy. Addition of new members in a subnetwork is done proactively. Omission of members from the subnetwork is done lazily during the anti-entropy process. So, when X eventually realizes that Y is no longer responsible for the same key-space partition (and vice-versa), the corresponding entry is dropped from the view of replica subnetwork. A peer which is not a replica is responsible for some other part of the network. Thus while the peer is dropped from the replica subnetwork view, the contact information can still be exploited by incorporating it as a redundant routing entry.

The data originally at a peer either resides at the same peer even after path extension, in which case, it continues to be accessible to all peers to which it was previously accessible. The data which however needs to be moved risks to become temporarily inaccessible. This risk is easily taken care of. The data is shipped to responsible peers following all available routes visible from the peer to which it originally belonged, i.e., using all its suitable new routing table entries. In our simplistic example, data with prefix 10 is shipped from Y to C, since Y has added C in its outing table. Thus, the data which was accessible to any peer (say Q) originally because it had a route to Y, will continue to be available, since Y will provide necessary forwarding information.

This also means that because of the merger process, only peers directly involved in the specific interaction need to proactively update their local routing table. Routing table of other peers continue to be usable, and there is no cascading effect of routing table maintenance.

Thus, peer Q referring to Y for prefix 1 continues to refer to it as such, and any query 10 from Q is routed first to Y, which then forwards it to - say C. Peers may however, over time, add more routing entries. For instance, Q adding a reference to D for redundancy in its routing table for the prefix 1. Such changes are normal in overlays and can be carried on in the background, without interrupting the functioning of the overlay and in fact instead making it more resilient to faults, churn and congestion.

Consequently, neither joining peers, nor merger of two existing overlay network disrupt the available functionality of the network members.[3]

Note that the merger process itself however needs to be performed in the whole network, and once the merger process starts, the first set of peers involved in the merger process can propagate the merger process rapidly within the rest of the network in a cascade, as will be discussed next.

4.1.3 Cascading new interactions among peers from the originally different networks

The first meeting of peers from originally two distinct overlay networks may happen because of whatsoever reasons, with or without the explicit knowledge and intention of the interacting peers. Once such a first interaction occurs, if the interacting peers have the same path or one has a path that is strictly a prefix of the other, then they can execute the

[3]Note that the above discussion is true only for write once and then onwards read-only data, since for read/write, it will be necessary to maintain the replicas more pro-actively.

merger process as described above. If peers with different paths meet each other, they need to do nothing (in terms of merger operations), though they can refer each other using their routing entries to peers with longer mutual match of path. Based on these references, each of the originally interacting peers will eventually discover peers from the other network, such that they have either the same path or one has a path which is strictly prefix of the other. Upon discovering such interaction partners, the peers can execute the merger operation as described above.

The merger operations are local. However, the same process needs to be executed over all the key space partitions. This is done by triggering new interaction among peers. Interacting peers can facilitate new interactions by informing all peers in their routing table about the new peer(s) they met. For example, A can inform B, C and D about U. Each of them can then use the pointers available at U to identify suitable interaction partners, e.g., W for B.

Spreading the information about the new network by flooding the local routing table is fast. All peers in the network gets informed in logarithmic time in terms of the network size (population). Moreover, many peers are subject to get multiple references. A final intuitive observation, also validated in simulations, is that a peer which has already executed the merger operation once does not need to initiate it again. However, if contacted by another peer from the originally different network, it may be required to perform again a merger operation.

5 Evaluation

The evaluations presented in this section are based on a discrete time simulator which models the peer interactions, routing table modification and data shipment. It also incorporates a modified version of the standard greedy prefix matching P-Grid routing algorithm to discriminate routing entries corresponding to peers from the originally different networks. Each of the experiments studied merger of two randomly generated P-Grid networks. Initially the networks were assumed to be in a consistent state. Particularly all replicas had consistent view of the stored content, and all routing entries at each peer was usable.

In real world P2P networks, these idealizing conditions do not hold due to continuous changes in the network membership (churn), and frequent addition of new content. These are important issues that have been extensively studied on their own right in the recent years. However in order to study only the effect of network merger, we conducted the current experiments ignoring these dynamics. Because of redundancy both in the routing entries as well as replication, it is expected that moderate level of churn will not affect the merger process, just like it does not affect normal operations in terms of recall (guarantee of success for a query) in the overlay, though it incurs additional maintenance overhead. This aspect is confessedly speculative and needs to be verified with further experiments. In that context, the current experiments are restricted to the primary focus of this paper - algorithms for, and effect of, merger of two originally isolated overlays, ignoring other influences.

In each time step, some peers perform some of the following actions as applicable. Peers interact and perform necessary changes in the routing table, ship content (key-values) and disseminate and obtain information about potential interaction partners for next interaction. Between two time rounds, the state of the network just after a round is evaluated by processing queries. The queries are originated at randomly chosen peers, and the keys being queried are also randomly chosen. The performance is quantified in terms of success rate of the queries measured in terms of the information retrieval measure of *recall*.

Performance metric: We use *recall* as the primary performance metric.[4] So to say, if a particular key-value pair is stored in either of the two original networks, what is the probability of locating this key (and the corresponding value) starting from any arbitrary peer. Before the merger process, keys originally stored only in the other network can not be located. Keys present in the same network are originally accessible from any peer in the same overlay network. At the end of the merger process, it should be possible to locate any key starting the search at any peer using the overlay's routing algorithm. We see from the experiments that it is indeed the case. We use $\mathcal{R}_{i/j}$ to denote the recall of keys originally stored in only network i (excluding common content), starting the query at a peer which originally belonged to network j. $\mathcal{R}_{\cap/j}$ is used to denote the recall of content originally stored in both the networks, when the query is started at a peer from network j.

The cost of overlay merger operation is measured in terms of the volume of data transfer during these interactions and anti-entropy based synchronization. Of further interest is the latency of the merger operation.

Parameter space explored in experiments: We evaluate the process of overlay network merger in different settings. Particularly we have studied the effect on the performance of the network merger along three critical axis - size of networks $|\mathcal{N}|$, duplication $\delta_{\mathcal{D}}$ of content in the original networks and the heuristic timeout $\mathcal{T}_{out}$ parameter after which peers from originally different networks are not discriminated during routing. The duplication factor $\delta_{\mathcal{D}}$ of content originally stored in the two networks is measured in terms of the fraction of keys stored originally in both the networks with respect to the ensemble of all keys stored in either of

[4]Precision is not an issue in the kind of search supported by structured overlays.

0-7695-2906-2/07 $25.00 © 2007 IEEE

the two networks $\delta_{\mathcal{D}} = \frac{|\mathcal{D}_1 \cap \mathcal{D}_2|}{|\mathcal{D}_1 \cup \mathcal{D}_2|}$ where $\mathcal{D}_i$ is the collection of all data (key-value pairs) originally stored in network i.

Workload: Network pairs of populations 17, 35; 132, 200; 723, 854 and 605, 612 were considered. All but in the last pair, the two networks had arbitrary and mutually different partitioning of the key-space. In the last case, both networks had arbitrary but exactly same key-space partitioning. For data duplication in the network $\delta_{\mathcal{D}}$, values of 0.1, 0.2, 0.4, 0.5 were used. Sufficiently low value of $\mathcal{T}_{out} = 3$ guaranteed perfect recall $\mathcal{R}_{j/j}$, and was used in most experiments. We also evaluate the behavior in the worst choice of $\mathcal{T}_{out} = 0$. In all the experiments, each key-space partition was originally replicated in between 3 to 5 peers. In each round, 2000 queries for keys present in at least one of the networks were issued, originating at random peers.

5.1 Recall and data transfer traffic

In the following plots, the *x-axis* represents the discrete time, and thus also indicates the rate and latency of the merger process. Recall of content originally present only in the other network $\mathcal{R}_{j/i}$ is shown in Figures 2(a) and 2(c) for different network sizes. We see that $\mathcal{R}_{j/i}$ rapidly climbs to 1, i.e., all keys even from the other network become accessible to all peers rather fast, and hence we can conclude that the merger process is also completed. All these experiments considered a value of $\mathcal{T}_{out}$ such that the merger process is completely transparent to end users in terms of accessibility of content, particularly any key that was accessible to a specific peer continue to be accessible throughout the merger process, i.e., $\mathcal{R}_{j/j} = 1$. Fairly low values of $\mathcal{T}_{out}$ sufficed for the purpose, e.g., 3. We also noticed that even in the worst case in terms of choice of $\mathcal{T}_{out}$, the performance of the overlays in terms of accessibility of keys is marginally affected. We elaborate this subsequently in Section5.2.

Volume of data transfer (normalized by the total number of unique data in both networks) is shown in Figures 2(b) and 2(d). Observe that in order to make all keys accessible to all peers, it is not needed that all keys which were not present in a particular network be shipped to peers in the other network. Instead often they become accessible simply because of the rewiring of the overlay. Thus the volume of data transfer (also accounting for the structural replica synchronization) is significantly lower than what would have been necessary if all data not present in the other network were to be transferred to some peers of the other network. Due to the infectious nature of triggering new interactions, most peers conduct the merger process rather fast, and the bulk of the data transfer is witnessed during these operations. Few peers actually need the background anti-entropy mechanism of replica subnetwork synchronization to obtain the keys from the other network.

As shown in Figure 3(a), for two networks with arbitrary and different partitioning of the key-space, the volume of data transfer increases if the two networks have originally more content in common, i.e., high $\delta_{\mathcal{D}}$. This is surprising since it may be expected that if more content is already present in both networks, it will need less data movement to make all keys available to all peers of both networks. Due to network merger the partition which individual peers are responsible for also changes, necessitating data movement as per the behavior described in Section 4.1.2. This data movement is actually a waste for duplicate content already present at the target peers, but is not known locally at the peers from which the data is being moved. This explanation of the counterintuitive behavior as observed in Figure 3(a) is also validated when we look at merger of two overlays with identical key-space partitions. In this case, there is no change of peers' partitions and thus no need to ship data away to other peers. The only data transfers in this case is because of anti-entropy based synchronization. We see that in this case the volume of data transferred decreases if the two networks originally had more content in common (Figure 3(b)). This observation is critical in that typically, two overlays are expected to originally partition the key-space arbitrarily, and hence differently. Thus in a typical situation, having less data in common in the original networks will make the merger process less expensive, in contrast to having more content in common, which will increase the data movement overheads of the merger process.

5.2 Other scalability issues

The latency of the merger process depends on the depth of the trees, and is essentially dictated by the smaller of the two networks involved in the merger. Route rewiring operations are also local.

Data transfer is bandwidth consuming, and is the greatest bottleneck for scalability. Moreover, its effect is not local among the interacting peers, and other peers are affected when a peer changes (extends) its path. However, it is an inevitable cost to incur if we want to merge two overlays. For practical purposes some optimizations are possible. For instance, if the data items themselves are rather large, one can reduce the actual traffic by sending first just the identifiers so that object already in the target peers is not transferred, as is happening with data items which were originally present in both networks. Since we measure the number of transfers, and not the absolute traffic, such implementation optimizations may have tremendous reduction of the absolute traffic, even though it does not change the fundamental findings of our experiments.

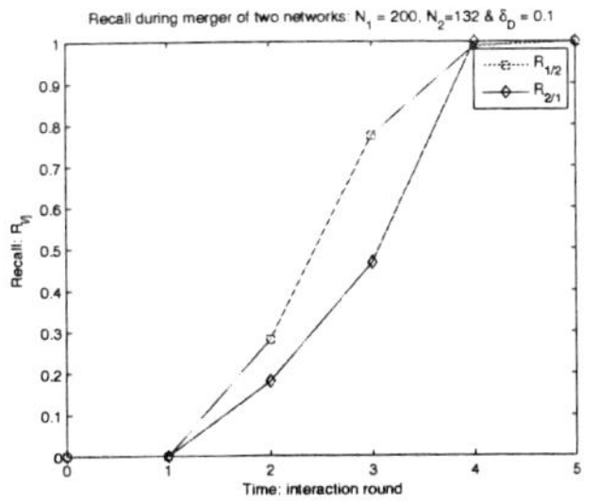

(a) Recall during the merger of two networks comprising 332 peers.

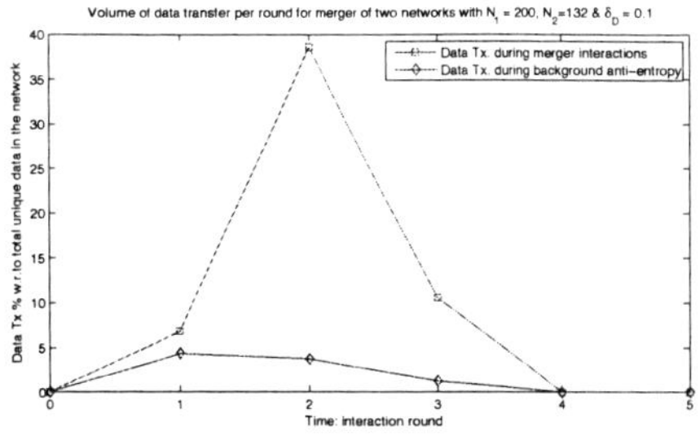

(b) Volume (normalized) of data transfer during the merger of two networks comprising 332 peers.

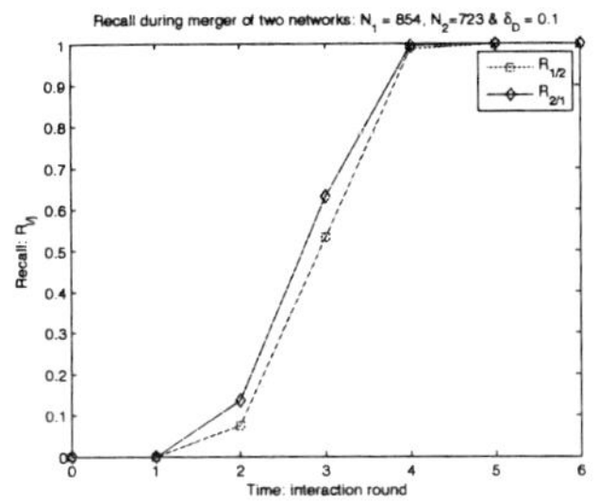

(c) Recall during the merger of two networks comprising 1577 peers.

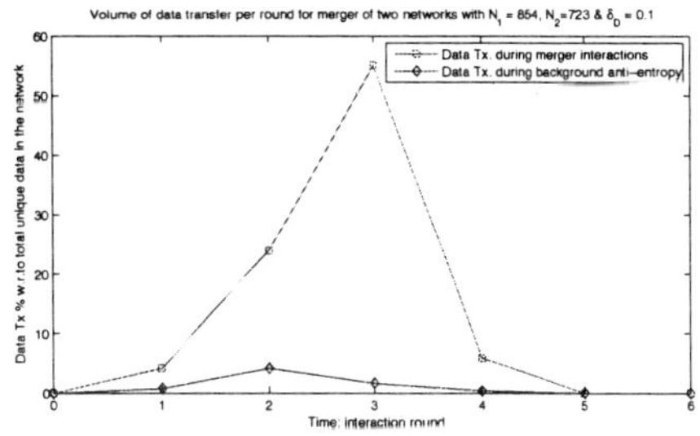

(d) Volume (normalized) of data transfer during the merger of two networks comprising 1577 peers.

Figure 2. Experiments based on merger of two P-Grid networks where $\mathcal{T}_{out}$ was such that $\mathcal{R}_{j/j}$ and $\mathcal{R}_{\cap/j}$ were always 1 for $j = 1, 2$.

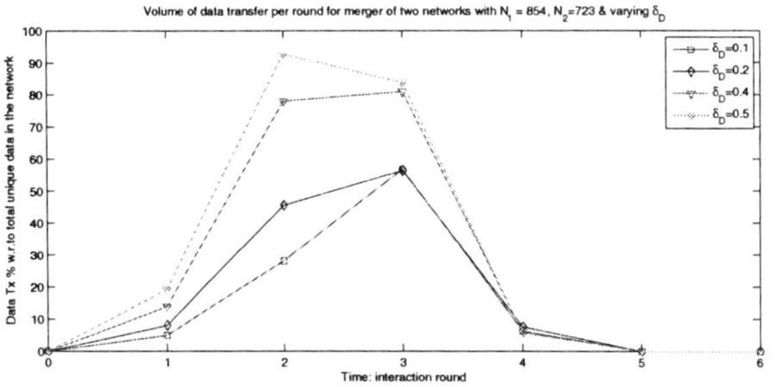

(a) Original networks had arbitrary key-space partitioning.

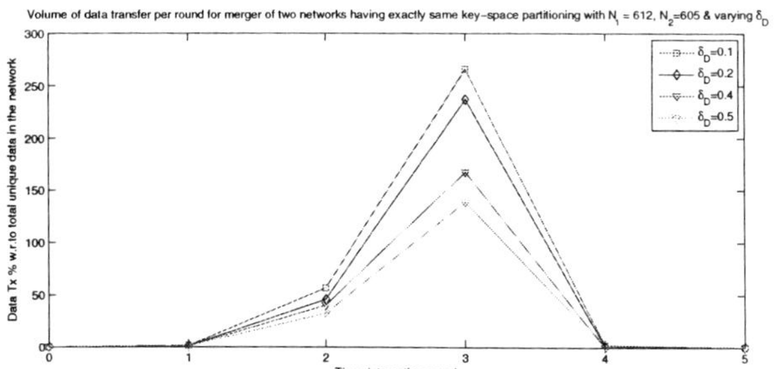

(b) Original networks had identical key-space partitioning.

Figure 3. Data transfer traffic for various values of $\delta_{\mathcal{D}}$.

5.2.1 Effect of $\mathcal{T}_{out}$

$\mathcal{T}_{out} = 0$ is the worst case scenario for routing while the merger process is not complete since the peers from two networks are never discriminated during routing. Even then, $\mathcal{R}_{j/j}$ is pretty high, though occasionally it is (slightly) less than 1 and this behavior holds for wide range of peer populations (Figure 4). Such a good worst case behavior in terms of choice of $\mathcal{T}_{out}$ is reassuring, since even if a proper value of $\mathcal{T}_{out}$ is not chosen, the performance deterioration is marginal. Since in large networks it is difficult to choose an appropriate $\mathcal{T}_{out}$, the merging networks' robustness against improper $\mathcal{T}_{out}$ is desirable for the scalability of the merger process. $\mathcal{R}_{\cap/j}$ was always 1 in all these experiments, thus content originally stored in both the networks always continued to be accessible.

6 Discussion

This paper provides rigorous evaluation of merger of two structured overlays, in the process validating some intuitions and speculations [4] - particularly we see that it is indeed possible to perform the merger process in a manner transparent to the end users, i.e., for any peer, keys which were accessible to it prior to the commencement of the merger process continue to be accessible to that peer.

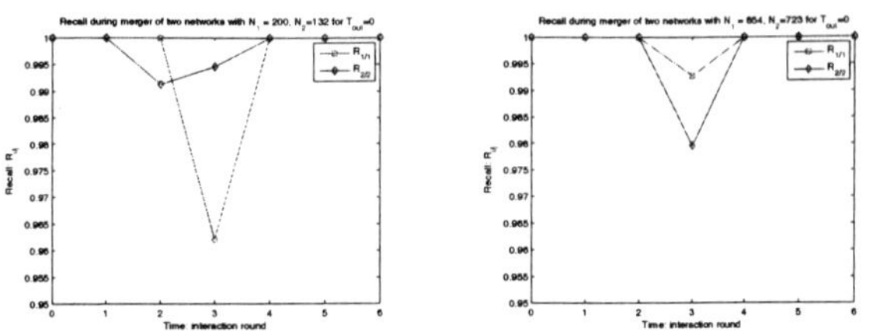

(a) Merger of two networks comprising 332 peers.

(b) Merger of 2 networks comprising 1557 peers.

Figure 4. $\mathcal{R}_{j/j}$ in the worst case choice of parameter $\mathcal{T}_{out} = 0$ (for $j = 1, 2$).

The experiments also give some results which are surprising at a first glance, particularly pertaining to the volume of data transfer. In a typical setting the original networks are expected to have different key-space partitioning to begin with, and in this case, less common data in the networks at the beginning will incur less data movement overhead than if there were more data already common in both networks. We also see that the ad-hoc parameter ($\mathcal{T}_{out}$) used in the algorithm for the merger/routing process have marginal effect, thus making the algorithm easy to use in real situations, without any need to determine an optimal parameter value. The current experiment results provide us a good insight into the merger process, however it also ignores the effect of churn in conjunction with the merger process, nor does it look into how multiple overlays may merge simultaneously. Since overlays should have sufficient redundancy to deal with churn in general, we expect that the merger process will stay rather unaffected by its influence. We assume peers locally discern between peers which are already part of its own network from peers from other networks, and use references from these alien peers to further propagate the merger process. Thus as long as we can ascertain a mechanism to distinguish normal churn (new node joining) from merger (meeting a node which is already part of another network), the merger mechanisms discussed in this paper are expected to work. These however remain speculations at the moment, and hence need to be verified. Besides more experiments to explore these aspects, theoretical results about the rate of convergence of the merger process, as well as overhead in terms of data movement estimated in terms of the initial conditions are required to completely understand the merger of overlays. Another aspect ignored in our current simulations is that the underlying physical network will have limited capacity, which may slow down the merger process since the merger process involves transfer of a huge volume of content. Furthermore, the routing on the overlays will be slowed in terms of real latency (not overlay hops), because of the high traffic and potential congestion caused due to data movement.

We argue that merger of structured overlays is a critical missing link, which facilitate decentralized bootstrapping and thus scalable deployment of such overlays in an organic fashion. In this paper we have a first concrete mechanism to merge a specific but important class of structured overlay - tree topology (prefix based routing) - and rigorous if not exhaustive simulation based evaluation of the merger process in diverse settings. Further evaluations, development of a more concrete theory of the merger process, integration of the merger algorithms in the current P-Grid software and algorithms for merger of other topologies, particularly ring, are some of the crucial next steps.

References

[1] K. Aberer, A. Datta, M. Hauswirth, and R. Schmidt. Indexing data-oriented overlay networks. *31st International Conference on Very Large Databases (VLDB)*, 2005.

[2] M. Caesar, T. Condie, J. Kannan, K. Lakshminarayanan, I. Stoica, and S. Shenker. ROFL: Routing on Flat Labels. In *SIGCOMM*, 2006.

[3] F. Dabek, M. F. Kaashoek, D. Karger, R. Morris, and I. Stoica. Wide-area cooperative storage with CFS. In *Proceedings of the 18th ACM Symposium on Operating Systems Principles (SOSP '01)*, 2001.

[4] A. Datta and K. Aberer. The challenges of merging two similar structured overlays: A tale of two networks. In *International Workshop on Self-Organizing Systems (IWSOS)*, 2006.

[5] P. Ganesan, M. Bawa, and H. Garcia-Molina. Online Balancing of Range-Partitioned Data with Applications to Peer-to-Peer Systems. In *VLDB*, 2004.

[6] P. Ganesan, P. K. Gummadi, and H. Garcia-Molina. Canon in G Major: Designing DHTs with Hierarchical Structure. In *ICDCS*, 2004.

[7] N. Harvey, M. B. Jones, S. Saroiu, M. Theimer, and A. Wolman. Skipnet: A scalable overlay network with practical locality properties. In *USITS 2003*, Seattle, WA, March 2003.

[8] M. Jelasity, A. Montresor, and O. Babaoglu. The bootstrapping service. In *ICDCSW '06: Proceedings of the 26th IEEE International ConferenceWorkshops on Distributed Computing Systems*, 2006.

[9] D. Joseph, J. Kannan, A. Kubota, K. Lakshminarayanan, I. Stoica, and K. Wehrle. OCALA: An Architecture for Supporting Legacy Applications over Overlays. In *USENIX/ACM Symposium on Networked Systems Design and Implementation (NSDI)*, 2006.

[10] J. Kubiatowicz, D. Bindel, Y. Chen, P. Eaton, D. Geels, R. Gummadi, S. Rhea, H. Weatherspoon, W. Weimer, C. Wells, and B. Zhao. Oceanstore: An architecture for global-scale persistent storage. In *Proceedings of ACM ASPLOS*. ACM, November 2000.

[11] A. Montresor, M. Jelasity, and O. Babaoglu. Chord on Demand. In *IEEE P2P*, 2005.

[12] C. G. Plaxton, R. Rajaraman, and A. W. Richa. Accessing Nearby Copies of Replicated Objects in a Distributed Environment. In *SPAA*, 1997.

[13] A. Rowstron and P. Druschel. Pastry: Scalable, distributed object location and routing for large-scale peer-to-peer systems. In *IFIP/ACM International Conference on Distributed Systems Platforms (Middleware)*, 2001.

[14] I. Stoica, R. Morris, D. Karger, F. Kaashoek, and H. Balakrishnan. Chord: A Scalable Peer-To-Peer Lookup Service for Internet Applications. In *ACM SIGCOMM, (Technical report version: http://pdos.csail.mit.edu/chord/papers/)*, 2001.

An Amortized Tit-For-Tat Protocol for Exchanging Bandwidth instead of Content in P2P Networks

Paweł Garbacki and Dick H.J. Epema
Delft University of Technology
The Netherlands
{p.j.garbacki,d.h.j.epema}@tudelft.nl

Maarten van Steen
Vrije Universiteit Amsterdam
The Netherlands
steen@cs.vu.nl

Abstract

Incentives for resource sharing are crucial for the proper operation of P2P networks. The principle of the incentive mechanisms in current content sharing P2P networks such as BitTorrent is to have peers exchange content of mutual interest. As a consequence, a peer can actively participate in the system only if it shares content that is of immediate interest to other peers. In this paper we propose to lift this restriction by using bandwidth rather than content as the resource upon which incentives are based. Bandwidth, in contrast to content, is independent of peer interests and so can be exchanged between any two peers. We present the design of a protocol called amortized tit-for-tat (ATFT) based on the bandwidth-exchange concept. This protocol defines mechanisms for bandwidth exchange corresponding to those in BitTorrent for content exchange, in particular for finding bandwidth borrowers that amortize the bandwidth borrowed in the past with their currently idle bandwidth. In addition to the formally proven incentives for bandwidth contributions, ATFT provides natural solutions to the problems of peer bootstrapping, seeding incentive, peer link asymmetry, and anonymity, which have previously been addressed with much more complex designs. Experiments with a real-world dataset confirm that ATFT is efficient in enforcing bandwidth contributions and results in download performance better than provided by incentive mechanisms based on content exchange.

1. Introduction

An important feature of peer-to-peer (P2P) architectures is that they allow to distribute the infrastructure setup and maintenance costs among the participating nodes. However, the competitive nature of P2P environments encourages selfish behavior of individual peers, which has been confirmed by a number of studies. For example, it has been shown in [22] that users of a P2P system should be seen as rational agents optimizing their own performance even if their actions adversely affect the performance of other peers. In [3] it has been observed that as much as 70% of the users of a popular file-sharing P2P network are freeriders who use the system resources without giving anything in return.

The poor performance of P2P networks caused by freeriding has stimulated research on incentives for resource sharing. All incentives in one way or another translate to constraining a peer's access to the resources of others with the contributions of that peer. The fairness enforcement mechanisms proposed to date build incentives on *content exchange*, as contributions are always expressed in terms of the local content made available by a peer. Content-exchange incentives establish a direct (e.g., exchange of content pieces between peers in BitTorrent [7]) or indirect (e.g., exchange rings in [4] or credit paths in [15]) bartering relationship between peers that are interested in each other's content. Then, the ability of a peer to contribute resources, and consequently also a peer's access to the resources offered by others, depends on the demand on the content possessed by the peer. As a result, peers that do not offer content of immediate interest to others cannot access resources of other peers.

In this paper we propose bandwidth rather than content as the resource upon which incentives are built. Bandwidth, in contrast to content, is unrelated to the interests or tastes of a peer, and is therefore potentially a more convenient unit of trade. In the *bandwidth-exchange* incentive model that we propose, any peer can contribute its currently idle bandwidth to assist other peers in their ongoing downloads, regardless of the actual content that is being downloaded.

As a proof of concept, we present the design of the ATFT protocol that employs mechanisms that are conceptually similar to those in BitTorrent [7] to enforce fairness in a P2P network where peers exchange (currently) unused bandwidth rather than content. ATFT *breaks the temporal nature* of BitTorrent tit-for-tat (TFT) that restricts current consumptions with current contributions by allowing bandwidth consumptions to be gradually amortized over time

0-7695-2906-2/07 $25.00 © 2007 IEEE

with bandwidth contributions. As a side effect, in addition to fairness enforcement, ATFT offers solutions to the four fundamental problems of P2P networks of bootstrapping newcomers, of seeding incentives, of efficient use of asymmetric links, and of anonymity.

In our ATFT protocol, each peer exchanges bandwidth with a limited number of bandwidth *borrowers*. The members of the borrowers set are selected in a fully decentralized manner, based on the amount of bandwidth contributed in the past to the peer performing the selection. A peer uses its currently idle bandwidth to assist its borrowers in their downloads. We perform an analytical study of the ATFT protocol, formally proving its incentive mechanism and determining the impact of the protocol parameters such as the size of the borrowers set on the sharing performance. The analytical results obtained in a simplified system model are confirmed with an experimental study using an 8-week trace of a popular file-sharing P2P community, filelist.org [2].

2. Content exchange vs bandwidth exchange

The amount of content transferred between peers in a P2P network translates directly into the amount of bandwidth required for the transfers. However, content and bandwidth are resources with very different properties. Content has a semantic meaning attached that makes it relevant to only those peers who are interested in it. One of the consequences of the semantic context of content is that a peer is a valuable contributor only if it has content requested by the others. In a system enforcing fairness in resource sharing, not being able to contribute decreases the chances of getting access to the shared resources. This property of the content-exchange model by definition discriminates peers that do not share popular content.

The bandwidth of a peer, on the other hand, can be used by any other peer to download the content it requests. However, in contrast to content, bandwidth is not a persistent resource and therefore it cannot be exchanged as easily as content. In our previous work [10] we have introduced the concept of collaborative downloads implemented by a data transfer protocol called 2Fast that allows peers to use bandwidth of others during their downloads. In 2Fast, a downloader utilizes the idle bandwidth of helper peers to fetch the content it requests more efficiently. Helper peers do not have to be interested in, or even know what they are downloading.

Despite its limitations, content exchange rather than bandwidth exchange is the basis of all incentive mechanisms commonly used in content-sharing P2P networks. Arguably the most well-known protocol providing incentives for resource contributions in content-exchange P2P networks is the BitTorrent protocol. BitTorrent uses a *tit-for-tat* (TFT) mechanism to prevent freeriding. BitTorrent TFT restricts access to locally stored file pieces based on the amount of data obtained recently from the accessing peer. There are several well-known limitations of BitTorrent TFT related to the fact that its applicability is restricted to peers downloading the *same* content at the *same* time. First, the newcomers are bootstrapped at the bandwidth cost of the existing peers. Second, no incentives for content injection (*seeding* in BitTorrent terminology) are provided. Third, peers with asymmetric Internet connections, which constitute a majority of P2P users [21], cannot fully utilize their download links as they are forced to download at the speed of their upload link.

The limitations of BitTorrent TFT are addressed to some extent in the design of credit-based systems such as [8, 11, 15, 23]. However, the ability of a peer to earn credits is heavily dependent on the popularity of the content possessed by the peer. Furthermore, the sophistication of the system mechanisms required to reliably account and validate credits prevents the credit-based systems from being widely used.

In this paper we show how the limitations of BitTorrent can be overcome avoiding the complexity of credit-based systems. We propose a simple protocol using mechanisms similar to those in BitTorrent, but based on bandwidth exchange rather than content exchange.

3 Design of ATFT

In this section we will describe our ATFT protocol, which builds incentives for contributions on the bandwidth-exchange concept. ATFT employs mechanisms similar to BitTorrent to account for a peer's bandwidth contributions and is based on those contributions to select the bandwidth borrowers with the highest chance of returning the borrowed bandwidth.

3.1 Mechanisms of ATFT

In this section we introduce the mechanisms of ATFT and set them off against the corresponding BitTorrent mechanisms (see Table 1). We assume here a basic knowledge of the BitTorrent mechanisms and accompanying terminology as described in, e.g., [13].

In BitTorrent, each peer maintains a limited-size set of peers interested in the file pieces possessed by the peer. The members of this set are candidates for content exchange. In ATFT, bandwidth exchange candidates are members of the *borrowers set*. A peer gives borrowers access to its idle bandwidth resources. The set of borrowers of a peer is not fixed, but rather it evolves based on the ability and willingness of the borrowers to return the consumed bandwidth.

A peer in BitTorrent keeps a set of peers that are potential sources of the missing pieces. The potential set is related to the interested set in the sense that peer p is in the potential

ATFT	BitTorrent TFT
borrowers set	interested set
contributors set	potential set
collaboration	active set
collaborative downloads	piece exchange
selection	choking
exploration	optimistic unchoking
local view	tracker

Table 1. The correspondence between the mechanisms of ATFT and BitTorrent TFT.

set of peer q if peer q is in the interested set of peer p. In ATFT, the equivalent of the potential set is the *contributors set*. Peer p is a contributor of peer q if peer q is a borrower of peer p.

At any time, a BitTorrent peer downloads file pieces from the members of its potential set that have the peer in their active sets. In ATFT, a peer downloading data forms a *collaboration* with those among its contributors that are on-line and are not requesting themselves, and so have idle bandwidth to spare. The peer forming the collaboration is called the *collector*, and the contributors in the collaboration are called the *helpers*. The goal of the collaboration is to assist the collector in downloading the requested data using the idle bandwidth of the helpers. The collaboration is established only for the time of a single download (e.g., transfer of one file). During consecutive downloads peer roles in a collaboration may be reversed, i.e., collectors may become helpers for peers that currently act as their helpers.

Data is transferred in BitTorrent by means of piece exchange between individual peers. ATFT replaces individual peers with collaborations of collectors and their helpers. The *collaborative download* protocol, described in more detail in Section 3.2, defines how the idle bandwidth of the helpers is used by (or transferred to) the collector. The collaborative download protocol establishes a tit-for-tat relation between peers inside the collaboration (collector and helpers) on the one hand and peers outside the collaboration on the other. Inside a collaboration, however, data is transferred only from helpers to the collector. The view of peer roles in the ATFT protocol from the perspective of a collector is presented in Figure 1. The collaborative download protocol guarantees only that the fairness in bandwidth contributions is preserved between peers in different collaborations. It is the role of the remaining mechanisms of ATFT to ensure that also the fairness between the collector and its helpers is preserved.

Peers in BitTorrent keep track of the amount of content contributed to them by the members of the potential set. The choking and optimistic unchoking mechanisms are employed by BitTorrent to select the peers to exchange content with that result in the highest download performance.

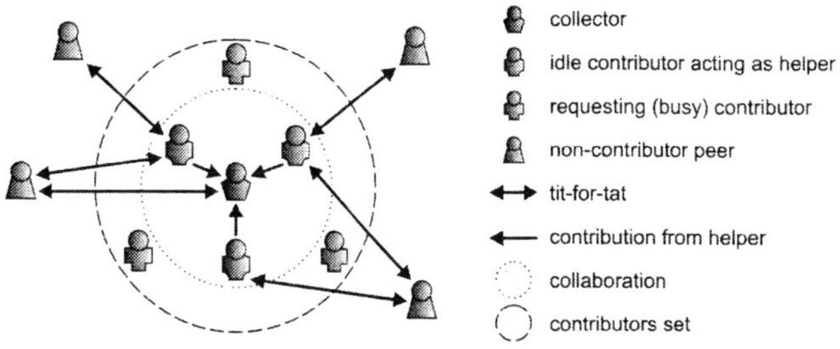

Figure 1. The collector-centric view of peer roles in the ATFT protocol.

In ATFT, peers account and maintain the amount of bandwidth obtained from their contributions. The *selection* and *exploration* operations, described in more detail in Section 3.3, are used to select as borrowers peers with the highest contributions.

The peer discovery functionality in BitTorrent is provided by the tracker, which is a central component maintaining the IP addresses and port numbers of all connectable peers downloading a certain file. BitTorrent peers can exchange data exclusively with peers downloading the same file, and so the tracker has to keep information only about downloaders of a single file. In ATFT, bandwidth can be exchanged between any two peers, and therefore a peer should be able to discover any other peer in the network. A central peer discovery component does not scale to the entire network. Instead, we assume that a peer in the ATFT network maintains a *local view* of the system, which contains information about a random subset of peers. New borrowers are selected from among the peers in the local view. As long as the randomness of the peers sample in the local view is preserved, ATFT is independent of the particular protocol used to update local views. Rather than proposing a new peer sampling protocol, we point to the extensive work done in this field [9, 12]. The size of the local view should be interpreted as the protocol configuration parameter.

3.2. Bandwidth transfer between helpers and collector

In BitTorrent, the (content) resource is transferred by means of transmitting pieces of a file between two peers downloading that file. In ATFT, the (bandwidth) resource transfer is handled by the collaborative download protocol that describes how the bandwidth of helpers is used by the collector. The realization of the collaborative download protocol generally depends on the type of a P2P network. Currently, the dominant P2P network types are file sharing and video streaming. Collaborative downloads integrate very naturally with P2P networks of both types.

In file sharing P2P networks, helpers can assist the collector simply by downloading file pieces that the collector misses. To obtain new data, helpers and collector trade locally possessed pieces for the pieces that have not yet been downloaded by any peer in the collaboration. The design of this simple protocol and its implementation in Tribler [19] P2P network client have been described in detail in our previous work [10].

P2P video streaming networks require that content pieces are transferred in a certain order allowing for video playback during the download. To increase the resilience to temporal bandwidth fluctuations, video streaming protocols make use of a buffer to prefetch pieces ahead of the current playback position. Protocols as BiToS [24] employ tit-for-tat bartering for the pieces in the buffer to guarantee fairness in peer data contributions. Similarly to file sharing networks, helpers in a video streaming network could use their bandwidth to obtain missing pieces, this time restricted to the contents of the buffer.

3.3. Forming peer relationships

Following a rational strategy of locally optimal choices, each peer in ATFT selects as borrowers peers with the highest bandwidth contributions. The process of choosing borrowers, presented in Algorithm 1, consists of the two operations of *exploration* and *selection*, which are repeated periodically but independently of each other. The exploration and selection operations are complementary in the sense that while exploration extends the borrowers set opening opportunities for bandwidth exchange, selection reduces the borrowers set by removing the least promising peers.

The exploration performed by peer p (line 1) is intended to expand its borrowers set up to the predefined size limit (line 2). New borrowers are selected randomly from the local view of peer p (line 3). If p selects peer q then q is added to the borrowers set of p (line 4) and p is added to the contributors set of q (line 5). Execution of line 5 requires network communication between p and q.

The selection operation (line 6) executed by peer p starts with replacing the borrowers set with peers that contributed a positive amount of bandwidth to p (line 7). By doing so, the peer follows the principle of reciprocation, giving access to the local bandwidth to those who contribute their own bandwidth. At this point the size of the borrowers set may be larger than allowed. In that case, we reduce the size of the borrowers set in two steps. First, we rank borrowers based on their bandwidth contributions (line 8). Second, we remove from the borrowers set all except at most $n_p - r_p$ peers with the highest contributions (lines 9 and 10).

Algorithm 1 provides high-level pseudocode that can be further customized by selecting values of the parameters n_x and r_x as well as the contributors ranking method. The selection of n_x is discussed in more detail in Section 4.3. The parameter r_x controls the "aggressiveness" of the exploration process. Generally, by setting r_x to a higher value, more peers can be probed for their suitability as desired borrowers in a shorter time, and consequently an optimal set of borrowers maximizing peer's gain can be found faster. On the other hand, however, increasing r_x gives more peers access to local bandwidth resources increasing the chance that the consumed bandwidth will not be returned. Therefore, the value of r_x should be customized depending on a peer's objective.

Algorithm 1: Exploration and selection operations.

```
   /* A_x is the set of borrowers of peer x          */
   /* C_x is the set of contributors of peer x       */
   /* n_x is the maximal number of borrowers of
      peer x                                         */
   /* r_x is the maximal number of randomly
      selected borrowers of peer x                   */
   /* V_x is the local view of peer x                */
1  explore(p : peer):
   begin
2      while |A_p| < n_p and V_p\A_p ≠ ∅ do
3          select randomly a peer q from V_p\A_p
4          add q to A_p
5          add p to C_q
       end
   end

6  select(p : peer):
   begin
7      A_p ← all peers in C_p with non-zero bandwidth
       contributions to p
8      rank peers in A_p according to increasing bandwidth
       contributions to p; peers with the same contributions are
       ranked randomly among each other
9      while |A_p| > n_p − r_p do
10         remove from A_p the peer with the lowest rank
       end
   end
```

The formula used to compute peer contributions in line 8 of Algorithm 1 defines the borrowers selection criterion. A simple formula could just compute the total amount of bandwidth contributed by a peer, giving more recent contributions a higher weight. More complex formulas could also interpret the reliability of the contributor expressed by the probability that the contributor will act as a helper for a longer period of time. Contributor reliability aspects are extremely important in case of video streaming protocols where not only the amount of available bandwidth but also the continuity of the contribution impacts the service quality.

3.4. Benefits of ATFT

After presenting the design of ATFT, we will discuss how the bandwidth exchange model of ATFT addresses the four limitations of the content exchange model of BitTorrent TFT briefly mentioned in Sections 1 and 2.

0-7695-2906-2/07 $25.00 © 2007 IEEE

The primary motivation behind the BitTorrent mechanism design is to prevent freeriding. Nonetheless, it has been shown that it is still possible to download data from the BitTorrent network at a reasonable speed without uploading any data in return [14]. As explained in [18], a fundamental flaw of BitTorrent's incentive mechanism is the presence of significant altruism in the protocol operation. A newcomer peer obtains the first few pieces from peers entrusting the newcomer to return the consumed bandwidth. The cost of bootstrapping is borne by the community, not the newcomer, as rationality would suggest. As part of the optimistic unchoking algorithm, peers donate usually 20% of their upload link capacity to bootstrap newcomers and find new peers to barter with. Although ATFT allows for bandwidth donation to randomly selected borrowers, the maximal number of random borrowers (r_x in Algorithm 1) is only a tuning parameter which can be set to 0 without affecting the principles of system operation. In case of r_x equal to 0, newcomers have to first prove themselves by contributing bandwidth to their borrowers before they will be offered access to bandwidth resources of the others. Hence, the cost of bootstrapping in ATFT is paid by the newcomers themselves, not the community.

Second, another well-known shortcoming of BitTorrent systems is the lack of incentives for seeding, i.e., for uploading content after completing a file download. Seeding is another, apart from bootstrapping of newcomers, altruistic type of behavior, which is crucial for BitTorrent system healthiness. In ATFT, seeding may be seen as a form of helping in download. The bandwidth used for seeding content to a borrower can be reclaimed in the future. Furthermore, if a helper already possesses the file requested by the collector, it does not have to reserve part of its upload capacity for tit-for-tat bartering in order to obtain file pieces from peers outside the collaboration. A seeding helper can transfer data to the collector at a speed of its upload capacity limit and be acknowledged for higher contribution than helpers that have to divide their upload link capacity between tit-for-tat and sending data back to the collector. In principle, a seeding helper contributes to the collector twice as much data as a helper using tit-for-tat to obtain missing file pieces. In conclusion, ATFT provides a clear incentive for content seeding.

Third, as explained in [10], BitTorrent cannot utilize the download link capacity of upload-capacity-limited peers. The temporal nature of BitTorrent TFT allows a peer to download only with the speed of its upload link capacity. ATFT detaches in time the periods when the bandwidth is contributed from the periods when the bandwidth is consumed. Consequently, peers can fill their down links completely with the bandwidth of the helpers.

Finally, the bandwidth-exchange model of ATFT can be used to provide a certain level of anonymity. A collector can decide not to expose its identity outside a collaboration by downloading data exclusively from the helpers. Since the identity of the collector is still known to members of the collaboration, helpers can be then seen as anonymizing proxies [1].

4. Analysis of ATFT

In this section we analyze the mechanisms of ATFT that provide incentives for bandwidth contributions and we investigate the impact of the size of the borrowers set on the bandwidth sharing performance. We start with a description of the P2P network model used in our analysis.

4.1. System model

In our model of a P2P system for analyzing ATFT, we denote by N the total number of peers in the system. All peers maintain a borrowers set of the same size n. We perform our analysis under steady state, assuming that all the peers have already found stable sets of borrowers. We do not study the impact of the number of borrowers that are selected randomly (r_x in Section 3.3) on the performance of ATFT.

We assume that peers are alternating between idle periods and request periods, and that the durations of both types of periods are exponentially distributed, with the same means for all peers. Let the average length of the idle periods and requesting periods be $1/\lambda$ and $1/\mu$, respectively. In this analysis we assume that the idle bandwidth of every helper is distributed evenly among its requesting borrowers.

The *contribution* of peer i, denoted by c_i, is equal to the average amount of bandwidth given to the borrowers during its idle periods. The contribution is bounded by a value dependent on the upload link capacity of the peer. The *gain* g_i of peer i is the average amount of bandwidth obtained by peer i from its contributors.

Furthermore, we assume that each peer can use as much help as it can get. Although the link capacity limit bounds the number of helpers that suffice to fill a peer's download link, using more helper peers improves the resilience to content availability changes caused by, e.g., transmission failures or peer leaves. This type of resilience is crucial in video streaming P2P networks.

4.2. Incentive for contribution

We prove analytically that in ATFT, a peer's gain grows when its own contribution grows. ATFT thus provides a direct incentive for bandwidth contributions. In our analysis, we exploit the fact that the mechanisms of ATFT closely resemble those of BitTorrent. Therefore we can directly apply the analytical methodology developed for BitTorrent-like systems to show certain properties of ATFT.

An analytical model of BitTorrent-like systems has been introduced in [20]. This model is based on assumptions analogous to those described by us in Section 4.1. Namely, the model in [20] assumes that peers request files to download according to a Poisson process and that they stay in the system for a random time which is exponentially distributed. BitTorrent peers have global knowledge about other peers in the system. The capacity of a BitTorrent peer is expressed by its upload link limit. No download bandwidth constraints are imposed. The contribution in BitTorrent is defined as the amount of data transferred to a peer in the active set in a recent time interval. The gain of a BitTorrent peer is the amount of data obtained from other peers in the same time interval.

ATFT extends the contribution accounting model of BitTorrent by allowing contributions to be maintained across multiple downloads. When peer contributions are computed, the mechanisms performing the selection of the best peers to barter with in BitTorrent and the selection of borrowers in ATFT operate on the same principles. Hence, also the incentive mechanisms built into the peer selection methods in BitTorrent and ATFT correspond to each other.

Before formulating the properties of the ATFT incentive mechanism, we introduce some conventions and notations in addition to those described in Section 4.1. Let's assume that peers are arranged in decreasing order according to their bandwidth contributions. Each peer is assigned a number in $1, 2, \dots, N$ representing its position in this ordering. Let $g(c)$ denote the average gain of peers with contribution c. The following corollary describes the correlation between the contribution and the gain of a peer in ATFT.

Corollary 1. *Suppose that peers $i, i+1, \dots, j$ have the same contribution c, where i (respectively j) is the first (respectively last) peer with this contribution. Then for any $k > j$, we have $g_i \geq g_{i+1} \geq \dots \geq g_j \geq g_k$. If additionally $j + i - 1 > n \geq 2$, then $g(c) > g_k$.*

Proof. Analogous to the proof of Lemma 2 in [20]. □

According to Corollary 1, the ATFT protocol guarantees that if the contribution of peer p is greater than the contribution of peer q, then the gain of peer p is at least as large as the gain of peer q. Furthermore, with the exception of a few special cases, the gain of peer p is greater than the gain of peer q. Hence, the ATFT protocol awards peers for their contributions by assigning better borrowers to the peers that contribute more.

We have shown that peers with higher contributions gain at least as much as peers with lower contributions. However, at this point it is not clear if a peer can preserve its current gain while decreasing its amount of contributed bandwidth. Now we will investigate how the *bandwidth sharing strategy*, i.e., the rules for choosing the amount of bandwidth contributed to borrowers, affects a peer's gain.

In [20], the problem of selecting the optimal bandwidth sharing strategy is modeled as a competitive game. A peer's goal in this game is to maximize its gain (primary objective) while minimizing its contribution (secondary objective). The set of optimal bandwidth sharing strategies for all peers joinly is given by a Nash equilibrium [16]. It is shown in [20] that if upload link capacities of peers are different, a Nash equilibrium may not exist. Therefore, let's consider a network with a finite number of peer *bandwidth groups* with all peers in a bandwidth group having the same upload bandwidth limit. Note that this is in fact a realistic assumption in the current Internet that consists of a limited number of link capacity classes. The following corollary characterizes the existence and the form of a Nash equilibrium.

Corollary 2. *If $n \geq 2$ and if the number of peers in each bandwidth group is greater than $n + 1$, there exists one and only one Nash equilibrium in which the contribution of each peer is equal to its upload bandwidth limit.*

Proof. A direct consequence of Proposition 1 in [20]. □

Corollary 2 states that the only optimal strategy for a peer maximizing its gain is to contribute the entire available upload bandwidth.

4.3. Borrowers set size

The size of the borrowers set is an important parameter of the ATFT protocol. We analyze the impact of the borrowers set size on the sharing performance.

As we have formally proven in Section 4.2, an optimal bandwidth sharing strategy for a peer is to contribute to its borrowers as much bandwidth as possible. So it is in the best interest of a peer to maximize the utilization of its idle bandwidth. The *utilization* of bandwidth is defined as the fraction of the idle time when the bandwidth is (completely) used by at least one borrower. It is obvious that the utilization depends on the size of the borrowers set. We denote by u_n the utilization when the borrowers set has size n.

Bandwidth utilization depends on the probability that at least one borrower requests bandwidth at a given time. The evolution of the number of requesting borrowers can be modeled as a birth-death process represented by a Markov chain, as depicted in Figure 2. The state of this process represents the number of requesting borrowers.

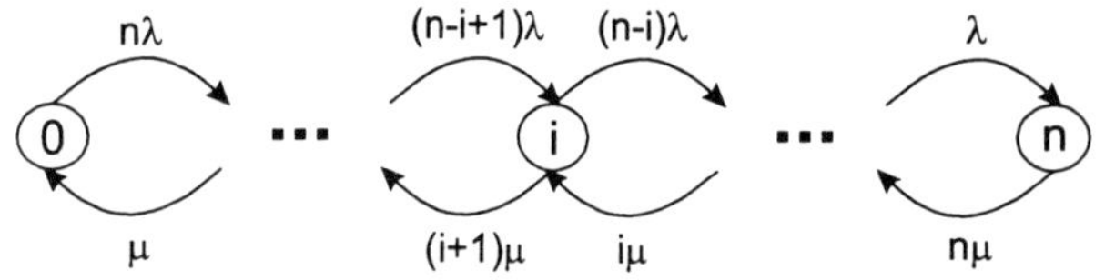

Figure 2. Evolution of the number of requesting borrowers.

If π_i is the probability of state i, then the balance equations of this Markov chain are

$$(n-i)\lambda\pi_i = i\mu\pi_{i+1}, \quad i = 0, \ldots, n-1,$$

from which we find:

$$\pi_i = \binom{n}{i}\left(\frac{\lambda}{\mu}\right)^i \pi_0.$$

The probability π_0 is determined by the normalization condition $\sum_{i=0}^{n} \pi_i = 1$:

$$\pi_0 = \left(1 + \frac{\lambda}{\mu}\right)^{-n}. \quad (1)$$

Since we assume that the bandwidth is fully utilized as long as there is at least one requesting borrower, the bandwidth utilization can be expressed as:

$$u_n = 1 - \pi_0.$$

Substituting for π_0 the value computed in Eq. 1 we get

$$u_n = 1 - \left(1 + \frac{\lambda}{\mu}\right)^{-n}. \quad (2)$$

According to Eq. (2), the bandwidth utilization converges very fast and is high even for small values of n. Keeping the borrowers set small has a practical reason discussed in [5]. Every new peer accepted as a borrower increases the chance that the contributed bandwidth will not be returned. A borrower refusing to return the contributed bandwidth will be eventually removed from the borrowers set, but the bandwidth it consumed cannot be recovered. It is therefore important for each peer to restrict the borrowers set to a number of valuable peers just large enough to fill the peer's download capacity.

5. Performance evaluation

In this section we present an experimental evaluation of the ATFT protocol. We first describe the experimental setup and then demonstrate the results of the experiments.

5.1. Experimental setup

We model the P2P network used in our experiments using a trace of a popular file-sharing P2P community, filelist.org [2]. The properties of the trace are presented in Table 2. Two reasons motivated the selection of the filelist.org trace as input for our experiments. First, filelist.org employs BitTorrent as the data distribution protocol. Because BitTorrent is currently the dominant P2P protocol [17], we believe that filelist.org users are representative of average P2P network users. Second, filelist.org provides detailed user information allowing us to track users across downloads of different files, a task that is generally hard for BitTorrent communities that do not provide such detailed user information.

Property	Value
trace start date	December 10, 2005
trace end date	January 31, 2006
number of peers (users)	91,169
number of files	4,021
average file size	1,084 MB
number of file downloads	2,326,187

Table 2. Filelist.org dataset properties.

Bandwidth capacity		Fraction of peers
Download	Upload	
784 kbps	128 kbps	0.2
1500 kbps	384 kbps	0.4
3 mbps	1 mbps	0.25
10 mbps	5 mbps	0.15

Table 3. Bandwidth distribution of peers used in our experiments.

The filelist.org dataset contains the meta-information describing the files requested by the peers, such as file size, and times of the requests. However, the dataset does not include the specification of peer bandwidth settings. We use the peer bandwidth distribution model introduced in [6]. According to this model, peers are divided into four bandwidth classes with probabilities as presented in Table 3.

We have developed a discrete time simulator of the ATFT protocol. In the simulations, we replay the system usage scenario of each peer, assuming that a peer is requesting bandwidth for a time period required to download the entire file, and is idle otherwise. The time when the file is requested and the size of the file are given in the filelist.org dataset. The download time depends on the download bandwidth of the peer during the requesting period. The download bandwidth of a collector is the sum of the bandwidths provided by the helpers and the bandwidth the collector obtains by bartering its upload bandwidth with peers outside the collaboration. Helpers divide their bandwidth resources evenly among the requesting borrowers. This means in particular that a peer can act as a helper for multiple borrowers at the same time, with each of those borrowers getting the same amount of the peer's bandwidth. In our simulations we assume a strict tit-for-tat so there are no altruistic peers such as seeds willing to donate their bandwidth.

In the beginning of the simulation, the borrowers set of each peer is filled with randomly selected peers. As motivated in Section 4, ATFT peers do not have to maintain large borrowers sets. In our simulation we set the borrowers set size to 30. The number of borrowers selected

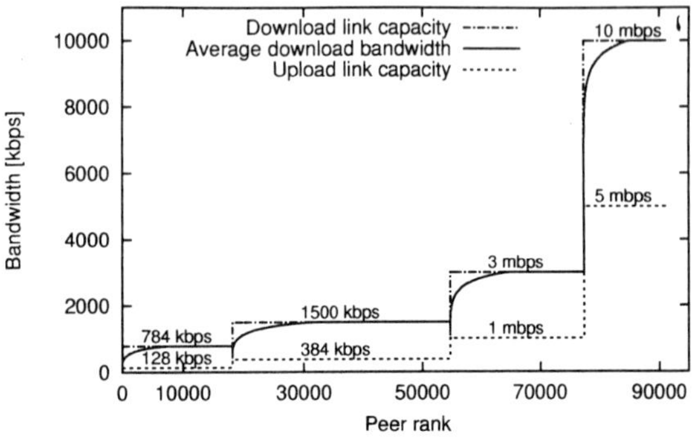

Figure 3. The average download bandwidth during request periods.

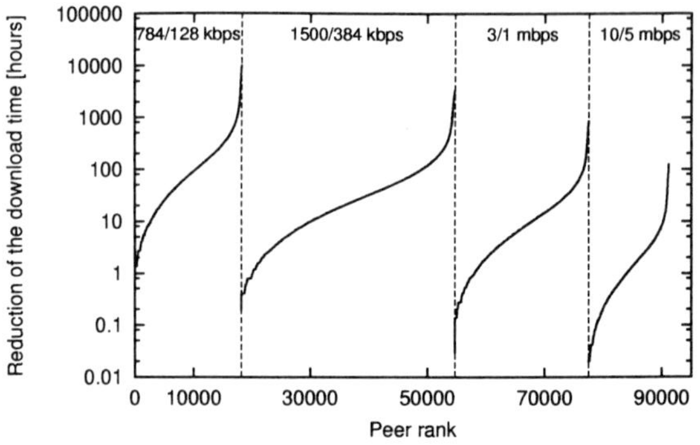

Figure 4. The reduction of the total download time when using ATFT instead of BitTorrent TFT.

randomly equals 3. The exploration and selection operations are performed every 10 minutes. To eliminate the bias caused by the random initialization of the borrowers sets, we start collecting data for a peer after its borrowers set has been updated 20 times.

As explained in Section 3.3, there are different ways of accounting for peer bandwidth contributions. In our simulations, a peer maintains a single value for keeping track of the bandwidth obtained from each contributor. This value is increased for every unit of bandwidth (e.g., one byte) received from the corresponding contributor, and it is cut in half every time the selection algorithm is executed to give a higher weight to more recent contributions.

5.2. Results of the experiments

We have conducted several experiments to assess different performance aspects of the ATFT protocol and compare it with the performance of BitTorrent-like systems. The results of our experiments allow us to quantify the performance improvement achieved by replacing the content-oriented incentive model of BitTorrent with the bandwidth-oriented model of ATFT.

5.2.1. Download performance

In the first series of experiments we investigate the download performance improvement by using the additional bandwidth offered by the contributors. All peers apply the optimal bandwidth sharing strategy as described in Section 4.2, giving their borrowers access to the entire upload bandwidth available during idle periods.

Figure 3 presents the average download bandwidth for each peer measured during its request periods. Here, peers are grouped according to their upload and download link capacities. The groups represent the link capacity classes described in Table 3. Obviously, the download bandwidth of a peer is always between its upload and download link capacity. Peers in each link capacity class are ranked according to their average download bandwidth. The results in Figure 3 indicate that ATFT leads to a high utilization of peer download links. On average, the download links of more than 90% of the peers are completely filled during more than 85% of the request periods. Note that in a system in which peers exchange content using BitTorrent TFT, a peer's download bandwidth is limited by its upload link capacity. We conclude that ATFT improves the average download bandwidth of a peer by a factor of 2 to 6, depending on the link capacity asymmetry.

The increase of the download bandwidth does not say much about the benefit in terms of the reduction in time spent downloading, which depends also on the amounts of data requested by peers. Therefore, in Figure 4 we present for each peer the difference between the time spent downloading requested files using the ATFT protocol and the time required to download the same files using BitTorrent TFT over the length of the entire trace. Also in this figure, the peers are grouped based on their bandwidth classes and ranked in each group according to the download time reduction. It can be observed that for some peers the reduction in download time is greater than the duration of the entire trace. To explain this anomaly we point out that the bandwidth limit assigned to a peer by the simulator may not match the actual bandwidth of the peer, which is impossible to extract from the filelist.org dataset. Nevertheless, the results presented in Figure 4 are still indicative if we assume that peers request files independently of their bandwidth limits, and that they are determined to wait until the requested files have been downloaded.

5.2.2. Contributing borrowers

In ATFT, peers contribute bandwidth to their borrowers with the intention to reclaim this bandwidth in the future. The exploration and selection algorithms of ATFT follow a simple strategy of giving access to local bandwidth to peers that contributed most in the past. In the ideal case, a peer should contribute bandwidth only to those peers that recip-

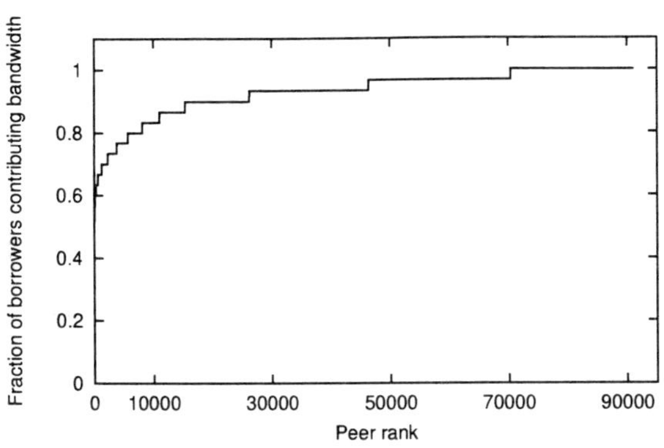

Figure 5. The fraction of borrowers contributing bandwidth averaged over peer requesting periods.

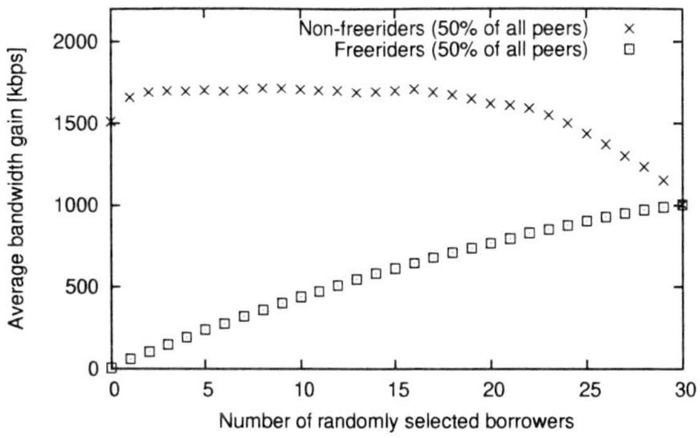

Figure 6. The average bandwidth gains of freeriders and non-freeriders as functions of the number of borrowers selected randomly.

rocate by giving the peer access to their own bandwidth resources. In other words, ideally the borrowers and the contributors sets of a peer should be the same. We evaluate experimentally how effective the exploration and selection mechanisms described in Section 3.3 are in finding borrowers that return the contributed bandwidth.

Figure 5 shows the average fraction of borrowers that are also contributors. The average has been computed by summing the fractions of contributing borrowers measured for all requesting periods and dividing the sum by the number of those periods. For 90% of peers, more than 25 out of the total of 30 (a fraction of 0.83) borrowers are contributing bandwidth. Furthermore, on average the number of contributing borrowers of a peer is equal to 27 which is also the number of non-randomly selected peers in Algorithm 1.

5.2.3. Freeriding

The main purpose of incentives in P2P networks is to stimulate contributions. In the following experiment we investigate the possibility of freeriding in ATFT. Freeriders consume the bandwidth resources of their contributors but refuse to help the others by keeping their borrowers sets empty. The bandwidth gain of a freerider obviously depends on the number of borrowers selected randomly by non-freeriding peers (see also Sections 3.3 and 3.4). We compare the bandwidth gain of freeriders and non-freeriders assuming that the role of freerider is assigned to 50% of randomly and uniformly selected peers.

Figure 6 presents the average bandwidth gain, i.e., the bandwidth contributed by helpers during requesting periods of freeriders and non-freeriders as it depends on the number of borrowers selected randomly (r_x). There are a few observations that can be made here. First, although setting r_x to 0 effectively reduces the gain of freeriders, it also negatively affects the gain of non-freeriders. In general, the process of finding optimal borrowers may be slow if r_x equals 0. Nonetheless, ATFT offers a reasonable performance to non-freeriders even when r_x equals 0. In contrast, BitTorrent TFT requires that the number of randomly selected peers to upload data to is always positive (see Section 3.4).

Second, the bandwidth gain of non-freeriding peers starts decaying only if r_x exceeds a certain threshold, in our experiment equal to 16. Until this threshold is reached, the gain of non-freeriders stays roughly at the same level. The system capacity expressed in terms of the bandwidth available during the idle periods of non-freeriders is sufficient to tolerate freeriding to some extent. The excess system capacity allows peers to set r_x higher, potentially increasing the chance of finding better borrowers faster, without decreasing their bandwidth gain, even in the presence of freeriding.

5.2.4. Sensitivity to the size of the borrowers set

In the final experiment we investigate the impact of the borrowers set size on the bandwidth gain. Based on the results of the analysis performed for a simplified system model we concluded in Section 4.3 that peer's gain is close to optimal already for small sizes of the borrowers sets. Here we validate the correctness of this conclusion in a system model derived from a real-world trace.

Figure 7 presents the correlation between the average bandwidth gain, computed in the same way as in Section 5.2.3, and the size of the borrowers set. Here the number of randomly selected borrowers is set to the smallest integer value larger than or equal to one tenth of the borrowers set size. The experimental evaluation confirms the results obtained analytically that the gain as a function of the borrowers set size converges quickly.

6. Conclusions and future work

In this paper we have proposed to replace the traditional incentive model of P2P networks which is based on content exchange with a novel incentive model based on bandwidth exchange. Bandwidth as a resource has a universal value for all the peers, unlike content, which is relevant only to

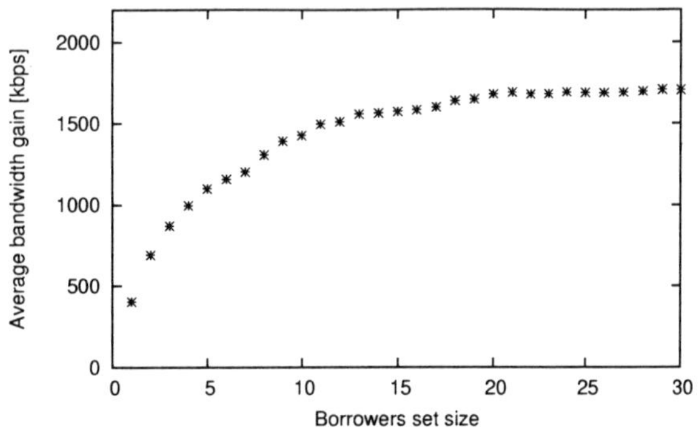

Figure 7. The average bandwidth gain as a function of the size of the borrowers set.

the group of peers interested in it. Therefore, the mechanisms for keeping track of the bandwidth exchanged between peers can be simpler than the mechanisms for maintaining the content contributions of peers across multiple downloads. As a proof of the bandwidth exchange concept, we have designed an ATFT protocol based on mechanisms employed by BitTorrent TFT for content exchange. ATFT offers an elegant solution to the problems encountered in BitTorrent including bootstrapping of newcomers, providing seeding incentive, efficient support of asymmetric links, and anonymity. We have formally proven that the ATFT protocol provides incentives for contributing bandwidth, discussed the selection of protocol parameters, and evaluated ATFT using a trace of a real-world P2P community.

We are currently working on the implementation of the ATFT protocol as part of the Tribler [19] system. This implementation will allow us to investigate the effect of the bandwidth-exchange incentive model on the behavior of users. In particular, it will be interesting to see if users leave their P2P software connected to the network in idle mode for periods longer than currently, to help their borrowers and consequently also to improve the performance of their own downloads.

References

[1] Anonymizer project page. http://anonymizer.com/.

[2] Filelist project page. http://filelist.org/.

[3] E. Adar and B. A. Huberman. Free riding on gnutella. Technical report, Xerox PARC, August 2000.

[4] K. G. Anagnostakis and M. Greenwald. Exchange-based incentive mechanisms for peer-to-peer file sharing. In *ICDCS'04*, Tokyo, Japan, March 2004.

[5] R. Axelrod. *The Evolution of Cooperation*. Basic Books, August 1985.

[6] A. R. Bharambe, C. Herley, and V. N. Padmanabhan. Analyzing and improving a bittorrent network's performance mechanisms. In *Infocom 2006*, Barcelona, Spain, April 2006.

[7] B. Cohen. Incentives build robustness in bittorrent. In *P2PEcon'03*, Berkeley, CA, May 2003.

[8] Y. Fu, J. Chase, B. Chun, S. Schwab, and A. Vahdat. Sharp: an architecture for secure resource peering. In *SOSP'03*, New York, NY, 2003.

[9] A. J. Ganesh, A. M. Kermarrec, and L. Massoulie. Peer-to-peer membership management for gossip-based protocols. *IEEE Transactions on Computers*, 52(2), 2003.

[10] P. Garbacki, A. Iosup, D. Epema, and M. van Steen. 2fast: Collaborative downloads in p2p networks. In *6th IEEE Int'l Conference on Peer-to-Peer Computing (P2P2006)*, Cambridge, UK, September 2006.

[11] M. Ham and G. Agha. Ara: A robust audit to prevent free-riding in p2p networks. In *5th IEEE Int'l Conference on Peer-to-Peer Computing (P2P2005)*, 2005.

[12] M. Jelasity, R. Guerraoui, and A.-M. Kermarrec. The peer sampling service: Experimental evaluation of unstructured gossip-based implementations. In *Middleware'04*, Toronto, Ontario, Canada, October 2004.

[13] A. Legout, G. Urvoy-Keller, and P. Michiardi. Rarest first and choke algorithms are enough. In *IMC'2006*, Rio de Janeiro, Brazil, October 2006.

[14] N. Liogkas, R. Nelson, E. Kohler, and L. Zhang. Exploiting bittorrent for fun (but not profit). In *IPTPS'06*, Santa Barbara, CA, February 2006.

[15] A. Nandi, T.-W. Ngan, A. Singh, P. Druschel, and D. S. Wallach. Scrivener: Providing incentives in cooperative content distribution systems. In *Middleware'05*, Grenoble, France, November 2005.

[16] J. F. Nash. Equilibrium points in n-person games. *Natl Acad Sci U S A*, 36(1), January 1950.

[17] A. Parker. The true picture of peer-to-peer file-sharing, panel presentation. In *IEEE 10th Int'l Workshop on Web Content Caching and Distribution (WCW 2005)*, Sophia Antipolis, France, September 2005.

[18] M. Piatek, T. Isdal, T. Anderson, A. Krishnamurthy, and A. Venkataramani. Do incentives build robustness in bittorrent? In *NSDI'07*, Cambridge, MA, April 2007.

[19] J. Pouwelse, P. Garbacki, J. Wang, A. Bakker, J. Yang, A. Iosup, D. H. J. Epema, M. Reinders, M. van Steen, and H. Sips. Tribler: A social-based peer-to-peer system. *Concurrency and Computation: Practice and Experience*, accepted 2007.

[20] D. Qiu and R. Srikant. Modeling and performance analysis of bittorrent-like peer-to-peer networks. *SIGCOMM Comput. Commun. Rev.*, 34(4), October 2004.

[21] S. Saroiu, K. P. Gummadi, and S. D. Gribble. A measurement study of peer-to-peer file sharing systems. In *MMCN'02*, San Jose, CA, January 2002.

[22] J. Shneidman and D. Parkes. Rationality and self-interest in peer to peer networks. In *IPTPS'03*, Berkeley, CA, February 2003.

[23] V. Vishnumurthy, S. Chandrakumar, and E. G. Sirer. Karma: A secure economic framework for p2p resource sharing. In *P2PEcon'03*, Berkeley, CA, June 2003.

[24] A. Vlavianos, M. Iliofotou, and M. Faloutsos. Bitos; enhancing bittorrent for supporting streaming applications. In *9th IEEE Global Internet Symposium (GI2006)*, Barcelona, Spain, April 2006.

0-7695-2906-2/07 $25.00 © 2007 IEEE

Aggregation Dynamics in Service Overlay Networks

Pietro Michiardi
Institut Eurecom, France
Email: michiardi@eurecom.fr

Paul Marrow, Richard Tateson and Fabrice Saffre
BT Group CTO, Pervasive ICT Research Center, UK
Email: First.Last@bt.com

***Abstract*—In this work we analyze the characteristics of service overlay networks generated by uncoordinated service providers that deploy different service replicas on overlay nodes across the Internet. Our approach differs from previous works, that generally rely on application-level routing, in that we allow nodes to autonomously re-wire the service overlay to make it capable of absorbing a heterogeneously distributed workload that would otherwise result in some nodes with a specific service being overloaded and others remaining idle. We provide a game theoretic model of the overlay creation process and propose several optimization methods to achieve Nash equilibrium topologies. Equilibrium overlays are characterized by interconnected clusters of nodes that instantiate the same service replicas. Hindered by the computational complexity of finding stable wirings, we propose a simple distributed heuristic that allows the study of overlay networks with a realistic size and with several service instances. We show the ability of our re-wiring strategy to promote the emergence of a clustered global topology whilst running locally. We also argue that the lack of incentives for nodes to participate in the overlay creation might lead to several types of misbehavior, of which some representative cases are analyzed. Finally, both scalability and diversity (in terms of service instances) issues that might affect our distributed heuristic are evaluated in detail.**

I. Introduction

In recent years, the Internet has witnessed an evolution towards a commercial infrastructure of service delivery, as opposed to its original intent of simply providing host connectivity. Different forms of overlay networks [1], [2], [4], [10], [14] have been developed to offer attractive service provisioning solutions, which are difficult to be implemented and deployed at the IP-layer. These networks not only provide application-level data routing but also value-added services, such as content distribution services, media compression/transcoding, language translation, encryption or decryption services, etc... In our work we address the realistic scenario where independent and uncoordinated economic entities such as service providers deploy and manage their service instances at multiple locations on the Internet.

We term the logical connections among service provider nodes a *service overlay network*. Overlay nodes offering one or more services receive and process user requests that are fulfilled until a finite service capacity that characterizes each node is reached. In this context, issues of scalability and load-balancing across service replicas become an important domain of research, that has been recently addressed in the literature for example in [16]. Although the literature is rich in examples [3], [5], [6], [15] that achieve load balancing in the traditional client-server model, in [16] the problem of how load can be shared across service replicas in an overlay network is treated as an overlay routing problem. On one hand, previous works do not consider the costs of relaying user traffic (requests and responses) that might affect the latency of the service overlay. On the other hand, all current efforts share a common characteristic that dictate an immutable service overlay network wherein links are created based on the existence of a service level agreement between overlay nodes. Instead, in this work we propose a different approach wherein each node participates to the construction (and maintenance) of the service overlay so that an unevenly distributed workload can be absorbed by the service overlay without relaying user traffic in the overlay.

In particular, the focus of this paper is to study the aggregation dynamics that arise in the context of service overlay networks when nodes are involved in the process of constructing the overlay in a distributed manner. We show that the problem of service overlay construction can be casted as a network creation game, first defined in [11]. We present an *overlay creation game* that accommodates the service load experienced by the nodes and we study equilibrium overlay topologies that are built through their uncoordinated interaction. In our work, we explore several methods for obtaining stable solutions ranging from the traditional iterated *best response* method (for which, inspired by the work in [12], we also give an integer linear programming formulation) to a constrained search method.

Our analysis on the service overlay creation game is hindered by the complexity of computing the best response of a node, which is proven to be NP-hard [11]. Hence, we present a simple heuristic introduced in [17] based on a randomized local algorithm that allows studying the *emergence* of service overlays for systems with a realistic size.

In this work we analyze the ability of a selected set of rules (based on our game theoretic formulation and on our local heuristic) to foster self-organization of what is originally a random graph into a structured network. Scalability issues with respect to the key parameters of system size and diversity (in terms of deployed services) are extensively discussed.

We demonstrate that both an overlay rewiring process based on selfish decisions and on purely local decisions and interactions can result in an efficiently organized structure prone to achieve load-balancing without central planning. We conclude by discussing the implications of some nodes acting maliciously by not following our prescribed local algorithm.

The contributions of this paper can be summarized as

0-7695-2906-2/07 $25.00 © 2007 Crown Copyright

follows:

- we suggest a novel approach that lets nodes self-organize in a service overlay network capable of absorbing a heterogeneous workload generated by clients using the overlay;
- we propose a game theoretic model of service overlay construction wherein the uncoordinated strategic actions of nodes result in a stable wiring of an initially random overlay;
- we evaluate a decentralized heuristic, designed to overcome the computational requirements of the game theoretic approach, that is capable of promoting the emergence of a global overlay topology characterized by clusters of nodes sharing similar traits;
- we study the impact of the lack of incentives for nodes to participate in the re-wiring process of the overlay, and suggest different misbehavior types.

The remainder of this paper is structured as follows: in Section II we detail the system model and architecture; in Section III we give a formal definition of the overlay creation game while in Section IV we present the randomized local search algorithm. In Section V we describe the numerical evaluation of our model and present our results. We illustrate related works in Section VI and conclude in Section VII.

II. UNCOORDINATED SERVICE OVERLAY CREATION

Inspired by the model proposed in [16], in Figure 1 we show an example of a service overlay network: individual service providers deploy their services at overlay nodes which establish logical links to form an overlay network. In the figure we show what we term *exit nodes*, that is those nodes that receive client requests for a service or a set of services.

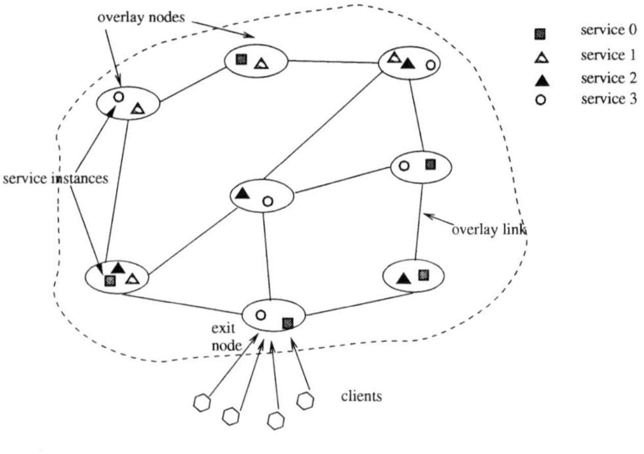

Fig. 1. System architecture under consideration with an example service level path.

While there are several challenges, for example, in the context of *service composition* [16] to enable rapid development of new applications, in this paper we focus on the construction and maintenance of the overlay network. We assume that overlay creation is achieved by the uncoordinated interaction of nodes that wish to minimize their cost, expressed in terms link, communication and load, incurred in the creation and maintenance of overlay links. Given a random unstructured overlay network, the problem we address in this paper is to find *stable* overlay configurations that take into account both load and connectivity constraints. Note that in this work we do not discuss mechanisms to *dispatch* user requests so as to achieve a fair load balancing: the overlay creation process should be seen as an optimization phase prior to the execution of such a mechanism.

A. Assumptions

To improve the tractability of the problem, we limit the scope of our study to physical topologies in which every node can communicate with every other node, that is the *communication graph* (i.e., the underlay physical network) is connected.

With the aim of simplifying the problem formulation we assume that only one service instance is deployed on each overlay node. Hence, in the following a node is equivalent to a service. We define a *type* t_i associated with a node i as the encoded description of the service that it can provide.

Every node i is characterized by a *nominal capacity* λ_n^i which defines the end-user request load a node can handle; λ_c^i identifies the current load experienced by node i. In the following we assume that:

$$\Lambda_n = \sum_{i=1}^{n} \lambda_n^i \, , \Lambda_c = \sum_{i=1}^{n} \lambda_c^i \, , \Lambda_c \leq \Lambda_n \qquad (1)$$

Equation 1 simply states that the system is able to support the requested load, that is, the system does not saturate. In this work we assume no additional end-user requests to be made at run-time.

III. OVERLAY CREATION GAME

In this Section we model overlay creation as a non-cooperative game with n nodes (i.e, players) whose strategies are to select which nodes to connect to. Our model extends the one presented by Fabrikant *et. al.* in [11]. Formally, there is a finite set of players $N = \{1, ..., n\}$, a finite set of player types $T = \{t_1, t_2, ..., t_n\}$ and the strategy space of player $i \in N$ is the list of other players to connect to, i.e., the set $S_i = \{(s_{ij})_{j \neq i} | s_{ij} \in \{0, 1\}\}$ where $|S_i| = 2^{(n-1)}$. Players simultaneously announce the list of other players with whom they wish to be connected. Their decisions generate a (directed) graph $G(s) = (N, s)$: the direction of a link from node i to node j indicates that node i will share its excess load with node j. However, for communication purposes, the link can be seen as bidirectional.

Note that this is a *single-stage* game with *simultaneous* announcements. Our game model requires complete information of the service overlay graph as well as node types and assumes players to be computationally unbounded. In the game, each player selects its strategy to minimize its cost.

The cost incurred by player i when all other players adopt strategy s_{-i} is additive in the cost l_j of a link to players of different type, in the cost l_j of a link to players of the same type modulated by a threshold function based on load information, as well as in the sum of the costs of reaching all other players:

$$c_i(s) = \alpha \sum_{j \in NB_i} (1 - \delta_{t_i,t_j}) l_j + \alpha\, \sigma(\lambda_c^i, \lambda_n^i) \sum_{j \in NB_i} \delta_{t_i,t_j} l_j + \sum_{j=1}^{n} d_{G(s)}(i,j) \quad (2)$$

where NB_i is the set of overlay neighbors for which a direct link exists, $d_{G(s)}(i,j)$ is the shortest path distance from node i to node j in the graph $G(s)$, and δ_{t_i,t_j} is the Dirac-Delta function $\delta_{t_i,t_j} = 1$ if $t_i = t_j$ and 0 otherwise.

The connection cost α represents the relative importance of player i's direct links to others and is the only parameter in the model.

The function $\sigma(\lambda_c^i, \lambda_n^i)$ is defined as follows:

$$\sigma(\lambda_c^i, \lambda_n^i) = 1 - \frac{1}{1 + e^{k(\lambda_c^i - \lambda_n^i)}} \quad (3)$$

$\sigma(\lambda_c^i, \lambda_n^i)$ is used to modulate the linking cost to a node running a replica of the service instantiated in i. When $\lambda_c^i \leq \lambda_n^i$, linking costs can be easily reduced to the model defined by Fabrikant in [11]. However, when $\lambda_c^i \geq \lambda_n^i$ link costs to other nodes with the same instance of the overloaded service in i significantly decrease. Hence, as long as node i can support its current load, it will seek at minimizing communication and linking costs; when the requests load λ_c^i approaches and exceeds the threshold λ_n^i, node i will prioritize the creation of links to overlay nodes that can support requests for the overloaded service.

The total cost of the graph G is then defined as:

$$C(G) = \sum_{i=1}^{n} c_i(s) \quad (4)$$

We now define what constitutes a solution of the game, that is, which overlay topologies result from the overlay creation game. When networks arise from the unilateral action of players, standard Nash equilibrium analysis can be informative about the structure of the networks that emerge. Let $s = s_N = (s_i, s_{N \setminus i})$ and let ζ designate the set of all undirected networks on N.

Definition 1: A network $G(s) \in \zeta$ is a Nash equilibrium network if there exists a strategy s that supports $G(s)$ where $c_i(s) \leq c_i(s'_i, s_{N \setminus i}) \forall i \in N$ and $s'_i \in S_i$.

A. Game optimization process

In this Section we describe three alternative methods that we used to find stable overlay configurations as described in Definition 1. The three methods under investigation share a common algorithmic structure shown in Algorithm 1[1]. The algorithm accepts as input the total number of nodes N that form the service overlay network, the number of edges E for each node i and the total number of types $\hat{T}$ in the overlay. We then generate a random initial overlay configuration and store it as an adjacency matrix. The algorithm outputs a selfishly optimized adjacency matrix where $Strategy^*$ indicates the best response for a node in each iteration. We use a stop criterion based on the definition of the Nash Equilibrium given in Section III.

Algorithm 1: Game Optimization Algorithm

```
Input: N, E, T̂
Output: UpdateAdj
Adj ← generateRandomOverlay(N, E);
TypeVector ← generateRandomTypes(T̂);
UpdateAdj ← Adj;
StopCriteria ← 0;
TotalCost ← 0;
iteration ← 0;
while StopCriteria = 0 do
    iteration ← iteration + 1;
    for i ← 1 to N do
        CurrentCost ← evaluateCost(i, UpdateAdj);
        StrategySpace ←
        generateSSpace(i, UpdateAdj);
        Strategy* ← −1;
        foreach Strategy ∈ StrategySpace do
            TmpMatrix ← UpdateAdj;
            TmpMatrix(i, :) ← Strategy;
            CostNew ← evaluateCost(i, TmpMatrix);
            if CurrentCost − CostNew > 0 then
                CurrentCost ← CostNew;
                Strategy* ← Strategy;
            end
        end
        if Strategy* ≠ −1 then
            UpdateAdj(i, :) ← Strategy*;
        end
        TotalCost(iteration) ←
        TotalCost(iteration) + CurrentCost;
    end
    if
    TotalCost(iteration) ← TotalCost(iteration − 1)
    then
        StopCriteria ← 1;
    end
end
```

In the following we detail three alternative approaches that differ in the way the strategy space available at each overlay node is generated. Our first method is based on an integer linear programming (ILP) formulation of the overlay creation game. This method provides exact solutions to the overlay creation game. In the second method we exhaustively explore all the possible strategies available to a player, which will then select the best response to all other players actions. Although

[1] For clarity of exposure nodes execute the algorithm sequentially. In our implementation nodes execute the algorithm in random order.

0-7695-2906-2/07 $25.00 © 2007 Crown Copyright

very simple to implement, the computational complexity of this approach is an obstacle the study of service overlay when the number of nodes is high. Lastly, we present a variation of the iterated best response method wherein we restrict the strategy available to a node at each round. This method allows to increase the number of nodes participating in the rewiring of the overlay at the cost of finding a selfishly optimized overlay which do not always meet the Nash condition given in Definition 1.

1) ILP formulation: In this Section we formulate of the overlay creation game based on the work presented in [12]. The following general method is used to obtain the best response of a node i when the degree of the connections established by that node (*i.e.*, the out-degree) is bounded by k_i. A wiring for a node i can be defined using $n-1$ binary unknowns Y_l, $1 \leq l \leq N$, $l \neq i$: $Y_l = 1$ iff i wires to l, and 0 otherwise. Define also the binary unknowns $X_{lj} : X_{lj} = 1$ iff i has l as a first-hop neighbor on a shortest path to j. Let $G(s)_{-i} = G(s) - s_i$ denote the *residual graph* obtained from $G(s)$ by taking away node i's outgoing links. A best response for node i under residual graph $G(s)_{-i}$ can be obtained by solving the following Integer Linear Program (ILP):

$$\texttt{minimize}:$$

$$c_i(G(S)_{-i}, X) = \sum_{j=1, j\neq i}^{n} p_{ij} \sum_{l=1, l\neq i}^{n} X_{lj} \cdot (\alpha + d_{G(s)_{-i}}(l,j))$$

$$\texttt{subject to}:$$

$$\sum_{l=1, l\neq i}^{n} X_{lj} = 1, \forall j \neq i; \sum_{l=1, l\neq i}^{n} Y_l = k_i; X_{lj} \leq Y_l, \forall l, j \neq i; \tag{5}$$

where $p_{ij} = 1$ iff $t_i \neq t_j$ and $p_{ij} = \sigma(\lambda_c^i, \lambda_n^i)$ iff $t_i = t_j$. Furthermore, $d_{G(s)_{-i}}(i,j)$ is the shortest path distance from node i to node j in the residual graph $G(s)_{-i}$.

Although the ILP formulation of the selfish optimization problem, as well as the limit on the out-degree of a node help in improving the algorithm execution time, we note that the overlay creation game is hindered by the number of times the Dijsktra algorithm needs to be executed for the evaluation of the cost associated to each feasible strategy. As a consequence, when the number of nodes that form the overlay and the number of service types instantiated on each node increase substantially, the optimization framework adopted in this Section cannot be used.

2) Exhaustive search, Iterated Best-response: Ideally, all of the strategy space available to a node should be examined to determine the action(s) yielding the lowest cost, as defined in Equation 2. The method presented in this Section enumerates for every node i, all the connection vectors that are within the feasible region of the optimization problem and associates a cost computed using Equation 2. Node i will select the connection vector (the strategy) that minimizes its cost. This simple approach limits the size of the network that can be studied, as the time complexity to find all possible strategies a node can have is exponential with the number of nodes (the problem is somehow similar to [11], where it is shown that computing the Nash equilibria for the network creation game is NP-hard).

3) Local search, Iterated Best-response: The following method builds on the Iterated Best-response approach but limits the strategy space of a node i to its (overlay) two-hop neighborhood. The function that associates a cost to each feasible strategy is the one defined by Equation 2. Node i will select the connection vector (the strategy) that minimizes its cost. It should be noted that this local search strategy may converge to overlay configurations that do not meet the Nash conditions. Each node periodically performs two operations: a *Link Drop* and a *Link Add* operations. The link drop procedure computes the cost for node i when each of its neighboring node is dropped. If the difference between the cost c_i of the current configuration and the new configuration without the dropped link is positive, node i updates its neighborhood by dropping the link to the node yielding the lowest cost. We describe the link drop procedure in Algorithm 2.

Algorithm 2: Link Drop procedure for node i

```
Input: i, OverlayAdjMatrix
Output: UpdateAdj
CurrentMatrix ← OverlayAdjMatrix;
NodeToDrop ← −1;
CurrentCost ← evaluateCost(i, CurrentMatrix);
MinCost ← CurrentCost;
foreach j ∈ CurrentMatrix(i, :) do
    tmpMatrix ← CurrentMatrix;
    tmpMatrix(i, j) ← 0;
    CostNew ← evaluateCost(i, tmpMatrix);
    if MinCost − CostNew > 0 then
        MinCost ← CostNew; NodeToDrop ← j;
    end
end
if NodeToDrop ≠ −1 then
    UpdateAdj(i, NodeToDrop) ← 0;
end
```

Using the link addition procedure node i randomly selects a 2-hop neighbor, that is the neighbor of a node to which she has a direct link, that is not the node dropped with the link drop procedure. If the cost c_i evaluated by adding a link to the randomly selected node decreases, then node i updates its current connections by adding a (direct) link to the randomly selected node. We describe the link addition procedure in Algorithm 3.

Note that, as opposed to the method described in Section III-A.2, the selfishly constructed overlay graph depends on the initial number of links E established by each node.

Algorithm 3: Link Add procedure for node i

```
Input: i, OverlayAdjMatrix
Output: UpdateAdj
CurrentMatrix ← OverlayAdjMatrix;
CurrentCost ← evaluateCost(i, CurrentMatrix);
j ←
rand(getTwoHopNeighbors(i, CurrentMatrix));
tmpMatrix ← CurrentMatrix;
tmpMatrix(i, j) ← 1;
CostNew ← evaluateCost(i, tmpMatrix);
if CurrentCost − CostNew > 0 then
  | UpdateMatrix(i, j) ← 1;
end
```

IV. Local Re-wiring of the Service Overlay

The optimization method exposed in Section III-A.3 appears to be very close to a local heuristic, given the structure of Algorithms 2 and 3. However, we cannot adopt this method for the implementation of a distributed algorithm to achieve overlay rewiring: indeed, the hidden characteristic of this method is that local decisions taken by the nodes depend on the cost function defined in Equation 2, which in turns depends on the *entire* overlay graph. In this section we design a completely distributed algorithm that mimics the behavior of the method discussed in Section III-A.3, but which uses local information only. Precisely, we focus on a a very simple algorithm that ignores the costs defined in Equation 2 and that is inspired by the procedures of adding and dropping one overlay link described in the previous Section.

Hence, the goal of this Section is to study the emergence of a given global topology arising from local decision-based rewiring of the service overlay. The literature is rich of local algorithms capable of promoting the emergence of networks characterized by some global properties, one of the most prominent examples being the "preferential attachment" rule proposed in [7] that produces scale-free topologies characterized by a power-law distribution of node degree. However, these algorithms often assume that global knowledge of the network topology (assumption that we also make in our game theoretical model) is available at each node.

In contrast, in this Section we assume that nodes do not have a global view of the system topology nor of the global service type distribution and we study the properties of overlay topologies obtained using a simple heuristic that stems from our game theoretic formulation of the problem.

In Section IV-A we detail our algorithm, called RLS (that we first introduced in [17]), based on *randomized local search* while in Section IV-B we outline possible attacks to the normal execution of the algorithm.

A. Randomized local search (RLS)

Given an initial service overlay configuration, nodes execute a distributed algorithm based on local information only, restricting the visibility of a node in a similar way to the one described in Section III-A.3. We introduce three node roles: the *initiator*, the *mediator* and the *target* role. Initiators and mediators interact so as to match the type associated to the initiator and the target nodes, at the expense of the mediator node that loses one connection. The effect of this rewiring strategy is that the node degree of the initial overlay configuration is preserved. The details of the randomized local search algorithm are given in Algorithm 4[2].

Algorithm 4: Randomized Local Search Algorithm

```
Input: N, E, T, MaxIterations
Output: UpdateAdj
Adj ← generateRandomOverlay(N, E);
Type_Vector ← generateRandomTypes(T);
UpdateAdj ← Adj;
StopCriteria ← 0;
while StopCriteria = 0 do
  | iteration ← iteration + 1;
  | for i ← 1 to N do
  |   | mediator ← rand(getOneHopNeighbors(i));
  |   | while isempty(target)&&TypeVector(i) ≠
  |   | TypeVector(target) do
  |   |   | target ←
  |   |   | rand(getOneHopNeighbors(mediator));
  |   | end
  |   | % Initiator adds link to Target
  |   | UpdateAdj(i, target) ← 1;
  |   | UpdateAdj(target, i) ← 1;
  |   | % V.1: Initiator removes link to Mediator
  |   | UpdateAdj(i, mediator) ← 0;
  |   | UpdateAdj(mediator, i) ← 0;
  |   | % V.2: Mediator removes link to Target
  |   | UpdateAdj(target, mediator) ← 0;
  |   | UpdateAdj(mediator, target) ← 0;
  | end
  | if iteration = MaxIterations then
  |   | StopCriteria ← 1;
  | end
end
```

In Algorithm 4 we sketch two variants of our method: in the first, the Initiator and Mediator nodes lose their connections when a matching node is found, in the second, the Mediator and the Target nodes lose their connections.

B. Rational attacks

Provided that there is no incentive for nodes to take up the role of Mediators, what is the impact of node misbehavior during the execution of the randomized local search algorithm? We try and address this question in the following.

Lack of incentives to follow the rules prescribed by the RLS algorithm are a direct consequence of the fact that a Mediator node might be reluctant to give up a connection (be

[2]For clarity of exposure nodes execute the algorithm sequentially. In our implementation nodes execute the algorithm in random order.

it with the Initiator or the Target) if this might be harmful for subsequent iterations of the algorithm in which the Mediator could switch to the role of Initiator. As an illustrative example consider the scenario in which two node types are present in the service overlay. If the Initiator and the Mediator share the same type, then there is no incentive for them to interact. If the Initiator and Mediator are of different type, for the simple fact of giving up a connection to the Initiator, the Mediator can preclude the possibility of gaining a new neighbor with the same type when its turn to be an Initiator arrives. The same apply if a connection with the Target node is lost.

We thus identified two simple mediator misbehaviors that we describe next:

- Misbehavior 1: the Mediator systematically ignores switch requests by Initiators;
- Misbehavior 2: the Mediator systematically fails in providing the Initiator with a Target sharing the same type.

We analyze the effects of these two node misbehavior when a fixed fraction of the overlay populations is misbehaving in Section V.

V. Numerical Evaluation

In this section we present the experimental setup used to characterize service overlays created both by the selfish optimization algorithm presented in Algorithm 1 (together with Algorithms 2 and 3) and by the RLS algorithm outlined in Algorithm 4. Our goal is to compute the Nash equilibria topologies of the overlay creation game and the stable topologies of the randomized local search algorithm using the methods described in Section III-A.2 and in Section IV. The overlay network graph $G(s)$ is represented by an adjacency matrix.

A. Experimental set-up

The initial conditions of the optimization problem are given by a set of N nodes, a node type vector that identifies which services are instantiated on the N nodes and a randomly generated service overlay. We used several models to generate an initial random deployment of the service overlay, but in this Section we will focus on *k-regular graphs* where the number of randomly chosen outgoing links E is a simulation parameter. We define a maximum number ($\hat{T}$) of different services available in the overlay and uniformly distribute them on the nodes. For every simulation run we randomize on the initial service overlay: in the following all plots are the results of several (50) algorithm executions, while the graphical representation of an overlay depicts an instance of a stable topology.

B. Metrics

In this work we are interested in studying the graph properties of the equilibrium service overlay. In Section V-C and Section V-D and we evaluate the *node degree distribution* that characterize the final stable configuration of the service overlay, when relevant. Furthermore, we study the *overlay homogeneity*, defined as the fraction of links connecting two overlay nodes of the same type. The homogeneity metric indicates to some extent the clustering degree of the overlay: values close to one are preferred over values close to zero.

C. Results for the selfish optimization algorithm

In this Section we discuss on the service overlay topologies that have been obtained with the local best response algorithm discussed in Section III-A.3. For illustrative purposes, we focus on overlay networks with $\hat{T} = 2$ types in the system and we assign equal nominal service capacities to each node, that is $\lambda_n^i = \lambda_n \forall i \in \{N\}\backslash\{i,j\}$, except for two nodes of each of the two types in the system that have a significantly higher nominal capacity. We expect these two nodes to have a high number of incoming links, as this implies current request load to be shared from an overloaded node to a high capacity node. The request load λ_c^i assignment is $\lambda_c^i = \lambda_c = 2 \cdot \lambda_n \forall i \in N$. We specify the linking cost defined in Equation 2.

Figure 2(a) shows the initial service overlay topology where $N = 30$ nodes are randomly deployed with $E = 4$ links per node. Node types are uniformly distributed, and two random nodes of different type are assigned a high nominal capacity, $\lambda_c = 100$: in Figure 2 node 1 and 16 are high capacity nodes. The wiring cost has been set to $\alpha = 100$.

Figure 2(b) shows that high capacity nodes have a high number of incoming links, while all other nodes sharing the same type are highly connected[3]. This is a direct consequence of the cost function of Expression 2: when a node is overloaded, the cost to connect to other nodes of the same type goes to zero, while communication costs still have an impact on the selection of which node is best to connect to. Figure 2(b) clearly shows two highly connected clusters of nodes sharing the same type. This new overlay configuration is prone to be used as a basis for a load dispatching mechanism and link directions indicate that excess load will flow towards nodes with high nominal capacity. It should be noted that the selfishly constructed overlay graph allows messages (*e.g.* maintenance or discovery signaling) to be exchanged by any node at a minimum cost.

The results presented in this Section are in line with those obtained using the simplified method (RLS), that are we extensively reported in the following Section.

D. Results for the randomized local search

This Section summarizes the results for the global self-aggregation dynamics arising from the RLS algorithm described in Section IV. Scalability issues with respect to key parameters such as system size and diversity (in number of types) are extensively studied. Lastly we show the impact of node misbehavior on self-aggregation dynamics.

1) Impact of the initial random overlay structure: Figure 3 show, for a sufficient number of time-steps for the graph to be stable, respectively the aggregated service overlay graph (Figures (a) and (d)), the node degree distribution (Figures (b) and (e)) and the homogeneity (Figures (c) and (f)) for

[3]In the Figure, a link without direction is a bidirectional link.

(a) (b)

Fig. 2. Rewiring process for the local iterated best response algorithm: initial (left) and equilibrium (right) topologies.

an overlay comprised of $N = 500$ nodes and $T = 3$ types. The simulation parameter is the number of random edges E assigned to each node during the system bootstrap.

Figures 3(c, f) show that the configuration of the initial overlay has a negligible impact on the convergence speed to a homogeneous network (in the sense of the definition given in section V-B) and the final homogeneity attained.

2) Impact of the system size and system diversity: In this section we show the sensitivity of the randomized local algorithm to variations in the system size and diversity, when $N = 500$, $T = 3$ and $E = 6$.

Figure 4 a) shows the impact of the system size on the dynamics of aggregation in terms of system homogeneity.

We observe that Algorithm 4 may support service overlay comprised of a very high number of nodes without the convergence speed being affected by the system size, confirming that our simple re-wiring strategy is highly scalable.

In Figure 4 b) we show the impact of the number of types in the system, that is the number of different services instantiated in the service overlay, on the homogeneity of the system.

Figure 4 b) indicates that increasing the number of service types deployed on the overlay may lead to very slow convergence times: results can improve when the initial random overlay is highly connected, at the risk of obtaining an final overlay with disconnected domains.

3) Impact of node misbehavior: In this section we assume a service overlay formed by $N = 500$ nodes (when not specified otherwise) with an initial number of edges $E = 6$ per node. We study the convergence speed of Algorithm 4 varying both the system size and diversity when a fraction of the population is misbehaving following the two models discussed in Section IV-B. In out analysis we vary the (fixed) fraction of misbehaving nodes m in the set $m = \{0.2, 0.5, 0.8\}$, but we plot only results for the two extreme cases for clarity of presentation.

In Figure 5(a,b) we show the impact of an increasing fraction of misbehaving nodes of type 1 when the number of nodes is a fixed parameter and we increase the number of service types instantiated in the overlay.

Figure 6(a,b) shows the impact of misbehaving nodes of type 2 under the same simulation settings described above.

When mediator nodes systematically fail in responding to requests made by initiators wishing to connect to nodes of similar type, the apparent effect as shown in Figure 5(a,b) is a slow convergence speed to a clustered overlay. Only when a very high fraction of nodes misbehave the performance degrades significantly from the case when no illegitimate node are present in the overlay.

The effects of a mediator providing a wrong target to the initiator are more pronounced: even a small fraction of misbehaving nodes of type 2 can disrupt the correct functioning of Algorithm 4, as shown in Figure 6(a,b). Clusters of nodes sharing the same service instance, thus being able to absorb the workload of overloaded nodes, are hardly formed.

In both cases of Figures 5 and 6, the negative effects of a malicious activity are proportional to the number of service types instantiated in the overlay.

In Figures 7(a,b) and 8(a,b) we show the impact on the system size of an increasing fraction of misbehaving nodes of type 1 and type 2 when we vary the (fixed) fraction of misbehaving nodes m.

By observing Figures 7(a,b) and 8(a,b), we conclude that when the system size scales up to a high number of participants, the effects of both types of misbehavior are less pronounced, although the second type of misbehavior is more disruptive.

VI. Related Work

Traditional load balancing has a long history in distributed systems literature. A small sample of previous results, that focus on coordinated and often centralized solutions, includes the following: [15] investigates the online assignment of unit length jobs under the L_∞ norm; [3] considers off-line assignments of unit length jobs; [5] consider greedy assignments of weighted jobs under the L_p norm, where the client-server graph is complete bipartite while [6] considers arbitrary client-server graphs and uses the L_2 norm.

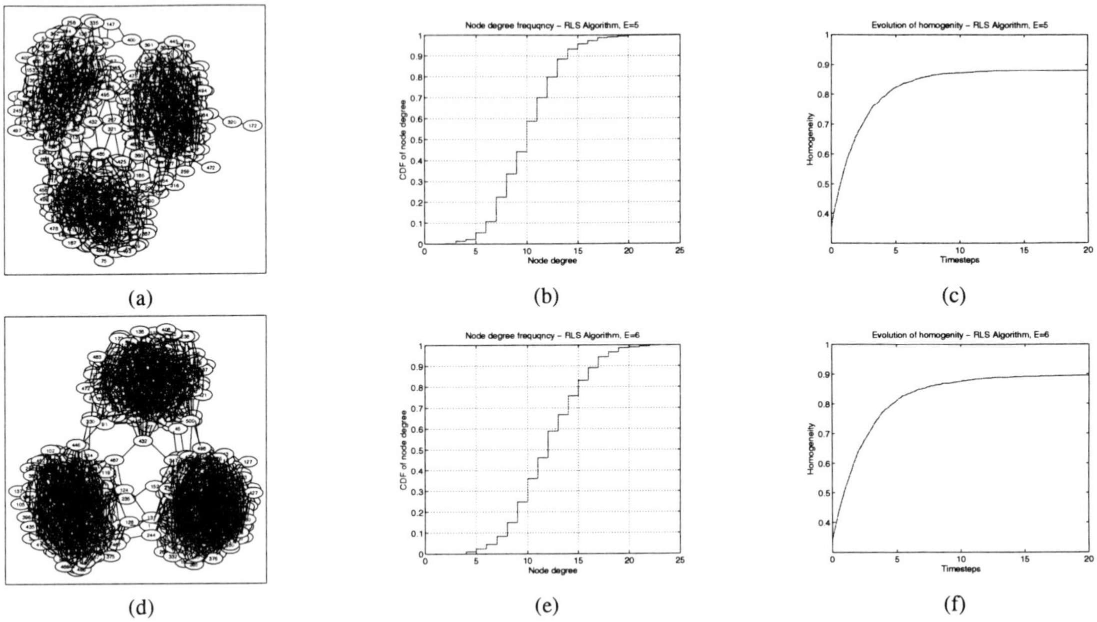

Fig. 3. Stable service overlays (left), Node degree distribution (middle) and Homogeneity plots for overlays with $E = 5$ (first row) and $E = 6$ (second row).

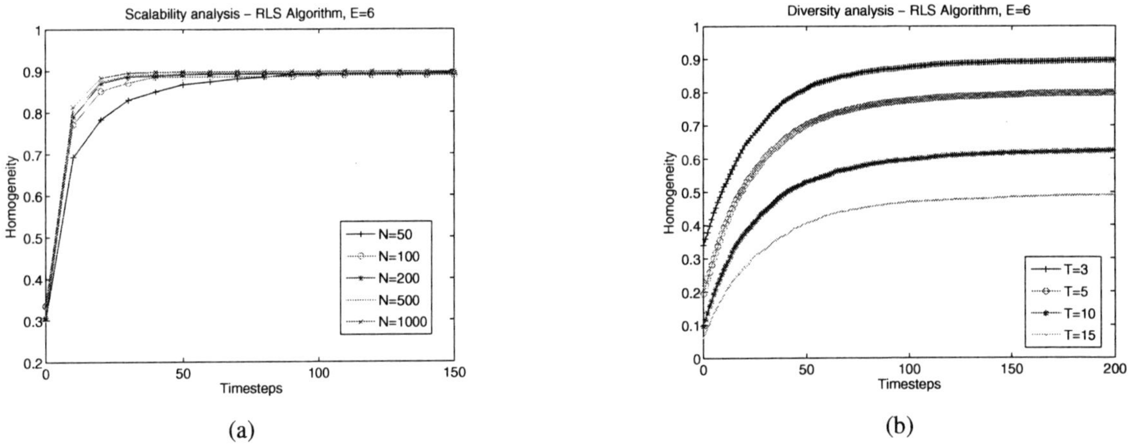

Fig. 4. Impact of system scalability (a) and diversity (b) on the randomized local search algorithm.

Uncoordinated load balancing has been studied, using game theory for example, in [18], [19]. Congestion games are at the heart of these works: uncoordinated, selfish clients compete to select servers providing the lowest response time (latency). Client latencies are related to the server loads. Server response time is assumed to be inversely proportional to the speed of the server, but grows with the p-th power of the number of users connected to the server. As we point out in Section I this framework is not suitable to meet the connectivity requirements of the service overlay.

The work presented in [16] from which we borrow the system model achieves load balancing among service replicas through overlay routing. The link metric adopted to select overlay service paths is inversely proportional to the capacity available at nodes on the service path. Note that load information is disseminated in the overlay so as to update the link cost metric.

The works that are closely related to ours are presented in [8], [9], [11], [13]. Fabrikant *et. al.* first present the network creation game that they use to characterize Internet topologies [11]. Their model accounts for link creation and communication costs and the resulting graph is generated by the unilateral interaction of selfish players. This model is extended in [9], where the authors consider equilibrium topologies that arise from the bilateral interaction of selfish players; in their model, link cost is paid by both vertices of an edge in the equilibrium graph. [8] presents an extension of the basic model in [11] wherein an application-level routing overlay is constructed by selfish overlay nodes. In [13], the authors study a class of simple protocols that aim to self-

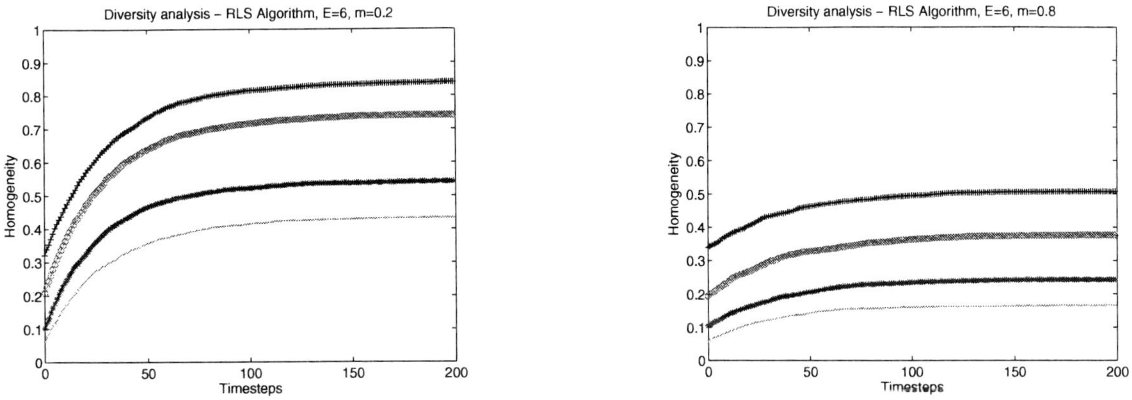

(a) (b)

Fig. 5. Impact of an increasing fraction of misbehaving nodes of type 1 on the randomized local search algorithm for a service overlay with different number of service types ($\hat{T}$).

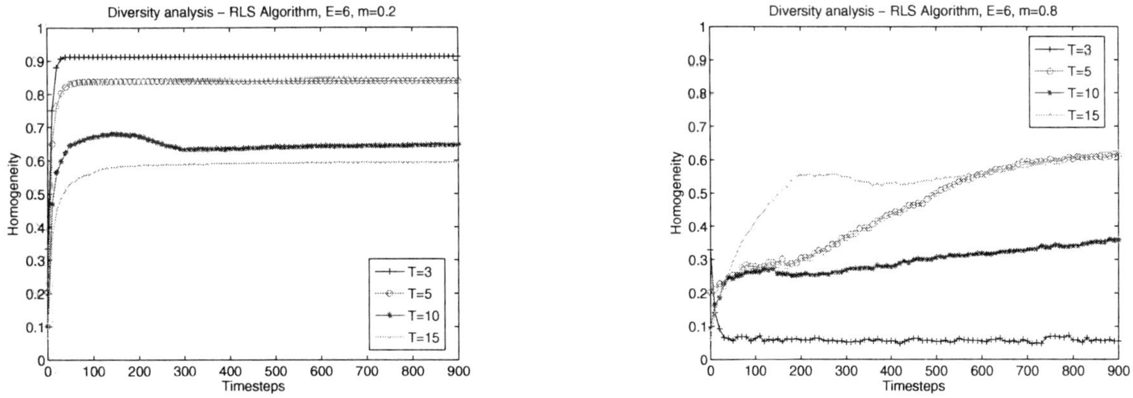

(a) (b)

Fig. 6. Impact of an increasing fraction of Misbehaving nodes of type 2 on the randomized local search algorithm for a service overlay with different number of service types ($\hat{T}$).

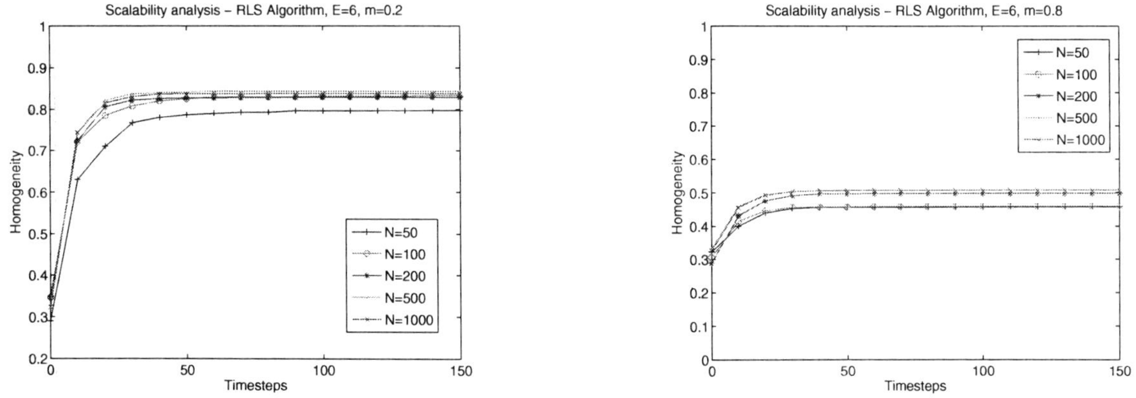

(a) (b)

Fig. 7. Impact of an increasing fraction of Misbehaving nodes of type 1 on the randomized local search algorithm for different sizes of the service overlay.

organize P2P networks into clusters of altruistic nodes that help each other to complete jobs requiring diverse skills. The authors also use a modeling approach akin to game theory, but explore the emergence of clusters when peers mimic the strategies of neighboring nodes. Our work is in line with [13] regarding the definition of a method where nodes select

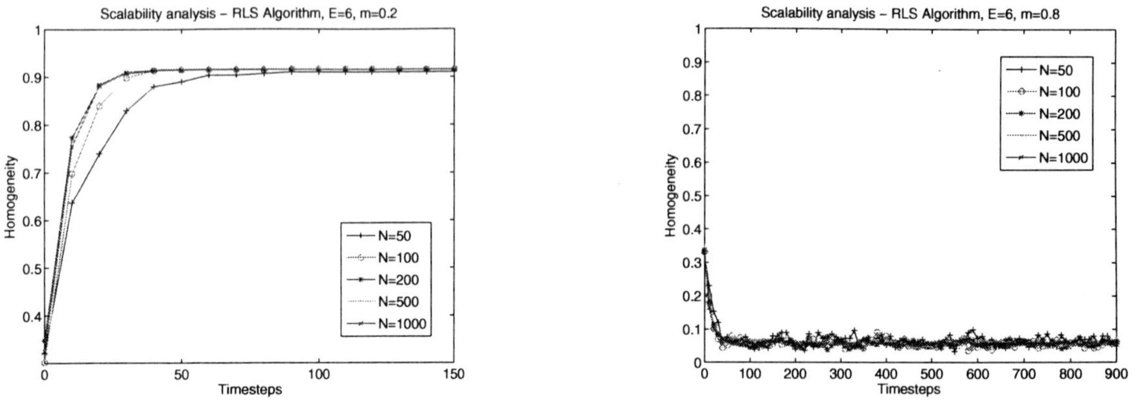

(a) (b)

Fig. 8. Impact of an increasing fraction of Misbehaving nodes of type 2 on the randomized local search algorithm for different sizes of the service overlay.

behaviors for the good of the overlay even though their actions are based on individual greedy utility maximization.

VII. Conclusion and Future Work

In this paper we presented a game theoretic model and a distributed algorithm for the formation of service overlay network. We analyzed three methods to attain equilibrium overlay topologies based on variants of the iterated best response algorithm and on an ILP formulation. The game theoretic analysis presented in the first part of this work allowed to formalize the problem of the overlay creation and characterize its structure, while providing intuitive results. However, the optimization methods proposed using the game theoretic framework had the underlying problem of requiring the global knowledge of the overlay graph. Hence, with the goal of presenting a fully distributed algorithm and improving the computational tractability of the service overlay formation process we proposed a local heuristic which mimics the game theoretic approach and studied the emergence of structured overlay topologies, wherein nodes sharing similar traits aggregated to form clusters. We studied the scalability of our heuristic and the impact of the system diversity, showing that node aggregation based on service types is efficient even when the system is large and when the number of different service instances is high. As a glimpse to another problem akin to a game theoretic formulation we studied aggregation dynamics when a fraction of overlay nodes misbehave following different models and showed that node misbehavior due to lack of incentives may jeopardize the aggregation process. As part of our future work, we seek to enrich our approach by assuming a time-varying workload and study overlay creation in the context of repeated games. We intend to explore incentive mechanisms to foster the participation of overlay nodes in the aggregation process.

Acknowledgments

This work has been partially funded by the Integrated Project CASCADAS (FET Proactive Initiative, IST-2004-2.3.4 Situated and Autonomic Communications) within the 6th IST Framework Program.

References

[1] Planet lab. http://www.planet-lab.org/.
[2] Snap: Structured overlay networks application platform. http://www.planet-lab.org/.
[3] N. Alon, Y. Azar, G. J. Woeginger, and T. Yadid. Approximation schemes for scheduling. In *Proc. of ACM SODA*, 1997.
[4] D. G. Andersen, H. Balakrishnan, M. F. Kaashoek, and R. Morris. Resilient overlay networks. In *Proc. of ACM SOSP*, 2001.
[5] A. Avidor, Y. Azar, and J. Sgall. Ancient and new algorithms for load balancing in the l_p norm. *Algorithmica*, 29:422–441, 2001.
[6] A. Awerbuch, A. Azar, E. F. Grove, P. Krishnan, M. Y. Kao, and J. S. Vitter. Load balancing in the l_p norm. In *Proc of IEEE FOCS*, 1995.
[7] A. L. Barbasi, R. Albert, and H. Jeong. Mean-field theory for scale-free random networks. *Physica*, A 272:173–187, 1999.
[8] B-G. Chun, R. Fonseca, I. Stoica, and J. Kubiatowicz. Characterizing selfishly constructed overlay routing networks. In *Proc. of IEEE INFOCOM*, 2004.
[9] J. Corbo and D. Parkes. The price of selfish behavior in bilateral network formation. In *Proc. of ACM PODC*, 2005.
[10] Z. Duany, Z. Zhangy, and Y. T. Houz. Service overlay networks: Slas, qos and bandwidth provisioning. In *Proc. of IEEE ICNP*, Paris, France, November 2002.
[11] A. Fabrikant, A. Luthra, E. Maneva, C. H. Papadimitriou, and S. Shenker. On a network creation game. In *Proc. of ACM PODC*, 2003.
[12] N. Laoutaris, G. Smaragdakis, A. Zestravos, and J. W. Byers. Implications of selfish neighbor selection in overlay networks. In *Proc. of IEEE Infocom*, 2007.
[13] A. Marcozzi and D. Hales. Emergent social rationality in a peer-to-peer system. Technical report, Department of Computer Science, University of Bologna, 2006.
[14] P. Maymounkov and D. Mazieres. Kademlia: A peer-to-peer information system based on the xor metric. In *Proc. of IPTPS*, Cambridge, MA, USA, March 2002.
[15] S. Philips and J. Westbrook. Online load balancing and network flow. In *Proc. of ACM STOC*, 1993.
[16] B. Raman and R. H. Katz. Load balancing and stability issues in algorithms for service composition. In *Proc. of IEEE INFOCOM*, 2003.
[17] F. Saffre, J. Alloy, M. Shackelton, and J. L. Deneubourg. Self-organized service orchestration through collective differentiation. *IEEE Transactions on Systems, Man, and Cybernetics - Part B: Cybernetics*, 26(6):1237–1246, 2006.
[18] S. Suri, C. D. Toth, and Y. Zhou. Selfish load balancing and atomic congestion games. In *Proc. of SPAA*, 2004.
[19] S. Suri, C. D. Toth, and Y. Zhou. Uncoordinated load balancing and congestion games in p2p systems. In *Proc. of HOT-P2P*, 2004.

Research Track, Session 5: Data Collection and Aggregation

Shruti: A Self-Tuning Hierarchical Aggregation System*

Praveen Yalagandula
HP Labs, Palo Alto, CA
praveen.yalagandula@hp.com

Mike Dahlin
The University of Texas at Austin
dahlin@cs.utexas.edu

Abstract

Current aggregation systems either have a single inbuilt aggregation mechanism or require applications to specify an aggregation policy a priori. It is hard to predict the read and write access patterns in large systems and hence applications built on such systems suffer from inefficient network usage. We present Shruti, a system that demonstrates a general approach for self tuning the aggregation aggressiveness to the measured workload in the system, thus optimizing the overall communication costs (e.g., the number of messages exchanged on read and write operations).

1 Introduction

Generic information aggregation frameworks such as Astrolabe [22], MDS-2 [6], and SDIMS [25] can serve as an important building block for constructing large-scale distributed services such as system management [9, 23], application placement [24], data sharing and caching [18, 20], sensor monitoring and control [11, 13], grid resource monitoring [6, 8], multicast tree formation [2, 14], and naming and request routing [5]. Such frameworks allow scalable information monitoring by forming one or more aggregation trees spanning machines in the system and by using an aggregation function at the root of each subtree to summarize the information in the subtree's leaves.

Unfortunately, existing aggregation systems use a static aggregation strategy that can perform well for some workloads but poorly for others, which prevents any system from being a truly general solution. For example, *read-dominated* attributes such as *numCPUs* tracking the number of CPUs on a physical node rarely change in value, while *write-dominated* attributes such as *numProcesses* tracking the number of processes running on a machine change quite often. An aggregation approach tuned for read-dominated attributes will consume high bandwidth when applied to write-dominated attributes. Conversely, an approach tuned for write-dominated attributes will suffer from unnecessary query latency or imprecision for read-dominated attributes. Also, the read-write access patterns may differ for different sets of nodes (spatial heterogeneity) and may change over time (temporal heterogeneity) requiring different aggregation strategies at different times and at different parts of the system [1, 19].

Most aggregation systems have a single fixed aggregation mechanism. For example, in Astrolabe [22], aggregation is performed at all levels in the aggregation tree and the aggregated values at each level are propagated to all nodes in the subtree on writes. Such a strategy might incur high communication overheads when aggregating attributes that change often. To limit the communication cost, Astrolabe throttles the rate at which information is propagated around in the system, which might lead to unnecessary inconsistency in probe responses for attributes that rarely change. In most tree based systems such as Ganglia [9] and most DHT-based systems [18, 20], aggregation is performed up to the root on writes. In MDS-2 [8], no aggregation is performed on writes but the information is aggregated on reads.

SDIMS [25] is the first aggregation framework that allows applications to control the aggregation aggressiveness in the system. SDIMS provides two knobs, `UP` and `DOWN`, that applications set at the installation phase of an aggregation function. These knobs denote how far up aggregation is performed in an aggregation tree and how far down the aggregate values at a level are propagated on updates in the system. SDIMS also allows applications to perform *continuous* probes to handle spatial and temporal heterogeneity. Though SDIMS exposes such flexibility to applications, it requires applications to know the read and write access patterns a priori to choose an appropriate strategy.

In this work, we present Shruti, a self-tuning system built on SDIMS that tracks reads and writes at different levels in an aggregation tree and dynamically decides how far up aggregation is performed and how far down aggregate values are propagated on writes. Shruti self-tunes the aggregation aggressiveness aiming to optimize the overall communication costs (the sum of read and write message costs). We

* This work is supported in part by the NSF Grant SCI-0438314 and by the University of Texas at Austin's Center for Information Assurance and Security.

0-7695-2906-2/07 $25.00 © 2007 IEEE

propose a *lease*-based mechanism in which a node grants a lease for an aggregate value to its parent or a child to denote that it will forward any changes to that aggregate value.

Our simulation results show that at any static globally uniform read-write operation ratio in the system, Shruti incurs similar cost as an optimal static UP and DOWN strategy for that ratio. Also, in contrast to SDIMS's policy of enforcing a single strategy across all attributes using same aggregation function, Shruti tunes to different strategies for different attributes and thus achieves half-an-order magnitude lower average messages per operation. Our results show that Shruti outperforms static aggregation strategies at almost all read-write ratios when there is a spatial heterogeneity in the access patterns. Finally, we also show that Shruti efficiently tunes to temporal heterogeneity in the read and write patterns and thus reduces communication costs by 50% in comparison to a static SDIMS policy.

2 Background: SDIMS

We base our system on SDIMS [25], the first aggregation framework that allows applications to control the aggregation aggressiveness in the system. In this section, we briefly describe the aggregation abstraction exposed by SDIMS and describe how it exposes flexible aggregation mechanisms to applications.

The aggregation abstraction in SDIMS is defined across a tree spanning all nodes in the system. An example aggregation tree is illustrated in Figure 1. Each physical node in the system is a leaf and each subtree represents a logical group of nodes. An internal non-leaf node is simulated by one of the physical nodes at the leaves of the subtree rooted at that node. Each physical node has *local data* stored as a set of (*attributeType*, *attributeName*, *value*) tuples such as *(configuration, numCPUs, 16)*, *(mcast membership, sessionfoo, yes)*, or *(file stored, foo, myIPaddress)*. The system associates an *aggregation function* f_{type} with each attribute type, and for each level-i subtree T_i in the system, the system defines an *aggregate value* $V_{i,type,name}$ for each (attributeType, attributeName) pair as follows. For a (physical) leaf node T_0 at level 0, $V_{0,type,name}$ is the locally stored value for the attribute type and name or NULL if no matching tuple exists. Then the aggregate value for a level-i subtree T_i is the aggregation function for the type, f_{type} computed across the aggregate values of each of T_i's k children. We illustrate a simple SUM() aggregation function in Figure 1.

Given this abstraction, SDIMS [25] leverages Distributed Hash Tables (DHTs) [18, 20] to construct multiple aggregation trees, and it maps different attributes to different trees. SDIMS leverages self-organizing properties of DHTs to repair the aggregation trees as reconfigurations happen in the system.

A major innovation of SDIMS is enabling flexible aggre-

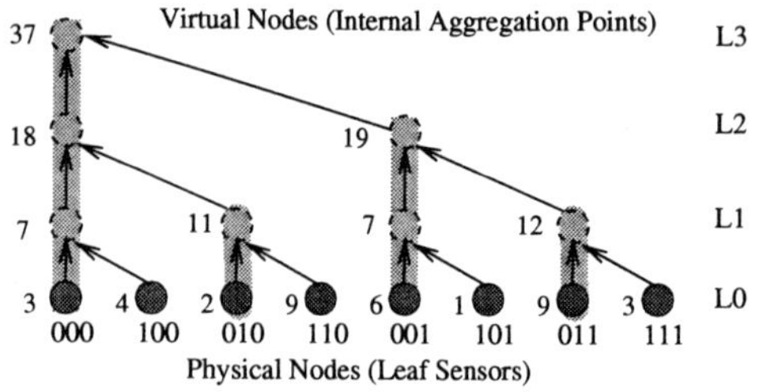

Fig. 1. An SDIMS aggregation tree in an eight node system aggregating values using SUM() aggregation function.

gate computation and propagation. While previous aggregation systems [9, 18, 20, 22] implement a single static strategy, SDIMS allows applications to choose an appropriate aggregation scheme by providing three functions: install, update, and probe. *Install()* installs an aggregation function for an attribute type and specifies the update strategy that the function will use, *Update()* inserts or modifies a node's local value for an attribute, and *Probe()* obtains an aggregate value for an attribute for a specified subtree level. The install interface allows applications to specify UP and DOWN parameters along with the aggregation function. The UP parameter denotes until how many levels aggregation is performed on update to an attribute. The DOWN parameter defines for how many levels downwards the aggregated value at a level is propagated. Figure 2 (from [25]) illustrates few interesting aggregation strategies for different values of UP and DOWN in SDIMS.

Need for Self-Tuning Aggregation: Though SDIMS allows applications to explicitly control aggregation aggressiveness, an application needs to know the update and probe patterns a priori to effectively set those knobs. But, predicting the operation patterns in advance might be impossible in real distributed applications. Consider a Content Distribution Network (CDN) serving webpages for a major sporting event. This CDN can leverage SDIMS to track copies of webpages on content servers. For each copy of webpage w on a content server, the server will perform an update for attribute *(CDN, w)* with tuple $\langle$*IP,TimeStamp*$\rangle$ as value where *IP* is the IP address of the content server and *TimeStamp* is the last modified timestamp of the webpage. The aggregation function is to choose tuples with the highest timestamp value so that the global aggregate value reflects the IP addresses of servers holding the most recent copies of a webpage. When contacted by a client, a content server performs a probe for the global aggregate to locate the recent copies.

In such a system, if we choose an aggregation strategy as in typical DHT based applications, UP=all and DOWN=0, then probes for an attribute from a node need to traverse the overlay path from that node to the root of that attribute's aggregation tree. During flash-crowds, this approach can imply a drastic increase in the probe traffic. Note that simple caching might not mitigate the problem in our exam-

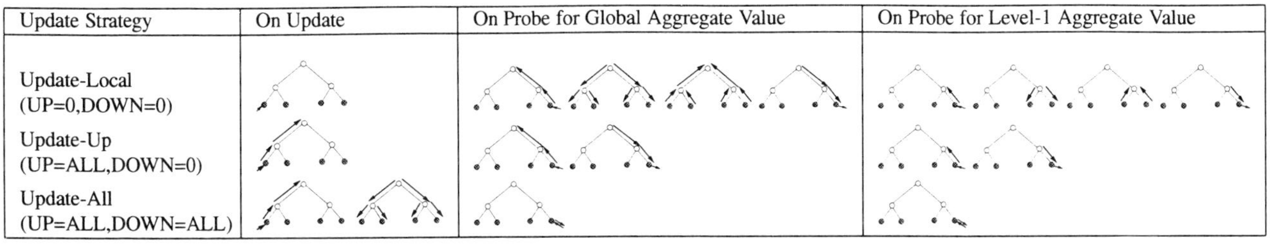

Fig. 2. Example strategies with SDIMS `UP` and `DOWN` knobs.

ple as the content of the webpages changes frequently (as scores change in a sports event). Also note that the probe patterns can drastically vary across the individual servers of the CDN serving different portions of the Internet. So, a static `UP` and `DOWN` parameter values can be insufficient for handling spatial and temporal heterogeneity in the access patterns. Also, the update and probe rates for different attributes can vary by a large magnitude because the read popularity of webpages typically follow a Zipf-like distribution independent of the update rates [1]. But, SDIMS's aggregation abstraction imposes same `UP` and `DOWN` strategy for all attributes of the same type.

3 Shruti: Architecture

Shruti dynamically alters the propagation of aggregate values on updates so that overall communication cost—the number of messages incurred on probes and updates—is minimized. Shruti tracks updates and probes happening at all nodes in an aggregation tree and chooses an appropriate aggregation strategy based on that information. Shruti runs on each node in the aggregation tree and decides when that node will send any updates in the aggregate value to the node's parent and children. We propose a *lease*-based architecture where a node conveys its intention to keep forwarding any updates for an aggregate to another node by granting a lease for that aggregate. In the following sections, we present more details about the lease architecture, data structures that Shruti maintains to track updates and probes, how Shruti makes leasing decisions, and how Shruti handles reconfigurations.

3.1 Leases

In SDIMS, applications let all nodes in the aggregation tree know how far to propagate the aggregate values on writes by setting `UP` and `DOWN` values at the install time of an aggregation function for an attribute type. All nodes need to know this information so that when a node gets a probe it can decide whether its local state includes the aggregate value needed for answering the probe. For example, consider an attribute with `UP`=all and `DOWN`=2. We illustrate how aggregates are propagated for a part of an aggregation tree in Figure 3. Since `UP` is set to all, the level-l node A

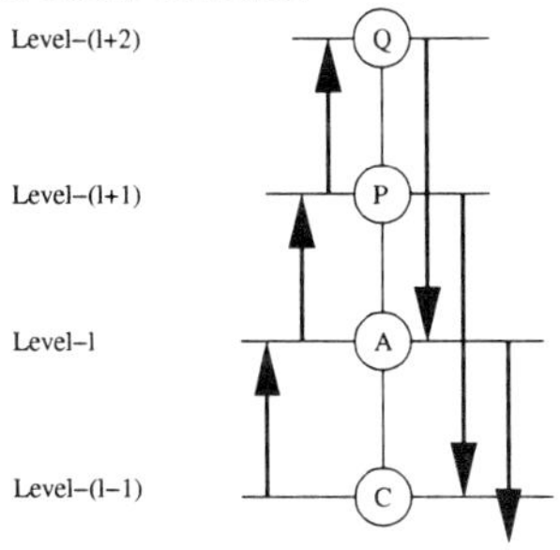

Fig. 3. Aggregate value propagation in a part of a tree for `UP`=all, `DOWN`=2.

knows that it has to propagate any updates to the level-l aggregate to its parent. Since `DOWN` is two, it propagates the level-l aggregate and also any updates it receives from its parent for the level-$(l+1)$ aggregate to its children. Similarly, this node's parent will propagate down any changes to either the level-$(l+1)$ aggregate or the level-$(l+2)$ aggregate. Now, if this node receives a probe for the level-$(l+2)$ aggregate, then it can respond without needing to further probe its parent. By knowing `UP` and `DOWN` a priori for an attribute, each node knows the rendezvous points between updates and probes for that attribute.

If we want to dynamically adapt the aggregation aggressiveness based on the workload for an attribute, then nodes in the tree need to have enough information for responding to probes. Shruti employs a *lease*-based scheme to control the level of aggregation upon updates and to let each node know how to respond to probes. A level-l node that has leases from all its children can respond to probes for the level-l aggregate without needing to probe its children. If it also has the lease from the parent for a level $l' > l$ aggregate, then it can respond to the probes for the level-l' aggregate without needing to send a probe to its parent. In Shruti, after a node A grants a level-l lease to another node B, then node A will send any changes to the level-l aggregate value until node B relinquishes that lease or node A revokes the lease.

Shruti does not exclusively work with leases to decide the propagation of aggregate values in an aggregation tree. Shruti also respects any application specified install time `UP` and `DOWN` parameters for an attribute type. Shruti uses the lease-based technique to extend the propagation of aggregate values in an aggregation tree beyond the amount of

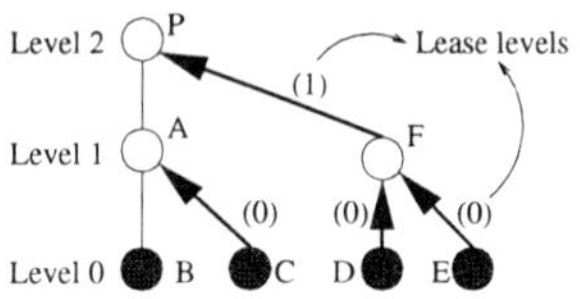

Fig. 4. An example lease state in an aggregation tree.

propagation an SDIMS static strategy allows. For example, if UP=all and DOWN=0 setting is chosen at install time of an attribute type, Shruti will always at least propagate changes in aggregate values up to the root of an aggregation tree. Shruti might further propagate aggregates down the tree to optimize communication bandwidth.

Invariants To respond correctly to probes, the leases that Shruti sets need to satisfy certain invariants. Consider the state of leases for an attribute in the Figure 4. We assume that the corresponding type is installed with UP=0 and DOWN=0. We show leases with thick arrows and denote the levels corresponding to leases in parenthesis next to the arrows. Note that in this state, node A cannot grant level-1 lease to its parent as it does not have the level-0 lease from one of its children B. Consider a situation where node A indeed granted the level-1 lease to its parent P. Since updates to the level-0 aggregate at node B are not propagated to node A, updates to the level-1 aggregate that node A propagates to its parent P will be incorrect. Any probe initiated at machines in the subtrees rooted at siblings of A (e.g., machine D) will receive an incorrect probe response. Another point to observe in Figure 4 is that node F cannot grant the level-2 lease to its children as it does not have the level-2 lease from its parent.

In the following, we present two invariants that Shruti maintains during setting up and tearing down leases to ensure correct rendezvous between probes and updates.

Invariant 1 *A level-l node can grant level-l lease to either parent or a child if and only if it has level-$(l-1)$ leases from all its children or if* UP$\geq l$.

Invariant 2 *A level-l node can lease level $l' > l$ to a child if and only if (i) it has the level-l' lease from its parent, (ii) if it has no parent, or (iii) if* UP $\geq l'$ *and* DOWN $\geq (l'-l)$ *holds.*

The above invariants also imply the following two conditions regarding when a node can relinquish a lease it has obtained from a neighbor of that node.

1. A node can relinquish a level-l' lease received from its parent only if it has not granted level-l' lease to any child.
2. A level-l node can relinquish a lease acquired from a child only if it has not granted a level-l lease to any other node.

3.2 Leasing Policy

Shruti keeps track of the updates and probes at each node and dynamically sets up and tears down leases between nodes to optimize overall communication costs. Briefly, it is useful for a node A to grant a level-l lease to another node B only if the number of messages that A and B exchange on probes when the lease is not granted is greater than the number of update messages that A has to forward to B after granting the lease. Note that each probe causes exchange of two messages between A and B—one for the query and one for a response; whereas each update causes only one message between two nodes. So a lease can be granted if we expect the number of probes to be even half of the number of updates. When the number of updates a node receives goes beyond two times the number of probes, then it is better to remove the lease.

We exploit dynamic adaptation of the aggregation strategies not only to optimize overall communication costs but also to trade-off bandwidth with probe response latencies. For example, if leases are set aggressively (say even when we expect probes to be far less than the half of the number of updates) but removed lazily (say remove only when the number of updates is four times more than the number of probes), then the average probe response times will be smaller but at the cost of increased communication costs. Shruti provides two knobs for the applications to control the lease aggressiveness: one knob to decide how leases are granted and another to decide how they are removed. Overall, Shruti supports and extends the flexibility provided by the static UP and DOWN SDIMS strategies.

In the following, we first describe the data structures that Shruti maintains on each node and then describe the knobs that Shruti exposes to the applications to set a leasing policy.

Data Structures Shruti maintains several logs for tracking updates and probes happening at each node. On a level-l node in an aggregation tree, Shruti maintains the following logs with timestamps:

- **LocalHistory** On each node, Shruti maintains timestamps of the most recent probe and update for each level from either its parent or any of its children. On a level-l node, the updates and probes for level $l' \geq l$ are accounted for the respective level l'. But updates received from the node's children for level-$(l-1)$ aggregate are accounted as updates for level l, since those updates affect the level-l aggregate.
- **NeighborHistory** This data structure on a node is used to track all probes and updates for all levels from each neighbor of a node (parent and children). A node maintains neighbor history for a level-l' aggregate with respect to another node B (aka history of updates and probes from node B for level l') only if node A can

Algorithm 1 OnProbe(*fromNode, reqLevel*)

```
timestamp ← current time
Add (probe, timestamp) to LocalHistory[reqLevel]
/* Check if invariants allow us to grant a lease for this level */
if canLease(reqLevel) then
    Add (probe, timestamp) to NeighborHistory[fromNode][reqLevel]
    lastUpdateTime ← timestamp of the most recent update from LocalHistory[reqLevel]
    numProbes ← number of probes in NeighborHistory[fromNode][reqLevel] with timestamp > lastUpdateTime
    if numProbes >= m then
        Grant lease for reqLevel aggregate to fromNode
else
    Clear all probes from NeighborHistory[fromNode][reqLevel]
```

Algorithm 2 canLease(*reqLevel*)

```
myLevel ← this node's level
if reqLevel > myLevel then
    if UP ≥ reqLevel AND DOWN ≥ (reqLevel−myLevel) then
        return true
    else if reqLevel ∈ LeasesReceived(parent) then
        return true
    else
        return false
else if reqLevel == myLevel then
    if UP ≥ myLevel then
        return true
    else
        for each child C ∈ children do
            if (reqLevel−1) ∉ LeasesReceived(C) then
                return false
        return true
return false
```

Algorithm 3 OnUpdate(*fromNode, level*)

```
timestamp ← current time
Add (update, timestamp) to LocalHistory[level]
/* Check if invariants allow us to relinquish a lease for this level. */
if level ∈ LeasedFrom(fromNode) AND canRelinquish(level) then
    Add (update, timestamp) to NeighborHistory[fromNode][level]
    checkLevel ← (level < myLevel)?myLevel:level
    /* Note that children of a level-l node send level-(l − 1) updates and affect level-l aggregate */
    lastProbeTime ← timestamp of the most recent probe from LocalHistory[checkLevel]
    numUpdates ← number of updates in NeighborHistory[fromNode][level] with timestamp > lastProbeTime
    if numUpdates >= k then
        Relinquish lease for level aggregate from fromNode
else
    Clear all updates from NeighborHistory[fromNode][level]
```

grant the level-l' lease or has received the level-l' lease from node B.

- **LeasesGranted** and **LeasesReceived** We maintain the leases a node acquired from and leases granted to either its parent or its children in these data structures. These data structures are indexed on the neighbor.

Granting and Relinquishing leases Shruti at a node uses the history of updates and probes from another node to predict the future update-probe patterns from that node. We assume that the patterns observed in the near past reflect the near future behavior. When invariants for granting a level-l lease are satisfied at a node A, we use the following

Algorithm 4 canRelinquish(*level*)

```
myLevel ← this node's level
if level < myLevel then
    level ← myLevel
if level ∈ LeasesGranted(parent) then
    return false
for each child C ∈ children do
    if level ∈ LeasesGranted(C) then
        return false
return true
```

general rule to decide whether to grant the level-l lease to a node B or not—grant the lease if m probes are received from node B while no updates happened to the level-l aggregate. In Algorithm 1, we present the pseudo-code for actions performed by Shruti on receiving a probe from another node. The pseudo-code for checking whether granting a lease would violate any invariant is shown in Algorithm 2.

Similar to the rule for setting a lease, we use the following rule for relinquishing a level-l' lease granted by a parent P to node A—relinquish the lease if k updates are received from the parent P while no probes are received for the level-l' aggregate. Similarly a level-$(l-1)$ lease granted by a child C is relinquished if k updates are received from the child C while no probes are received for the level-l aggregate. Note that updates for level-$(l-1)$ from a node's children affect the value of level-l aggregate at the node. The pseudo-code for Shruti's actions on receiving an update is shown in Algorithm 3. We present pseudo-code checking whether relinquishing a lease violates any invariant in Algorithm 4.

Consider an example with k=2 and m=1. A node A that can grant a level-l lease to node B grants that lease to B as soon as it gets a probe from B. And node B relinquishes that lease if it gets two updates from node A for that aggregate while not receiving any probes for that aggregate.

The two knobs k and m control how aggressively leases are set and how aggressively they are removed. A setting where k is about twice the value of m performs optimally in terms of number of messages. A large value for k and a small value for m cause leases to be set aggressively but to be removed lazily leading to better probe response times but at increased bandwidth.

3.3 Default Lease State

To be efficient and be scalable with *sparse attributes*, Shruti on each node at level-l for an attribute starts with a state where it assumes that it has level-$(l-1)$ leases from all its children and has granted a lease for the level-l aggregate to its parent.

Sparse attributes are attributes that are of interest to only few nodes in the system and only those nodes perform update or probe operations for that attribute. In most practical systems with a large number of attributes, all nodes will likely not be interested in all attributes. For example, up-

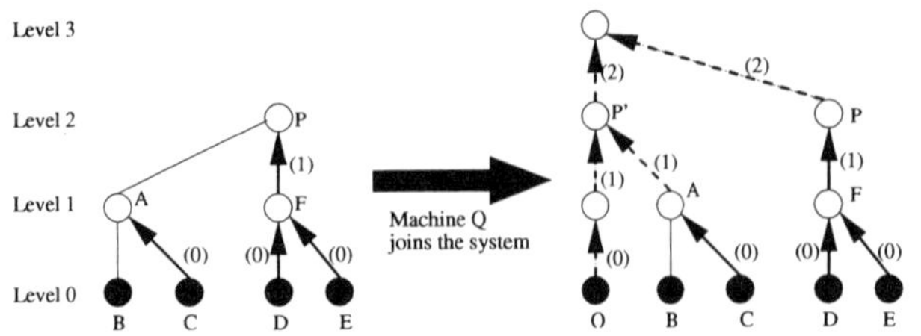

Fig. 5. Violation of Invariant 1 on reconfiguration: Node A does not have lease from B while it has lease granted to its parent. The dotted arrows represents the default leases assumed for new nodes.

dates and probes to an attribute corresponding to a multicast session with small membership will generally be done only by its members.

If nodes were to start in a state where no leases are granted for an attribute and with default UP=0 and DOWN=0, the first probe operation would incur $2.N$ messages in an N node network, as the probe would have to collect information from all nodes in the system. Thus, even for sparse attributes that are of interest to only a handful of nodes, all nodes in the system would be touched by the first few probes for that attribute until leases are set. Once leases are set, those uninterested nodes would not receive any more messages regarding the attribute. But explicitly setting leases implies that all nodes have to maintain some information about all attributes whether they are interested in that attribute or not. Hence this hypothetical initial state would undermine Shruti's ability to scale to large numbers of attributes.

Instead, by starting in a lease state in which Shruti on each node for all attributes assumes that it has leases granted from all its children and has granted a lease for the local aggregate to its parent, the unnecessary leasing information need not be explicitly maintained. Hence only nodes that are interested in an attribute and nodes helping these interested nodes in aggregation of the attribute will ever maintain any explicit information about the leases (when leases are relinquished or when leases are further granted down to children), thus achieving scalability with sparse attributes.

3.4 Reconfigurations

Reconfigurations will be a norm in any large distributed system, and in the face of reconfigurations, the invariants for leases might not continue to hold at one or more nodes in the system. Invariant 1 is violated when a level-l node in an aggregation tree acquires a new parent when it does not have level-$(l-1)$ lease from one of its children. For example, consider an aggregation tree in a four machine system shown on the left in Figure 5. In this aggregation tree, all invariants are satisfied. Suppose machine Q joins and the aggregation tree reconfigures as shown on the right in the

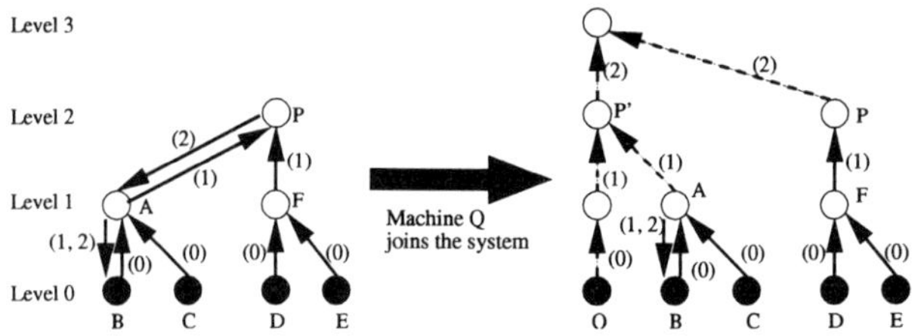

Fig. 6. Invariant 2 violation on reconfiguration. A has granted a level-2 lease to its child but does not have level-2 lease from its parent.

figure. As discussed in the previous section, new nodes start with a lease state where each level-l node assumes that it has level-$(l-1)$ lease from all its children. The dotted arrows show the default leases assumed when machine Q joins the system. At node A, Invariant 1 is violated. The parent of node A, node P', has level-1 lease from node A while node A does not have level-0 from one of its children B.

Similar to the violation of Invariant 1, Invariant 2 might be violated during reconfigurations. We show an example case where such violation occurs in Figure 6. Note that node A before reconfiguration has the level-2 lease from its parent P which it granted further down to one of its children B. When it acquired a new parent P', node A no longer has the level-2 lease from its parent but still has an outstanding level-2 lease to its child, violating Invariant 2.

In the face of reconfigurations, the goal of Shruti is to revert to a state conforming to all invariants. Observe that invariant violations occur only when a node gets a new parent. Acquiring a new child or losing an existing child does not affect the consistency of leases at a node. At a node where an invariant violation occurs, Shruti revokes leases that violate invariants. For example, when Invariant 1 is violated at a node due to acquiring a new parent, that node revokes the lease to its parent. In the example shown in Figure 5, node A revokes the level-1 lease to its new parent P'. Similarly, when Invariant 2 is violated at a node, that node revokes leases it granted to its children that violate invariants. For example, node A in Figure 6 revokes its level-2 lease to node B after it gets new parent P'.

A node that receives revocation of a lease from its parent or one of its children might have to further revoke some leases that this node granted to other nodes. For instance, when a node receives revocation of a level-l lease from its parent, it has to further revoke any level-l leases it has granted to its children. Also, when a node at level-l receives revocation of level-$(l-1)$ lease from one of its children, then it should revoke any level-l leases it has granted.

Note that while lease revocation is in progress, some of the probes might receive incorrect responses. But once the system becomes stable (no machine or network failure events or no new machine join events), Shruti on each node attains a state satisfying invariants through revoking zero

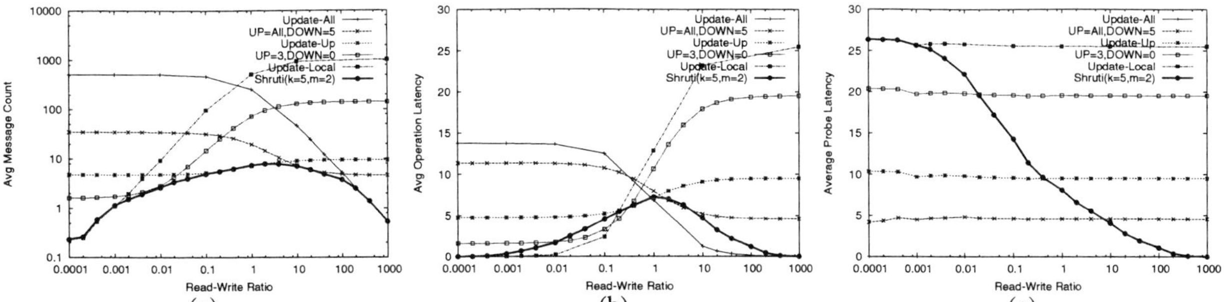

(a) (b) (c)

Fig. 7. Shruti vs. SDIMS static `UP` and `DOWN` for a wide range of read-to-write ratios: (a) Average message cost per operation, (b) Average latency per operation, and (c) Average probe latency.

or more leases it has granted to other nodes. Once invariants are satisfied in the lease state, all probes receive correct responses. In a separate effort [12], we address how an aggregation system can expose *network imprecision* so that a probe response can explicitly indicate whether a system is sufficiently stable for invariants such as this to hold.

4 Experimental Evaluation

We present our experimental results on Shruti comparing its performance to static up and down strategies for a wide range of update and probe patterns, referred to as read-write ratios, and with spatial and temporal heterogeneity in the access patterns. We focus on two metrics—communication cost and operation latency. Our evaluation shows that Shruti (i) adapts to the access patterns and approximates the optimal static strategy for a static and globally uniform read-write ratio, (ii) adapts to spatial heterogeneity in the access patterns across nodes to outperform any single static strategy, and (iii) quickly adapts to temporal heterogeneity such as changing access patterns.

We simulate a 512-node aggregation system, and we install a simple summation operation as the aggregation function. A write at a node for an attribute increments the previous value for the attribute at that node. We initially update each attribute at each node with a value of one. All probes are for the global aggregate value. We simulate 50000 operations for each aggregation strategy in each experiment.

Single attribute, uniform read-write ratios across nodes In this first set of experiments, we consider a single attribute and uniform read-write ratios across all nodes. For such a workload, there exists an optimal static `UP/DOWN` strategy, and we examine whether Shurti's self-tuning succeeds in balancing costs and benefits to match that strategy. In Figure 7(a), we plot the measured average message cost per operation in Shruti comparing it to different static up and down strategies in SDIMS. We use values of 5 and 2 for *k* and *m* (recall that *k* and *m* determine the aggressiveness with which leases are set and removed as explained in Section 3.2), respectively, in Shruti. Observe that at each read-write ratio, Shruti approximates the behavior of an optimal up-down SDIMS strategy at that ratio.

In Figure 7(b), we plot the average latency per operation (both updates and probes considered) in Shruti and in SDIMS. We consider each overlay hop to consume a unit of latency. Note that whereas any static strategy that behaves well at some read-to-write ratios incurs a high operation latency at other read-to-write ratios, Shruti performs well at all read-to-write ratios. For example, although the Update-all strategy performs optimally in terms of operation latency for read-to-write ratios greater than one, it incurs a high communication cost for read-write ratios less than one when compared to Shruti (Figure 7(a)).

In Figure 7(c), we plot the average probe response latencies with different read-to-write ratios for static up-down strategies and Shruti. We assume that each overlay hop has unit latency. Note that Shruti adapts to reduce overall communication bandwidth and hence incurs different latencies at different read-write ratios. When probes are rare (e.g., low read-write ratio), Shruti minimizes update cost, which increases probe latency, but as probes become more frequent, Shruti's self-tuning algorithm shifts work to the updates reducing probe latencies. All static strategies have fixed average probe response latencies.

Varying *k* and *m* in Shruti In Figure 8, we plot the average message cost observed for different values of *k* and *m* in Shruti while varying the read-to-write ratios. As expected, for large values of k and small values of m, the system adapts quickly to probes but slowly to writes; hence, it performs better at large read-write ratios but suffers at small read-write ratios. In Figure 9, we compare the average probe latency for these different strategies. Observe that the probe-favoring higher *k* compared to *m* strategies result in smaller probe latencies. We conclude two key points from these set of results: (1) *k*=5 and *m*=2 or *k*=5 and *m*=3 are good default values for *k* and *m* as Shruti performs better with these values than with any other settings and (2) applications that intend to reduce the response latency at the cost of higher bandwidth can use a more aggressive leasing

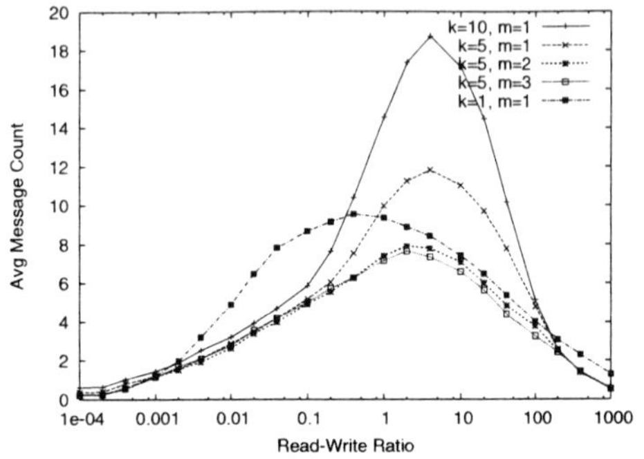

Fig. 8. Average message cost per operation in Shruti for different values of k and m.

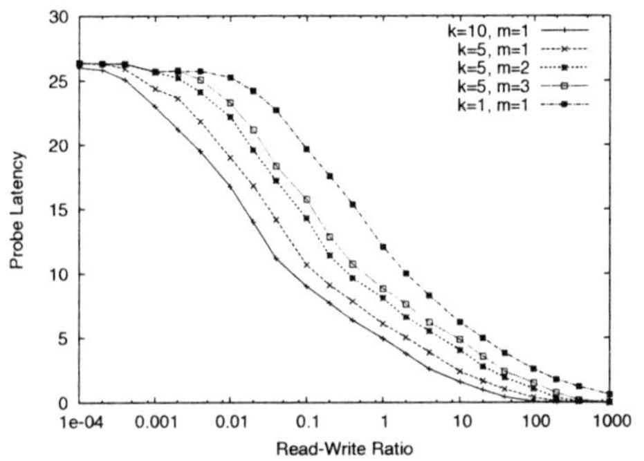

Fig. 9. Average probe latency in Shruti for different values of k and m.

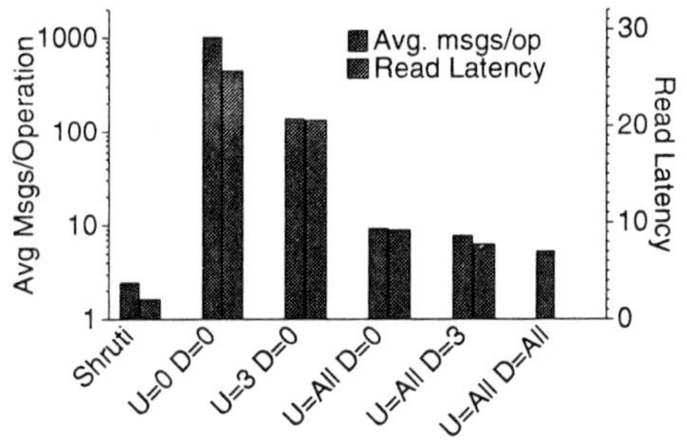

Fig. 10. Multiple attributes case: Shruti (k=5, m=2) vs SDIMS static `UP` and `DOWN` strategies.

policy by setting a high value for k and a small value for m.

Multiple attributes, Zipf-like distribution in probes Studies have shown that web accesses and P2P queries follow Zipf-like distribution [1, 19] with respect to the objects. Here, we study the performance of Shruti when probes to attributes follow Zipf-like distributions [1] (the ith popular attribute gets C/α^i fraction of probes) with $\alpha = 1.3$. The write operations are assigned to different attributes in a uniform way. We simulate 100 attributes, all of same type, with a global average read-to-write ratio of 100. In Figure 10, we present the average number of messages per operation and average probe latency incurred by Shruti compared to a set of SDIMS strategies with different static up and down values. Clearly, Shruti achieves both lower communication cost and smaller average probe response time than SDIMS's

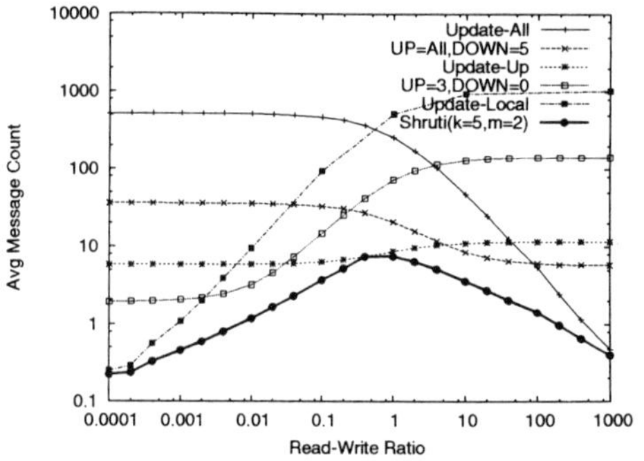

Fig. 11. Spatial heterogeneity: Average message count – Shruti vs. SDIMS strategies

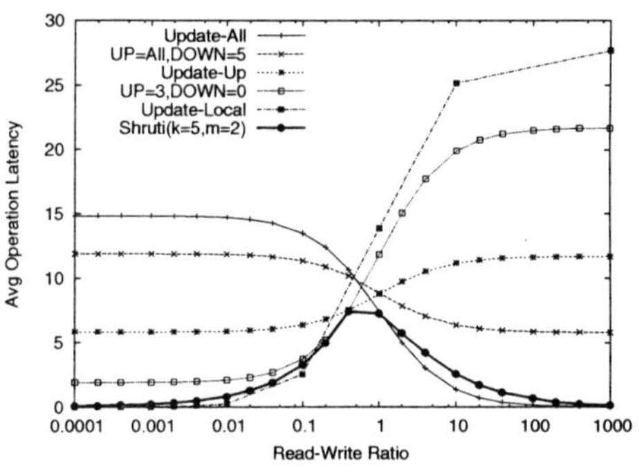

Fig. 12. Spatial heterogeneity: Average operation latency – Shruti vs. SDIMS strategies

static strategy through adapting aggregation aggressiveness separately for each individual attribute.

Spatial heterogeneity The distribution of updates and probes for an attribute will not be uniform across nodes in a real system. For example, for an attribute corresponding to a multicast session, typically only members of that multicast session perform most update and probe operations. We simulate a single attribute operation rates at nodes following a Zipf-like distribution with $\alpha = 1.3$. In Figures 11 and 12, we plot the average number of messages per operation and average operation latency incurred in Shruti in comparison to that incurred by a set of SDIMS strategies for different read-to-write ratios. Note that Shruti achieves lower communication costs compared to the first set of results in Figure 7(a) as it exploits the spatial heterogeneity to set leases such that updates and probes are propagated to only nodes interested in that attribute.

Temporal heterogeneity The read-write ratio for attributes change over time as attributes become popular and then as popularity fades. In this experiment with three phases each with 20000 operations, we start with a read-to-write ratio of 0.01 in the first phase, change it to 100 in the second phase, and revert back to 0.01 in the final phase. We measure the number of messages incurred per each operation and compare Shruti with a SDIMS Update-UP (`UP`=all and `DOWN`=0) strategy. In Figure 13, we compare the per-phase and overall average message cost for Shruti

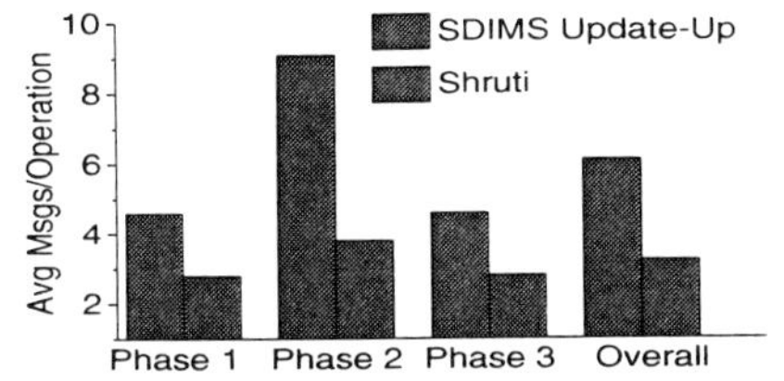

Fig. 13. Temporal heterogeneity: Average message count per operation in Shruti vs. SDIMS for three phases of the experiment.

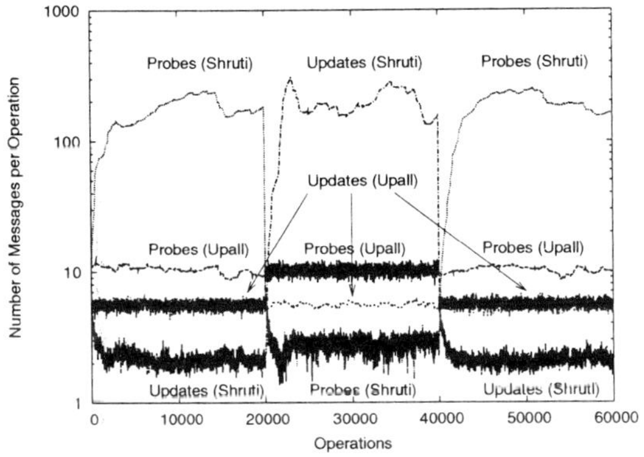

Fig. 14. Temporal heterogeneity: Number of messages per operation in Shruti vs. SDIMS `UP`**=all and** `DOWN`**=0.**

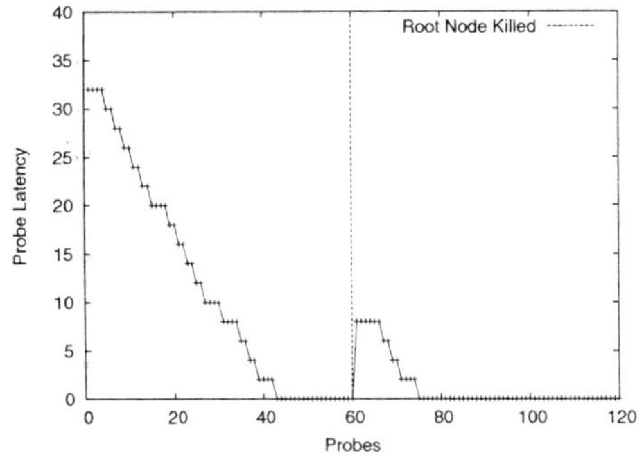

Fig. 15. Reconfiguration handling: Latency of probe operations. After sixty probes, we kill the root node of the aggregation tree.

with the SDIMS strategy. We also plot number of messages incurred per each operation in Figure 14. Note that whereas the SDIMS static scheme incurs a similar number of messages on every operation irrespective of the read-write-ratio, Shruti adapts to the observed read-write ratios and thus incurs lower communication costs.

Reconfigurations We demonstrate Shruti's reconfiguration handling capability in this experiment. As described in Section 3.4, when a virtual node in an aggregation tree loses its parent or obtains a new parent during a reconfiguration event, then the virtual node might revoke some of the leases it has granted to other nodes so that invariants are satisfied. As leases are revoked, probes might experience increased latency. With Shruti running on 1024 nodes, we first perform several write operations for an attribute at all nodes so that all leases are removed. We then perform several probes from a machine so that leases are set from all leaves to the root of the aggregation tree and on the path from the root to the probing leaf. In Figure 15, we plot the response latency of probe operations. After sixty probes, we kill the root node which causes revocation of leases on the path from the root node to the probing node. Hence the following probes suffer higher latency until the leases are set again from the new root down to the probing node.

5 Related Work

Existing aggregation systems use a static aggregation strategy that can perform well for some workloads but might perform poorly for others. Astrolabe [22] employs an *Update-All* type aggregation mechanism, DHTs and DHT based systems(e.g., [18, 20]) use an *Update-Up* mechanism, and Globus' MDS-2 [6] uses an *Update-None* mechanism.

The Controlled Update Propagation (CUP) protocol by Roussopoulos et al. [17] and Overlook [21], a name service system, are closely related to Shruti. CUP addresses a similar problem in the context of updating cached results of *get* operations in DHTs and Overlook replicates name service content along a tree to reduce lookup latency of DNS resolve queries. Though CUP, Overlook, and Shruti share the idea of using lease-based techniques, they differ in the design choices leading to different tradeoffs. First, CUP and Overlook only consider replicating the root content at other nodes; they build upon the DHT architecture and hence assume that aggregation is performed up to the root on writes. So they dynamically control the propagation of updates only downwards where as Shruti controls update propagation even towards the root. For Overlook, which is a naming service where the number of updates will be far less than the number of probes for any entry, such downward only propagation control is appropriate. In SDIMS, we consider different attributes with different behaviors. For an attribute that is updated by only a single node and no other node probes for that attribute, it is inefficient to even aggregate the data up to the root in the corresponding aggregation tree. Second, the maintenance overheads are different in these three systems. In CUP, each replicated object at a node expires unless refreshed by the parent for that object. So, the maintenance overhead is on the order of the number of objects. In Overlook and Shruti, a replicated object at a node expires if the parent that gave the lease fails. So, lease maintenance overhead involves tracking liveness of the parents of a node; hence an overhead in the order of the number of parents a node has. Whereas a node might have $O(N)$ parents in the worst case in Overlook, each node in Shruti has to track only $O(\log N)$ other nodes, where N is the number of nodes in the system.

Other closely related projects are Beehive by Rama et al. [16] and SCAN by Chen et al [3]. In Beehive, no updates are considered and the goal is to place a minimum number of replicas such that all queries are satisfied with a constant communication cost, assuming queries follow a Zipf distribution. Chen et al. solve a similar problem of placing a minimum number of replicas while satisfying client QoS requirements and server constraints. Cohen et al. study replication strategies in unstructured P2P networks [4].

Lease-based techniques are employed in many distributed systems such as replicated file systems [10] and web caching and replication [7, 26]. All web replication research consider the case where updates to objects happen at a single server. Yin et al. propose volume leases [26] where a server issues a volume lease with a short timeout period and object leases with a long timeout period. This helps in reducing the communication from the server to the replicas while ensuring strong consistency guarantees. In Shruti, each node pings its neighbors frequently to check their liveness (similar to short volume lease timeout) and considers all leases that a neighbor issued to be valid as long as the neighbor is alive or the lease is either relinquished or revoked (similar to long object lease timeout).

6 Conclusions

Current aggregation systems either have single inbuilt aggregation mechanism or require applications to specify aggregation policy a priori. It is hard to predict the read and write access patterns in large systems in advance and hence such systems suffer from inefficient network usage. We present Shruti, a system that demonstrates a general approach for self-tuning the aggregation aggressiveness to the measured workload in the system optimizing the overall communication costs (e.g., the sum of costs for reads and writes). Our simulation studies demonstrate the effectiveness of dynamic adaptation in reducing communication costs for wide range of workloads. In a separate effort [15], we explore theoretical bounds for the efficacy of our tuning algorithm with leases.

References

[1] L. Breslau, P. Cao, L. Fan, G. Phillips, and S. Shenker. Web caching and zipf-like distributions: Evidence and implications. In *Proceedings of IEEE Infocom*, 1999.

[2] M. Castro, P. Druschel, A.-M. Kermarrec, A. Nandi, A. Rowstron, and A. Singh. SplitStream: High-bandwidth Multicast in a Cooperative Environment. In *SOSP*, 2003.

[3] Y. Chen, R. H. Katz, and J. D. Kubiatowicz. SCAN: a Dynamic Scalable and Efficient Content Distribution Network. In *First Intl. Conf. on Pervasive Computing*, Aug 2002.

[4] E. Cohen and S. Shenker. Replication strategies in unstructured peer-to-peer networks. In *SIGCOMM*, 2002.

[5] R. Cox, A. Muthitacharoen, and R. T. Morris. Serving DNS using a Peer-to-Peer Lookup Service. In *IPTPS*, 2002.

[6] K. Czajkowski, S. Fitzgerald, I. Foster, and C. Kesselman. Grid information services for distributed resource sharing. In *Proc HPDC*, Aug 2001.

[7] V. Duvvuri, P. Shenoy, and R. Tewari. Adaptive leases: A strong consistency mechanism for the world wide web. In *Proceedings of IEEE Infocom*, Mar. 2000.

[8] I. Foster, C. Kesselman, C. Lee, R. Lindell, K. Nahrstedt, and A. Roy. A distributed resource management architecture that supports advance reservations. In *IWQoS*, 1999.

[9] Ganglia: Distributed Monitoring and Execution System. `http://ganglia.sourceforge.net`.

[10] C. Gray and D. Cheriton. Leases: An Efficient Fault-Tolerant Mechanism for Distributed File Cache Consistency. In *Proc. SOSP*, pages 202–210, 1989.

[11] C. Intanagonwiwat, R. Govindan, and D. Estrin. Directed diffusion: a scalable and robust communication paradigm for sensor networks. In *MobiCom*, 2000.

[12] N. Jain, D. Kit, P. Mahajan, P. Yalagandula, M. Dahlin, and Y. Zhang. PRISM: Precision-aware Aggregation for Scalable Monitoring. Technical Report TR-06-22, Department of Computer Sciences, UT Austin, 2006.

[13] S. R. Madden, M. J. Franklin, J. M. Hellerstein, and W. Hong. TAG: a Tiny AGgregation Service for Ad-Hoc Sensor Networks. In *OSDI*, 2002.

[14] A. Nandi, A. Ganjam, P. Druschel, T. E. Ng, I. Stoica, H. Zhang, and B. Bhattacharjee. SAAR: A Shared Control Plane for Overlay Multicast. In *NSDI*, 2007.

[15] C. G. Plaxton, M. Tiwari, and P. Yalagandula. Online Aggregation over Trees. In *IPDPS*, 2007.

[16] V. Ramasubramanian and E. G. Sirer. Beehive: O(1) Lookup Performance for Power-Law Query Distributions in Peer-to-Peer Overlays. In *NSDI*, March 2004.

[17] M. Roussopoulos and M. Baker. CUP: Controlled Update Propagation in Peer-to-Peer Networks. In *USENIX*, 2003.

[18] A. Rowstron and P. Druschel. Pastry: Scalable, Distributed Object Location and Routing for Large-scale Peer-to-peer Systems. In *Middleware*, 2001.

[19] K. Sripanidkulchai. The popularity of gnutella queries and its implications on scalability, 2001. White Paper.

[20] I. Stoica, R. Morris, D. Karger, F. Kaashoek, and H. Balakrishnan. Chord: A scalable Peer-To-Peer lookup service for internet applications. In *ACM SIGCOMM*, 2001.

[21] M. Theimer and M. B. Jones. Overlook: Scalable Name Service on an Overlay Network. In *ICDCS*, 2002.

[22] R. VanRenesse, K. P. Birman, and W. Vogels. Astrolabe: A Robust and Scalable Technology for Distributed System Monitoring, Management, and Data Mining. *TOCS*, 2003.

[23] M. Wawrzoniak, L. Peterson, and T. Roscoe. Sophia: An Information Plane for Networked Systems. In *HotNets'03*.

[24] R. Wolski, N. Spring, and J. Hayes. The network weather service: A distributed resource performance forecasting service for metacomputing. *Journal of Future Generation Computing Systems*, 15(5-6):757–768, Oct 1999.

[25] P. Yalagandula and M. Dahlin. A scalable distributed information management system. In *SIGCOMM 2004*.

[26] J. Yin, L. Alvisi, M. Dahlin, and C. Lin. Volume Leases to Support Consistency in Large-Scale Systems. *IEEE Transactions on Knowledge and Data Engineering*, Feb. 1999.

An Autonomy Oriented Computing (AOC) Approach to Distributed Network Community Mining

Bo Yang[1,2], Jiming Liu[2]
[1] College of Computer Science and Technology, Jilin University, Changchun, P.R.China
[2] Department of Computer Science, Hong Kong Baptist University, Kowloon, Hong Kong
ybo@jlu.edu.cn, jiming@comp.hkbu.edu.hk (corresponding)

Abstract

A network community is a special sub-network that contains a group of nodes sharing similar linked patterns. A distributed network community mining problem (D-NCMP) is concerned with finding all such communities from a distributed network. A variety of applications in WWW and ad-hoc networks such as P2P and sensor networks can be formulated into D-NCMPs, in which both resources and controls are distributed and/or decentralized. The problem is difficult for some existing methods to deal with because of the fact that their required global topological representations of distributed networks are hard to obtain. In this paper, we present an autonomy oriented computing (AOC) approach [15], in which the nodes and links of a distributed network are distributed among a group of autonomous agents that collectively find global communities hidden in the network. In doing so, the agents maintain only their respective local views and update them through a proposed self-organization process. The effectiveness of the AOC based approach has been validated using network examples.

Keywords: *Autonomy Oriented Computing (AOC), Self-organization, Distributed Network Community Mining*

1. Introduction

A network community corresponds to a group of nodes, within which the links are dense but between which they are sparse, as illustrated in Fig.1. A network community mining problem (NCMP) is essentially a problem of finding all such communities from a given network.

A wide variety of problems can be formulated into NCMPs. They include social network analysis [1,2], biological network analysis [1,2,4], Web page clustering [5,6], and image segmentation [7]. So far many algorithms have been proposed to address NCMPs. These algorithms generally fall into three main categories: (1) bisection methods such as spectral methods [7,8] and the Kernighan-Lin algorithm[9]; (2) hierarchical methods, such as agglomerative methods based on structural metrics [10] and divisive methods based on betweenness metrics, such as the GN algorithm [1] and the Radicchi algorithm [11]; and (3) methods for mining hyperlink-based Web communities, such as the HITS algorithm [5] and the MFC algorithm [6].

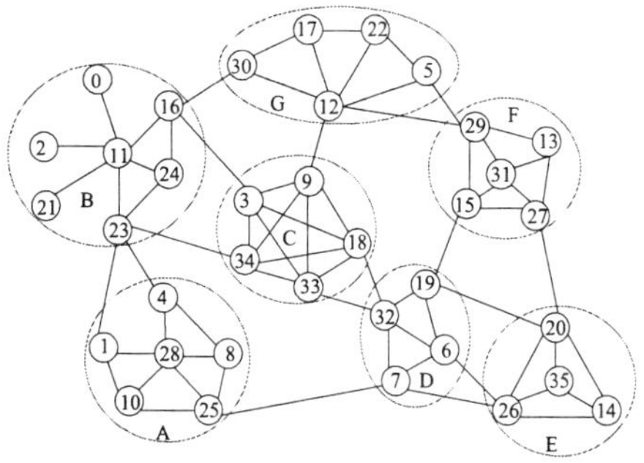

Figure 1 A representation of network communities as inspired by [3]. The simple network describes the communication relationships between 32 mobile agents running in an ad-hoc network containing seven portable computers. Seven communities denoted by A to G are detected based on their communication relationships. Within each community, the communications between agents are frequent, whereas between them, the communications are rare. In order to improve the efficiency of the entire network, those agents belonging to the same communities should autonomously move to and/or share the same computers.

Hyperlinked-based Web communities are groups of Web pages, in which pages are highly linked to each other. Finding such a kind of Web communities is very useful for foraging information on the Web. This is because such self-organized Web communities are often highly special topic-related [6]. The MFC algorithm tries to find Web communities based on the Max Flow-Min Cut theorem through iteratively finding and cutting the “bottleneck edges” between two communities. The HITS aims to find a special hyperlinked community that is defined as a collection of authorities and hubs mutually linked together.

However, the networks concerned by most of the existing methods or algorithms as mentioned above are centralized rather than distributed and dynamically updating. In fact, in the areas of WWW and ad-hoc networks, many applications involve distributed and dynamic networks where resources and controls are not only distributed and/or decentralized, but also frequently updated. These applications call for new approaches to a new type of NCMP, which we refer to as distributed NCMP (or D-NCMP). In short, the D-NCMP is concerned with finding all communities from a distributed and dynamically evolving network.

For instance, one of the tasks in building an online enterprise system is to efficiently manage and utilize the vast amount of information about customers. The information may be distributed and dynamically updated, and can be represented into semantically meaningful networks. Such distributed, dynamically evolving complex networks contain different types of virtual communities with respect to different semantic attributes, such as IP addresses, users’ profiles, interests, and contacts. In these networks, individuals within the same community are most likely to share similar interests. Therefore, being able to discover such communities can greatly help an enterprise to effectively segment its customers into different groups and hence to provide corresponding personalized services based on such hidden knowledge.

In this paper, we will formally define the D-NCMP and present an autonomy oriented computing (AOC) approach to solving it [15]. In our approach, a group of computational entities or agents are dispatched into a distributed network; they autonomously work with and update their local views and collectively partition the complete network into various natural communities, by means of local view self-organization. The AOC approach is applicable in two situations: (1) the network to be processed is distributed and/or decentralized in nature, e.g., WWW, and its complete topological representation is either unavailable or too difficult to obtain because of its distributed nature and/or large scale, and (2) the computation has to be carried out in a distributed fashion, because a centralized control is not feasible, e.g., in an ad-hoc sensor network or in a privacy-preserved environment.

Recent research on sensor networks has addressed the problem of autonomous clustering, in an attempt to reduce the energy consumption of sensors or to easily control a group of homogenous sensors. For instance, Bae and Yoon have proposed an algorithm that can autonomously cluster geographically adjacent sensors into groups and specify a head for each group at the same time [12]. In their approach, the data to be transmitted to sinks will first be aggregated at each cluster head. This significantly decreases the data volume to be sent and thus cut down the energy consumption in data communication. Other related studies can be found in [13,14], which are concerned with clustering a sensor network into groups, where the variables monitored by sensors, such as the temperature and pressure of different sites on ocean surface, show similar changing patterns (called trend in [13] or gradient in [14]). Based on these clusters, remote users can discriminatively distribute different commands to sensors in different clusters. It can be noted that in some of the studies [12], the clusters concerned in a sensor network are defined in terms of spatial relationships as each sensor can only sense its adjacent area and also the monitored signals tend to be similar if their spatial sites are close to each other. In other words, the problem definition and the motivation of mining network communities based on pure link structures, as to be discussed in this paper, are different from those of clustering sensor networks based on spatial locations. In addition, the self-organization ideas adopted in our work, i.e., AOC based self-aggregation and propagation in local views, are different from those in the above mentioned methods, i.e., self-declaration and self-pruning [12], asynchronous signaling [13], and quorum sensing [14].

The remainder of the paper is organized as follows: Section 2 gives a formal definition of the D-NCMP, and the basic ideas behind our approach. Section 3 presents an autonomy oriented computing (AOC) based approach to solving the D-NCMP. In Section 4, we validate the approach using some network examples, and examine its performance in detail. Finally, Section 5 concludes the paper and discusses future work.

2. Formal definition of the D-NCMP

Definition 2.1 Let $N=(V,A)$ be a distributed network, where $V=\{v_1,\cdots,v_n\}$ is the set of nodes and $A=\{<v_i,v_j,w_{ij}>|1\le i,j\le n\}$ is the set of directed links that connect a pair of nodes with weight w_{ij}. N is distributed among m autonomous agents, and the *local view* (or view for short) of each agent p ($1\le p\le m$) is made up of (V_p,A_p), satisfying the following conditions:

(1) $\bigcup_{1 \le p \le m} V_p = V$ and $V_p \cap V_q = \phi, for\ p \neq q$

(2) $A_p = \{<i, j, w_{ij}> | <v_i, v_j, w_{ij}> \in A \wedge v_i \in V_p\}$

Let $NC(v_i) \subseteq V$ be the *network community* (as mentioned in the introduction) containing node v_i. Then, a D-NCMP can be stated as follows: For each agent p ($1 \le p \le m$), compute $NC(v_i)$ for all $v_i \in V_p$ based on its local view, (V_p, A_p).

From the above definition, we can see the essential distinction between a typical NCMP and a D-NCMP. In the former, we wish to find all natural communities of a given network correctly and efficiently based on its given global topological structure. While in the latter, we are especially interested in how to find such communities from a distributed network based only on a set of local views of the network.

As an example, let us observe the network as shown in Fig.1. We assume that the nodes are distributed among five agents, as illustrated in Fig.2.

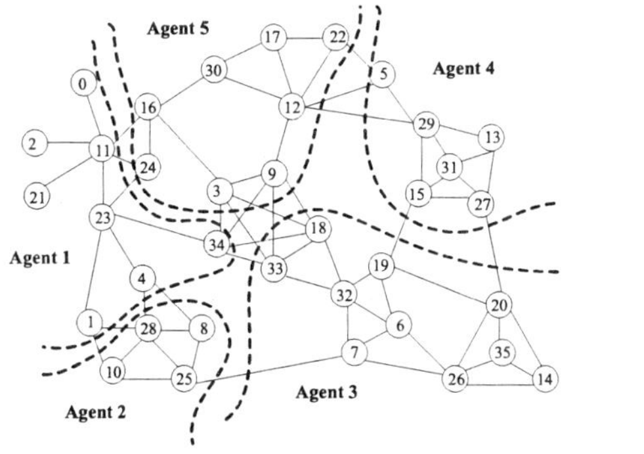

Figure 2 A schematic illustration of the D-NCMP. The network, as shown in Fig.1, is distributed among five agents at different locations. Each of them only has a local view of the network, including the nodes that they control and the links going out from these nodes. The task of the D-NCMP is to find all seven network communities denoted by A to G, as shown in Fig.1, through the self-aggregation and propagation of local views by the five agents.

As shown in Fig.2, initially the local view of agent 2 is (V_2, A_2), where $V_2 = \{8, 10, 25, 28\}$, $A_2 = \{<28,4>, <28,1>, <28,8>, <28,10>, <28,25>, <8,4>, <8,28>, <8,25>, <10,1>, <10,28>, <10,25>, <25,10>, <25,28>, <25,8>, <25,7>\}$. Note that w_{ij} in the set A_2 is omitted since all weights of this network are assumed to be equal to 1. The objectives of the five agents are to discover all the community members for their respectively governed nodes. For instance, agent 1 manages to compute all $NC(v_i)$ for each $v_i \in V_1 = \{0,2,11,21,23,34,4,1\}$ based on its local view (V_1, A_1). As shown in Fig.1, the objective of agent 1 is to find: $NC(0) = NC(2) = NC(21) = NC(11) = NC(23) = \{0,2,11,21,23,24,16\}$; $NC(1) = NC(4) = \{1,4,8,28,10,25\}$; $NC(34) = (3,9,18,34,33)$.

One immediate approach to solving such a D-NCMP is to introduce an administrative agent, who will reconstruct a global view of the entire distributed network based on the patched local views provided by all other agents. After that, the administrative agent will apply one of the algorithms designed for the NCMP to discover all communities hidden in the network. The final results are then sent to each agent from this agent. Obviously, this approach is not distributed and has several limitations, as discussed in the introduction. In the following sections, we will present a completely distributed approach to addressing this issue based on the methodology of *Autonomy Oriented Computing* (AOC).

As Liu et al. have stated [15,16], AOC is a new computing paradigm for solving hard computational problems and for characterizing the behavior of a complex system though emphasizing the modeling of autonomy in the entities of a complex system and their self-organization. AOC is especially suitable for addressing large-scale, distributed, dynamically evolving, and locally interacting problems, such as D-NCMPs.

For the clarity of description, in the presentation of our AOC-based approach, we will make the following assumption: Each agent controls only one node. Note that this assumption will not lower the degree of difficulty of a D-NCMP, and our approach described based on the assumption can readily be modified to suit for general cases, where each agent controls multiple nodes, as stated in Definition 2.1.

3. AOC-based approach to D-NCMP

A typical AOC system is composed of three main elements: a group of autonomous entities or agents, an environment where agents reside, and the system objective [15,16]. A distributed NCMP can be instantiated as an AOC system, named AOC-0 here, as follows: (1) the environment of the AOC-0 is the distributed network to be processed; (2) for each node of the distributed network, there is one autonomous agent residing on it; and (3) the system objective of the AOC-0 is to find the solution of the D-NCMP, that is, to discover all natural communities hidden in its environment through the self-organization of autonomous agents. In this section, we will describe the basic formulations and algorithms in the AOC-0 for solving the D-NCMP.

3.1 Environment of the AOC-0

The environment of the AOC-0 is defined as a distributed network, in which a group of nodes are distributed geographically and each node only stores the links associated to its direct neighbors. Node i is the neighbor of node j if there is a link from j to i. Formally, each node is defined as $<ID, NL, MP, DP>$, where the components respectively denote the identifier, neighbor list, message pool, and data pool of the node. After knowing the identifier of a node, agents in the environment can send messages to it. All messages received by a node will be stored in its messages pool. The data produced by agents will be stored in the data pools of the nodes that they respectively control. Given a distributed network, $N = (V, A)$, node v_i is initialized as: $v_i.ID = i$, $v_i.NL = \{<i,j,w_{ij}> | <v_i,v_j,w_{ij}> \in A\}$, $v_i.MP = v_i.DP = \phi$ (i.e., *null*).

3.2 System objective of the AOC-0

The system objective of the AOC-0, Ψ, is defined as: $\Psi = \psi_1 \wedge \cdots \wedge \psi_n$, where ψ_p ($1 \leq p \leq n$) is the objective of agent p, defined as $\psi_p = NC(v_p)$, where v_p is the node controlled by agent p. In other words, we assume that the objective of the overall AOC system will be achieved after all the distributed agents in it have completed their respective objectives.

3.3 Agent model of the AOC-0

The agent of the AOC-0 is characterized by five attributes including: identifier, clock, objective, local view, and actions, as denoted by $<ID, t, \psi, view(t), actions>$. The agent on node v_p is initialized as follows: $agent.ID = v_p.ID = p$; $agent.t = 0$; $agent.\psi = NC(v_p)$; $agent.view(0) = v_p.NL$; $agent.actions = <$*get_view, evaluate_view, shrink_view, enlarge_view, balance_view, sleep*$\}$. Variable t denotes the clock maintained by agent p ($agent_p$), which is used to implement the synchronization between $agent_p$ and other agents. After taking each action, $agent_p$ will adjust its clock by $t \leftarrow t+1$. Agent will become inactive after its clock reaching the final time or taking *sleep* action.

Agent view is a critical concept in our purposed AOC-based approach, in which agents update their respective views autonomously and asynchronously by taking some predefined actions. $agent_p.view(t)$ denotes the view of $agent_p$ at time t. Initially, the view of each agent, $agent.view(0)$ is set to the NL value of the node it controls. That is to say, at the beginning, each agent can only see the adjacent area of the node. Then, each agent starts to update (shrink or enlarge) its own view based on the information it gathers from its local environment, until its view cannot be changed any more. During the course, for $agent_p$, the nodes belonging to the network community, $NC(v_p)$, will be added into its view, one by one, and those nodes not belonging to $NC(v_p)$ will be gradually excluded from its view. At the convergent time, T, all the nodes remaining in the set of $agent_p.view(T)$ are regarded as the members of the network community, $NC(v_p)$. In other words, we have: $agent_p.\psi = NC(v_p) = \{v_i | <p,i,w_{pi}> \in agent_p.view(T)\} \cup \{v_p\}$.

$Agent_p$ takes action $agent_p.get\_view(q,t)$ to get the view of $agent_q$ at time t through a synchronized message communication between two agents. We assume that in the environment, there exits a message passing mechanism which guarantees that each message will be delivered to its destination.

3.3.1 Evaluating agent view

$Agent_p$ takes action $agen_p.evaluate\_view(t)$ to evaluate its current view, that is, to calculate the similarities between node v_p and other nodes in its current view. The nodes with larger similarity values are more likely to belong to community $NC(v_p)$. Based on the similarity presented here, $agent_p$ can determine which nodes will be kept in and which ones will be excluded from its current view.

In an centralized network, the similarity of node v_i and node v_j is defined:

$$s_{ij} = \frac{|K(i) \cap K(j)|}{|K(i)|} \cdot \frac{|K(i) \cap K(j)|}{|K(j)|} \quad (3.1)$$

where $K(i)$ is the set of neighbors of node v_i. The main idea behind this definition is inspired from the human society, in which two individuals sharing more acquaintances are more likely in the same social community. s_{ij} actually indicates the probability of two individuals belonging to the same community. Based on Eq.(3.1), we can define the similarity between two nodes in a weighted, directed, and distributed network.

Definition 3.1 Let v_p and v_q are two nodes in a distributed network. Agents p and q are on the nodes v_p and v_q, respectively. The *similarity* between the nodes v_p and v_q at time t is defined as follows:

$$s^t_{pq} = S(agent_p.view(t), agent_q.view(t)) = \frac{\sum_{k \in K_p(t) \cap K_q(t)} w^*_{pk}}{\sum_{k \in K_p(t)} w^*_{pk}} \cdot \frac{\sum_{k \in K_p(t) \cap K_q(t)} w^*_{qk}}{\sum_{k \in K_q(t)} w^*_{qk}} \quad (3.2)$$

where $K_i(t) = \{i\} \cup \{k | <i,k,w_{ik}> \in agent_i.view(t)\}$; $w^*_{ik} = agent_i.view(t).<i,k,w_{ik}>.w_{ik}$. The action is presented in Fig.3. In the last step, agent p submits its new view at time $t+1$ to the data pool on node v_p.

$agent_p.view(t+1) \leftarrow \phi$;

for $\forall <p,q,w_{pq}> \in agent_p.view(t)$

$\quad agent\_q\_view\_t \leftarrow agent_p.get\_view(q,t)$;

$s^{t}_{pq} \leftarrow S(agent_p.view(t), agent\_q\_view\_t)$;

$agent_p.view(t+1) \leftarrow agent_p.view(t+1) \cup \{< p, q, s^{t}_{pq} >\}$;

end

$v_p.DP \leftarrow v_p.DP \cup agent_p.view(t+1)$;

Figure 3 The action of evaluating agent view

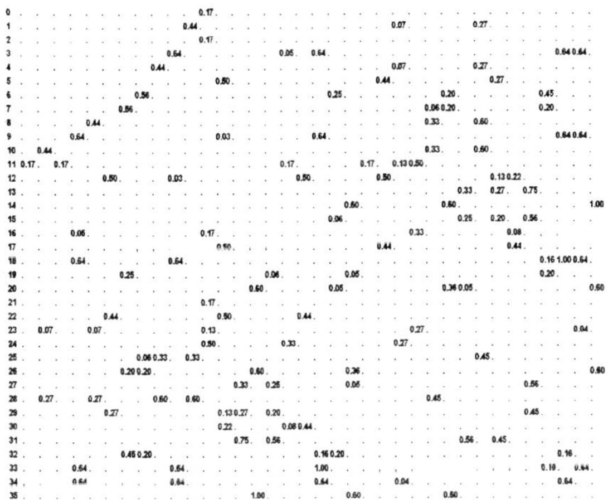

Figure 4 $AVM^{(1)}$ with respect to the network shown in Fig.1

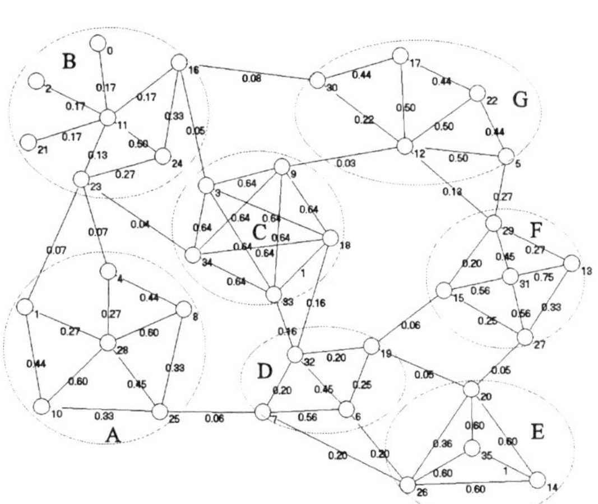

Figure 5 $AN^{(1)}$ with respect to the network shown in Fig.1

For the sake of description, the *views of all agents* are here represented in terms of a *matrix*, called *agent view matrix* at time *t* or $AVM^{(t)}$, which is defined as:

$$AVM^{(t)}(i,j) = \begin{cases} w_{ij}, if < i, j, w_{ij} > \in agent_i.view(t) \\ 0 \quad , else \end{cases} \qquad (3.3)$$

$AVM^{(0)}$ is the adjacency matrix of a network. After each agent$_p$ completes action *evaluate_view*(0), we get $AVM^{(1)}$. As an example, $AVM^{(1)}$ with respect to the original network of Fig.1, is given in Fig.4. In what follows, we refer to the network whose adjacency matrix is given by $AVM^{(t)}$ as an *agent network* at time *t*, denoted as $AN^{(t)}$, where each node denotes an agent and the links describe the relationships among these agents in terms of their similarities. Corresponding to $AVM^{(1)}$ of Fig.4, $AN^{(1)}$ is shown in Fig.5, from which we observe that the similarity values between the nodes belonging to different communities are much less than those belonging to the same communities.

We can prove that the time complexity of action *agen$_p$.evaluate_view* is $O(d_t^2)$, where d_t is the average degree of the *agent network* at time *t*.

3.3.2 Shrinking agent view

Agent$_p$ takes action *agent$_p$.shrink_view(t)* to exclude those nodes that may not belong to its network community, $NC(v_p)$, based on its current view at time *t*. The action is defined in Fig.6, in which ω_1 and ω_2 are two predefined constants.

$agent_p.view(t+1) \leftarrow \phi$;

$$\mu^{t}_{p} \leftarrow \frac{w^{*}_{pq}}{|agent_p.view(t)|}; \quad \sigma^{t}_{p} \leftarrow \left(\frac{\sum_{q} (w^{*}_{pq} - \mu^{t}_{p})^2}{|agent.view(t)|} \right)^{1/2};$$

for $\forall < p, q, w_{pq} > \in agent_p.view(t)$

if $w_{pq} \geq \omega_1 \cdot (\mu^{t}_{p} + \omega_2 \cdot \sigma^{t}_{p})$

$agent_p.view(t+1) \leftarrow agent_p.view(t+1) \cup \{< p, q, w_{pq} >\}$;

endfor

$v_p.DP \leftarrow v_p.DP \cup agent_p.view(t+1)$;

Figure 6 The action of shrinking agent view

We can also prove that the time complexity of action *agent$_p$.shrink_view* is $O(d_t)$, where d_t is the same as before. Note that the shrinking view action will not lead to losing nodes because those excluded nodes will still be kept in the views of other agents and may be included back again through an enlarging view action in the subsequent iterations.

3.3.3 Enlarging agent view

Agent$_p$ takes action *agent$_p$.enlarge_view(t)* to incorporate those nodes that may belong to network community $NC(v_p)$ into its current view at time *t*. This action is inspired by the human society in which an individual is likely to make new friends out of his/her old friends' friends. The action is specified in Fig.7, where *rand*(*S*) randomly selects an element from a set, *S*, and returns it. We can show that its time complexity is $O(d_t)$.

$agent_p.view(t+1) \leftarrow agent_p.view(t)$;

$q \leftarrow rand(\{i \mid < p, i, w_{pi} > \in agent_p.view(t+1)\})$;

$agent\_q\_view\_t \leftarrow agent_p.get\_view(q,t)$;

$w_{pq} \leftarrow agent_p.view(t+1).< p, q, w_{pq} >.w_{pq}$;

for $\forall < q,i,w_{qi} > \in agent\_q\_view\_t$

  if $< p,i,w_{pi} > \in agent_p.view(t+1)$ then

    $w_{pi} \leftarrow agent_p.view(t+1). < p,i,w_{pi} > .w_{pi}$;

  else $w_{pi} \leftarrow 0$;

  $s_{pi} \leftarrow \max(w_{pi}, w_{pq} \cdot w_{qi})$;

  $agent_p.view(t+1) \leftarrow agent_p.view(t+1) - \{< p,i,w_{pi} >\} \cup \{< p,i,s_{pi} >\}$;

end

for $\forall < p,q,w_{pq} > \in agent_p.view(t{+}1)$

  if $w_{pq} < \omega_1 \cdot (\mu_p^{t+1} + \omega_2 \cdot \sigma_p^{t+1})$ then

    $agent_p.view(t+1) \leftarrow agent_p.view(t+1) - \{< p,q,w_{pq} >\}$;

end

$v_p.DP \leftarrow v_p.DP \cup agent_p.view(t+1)$;

Figure 7 The action of enlarging agent view

Considering the network shown in Fig8.(a), in which there are in total seven agents on seven nodes. At time t, the view of agent$_i$ is: {<i, 1, 0.3>, <i, j, 0.5>, <i, 5, 0.15>}. After agent$_i$ completes the action, the view of agent$_i$ at time t+1 becomes {<i, 1, 0.3>,<i, 2, 0.3>,<i, j, 0.5>, <i, 4, 0.25>}; two new nodes, nodes 2 and 4, are added, and node 8 is deleted.

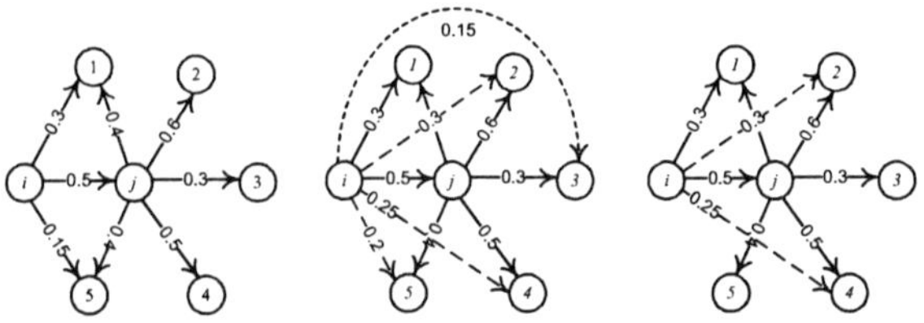

(a) (b) (c)

Figure 8 The schematic illustration of the enlarging view action. (a) presents the original network in which agent$_i$ will apply the action. First, agent$_i$ randomly selects one neighbor out of its three neighbors, denoted as agent j. Then, agent$_i$ chooses all the neighbors of agent$_j$ as its new neighbors, as illustrated in (b), where the dashed lines denote the newly created links. Finally, agent$_i$ evaluates its current neighbors and abandons those with low similarity values, as illustrated in (c).

3.3.4 Balancing agent view

Finally, let us take a look at action *agent$_p$_balance_view(t)* as performed by agent$_p$. This action will enable the agent to average the similarity values between v_p and the nodes in its view at time t. Its time complexity is O(d_t^2).

$agent_p.view(t{+}1) \leftarrow \phi$;

for $\forall < p,q,w_{pq} > \in agent_p.view(t)$

  $agent\_q\_view\_t \leftarrow agent_p.get\_view(q,t)$;

  if $< q,p,w_{qp} > \in agent\_q\_view\_t$ then

    $s_{pq} \leftarrow (w_{pq} + w_{qp})/2$;

  else $s_{pq} \leftarrow w_{pq}/2$;

  $agent_p.view(t+1) \leftarrow agent_p.view(t+1) \cup \{< p,q,s_{pq} >\}$;

end

$v_p.DP \leftarrow v_p.DP \cup agent_p.view(t+1)$;

Figure 9 The action of balancing agent view

3.3.5 The life-cycle of an agent

Based on the actions discussed above, the life-cycle of agent$_p$ is given in Fig.10.

/* initialization phase */
1. $agent_p.t \leftarrow 0$;
2. $agent_p.view(0) \leftarrow v_p.NL$;
3. $v_p.DP \leftarrow v_p.DP \cup agent_p.view(0)$;
/* action phase */
4. while $agent_p.t<T$ do
5. $agent_p.evaluate\_view(agent_p.t)$;
6. $agent_p.shrink\_view(agent_p.t+1)$;
7. $agent_p enlarge\_view(agent_p.t+2)$;
8. $agent_p.balance\_view(agent_p.t+3)$;
9. $agent_p.t \leftarrow agent_p.t+4$;
10. if $agent_p.view(agent_p.t) = agent_p.view(agent_p.t-4)$ then
11.   goto 12;
/* inactive phrase */
12. $agent_p.\ \psi = \{v_i | <p,i,w_{pi}> \in agent_p.view(agent_p.t)\} \cup \{v_p\}$;
13. $agent_p.sleep$;

Figure 10 The life-cycle of agent$_p$

The life-cycle of an agent in AOC-0 can be divided into three main phases: initialization phase, action phase, and inactive phase. In the initialization phase, agent$_p$ initializes itself by setting its starting clock and its initial view, and putting the view into the data pool of the node it resides on. In the action phase, agent$_p$ takes its actions, as a sequence of *evaluate_view*, *shrink_view*, *enlarge_view,* and *balance_view*, to repeatedly update its view until it becomes stabilized or its clock reaches a predefined threshold. After the view of agent$_p$ become stabilized, i.e., its current view is identical to its previous view, we say that a convergent view has been reached. At this time, the current value of t is denoted as t_c and the current view is called the *convergent view* of agent$_p$. After agent$_p$ finds all members belonging to its network community *NC*(v_p) based on its convergent view, it will become inactive.

3.4 AOC-d algorithm for solving D-NCMP

A given D-NCMP can be modeled as an AOC system, in which a distributed network is considered as the environment of the AOC system, and the solution of the D-NCMP is the objective of the AOC system. The nodes in the distributed network are controlled by a group of autonomous agents running asynchronously. The collaborations between them are implemented with the aid of a distributed clock mechanism, in which each agent maintains its own clock. Each agent only has a local view of the environment where it resides. During its life-cycle, each agent repeatedly updates its view by taking some predefined actions. After the updating process converges, the final view of each agent contains exactly the members belonging to the network community. The agents that have achieved their objectives suspend their actions and become inactive. The objective of the AOC system is thus achieved when all its agents become inactive.

We illustrate how the AOC-d algorithm works using the network shown in Fig.1. We will focus on $agent_0$. Three parameters involved are set as follows: $T = 100$, $\omega_1 = 0.4$, and $\omega_2 = 0.3$.

First, $agent_0$ initializes itself at t=0, Its view is set to: $agent_0$.*view*(0) = {<0, 11, 1>}.

Then, $agent_0$ starts its action phase. It takes *evaluate_view* in Step 5, and its view becomes: $agent_0$.*view*(1) = {<0, 11, 0.17>}. After *shrink_view* in Step 6, its view becomes: $agent_0$.*view*(2) = {<0, 11, 0.17>}. After *enlarge_view*, it becomes: $agent_0$.*view*(3) = {<0, 11, 0.17>, <0,24,0.08>}. After it performs *balance_view*, its view becomes: $agent_0$.*view*(4) = {<0, 11, 0.17>, <0,24,0.04>}.

Next, in Step 9, $agent_0$ updates its clock, i.e., t=4. In Step 10, $agent_0$ checks whether it has reached a convergent view by comparing its current view, $agent_0$.*view*(4), with its previous view, $agent_0$.*view*(0). Because $agent_0$.*view*(4) is not equal to $agent_0$.*view*(0) and the current time is less than T, $agent_0$ goes to Step 4 and starts a new iteration. After finishing the second iteration, $agent_0.t$ = 8, and $agent_0$.*view*(8) = {<0, 2, 0.26>, <0,21,0.26>, <0,23,0.25>, <0,11,0.51>, <0,24,0.51>, <0,16,0.26>}.

After $agent_0$ completes the third iteration and reaches the fourth, its view at time 16 becomes: $agent_0$.*view*(16) = {<0, 2, 1>, <0,21,1>, <0,23,1>, <0,11,1>, <0,24,1>, <0,16,1>}. At this time, $agent_0$ has reached its convergent view, since $agent_0$.*view*(16) is exactly equal to $agent_0$.*view*(12). Thus, it quits the cycle of view updating.

In the inactive phase, $agent_0$ obtains all the members belonging to network community *NC*(0), by taking the action in Step 12:

$$agent_0.\psi = \{i \mid (p,i,w_{pi}) \in agent_0.view(16)\} \cup \{0\}$$
$$= \{2,21,23,11,24,16,0\} = NC(0)$$

Finally, $agent_0$ becomes inactive, taking *sleep* in Step 13.

Using the representation of *agent network*, as introduced in Section 3.3.1, we can easily visualize the dynamic process of view updating by all agents in the AOC system. At time 24, i.e., after six iterations, all agents in the AOC system find their respective network communities, and become inactive, as shown in Fig.11.

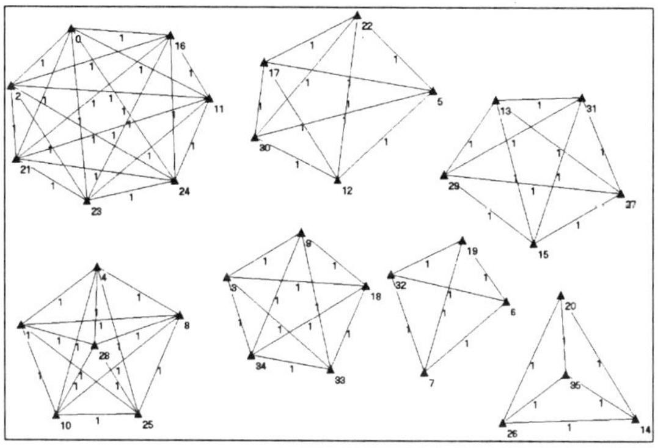

Figure 11 The finally evolved *agent network* with respect to the distributed network of Fig.1

3.5 Positive feedback in the self-organizing agent network

It can be noted that in the AOC-0 system, there are two types of networks, which form a two-layer structure. The bottom layer is the distributed network (i.e., physical network) to be mined, and the top layer is the agent network (i.e., conceptual network) consisting of the views of all agents upon the bottom layer. The agent network is dynamically updated, as the views of agents keep on evolving during their life-cycles.

When $agent_p$ appears in the view of $agent_q$, a new link from q to p will be added to the agent network. In contrast, when $agent_p$ is excluded from the view of $agent_q$, the existing link from q to p will be deleted from the agent network. As directed by the predefined actions, the agent network evolves continuously, from an old structure to a new one, similar to such dynamic systems as human societies and ecosystems.

The evolution of the agent network is, in fact, a positive feedback process, in which the links between agents corresponding to the nodes in the same network communities will gradually emerge, while the links between agents corresponding to the nodes in different network communities will gradually disappear. Regulated by this feedback mechanism, agents can self-organize themselves into a number of separated groups; each group corresponds to one network community of the distributed network in question. The finally evolved agent network comes into being when all its agents become inactive, which is made of a set of separated cliques, and each of them corresponds to one network community. For example, in Fig.11, there are seven cliques in the finally evolved agent network, each of which corresponds to a network community of the distributed network as shown in Fig.1.

Now let us examine the positive feedback mechanism of the AOC-d algorithm with the aid of *agent view matrix* (*AVM*), as introduced in Section 3.3.1. The network to be discussed here is a randomly generated network, as commonly used to test the performance of algorithms for mining a community structure [1,11]. The community structure of the random network is known beforehand. But, it is stochastic in other respects as regulated by parameters. The random network is defined as $G(c,n,k,p_{in})$, where c is the number of communities in the network, n is the number of nodes in each community, k is the degree of each node, and p_{in} is the probability of each node connecting other nodes in the same community. Obviously, as $p_{in} \to 0$, the community structure of the random network becomes increasingly ambiguous. In our example, the random network to be processed is $G(4,64,30,0.5)$, and we set T =50, $\omega_1 = 0.3$ and $\omega_2 = 0.2$.

Fig.12 presents the *agent view matrices* for the random network at different time steps, in which each dot "." denotes a non-zero element, i.e., a non-zero weight associated with a link between two agents. The nodes belonging to the same community are arranged together. We can see four dense areas along the diagonal in these matrices. Each of them corresponds to a community. The evolving process of the agent network converges after 28 time steps, as shown in Fig.12(a)~(f). From them, we can see that, as the agent network evolves, the links between communities (i.e., the dots outside the four dense areas) gradually disappear, while those within communities (i.e., the dots inside the four dense areas) gradually increase. Finally, the agent network evolves into a new network containing four separated cliques, each of which corresponds to a community of the random network, as shown in Fig.12(h).

3.6 Time complexity of the AOC-d algorithm

We have proved that the worst case time complexity of the AOC-d algorithm is $WT = O(d_{t_c}^2) = O(n^2/k^4)$ where k is the number of communities in the distributed network. In the case of, $k<<n$ we have:

$$WT = O(d_{t_c}^2) = O(n^2/k^4) = O(n^2).$$

While in the case of $k \geq \sqrt{n}$, we have:

$$WT = O(d_{t_c}^2) = O(n^2/k^4) = O(1).$$

That is to say, each agent will quickly complete its task within a constant time. From the above analysis, we can see that, given a network, the efficiency of the AOC-d algorithm is related to the community structure of the network. Generally speaking, the more communities the network contains, the more efficient the AOC-d algorithm will be.

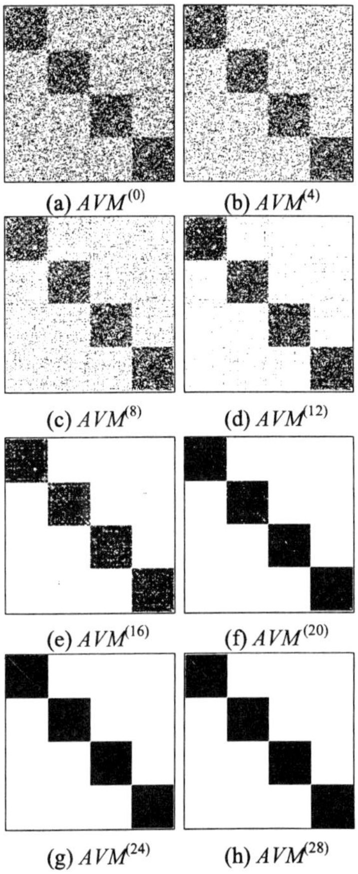

Figure 12 Examining the positive feedback mechanism of the AOC-d algorithm, in terms of a series of evolving agent view matrices with respect to a random network, G(4,64,30,0.5)

4. Evaluation of the AOC-d algorithm

In this section, we validate the effectiveness of the AOC-d algorithm using two networks. Although the networks are presented in centralized styles, for the purpose of testing our AOC-based, distributed approach, we treat them as distributed networks, i.e., we consider that their nodes and links are distributed over different sources or geographical locations.

4.1. Applying AOC-d to a semantic social network

Flink is a weighted and directed social network that describes the scientific collaborations among 681 researchers in the Semantic Web area [17]. It contains rich information such as personal profiles and centrality distribution, which is useful for understanding the real meaning of a detected community.

In Fig.13, the top panel presents the final result of the AOC-d algorithm, in terms of an agent view matrix, in which each block along the diagonal line is a community. Altogether, 148 communities were detected with $\omega_1 = 0.6$ and $\omega_1 = 0.4$. As an example, we discuss the second largest community, as circled in the agent view matrix and as shown in the bottom panel, which contains Steffen Staab with the biggest centrality values such as indegree, closeness, betweenness, and publications.

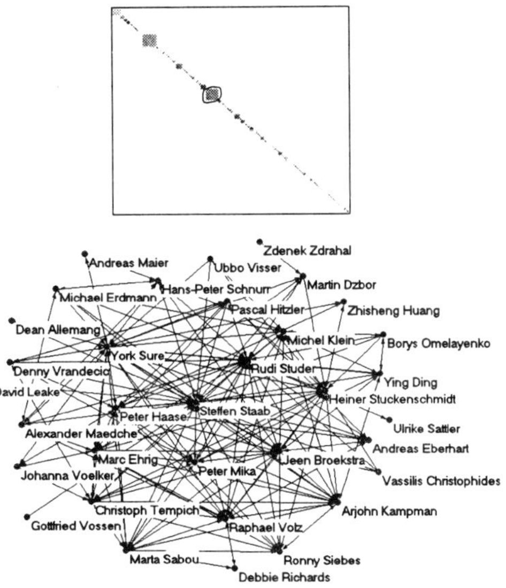

Figure 13 Mining communities form Flink with AOC-d.

After checking their profiles, we note that the detected community is highly location related. In it, 18 out of 34 come from Germany, 14 out of 18 come from the same city, Karlsruhe, and 11 out of 14 come from the University of Karlsruhe. We also note that the community is research interest related. For examples, 19 out of 34 persons share the topic of "knowledge management", and 16 persons share the topic of "ontology edit/extraction".

4.2 An application of the AOC-d algorithm in iPDA

iPDAs (intelligent Portable Digital Assistants) carried by peoples form a distributed communication network in which people communicate with each other through calls or messages as shown in Fig.14. One useful function of such an iPDA is to find and recommend new friends with similar interests or promising partners in research or business to its owners, in terms of the accumulated communication records during a certain period. To implement that, each iPDA does three things: 1) selecting people who have communicated at least a certain number of times (i.e., above a threshold) as its initial local view; 2) finding the community containing its owner based on the AOC-d algorithm; and 3) reporting new persons to its owner. For example, for the network shown in Fig.14, 16 communities were detected with $\omega_1 = 0.3$ and $\omega_1 = 0.4$. For the user Neumann in the circled community, its iPDA will recommend 5 new people to him as new partners, including Gao, Zhou, Zhu, Yu, and Roberts.

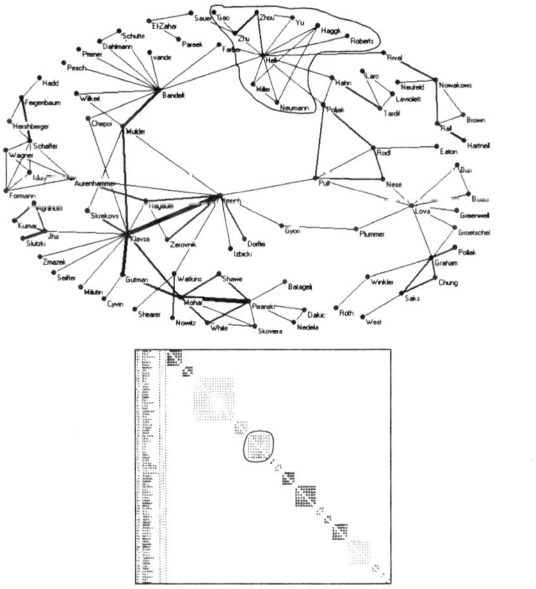

Figure 14 An illustrative iPDA network distributed at a certain time in terms of communications between individuals, in which the width of an edge denotes the frequency of communications. The bottom panel is the agent view matrix of the finally evolved agent network.

5. Discussions and conclusion

In this paper, we have presented a distributed network community mining problem (D-NCMP), and have given an AOC-based approach to solving it. In this approach, the nodes and links of distributed networks are distributed among a group of autonomous agents, who are responsible for finding all natural communities hidden in distributed networks, based on their respective local views. Agents in the AOC-based approach act asynchronously and concurrently without any global control, while being able to achieve their respective objectives through self-aggregation and propagation in local views. We have validated the effectiveness of this approach using some network examples, and have illustrated a promising application of intelligent PDAs.

Two parameters, ω_1 and ω_2, are involved in the AOC-d algorithm, which are used to control the granularity of network communities. More communities with smaller sizes can be obtained under larger ω_1 and ω_2. Through experiments, we have found that, for most networks, the mining results, such as the number of communities and the modularity of a network (for the definition of modularity, refer to [18]), are related but not sensitive to the values of ω_1 and ω_2 if they are within the range of [0.2,0.6]. Generally speaking, individual agents can choose different parameters according to their specific requirements. For instance, those agents who want to find coarse communities with larger sizes may set smaller parameters.

It should be mentioned that our AOC-based, distributed approach can readily be modified to perform *incremental* distributed network community mining, and hence to address large-scale, *locally interacting,* and *highly dynamic* networks. In doing so, each agent monitors and reacts to a new update happening in its local view. That is, it computes its new convergent view through local interactions with other agents, based on its previous view and the new update. Limited by the space, we will not present the details here.

So far, we have only demonstrated our approach using some simulated distributed networks with relatively small sizes. In our future work, we plan to extend our approach to real-world distributed networks. A related study would be to further analyze the performance of this approach, such as general conditions for its convergence, and sensitivity to agent communication failures or other noises.

References

[1] M.Girvan, M.E.J.Newman, "Community structure in social and biological networks," Proceeding of National Academy of Science, 2002(9):7821-7826.

[2] G. Palla, I. Derenyi, I. Farkas, T. Vicsek, "Uncovering the overlapping community structure of complex networks in nature and society," Nature, 2005(435): 814-818.

[3] V. Batagelj and A. Mrvar, "Analysis and visualization of large networks," in Graph Drawing Software, Springer, Berlin, 2004: 77-103.

[4] D.M.Wilkinson, B.A.Huberman, "A method for finding communities of related genes," Proceeding of National Academy of Science, 2004(101): 5241-5248.

[5] J.M. Kleinberg, "Authoritative sources in a hyperlinked environment," J. ACM, 1999(46): 604-632.

[6] G.W.Flake, S.Lawrence, C.L.Giles, F.M.Coetzee, "Self-organization and identification of Web communities," IEEE Computer, 2002(35): 66-71.

[7] J.Shi, J.Malik, "Normalized cuts and image segmentation", IEEE Trans. on Pattern Analysis and Machine Intelligence, 2000(22): 888-904.

[8] M.Fiedler, "Algebraic connectivity of graphs," Czechoslovakian Math. J., 1973(23): 298-305.

[9] B.W.Kernighan, S.Lin, "An efficient heuristic procedure for partitioning graphs," Bell System Technical, 1970(49): 291-307.

[10] J.Scott, Social Network Analysis: A Handbook, 2nd edn. Sage Publications, London, 2000.

[11] F.Radicchi, C.Castellano, F.Cecconi, V.Loreto, D.Parisi, "Defining and identifying communities in networks," Proceeding of National Academy of Science, 2004(101):2658-2663.

[12] K. Bae, H.Yoon, "Autonomous clustering scheme for wireless sensor networks using coverage estimation-based self-pruning," IEICE Trans. Comm., 2005(3): 973-980.

[13] A.Meka, A.K.Singh, "Distributed spatial clustering in sensor networks," LNCS, 2006(3896):980-1000.

[14] I.Wokoma, L.L.Shum, L.Sacks, I.Marshall, "A biologically-inspired clustering algorithm dependent on spatial data in sensor networks," Proceeding of the Second European Workshop on Wireless Sensor Networks, Istanbul, Turkey, 2005:386- 390.

[15] J. Liu, X.L. Jin, K.C. Tsui. Autonomy Oriented Computing. Springer/Kluwer Academic Publishers, 2004.

[16] J. Liu, X.L.Jin,, K.C. Tsui. "Autonomy Oriented Computing (AOC): Formulating computational systems with autonomous components," IEEE Trans. on Systems, Man, and Cybernetics, Part A: Systems and Humans, 2005(35):879- 902.

[17] http:// flink.semanticweb.org/

Acknowledgements

The work reported in this paper was carried out in e-Transformation Research Centre at Hong Kong Baptist University and supported by a Hong Kong RGC Central Allocation grant (HKBU 2/03/C). The first author has been supported by a National Natural Science Foundation of China grant (No. 60503016).

Self-Organized Data-Gathering Scheme for Multi-Sink Sensor Networks Inspired by Swarm Intelligence

Yuichi Kiri†, Masashi Sugano‡ and Masayuki Murata†

† *Graduate School of Information Science and Technology, Osaka University*
1–5 Yamadaoka, Suita, Osaka 565–0871, Japan
{y-kiri,murata}@ist.osaka-u.ac.jp

‡ *School of Comprehensive Rehabilitation, Osaka Prefecture University,*
3–7–30 Habikino, Habikino, Osaka 583–8555, Japan
sugano@rehab.osakafu-u.ac.jp

Abstract

We propose a new system of gathering data from sensor networks with multi-sink configurations inspired by the swarm intelligence of ants. It is a novel solution developed to achieve reliable data gathering over extended periods of time. Each sensor node determines its next action through repeated interaction and feedback from its neighbors. Beneficial clustering and routing emerge in a self-organized way from these actions, and this leads to a robust and dependable data-gathering system. Our simulation results revealed that the proposed system can reliably deliver event information to the sink nodes, is robust over very-poor-quality wireless channels, and has self-recovery capabilities to deal with failures of sensor nodes including the sink nodes.

1. Introduction

Sensor networks have become one of the hottest areas of research and a lot of research has focused on this topic. The nodes in these networks sense their ambient surroundings or events, and transmit the information they obtain via wireless channels to sink nodes, which gather the data from all sensor nodes. Because sensor networks can cover large areas and extract localized features, they have been attracting increased attention from a wide variety of areas such as medical fields, welfare, security, and disaster prevention.

It is difficult to achieve longer and more reliable monitoring of regions. The sensor nodes' memory capacity, processing power, and countermeasures against error in wireless channels inevitably need to be sacrificed for economic efficiency where their production cost should be lower than 1$ to attain affordable sensor networks [2]. Sensor nodes in some applications being considered today are outdoors and in environments that vary a great deal according to the location. Therefore, we need to take poor quality in communication channels and even sink node failure into account according to the circumstances. Although a great deal of conventional research has emphasized that battery power is one of the most important resources in sensor networks, robustness and dependability should be valued more for the environments.

Sensor networks also suffer from scalability problems. Although the number of sensor nodes deployed within the region being monitored depends on a network's applications, the total number can reach hundreds or thousands. The common method of communication used by sensor networks is converge-cast (many-to-one) in which all packets transmitted from sensor nodes concentrate on a sink node, because the purpose of the network is usually to collect information. Thus, as the number of sensor nodes increases, those nodes located near the sink node consume large amounts of power. The sink node is then isolated once they deplete their batteries, and the sensor network fails to function.

Considering that an enormous number of sensor nodes can be deployed, it is widely said that concentrated controlling systems do not fit well to sensor networks. The difficulty to obtain information over the entire network is caused by the number of sensor nodes. From that standpoint, autonomous distributed systems hold great promise. In such systems, sensor nodes must determine their next actions based on limited information. Each of their actions must lead to the most beneficial action for the network as a whole without external management. Therefore, self-organized behavior is strongly desired for sensor networks.

We propose a novel solution to these problems with sensor networks detecting events in this paper. Our scheme does not require geographical information or synchronization between sensor nodes. The most significant characteristic of our scheme is the application of the swarm intelli-

0-7695-2906-2/07 $25.00 © 2007 IEEE

gence of ants to sensor networks with multi-sink configurations. Each ant determines what it should do through estimating its surroundings, interacting with neighboring ants, and obeying the local rules it has as a species. Although an individual ant is simple and unintelligent, their collective action creates biological order and results in them heading toward a beneficial direction on the system level. This feature of ant swarming is highly concurrent, adaptable to changes in the environment, and has been attracting a great deal of attention. The model of swarming is well suited to sensor networks composed of nodes with only simple functional capabilities.

Our scheme, which adopts swarm intelligence, achieves long-term data gathering in a different way to much of the conventional research, i.e., it is robust and adaptable to environmental changes. Most of the past research has only focused on reducing the imbalances in power consumption over the region being monitored or power consumption itself. Of course as we previously mentioned, although power is one of the most valuable resources of battery-operated sensor nodes, we urgently require robustness against poor quality in communication channels, sensor node failure, and even sink node failure. We resolved such critical demands using swarm intelligence such as *ant-based clustering* and *Ant Colony Optimization* (ACO). We show that our new scheme enables high degrees of data gathering and attains self-recovery capabilities and robustness through the simple actions of individual sensor nodes.

The remainder of the paper is organized as follows. Section 2 presents related work that has taken multi-sink sensor networks and swarm intelligence into consideration. The details on our proposed scheme and its operation are described in Section 3 and the simulation results are provided in Section 4. The paper concludes with an outlook toward our future research.

2. Related work

Our proposed scheme includes many concepts within its design. Multi-sink sensor networks, which are the target of this paper, have been actively discussed lately. Swarm intelligence has also drawn a great deal of interest from a variety of areas, other than networking, due to its self-organized behavior.

2.1. Sensor networks with multiple sink nodes

Although much research has set its target on sensor networks with a single-sink configuration, a not negligible amount of work has addressed multi-sink sensor networks. The motivation for studying multiple-sink nodes has been to improve scalability. For example, Oyman and Ersoy [12] stated that in a network with thousands of sensor nodes, they should be grouped into several clusters and sink nodes should be individually dedicated to a single cluster in view of scalability. They solved problems by finding the best sink locations on that basis and determining the minimum number of sinks for a predefined number of operation periods.

There has been some research on the routing problem in multi-sink sensor networks. Chen et al. [5] deployed multi-sink nodes taking into account that sensor nodes around a sink node consume a large amount of power in relaying the packets destined for that sink node. Multi-path Routing in large-scale sensor networks with Multiple Sink nodes (MRMS) has been proposed on that basis. MRMS takes a multi-path routing approach, in which sensor nodes shift a primary path to an alternative one when the residual power of the sensor nodes on the primary path falls below a predefined threshold. Kalantari and Shayman [8] analytically derived the optimal-routing direction for an arbitrary point over a region being monitored for both single-sink and multi-sink configurations based on electrostatic theory. Using their results, we can equalize the power consumption of sensor nodes as much as possible. The results are represented in the form of partial differential equations; however, whether the equations can be solved depends on the sensor-network model.

The proposal by Lee *et al.* [10] is close to our idea in terms of applying the multi-sink configuration to improve robustness against sink-node failure as well as scalability. They established the same number of routing trees as sink nodes, with the sink nodes acting as roots using the concept of *De Bruijn digraphs*. When there is sink-node failure, the sensor nodes in the failed sink-node's tree can move into another tree, so their scheme was robust against sink failure. However, they did not evaluate how robust it was or clarify how this mechanism would affect sensor networks.

2.2. Swarm intelligence

One of the most frequently used forms of swarm intelligence in the networking area is probably ACO, which is observed in ants foraging for food. Although the ACO approach will be described in detail in Section 3.3, we also utilized ACO's idea in our routing along with some trailblazers. For example, AntNet [3] applied ACO to packet-switching networks such as the Internet, and AntHocNet [4] applied it to Mobile Ad-hoc Network (MANET). Although differing in the details, BeeAdHoc [14] was also proposed for MANET, which also provided positive feedback inspired by the swarm intelligence of honey bees. Zhang *et al.* [16] found that AntNet does not perform sufficiently well in sensor networks and, therefore, improved it. However, their improved version only considered single-sink sensor networks as the target and they did not discuss robustness.

Some species in the world of ants divide their eggs and larvae based on their size. A clustering algorithm called ant-based clustering was studied [15, 13] inspired by such behavior. Ant-based clustering is characterized by a probabilistic approach, where clustering is repeatedly realized by ants and stochastically selected eggs are picked up or dropped. We introduced such a probabilistic approach to the clustering of sensor nodes in our scheme. Dynamic clustering adapting to changes in the environment can accommodate sink-node failures.

3. Design of proposed scheme

3.1. Design consideration

Scalability is critical in sensor networks incorporating a number of sensor nodes. However, converge-cast constrains scalability in sensor networks.

The transmission range by sensor nodes needs to be short to reduce the amount of power consumed by their limited batteries. Therefore, multi-hop communication is necessary for sensor networks. All the packets transmitted by sensor nodes, on the other hand, are destined for sink nodes to enable information to be gathered. The sensor nodes near a sink node must relay all packets and, therefore, run out of power earlier than the others. As a result, the network is partitioned and packets cannot reach the sink node. The area around the sink node is a bottleneck for sensor networks. We previously pointed out this problem in previous work [9]. A wide variety of energy-aware routing protocols has been proposed thus far to resolve these imbalances in power consumption. However, these approaches are not essential solutions as long as converge-cast is used in a multi-hop way. We believe that we must adopt a multi-sink configuration to improve the scalability of sensor networks.

The benefits that can be gained from a multi-sink configuration are not limited to scalability. Conventional research has actively discussed sensor node failure, but only a few have discussed sink node failure. It is necessary to continue data collection if a sink node fails, especially in sensor networks deployed in areas people cannot access. If we could prevent a sink node from becoming a single point of failure by applying a multi-sink configuration to a sensor network, and if we could also maintain performance the same as it was before the sink node failed, we can say it is a self-recovering sensor network. Such a system would greatly contribute to dependability and robustness.

Our sensor network model is outlined in Fig. 1. A number of sensor nodes are placed over the region being monitored as well as multiple sink nodes. These sink nodes behave as gateways to other networks such as the Internet and dedicated networks. Packets received at the sink nodes are processed and transmitted to data servers. We only focus on

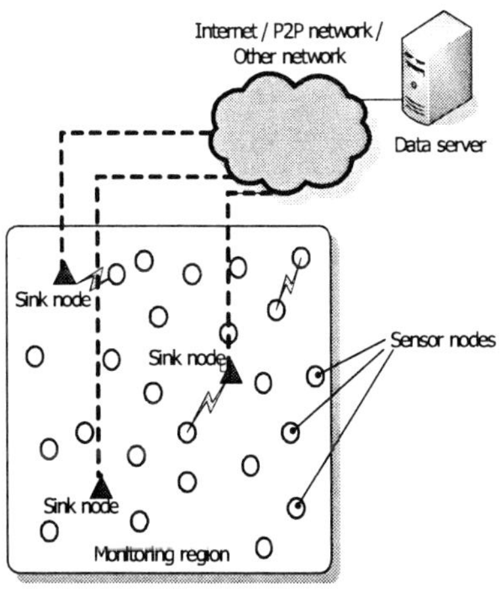

Figure 1. Network architecture model

communications from sensor nodes to sink nodes, and other communications and data processing are beyond the scope of this paper.

3.2. Overview of proposed scheme

We propose dividing a sensor network into as many clusters as there are sink nodes, and sensor nodes that transmit packets to sink nodes are dedicated to that cluster. In terms of clustering, one option is to optimally split sensor nodes into clusters and retain them for the lifetime of the sensor networks. Data collection over an area may be impossible due to cluster-level power depletion where a number of events, which the sink node should be notified of, only occurs in the area of a particular cluster. If a sink node fails, its cluster cannot collect information, either. Clusters in our proposed scheme dynamically expand and shrink by applying ant-based clustering depending on the situation. Such behaviors by clusters adapt to the varieties of patterns for occurring events and contribute to longer operating times. Even when a sink node fails, dynamic clustering enables sensor networks to work well with the failure having only a slight influence.

We apply the principle of ACO to hop-by-hop routing in our proposed scheme. Each sensor node has a *pheromone table*, and the benefit of selecting a neighbor as next-hop node are stored in the form of pheromones. When a sensor node transmits a packet to notify the sink node of event, it refers to its pheromone table, and stochastically selects the next-hop node based on the pheromone value. Thus, each sensor node selects a next-hop node with greater probability of having a higher pheromone level. A sensor node with more pheromone value means preferable next-hop node. Furthermore, if some neighboring nodes have almost the same pheromone value, they are selected as next-hop nodes with almost the same frequency and the number of packets

0-7695-2906-2/07 $25.00 © 2007 IEEE

that must be relayed is distributed among them. This leads to load sharing.

3.3. Details on ant routing in our scheme

The basic concept underlying ACO in the routing algorithm is outlined in Fig. 2. A source node transmits small control packets called "ants" to the destination node to construct paths. In sensor networks, destination node corresponds to sink node. Each ant wanders randomly over the network to find its destination, collecting information on the quality of the trail it walked through (e.g., hop count, delay, and the residual power of nodes on the trail). Once the ant reaches its destination, it follows the trail back to the source node, leaving some pheromone along the trail. The amount of pheromone it leaves depends on the quality of the path. Ants that are transmitted later from the source node stochastically select a path on which more pheromones remain, and more effectively arrive at the destination following better paths. These ants also leave pheromones on their return journey. Application packets are likely to follow a beneficial path due to such a positive-feedback approach.

Unlike the Internet or MANET that mainly use unicast communication, a "good path" in the sensor network is:

- A path leading to a sink node without any unnecessary circumvention and
- One whose sensor nodes have sufficient residual power.

It is not necessary for each source node to find good paths to a sink node by flooding them with ants. Such flooding beginning from the source node could cause unnecessary power consumption and needlessly occupy wireless channels, because of ants traveling back and forth over the network. Thus, we choose sink nodes to flood the ants, which we called *backward ants*. Backward ants do not go back into the sink. As we previously pointed out, the required next-hop node is a sensor node located nearer to the sink node, which has enough residual power. With that in mind, the role of backward ants is to establish a pheromone distribution in which the required next-hop node has a higher pheromone value.

Let us introduce the following terms to simplify our explanation of routing.

n_i:	ID of sensor node.
S_k:	ID of sink node. At the same time, S_k also represents the ID of a cluster to which sink node S_k is dedicated.
$Pb_{n_i}(S_k)$:	Pheromone value that n_i assigns to a backward ant, which is transmitted by S_k.
S_{n_i}:	ID of sink node that n_i belongs to.
$P_{n_i}(n_i)$	Pheromone value for n_i which is declared by n_i.
$P_{n_i}(n_j, S_k)$:	Pheromone value that represents benefits of using n_j as next-hop node for n_i to transmit packet whose destination is S_k.
$C_{n_i}(S_k)$:	Cluster pheromone of S_k, which means benefits of belonging to the cluster S_k, estimated by n_i.
E_{r_i}:	Residual power of n_i.
E_{m_i}:	Initial power of n_i.

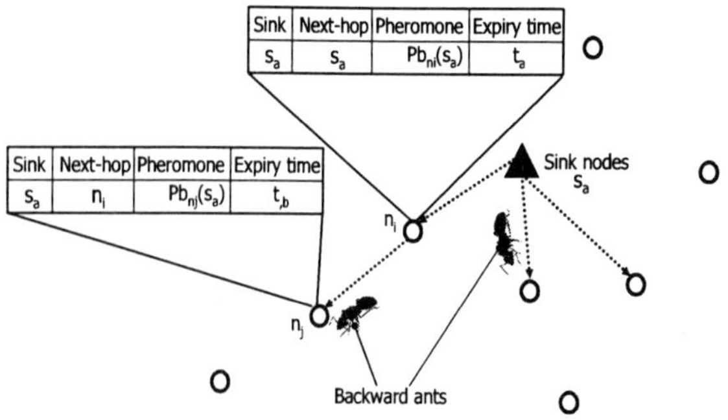

Figure 3. Updating pheromone table on receiving backward ants.

S_a broadcasts backward ant B with maximum pheromone value $Pb_{S_a}(S_a) = P_{\max}$. On receiving B, sensor node n_i stores its pheromone value ($Pb_{S_a}(S_a)$), its source node (S_a), and sensor node which relays B immediately before (S_a) in its own pheromone table as an entry. Thus, n_i memorizes that the benefit of selecting S_a as a next-hop node for transmitting packets to S_a is $P_{\max}$. After that, n_i relays B, making B carry a new pheromone value. This new pheromone value $Pb_{n_i}(S_a)$ is calculated according to:

$$Pb_{n_i}(S_a) = \alpha \left(1 - \exp\left(-\beta \frac{E_{r_i}}{E_{m_i}}\right)\right) Pb_{S_a}(S_a) \quad (1)$$
$$0 < \alpha < 1, \beta > 0$$

After receiving B, which is relayed by n_i, n_j creates a new entry for it, as in the case of n_i. Then, n_j calculates a new pheromone value according to Eq. (1), and forwards B with a new pheromone again. An ideal pheromone distribution emerges through frequent repetitions of these behaviors.

Although the entities of backward ants are merely small control packets, flooding them consumes vast amounts of power in relaying and occupies wireless channels. Thus, the frequency with which backward ants are transmitted should be as low as possible. However, the pheromone table must reflect current changes to the network to construct an efficient path to sinks where changes to the network topology occur during the intervals backward ants are

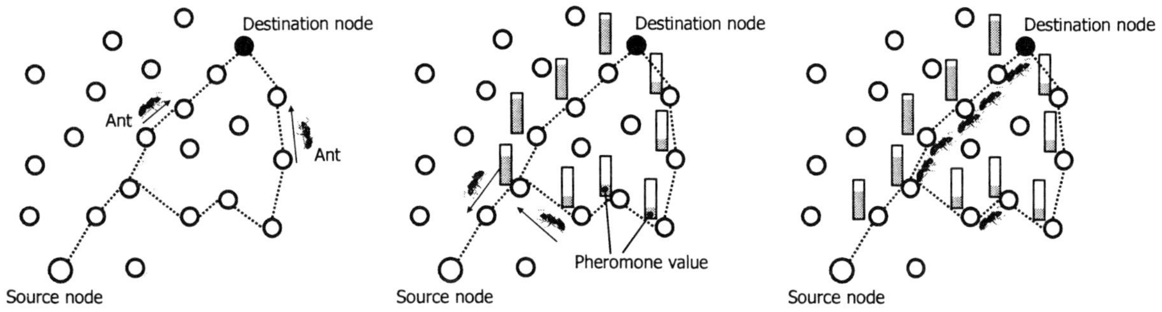

(a) Source node transmits ants to its destination.

(b) Once an ant arrives at destination, it returns to the source node, leaving pheromones on its return path.

(c) More ants and application packets are attracted to a path with more pheromones.

Figure 2. Principle underlying the routing algorithm using ACO.

transmitted. We decided to assign the role of updating the table to *hello ants*, which are broadcast packets transmitted more frequently at fixed intervals than backward ants. They do not cause flooding with a TTL of 1. Hello ants carry pheromone value P_{n_i} of source node n_i, the ID of sink node S_{n_i} to which n_i belongs, and the pheromones of cluster $C_{n_i}(S_{n_i})$ to which S_{n_i} is dedicated. We will describe cluster pheromones in detail in Section 3.4. The exchange of hello ants by neighboring nodes reflects an up-to-date state in the pheromone table of each sensor node. On receiving a hello ant from n_i, and only if it has an entry for n_i stored in its pheromone table, n_j updates the pheromone value of its entry as follows

$$P_{n_j}(n_i, S_{n_i}) = \gamma P_{n_j}(n_i, S_{n_i}) + (1-\gamma) P_{n_i}(n_i) \quad (2)$$

with $\gamma \in [0, 1]$. When n_j broadcasts a hello ant, n_j makes it carry its pheromone value, P_{n_j}, which is defined as follows.

$$P_{n_j} = \frac{\sum_l \sum_m P_{n_j}(l, m)}{l \cdot m} \quad (3)$$

This is the average pheromone value for entries in its pheromone table.

Sending event information to sink nodes is not a difficult task if pheromone distribution is properly constructed. When sensor node n_i transmits a packet, it sets the destination of the packet to the sink node S_{n_i} to which it belongs, and stochastically selects the next-hop node by referring to pheromones in its pheromone table. The probability of n_i selecting n_j as a next-hop node is represented as:

$$p_{n_i}(n_j) = \frac{P_{n_i}(n_j, S_{n_i})^2}{\sum_{k \in N_{n_i}} P_{n_i}(k, S_{n_i})^2} \quad (4)$$

where N_{n_i} means the candidate set of next-hop nodes for n_i.

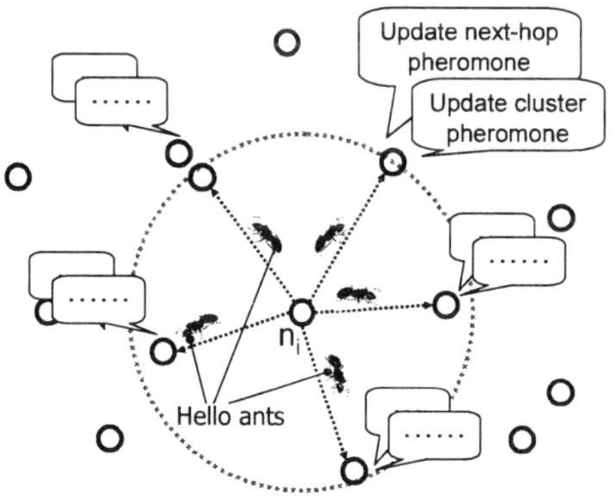

Figure 4. Sensor nodes receiving hello-ant update the pheromone values in their pheromone table.

3.4. Ant-based clustering in our system

How to select a sink node for each sensor node still remains a question in multi-sink sensor networks. One option is setting a sink for all sensor nodes when deploying a sensor network and keeping them for as long as the sensor network continues to operate. However, sensor nodes near the sink node, which is responsible for that area, may deplete their power when relaying numerous packets when events frequently occur in a specific area of the region being monitored. As a result, collecting information from that area becomes impossible. Otherwise, sensor nodes belonging to that sink node may blindly send packets to it when failure occurs. We introduced an ant-based method of clustering to solve these problems.

Ant-based clustering was originally a method of swarm

intelligence by ants grouping eggs or larvae according to their size. Ants repeatedly pick up and drop larvae based on their degree of similarity while wandering around a certain neighborhood. Clusters of different-sized larvae emerge in a self-organized way based on their behavior. We substitute similarity with the advantage of belonging to a cluster, and perform clustering to suit the network situation.

A cluster is a set of sensor nodes. Therefore, we should consider the state of sensor nodes in a cluster, such as residual power and distance from the sink node to define the advantages a cluster gains by behaving in the proposed way. These situations have already been reflected in the pheromone value introduced in Section 3.3, but this pheromone value mostly depends on neighboring sensor nodes and does not necessarily indicate the situations on a cluster level. To overcome this limitation, we introduce a *cluster pheromone*. The value of a cluster pheromone is calculated based on the pheromone of sensor node, and reflects the attractiveness of a cluster.

When sensor node n_i belongs to cluster S_j, n_i generates hello ants to carry the cluster pheromones of $C_{n_i}(S_j)$, which n_i considers, as well as cluster ID S_j. Sensor node n_k, which receives a hello ant transmitted by n_i, memorizes the n_i that says its cluster is S_j and its cluster pheromone is $C_{n_i}(S_j)$ in its *neighbor table* (This is currently a separate table from the pheromone table, but these are easily integrated into one). $C_{n_i}(S_j)$ is defined as:

$$C_{n_i}(S_j) = \frac{\sum_{k \in belong_{n_i}(S_j)} C_k(S_j) + avg\_ph_{n_i}(S_j)}{|belong_{n_i}(S_j)| + 1} \qquad (5)$$

where $belong_{n_i}(S_j)$ represents a set of nodes which are neighbors of n_i that participate in cluster S_j. $avg\_ph_{n_i}(S_j)$ is represented in Eq. (6) and is the average amount of pheromones in the entries which has the destination sink S_j.

$$avg\_ph_{n_i}(S_j) = \frac{\sum_{k \in belong_{n_i}(S_j)} P_{n_i}(k, S_j)}{|belong_{n_i}(S_j)|} \qquad (6)$$

Eq. (5) merely calculates the average value for the cluster pheromones of S_j, which is given by n_i and neighbors of n_i belonging to S_j.

Because hello ants also convey the cluster ID of the source node, sensor nodes can learn which cluster the neighboring nodes belong to, and whether they are on the boundaries of clusters. Sensor nodes on boundaries stochastically select whether they will transfer their membership from their cluster to another, just like real ants that pick up larvae to carry them elsewhere. Actual ants determine whether to pick up larvae based on similarities between these and neighboring larvae. We uses this feature of belonging to a cluster instead of similarity. The probability of n_i changing membership from cluster S_j to cluster S_k is defined in Eq. (7)

$$p_{n_i}(S_j \to S_k) = \left(\frac{f_{n_i}(S_j, S_k)}{k + f_{n_i}(S_j, S_k)} \right)^2, \qquad (7)$$

where k is a threshold parameter which controls probability of changing cluster membership. $f_{n_i}(S_j, S_k)$ is calculated as

$$f_{n_i}(S_j, S_k) = \max\left(0, \frac{|belong_{n_i}(S_k)|}{N_{n_i}} \frac{C_{n_i}(S_k) - C_{n_i}(S_j)}{C_{n_i}(S_k)}\right) \qquad (8)$$

In this equation, we consider the ratio between the number of neighbors participating in a certain cluster and the number of all neighbors. This term reflects our idea that sensor nodes on cluster boundaries should have a higher tendency to change their membership than others in view of connectivity among sensor nodes inside clusters. The cluster gradually changes according to the probability $P_{n_i}(S_j \to S_k)$.

3.5. Detection of sensor-node and sink-node failures

Sensor nodes are prone to fail due to their cheap production costs. Moreover, power is inevitably depleted during the long periods of operation of a sensor network. Sink nodes are no exception in that they can fail. Therefore, it is necessary to detect these failures and take appropriate countermeasures in order to be able to gather data over long term.

We applied a soft-state model to detect failures using hello ants transmitted by all sensor nodes at fixed intervals. As seen in Fig. 3, each entry in the pheromone table has a field for expiry time. At each time a sensor node receives a hello ant from n_i, it updates the expiry time field in the entry whose next-hop node field is n_i in its pheromone table. If n_i fails or experiences depleted power, neighboring sensor nodes cannot receive hello ants from n_i. After expiry time δ_n, neighboring sensor nodes delete the entry for n_i. Thus, as we use a soft-state model, we do not need to take explicit measures to detect failure. Sensor nodes select appropriate next-hop nodes according to Eq. (4) without any special handling.

Detecting sink node failure is also based on the same soft-state model. That is, the sink node periodically broadcast hello ants as well as sensor nodes. Sensor nodes around the sink node determine that the sink has failed if they have not received hello ants from it for a predefined time, δ_S. The cluster is no longer preferable in sink node failure. Thus, sensor nodes detecting sink node failures only stored a small value for the cluster pheromones in their hello ants. As these hello ants propagate over the network, sensor nodes participating in the failed sink's cluster abandon their membership, and join other clusters.

Detecting failure in sink nodes differs vastly from that in sensor nodes in that false detection is unacceptable. If hello ants cannot reach a neighboring node due to packet loss, the neighboring node mistakenly detects failure. Detecting failure incorrectly at a sensor node has an insignificant local effect; however, detecting failure in a sink node causes a transition in membership on the cluster level. We therefore decided to set δ_S for a longer duration than δ_n. The longer the expiry interval is, the lower the probability of incorrect detection is. A shorter expiry interval is preferable to enable adaptation to rapidly changing situations. Balancing this tradeoff is an important challenge that remains for the future.

4. Evaluating our proposed scheme

4.1. Simulation environment

We implemented our proposed scheme for the ns–2 [1] network simulator. In all the following experiments, we randomly place 200 sensor nodes over a region monitoring a square, 100 m per side. We assume that there are four sink nodes, and prepare three scenarios for a series of coordinates for the sinks as follows.

- *Scenario 1*: $(25, 25), (75, 25), (25, 75), (75, 75)$
- *Scenario 2*: $(15, 75), (38, 20), (60, 85), (85, 50)$
- *Scenario 3*: $(10, 10), (90, 10), (10, 90), (90, 90)$

Each plot below was made from the average of 15 simulations. We used IEEE 802.15.4 [7] in the simulation experiments, which is well known for its energy efficiency and low-rate communication. We applied a two-ray ground reflection the radio propagation model to simulate the signal power received for each packet. The parameter settings of the sensor nodes from [11, 6] were used in Table 1. Further simulation parameters are also shown in Table 2. We are currently investigating the individual influences of these parameters, but the values in the table were chosen because they yielded a good performance.

Our target was detecting event in sensor networks. Sensor nodes detect various kinds of events such as increase in temperature, and each node generates a packet to notify its sink of these events. These packets are relayed by other sensor nodes and arrive at the sinks. Events in our simulation experiments occurred at random points per second.

4.2. Event notification rate

Reliability of communication is one of the most important metrics in sensor networks whose purpose is to collect

Table 1. Parameters for sensor nodes

Power consumption for transmission	40.95 mW
Power consumption for reception	45.78 mW
Transmission power	0 dB
Transmission distance	10 m
Interference distance for transmission	16.8 m
Frequency	2450 MHz
Radius of sensing area	10 m
Transmission rate	250 kbps

Table 2. Simulation Parameters

Initial power	1 J
α	0.7
β	7
δ_n	3 s
δ_S	9 s
Interval in transmitting hello ants	0.5 s
Interval in transmitting backward ants	10 s

event data. We, therefore, define a metric to reflect that idea, the event-notification rate. The event-notification rate is defined as r_e/s_e, where s_e is the number of packets generated by sensor nodes which detect event e, and r_e is the number of packets carrying information on e and arriving at sink nodes. The plots in Fig. 5 are the results obtained with 200 sensor nodes in all three scenarios. PER is the packet error rate. The packet is randomly dropped depending on value of the PER. As we can see from these figures, the proposed scheme achieves a high event-notification rate of about 90%. The sensor network can carry event information to the sink nodes without the harmful effects of notification errors even when the wireless channels are of very poor quality. This is because the control packets are broadcast packets and interaction between neighboring sensor nodes compensates for the dropped packets. The pheromone distribution over the region being monitored using *Scenario 1* at $t = 400$ s with PER $= 0$ and PER $= 0.3$ is plotted in Fig. 6. We can see that the pheromone distribution is almost the same regardless of PER or the quality of the wireless channels. This is the advantage of the self-organized scheme, which solves difficult problems through iterating the simple actions of agents.

Fig. 7 plots the event-notification rate for Scenario 1 with 400 sensor nodes and looks about the same as in Fig. 5(a). The reason the event-notification rate is slightly reduced is due to the interference between packets carrying event information and backward ants, which increase in number while propagating in the network. Controlling the number of backward ants remains a serious challenge for future work.

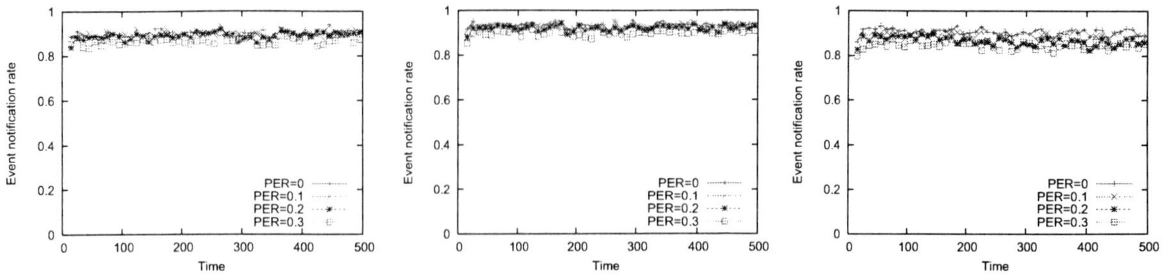

(a) Scenario 1 (b) Scenario 2 (c) Scenario 3

Figure 5. Event notification rate over time for all three scenarios

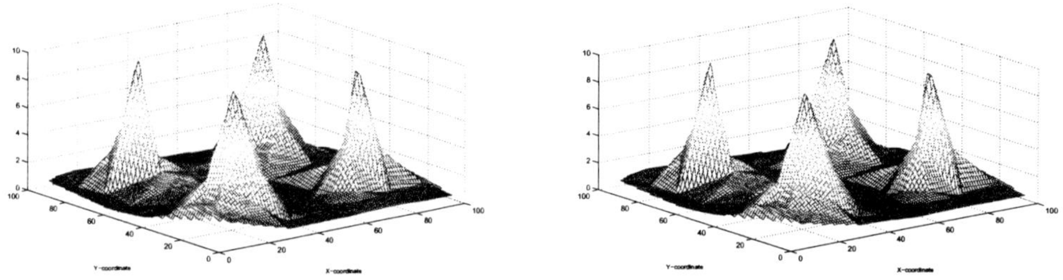

(a) PER=0 (b) PER=0.3

Figure 6. Pheromone distribution over region being monitored at $t = 400$ s for Scenario 1.

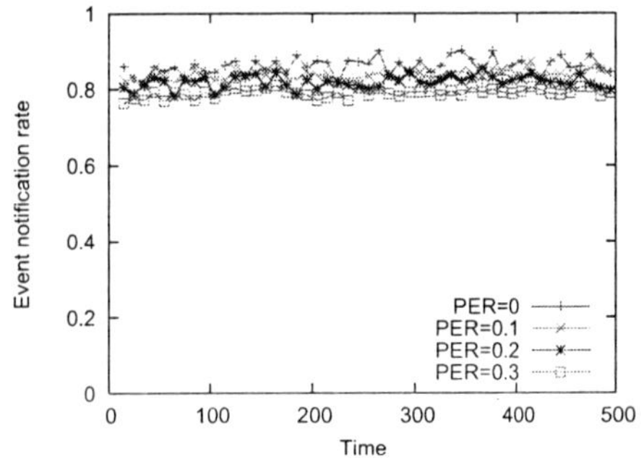

Figure 7. Event-notification rate with 400 nodes for Scenario 1.

4.3. Self-recovery from node failure

We simulated sensor node failure as follows to study the robustness of our proposal. Failure in this paper is defined as a state in which neither transmission nor reception is possible. We randomly selected $200 \times p_{\text{fail}}$ ($p_{\text{fail}} \in [0, 1]$) sensor nodes and made them fail at $t = 100$ s simultaneously in sensor networks where 200 sensor nodes had been deployed. This is far more serious than what can actually happen in reality. We set the PER to 0.1 and consider Scenario 1. We are interested in observing how soon and to what extent the event-notification rate would immediately recover from a decline after $t = 100$ s.

The results we obtained are shown in Fig. 8. The event-notification rate hovers at about 90% until $t = 100$ s, and then experiences a sudden drop just after $t = 100$ s. However, the event notification rate recovers within the short time to its previous state. That is, a certain degree of sensor node failures has little influence on the event-notification rate in our scheme, and it continues to collect event information. Most sensor nodes have some candidates for the next-hop node in their pheromone table and they stochastically select the next-hop node from these due to our ACO approach. When a sensor node detects failure in a neighboring node, it only eliminates the entry for the failed node, and the event-detection rate quickly recovers. These actions do not require global information or coordination, but the current state of neighbors which is easily acquired. With

0-7695-2906-2/07 $25.00 © 2007 IEEE

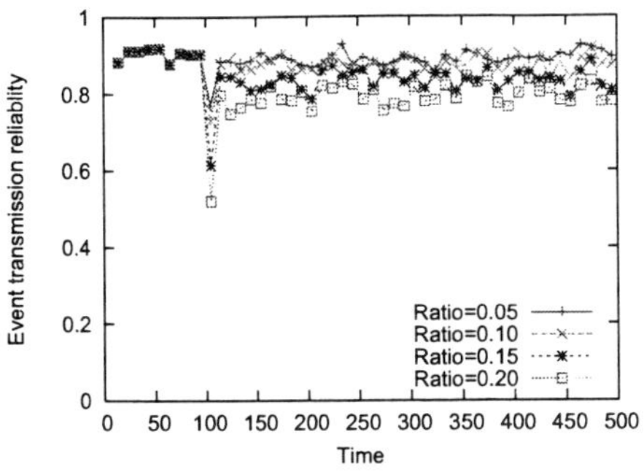

Figure 8. Self-recovery feature when sensor nodes fail simultaneously.

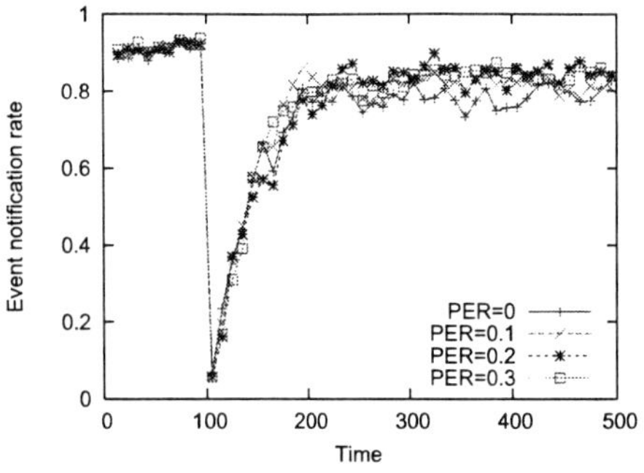

Figure 9. Self-repair features when sink node fails.

efficient combination of node-failure detection using a soft-state model and an ACO approach which selects the next-hop node stochastically, we can achieve self-recovery capabilities and it largely contributes to the attainment of more reliable sensor networks.

4.4. Self-Recovery after Sink Failure

Sink nodes can obviously fail as well. Most studies with single-sink configurations do not accommodate sink node failures, and in addition, only a few countermeasures against such failures have been mentioned even in multi-sink configuration sensor networks thus far. We took sink node failures into account, and proposed that sensor nodes belonging to the failed sink node transfer their membership to another cluster and continue to collect event information. We conducted new simulation experiments as follows to demonstrate the effectiveness of this proposal. Using Scenario 1, we made sink node S_1 located at the point of $(25, 25)$ fail at $t = 100$ s with PER $= 0.1$. However, it was difficult to interpret the effectiveness when events occur far from S_1. Therefore, we limited the area where events occurred to a circular area with a radius 20 m at the center of S_1 in our simulations.

Fig. 9 shows the experimental results. At $t = 100$ s, the event-notification rate falls steeply to almost 0% because all the packets are destined for S_1. However, after that, it recovers rapidly to the same rate as before S_1 failed. The state of the clusters is shown in Fig. 10. The single circles represent sensor nodes and the double circles are sink nodes. The gauge located to the upper right of a sensor node shows its residual power of the sensor node. Before S_1 failed, four clusters emerged, for each sink node. After S_1 failed, the clusters converge to three. We can achieve about the same event-notification rate as that before sink failure, through all sensor nodes repeating interactions with their neighbors and changing the shapes of clusters in a self-organized way. This strongly indicates our proposal is extremely robust and has strong self-recovery capabilities.

5. Conclusion

We described sensor networks with multi-sink configurations in this paper that were preferable in terms of scalability and fault tolerance and proposed a novel data-gathering scheme suited to these types of networks. It was inspired by the swarm intelligence of ants such as that found in ant-based clustering and ant-colony optimization. Each sensor node determines its next action through repeating interactions with neighboring nodes, and these actions enable the sensor network to evolve toward an optimal state. This data-gathering scheme, which splits sensor nodes into various clusters using ant-based clustering and conveys packets to the sink nodes with ACO routing, had a high event-notification rate and was stable and robust against poor-quality channels. It also had good self-recovery capabilities. In the case that sensor or sink node failure occurs, our scheme detects it properly, recovers from it, and can continue data collection in the way same as it was before the failure. Especially, as far as we know, there are no papers that deal with any countermeasures against sink node failure and evaluate it.

Our proposed data-gathering scheme, which is a combination of self-organization and self-recovery, is preferable for sensor networks because it can be deployed under harsh conditions. We did notice, however, that backward ants frequently interfered with packets conveying event information, and robustness gradually decreased with longer intervals between transmissions between backward ants. So far we have not fully examined the influences of the parameters. We adopt a probabilistic approach on clustering, but a deterministic approach might show better properties. We intend to tackle these issues, and would like to clarify the differences in characteristics between self-organized and centrally controlled sensor networks.

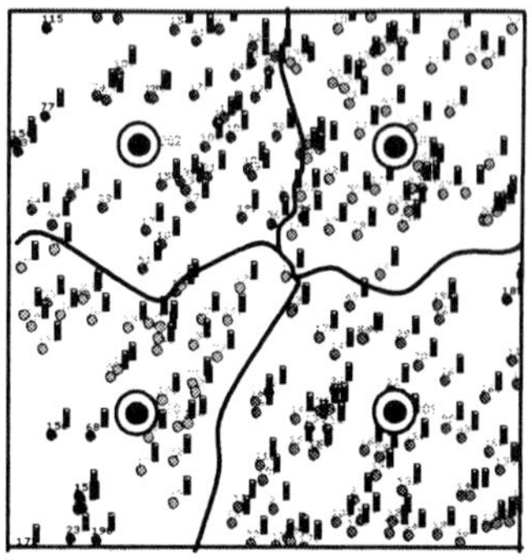

(a) $t = 99$

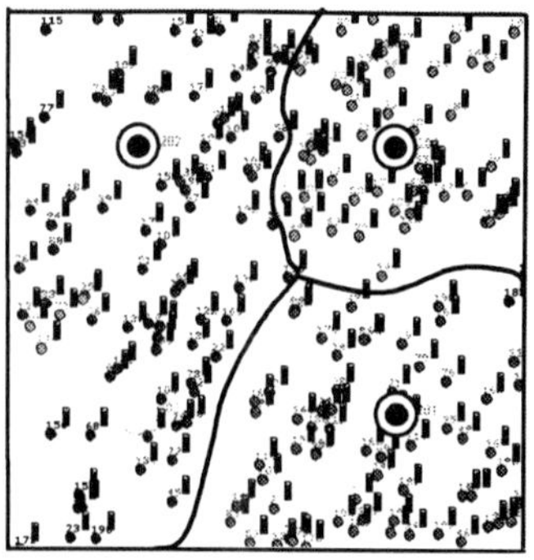

(b) $t = 120$

Figure 10. Cluster shapes over time when sink node fails

Acknowledgements

This research was supported in part by "Special Coordination Funds for Promoting Science and Technology: Yuragi Project" of the Ministry of Education, Culture, Sports, Science and Technology, Japan, Grant-in-Aid for Scientific Research (A) 16200003 and (C) 19500060. We also would like to especially thank Kenji Leibnitz and Shin'ichi Arakawa of Osaka University for their constructive comments throughout this work.

References

[1] ns-2 – the network simulator. online available at http://www.isi.edu/nsnam/ns.

[2] I. F. Akylidiz, W. Su, Y. Sankarasubramaniam, and E. Cayirci. A survey on sensor networks. *IEEE Communications Magazine*, Aug. 2002.

[3] B. Barń and R. Sosa. AntNet: Routing algorithm for data networks based on mobile agents. *Inteligencia Artificial, Revista Iberoamericana de Inteligencia Artificial*, 12:75–84, 2001.

[4] G. D. Caro, F. Ducatelle, and L. M. Gambardella. AntHocNet: an ant-based hybrid routing algorithm for mobile ad hoc networks. *European Transactions on Telecommunications*, 16, Oct. 2005.

[5] Y. Chen, E. Chan, and S. Han. Energy efficient multipath routing in large scale sensor networks with multiple sink nodes. In *Proceedings of the Sixth International Workshop on Advanced Parallel Processing Technologies*, Hong Kong, China, Oct. 2005.

[6] Chipcon. *Chipcon AS SmartRF®CC2420 Preliminary Datasheet*, 1.2 edition, June 2004.

[7] IEEE. *802.15.4–2003 IEEE Standard for Information Technology–Part 15.4: Wireless Medium Access Control (MAC) and Physical Layer (PHY) Specifications for Low-Rate Wireless Personal Area Networks (LR-WPANs)*, Oct. 2003.

[8] M. Kalantari and M. Shayman. Design optimization of multi-sink sensor networks by analogy to electrostatic theory. In *Proceedings of the Wireless Communication and Networking Conference*, Las Vegas, Nevada, USA, Apr. 2006.

[9] Y. Kiri, M. Sugano, and M. Murata. On characteristics of multi-hop communication in large-scale clustered sensor networks. *IEICE Transactions on Communications*, E90-B(2):228–238, Feb. 2007.

[10] H. Lee, A. Klappenecker, K. Lee, and L. Lin. Energy efficient data management for wireless sensor networks with data sink failure. In *Proceedings of the Workshop on Resource Provisioning and Management in Sensor Networks (RPMSN 2005)*, Nov. 2005.

[11] Moteiv Corporation. *Telos (Rev B): PRELIMINARY Datasheet*, May 2004.

[12] E. I. Oyman and C. Ersoy. Multiple sink network design problem in large scale wireless sensor networks. In *Proceedings of the IEEE ICC 2004*, Paris, France, June 2004.

[13] A. L. Vizine, L. N. de Castro, E. R. Hruschka, and R. R. Gudwin. Towards improving clustering ants: An adaptive ant clustering algorithm. *Informatica Journal*, 29, 2005.

[14] H. F. Wedde, M. Farooq, T. Pannenbaecker, B. Vogel, C. Mueller, J. Meth, and R. Jeruschkat. BeeAdHoc: An energy efficient routing algorithm for mobile ad hoc networks inspired by bee behavior. In *Proceedings of the 2005 conference on Genetic and evolutionary computation*, pages 153–160, Washington DC, USA, June 2005.

[15] D. Zaharie and F. Zamfirache. Dealing with noise in ant-based clustering. In *Proceeding of IEEE Congress of Evolutionary Computation*, pages 2395–2402, Edinburgh, UK, Sept. 2005.

[16] Y. Zhang, L. D. Kuhn, and M. P. Fromherz. Improvements on ant routing for sensor networks. In *Proceedings of the Fourth International Workshop on Ant Colony Optimization and Swarm Intelligence*, Brussels, Belgium, Sept. 2004.

Research Track, Session 6: Combinatorial Optimization

On Scaling Multi-Agent Task Reallocation Using Market-Based Approach *

Rajesh K. Karmani   Timo Latvala   Gul Agha
Department of Computer Science
University of Illinois at Urbana-Champaign
Urbana, IL 61801 USA
{rkumar8,tlatvala,agha}@uiuc.edu

Abstract

Multi-agent systems (MAS) provide a promising technology for addressing problems such as search and rescue missions, mine sweeping, and surveillance. These problems are a form of the computationally intractable Multi-Depot Traveling Salesman Problem *(MDTSP). We propose a novel market-based approach, called Market-based Approach with Look-ahead Agents (MALA), to address the problem. In MALA, agents use look ahead to optimize their behavior. Each agent plans a preferred, reward-maximizing tour for itself using our proposed algorithm which is based on the Universal TSP algorithm. The agent then uses the preferred tour to evaluate potential trades with other agents in linear time – a necessary prerequisite for scalability of market-based approach. We use simulations in a two dimensional world to study the performance of MALA and compare it with* O-contracts *and* TraderBots, *respectively, a centralized approach and a distributed approach. Experiments suggest that MALA efficiently scales to thousands of tasks and hundreds of agents in terms of both computation and communication complexity, while delivering relatively good-quality but approximate solutions.*

1. Introduction

Multi-agent systems have been proposed as a promising technology to address problems such as *search and rescue missions*, *sensing and data collection*, *mine sweeping*, *surveillance*, etc. We motivate the problem with two examples. Consider a team of robots is dropped from a helicopter for mine-sweeping. The robots know the suspected locations of the mines. The mission of the team is to visit the sites, and detect and disable mines that are found. Each robot has limited battery power. The problem is to find an allocation of mines to robots so that each mine gets visited once by some agent and the mission is accomplished in the shortest time feasible. As another example, consider millibots [10] launched from different points in order to monitor the structural health of a building. For such monitoring, vibration and strain need to be measured at hundreds and thousands of points of interest.

One way to address the problem described above is by using a group of robotic agents to visit a set of pre-selected observation points and accomplish an objective such as taking a measurement. We'll call such a 'visit' to an observation point, a *task*. We assume that we are working with a 'known' world: each agent knows the position corresponding to the tasks but need not know the position of other agents.

An agent's *mission* consists of a set of tasks that are assigned to it, together with the agent's plan to visit these tasks (a tour). A mission is complete when every task in the set has been performed, i.e., the tour is complete. Observe that computing optimal mission plans corresponds to solving the *Multi-Depot Traveling Salesman Problem* (MDTSP), and is thus a generalization of the classic *Traveling Salesman Problem* (TSP). The MDTSP problem is computationally intractable; it involves computing multi-agent TSP solutions. A naïve solution would be to exhaustively enumerate the possible allocations and compute a tour for each allocation. However, this approach is not computationally feasible: given m agents and n tasks, there are m^n allocations. Each allocation requires computing m NP-Hard TSPs, where the size of a TSP varies from 0 to n.

To systematically tackle the problem, we model our agents in the following way. First, each agent is rational but has bounded computational power. Second, an agent is self-interested but cooperative: it wants to maximize the number of tasks that it performs. Finally, each agent is capable of covering only a fixed total distance (corresponding to its fuel). Given this constraint, the global objective becomes that of servicing maximum number of tasks.

We propose a distributed, market-based approach to find

*This research has been supported in part by NSF under grant CNS 05-09321 and by ONR under DoD MURI award N0014-02-1-0715.

reasonably efficient, but not optimal, solutions to the task allocation problem. Market-based approaches have been successfully used to solve co-ordination problems for multi-agent systems [1, 5, 8, 17]. They naturally form a distributed framework, and offer a good way of sharing information between agents. The challenge faced by economic approaches, including market-based ones, is to design *efficient* algorithms for the behavior of individual agents.

Our approach *Market-based Approach with Look-ahead Agents* (MALA) works as follows. We start the process by randomly allocating each task to some agent. The problem then becomes one of task reallocation. Each agent then computes a tour on the set of tasks within its fuel range using a modified *Universal TSP (U-TSP)* algorithm [9]. Specifically, we use a 2-approximation TSP tour [3] to guide the non-deterministic choices that are inherent in the original U-TSP algorithm. Our simulations suggest that the use of 2-approximation TSP tour significantly reduces the cost of tours obtained using the original U-TSP algorithm. Note that the 2-approximation tour is only used for resolving the non-determinism, and this does not modify the properties of a U-TSP tour.

The U-TSP based algorithm is desirable due to two reasons. First, observe that some tours computed over the tasks within the fuel range may still exceed the given fuel budget. We propose a greedy pruning strategy which exploits the representation and properties of U-TSP tour, and allows agents to compute their desired tour for a given fuel budget. Second, a U-TSP tour allows linear time computation of the cost of subtours while guaranteeing a good approximation on the cost.

The desired tour approximates the maximization of agents' reward for given fuel constraint. Once an agent has computed a desired tour, it negotiates with other agents to get as close as possible to their desired tour. Myopic agents run the risk of getting stuck on a local optimum. Performing a full look ahead in the future would address this problem. In an agent-based decentralized solution, such a look ahead requires each agent to estimate other agents' preferences. This is prohibitively expensive for large instances [12]. We conjecture that a partial look ahead reduces the chances that the solution gets stuck in a local optimum.

We evaluate MALA by means of simulations and compare it with two existing approaches specifically the centralized O-contracts approach [11] and the distributed, multi-agent Traderbots approach [7] . Results suggest that MALA outperforms the centralized approach in solution quality as well as computation time, while the Traderbots approach suffers from higher communication cost.

2. Related Work

Different approaches such as linear programming, mixed integer linear programming and iterative network flow have been adopted to overcome the computational challenge in solving MDTSP. In this paper, we will compare our approach to other market-based approaches–not only because such approaches are the most closely related to our approach, but also because they show considerable improvement in solution quality over the other approaches.

One approach that has been proposed to avoid the intractability of full look ahead may be termed the *instantaneous assignment* (IA) (e.g. [1]). In the IA approach, agents do not plan for tasks beyond the immediate one; instead they focus on the one task they are carrying out or they are bidding for. Predictably, IA can lead to poor solution quality due to local optima.

Sujit et al. [15] restrict the scope of the problem by assuming that the field is unknown, and hence the agents cannot plan ahead. In their work, agents can communicate within a limited range (global broadcast is not feasible). Their approach has been tested for small scale multi-agent systems: their experiments use 7 agents and up to 50 tasks. Note that we experiment with hundreds of agents and thousands of tasks.

An alternative approach is to use a central mediator. An example of these approaches is *auction* mechanism which has been very popular recently. In auctions, a central auctioneer puts tasks in a market and agents can bid for them according to their cost functions. Auctions come in two flavors: single-task and combinatorial. In *single-task auctions*, agents are uncertain about the preferences of other agents and about future contracts. Hence, agents make short-sighted commitments. *Combinatorial auctions* [14] can theoretically find optimal solutions but they suffer from some major deficiencies: an agent needs to compute a strategy for bidding, and the number of combinations of items (known as bundles) grows exponentially as a function of the size of a bundle, which makes the cost calculation for large instances intractable–both at the bidder's end and at the seller's end (where winners are chosen in the auction clearance).

Reallocation mechanisms are generally used to improve the quality of solutions obtained through centralized approaches. Peer-to-peer task reallocation is equivalent to a local search where every move or exchange between the agents decreases the cost or increases the utility. It has been shown that global optimum can be reached in finite number of steps if the agents could have a complete look ahead [11], where each step is an *O-contract* which moves a single task possibly with some payment. However, as we mentioned earlier, complete look ahead is computationally intractable.

An alternative is to use *OCSM-contracts*: an OCSMcontract is a member of the set formed by the cross-product of a number of different types of contracts: original contracts, cluster contracts, swap contracts and multi-agent contracts. For detailed explanation of these contracts, see [11]. Globally optimal solution can be reached in a finite number of steps using OCSM-contracts and a simple greedy strategy without requiring look ahead [11]. The problem with this approach is two fold: the number of steps required is exponential and evaluating contracts at each step is computationally intractable. There is a need to study strategies for distributed negotiation short of exhaustive enumeration and greedy exchange.

It is interesting to note that Sandholm and his group, who have done considerable research in contract evaluation based on marginal costs, suggest a paradigm shift to centralized or mediated clearing to overcome the inefficient solutions negotiated by myopic agents [12]. However, our work is motivated by the conjecture that complete look ahead may not be necessary for efficient solutions; we conjecture that approximate, partial lookahead will support a decentralized approach that is both scalable and efficient.

3. Approach

MALA works in two-phases (see Figure 1):

Planning Phase: In the planning phase, each agent computes a preferred tour. Such a tour provides the agent a means of doing a look ahead to determine its utility for a potential task.

Negotiation Phase: In the negotiation phase, an agent attempts to trade tasks with other agents in order to sell unwanted tasks and acquire preferred tasks. Each trade is pair-wise and is evaluated based on a marginal cost analysis done by the two agents involved in the trade.

We now define the problem formally and provide the details of the U-TSP based algorithm and the negotiation strategy.

3.1. Problem Definition

Let T be a set consisting of n tasks, and A be a set consisting of m agents such that $n \gg m$. Assume a k-dimensional Euclidean field on which the tasks in T and the agents in A are located. Their distribution across the field is uniform random. Let T^* be the set consisting of finite sequences of tasks. Each sequence corresponds to a possible tour for an agent, and the tasks in a sequence are said to be assigned to the agent. A task allocation is a mapping $A \rightarrow T^*$ such that the intersection between each of the sequences in the range is empty. In other words, each task is uniquely assigned to an agent.

According to the taxonomy presented in [6], the problem we are addressing may be characterized as follows. Tasks are *single-agent*, i.e., tasks require just one single agent to service. Agents are *single-task*, i.e., agents can service only one task at a time. The approach is *time-extended* since the agents plan ahead and may include more than one task in their schedule.

We start with a random allocation R. The goal is to find a task allocation O such that the maximum number of tasks can be serviced by the agents. Note that starting with a random allocation ensures that each task is initially allocated to some agent. Each agent is subject to a fuel constraint which limits the total distance it can travel. It is obvious that some tasks may be impossible to service due to the fuel constraint, even given an optimal allocation.

We assume that the field is static in the sense that neither the agents, nor the tasks, move, appear or disappear; the communication between agents is reliable; and there is no central mediator. These assumptions ensure that the only uncertainties agents face are those related to other agents' preferences. The simplification enables us to focus on the effect of limited look ahead, measured in terms of scalability and quality of solution metrics.

3.2. Mechanism Design

A market-based approach has to fix the rules of the game (mechanism). Mechanism design critically affects potential outcomes: properly designed mechanisms play a significant role in restricting the solution space to a space that mostly contains desirable outcomes [16]. Our market uses the following mechanism:

- Each task has a constant utility associated with it. This provides each agent the incentive to maximize the number of tasks it services.
- Each task which remains un-serviced incurs a penalty (constant p here) for the agent assigned to it. Thus, an agent has the incentive to actively sell-off tasks which it does not expect to be able to service.
- Agents *offer* tasks which they own to the market. Such offers may include side-payments as inducements.
- Agents may *bid* for tasks that are available in the market.
- Agents may *accept* a bid.
- Agents can express their interest in buying a task which is owned by some other agent but is not available in the market. Such offers are called *hostile offers*. Hostile offers are accompanied by the offer of a payment as inducement.

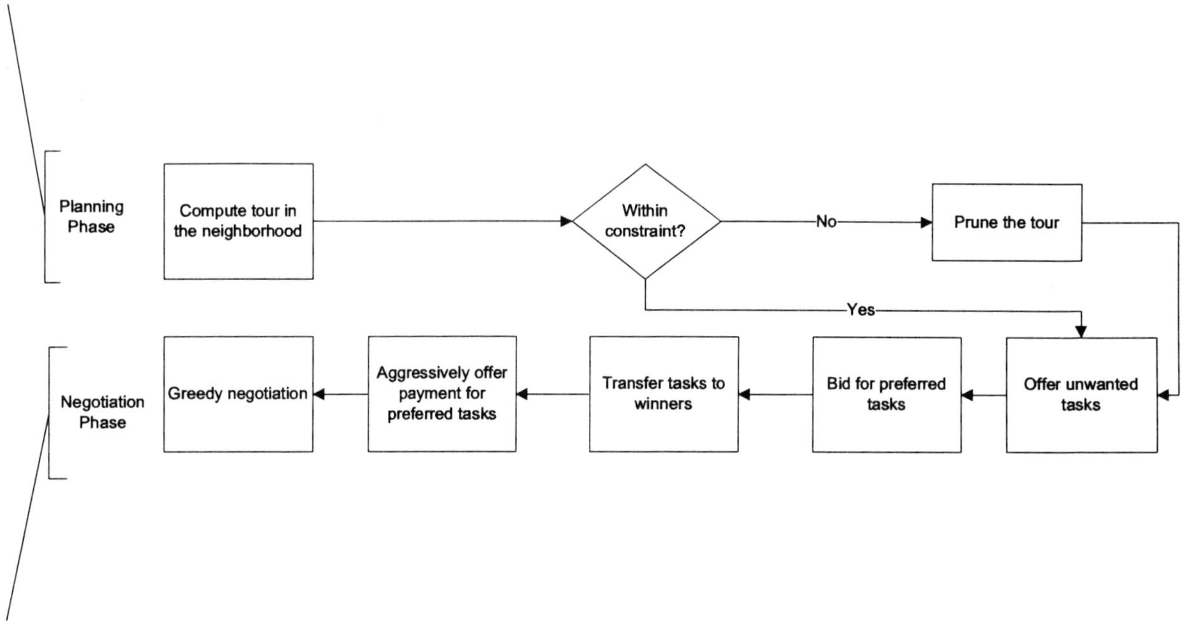

Figure 1. Overview of the approach.

3.3. Modified Universal TSP

In the planning phase, each agent computes a preferred tour in its neighborhood using the Universal TSP (U-TSP) algorithm [9] such that the tour maximizes its reward for the given fuel constraint. We express the fuel constraint in terms of total distance an agent may travel. Since the agent is required to return to its origin, an agent's neighborhood is defined as the region within the radius $d/2$, where d is the agent's fuel constraint. Once a tour for all destinations in the neighborhood has been computed, the U-TSP algorithm enables a linear time computation of the cost of a subtour. This enables a marginal cost analysis in linear time.

Using the U-TSP algorithm provides an $O(\log n)$ approximation for the cost of a the subtour. On the other hand, using a 2-approximation TSP algorithm would produce an approximation that is at most two times from the optimum cost of the tour. However, in this case evaluating each trade requires up to four computations, each of which costs $O(n \log n)$ [2, 4]. This is a significant cost for large problem instances and hinders scalability. Thus we have to make a trade-off between solution quality and scalability.

In order to try to reduce the error in the U-TSP approximation, we modify it as follows. Note that the U-TSP algorithm is based on a tree data structure and involves some nondeterminism during its computation. In order to improve the tours, an agent computes a tighter tour *on the same points* using the 2-approximation algorithm [3]. This computation is used to heuristically guide the U-TSP algorithm's initial computation. With such guidance, we observed significant improvements in the quality of the solutions provided by the U-TSP algorithm.

The need for tight tours is fairly obvious. Our global objective is to maximize the number of tasks carried out given that each agent has a fuel constraint. This is helped by finding low-cost tours for each agent: in general, the global objective is positively correlated with agent allocations which minimize the cost of its tour.

The complete algorithm is described in Algorithm 1.

Algorithm 1 - Modified Universal TSP Algorithm

```
T = Tree structure from U-TSP algorithm
R = 2-approximation tour

makeTour (Node T)
  if (T.hasChildren)
     for all (v in t.children)
        - w = makeTour(v)
        - rank(w) = arg max_{wi∈w} (indexOf(wi, R))
        - list.add(w)
     sort list in ascending order of rank
     for all (v in list)
        add elements of v to the list Tour
     return Tour
  else
     return list containing T
```

While we constrain an agent's tour to tasks within its

radius, the tour obtained by our modified U-TSP may exceed the agent's fuel constraint (and generally will). To prune this tour, we experimented with two approaches. We first tried a greedy algorithm: find a task with the highest marginal cost at each step and remove it from the tour; repeat until the tour cost is just within the agent's fuel constraint.

We then tried a more sophisticated approach which exploits the tree-based data structure of the U-TSP algorithm. The core idea behind U-TSP algorithm is to divide the field into small regions and progressively build a tree of tasks bottom-up by selecting coarser regions at each subsequent level. The intuition behind our algorithm is to exploit the structure provided by this tree to remove the smallest region from the tour such that the resulting tour is just within an agent's fuel constraint.

Specifically, our algorithm starts from the root of the tree and removes branches which correspond to chunks of region from the tour until the tour cost falls below the agent's fuel constraint. At this point, it "zooms down" on that chunk, keeps removing finer chunks until the tour cost falls below d. This repeats until it finds a tour such that the tour's cost is just below the fuel constraint d. From experiments, we found that the second algorithm produces marginally better tours than the first one. The second algorithm is described in Algorithm 2.

Algorithm 2 - Pruning Tours

```
pruneTree (Node T)
  if (T is leaf)
      remove T from tour
  while(cost > CONSTRAINT)
      - Find the branch j having the least
          reward with respect to cost
      - Remove tasks in the branch from tour
      - Compute cost of the remaining tour
  Restore the tasks in branch j to the tour
  pruneTree (j)
```

3.4. Negotiation Strategy

Once all agents have computed a preferred tour, they negotiate with each other towards their preferred tour. At step 1, agents put tasks they do not want in the market (recall that an agent will be penalized for not servicing tasks assigned to it in the final allocation). Let the set of tasks that were initially assigned (by random allocation) to an agent be RA, and the set of tasks in its preferred tour be PT. Then the agent wants to get rid of $RA \setminus PT$, and acquire $PT \setminus RA$ from the market.

If only one agent is interested in an offered task, it simply takes the task. If multiple agents are interested in a task, the owner agent starts an auction realizing the potential to gain utility. After such tasks have been moved, we have one the following situations for each task t:

1. Only one agent prefers t and the task is assigned to that agent. In this case, no further action is necessary.
2. No agent prefers to have t but it is assigned to one of them. In this case, the owner computes the maximum side-payment it can offer for t and puts this offer into the market. Each agent for whom the task is in its range uses this side-payment to compute its marginal gain.
3. Multiple agents prefer t and one of them owns it. Observe that t may not be available in the market if random allocation assigns it to an agent that prefers t. This agent may not have the highest incentive to service t, though. Each of the remaining interested agents puts a hostile bid in the market offering a price it is willing to pay based on its marginal cost analysis. The owner decides whether to accept the offer based on its own marginal cost analysis.

Thus far marginal cost analysis has been based on agents' preferred tours (See Figure 1: we are now at the point just before the box 'Greedy negotiation'). We assume that in the face of uncertainty, agents remain "optimistic" about reaching their preferred tour. Now the agents realize that they may not reach the preferred tour and become "pessimistic." In this case, we assume agents resort to a greedy strategy and analyze contracts myopically, based on their current assignment.

4. Results

We tested the effectiveness of using MALA by experiments done on a custom-designed simulator. The simulator is synchronous: at each time step, every agent is allowed to execute some action. We generated 1730 problem instances, each representing a different combination of number of agents (from 20 to 200 in increments of 20), number of tasks (from 100 to 2000 in increments of 100) and fuel constraint (from 100 to 1900 in increments of 200). We also imposed the requirement that the number of tasks must be at least three times the number of agents in every instance.

We ran the simulations on the same test instances for each of three approaches: MALA, centralized O-contracts, and Traderbots. We measured the (simulated) computation time, the number of messages required, the number of broadcasts required, coverage and cost of the tours. Our definition of coverage is as follows. Let d be the fuel constraint for an agent. Then every task located outside the radius $d/2$ of that agent is trivially infeasible (for the agent).

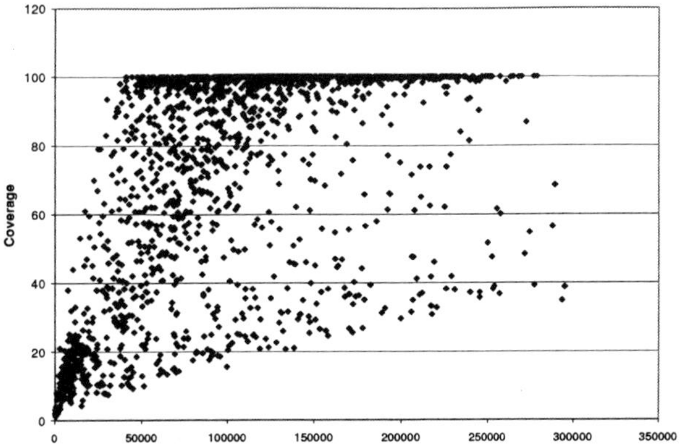

(a) Traderbots approach.

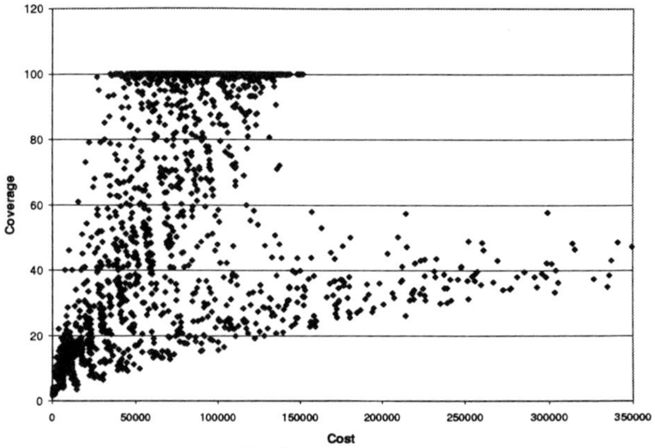

(b) O-contracts.

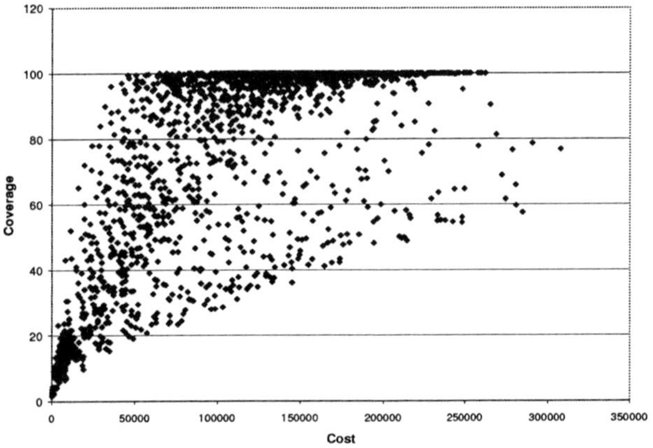

(c) MALA.

Figure 2. Solution quality as coverage vs cost for all instances.

Coverage is the number of not trivially infeasible tasks that have been allocated to some agent as a fraction of the total number of tasks. Note that servicing a task may be infeasible but not trivially unfeasible. In MALA, this may happen in two ways: firstly, because the initial random allocation assigns an infeasible task to an agent which the agent is not able to subsequently get rid of; or secondly, because of the use of the greedy strategy by a pessimistic agent. This means that our coverage metric introduces a possible bias against MALA: unlike MALA, neither of the other approaches prunes tasks within the fuel range of agents to arrive at their tours. Thus the tours proposed by the other approaches may be more likely to be infeasible, which would make our estimate of their coverage relatively generous. We have not studied the results for this bias.

Figure 2 (a,b,c) shows scatter plots of coverage against cost representing all problem instances. Essentially, this plot represents the quality of solution. High-quality solutions provide high coverage for lowest possible cost (the upper-left portion of the graph) and this is where we would like more points to appear.

The O-contracts approach results in a significant number of points in the high cost, low coverage (lower-right) section of the graph. The greedy, multi-agent approach does better than the O-contracts approach but MALA fares significantly better than both–as evident by the density of points in the upper-left section of the graph. The lower periphery of the plots warrants careful observation. In plot (c), the lower periphery has a higher slope compared to those in plots (a) and (b) and thus, seems to evade the lower-right region. For example, at 100000 units of cost, the lowest point in (c) is at around 28% coverage while corresponding numbers for (a) and (b) are 15% and 16%. Similarly, at 150000 units of cost, the lowest point in (c) is at around 41% coverage while corresponding numbers in (a) and (b) are 22% and 23%. This observation supports our hypothesis that the approximate look ahead helps in avoiding the worst solutions.

Figure 3 (a) shows a plot of coverage versus number of tasks, for a specific combination of number of agents and fuel constraint (100 and 1100 respectively) while (b) shows the same for 60 agents and fuel constraint of 1300. Intuitively, coverage will decrease with increasing number of

0-7695-2906-2/07 $25.00 © 2007 IEEE

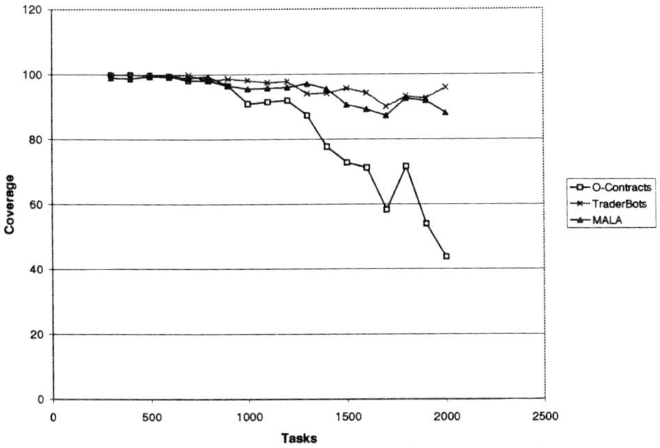

(a) 100 agents - 1100 units fuel constraint

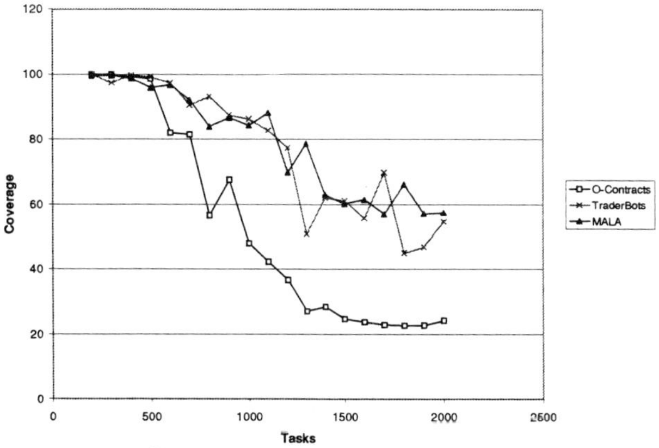

(b) 60 agents - 1300 units fuel constraint

Figure 3. Behavior of coverage with respect to tasks.

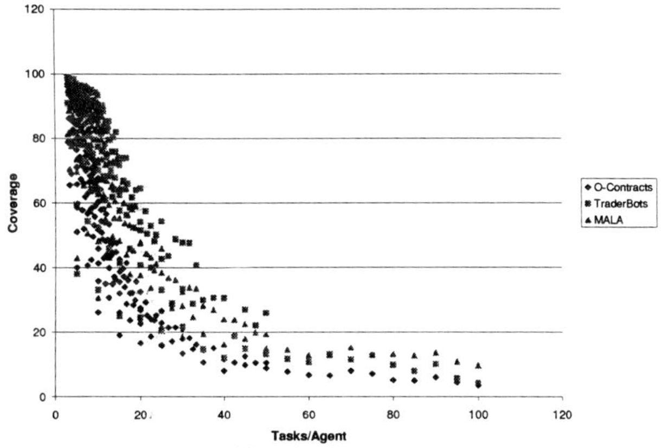

(a) 500 units fuel constraint

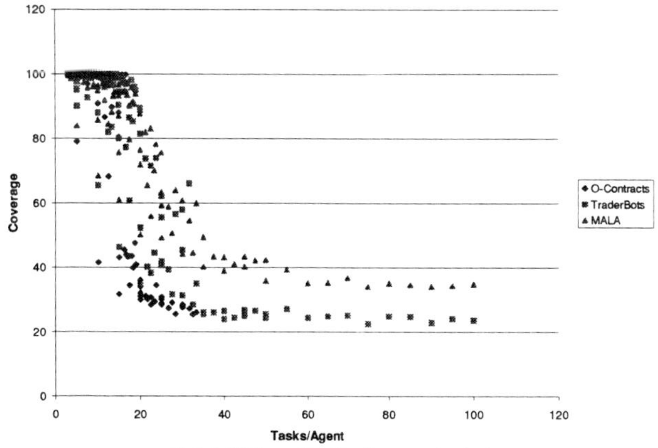

(b) 1500 units fuel constraint

Figure 4. Behavior of coverage with respect to the ratio tasks/agents.

tasks keeping other factors constant, and this plot indicates how different approaches fare relative to each other. Coverage drops rapidly for O-contracts based approach as number of tasks increase. This suggests that O-contracts based approach is more likely to get stuck in local optimum. The curve for MALA shows a much lower slope. Interestingly, the other distributed approach has a very similar curve to that of MALA.

We analyzed coverage as a function of the ratio of tasks per agent, keeping the agents' fuel constraint constant. The difficulty of satisfying a problem instance increases as a function of this ratio (given constant fuel), and therefore the coverage drops. Figure 4 shows a scatter plot for all three approaches for two different fuel constraints. It is quite clear that both the distributed approaches provide better solutions than the central approach. For the most difficult instances–those with a density ratio of 50 or more–MALA dominates the other two approaches in both the plots. This again suggests that MALA avoids the worst solutions.

Figure 5 shows the average coverage as a function of the fuel constraint (the average is taken across all combinations of numbers of agents and tasks). The best fit model for these curves appear to be a power law (R-squared for the best fits: 0.45 for O-contracts, 0.44 for TraderBots, and 0.60 for MALA).

To analyze these results statistically, we performed a number of paired t-tests (recall that we ran simulations for all approaches for the *same* problem instances). For coverage as a function of fuel, the TraderBots approach does better than MALA for fuel constraints below 900 ($p < .001$), while MALA outperforms TraderBots for fuel constraints greater than 1500 ($p < .001$). The two approaches are comparable between fuel constraint of 900 and 1500. Observe that MALA provides good solutions in comparison to the other two approaches despite them employing a 2-approximation TSP algorithm for evaluating contracts.

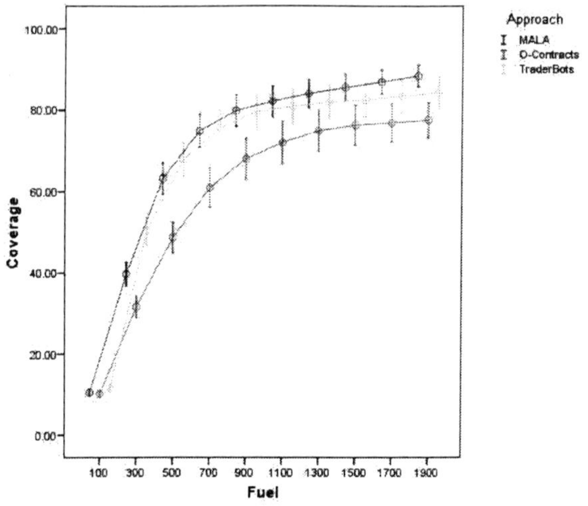

Figure 5. Coverage vs Fuel across all combinations of number of agents and number of tasks. 95% Confidence Intervals around the mean are shown.

Figure 6 compares the communication cost of the two distributed approaches, MALA and TraderBots, in terms of messages (point-to-point) and broadcasts (offers made in the market). Clearly, MALA requires fewer messages and broadcasts to reach its solution: a paired t-test shows that the difference is significant ($t = 42, p < .001$ for messages, and $t = 37, p < .001$ for broadcasts). These results can be explained by observing that in the planning phase of MALA, agents are selective in determining their preferred trades, and therefore require less communication. The result supports the importance of look ahead. Because the O-contracts approach is a centralized approach, obviously there is no communication overhead during the computation. However, a burst of communication is expected in the beginning to gather preferences from agents, and after the computation in order to propagate the allocation to agents. Gathering preferences requires scheduling messages of all the agents; this could be quite expensive and involve a lot of messages. Moreover, communication with the centralized server are also likely to be expensive as the server could be a hotspot.

We did all our simulations on a single machine. In our approach, we observed that significant computation time is spent in computing U-TSP based tours. In a real distributed environment, this time would be spread across all agents executing in a parallel fashion. On the other hand, the O-contracts based approach is completely centralized and has a very high computation time. The TraderBots approach does not involve computing tours and does better in terms of computation time per agent. In real settings, though, the TraderBots approach would suffer from high convergence time due to very high volume of messages and broadcasts required. We believe there is ample evidence from the results that the investment in computing a preferred tour ahead pays off significantly both in terms of solution quality and the number of messages exchanged.

5. Conclusion and Future Work

We proposed a novel market-based approach to solve multi-agent task allocation, whereby an agent has a limited look ahead. Agents trade tasks based on their estimates of the marginal cost or payoff of a trade. We proposed using a modified U-TSP algorithm to enable agents to achieve such look ahead because U-TSP based marginal cost computations are linear in time and hence allow the agents to process large number of messages at each step. This enables our algorithm to be scalable to large instances of the problem. The results of our simulations support the conjecture that such limited look ahead may provide an effective and scalable solution to the problem.

By using an initial allocation, we defined the problem as one of task reallocation. However, the choice of random allocation may not be the best. An alternative initial allocation could be obtained by using an auction mechanism. It is possible that such an allocation could further improve the solution quality while lowering computation and communication cost. Furthermore, an allocation obtained through auctions allows us to relax the assumption of 'known' world, and reliable communication in the whole field. Each agent will bid for and trade tasks, and communicate with other agents located only in its neighborhood.

To evaluate the pay-off from look ahead, we assumed a two dimensional world and reliable communication. We believe this work can be readily extended to a k-dimensional Euclidean world. However, in certain applications, such as search and rescue operations in an urban terrain, Euclidean metric may be inapplicable. In some cases, a City Block or *Manhattan metric* may be more appropriate. In this case, using the Euclidean assumption in MALA may still provide a reasonable approximation that may be adjusted: the Manhattan distance between two points is at most $\sqrt{2}$ times the Euclidean distance between them, and on average, as a simple calculation shows, it is 1.28 times the Euclidean distance. However, note that obstacles could introduce a complex topology that cannot be captured by the Manhattan metric; in this case, our results may not hold.

It is important to reiterate that MALA does not lead to optimal solutions as the look ahead itself is approximate. Even if the look ahead were optimal, this preference would be unknown to other agents. Moreover, multiple agents may have conflicting preferences, making global optimization difficult. In our approach, look ahead provides temporary "optimism" to the agent (in terms of allocation they

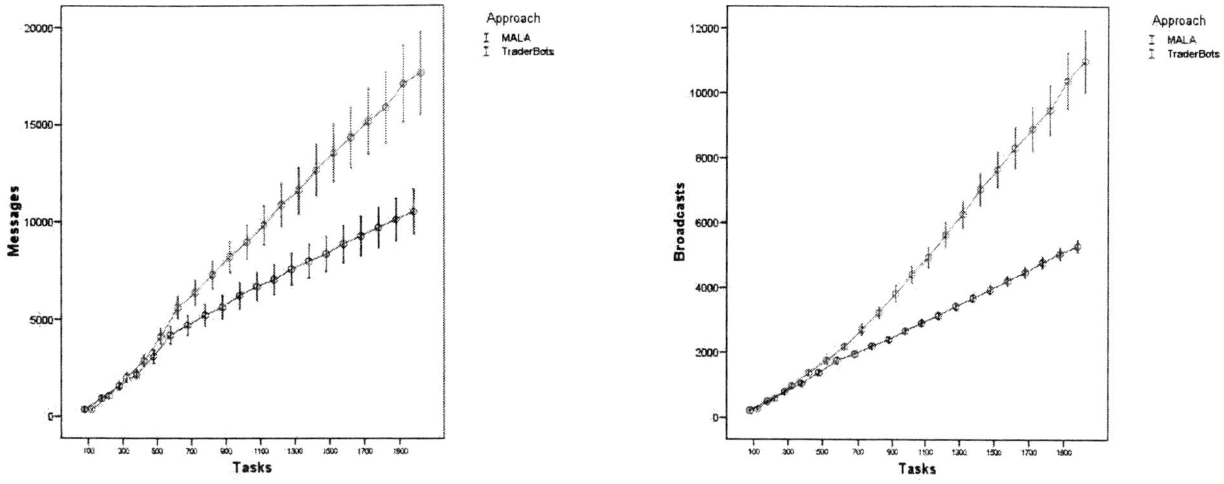

Figure 6. Number of messages and broadcasts required vs the number of tasks across all combinations of number of agents and fuel constraint. 95% Confidence Intervals around the mean are shown.

have reached a milestone or a higher level); once they realize that they may not have what they prefer, agents switch to "pessimism" as a fall-back strategy. In our implementation, pessimistic agents adopt a greedy approach. We found some literature in economics on modeling optimism or pessimism due to uncertainty in game-theoretic settings [13]. We believe there is potential future work in this direction.

We plan to extend our approach to handle dynamic environments where tasks are allowed to appear and disappear, and agents may have limited mobility. Also, there are quite a few applications which impose constraints or dependencies between the tasks. The challenge in this case is to represent and evaluate bids for interdependent tasks. Another generalization of the current problem is as follows: instead of each task requiring a single agent, a task may require multiple agents to service it. Finally, we plan to test the behavior of MALA with imperfect communication and heterogenous agents (such as agents having different fuel constraint) which can introduce further uncertainties into the problem.

Acknowledgements

We would like to thank Chandra Chekuri for suggesting the use of the Universal TSP algorithm and for providing useful insights into alternative approaches for planning tours. We would also like to thank Vijay Anand Reddy for suggestions about the relation between Manhattan and Euclidean metrics.

References

[1] A. Ahmed, A. Patel, T. Brown, M. Ham, M.-W. Jang, and G. Agha. Task assignment for a physical agent team via a dynamic forward/reverse auction mechanism. In *The International Conference of Integration of Knowledge Intensive Multi-Agent Systems KIMAS '05: Modeling, Evolutions and Engineering*, pages 311–317, April 2005.

[2] M. Andersson and T. Sandholm. Time-quality tradeoffs in reallocative negotiation with combinatorial contract types. In *AAAI/IAAI*, pages 3–10, 1999.

[3] T. H. Cormen, C. E. Leiserson, R. L. Rivest, and C. Stein. *Introduction to Algorithms, 2nd edition.* MIT Press, McGraw-Hill Book Company, 2000.

[4] M. B. Dias, B. Ghanem, and A. T. Stentz. Improving cost estimation in market-based coordination of a distributed sensing task. In *2005 IEEE/RSJ International Conference on Intelligent Robots and Systems*, pages 3972 – 3977, August 2005.

[5] M. B. Dias and A. T. Stentz. Opportunistic optimization for market-based multirobot control. In *Proceedings of the 2002 IEEE/RSJ International Conference on Intelligent Robots and Systems (IROS '02)*, volume 3, pages 2714 – 2720, September 2002.

[6] M. B. Dias, R. M. Zlot, N. Kalra, and A. T. Stentz. Market-based multirobot coordination: A survey and analysis. Technical Report CMU-RI-TR-05-13, Robotics Institute, Carnegie Mellon University, Pittsburgh, PA, April 2005.

[7] M. B. Dias, R. M. Zlot, M. B. Zinck, J. P. Gonzalez, and A. T. Stentz. A versatile implementation of the traderbots approach for multirobot coordination. In *Proceedings*

of the International Conference on Intelligent Autonomous Systems (IAS), March 2004.

[8] B. P. Gerkey and M. J. Matarić. Sold!: Auction methods for multi-robot coordination. *IEEE Transactions on Robotics and Automation*, 18(5):758–768, Oct. 2002.

[9] L. Jia, G. Lin, G. Noubir, R. Rajaraman, and R. Sundaram. Universal approximations for TSP, Steiner tree, and set cover. In *Proceedings of the thirty-seventh annual ACM symposium on Theory of computing*, pages 386–395, 2005.

[10] L. Navarro, R. Grabowski, C. Paredis, and P. Khosla. Millibots. *IEEE Robotics and Automation Magazine*, pages 31 – 40, December 2002.

[11] T. Sandholm. Contract types for satisficing task allocation: I theoretical results. In *AAAI Spring Symposium: Satisficing Models*, 1998.

[12] T. Sandholm. Making markets and democracy work: A story of incentives and computing. In *Proceedings of the International Joint Conference on Artificial Intelligence (IJCAI)*, pages 1649–1671, 2003.

[13] B. C. Schipper. The evolutionary stability of optimism, pessimism and complete ignorance. Discussion Papers 68, SFB/TR 15 Governance and the Efficiency of Economic Systems, Free University of Berlin, Humboldt University of Berlin, University of Bonn, University, Nov. 2005. available at http://ideas.repec.org/p/trf/wpaper/68.html.

[14] T. Smith, T. Sandholm, and R. Simmons. Constructing and clearing combinatorial exchanges using preference elicitation. In *Proceedings of the AAAI workshop on Preferences in AI and CP: Symbolic Approaches*, 2002.

[15] P. B. Sujit, A. Sinha, and D. Ghose. Multiple uav task allocation using negotiation. In *AAMAS '06: Proceedings of the fifth international joint conference on Autonomous agents and multiagent systems*, pages 471–478, New York, NY, USA, 2006. ACM Press.

[16] H. Varian. Economic mechanism design for computerized agents. In *Proceedings of the First USENIX Workshop on Electronic Commerce*, July 1995.

[17] R. Zlot, A. Stentz, M. Dias, and S. Thayer. Multi-robot exploration controlled by a market economy. In *Proceedings of the IEEE International Conference on Robotics and Automation*, 2002.

Distributed Frequency Assignment Using Cooperative Self-Organization

Gauthier Picard, Marie-Pierre Gleizes and Pierre Glize
IRIT - Université de Toulouse III
118, route de Narbonne, F-31062 Toulouse cedex 9 FRANCE
{picard, gleizes, glize}@irit.fr

Abstract

This paper presents an approach using self-organizing multi-agent systems to solve distributed constraint satisfaction problems (DCSP), which concerns distribution among agents which task is to assign personal variables to values with respect with known constraints. Agents only know their variables and the constraints affecting them, and have to negotiate to find a collective solution. The proposed approach defines cooperative self-organization as the process leading the collective to the solution: agents can change the organization by their own decision to improve the state of the system. This work is illustrated on distributed frequency assignment, a classical constraint-based problem.

1. Introduction

Multi-agent systems are a design paradigm to tackle distributed and difficult problems such as autonomic computing, ad-hoc networks, manufacturing control or supply chaining [10, 4]. Once plunged in dynamic environments, such systems have to respond to changes and pressure. Since centralized methods can no longer provide answers for really distributed and huge problems, the adaptive multi-agent system (AMAS) approach considers that decision to change the function of the system is owned by the parts of the system (the agents). These agents are then able to change the organization of the system to modify the behavior of the whole system [1].

For agents, the trigger to decide when to change the organization locally is *cooperation*. Cooperation is considered as the boundary between two kinds of behaviors: "less altruistic as possible" and "less selfish as possible" [12]. Once an agent is no more cooperative (conflict, uselessness, concurrency, etc.) it modifies the organization of the system by changing its position within the environment and the other agents it knows. This approach, called *cooperative self-organization*, has already been applied to difficult problems such as distributed university time tabling [11, 12].

This paper presents a new solution for distributed constraint-based problems using cooperative self-organization. This work is close to well-known ABT (Asynchronous Back-Tracking), ADOPT (Algorithm for Distributed Constraint Optimization) or AWC (Asynchronous Weak Commitment) algorithms [14, 9], but does not require a total order among agents, and is comparable to local search-based algorithms such as tabu search. The AMAS approach is here applied to a distributed *frequency assignment with polarization problem* (FAPP) which is a distributed version of the classical frequency assignment problem [2].

This document is structured as follows. First, the existing multi-agent-based approaches to tackle distributed constraint satisfaction and optimization problems are presented. In section 3, the FAPP is formally described. The proposed approach and algorithms are then presented in sections 4 and 5, and some results are shown in section 6 and discussed in section 7. Finally, section 8 concludes the paper and draws some perspectives to this work.

2. Multi-Agent Constraint Solving

Many decision problems can be expressed as *constraint satisfaction problems* (CSP). A problem is there expressed as a set of variables (the objectives) which can be assigned to values in given domains with respect to a set of constraints. A CSP is a triplet $\langle X, D, C\rangle$ such that: $X = \{x_1, \ldots, x_n\}$ is a finite set of variables to assign values to, $D = \{D_1, \ldots, D_n\}$ is a finite set of domains for each variable, $C = \{c_1, \ldots, c_m\}$ is a finite set of constraints on the values of variables. Domains D_i can be finite or infinite, and discrete or continuous. Moreover constraints from C can be expressed as tuples of impossible values or as predicates on several variables. This implies several way to model a problem into a CSP, and therefore several kinds of solvers to support them.

A *distributed constraint satisfaction problem* (DCSP) is a quintuplet $\langle A, X, D, C, f\rangle$ such that: $\langle X, D, C\rangle$ is a CSP, A is a finite set of agents, $f : A \times X \mapsto \{true, false\}$ is a predicate which assigns variables to agents. Solving a DCSP requires providing agents with behavior as to negotiate to find a solution. In fact, agents do not know the whole problem and must interact to get some information useful for solving their constraints. DCSP framework was firstly introduced by Yokoo et *al.* who propose asynchronous algorithms inspired from non-distributed search algorithms [14]. ABT (Asynchronous Back-Tracking) is an asynchronous version of a backtrack algorithm with a *predefined order* on agents to ensure consistency and exchange of nogoods. AWC (Asynchronous Weak Commitment) is an enhancement of ABT with two main extensions: *min-conflict* heuristic and dynamic agent ordering depending on agents' nogoods and their neighborhood. AWC is faster than ABT to find a solution, but ABT is faster to prove a solution is not satisfiable. These two algorithms are complete. Other works inspired from on DCSP are based on more local view for agents, but are not complete such as DynDBA (Dynamic Distributed Breakout Algorithm) [8].

There exist problems for which no solution is satisfiable. But, by defining a cost function for each constraint, the problem becomes an optimization problem in which the objective function to optimize (maximize or minimize) is a combination of the cost functions, such as the sum or a weighted sum, for example. These problems, once distributed among agents, are called *distributed constraint optimization problems* (*DCOP*). The most popular multi-agent algorithms to solve such optimization problems are ADOPT (Algorithm for Distributed Constraint Optimization) [9] and its successors, and the ERA (Environment, Reactive rules, and Agents) approach [6], in which agents evolve within the domains of their variables and follow different stochastic behaviors to converge towards a solution.

In this paper, only the satisfaction part of the frequency assignment problem with polarization is expounded, within a potential dynamic environment. Still, ERA is kept in mind for their approach by positioning.

3. Frequency Assignment Problem

3.1. Presentation

The frequency assignment with polarization problem (FAPP) consists in finding frequency allocation within a hertzian telecommunication network, which is composed of several transmitter and/or receiver sites [2]. A hertzian connection can be constituted of one or more radioelectrical unidirectional paths between antennas of distinct geographical sites. Each path is characterized by its frequency and its polarization, which can get values within predefined domains.

Let T be the set of paths. Let $F_0, F_1, ..., F_n$ be the n domains of frequencies. Let $P_{-1} = \{-1\}, P_1 = \{1\}, P_0 = \{-1, 1\}$, the three possible domains of polarization. At each $i \in T$, we associate (f_i, p_i) such that $f_i \in F_{\varphi(i)}$ and $p_i \in P_{\pi(i)}$, where $\varphi(i)$ and $\pi(i)$ indicate respectively the frequency and polarization domain numbers of i.

There exist two types of constraints on these networks. Physical constraints related to the proximity or, at the contrary, to the geographical distance. These interference constraints are called electromagnetic constraints (CEM), and are soft constraints. The difference of polarization is a technical means to diminish interference problems between frequencies caused by these constraints. The second type of constraints are imperative technological hard constraints (CI), which impose a distance between the frequencies of two paths. In matrix form, the constraints are:

$$\begin{cases} (CEM) & |f_i - f_j| \geq \frac{|p_i+p_j|}{2}\gamma_{ij}^{(k)} + \frac{|p_i-p_j|}{2}\delta_{ij}^{(k)} \\ & \text{with } k = 0 \text{ to } 10 \\ (C2) & |f_i - f_j| = \epsilon_{ij} \\ (C3) & |f_i - f_j| \neq \epsilon_{ij} \\ (C4) & f_i = f_j \\ (C5) & f_i \neq f_j \\ (C6) & p_i = p_j \\ (C7) & p_i \neq p_j \end{cases}$$

where γ_{ij} and δ_{ij} indicate required frequency distance as a function of polarization.

A feasible solution corresponds to the assignment of a frequency and a polarization to each path by satisfying the set of given constraints. The problem being often over constrained, CEM can be relaxed over 11 levels (from 0 for satisfaction to 10). The objective is therefore twofold:

1. to satisfy the constraints C2, C3, C4, C5, C6 and C7,
2. to minimize a cost function, which is not described here, since the paper only addresses the satisfaction part of the FAPP. More details on this function are available in [2].

Halfway between real problems and case studies (such as graph coloring or n queens problems), the study of FAPP represents an interesting step towards the resolution of real constraint-based problems. The heterogeneity of the constraints and the large sizes (up to 3,000 paths) make the FAPP be an interesting challenge. Nevertheless, two characteristics make its study easier: finite and discrete domains and binary constraints. The originality of the FAPP also lies in the melting of hard and soft constraints. The question is both a constraint satisfaction problem and an optimization one. Therefore, this implies modeling and implementing bivalent algorithms to *necessarily* process a set of hard constraints and next to *possibly* improve the global state by focusing on soft constraints. This paper only focuses on the first objective.

3.2. Towards the Distribution of FAPP

There exist several efficient solutions to tackle the FAPP: local search and tabu search [3], lower bounding and tabu search procedures [5], or arc-consistency and tabu search [13]. All these approaches are based on tabu search and are not distributed, nor adaptive. These algorithms are centralized and manage all the network. If a change occurs during the solving process, all the process must be relaunched. For example, if a site disappears (transmitter/receiver dysfunction), these systems are not able to respond by providing a new assignment from the current one.

Several constraints naturally appear when using the agent paradigm, from the viewpoint of dynamic and distributed problems solving. First, the absence of global control makes difficult the separation into phases, as it appears in the three previously quoted algorithms. Second, the dynamical aspects, i.e. the capability to add or remove constraints or paths in a FAPP during the solving process, prevents using arc-consistency pre-processing.

However, several concepts can be reused at the agent level:

- the concept of *penalty* on values used by [13] to force exploring the domain of a path,
- the concept of *criticity* of a variable or a value, used by [3] to favor, at the contrary, some values or to make some agents have priority,
- the concept of *pairs of paths* linked by C2 or C4 constraints (cf. 3.1) used by [5], which can be implemented as a dialog between agents,
- the concept of *tabu*, in general, and forbidding some paths to modify their values, in particular, can be transposed at the agent level.

Besides the fact that tabu approaches are outstanding to solve the FAPP, this approach can be reused at the agent level, at the contrary of methods using variable neighborhood on the search space. The multi-agent approach presented in the next sections, based on AMAS, brings a novel point of view, different from the previous approaches, since agents self-organize to find a solution.

4. Self-Organizing Multi-Agent Modeling

In this section, a multi-agent system to solve the FAPP, by using cooperative self-organization, is described.

4.1. Problem Specification

To describe the MAS, here are some characteristic data of the FAPP:

- T, the set of paths,
- $\forall t \in T,\ F_t$ the frequency domain associated to t,
- $\forall t \in T,\ P_t$ the polarization domain associated to t,
- C, the set of constraints,
- CI, the set of hard constraints,
- CEM, the set of soft constraints (CEM),
- $\forall t \in T,\ C_t = CI_t \cup CEM_t$, the set of constraints of path t,
- $\forall c \in C,\ t_1(c)$ and $t_2(c)$, the two paths linked by the constraint c,
- $\forall t, u \in T,\ v(t, u) \equiv \exists c \in (C_t \cap C_u)$, the neighborhood relation between two paths,
- $\forall t \in T,\ V_t = \{u \in T \mid v(t, u) = true\}$, the set of neighbors of the path t, called *neighborhood*.

The system to model includes a set of autonomous agents, which are homogeneous concerning their representations and behaviors. A distinct agent is associated with each path (or variable). Let A be the set of agents of the system and let T be the set of paths. For all agent $x \in A$, we note $t_x \in T$ the path associated to the agent. So, $f(x, t_x) = true$, by using the notation of DCSP in section 2. An agent x is the neighbor of an agent y if and only if their paths are neighboring (they share a constraint). The neighborhood of an agent, i.e. the social environment, is defined as the set of its neighbors:

$$\forall x, y \in A,\ v(x, y) \equiv v(t_x, t_y)$$
$$\forall x, y \in A,\ y \in V_x \equiv t_y \in V_{t_x}$$

An agent has the same frequency domain than the variable its represents:

$$\forall x \in A,\ F_x = F_{t_x}$$
$$\forall x \in A, P_x = P_{t_x}$$

Hard constraints and CEM are known by each agent the variable depends on. Let C_x be the set of constraints known by an agent:

$$\forall x \in A,\ C_x = C_{t_x}$$

A satisfied constraint $c \in CI_x$ is noted $c = true$.

As this paper only deals with hard constraints, CEM are not formally presented here.

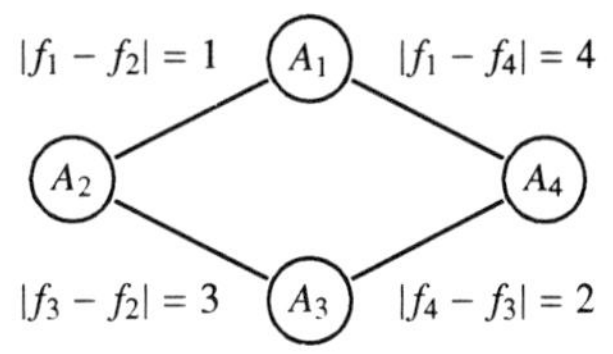

Figure 1. Simple example with 4 agents and 4 hard constraints

In the example of fig. 1, $A = \{A_1, A_2, A_3, A_4\}$. The agents have the same domains $D_f = \{1, 2, 3, 4, 5, 6\}$ and $D_p = \{1\}$. The problem is simplified by putting aside the polarization. There are only two types of constraints: C2 and C4, i.e. distance constraints. For example, a constraint exists between A_1 and A_2: $|f_1 - f_2| = 1$. It is easy to find solutions for this FAPP, which are, for $(f_{A_1}, f_{A_2}, f_{A_3}, f_{A_4})$: $(2, 1, 4, 6)$ and $(5, 6, 3, 1)$.

Therefore, the problem of frequency assignment can be viewed as a positioning problem in which agents represent frequencies, as viewed in ERA [6]. Each agent must find a right position (value) within their domain, by following a self-organizing process. At the beginning of the process, agents are randomly positioned, as follows, for example, with a shared domain:

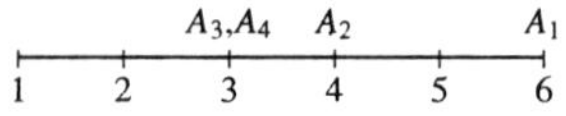

One possible solution is therefore:

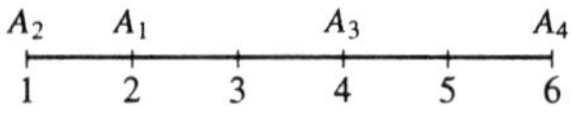

To pass form the initial state to the solution, we propose to use self-organization and negotiation between agents. Each agent aims at finding the right place within the organization by using only local interactions with its neighbors (agents linked by constraints) and deciding by itself to move from one position to another. Local criteria, inspired by *cooperation*, are embedded in agents to implement their decision making. This notion is here more than sharing resources or skills to perform a common task, but it also encapsulates the capability to anticipate conflicts and to act to repair or to remove non cooperative situations, such conflicts.

4.2. Cooperative Agents' Characteristics

Agents are the only active entities of the system, which interact to cooperatively solve the FAPP. Two main data characterize an agent, except its environment: its *value* and its *difficulty*. The value of an agent x is the current pair $(f, p)_x$ with $f \in F_x$ and $p \in P_x$. The difficulty d_x of an agent x is a quantitative measure which take into account the current environment and value of an agent. The higher it is, the more the agent believes it is far from a solution, as a heuristic does. This measure is the basis for cooperative mechanisms. For an agent, the difficulty is its own and is more detailed in section 5.

In addition to these two values, the agent has a view on its environment. This view is partial. An agent only knows the value and the difficulty of each of its neighbor, but does not know constraints, views, nor domains. The communication between agents is implemented with messages.

Each agent evolves within an own *physical* environment which consists in the domains of frequency and polarization. These domains, even if possibly identical, are not shared. In the same manner, each constraint is duplicated for each agent knowing it.

The coherence between an agent's view and its constraints is always ensured. Every changes of the view implies changes of the state of the constraints (satisfied or not satisfied). However, the global coherence between the views of different agents is not guaranteed since messages still flow. In fact, the view of a neighbor on an agent can differ from the current state of the agent. Therefore, constraints between two agents can be in different state. To ensure the global coherence once the system is stopped, some hypothesis, raised by Yokoo et *al.* for DCSP solving, must be assumed [14]:

1. messages are received in a finite time,
2. messages are not lost or changed during transmission,
3. messages are always processed by the agent receiving it.

To avoid ambiguity concerning the views of agents:

- let $c^x \in C_x$ be the constraint c from the point of view of x,
- let d_x^y be the difficulty of x from the point of view of y,
- let $(f, p)_x^y$ be the current value of x from the point of view of y.

4.3. Cooperative Agents' Behavior

The behavior of the cooperative agent is composed of 4 steps, as shown in fig. 2. This algorithm is common to all the agents which run it concurrently.

Initialization consists in choosing (randomly, for example) a value within the domains (line 1) and informing the neighborhood that the agent is running (line 2).

As communication is implemented with messages, each agent owns a mailbox it *checks* eventually. Messages are

```
   // Step 1: Initialization
1  selectValue;
2  sendValuesToNeighbourhood;
3  while isRunningSystem do
       // Step 2: Check
4      checkMessages;
       // Step 3: Decision
5      if receivedAllValues then
6          evalDifficulty;
7          if isDifficultyChange then
8              sendValuesToNeighbourhood;
9          end
10         if receivedAllDifficulties then
11             if mostDifficult then
                   // Step 4: Assignment
12                 assignment;
13             end
14         end
15     end
16 end
```

Figure 2. The 4-step behavior of an agent

processed consequently to the check from the oldest to the newest. This phase ends when the mailbox is empty (line 4).

Decision leads to choose the agent that will act to change the global solution by assigning a new value (line 11), in a given neighborhood. An agent decides only if it knows the difficulties of its neighborhood (line 10). Moreover, an agent can only calculate its difficulty (line 6) if it knows the values of its neighbors (line 5). These are not blocking conditions since agents communicate data as soon as they get them (cf. section 4.4). From its point of view, if an agent has the highest difficulty, for a given neighborhood[1], it is *elected* as the agent that have to act for the neighborhood. With equal maximum difficulties, the agent is randomly elected.

For $x \in A$, we define $e(x)$ the fact that x is eligible:

$$\forall x \in A,\ e(x) \equiv \forall y \in V_x,\ d_x^x \geq d_y^x$$

Therefore, this is the agent that has the highest difficulty which will try to improve the current situation. This approach is preferred to an approach considering this is a neighbor of the agent with the maximum difficulty that is chosen. In fact, a neighbor has only a limited number of constraint with an agent, and therefore is not well placed to help it. This phase underlines a first aspect of the cooperation notion: *agents let neighbors with more difficulty than themselves act*. It is a self-organized process.

Assignment is only accessible to elected agents. The elected selects, for its current value in its domain, a value it believes being the best one for itself and its neighborhood. There is no way for an agent to force other agents to change their values. If more than one value seems correct, the final value is randomly chosen. At the end of the assignment phase, the agent disables itself (only for decision): it informs its neighborhood that it will not participate to the next elections until another agent is elected. This is an *egalitarian* policy that allows other agents to act. A disabled agent can however be invited to an assignment session (cf 4.4). The state (enable/disable) of an agent is known by its neighbors and can be interpreted as a *local tabu*.

Once the system is running, all the agents follow the *check-decision-assignment* cycle without being able to stop the process by themselves.

[1]Therefore, there may be several elected agents within the system.

4.4. Communication Protocol

An agent only communicates with its neighbors, by using direct messages containing the view (i.e. the displayed values) of the sender, the view of the receiver, and the assignment session if necessary (cf. next paragraphs). Moreover, an agent systematically informs its neighbors if changes of value or difficulty occur, not to distort the views and the decisions of its neighbors.

Not to overload the communication network, here are the triggers to send messages:

- after *initialization*,
- during *check*, at each message reception:
  - either the value of the neighbor has changed, therefore the difficulty must be calculated,
  - or the neighbor is disabled, therefore the view of the state must be changed,
  - or the difficulty of the neighbor has changed or it is enabled.
- at the end of the *check* step, the agent sends a message to its neighborhood only if a change of difficulty occurred consequently to the change of a value of a neighbor or if it changed its state (lines 7-8).
- at the end of the *assignment* step, the agent disables itself and informs its neighbor of the change of values, state or difficulty.

To prevent *deadlocks*, it is necessary to introduce a synchronization point during the assignment. This is implemented by using the notion of *assignment session*. For a given neighborhood, an elected agent first creates an assignment session, which is a synchronized object (monitor or equivalent). Then, it sends invitations to its neighbors, with its last value, state and difficulty. A neighbor can then accept or reject the invitation if either it is already within an assignment session for which the elected is more in difficulty or it has itself a higher difficulty than the elected. Once the elected has received all the answers, it begins the assignment. Once finished, it informs its invited neighbors that the session is correctly ended by sending its new value. Until the session is not ended, the *invited agents* do not process the messages coming from the elected agent.

5. Cooperative Criteria for Hard Constraints

5.1. Difficulty Measurement

Difficulty is the decision criterion for electing an agent. It is a sorted tuple of sub-criteria. The difficulty for an agent $x \in A$ viewed by an agent $y \in A$ is noted:

$$d_x^y = [Im_x^y, Po_x^y, NS_x^y, Ag_x^y]$$

The *improvement* (or Im), of an agent is the best possible improvement for this agent considering the current situation by counting the number of unsatisfied hard constraints. For all $x \in A$, for all $(f, p) \in F_x \times P_x$, $NS_x(f, p)$ is the number of unsatisfied hard constraints with the value (f, p). With $NS_x \equiv NS_x(f, p)_x$, we note:

$$\forall x \in A,$$
$$Im_x = NS_x - min\{NS_x(f, p),\ (f, p) \in F(x) \times P(x) \setminus (f, p)_x\}$$
$$\text{and}$$
$$\forall x \in A, \forall y \in V_x,$$
$$Im_x^x > Im_y^x \Rightarrow d_x^x > d_y^x$$

The cost to calculate this criterion is $|F_x \times P_x - 1|$ since the current value is not included. The idea of this criterion is to consider that the agents, that know they can strictly improve their local situation, know they are not well positioned. This requirement of projecting forward, even if costly, significantly improves the search for solutions.

Contrary to Im, the next criteria are not based on domains but on constraints. For all $x \in A$, for all $c^x \in CI_x$, let $FPS(c^x)$ be the set of pairs $(f, p) \in F_x \times P_x$ which satisfy c^x from the current view of x.

The second criterion, *possibilities* (or Po), expresses the fact that a constraint is difficult if there only exist few possible assignments that satisfy the constraint:

$$\forall x \in A,$$
$$Po_x = min\{|FPS(c^x)|,\ c^x \in CI_x \text{ and } c^x = false\}$$

and in case of equality of the previous criterion (Im):

$$\forall x \in A,\ \forall y \in V_x,$$
$$\text{s.t. } Im_x^x = Im_y^x,$$
$$Po_x^x < Po_y^x \Rightarrow d_x^x > d_y^x$$

The third criterion is the *number of unsatisfied hard constraints* (or NS_x). This criterion assumes that an agent having more unsatisfied constraints has more difficulties, in case of equality of the previous criteria (Im then Po):

$$\forall x \in A,\ \forall y \in V_x,$$
$$\text{s.t. } Im_x^x = Im_y^x \text{ and } Po_x^x = Po_y^x,$$
$$NS_x^x > NS_y^x \Rightarrow d_x^x > d_y^x$$

Finally, the last criterion to measure the difficulty is the *oldness* (or Ol). For all $x \in A$ and for all $c^x \in CI_x$, let $TI_x(c^x)$ be the number of assignments performed by x or its neighborhood since the last satisfaction it knows. This represents the oldness of constraints and we set:

$$\forall x \in A,\ Ol_x = max\{\ TI_x(c^x,\ c^x \in CI_x|)\}$$

The agent having the oldest constraint is in the more difficulty, in case of equality of the previous criteria:

$$\forall x \in A, \forall y \in V_x,$$
$$\text{s.t. } Im_x^x = Im_y^x \text{ and } Po_x^x = Po_y^x \text{ and } NS_x^x = NS_y^x,$$
$$Ol_x^x > Ol_y^x \Rightarrow d^x > d^y$$

5.2. Other Decision Criteria

Besides the difficulty notion, there exist two other criteria to elect agents. First, an agent will try to be elected if and only if it owns unsatisfied constraints, not to elect agents that will not change the current state of the system:

$$\forall x \in A, solved(x) \equiv \forall y \in V_x \cup \{x\},\ NS_y^x = 0$$

If two agents have the same difficulty at this time of the comparison, an agent is randomly chosen (Eq).

The last criterion is the fact that an agent which is the only active agent for a given neighborhood is automatically elected (De).

5.3. Choosing Values

The key idea for choosing values in a cooperative manner is that an agent will select the value to assign as a function of the criterion that trigger its election. This criterion, called *discriminant criterion*, that discriminates agent x from agent y, is noted cd_y^x. The criterion for x to select the action to perform is called *selection criterion* and noted cs^x:

$$\forall x \in A,\ cs^x = min\{cd_y^x,\ y \in V_x\}$$

A different manner of choosing possible values is associated to each decision criterion:

- $cs^x = Im$: select the values that maximize the improvement,
- $cs^x = Po$: select the set of constraints with the minimum of possibilities,
- $cs^x = NS$: select the set of constraints with the maximum of possibilities,
- $cs^x = Ol$: select the oldest constraints,
- $cs^x = Eq$: select the constraints shared with the agents having a difficulty equal to the agent's difficulty,

- $cs^x = De$: select the set of all the constraints for the agent.

Let VEl_x be the set of values chosen by x.

Nevertheless, there is a drawback to make this choice using the sets of constraints: all the constraints can be unsatisfiable in the situation and therefore, all the values are possible except the current one. It implies implementing some dialog capabilities between an elected and the invited agents.

5.4. Dialog with Invited Agents During a Session

An assignment is useful for a neighbor in two situations:

- this assignment improves *immediately* the situation of the neighbor,
- this assignment improves *possibly* the situation of the neighbor, by leading it, for example, to assign a value that decreases its number of unsatisfied constraints, if the neighbor is elected in the future.

Let $S_x(f, p)$ be the number of satisfied hard constraints of the agent x with the value (f, p). The exchanged data to represent the utility of a value (f_x, p_x) of an elected agent x for a neighbor y is:

$$u_x^y(f_x, p_x) = \\ max\{|S_y(f_y, p_y)|,\ (f_y, p_y) \in F_y \times P_y \text{ and } (f, p)_x^y = (f_x, p_x)\}$$

The cost of this calculus is initially high: for each value of the elected, a matrix of the number of constraints satisfied must be calculated. But once calculated a first time, it only requires updates.

With this utility for each value and each neighbor, the elected agent x selects the values that maximize the sum of the utilities of its neighbors:

$$VNe_x = max\{\sum_{y \in V_x} u_x^y(f, p) \mid (f, p) \in VEl_x\}$$

If there still exist several equivalent values, x does the same process by only selecting values in VNe_x. This last selection is possible because it appends after the choice of values relatively to the selection criterion and before the participation of its neighbors: the agent has achieved its tasks, has requested its neighbors' proposals and thus it can satisfy its own needs. This represents the *equilibrium between altruism and selfishness* that defines the notion of cooperation, as presented in [12].

Finally, if there still exist equivalent values after this selection, one of them is chosen *randomly*.

Table 1. Solving trace for the FAPP of fig. 1

	Step 1		Step 2		Step 3		End
A_1	*3* [1,0,2,1]	1,2,4,*5*,6	5 [1,0,2,2]	0	5 [0,0,1,3]	1 (5)	5
A_1-A_2	[2,1] (2,4)		[2,2] (2,4)		[1,0] (5)		
A_1-A_4	[0,1]		[0,2]		[0,3]		
A_2	3 [1,1,2,1]	0,0,0,1(6),0	*3* [2,1,2,2]	6	6 [0,1,0,0]	n/a	6
A_2-A_1	[2,1] (2,4)		[2,2] (4,6)		[2,0] (4,6)		
A_2-A_3	[1,1] (6)		[1,2] (6)		[1,0] (6)		
A_3	3 [1,1,2,1]	n/a	3 [1,1,2,1]	0	3 [0,1,1,2]	1 (3)	3
A_3-A_2	[1,1] (6)		[1,1] (6)		[1,0] (3)		
A_3-A_4	[2,1] (1,5)		[2,1] (1,5)		[2,2] (1,5)		
A_4	3 [1,0,2,1]	1(5),0,0,1(1),0	3 [2,1,2,2]	n/a	*3* [2,1,2,2]	1	1
A_4-A_1	[0,1]		[1,2] (1)		[1,2] (1)		
A_4-A_3	[2,1] (1,5)		[2,2] (1,5)		[2,2] (1,5)		

5.5. Example

Table 1 shows an example of solving trace for the FAPP presented in fig. 1. $(f_{A_1}, f_{A_2}, f_{A_3}, f_{A_4}) = (3, 3, 3, 3)$ is the initial state. Three steps are required to achieve a solution. Since all the agents are in a same neighborhood, there is no concurrent solving, contrary to larger problems.

For each step, data are presented as follows. A *decision part* (sub-column at left of each step), for each agent, is composed of the frequency, followed by the difficulty vector, and for each constraint (noted as $A_x - A_y$) a vector $[possibility, age]$ followed by the frequencies that can satisfy the constraint. For example, at the beginning, A_1's frequency is 3, its difficulty is $[1, 0, 2, 1]$, and the constraint $A_1 - A_2$ from A_1's viewpoint has two possibilities which are $(2, 4)$ and its age is 1.

An *invitation part* (sub-column at right of each step) for the elected agent shows the frequencies it believes as being possible. Its neighbors send, for each of these frequencies, the sum of possible improvement and the immediate improvement, with the frequency that implies this improvement (if any). For example, at step 1, A_1 is elected (frequency in italics) and presents the set of possible frequencies $VEl_{A_1} = \{1, 2, 4, 5, 6\}$ to its neighbors. A_2 sends $\{0, 0, 0, 1(6), 0\}$ to A_1, in order to inform that if A_1 chooses the frequency 5 then A_2 has a possible improvement of 1 by choosing the frequency 6. At step 2, A_1 is disabled (gray background) because it just assigns a new value.

At step 1, two agents are equivalent: A_1 and A_4. A_1 is randomly chosen and his discriminant criterion is therefore $cs^{A_1} = Eq$. A_1 looks at the constraint it shares with A_4: $A_1 - A_4$. As there is no possibility to satisfy this constraint, A_1 is not able to choose a good value, and it selects the whole domain except its current value: $\{1, 2, 4, 5, 6\}$. The answer of its neighbors is that the best choice is 5. That lets only one possible assignment for A_2 to 6 and for A_4 to 1.

Table 2. Experimental setup

FAPP Instance	01	11	22	33	38
Agents	200	1000	1750	650	2500
CI	168	978	1799	578	3112
Runs	400	400	67	400	48
Time limit (s)	60	160	1000	150	1400

Table 3. Percentage of unsatisfied CI

FAPP Instance	01	11	22	33	38
CI	168	978	1799	578	3112
% Unsatisfied	0	0,015	3,49	0,004	6,82

Table 4. Assignments

FAPP Instance	01	11	22	33	38
Assign.	107.24	547.02	964.81	338.35	1146.18
Assign./CI	0.64	0.56	0.54	0.59	0.37
Assign./Time(s)	17.87	3.42	0.96	2.26	0.82
σ	5.33%	6.89%	5.36%	2.28%	3.88%

At step 2, A_1 is disabled and A_2 and A_4 are elected with the criterion *Im*. Since agents can only be invited at one session at a same time, A_1, for example, rejects the invitation of A_4, which will wait until the assignment session of A_2 ends, to send another invitation. A_2 performs the assignment, for the criterion *Im*, and it looks at the values that imply the highest improvement, i.e. 6 which satisfies the two constraints of A_2. The dialog with its neighbors is useless since there is only one possible value: 6.

At step 3, A_4 is elected despite the difficulty changes for A_1 and A_3, and it reasons as A_2 did by choosing the value 1 that satisfies its two constraints. Once the assignment done, all the agents are solved: a solution has been found.

6. Results and Analysis

The different instances referred in this paper come from the ROADEF challenge 2001[2], have been ran on one computer several times, with specific time limits shown in table 2.

6.1. Convergence

The convergence towards solutions is shown in fig. 3. The important initial decreasing is due to the fact that some constraints are satisfied as soon as the random initialization is done. These constraints are often C3 or C5 constraints, since they are easier to satisfy. The decreasing appearing once the time limit is reached corresponds to the termination of agents that process their remaining messages before ending, without beginning new assignment sessions: they

[2]http://uma.ensta.fr/conf/roadef-2001-challenge/index_main.html

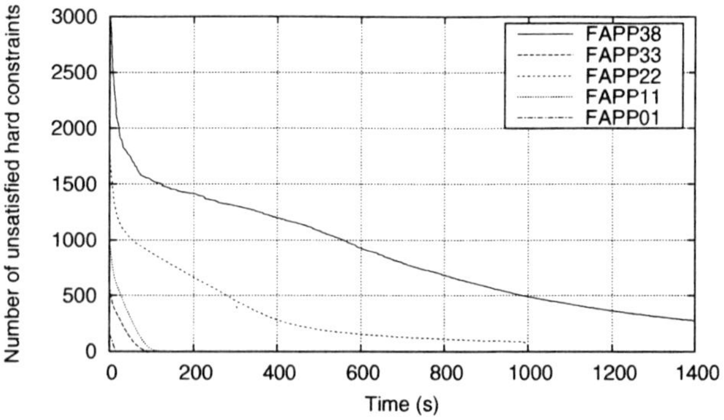

Figure 3. Convergence to solutions

reached a stable situation. But results for FAPP22 shows a stagnation: a local minimum is reached, and it remains, on average, 3.49% of unsatisfied constraints, as shown in table 3. Another problem is the time to solve a non complete problem (there is no CEM), which depends on the number of agents. Therefore, even if performing on small instances (200 agents), the approach does not manage to find solutions systematically.

6.2. Assignments and Messages Traffic

Table 4 shows there is only few assignments. Considering the size of the search space, the exploration is limited. In fact, the main idea behind the notion of cooperation is to make the good choices upstream to ensure a quick convergence, instead of exhaustively explore the search space: cooperation is here a *meta-heuristic*, in the sense criteria are not problem-specific. The small ratio between the number of assignments and the number of hard constraints confirms the process is strongly guided. The standard deviation σ is small too, in the order of 5%, which emphasizes the adaptation capability of the algorithm, independantly of the initial situation, and therefore adaptation to changes during the solving process.

However, the speed of assignment is low, and this ratio decreases with a great number of agents. But, at each time, there is more than one assignment session, and since the behavior is completely concurrent, the time, on distributed environment is far better, even by taking into account the message traffic, shown in table 5: there are few messages sent by agents. Moreover, there are few situations of conflict (assignment session canceling), as shown in table 6.

6.3. Decision Criteria Relevance

Among the criteria presented in section 5, fig. 4 shows which ones are used by the agents during the solving process. The value for the criterion *De* (when neighbors are already elected) is very small. But, the criterion *NS* (number

Table 5. Message traffic

FAPP Instance	01	11	22	33	38
Agents	200	1,000	1,750	650	2,500
Total Messages	2,335	15,841	33,247	8,348	48,727
Messages/Agent	11.7	15.8	19	12.8	19.5

Table 6. Percentage of canceling messages

FAPP Instance	01	11	22	33	38
% canceling	4.21	6.02	13.56	5.22	10.28

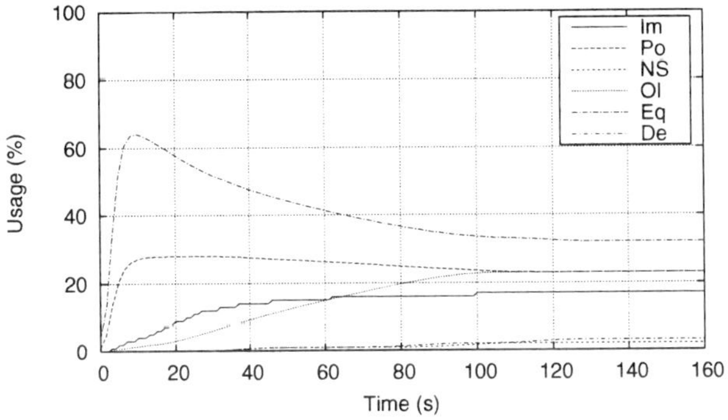

Figure 4. Distribution of the discriminant criteria for the instance FAPP11

of unsatisfied constraints) is not frequently triggered, contrary to *Ol*, *Im* and *Po* which are eventually used. Finally, average 30% of agents evaluate one of their neighbors as equal (*Eq*).

7. Discussion

7.1. Communication

Although there are few sent messages by agent, information updates can be limited even more outside of the assignment sessions. It is possible to only keep necessary updates (e.g. during initialization) and let the agents share and commit their views during assignment sessions during which canceling messages are more numerous: the system will become more synchronous. On the other side, to obtain more flexibility, invitations to assignment sessions which are blocking points may be limited too. But, without this synchronization point, the system is unable to stabilize since views constantly change. However, modifications can be considered: either reducing the time an invitation requires, because once the dialog is done it is no more needed to wait; or, limiting the number of invited neighbors, by using some preference measure and memory. Another approach can also be to allow agents to participate to more than one session at a time, while keeping them still blocked. In fact, there are only few sessions at a time.

7.2. Difficulty Evaluation

A first observation is that the criteria are *generic*: they are not relative to FAPP, even if *Po* is close to the FAPP notions. Moreover, the concept of pair of paths, introduced by [3] to manage particular cases of paths sharing C2 or C4 constraints, does not appear in the decision, even if it partially impacts on *Po*.

Second, sorting the criteria is one remaining open question, which validity is more complex to observe. Even if it seems relevant to position *Im* at the head (by analyzing the results of section 6.3), the other criteria can be discussed and experimented more precisely.

7.3. Soft Constraints and Optimization

Tackling CEM soft constraints is one perspective of this work. These constraints are far more numerous and increase the neighborhoods, and will put the communication protocol on the spot by imposing a great number of invited during sessions. To solve this problem, a possible track is to consider two kinds of neighborhoods: CI and CEM.

Afterwards, another problem is to include soft constraints in the difficulty measure. If it seems relevant to position them after the criteria for hard constraints to discriminates the numerous equality cases, as emphasized in section 6.3, it must not corrupt the solutions for CI. For that, new criteria must be modeled and new relative actions must be implemented.

7.4. Dynamic Problems

Introducing dynamics within the system, by adding or removing agents and constraints during the solving process is another interesting point to discuss and may be the easier one. This is possible thanks to the self-organization mechanisms, which are implemented as local and asynchronous, among agents. This algorithm can easily adapt to changing environments. The only point to warn is the assignment session: deleting agents which invited in sessions must be carefully studied. Results on the standard deviation (cf. section 6.3) comfort this idea.

Nevertheless, a drawback is the fact that the solving process relies on communication of information between agents, relatively to the assumptions of section 4.2. What if the communication network breaks down? By now, the system is robust because the problem can change in runtime, but it is not robust if the communication network is not reliable. One solution is to manage uncertainty on neighbor's information to tackle the approximative rightness of information, for example. This subject will be prospected in future works.

7.5. Comparison to Other Approaches

Contrary to APO [7] or ABT [14] algorithms, there is no addition of new virtual neighborhood links and therefore new virtual neighbors during the process to solve a static problem, which forbids increasing the link density and then harms the notion of locality.

The termination criteria is only a time limit. This is due to the fact that agents are unable to terminate by themselves because of their limited view, and because of the absence of hierarchy, contrary to ADOPT algorithm [9], but similarly to ERA approach [6].

Because this work only addresses the hard constraints of the FAPP, it is not possible to directly compare our algorithm to existing ones, in terms of performance. But, to validate our approach, several comparisons have been done by translating graph-coloring problems into FAPP, as ADOPT presents some results for these problems [9]. Results are not really good (up to 2 times less efficient), even if these two kinds of problems are CSP, because they are slightly different. First, instances for graph-coloring involve domains with only 3 values, when domains of FAPP contains to 100 times more values. Moreover, in graph-coloring, there are few variables/agents (some tens), when FAPP requires at least 200 agents. Finally, and this is the most important difference, graph-coloring is more constrained (even over constrained) than FAPP. There are numerous constraints per agent. Therefore, the order on criteria we used may be not adapted to this kind of problems.

8. Conclusion

In this paper, a multi-agent system, using self-organization mechanisms, has been developed to tackle a frequency assignment problem (FAPP). The local algorithm we present is based on cooperation between agents which elect and negotiate during assignment sessions to improve the global satisfaction, by reasoning on their difficulties. The main outcome is to produce adaptive systems able to respond to environmental changes. The systems find solutions for large FAPP, even if the performance are not high, compared to other algorithms. Two major perspectives are emphasized. First, improving the global behavior by studying other decision criteria and sorting them within the difficulty measure. Second, enhancing the system to take into account soft constraints such CEM for the FAPP.

Acknowledgments

We would like to thank Florian Cornet for his contribution to the development of the solver, and Gérard Verfaillie for his enlightened advices.

References

[1] D. Capera, J. Georgé, M.-P. Gleizes, and P. Glize. The AMAS theory for complex problem solving based on self-organizing cooperative agents. In *1st Int. TAPOCS Workshop at 12th IEEE WETICE*, pages 383–388. IEEE, 2003.

[2] T. Defaix. FAPP: Frequency Assignment with Polarization Problem - ROADEF Challenge 2001. Technical Report Revision 2, CELAR/TCOM, 2000.

[3] P. Galinier, M. Gendreau, and P. Soriano. Solving the Frequency Assignment Problem with Polarization by Local Search and Tabu. *4OR*, 3(1):59–78, 2005.

[4] K. H., P. Valckenaers, B. Saint-Germain, P. Verstraete, C. B. Zamfirescu, and H. Van Brussek. Emergent Forecasting Using Stigmergy Approach in Manufacturing Coordination and Control. In *Engineering Self-Organizing Applications (ESOA'04)*, pages 210–226. Springer, 2004.

[5] A. Hertz, D. Schindl, and N. Zufferey. Lower bounding and tabu search procedures for the frequency assignment problem with polarization constraints. *4OR*, 3(2):139–161, 2005.

[6] J. Liu, H. Jing, and Y. Y. Tang. Multi-agent Oriented Constraint Satisfaction. *Artificial Intelligence*, 136(1):101–144, 2002.

[7] R. Mailler. Using Cooperative Mediation to Solve Distributed Constraint Satisfaction Problems. In *AAMAS'04*, pages 446–453. ACM, 2004.

[8] R. Mailler. Comparing two approaches to dynamic, distributed constraint satisfaction. *AAMAS'05*, 2005.

[9] P. J. Modi, W. Shen, M. Tambe, and M. Yokoo. ADOPT: Asynchronous Distributed Constraint Optimization with Quality Guarantees. *Artificial Intelligence*, 161(2):149–180, 2005.

[10] P. Peeters, P. Valckenaers, J. Syns, and S. Brueckner. Manufacturing Control Algorithm and Architecture. In *2nd International Workshop on Intelligent Manufacturing Systems*, pages 877–888, 1999.

[11] G. Picard, C. Bernon, and M.-P. Gleizes. ETTO : Emergent Timetabling by Cooperative Self-Organization. In *Engineering Self-Organizing Applications (ESOA'05)*, pages 31–45. Springer, 2005.

[12] G. Picard and P. Glize. Model and Analysis of Local Decision Based on Cooperative Self-Organization for Problem Solving. *Multiagent and Grid Systems (MAGS)*, 2(3):253–265, 2006.

[13] M. Vasquez. Arc-consistency and tabu search for the frequency assignment problem with polarization. In *CP-AI-OR'02*, pages 359–372, 2002.

[14] M. Yokoo, E. H. Durfee, T. Ishida, and K. Kuwabara. The Distributed Constraint Satisfaction Problem : Formalization and Algorithms. *IEEE Transactions on Knowledge and Data Engineering*, 10(5):673–685, 1998.

An Adaptive Strategy for Resource Allocation Modeled as Minority Game

Ka-man Lam and Ho-fung Leung
Department of Computer Science and Engineering
The Chinese University of Hong Kong
{kmlam, lhf}@cse.cuhk.edu.hk

Abstract

In a computer system, different agents need different resources to complete their tasks. The objective of resource allocation is to allocate the resources to the agents so that they can complete their tasks and at the same time make good utilization of resources. In this paper, we model the resource allocation problem as a Minority Game. In this way, the system has the advantages of a distributed system but with reduced overhead. Also, this approach is autonomous and adaptive. We design an adaptive strategy for agents to play in the game model. We perform simulations of a single-choice model, a multi-choice model in which agents have (and do not have) preferences over the resources. Simulations show that agents with the proposed adaptive strategy are able to make more right decisions and better resource utilization than previous work.

1. Introduction

Resource allocation is an important subject in Computer Science. In a computer system, different agents, or programs, need different resources to complete their tasks. However, each resource has a maximum capacity. Obviously, a system is not efficient if some resources are overloaded while others are left idle. So, the objective of resource allocation is not only to allocate the resources to the agents so that they can complete their tasks but also to find an allocation which can make good utilization of resources.

There are two approaches for resource allocation, *centralized* [4, 9] and *distributed* [6, 15]. In centralized approaches, a central entity is responsible for allocating the resources to the agents. The advantage of this approach is that the communication protocol between the central entity and other agents is rather simple. However, the disadvantage is that a centralized allocating mechanism is very complex and the problem can be NP-complete [10]. In distributed approaches, agents negotiate with each other to meet an agreement on the allocation of resources. Although in this approach a centralized allocating mechanism is not needed, more complicated issues need to be addressed: the system needs to have a negotiation protocol for the agents, the agents need to decide what negotiation strategies to use, and a large number of deals as well as communication may be needed in order to finalize an allocation.

Galstyan *et al.* [12] propose another approach to the resource allocation problem: modelling the situation as a *Minority Game*. There are several advantages for this approach. First, the system is distributed. A central entity or a centralized allocating mechanism is not needed. Second, there is no communication or negotiation among agents. The system thus has reduced overhead in communication. Third, the agents are autonomous. Agents individually maximize their own payoffs, an agreement on the allocation is reached automatically after all agents have chosen their actions. The most important, the agents can be adaptive. As we shall show in this paper, agents using adaptive strategies have improved performance.

However, there are several inadequacies in Galstyan's model. First, the strategies that the agents used are randomly generated, which is not intuitive. Second, agents in their model have no preference over the resources, which is not true in some resource allocation problems [7]. Third, as we shall show in this paper, the performance of their model can be improved. In this paper, we solve these problems.

A famous and widely used decision-making method is to maximize expected utility [17]. However, many experiments show that humans violate the Expected Utility Theory [1, 13]. Prospect Theory [13] suggests that is because people have their own attitudes towards risk. According to the theory of *Conditions of Learning* in psychology [11], such attitude will be changed by favorable or unfavorable experiences. In this paper, we design an adaptive strategy, based on these two theories, for agents to play in the game model. Simulations show that the proposed adaptive strategy has better performance than Galstyan's model in terms of individual payoffs as well as resource utilization.

The rest of the paper is structured as follows. In section 2 and 3, we model the resource allocation problem as Mi-

0-7695-2906-2/07 $25.00 © 2007 IEEE

nority Game and present our adaptive strategy. We give the simulation results in section 4. In section 5, we compare our results with a related work. In the last section, we conclude the paper and suggest possible future work.

2 Resource Allocation and Minority Game

2.1 Resource Allocation Problem (RAP)

In a computer system, there are a number of resources and there is a number of agents or programs. Each agent or program is responsible for a task. For an agent or a program to complete its task, one or more resources are needed. Resource Allocation Problem refers to the problem of distributing a number of resources among a number of agents [7]. There are two objectives of resource allocation. First is to allocate the resources to the agents so that they can complete their tasks. Second is to make good use of resources. That is not to overload or under load a resource.

There are two types of resources: divisible resources and indivisible resources. The difference between the two types is that a divisible resource (with a certain capacity) can be shared by a number of agents while an indivisible resource cannot. In this paper, we consider only divisible resources.

An allocation is a particular distribution of resources among the agents. One or more resources may be allocated to an agent. In this paper, only one resource is allocated to an agent at a time. In some systems, agents may have preferences over the resources they receive. In other systems, agents may not have such preferences. In this paper, we perform simulations on both of these two kinds of resource allocation problems.

2.2 Minority Games (MG)

Minority Games originated from the El Farol Bar problem raised by Arthur [3]. In the Bar problem, n people decide independently each week whether to go to a bar. Going to the bar is enjoyable only if the bar is not too crowded, say $n < 60$. Arthur suggested players to use predictors to make decisions based on the attendance of the past d weeks. A predictor might be: to predict next week's attendance to be 50, etc. Arthur suggested that each player should possess and keep track of a number of predictors and always use currently the most accurate predictor. Arthur performed a set of experiments and found that the attendance number fluctuated around the capacity of the bar.

Later, Challet and Zhang [5] formalized the El Farol Bar problem as Minority Games. In Minority Games, n players choose to be on side A or side B. After all players have made their decisions, each of those who are on the minority side wins and gets a point. Challet and Zhang record the winning side in each time step instead of the actual attendance number. In this way, for a record of winning sides in the past H rounds, there will be 2^H possible histories of winning sides. Each strategy (or predictor) basically is a lookup table matching each of the 2^H possible histories to a prediction. Note that these predictions are just some random predictions. An example of a strategy (or predictor) for $H = 3$ is shown in Table 1. As the total number of strategies (2^{2^H}) is too large for players to handle, each player randomly draws S strategies to use and keep track of. Given a history of winning sides, players use currently the most accurate predictor to choose their actions. For example, if a player uses the predictor as shown in Table 1 and the history is BBA, then the player will choose B in this round. At the end of each round after the winning side is announced, the predictors which have made correct predictions gain a virtual point. The predictor with the most virtual points is thus the most accurate one. Players always use the most accurate strategy to decide their action.

Table 1. An example of predictor for $H = 3$.

Histories	Predictions	Histories	Predictions
AAA	B	BAA	B
AAB	A	BAB	A
ABA	A	BBA	B
ABB	B	BBB	A

2.3 Modelling of RAP as a MG

In this paper, following [12], we model the resource allocation problem as a Minority Game. n agents need to use resource R to complete their tasks. As resource R has a fixed capacity C, the n agents need to decide whether or not to use the resource R in each round of the game. The resource is overloaded if the number of agents choosing to use the resource exceeds its capacity. After all agents have made their decisions, if resource R is not overloaded, those agents who has chosen to use the resource get a point. Otherwise, those agents who have chosen not to use the resource get a point. At the end of each round, the agents are informed whether the resource is overloaded or not.

The single-choice model can be extended to a multi-choice model. Suppose n agents, each of them need to use one of the k resource (R_1, R_2, ..., R_k) to complete their tasks. In each round of a multi-choice game, n agents decide to use one of the k resources (R_1, R_2, ..., R_k). Each resource R_i has a fixed capacity C_i, where $i \in [1, k]$. In resource allocation problems, agents may have preferences over the resource assigned to them. To model this, an agent gets a payoff of p_i if the agent chooses to use a resource R_i and that resource is not overloaded, after all agents have made their decisions.

Table 2. An example of predictor for $H = 3$ in a resource allocation game, where O represents that the resource is overloaded, U represents that the resource is not overloaded, A represents an action of using the resource and N represents an action of not to use the resource.

Histories	Actions	Histories	Actions
OOO	A	UOO	A
OOU	N	UOU	N
OUO	N	UUO	A
OUU	A	UUU	N

In previous work of resource allocation [4, 6, 9, 15], resources are allocated to the agents through a central entity or through negotiations. In this paper, we try to design an autonomous system in which agents choose which resource(s) to use. Our objective is to design a strategy for the agents so that the agents can maximize their own payoffs and the resource has good utilization most of the time (that is the number of agents choosing to use the resource is close to its capacity but the resource is not overloaded).

3 Adaptive Strategy

A traditional way to play in Minority Games is to use predictors which assign an action to each of the possible histories. In previous studies of Minority Games [2, 5, 14], the predictors of the players are randomly generated, which means the actions assigned are also generated randomly. In Galstyan's minority game model of resource allocation problem [12], similar predictors which randomly assign actions to the histories are also used. Take the predictor as shown in Table 2 as an example, it is counterintuitive why the action for history OOO is A but not N.

To assign actions in a more intuitive way and to improve the performance of traditional predictors, we designed *Behavioral Predictors* for Minority Games [16]. Similar to Prospect Theory [13], each agent has an *attitude* towards a choice. We use attitudes of an agent, in addition to histories and the payoff of an action, to calculate the *attractiveness* of an action. Then we assign the action with higher attractiveness to the corresponding history in the Behavioral Predictor. We showed that the Behavioral predictors improve the performance of traditional predictors which randomly assign actions to the histories. We also show that agents can make decisions with an adaptive strategy instead of using predictors. Yet, both resource utilization and individual payoffs are improved compared to previous work [2, 5, 12, 14] in Minority Games.

Following [16], we associate an attitude $a_x \in [0, 1]$ for choice x to each agent. In a single-choice model, agents choose whether or not to use a resource R. So, $x \in \{A, N\}$, where A represents an action of using the resource in the next round and N represents not to use the resource in the next round. In a multi-choice problem, agents choose to use one of the k resources (R_1, R_2, ..., R_k). So, $x \in \{R_1, R_2, \ldots, R_k\}$.

We use the attitude a_x as a weight to calculate the weighted average of the ratio that resource R is overloaded (or not overloaded) in a history and the payoff of the choice. Formally, an agent chooses an action by calculating the *attractiveness* $attr_x$ of choice x:

$$attr_x = (1 - a_x) \times h + a_x \times u_x \qquad (1)$$

where a_x is the attitude of the predictor for choice x and u_x is the payoff (normalized to the range $[0, 1]$) of choice x. In calculating the attractiveness of using a resource, $h = \frac{\text{the number of times that the resource is not overloaded}}{\text{size of the history}}$.
In calculating the attractiveness of not using the resource, $h = \frac{\text{the number of times that the resource is overloaded}}{\text{size of the history}}$.
An agent chooses an action with the highest attractiveness or chooses randomly in case of a tie.

An agent with $a_x = 0$ is the most *history-relying*. Such agent considers only the history of whether the resource is overloaded when making decision. For example, in a single-choice model, such agent chooses an action of A (using the resource in the next round) given a history of UUO because the resource is not overloaded most of the time. An agent with $a_x = 1$ is the most *payoff-seeking*. Such agent considers only the payoff when making decision. For example, in a multi-choice problem, suppose the payoff of choosing resource R_1 is 0.1, the payoff of choosing resource R_2 is 0.2, and the payoff of choosing resource R_3 is 0.3 if that resource is not overloaded, then this agent will always choose resource R_3 as it does not consider the history of whether the resource is overloaded in decision-making. In this way, a more history-relying agent tends to use the resource which is not overloaded most of the time. On the other hand, a more payoff-seeking predictor tends to choose an action which brings a higher payoff.

For example, in a single-choice model, suppose the attitudes $a_A = 0.9, a_N = 0.3$, the history of whether the resource R is overloaded in the past three rounds is OOU, the payoff of choosing to use the resource is 1, then using Equation 1 to calculate the attractiveness of the choices:

- $attr_A = (1 - 0.9) \times \frac{1}{3} + 0.9 \times 1 = 0.933$
- $attr_N = (1 - 0.3) \times \frac{2}{3} + 0.3 \times 0 = 0.467$

As $attr_A > attr_N$, the agent will choose to use the resource in the next round.

Another example, in a multi-choice problem, suppose the attitudes $a_{R_1} = 0.9, a_{R_2} = 0.3, a_{R_3} = 0.5$, the histories of whether the resources R_1, R_2 and R_3 are overloaded in the past three rounds are OOU, OUO OOO respectively, the payoffs of choosing to use the resources are 0.1, 0.5 and 0.2 respectively, then using Equation 1 to calculate the attractiveness of the choices:

- $attr_{R_1} = (1 - 0.9) \times \frac{1}{3} + 0.9 \times 0.1 = 0.123$
- $attr_{R_2} = (1 - 0.3) \times \frac{1}{3} + 0.3 \times 0.5 = 0.383$
- $attr_{R_3} = (1 - 0.5) \times 0 + 0.5 \times 0.2 = 0.1$

As $attr_{R_2}$ is the maximum, the agent will choose to use resource R_2 in the next round.

According to the theory of *Conditions of Learning* in psychology [11], attitudes will be changed by favorable or unfavorable experiences. So, agents change the attitudes a_x adaptively. At the end of each round, an agent updates its attitudes: if the agent has chosen to use a resource R and the resource is not overloaded, then a_x is increased by a_+; if the agent has chosen use a resource R and the resource is overloaded, then a_x is decreased by a_-. Intuitively, an agent using the adaptive strategy should perform better. This is confirmed by the simulations described in the following section.

4 Simulations

In this section, we perform two sets of simulation on single-choice model and multi-choice model. There are two objectives in these simulations. First, we want to show that the system has good resource utilization when agents use the proposed adaptive strategy. Here, good resource utilization means the number of agents choosing a particular resource does not exceed the capacity of the resource but it is always close to the capacity so that the resource is fully utilized. The second objective is to show that agents with the proposed adaptive strategy have good individual payoff. This means that in real resource allocation problems, agents with the adaptive strategy are able to choose the right resource at the right time so that they can complete their tasks on time. It is important because if an agent always chooses to use a resource at the wrong time (that is the resource is overloaded), the agent can never get its tasks done.

4.1 Single-choice Model

In the single-choice model, n agents decide whether or not to use a resource R in each round. The resource R has a fixed capacity C. In this simulation, we use $C = \frac{n}{2}$. The resource is overloaded if the number of agents choosing to use the resource exceeds its capacity. After all agents have made their decisions, if resource R is not overloaded, those agents who has chosen to use the resource get a point. Otherwise, those who have chosen not to use the resource get a point. At the end of each round, the agents are informed whether the resource is overloaded or not. Then, they adjust their attitudes according to the adaptive strategy.

We perform simulations for history size $H = 1, 3, 7$. For each history size, we perform simulations for $n = 100, 500, 1000$. In all simulations, all agents have initial attitudes $a_A = a_N = 0.5$. The reason of using 0.5 as initial attitudes is that this value means a neutral attitude: agents with 0.5 as their attitudes have equal weight on history as well as on payoff. In all simulations, agent i has adaptive parameters $a_+ = a_- = \frac{i-1}{n}$. In each game, there are 1000 rounds. The results are shown in Figure 1 to Figure 9.

We perform simulations for different population sizes and different history sizes. From Figure 1(a) to Figure 9(a), we can see that the number of agents choosing to use the resource only has little fluctuation around the capacity of the resource. The fluctuation is low in all cases. Although the fluctuation is large in the first few rounds, the fluctuation reduces very soon. This is because it takes some time for the agents to learn and adapt.

From Figure 1(b) to Figure 9(b), we can see that in all cases, one of the agents has particularly low payoff. This agent has adaptive parameters $a_+ = a_- = 0$, which effectively has no adaptation. So, agents can get higher payoff by using the adaptive strategy than not using it.

There are 1000 rounds in each of the simulation. An agent gets a point if it chooses to use the resource and the resource is not overloaded or if the agent chooses not to use the resource and the resource is overloaded. So, the maximum payoff that an agent can get is 1000. This happens when the agent makes the right decision in all 1000 rounds. From Figure 1(b) to Figure 9(b), we can see that most of the agents can get a payoff of about 500, which means most of the agents can make right decisions about half of the time.

From Figure 1(b) to Figure 9(b), we can see that agents with adaptive parameters $0.2 < a_+, a_- < 0.7$ have higher payoffs than other agents. The difference is more significant in larger population size. This is because agents with adaptive parameters lower than 0.2 adapt too slowly. On the other hand, agents with adaptive parameters larger than 0.7 changes their attitudes too rapidly. They may be history-relying in one round and become payoff-seeking in the next round. As a result, they may make a right decision in one round and unnecessarily change to a wrong decision in the next round.

These results suggest that the adaptive strategy should enable agents to make good use of the resource in systems with different population sizes. At the same time, agents with the adaptive strategy can make the right decisions about half of the time, which is a lot better than the agent without adaptation. Also, the performance in resource utilization is independent of the history sizes that the agents use.

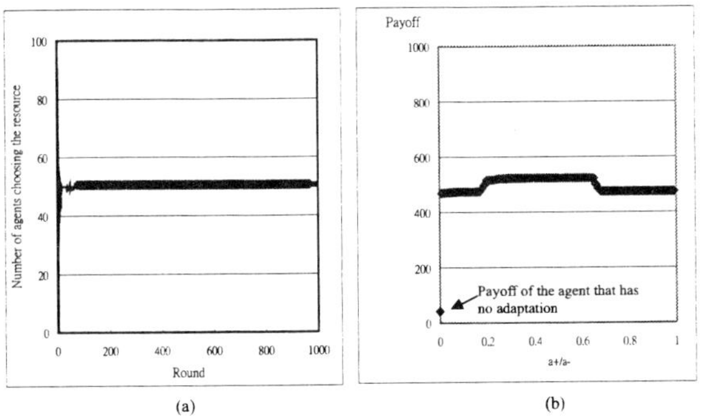

Figure 1. $H = 1$, $n = 100$: (a) Number of players choosing the resource in each round (b) Payoff of each player.

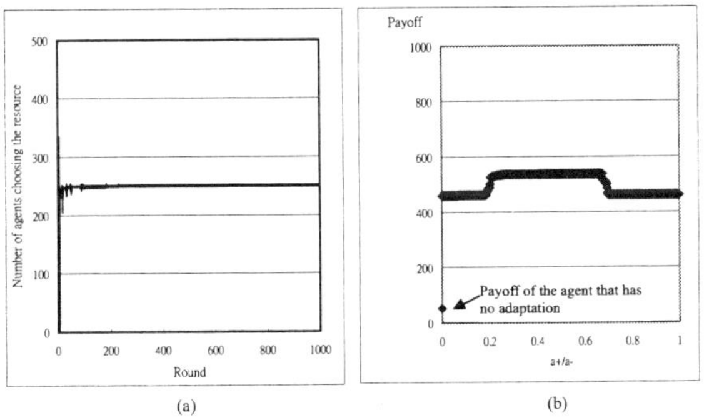

Figure 2. $H = 1$, $n = 500$: (a) Number of players choosing the resource in each round (b) Payoff of each player.

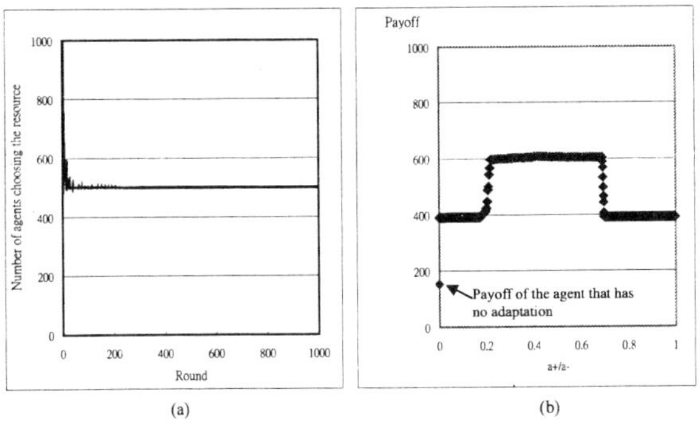

Figure 3. $H = 1$, $n = 1000$: (a) Number of players choosing the resource in each round (b) Payoff of each player.

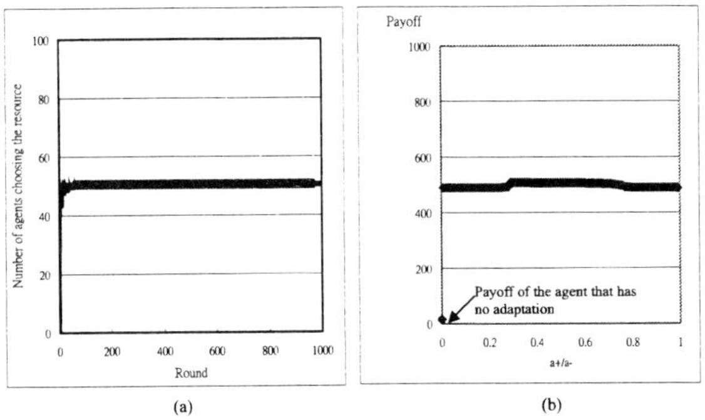

Figure 4. $H = 3$, $n = 100$: (a) Number of players choosing the resource in each round (b) Payoff of each player.

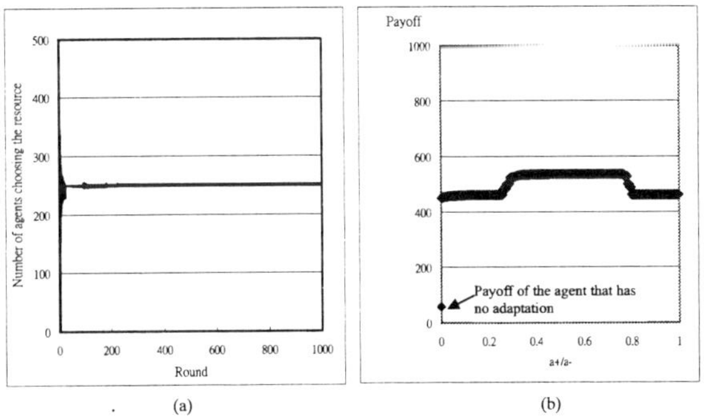

Figure 5. $H = 3$, $n = 500$: (a) Number of players choosing the resource in each round (b) Payoff of each player.

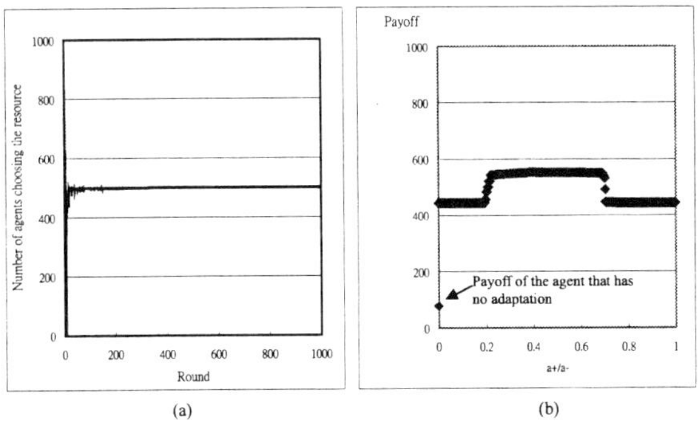

Figure 6. $H = 3$, $n = 1000$: (a) Number of players choosing the resource in each round (b) Payoff of each player.

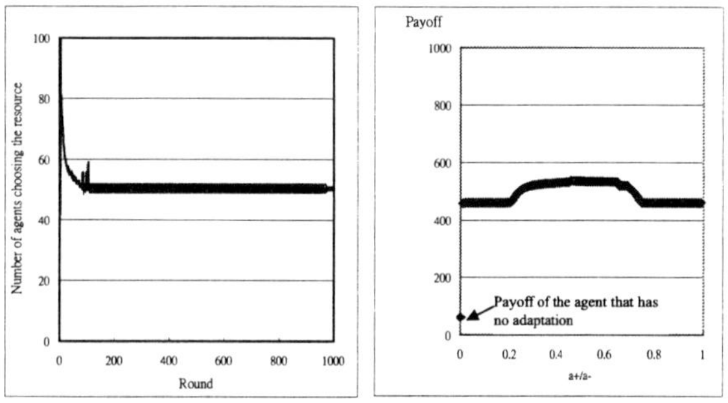

(a) (b)

Figure 7. $H = 7$, $n = 100$: (a) Number of players choosing the resource in each round (b) Payoff of each player.

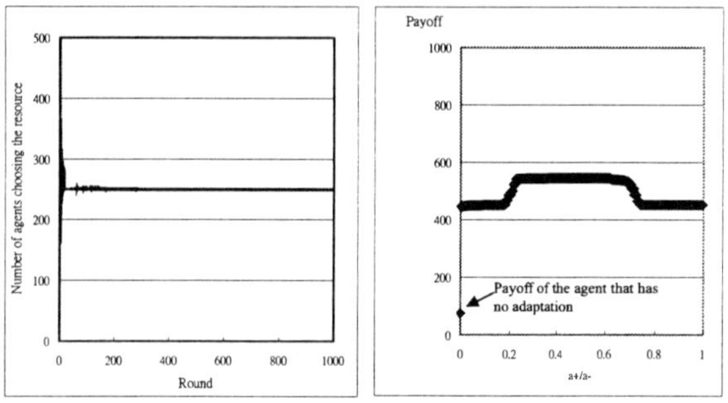

(a) (b)

Figure 8. $H = 7$, $n = 500$: (a) Number of players choosing the resource in each round (b) Payoff of each player.

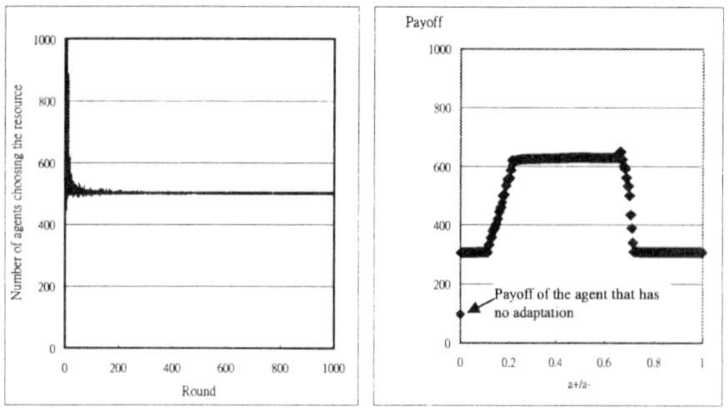

(a) (b)

Figure 9. $H = 7$, $n = 1000$: (a) Number of players choosing the resource in each round (b) Payoff of each player.

4.2 Multi-choice Model

In most systems, more than one resource is available to the agents. An agent may be able to complete its tasks with one of the available resources. So, we extend the single-choice model to a multi-choice model. In each round of a multi-choice game, n agents decide to use one of the k resources (R_1, R_2, ..., R_k). Each resource R_i has a fixed capacity C_i, where $i \in [1, k]$.

In some systems [6, 10], agents have no preference over the resources, which is similar to Galstyan's model [12]. We model this in the first simulation. As agents have no preference over the resources, agents choose whether to use a resource or not based on past histories whether the resource is overloaded or not.

In other systems [4, 8], agents may have preferences over the resources. We model this in the second simulation. In this case, agents choose whether to use a resource or not based on their preferences as well as past histories whether the resource is overloaded or not.

4.2.1 Without preference over the resources

As agents have no preference over the resources, an agent gets a point if it chooses resource R_i and the resource is not overloaded after all agents have made their decisions. This is the same as that in the single-choice model. We perform simulation for $k = 3, 10$ and history size $H = 3$. For $k = 3$, we have $n = 1000$, $C_1 = 200$, $C_2 = 300$, $C_3 = 500$. For $k = 10$, we have $n = 5500$, $C_i = 100i$. Same as previous simulations, all agents have initial attitudes $a_{R_i} = 0.5$ and agent i has adaptive parameters $a_+ = a_- = \frac{i-1}{n}$. We perform simulation for 1000 rounds. The results are shown in Figure 10 and Figure 11.

From Figure 10(a) and Figure 11(a), we can see that the number of agents choosing a particular resource fluctuates around the capacity of the resource. For $k = 3$, fluctuation is large in the first 30 rounds. For $k = 10$, fluctuation is large in the first 100 rounds. Also, the fluctuation is lower for $k = 3$ than for $k = 10$. This is because agents need more time to learn and adapt if there are more resources. Although fluctuations are large in the first few rounds, fluctuations soon become lower.

In Figure 10(b) and Figure 11(b), we plot the number of right decisions that the agent made instead of the payoffs of the agents. However, both are the same because an agent can get a point if it has chosen a resource and that resource is not overloaded, which means the agent has made a right decision. In these two graphs, we can see that agents with adaptive parameters $0.3 < a_+, a_- < 0.6$ make more right decisions. Also, the agent with $a_+ = a_- = 0$ makes particularly few right decisions as this agent has no adaptation at all.

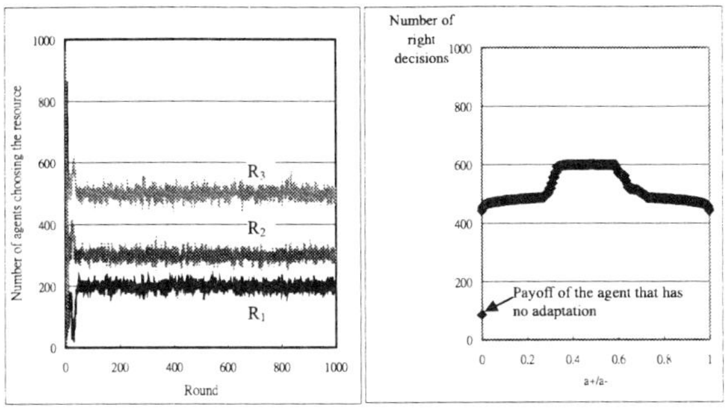

(a) (b)

Figure 10. $k = 3$, $n = 1000$, $H = 3$, Without preference over the resources: (a) Number of players choosing resources R_1 to R_3 in each round (b) Number of right decisions each agent made.

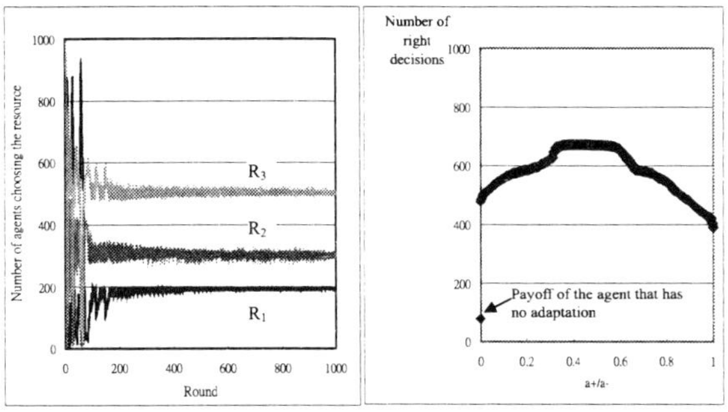

(a) (b)

Figure 12. $k = 3$, $n = 1000$, $H = 3$, With preference over the resources: (a) Number of players choosing the resources R_1 to R_3 in each round (b) Number of right decisions each agent made.

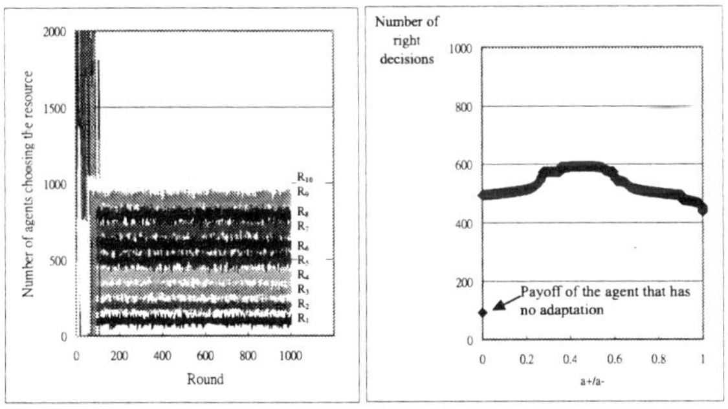

(a) (b)

Figure 11. $k = 10$, $n = 1000$, $H = 3$, Without preference over the resources: (a) Number of players choosing the resources R_1 to R_{10} in each round (b) Number of right decisions each agent made.

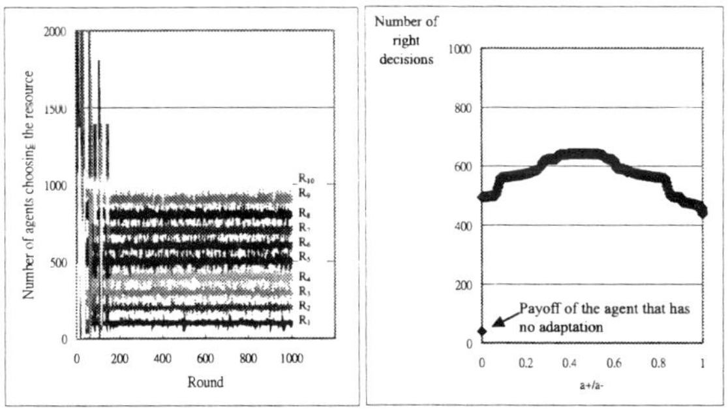

(a) (b)

Figure 13. $k = 10$, $n = 5500$, $H = 3$, With preference over the resources: (a) Number of players choosing the resources R_1 to R_{10} in each round (b) Number of right decisions each agent made.

4.2.2 With preference over the resources

In resource allocation problems, agents may have preferences over the resource assigned to them. To model this, an agent gets a payoff of p_i if the agent chooses to use a resource R_i and that resource is not overloaded, after all agents have made their decisions. As different agents have different preferences over the resources, in the following simulations we randomly generate p_i for each agent, where $0 < p_i \leq 1$.

We perform simulations for $k = 3, 10$. For $k = 3$, we have $n = 1000$, $C_1 = 200$, $C_2 = 300$, $C_3 = 500$. For $k = 10$, we have $n = 5500$, $C_i = 100i$. In these simulations, we use history size $H = 3$. Same as previous simulations, all agents have initial attitudes $a_{R_i} = 0.5$ and agent i has adaptive parameters $a_+ = a_- = \frac{i-1}{n}$. In each game, there are 1000 rounds. The results are shown in Figure 12 and Figure 13.

From Figure 12(a) and Figure 13(a), we can see that the number of agents choosing a particular resource fluctuates around the capacity of the resource although fluctuation is large in the first 60 rounds and in the first 150 rounds respectively. This is because agents need more time to learn and adapt if there are more resources. Also, the fluctuation is lower for fewer numbers of resources.

By comparing Figure 10(a) with Figure 12(a) and Figure 11(a) with Figure 13(a), we can see that the number of agents choosing a particular resource has less fluctuation if agents' preferences over the resources are taken into account in decision-making. This is because agents make more right decisions if they take into account their preferences over the resources in making decisions. As agents make more right decisions, the fluctuations are lower. This means that resources are better utilized.

In Figure 12(b) and Figure 13(b), we again plot the number of right decisions that the agent made instead of the payoffs of the agents. In this simulation, agents have preferences over the resources which are modeled as payoffs. We use the payoffs for decision-making. In this way, payoff-seeking agents tend to choose the resource that they prefer more while history-relying agents tend to choose the resource that is less overloaded in the history. As the payoffs p_i are randomly generated, an agent getting a higher payoff does not mean that the agent has made more right decisions. So, we plot the number of right decisions that the agent made instead of the payoffs that the agents got. Same as before, agents with adaptive parameters $0.3 < a_+, a_- < 0.6$ make more right decisions. Also, the agent which has no adaptation, that is $a_+ = a_- = 0$, makes particularly few right decisions.

By comparing Figure 10(b) with Figure 12(b) and Figure 11(b) with Figure 13(b), we can see that agents generally make more right decisions in the case where their preferences over the resources are modeled. This is because history-relying agents tend to choose the resource that is less overloaded in the history while payoff-seeking agents tend to choose the resource according to their preferences.

In this subsection, simulations show that the adaptive strategy can also work in systems with multiple resources. Besides, the adaptive strategy can work in systems in which agents have or do not have preference over the resources.

5 Comparison with Related Work

Galstyan *et al.* [12] also model the resource allocation problem as a Minority Game. Similar to the traditional minority game model [5], Galstyan *et al.* also use predictors. Each agent uses and keeps track of a number of predictors. At the end of each round, the predictors which have made correct predictions gain a virtual point. The predictor with the most virtual points is thus the most accurate one. Agents always use the most accurate strategy to decide their action.

Different from the traditional minority game model [5], the agents record the actions of m neighbors in the previous round instead of recording the winning sides in the past H rounds. So, instead of using a history of winning sides to choose an action for the coming round, agents use a profile of actions chosen by their neighbors in the previous round. Galstyan *et al.* find that fluctuation of the number of agents choosing a particular resource is the lowest with connectivity $m = 2$.

For example, if an agent use the actions of 2 neighbors to choose its action in the coming round, a predictor in a single-choice game will look like the one shown in Table 3, where A represents an action of using the resource and N represents an action of not to use the resource.

Using the predictor shown in Table 3, if both of the two neighbors chose A (to use the resource) in the previous round, then an agent will choose A in the coming round.

Table 3. An example of Galstyan's predictor for $m = 2$ in a single-choice game.

Actions of 2 neighbors	Actions to choose
AA	A
AN	N
NA	N
NN	A

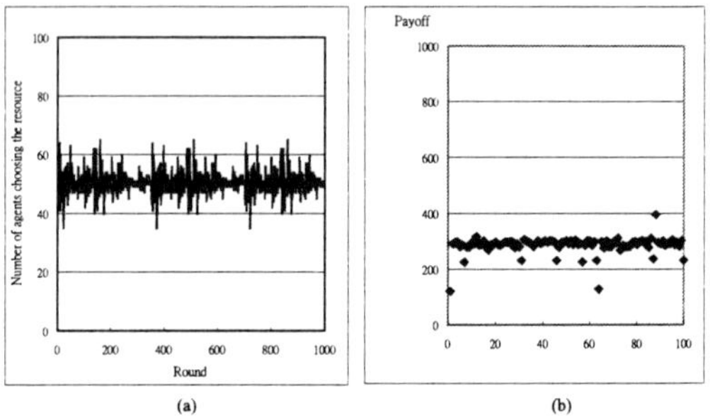

Figure 14. $m = 2$, $n = 100$: (a) Number of players choosing the resource in each round (b) Payoff of each player.

Similar to previous studies of Minority Games [2, 5, 14], the predictors of the players are randomly generated, which means the actions to choose in the coming round are also generated randomly. So, there is no reason why an agent should choose A if both of its two neighbors chose A in the previous round.

We perform simulations of a single-choice model for $m = 2$ and $n = 100, 500, 1000$. In each game, there are 1000 rounds. Following [12], each agent has 2 predictors to use and keep track of. The results are shown in Figure 14 to Figure 16.

From Figure 14(a) to Figure 16(a), we can see that the

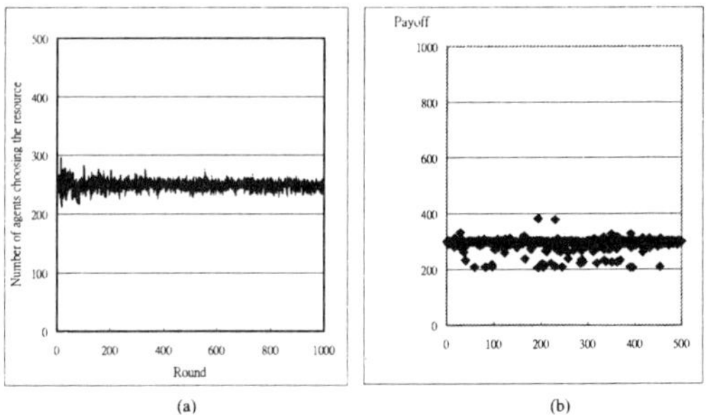

Figure 15. $m = 2$, $n = 500$: (a) Number of players choosing the resource in each round (b) Payoff of each player.

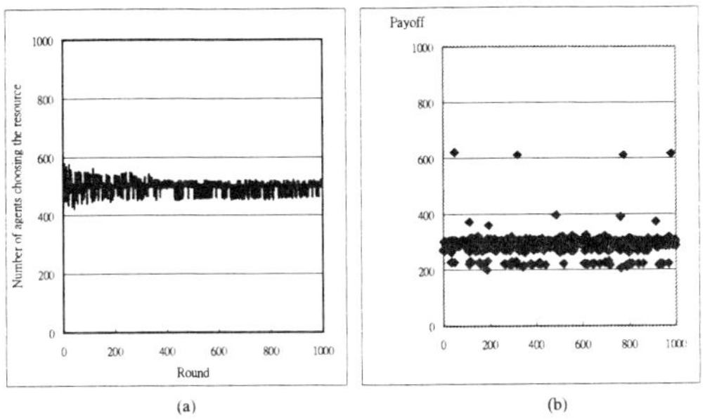

Figure 16. $m = 2$, $n = 1000$: (a) Number of players choosing the resource in each round (b) Payoff of each player.

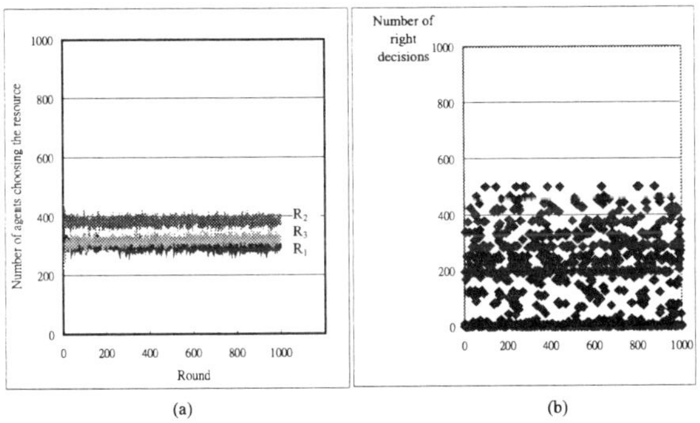

Figure 17. $k = 3$, $n = 1000$, $m = 2$: (a) Number of players choosing the resources R_1 to R_3 in each round (b) Number of right decisions that the agent made.

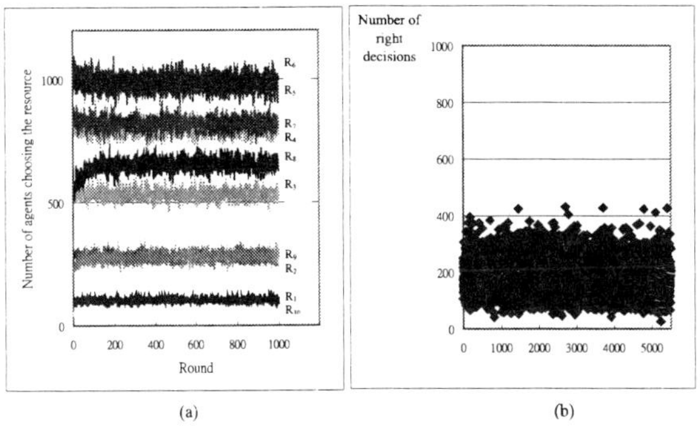

Figure 18. $k = 10$, $n = 5500$, $m = 2$: (a) Number of players choosing the resources R_1 to R_{10} in each round (b) Number of right decisions that the agent made.

Table 4. Fluctuations of the number of agents choosing a particular resource in Figure 18.

Resource	Capacity	Fluctuation around
R_1	100	100
R_2	200	250
R_3	300	500
R_4	400	800
R_5	500	1000
R_6	600	1000
R_7	700	800
R_8	800	650
R_9	900	300
R_{10}	1000	60

fluctuation of the number of Galstyan's agents choosing to use the resource is large. By comparing with Figure 1(a) to Figure 9(a), the fluctuation is much lower in cases where agents use the proposed adaptive strategy.

From Figure 14(b) to Figure 16(b), we can see that the payoffs that most Galstyan's agents get are below 400. By comparing with Figure 1(b) to Figure 9(b), the payoffs that most agents (using the adaptive strategy) get are above 400, except the one without adaptation. This result shows that agents using the proposed adaptive strategy are able to make more right decisions than Galstyan's agents.

We also perform simulations of a multi-choice model for $m = 2$. Same as the simulations in section 4.2, we perform simulations for number of resources $k = 3, 10$. For $k = 3$, we have $n = 1000$, $C_1 = 200$, $C_2 = 300$, $C_3 = 500$. For $k = 10$, we have $n = 5500$, $C_i = 100i$. Again, each agent has 2 predictors to use and keep track of. In each game, there are 1000 rounds. The results are shown in Figure 17 and Figure 18.

From Figure 17(a), we can see that the number of agents choosing R_1 (with $C_1 = 200$), R_2 (with $C_2 = 300$), and R_3 (with $C_1 = 500$) fluctuate around 300, 400 and 300 respectively. This means that R_1 and R_2 are overloaded most of the times while R_3 is always under loaded. From Figure 18(a), we can see that the fluctuations of the number of agents choosing a particular resource, which is shown in Table 4. From the table, we can see that R_1 to R_7 are overloaded most of the times while R_8 to R_{10} are always under loaded.

By comparing with Figure 10(a) and Figure 11(a), we can see that the number of agents choosing a particular resource fluctuates around the capacity of that resource when agents use the adaptive strategy. This suggests that agents using the proposed adaptive strategy make much better resource utilization.

Again, by comparing Figure 17(b) and Figure 18(b) with Figure 10(b) and Figure 11(b), we can see that agents with the adaptive strategy generally make more right decisions than agents using Galstyan's model.

From the above comparisons, we can see that the adaptive strategy improves the performance of Galstyan's model.

The reason behind is that Galstyan's agents only use their neighbors' previous actions to make decisions. These agents do not choose their actions based on whether the resource is overloaded in the previous round. Also, the predictors that these agents used are randomly generated. So, these agents are actually switching between some random actions. On the other hand, agents using the proposed adaptive strategy choose their actions based on the history whether the resource is overloaded in the previous round. Also, these agents learn whether they have made a correct decision in the previous round and change their attitudes adaptively. As a result, agents using the proposed adaptive strategy are able to make more right decisions and better resource utilization.

6 Conclusions and Future Work

Many studies [4, 6, 9, 15] have been carried out for resource allocation. In many cases, there is a large overhead to the system due to the complexity of the design.

In fact, resource allocation problem can be modeled as a Minority Game. In this way, the system is distributed with reduced overhead. Also, the system is autonomous and can be adaptive.

In this paper, we model the resource allocation problem as a Minority Game. We design an adaptive strategy for agents to play in the game model. We perform simulations of a single-choice model, a multi-choice model in which agents have no preferences over the resources and a multi-choice model in which agents have preferences over the resources. We also compare our results with a related model. Simulations show that agents with the proposed adaptive strategy are able to make more right decisions and better resource utilization.

In this paper, we only model resource allocation problems in which resources have fixed capacities. In some resource allocation problems, the capacities of resources may change over time. As future work, we are going to extend our model to due with resources having time-dependent capacities.

In real resource allocation problems, agents often need a bundle of resources in order to complete their tasks. However, this is not modeled in this paper. In this paper, agents choose only one resource at a time. Another possible future work is to extend our model so that agents can choose a bundle of resources at a time. Add to this, we can compare the extended model with existing resource allocation methods.

7 Acknowledgments

The work described in this paper was partially supported by a grant from the Research Grants Council of the Hong Kong Special Administrative Region, China (Project No. 413306).

References

[1] M. Allais. Le comportement de l'homme rationnel devant le risque: 367 critique des postulats et axiomes de l'ecole americaine. *Econometrica*, 21:503–546, 1953.

[2] R. M. Araujo and L. C. Lamb. Towards understanding the role of learning models in the dynamics of the minority game. In *Proceedings of The 16th IEEE International Conference on Tools with Artificial Intelligence*, pages 727–731, 2004.

[3] W. B. Arthur. Inductive reasoning and bounded rationaliy. *The American Economic Review*, 84(2):406–411, 1994.

[4] C. Boutilier, M. Goldszmidt, and B. Sabata. Sequential auctions for the allocation of resources with complimentarities. In *International Joint Conference on Artificial Intelligence*, pages 527–523, 1999.

[5] D. Challet and Y. Zhang. Emergence of cooperation and organization in an evolutionary game. *Physica A*, 246:407–418, 1997.

[6] A. Chavez, A. Moukas, and P. Maes. Challenger: A multi-agent system for distributed resource allocation. In *Proceedings of the First International Conference on Autonomous Agents*, pages 323–331, 1997.

[7] Y. Chevaleyre, P. E. Dunne, and et al. Issues in multiagent resource allocation.

[8] Y. Chevaleyre, U. Endriss, S. Estivie, and N. Maudet. Multi-agent resource allocation with k-additive utility functions. In *Workshop on Computer Science and Decision Theory*, pages 83–100, 2004.

[9] P. Cramton, Y. Shoham, and R. Steinberg. *Combinatorial Auctions*. MIT Press, 2006.

[10] S. S. Fatima and M. Wooldridge. Adaptive task and resource allocation in multi-agent systems. In *The Fifth International Conference on Autonomous Agents*, pages 537–544, 2001.

[11] R. Gagne. *The Conditions of Learning (4th ed.)*. New York: Holt, Rinehart and Winston, 1985.

[12] A. Galstyan, S. Kolar, and K. Lerman. Resource allocation games with changing resource capacities. In *Proceedings of The Second International Joint Conference on Autonomous Agent and Multiagent Systems*, pages 145–152, 2003.

[13] D. Kahneman and A. Tversky. Prospect theory: An analysis of decision under risk. *Econometrica*, 47(2):263–291, 1979.

[14] H. Kimura and E. Akiyama. Grand canonical minority games with variable strategy spaces. In *Proceedings of The 19th Annual Conference of The Japanese Society for Artificial Intelligence*, pages 291–301, 2006.

[15] J. Kurose and R. Simha. A microeconomic approach to optimal resource allocation in distributed computer systems. *IEEE Transactions on Computers*, 38(5):705–717, 1989.

[16] K. Lam and H. Leung. An adaptive strategy for minority games. In *International Conference on Autonomous Agents and Multiagent Systems*, 2007.

[17] J. von Neumann and O. Morgenstern. *Theory of Games and Economic Behavior*. Princeton University Press, 1944.

Research Track, Session 7: Management and Control

Controlling Access to Preserve QoS in a Self-Aware Network

Erol Gelenbe
Imperial College London
Intelligent Systems and Networks Group
Electrical & Electronic Engineering Dept.
SW7 2BT London, UK
e.gelenbe@imperial.ac.uk

Georgia Sakellari
Imperial College London
Intelligent Systems and Networks Group
Electrical & Electronic Engineering Dept.
SW7 2BT London, UK
g.sakellari@imperial.ac.uk

Maurizio D'Arienzo
Seconda Università degli studi di Napoli
Via del setificio 15
San Leucio (CE)
81020, Italy
maudarie@unina.it

Abstract

Multimedia traffic and real-time applications created a need for network Quality of Service (QoS). This demand led to the development of autonomous networks that use adaptive packet routing in order to provide the best possible QoS. Admission Control (AC) is a mechanism which takes those networks a step further in guaranteeing packet delivery even under strict QoS constraints. This paper describes a measurement-based admission control algorithm which decides whether a new connection can be served without affecting the existing users of the network, based on the multiple QoS metrics that the users of a Self-Aware Network have specified. Our algorithm promises QoS throughout the lifetime of all accepted connections in the network. The impact that the new call will have, on the QoS of both the new and the existing users, is estimated by sending probe packets and monitoring the networks by exploiting its self-awareness. The decision of whether to accept a new call is made using a novel algebra of QoS metrics, inspired by Warshall's algorithm, which looks for a path with acceptable QoS values that can accommodate the new flow. In this paper we describe the underlying mathematical principles and present experimental results obtained by evaluating the method in a large laboratory test-bed operating the Self-Aware Cognitive Packet Network (CPN) protocol.

1. Introduction

The current "best effort" Internet architecture does not secure the Quality of Service (QoS) that multimedia traffic and real-time applications, such as video on demand, Internet telephony (Voice-over-IP), remote medical diagnosis and treatment, and online trading systems require in order to function properly. This need led to the development of Self-Aware Networks [13] that use adaptive packet routing protocols, like the Cognitive Packet Network (CPN) [18], to address QoS and provide reliable service to their users. But even in these networks, congestion is a factor that can lead to unstable and unreliable situations which will affect the service quality. Admission Control (AC) provides a solution to traffic congestion and promises a stable and reliable network which will guarantee packet delivery under QoS constraints. A proposal of a measurement-based AC, which exploits the ability of CPN to collect QoS information on all links, is the purpose of the work presented in this paper. Our scheme bases its decision of whether to accept a new connection in the network by estimating both the resources it will need and the impact it will have on the ongoing connections.

2. AC Algorithms - Types and History

According to whether the traffic parameters are specified a priori or whether the admission decisions rely on measurements of the actual traffic load, Admission Control Algorithms can be classified in two categories: parameter-

0-7695-2906-2/07 $25.00 © 2007 IEEE

based and measurement-based. The parameter-based AC algorithms can be analysed by formal methods, while the measurement-based ones can only be analysed through experimentation on real networks or with simulation or emulation.

2.1. Parameter-based AC

These algorithms compute the amount of network resources required to support new flow by given a priori flow characteristics. They can be further classified as non-statistical and statistical allocation algorithms. The **Non-statistical allocation or deterministic** (also called Peak Bandwidth Allocation) is the simplest form among all admission control algorithms. The only knowledge it uses is the peak rate or worst-case parameter to compare against the network's available bandwidth and make a decision on whether to accept the new connection request or not. The algorithm ensures that the sum of requested resources and the existing connections is bounded by the physical link capacity. The most significant disadvantage of this type is that they assume that connections transmit at their peak rates all the time, thus they allocate more bandwidth than it is required to provide QoS guarantees for the existing connections, and the network resources are under-utilised. An other drawback is that there is no multiplexing gain among the sessions admitted into the network, since it works on a flow by flow basis and does not consider sharing bandwidth resources between connections. **Statistical allocation** is a group of much more complicated admission control algorithms. It does not admit new connection requests on the basis of their peak rates; rather the bandwidth for a connection is assigned at less than the peak bandwidth of the connection, depending on the statistical distribution of the arriving cells in the connection [25]. Statistical allocation results in statistical multiplexing gain, when dealing with sources that arrive in "bursts", since it assumes sharing bandwidth resource with other connections and thus the sum of all peak rates may be greater than the capacity of the output link. This type is difficult to be implemented effectively because of the uncertainty in the distribution of the incoming traffic and the inaccurate and difficult-to-calculate statistical information of the traffic arrival process.

Following are the most well-known parameter based algorithms.

Rate or Simple Sum is the simplest parameter-based algorithm, and the most widely implemented by switch and router vendors [24]. It ensures that the sum of requested resources does not exceed the link capacity. The Simple Sum algorithm does not take into account QoS metrics other than bandwidth, and it assumes that every user will use all of its reserved bandwidth.

Acceptance Region schemes decide whether to admit a new flow according to the current state of the system and whether the state lies within the "acceptance" or "rejection" region. The acceptance region is calculated in order to maximize the line utilisation for a nominal packet loss, given a set of flows with a given declaration of peak and mean rates. The calculation in both [20] and [27] assumes that calls arrive according to a Poisson process, that the calls admitted are independent and stay in the network for exponentially distributed time, that they have identical bandwidth requirement statistics and they are described by a Markov fluid process. The model in [20] tries to deal with high offered load situations by not considering for acceptance any call, every time an arriving call is rejected, until after a call currently in progress has ended.

Though the acceptance region algorithms are quite simple, this simplicity comes as a result of simplifications of the network model, which results in limitations in such algorithms. For instance, they perform quite poorly at low link capacity. Another limitation is related to the often made assumption of homogeneous on-off sources. Thus it may not be clear whether such algorithms are still applicable when the traffic sources do not fit this model.

Equivalent Bandwidth (also known as equivalent capacity or efficient bandwidth) is the minimum bandwidth that is needed to carry the traffic that is generated by a source in isolation, without violating the QoS requirements. In this approach, each source is assigned an equivalent bandwidth and a new call is accepted if the sum of these equivalent bandwidths is less than the capacity of the links.

The schemes of [21] and [22] uses a fluid-flow model for the source and a bandwidth allocation process to calculate the equivalent bandwidth by taking into account the impact of source characteristics (the duration of the burst period) either when the impact of individual connection characteristics is critical or when the effect of statistical multiplexing is of significance. The idle periods and burst lengths are assumed exponentially distributed and independent from each other, so that the source statistics can be fully characterised by the peak rate of a connection the mean rate of a connection, and the average duration of a burst period. The equivalent capacity is the minimum value of two parameters. The first relies on a Gaussian approximation for the aggregate bit rate of the network connections routed over a link and is representative of bandwidth requirements when the effect of statistical multiplexing is of significance and the second represents the impact of source characteristics (the duration of the burst period) on the required bandwidth and estimates the equivalent capacity when the impact of individual connection characteristics is critical.

[6] proposes an admission control algorithm, based on [21] scheme, which estimates the equivalent capacity of a class using the Hoeffding Bound, a looser bound of the sum of N independent, random variables. The Hoeffding

0-7695-2906-2/07 $25.00 © 2007 IEEE

Bound does not assume normal distribution of the aggregate traffic, so this model does not assume a normal approximation of the arrival rate distribution, and thus is preferable for classes with either a moderate number of admitted connections or for traffic from heterogeneous sources with wide range in the peak rates.

Equivalent bandwidth schemes are characterised by their simplicity, since determining whether a given set of traffic sources can be accommodated without any QoS violation comes down to comparing the sum of the equivalent bandwidths of individual sources to the link capacity. This approach does not consider the effect of buffering which increases the effective capacity of a system. Of course, since Equivalent Capacity AC algorithms are parameter-based, they reserve the resources that are specified by the source traffic description, which could lead to low network utilisation since users could request more resources than they require.

The **Diffusion based statistical AC** uses statistical bandwidth based on closed-form expressions that use diffusion approximation models. It exploits information about buffer sizes and the multiplexed traffic that shares a common link to obtain a diffusion approximation based cell loss estimate and assumes that traffic follows an "On-Off" behaviour.

The scheme in [17] uses two diffusion models: one for a finite buffer (FB) ATM multiplexer and another for an infinite buffer (IB) ATM multiplexer. The cell loss probability is estimated by the overflow probability, which is the overall probability of exceeding the actual buffer capacity B.

A new connection is admitted if the statistical bandwidth on every intermediate link along the selected path is less than the link capacity. The use of diffusion-based techniques has been shown to be conservative with respect to cell loss, but more economical in bandwidth allocation, and has the disadvantages of the parameter-based algorithms.

2.2. Measurement-based AC (MBAC)

This approach relies on measurements of actual traffic load in making admission decisions. It uses these network measurements to estimate the current load of existing traffic, instead of computing the traffic characteristics out of the user specified connection's parameters. It has no prior knowledge of the traffic characteristics and makes the admission decisions based only on the current state of the network. The measurement-based schemes alleviate the burden on the users to accurately specify the parameters for their traffic flow, and thus is a more practical approach for achieving statistical multiplexing gain with variable-rate traffic.

Following are the most well-known MBAC mechanisms which have been proposed for conventional networks.

Measured Sum [24] is the measurement-based version of the Simple Sum algorithm. It tries to increase the network utilisation by measuring the actual network load and substituting the reserved rates of the existing users with the measured load. Again the admission decision is based only on the availability of bandwidth and does not consider any other QoS metric.

Measurement Based Admission Control with Delay and Bandwidth Constraint schemes do both delay and bandwidth checking and are used with predictive service for "tolerant" applications which allow a certain degree of QoS violations. When a new flow requests service the network must characterise its traffic. The algorithm described in [23], is designed for predictive service which approximates the maximum delay of predictive flows by replacing the worst-case parameters in the analytical models with measured quantities. The computation of worst-case queueing delay is different for guaranteed and predictive services. Such algorithms cannot be used in networks with strict QoS requirements and are only applicable in networks with predictive service. Also the schemes tend to exceed the needed bandwidth reservation, since they use worst-case delays, which is rarely the case since multiple sources will rarely simultaneously transmit packets at peak rate.

The **Endpoint Admission Control** [2, 1, 4, 19, 3] is a measurement-based scheme in which the end host (endpoint) probes the network by sending probe packets at the data rate it would like to reserve and records the resulting level of packet losses, specially marked packets, or other QoS criteria. The host then admits the flow only if the loss or marking percentage is below some threshold value. Endpoint admission control requires no explicit support from the routers that do not need to keep a per-flow state or process reservation requests. This approach simply uses the fact that routers may drop or mark packets in a normal manner. In some cases the probe packets are treated equally with the data packets and in others they are sent at a different priority level.

When a new user requests to enter the network, a probe is sent from the source to the destination. The destination counts the received packets until the probe time period expires and sends a measurement report, under high priority, to the source with the number of probe packets received. Based on that report, if the calculated probe loss probability is less than a threshold the source decides to accept the new call. If he probe does not succeed on reaching the destination, due to temporal network overload or opposing probe processes, the session establishment fails and the source must wait for a random time (back-off time) before issuing a new probe. The back-off time is calculated from a uniform distribution of some width, which is doubled for each consecutively blocked attempt to reach the same receiver.

[7] assumes that call requests arrive according to a Poisson process of rate λ. A new call sends w probe packets

and is admitted if and only if the number of marked probe packets is less than or equal to a threshold r.

End-point admission schemes suffer from the shortcomings of any measurement based scheme where estimates may not be in line with what will be observed when the real traffic is sent instead of the probe traffic.

Measurement-based AC algorithms are shown to achieve much higher utilisation than parameter-based [23], and the more accurate and up-to-date the measurements the better the algorithm. So the last few years the research is focused on accurate network monitoring tools and as admission control is concerned it is turned towards measurement-based approaches.

3. Self Aware Networks

Self Aware Networks (SAN) is a proposal of QoS enabled networks with enhanced monitoring and self improvement capabilities that use adaptive packet routing protocols, such as Cognitive Packet Network (CPN) ([18], [14], [15], [12], [11], [10], [9], [16]) and address QoS by using adaptive techniques based on on-line measurements. In CPN, users declare their QoS requirements (QoS Goals) such as minimum delay, maximum bandwidth, minimum cost, etc. It is designed to perform Self-Improvement by learning from the experience of smart packets, using random neural networks (RNN) [8] with reinforcement learning (RL), and genetic algorithms. RL is carried out using a QoS Goal defined by the user, who generated a request for the connection, or by the network itself. The decisional weights of a RNN are increased or decreased based on the observed success or failure of subsequent smart packets to achieve the Goal. Thus RL will tend to prefer better routing schemes, more reliable access paths to data objects, and better QoS.

More analytically, CPN makes use of three types of packets: smart packets (SP) for discovery, source routed dumb packets (DP) to carry payload, and acknowledgements (ACK) to bring back information that has been discovered by SPs which are used in nodes to train neural networks. Conventional IP packets may tunnel through CPN to seamlessly operate mixed IP and CPN networks. SPs are generated either by a user requesting to create a path to some CPN node, or by a user requesting to discover parts of network state, including location of certain fixed or mobile nodes, power levels at nodes, topology, paths and their QoS metrics.

SPs discover routes by using random neural networks (RNN) [8] with reinforcement learning (RL). RL is carried out using a QoS Goal (such as packet delay, loss, hop count, jitter, etc) which is defined by the user who generated a request for the connection, or by the network itself. The decisional weights of a RNN are increased or decreased based on the observed success or failure of subsequent SPs to achieve the Goal. Thus RL will tend to prefer better routing schemes, more reliable access paths to data objects, and better QoS.

When a Smart Packet arrives to its destination, an ACK is generated and heads back to the source of the request, following the reversed path of the SP. It updates mailboxes (MBs) in the CPN nodes it visits with the information which has discovered, and provides the source node with the successful path to the node. All packets have a life-time constraint based on the number of nodes visited, to avoid overburdening the system with unsuccessful requests or packets which are in effect lost. A node in the CPN acts as a storage area for packets and mailboxes (MBs). It also stores and executes the code used to route smart packets. It has an input buffer for packets arriving from the input links, a set of mailboxes, and a set of output buffers which are associated with output links. The route brought back by an ACK is used as a source route by subsequent DPs of the same QoS class having the same destination, until a newer and/or better route is brought back by another ACK. ACK messages also contain timestamp information that can be used to monitor the QoS metrics on a single link and/or partial or complete paths.

Each node stores a specific RNN for each active source-destination pair, and each QoS goal. The number of neurons in an RNN corresponds to the number of routing outputs of a node. Each output link of a node is represented by a neuron in the RNN. The arrival of Smart Packets(SPs) triggers the execution of RNN and the routing decision is the output link corresponding to the most excited neuron. CPN reinforcement learning changes neuron weights to reward or punish a neuron according to the level of goal satisfaction measured on the corresponding output.

The level of goal satisfaction is expressed by a reward. Given some goal G that a packet has to minimize, the reward R is formulated simply as $R = 1/G$. The state q_i of ith neuron in the network is the probability that it is excited. The q_i, $1 < i < n$ satisfy the following system of nonlinear equations:

$$q_i = \frac{\lambda^+(i)}{r(i)+\lambda^-(i)}$$

where $\lambda^+(i) = \sum_j q_j w^+_{ji} + \Lambda_i$ and $\lambda_-(i) = \sum_j q_j w^+_{ji} + \lambda_i$

w^+_{ji} is the rate at which neuron j sends "excitation spikes" to neuron i when j is excited, w^-_{ji} is the rate at which neuron j sends "inhibition spikes" to neuron i when j is excited, and $r(i)$ is the total firing rate from the neuron i. For an n neuron network, the network parameters are these n by n "weight matrices" $W^+ = \{w^+(i,j)\}$ and $W^- = \{w^-(i,j)\}$ which need to be "learned" from input data.

The RNN weights are updated based on a threshold T:

$$T_k = \alpha T_{k-1} + (1-\alpha) R_k$$

where R_k, k = 1, 2, ... are successive measured values of reward R and α is some constant ($0 < \alpha < 1$) that is used to tune the responsiveness of the algorithm: for instance $\alpha = 0.8$ means that on the average five past values of R are being taken into account. Neurons are rewarded or punished based on the difference between R_k, the current reward, and T_{k-1}, the last threshold.

4. Our proposed multiple criterion AC algorithm

The measurement-based AC algorithm we propose [26] is based on measurements of the QoS metrics on each link of the network before and after the transmission of probe packets. This does not require any special monitoring mechanism since the CPN already collects QoS information on all links and paths that the SPs have explored and on all paths that any user is using in the network. Furthermore, since it is the users that determine the QoS metrics that interest them, CPN collects data for the different QoS metrics that are relevant to the users themselves.

The proposed AC scheme consists of two stages. The fist one is called Probing Stage and is the stage where the impact of the new flow is estimated by probing the network. In the second stage (Decision Stage) the AC decides on whether to accept a new call into the network based on whether there is a feasible path which can accommodate the new call without affecting the quality of formerly accepted flows.

4.1. Probing Stage - Estimation of the impact of a new flow

Every QoS metric can be considered as a value which increases as the "traffic load" increases. A new connection will increase the load of the paths it may be using so it is assumed that the value taken by the QoS metrics will increase. For example, delay increases as the network traffic load increases.

Let as consider some link (i, j). A small increase x in the load that is obtained in a controlled manner, e.g. by sending probe packets at rate x, generates an estimate of the manner in which the QoS metric q varies around the current load point Y:

$$\hat{q}' = \frac{q(Y + x) - q(Y)}{x}. \quad (1)$$

The impact of a new flow with total traffic rate X can then be evaluated by using the estimate and the measured derivative from (1):

$$\hat{q}(Y + X) = q(Y) + \hat{q}'X, \quad (2)$$

without having to know the initial load Y. This estimate may be optimistic or pessimistic. However it is likely that

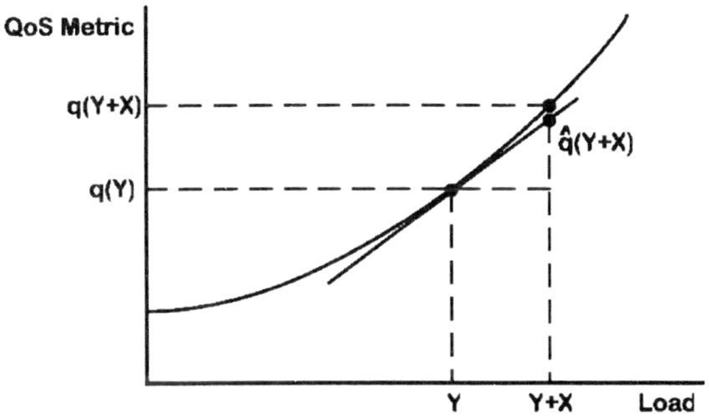

Figure 1. QoS metric vs Load

the path that CPN will select for the probe traffic, because it provides the most favorable impact on current flows and because it satisfies the QoS needs of the new flow. It is also likely that this path is also the best path in terms of actual observed QoS after the new user's full traffic is inserted. Contrary to the existing measurement-based AC schemes that use probing, in our scheme, it is not required to send the probe packets at the same rate as the new call's requested rate. Instead we can send them at a much lower rate and still have an accurate estimation. This is a major advantage since this way the probing process has no significant impact on the network's congestion.

4.2. Decision Stage

Let us assume that the users may be concerned with m distinct QoS metrics $q_v \in R$, $v = 1, ...m$ that are specified in terms of QoS constraints $[q_v \in C_v(u)$ for each user $u]$, where $C_v(u) \subset R$ is typically an interval of acceptable values of the QoS metric v for user u. We will detail the AC algorithm in terms of forwarding packets from some source s to a destination d. However this approach can be generalised to the case where u is requesting some service S.

A network can be considered as a network graph $G(N, E)$ with nodes N, $n = |N|$, and a set E of directional links (i, j), where $i, j \in N$. The CPN algorithm explores $G(N, E)$ and collects QoS data about the parts of the network that are being currently used, or which have been explored by SPs. We assume that this data is available in one or more locations in the form of $n \times n$ *link QoS matrices* Q_v with elements:

- $Q_v(i, j) = r$ where $r \geq 0$ is a real number representing the QoS of link (i, j) which has been measured at some recent enough time, and
- $Q_v(i, j) = unknown$ if i and j are not directly connected or if either a SP has not explored the link for

QoS metric v or if this happened so long ago that the value could be inaccurate.

From the link matrices Q_v we can compute:

- The set of known (explored) paths $P(s, d)$ from s to d, and
- The *path QoS matrices* K_v, where $K_v(s, d)$ is the *known best value* of the QoS metric v for any *path* going from s to d if such a path exists and if the links on the path have known entries in the link QoS matrices. Other entries in K_v are set to the value "unknown".

By "best value" we mean that several paths may exist for the source-destination pair (s, d), but $K_v(s, d)$ will store, for instance, the smallest known delay for all paths going from s to d if q_v is the delay metric. We will discuss below how the path QoS matrices are computed from the link matrices.

4.3. The AC Algorithm

Let us assume that the network is currently carrying z users, any one of which will be generically represented by some QoS constraint $q_w(z)$ and a new user u requests admission for a connection from source s to destination d carrying a traffic rate X and with QoS constraint $q_v(u)$. The proposed AC algorithm proceeds as follows:

- Find the set $P(s, d)$. If it is empty, send SPs to discover paths. If unsuccessful, reject the request. Otherwise monitor the current network, create the $Q_w(i, j)$ matrices for all discovered links and all QoS metrics (including $w = v$), and then send probe traffic at rate x along the network.
- Use the probe traffic to obtain $\hat{q}'_w(i, j)$ for each QoS metric w of interest, including $w = v$, and for all links (i, j). Note that some links may not be concerned by the probe traffic so for that links we take $\hat{q}'_w(i, j) = 0$. The path that the probe packets will follow, will be the one that the SPs have chosen as more appropriate so that it satisfy the QoS needs of the new flow, so, it is very likely to also be the path that will be followed after the new user's full traffic is inserted.
- Afterwards compute the estimation

$$\hat{Q}_w(i, j) = Q_w(i, j) + X\hat{q}'_w(i, j) \tag{3}$$

  for all concerned links and all QoS metrics. For unconcerned links we take $\hat{Q}_w(i, j) = Q_w(i, j)$.
- Compute $\hat{K}_w$ from $\hat{Q}_w$ (to be detailed below) for all the QoS metrics of interest, including v.
- Finally, if $\hat{K}_v(s, d) \in C_v(u)$ AND $\hat{K}_w(s', d') \in C_w(z)$ for all other current users z with source-destination pair (s', d') and QoS metric $q_w \in C_w(z)$, then accept u; else reject the request.

4.4. Computing the QoS matrices

For each $i, j \in N$ of a network graph $G(N, E)$ with nodes N, $n = |N|$, and a set E of directional links (i, j). the well known "Warshall's algorithm" [28] determines whether there is a path from node i to node j by computing the Boolean matrix K, the transitive closure of the graph's adjacency matrix Q, in less than n^3 Boolean operations.

$$K = \bigcup_{k=1}^{n} Q^k \tag{4}$$

or

$$K^n[i, j] = K^{n-1}[i, j] \bigvee \left(K^{n-1}[i, n] \bigwedge K^{n-1}[n, j]\right) \tag{5}$$

where $K^1[i, j] = Q[i, j]$ and the matrix elements are treated as boolean values with $\bigvee$ being the logical "OR" and $\bigwedge$ the logical "AND".

Floyd's algorithm [5] extends Warshall's algorithm to obtain the cost of the "smallest cost path" between any pair of vertices in the form of a real-valued matrix.

$$K^n[i, j] = min\left\{K^{n-1}[i, j], \left(K^{n-1}[i, n] + K^{n-1}[n, j]\right)\right\} \tag{6}$$

Thus, our algorithm can use Floyd-Warshall's technique to construct K_v from Q_v, and hence $\hat{K}_v$ from $\hat{Q}_v$ if the QoS metric q_v is additive, so that $K_v(i, j)$ is the smallest value of the QoS metric among all known paths from i to j. Note that delay and the variance of delay, are both additive metrics. Although loss rate is not additive, the number of lost packets is an additive metric.

For non-additive metrics we have developed a generalisation of the Floyd-Warshall, which is described next.

4.5. Generalisation of the Floyd-Warshall algorithm to non-additive QoS metrics

Consider the matrix Q_v mentioned above, whose entries are the measured QoS values $r \geq 0$ over links (i, j) whenever such a link exists, or otherwise have the value "unknown".

The matrix K_v which is calculated as shown below, provides us with the "best QoS value" for every path between every pair of vertices (i,j).

$$K_v = \bigoplus_{k=1}^{n} [Q_v]^k \tag{7}$$

or

$$K_v^n[i,j] = K_v^{n-1}[i,j] \otimes \left(K_v^{n-1}[i,n] \oplus K_v^{n-1}[n,j]\right) \quad (8)$$

where in (8) $K_v^1 = Q_v$ and in (7) the operator $\bigoplus$ between two real valued matrices B, C ($D_v = B_v \bigoplus C_v$) is defined as $D_v(i,j) = \otimes_{t=1}^{n}\left[B_v(i,t) \oplus C_v(t,j)\right]$. The operator $\oplus$ between two QoS parameters depends on the QoS metric that is being considered and can be the addition (+) for delay and variance, the minimum (min) for bandwidth etc. The $\otimes$ is also an operator that depends on the specific QoS metric q, and selects the "best value" among the elements on which it operates, e.g. in case of the delay, loss or variance metric it will obtain the minimum value, while for bandwidth or security it will select the maximum value for all paths going from i to j.

5. Experimental results

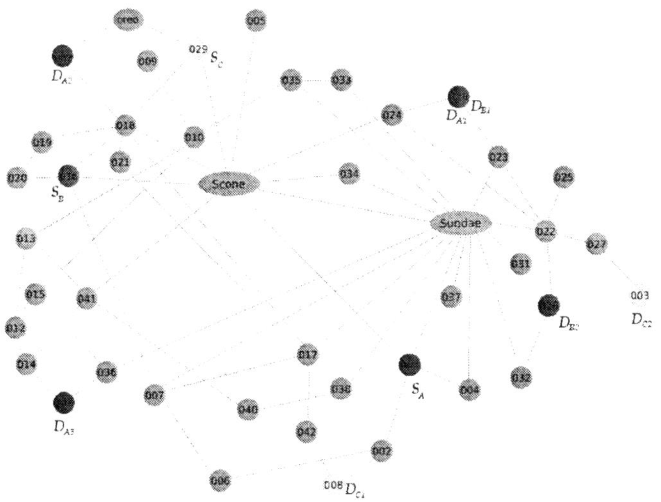

Figure 2. The CPN testbed used in our experiments

Configuration of the experiments:

- The experiments where conducted in a 44-node testbed representing the SwitchLAN network topology[1].
- All links have the same capacity ($10\,Mbits/s$)
- All users have the same QoS requirements: $delay \leq 50\,ms$, $jitter \leq 5\,ms$, $bandwidth \geq 3\,Mbits/s$, and $packetloss \leq 5\,\%$. These values are quite fastidious (for high-quality video the delay should be only less than $150ms$) and are chosen in order to evaluate our algorithm for very demanding requests.
- There are 7 Source-Destination (S-D) pairs ($S_A - D_{A1}, S_A - D_{A2}, S_A - D_{A3}, S_B - D_{B1}, S_B - D_{B2}, S_C - D_{C1}, S_C - D_{C2}$, that correspond to 7 users $(A1, A2, A3, B1, B2, C1, C2)$.
- In order to avoid having more than one users requesting to enter the network at the same time which would lead to multiple flows of probe traffic and misleading measurements, each user enters a queue ("request queue") at the data gathering point.
- The users that are denied access, instead of being considered rejected, they enter another queue ("reject queue") and request to enter again. This process continues until they are finally accepted or a specific period of time ("user lifetime") has past. In our experiments the user lifetime of each user is $150\,s$, meaning that every user will wait to be served for at most $150\,s$ and if that time expires the user will leave the network and will be considered rejected. The "reject queue" has bigger priority than the "request queue" and is served first.
- After making a request, if the request is satisfied then the user will wait for a constant time W and then make another request. The same is true if its request is not satisfied.
- Our experiments covered three cases:
  - The Admission Control is disabled (NO AC).
  - The AC is enabled (WITH AC).
  - The AC is enabled but also the length of the feasible paths is restricted (WITH AC & MPL).

  The third approach tries to take under consideration the fact that the algorithm may accept a very long feasible path which CPN would possibly not use for the new traffic. To avoid this conflict of the two intelligent mechanisms, we set a maximum path length (MPL) limit for the length of the feasible path. In our experiments the limit of the feasible path length was set to 6.
- In total 99 experiments were conducted (33 for each case), lasting $15\,min$ each.
- In all cases each experiment has a time W in the $(150, 120, 90, 80, 70, 60, 50, 40, 30, 20, 15)\,s$ range which correspond to total arrival rate λ for all three users of $(2.8, 3.5, 4.67, 5.25, 6, 7, 8.4, 10.5, 14, 21, 28)\,rqsts/min$ respectively. Thus the load on the system is increased

[1]The Swiss Education & Research Network, http://www.switch.ch/network/

in each of the successive experiments. Each experiment was conducted 3 times and the results presented in this paper are the average value of those three runs.

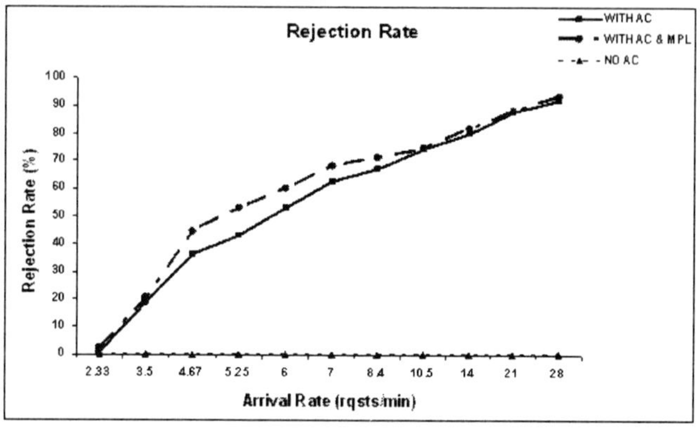

Figure 3. Average rejection rate

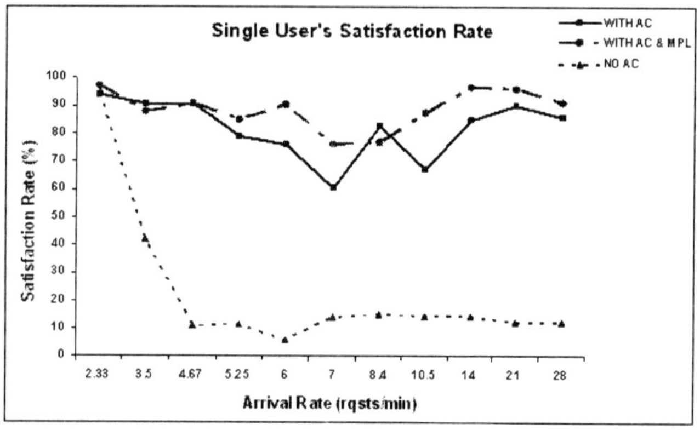

Figure 4. Average user satisfaction

The experimental results are summarize by figures 3, 4, 5. In figure 3 we compare the total rejection rate for the connection requests in all three cases, while figure 4 reports the satisfaction rate of a user (here user $A1$) in all three cases described above. Satisfaction of a user means that all four QoS requirements of that user are fulfilled at all times. Of course when the AC is disabled all users are immediately accepted and so the rejection rate is zero. Figure 5 shows the average time a user has to wait until it is served or the user lifetime expires, when the AC is enabled. In the case where the AC is disabled all users are served the moment it is possible.

We observe that when the AC algorithm is enabled the satisfaction of user $A1$ is much higher than when there is no AC. When the feasible path's length is limited the percentage of the user traffic that is led through the feasible path increases so the results are more accurate and the satisfaction rate is better than when only the AC is enable without

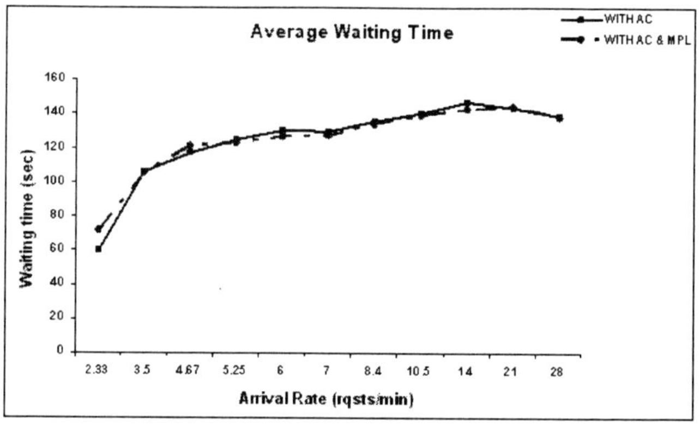

Figure 5. Average time a user waits before he is served

path length restrictions (figure 4). Of course restricting the length of the feasible path which is used to make the decision, makes the algorithm more strict, and thus the rejection rate should increase, as figure 3 confirms. Finding the optimal limit of the feasible paths length is something that could further improve our algorithm and should therefore be further investigated.

6. Conclusions

This paper proposes a measurement based AC algorithm that uses measurements to estimate the impact that a new connection will have on the QoS of both the new and the existing users. The monitoring of the system is being done by exploiting the Self-Aware CPN architecture. We provide a description of the algorithm and some experimental results conducted in a laboratory test-bed showing the effectiveness of the AC by studying the satisfaction throughout a user's lifetime.

A basic difference between our algorithm and other measurement-based AC schemes that use probing is that our algorithm estimates the new flow's impact by probing at a small rate, so that probe packets will not contribute noticeably to the network's congestion. Also the users are the ones that specify the QoS constraints they need in order to obtain the network service they require for a successful connection. The decision of whether to accept a new user is based on a novel algebra of QoS metrics which investigates whether there is a feasible path which can accommodate the new request without affecting the ongoing connections.

Further work following this paper will provide experimental results showing the effectiveness of the algorithm compared to other measurement-based algorithms. Also experiments with different non-additive QoS metrics should be conducted. Finally optimising the rate and duration of the probing would most probably lead to more accurate estimations and further improve our algorithm.

References

[1] G. Bianchi, A. Capone, and C. Petrioli. Throughput analysis of end-to-end measurement-based admission control in ip. In *Proceedings of IEEE INFOCOM 2000*, pages 1461–1470, Tel Aviv, Israel, Mar. 2000. IEEE.

[2] L. Breslau, E. W. Knightly, S. Shenker, I. Stoica, and H. Zhang. Endpoint admission control: Architectural issues and performance. In *Proceedings of ACM SIGCOMM 2000*, pages 57–70, Stockholm, Sweden, Oct. 2000. Acm.

[3] C. Cetinkaya and E. W. Knightly. Egress admission control. In *Proceedings of IEEE INFOCOM 2000*, volume 1, pages 1471–1480, Tel Aviv, Israel, Mar. 2000. IEEE.

[4] V. Elek, G. Karlsson, and R. Ronngren. Admission control based on end-to-end measurements. In *Proceedings of IEEE INFOCOM 2000*, volume 2, pages 623–630, Tel Aviv, Israel, Mar. 2000.

[5] R. W. Floyd. Algorithm 97: Shortest path. *Communications of ACM*, 5(6):345, June 1962.

[6] S. Floyd. Comments on measurement-based admissions control for controlled-load services. *Submitted to Computer Communication Review*, July 1996.

[7] A. J. Ganesh, P. Key, D. Polis, and R.Srikant. Congestion notification and probing mechanisms for endpoint admission control. *IEEE/ACM Transactions on Networking*, 14(3):568–578, June 2005.

[8] E. Gelenbe. Learning in the recurrent random neural network. *Neural Computation*, 5(1):154–164, Jan. 1993.

[9] E. Gelenbe, M. Gellman, R. Lent, P. Liu, and P. Su. Autonomous smart routing for network qos. In *Proceedings of the First International Conference on Autonomic Computing (ICAC)*, pages 232–239, New York, NY, USA, May 2004.

[10] E. Gelenbe, M. Gellman, and P. Su. Self-awareness and adaptivity for quality of service. In A. Tantawy and K. Inan, editors, *Proceedings of the IEEE International Symposium on Computers and Communications (ISCC'03)*, pages 3–9, Kemer-Antalya, Turkey, June/July 2003. IEEE Computer Society. Invited Paper.

[11] E. Gelenbe, R. Lent, A. Montuori, and Z. Xu. Towards networks with cognitive packets. In *Proceedings of the International Conference on Performance and QoS of Next Generation Networking*, pages 3–17, Nagoya, Japan, Nov. 2000. Opening Invited Paper.

[12] E. Gelenbe, R. Lent, A. Montuori, and Z. Xu. Cognitive packet networks: Qos and performance. In *Proceedings of the 10th IEEE International Symposium on Modeling, Analysis, and Simulation of Computer and Telecommunications Systems (MASCOTS'02)*, pages 3–12, Fort Worth, TX, Oct. 2002. IEEE Computer Society. Opening Keynote Paper.

[13] E. Gelenbe, R. Lent, and A. Nunez. Self-aware networks and qos. *Proceedings of the IEEE*, 92(9):1478–1489, Sep. 2004.

[14] E. Gelenbe, R. Lent, and Z. Xu. Design and performance of cognitive packet networks. *Performance Evaluation*, 46(2-3):155–176, Oct. 2001.

[15] E. Gelenbe, R. Lent, and Z. Xu. Measurement and performance of a cognitive packet network. *Computer Networks*, 37(6):691–701, Dec. 2001.

[16] E. Gelenbe and P. Liu. Qos and routing in the cognitive packet network. In *Proceedings of the IEEE International Symposium on a World of Wireless, Mobile and Multimedia Networks*, pages 517–521, Taormina, Italy, June 2005.

[17] E. Gelenbe, X. Mang, and R. Oenvural. Diffusion based statistical call admission control in atm. *Performance Evaluation*, 27/28(Com):411–436, Oct. 1996.

[18] E. Gelenbe, Z. Xu, and E. Seref. Cognitive packet networks. In *Proceedings of the 11th International Conference on Tools with Artificial Intelligence (ICTAI '99)*, pages 47–54, Chicago, IL, Nov. 1999. IEEE Computer Society Press.

[19] R. J. Gibbens and F. Kelly. Distributed connection acceptance control for a connectionless network. In *Proceedings of the 16th International Teletraffic Congress (ITC 99)*, volume 2, pages 941–52, Edinburgh, UK, Feb. 1999.

[20] R. J. Gibbens, F. P. Kelly, and P. B. Key. A decision-theoretic approach to call admission control in atm networks. *IEEE Journal on Selected Areas of Communications*, 13(6):1101–1114, Feb. 1995.

[21] R. Guerin, H. Ahmadi, and M. Naghshineh. Equivalent capacity and its application to bandwidth allocation in high-speed networks. *IEEE Journal on Selected Areas in Communications*, 9(7):968–981, Sep. 1991.

[22] R. Guerin and L. Gun. A unified approach to bandwidth allocation and access control in fast packet-switched networks. In *Proceeding of INFOCOM'92*, volume 1, pages 1–12, Florence, Italy, May 1992.

[23] S. Jamin, P. Danzig, S. Shenker, and L. Zhang. A measurement-based admission control algorithm for integrated services packet networks. *IEEE/ACM Transactions on Networking*, 5(1):56–70, Aug./Sep. 1997.

[24] S. Jamin, S. J. Shenker, and P. B. Danzig. Comparison of measurement-based admission control algorithms for controlled-load service. In *Proceedings of the Conference on Computer Communications (IEEE INFOCOM '97)*, volume 3, pages 973–980, Kobe, Japan, Apr. 1997. IEEE Computer Society Press.

[25] H. G. Perros and K. M. Elsayed. Call admission control schemes: A review. *IEEE Communications Magazine*, 34(11):82–91, Nov. 1996.

[26] G. Sakellari, M. D' Arienzo, and E. Gelenbe. Admission control in self aware networks. In *Proceedings of the 49th annual IEEE Global Telecommunications Conference, GLOBECOM 2006*, San Francisco, CA, USA, Nov./Dec. 2006.

[27] D. Tse and M. Grossglauser. Measurement-based call admission control: Analysis and simulation. In *Proceedings of the INFOCOM '97*, volume 3, pages 981–989, Kobe, Japan, Apr. 1997. IEEE Computer Society Press.

[28] S. Warshall. A theorem on boolean matrices. *Journal of the ACM*, 9(1):11–12, Jan. 1962.

Leveraging Resource Prediction for Anticipatory Dynamic Configuration

Vahe Poladian, David Garlan, Mary Shaw, M.Satyanarayanan, Bradley Schmerl, João Sousa[†]
School of Computer Science, Carnegie Mellon University
Information and Software Engineering, George Mason University[†]
{poladian, garlan, mary.shaw, satya, schmerl}@ cs.cmu.edu, jpsousa@gmu.edu

Abstract

Self-adapting systems based on multiple concurrent applications must decide how to allocate scarce resources to applications and how to set the quality parameters of each application to best satisfy the user. Past work has made those decisions with analytic models that used current resource availability information: they react to recent changes in resource availability as they occur, rather than anticipating future availability. These reactive techniques may model each local decision optimally, but the accumulation of decisions over time nearly always becomes less than optimal.

In this paper, we propose an approach to self-adaptation, called anticipatory configuration that leverages predictions of future resource availability to improve utility for the user over the duration of the task. The approach solves the following technical challenges: (1) how to express resource availability prediction, (2) how to combine prediction from multiple sources, and (3) how to leverage predictions continuously while improving utility to the user. Our experiments show that when certain adaptation operations are costly, anticipatory configuration provides better utility to the user than reactive configuration, while being comparable in resource demand.

1. INTRODUCTION

Predictive resource management has gained increasing mindshare in the pervasive computing research community over the past decade. For example, Satyanarayanan's 2001 paper on the challenges of pervasive computing [15], identifies prediction as an important desired feature of systems that aim to provide an improved and seamless user experience. One of the scenarios describes how the user's intelligent virtual assistant makes anticipatory decisions based on predictions of available wireless bandwidth in different locations of an airport concourse and helps the user complete her communication tasks on time for her departure.

With the goal of seamless user experience in mind, recent self-adaptive systems improve quality of service despite resource shortage by using models of user preferences, historical profiles of application resource intensity, and estimates of current resource availability. Such systems partially automate various system decisions, such as which suite of applications to run and how to allocate scarce resources among concurrent applications with the objective of best satisfying the individual preferences of the user. These systems may also guide the adaptation of resource-aware applications, when more than one dimension of quality is of concern to the user, perhaps using a set of preference functions explicitly specified by the user for a given task and context.

A common shortcoming in the behavior over time of such self-adaptive systems arises from their purely reactive adaptation policies. The analytical models in such systems consider a very small horizon of time for both predictions. As a result, when dealing with changes in the operating environment, e.g., changes in resource availability, these systems make decisions based only on recent data, often resulting in suboptimal decisions over time. For example,

- Aura ([4][12][16]) achieves dynamic behavior by performing re-configurations, which are costly in terms of both resource usage and user disruption. Multiple costly re-configurations in response to several changes add up to a globally suboptimal utility to the user over time.
- QRAM [8] admits tasks and allocates resources among them based on their utility to the system and resource demand intensity. Running tasks have a priority over new ones. If available resource levels are not sufficient, the system will not admit new tasks, even though there might be a resource allocation using both running and new tasks that improves utility.

Thus, making decisions without considering future changes is myopic and can be suboptimal over the long term.

Recent results in resource prediction offer an alternative to reactive adaptation. For example, Qiao et al [13] and Sang et al [14] have analyzed a significant number of traces and have concluded that in many cases, network traffic has good predictability. Using relatively inexpensive linear time series models, predictions of network traffic can be done in near real time for a meaningful future horizon, e.g., a few dozen seconds, or even minutes. Other sources of predictive information are also available, e.g., administrator-announced network, CPU and service outages, recurring patterns of resource usage that have weekly or daily periods, remaining battery level, and models of battery drainage.

Predictions of resource availability over a meaningful horizon naturally lead to uncertainty because of randomness inherent in the predicted variables and the noisy nature of the predictors. A system that uses long-term predictors must explicitly deal with the uncertainty in such predictions.

In this paper, we propose an anticipatory approach to self-adaptation, which combines the benefits of resource prediction research into an existing framework of dynamic configuration. Specifically, we present an enhanced analytical model of configuration that improves upon existing reactive models of resource allocation by taking advantage of resource predictions from multiple sources. We also present a set of resource allocation algorithms that leverage predictive information to the benefit of the user. We demonstrate that these new algorithms improve upon the earlier reactive algorithms while remaining feasible for real time evaluation.

In this work three main results address key challenges in engineering a system for anticipatory configuration. First,

0-7695-2906-2/07 $25.00 © 2007 IEEE

we define a mathematical notation for expressing uncertainty in predictors that is consistent with resource prediction literature. Next, we define a calculus for combining predictions from multiple sources into an aggregate prediction. Third, we present an efficient online algorithm of anticipatory configuration that leverages predictive information. Theses results constitute a modest contribution towards the challenges identified by Satyanarayanan.

The rest of the paper is structured as follows. Section 2 surveys related work and highlights the novelty of this work. Section 3 defines important terms, enumerates the requirements for anticipatory configuration, and presents our approach, including a notation for predictors and combining calculus. In Section 4, we describe the algorithms for anticipatory configuration and analyze their theoretical running times. Section 5 presents the results of runtime experiments comparing several approaches to configuration, including anticipatory and reactive. The evaluation of our approach and enumeration of software engineering benefits in Section 6. We summarize the conclusions in Section 7.

2. RELATED WORK

Self-adaptive systems such as QRAM [8], Aura [12][16], Nemesis [10], and Odyssey [9][11], incorporate models of user preferences, application behavior, and resource availability to optimize some measure of user satisfaction. QRAM is a general framework for quality of service management, while Aura is a configuration (self-adaptation) infrastructure for pervasive computing. Both systems implement a centralized resource arbiter that makes resource allocation decisions. Nemesis employs a decentralized approach based on congestion pricing to optimize resource allocation among concurrent applications. Initial work on Odyssey addressed *agile* adaptation mechanisms [11]. Later, Narayanan et al [9] demonstrated how instantaneous predictions can help improve the response times of interactive applications.

All of the above systems are reactive in adaptation policies. These systems have short prediction horizons and consider the predictions to be exact. Our approach differs from the above systems in three respects. Our model has a prediction horizon of dozens of seconds or minutes, deals with uncertainty of predictions, and makes anticipatory decisions.

NWS [17] and RPS [1] are tools for gathering and analyzing resource demand and supply. Dinda [3] presents a comprehensive overview of prediction using linear time series models. A number of studies (Qiao [13], Sang [14], Wolski [18]) have demonstrated that: (1) resources have good predictability and (2) when resources are predictable, inexpensive models with autoregressive (AR) components work just as well as more complex schemes. Qiao et al [13] conjecture that resource prediction can be done online, using software running on routers or compute servers. Gurun et al designed a lightweight version of NWS called NWSLite suitable for mobile and pervasive devices [6].

Anticipatory configuration is similar to online stochastic combinatorial optimization (OSCU) problems such as packet routing and vehicle dispatch ([2][6]). While the problem domains are different, each dynamic configuration algorithm has an analog in OSCU. The Reactive, Perfect, and Expectation algorithms in dynamic configuration are respectively called Local, Offline, and Expectation in OSCU.

3. APPROACH

We now introduce the problem of anticipatory dynamic configuration, discuss the specific technical challenges that we addressed in this work, and describe our approach. Because anticipatory configuration builds on an earlier model of reactive configuration, we briefly review the pertinent details of that model first.

3.1 Terminology

Following [16], we define the set of computational devices, applications, and resources available to a user in a location as the *environment*. Applications and devices provide *services*, which are abstract descriptions of the application capabilities, identified by service type, e.g. "play video", "edit text", "browse web". A specific application on a specific device is called a *supplier*. Users carry out *tasks* to work on their everyday projects, e.g., plan a vacation, produce a report, or review a video clip. A task specifies the use of one or more simultaneous services for the *duration* of the *activation* of the task. Each task might be activated several times, possibly in different locations.

Applications use computational *resources* (such as CPU cycles, network bandwidth, disc, memory, and battery energy) to provide service to the user. In many environments resources are scarce and can change over time. Some applications are resource and fidelity aware, able to provide lower level of service in one or more *quality of service* (QoS) *dimensions* while consuming fewer resources. Lower quality service allows the user to make progress on his task, although his satisfaction from the task might be lower.

A suite of applications that can satisfy a task is called a *supplier assignment*. There might be multiple *candidate* assignments for a task in an environment, because each service in the task might be satisfied by alternative available applications. A resource *allocation* is a set of resource vectors, one per supplier in an assignment. Each of these vectors specifies the maximum amount of a resource that the application should consume. A QoS *set-point* is a vector of QoS levels that the application should meet. A *configuration* is a triple of supplier assignment, resource allocation and QoS set-points.

The problem of configuration is to find a configuration that maximizes user's *utility*. Utility depends on the suppliers in the assignment as well as QoS set-points.

In the earlier model of configuration [12], utility is an instantaneous measure of a user's satisfaction. That model works *reactively*, by considering only snapshots of current resource availability in the resource allocation and configuration selection. As resource availability changes, the reactive model performs reconfiguration, changing the previous configuration if there is gain in instantaneous utility. Thus the solution in the reactive model maximizes instantaneous utility in a series of locally optimal decisions.

0-7695-2906-2/07 $25.00 © 2007 IEEE

In contrast, an *anticipatory* model of configuration considers future resource availability predictions, and chooses *sequences* of configurations over the duration of the task, and maximizes the expected value of utility *accrued* over the duration of the task.

3.2 Challenges

The principal goal in this work is to improve the quality of service to the user in an existing framework of dynamic configuration by leveraging resource predictions. To do so, we must address the following three requirements:

R1. *Define a measure of accrued utility that captures the temporal dimension of anticipatory configuration.*

To make globally optimal decisions, the utility function of the user needs to be enhanced. The enhanced notion of utility should: (1) incorporate the temporal dimension of the anticipatory configuration and guide globally optimal decision-making, (2) represent a user's satisfaction with service quality over a period of time, while capturing the relevant attributes of a task, as before, and (3) allow for comparison of anticipatory and reactive configuration models.

R2. *Express and combine predictive information about future resource availability from multiple predictors.*

One part of the challenge here is to express predictive information in a way that is consistent with existing prediction literature. Second part of the challenge is to aggregate predictions from multiple sources.

R3. *Design efficient on-line algorithms for anticipatory configuration that improve expected utility for the user.*

The new algorithms for anticipatory configuration must make online decisions under uncertainty. Such algorithms must balance the runtime resource overhead and latency with optimal decision making. These algorithms should demonstrate improvement over those in the reactive model under reasonable assumptions of predictor accuracy.

3.3 Utility

3.3.1 Utility in the Reactive Model

Utility is a measure of user satisfaction with respect to the running state of the systems. In the model of reactive configuration, the system is concerned with *instantaneous utility* (IU), which has three parts: affinity for applications, preference for quality of service, and penalty for switching. The first part in the instantaneous utility allows the user to express his preference for specific applications. For example, the user might specify that among video players he strongly prefers Windows Media Player, but might also be happy with QuickTime or RealOne Player by giving scores to each of these choices. Furthermore, he might also accept any other video player, but score them below either QuickTime or RealOne.

The second part in the utility is collection of preference functions and weights that allow the user to express a desired level of service in each QoS dimension as well as trade-offs among different dimensions. Using a preference function for each QoS dimension, the user specifies how much he values improvement or deterioration of service along that dimension. Using a scalar weight, the user specifies how important that dimension is relative to others.

The third part in the utility allows the user to specify penalties for disruptive changes. This is to discourage the system from switching currently running applications, unless the gain in utility is sufficiently large. For each service in the task, switching of applications is penalized by a scalar amount.

The instantaneous utility is combination of the three parts. Appendix A has the formal expression of IU.

3.3.2 Utility in the Anticipatory Model

In the model of anticipatory configuration the objective of the system is to maximize the *accrued* utility. We use a discrete time model by dividing the duration of the task into T equal windows, and index each using variable t, $0 \le t < T$. Let *Seq* denote a sequence of T-1 configurations, one per each window in the duration of the task: $Seq = \{Seq_0, Seq_1, \ldots, Seq_{T-1}\}$, where each Seq_s is a configuration chosen to run during period s. The accrued utility (AU) of the sequence *Seq* is defined as:

$$AU(Seq) = IU(Seq_0, \phi) + \sum_{s=1}^{T-1} IU(Seq_s, Seq_{s-1})$$

where in the expression of the instantaneous utility we include both the current and previous configuration. In other words, the accrued utility over a time period is the sum of instantaneous utilities during that time period.

3.4 Supplier (Application) Profiles

Applications use resources to provide service. Typically, providing a better level of service requires the use of more resources. Using historical profiling [9], it is possible to find an application's resource requirement for each level of quality of service. An *application profile* is an enumeration of resource and QoS vector pairs, where the resource vector is the required level of resources for providing the level of service specified by the QoS vector.

In the anticipatory configuration model we continue to assume that application profiles are static, i.e. they are computed using offline profiling, don't change over time, and are sufficiently accurate.

3.5 Resource Availability Predictions

3.5.1 Resource Availability in the Reactive Model

In the reactive models of configuration, only the current level of resource availability is modeled.

The anticipatory model explicitly incorporates predictions of future resource availability. Next we discuss the details of resource prediction.

3.5.2 Resource Prediction

Ideally, a prediction for the available level of a resource is a probability density function for a future time of prediction s and the current time, t. For each possible level r of the resource, the function predicts the probability that the resource will be at that level at time t. Thus, the available level of resource R at time s is a random variable, R_s. To capture the fact that the prediction is made at time t, we use the following notation: $R_{s|t}$, which is the conditioning of the random variable R_s based on the information available at time t.

A *generalized predictor* for resource R at time t, $0 \leq t < T$, is a set of probability density functions, one for each s, $s \geq t$, of the random variable $R_{s|t}$.

In practice, a predictor might not provide the complete distribution of the resource for all future times s. For example, a prediction from one source might be that with 100 percent probability, the available resource level can not exceed a certain threshold. Another source might predict a surge or drop in the resources around a specific time.

3.5.3 Types of predictors

We define three types of resource predictors: linear recent history, relative move, and bounding predictors.

A *linear recent history predictor* is any predictor that uses recent history and a linear time-series model to predict the next value in the series of resource availability. This predictor is motivated by existing literature [3]. We consider autoregressive (AR) models of low orders. Moving Average (MA) and auto-regressive moving average (ARMA) models can be easily handled in a similar manner by the anticipatory configuration algorithms.

Formally, an autoregressive linear recent history predictor of order p for resource R is an equation of the form:

$$R_{t+1|t} = \varphi_1 r_t + \varphi_2 r_{t-1} + \ldots + \varphi_p r_{t-p+1} + Z_{t+1},$$

where r_i are the previous p observations of the resource (the small letters indicate that these numbers are not random), φ_i are parameters of the model and are known at prediction time, and Z_{t+1} is a normal random variable with mean 0 and variance σ, $Z_{t+1} \sim N(0, \sigma)$.

Notice that the prediction we have is only one step ahead. However, we can easily express $R_{t+2|t}$ using $R_{t+1|t}$, the previous p-1 observations, and Z_{t+2}, an additional normal random variable which is independent of Z_{t+1}.

There might be opportunities for prediction that are not captured by a linear predictor. For example, by observing resource demand changes (surges and drops) and correlating these with calendar information, it might be possible to predict such changes and their length in the future.

The second, *relative move predictor* predicts step-up or step-down changes in resource availability. Formally, a relative move predictor is a set of tuples $<s, M>$, where s is the time of prediction and M is the possibly random magnitude of the predicted move. For the purposes of this work, we will assume that M is normally distributed, $M \sim N(\mu,\sigma)$. Formally, if rm is a relative move predictor, then $rm = \{<s,M>\}$.

The third, *bounding* predictor specifies the maximum and minimum possible level of resource availability for a union of time intervals. A bounding predictor is motivated by the availability of various sources of information, such as the maximum bandwidth specification of a DSL line, signal strength and type of WiFi network. In case of CPU, the maximum available level is available from hardware specification and from the power saving settings.

3.5.4 Predictor Calculus

We now define a calculus for combining multiple predictors into an aggregate prediction. Let L denote the set of all linear predictors, RM denote the set of relative move predictors, B denote the set of bounding predictors. We define operations on predictors as follows.

<u>Boosting</u> of two linear predictors: if $l1$ and $l2$ are predictors in L, then $l3 = l1 \times l2$ is a linear predictor. The term *boosting* refers to the machine learning technique that allows improved prediction or classification by combining multiple predictors or classifiers. Simple averaging is boosting, although a good booster should reduce the prediction error by finding correlations among the predictors.

<u>Concatenation</u> of two relative move predictors: if $rm1$ and $rm2$ are predictors in RM, then $rm3 = rm1 \cdot rm2$ is also a relative move predictor. If $rm1$ and $rm2$ have conflicting predictions, i.e. one of the predictions in $rm1$ is for the same time period as another prediction in $rm2$, we can simply combine those two predictions by adding the random moves. Otherwise, the predictions are combined by taking the union of the two sets of predictions.

<u>Addition</u> of a relative move predictor to a linear predictor: if $rm1$ is in RM and $l1$ is in L, then $gp1 = l1 + rm1$ is a generalized predictor that combines the relative moves predicted by $rm1$ into the linear prediction of $l1$.

<u>Bounding</u> of a generalized predictor by a bounding predictor: if $gp1$ is a generalized predictor and $b1$ is a bounding predictor in B, then $gp2 = gp1 \,||\, b1$ is a generalized predictor that is the bounding of $gp1$. Bounding limits the support of any probability density function to the interval specified by $b1$.

Intuitively, a linear predictor finds self-correlations in the recent history of resource availability. A relative move predictor finds periodic patterns of resource increases or decreases that are not reflected in the recent history. The effect of a relative move is in addition to the prediction of a linear predictor (hence justifying the operation of addition). A bounding predictor limits the range of resource availability.

Let's see the predictor calculus in action by the way of a

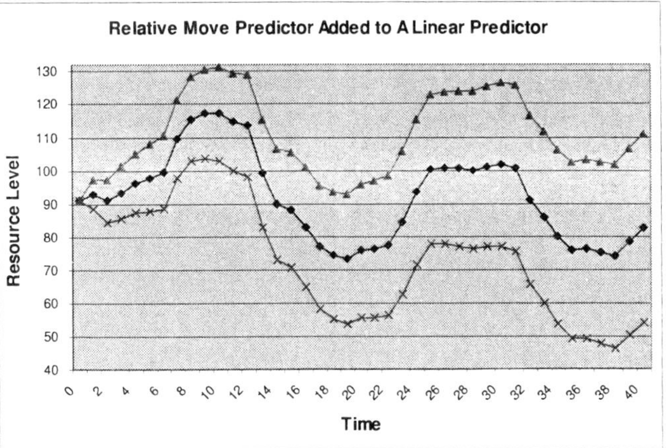

Figure 1: The mean and one standard deviation band of the sum of linear and relative move predictors. The Y axis is in abstract units of resource.

simple example. Suppose $l1$ and $l2$ are linear predictors, $rm1$ and $rm2$ are relative move predictors and $b1$ is a bounding predictor. Then $l1 \times l2 + rm1 \cdot rm2 \,||\, b1 = \{(l1 \times l2) +$

$(rm1 \cdot rm2)\} \| b1$. In other words, we first apply all boosting operations to obtain one linear predictor. Next we apply all the concatenation operations until one relative move predictor remains. Then we perform addition with the only resulting linear predictor and the only resulting relative move predictor. After that, we apply as many bounding operations as there are bounding predictors.

Figure 1 shows resource predictions using 3 curves. The middle curve is the expected value (mean) of the predicted level of the resource. The top curve is one standard deviation above the mean and the bottom curve is one standard deviation below the mean. This predictor was obtained by the addition of a relative move predictor (*rm1*) to a linear predictor (*l1*).

3.6 The Formal Optimization Problem

Informally, the optimization problem at hand is one of choosing a sequence of configurations over the duration of the task, such that the expected value of accrued utility is maximized given the aggregate knowledge of all resource predictors. There are two constraints to the optimization problem: (1) the level of quality of service of each supplier is bound by the supplier's historical QoS vs. resource profile, and (2) the sum of resource demands of the suppliers in the running configuration in each time period can not exceed the actual resource supply.

Let *Set(Seq)* be the set of all possible configuration sequences. Let $QoSProf_{\text{supp}}$ denote the QoS vs. resource profile for the supplier identified by *supp*. Let $rr_{s|s}$ denote the actual resource availability vector for each time period s, $0 \leq s<T$. Let *Seq* denote a sequence of configurations: $Seq = \{Seq_0, Seq_1,\ldots,Seq_{T-1}\}$, where each Seq_s specifies a supplier assignment. Then the objective of anticipatory configuration is to maximize:

$$\underset{Seq \in Set(Seq)}{\arg\max}\; E\left[IU(Seq_0, \phi) + \sum_{s=1}^{T-1} IU(Seq_s, Seq_{s-1}) \right]$$

given the knowledge of all the resource predictors and subject to the following constraint for each s, $0 \leq s<T$:

$$\sum_{Supp \in Seq_S} QoSprof_{Supp}(f_{Supp}) \leq \left\| rr_{s|s} \right\|$$

The inequality in the above constraint is understood for each resource dimension separately and must hold for *any* combination of quality set-point choices (denoted by of f_{Supp}) among the suppliers of Seq_s.

4. ALGORITHMS AND ANALYSIS

An algorithm for anticipatory configuration should maximize the expected accrued utility over the duration of the task. At each time step, an algorithm decides which assignment of the suppliers to choose as well as how to allocate resources among them. First we describe some prerequisite computation. Next, we describe two different algorithms for anticipatory configuration.

4.1 Prerequisite Algorithms

4.1.1 Resource sieve and resource scenarios

For tractability purposes, we discretize the available levels of resources. For each resource, we enumerate the possible available levels of that resource. Then we consider the Cartesian combinations of the available levels of all the resources. We call this the resource sieve. And we call each point in the sieve a resource scenario.

For example, if the environment includes one laptop, and one of the resources under consideration is the CPU of the laptop, then the possible available levels of the CPU can be anywhere from 0 to 100 percent of the maximum, in 4 percent increments.

Another resource of interest, downstream TCP bandwidth, might have 13 levels: 100, 150, 200, 250, 300, 350, 400, 500, 600, 700, 800, 900, 1000 (all in kbps). These levels are based on the available suppliers and their resource intensity for various levels of quality of service.

With two resources, CPU and bandwidth, as described above, the resource sieve will have 26 * 13 = 338 resource *scenarios*. We generate resource scenarios using an ad-hoc enumeration and call this algorithm GenResourceSieve.

4.1.2 Supplier assignments

For each service in a task, there may be multiple available suppliers in the environment that can satisfy that service. For example, for a "play Video" service, on a typical Windows system there might be as many as 4 applications to choose from: Windows Media Player, RealOne Player, Apple QuickTime, iTunes. The same applies for browsers, e-mail readers, text editors, compilers, etc.

Recall that a supplier assignment is an assignment of one application for each service in the task. A task can have multiple supplier assignments. We generate all possible supplier assignments using ad-hoc enumeration and call this algorithm GenSuppAssignments.

We now present three lemmas that help in computing instantaneous utility and designing the algorithms:

Lemma 1: affinity for applications depends only on the choice of a supplier assignment and does not depend on the level of available resources in the past, present, or future.

Lemma 2: the switching penalty depends only on the supplier assignments in the previous and in the current time period.

Lemma 3: QoS utility depends only on the current assignment of suppliers and current resource availability.

These lemmas follow directly from the definition of instantaneous utility. Armed with these three lemmas, we perform the following computations.

Penalty(SA1, SA2): for each pair of candidate supplier assignments, SA1 and SA2, compute the penalty in the hypothetical situation when switching from SA1 to SA2 by complete enumeration of all pairs and store the result in a two-dimensional array.

SuppPrefScore(SA): for each candidate supplier assignment, SA, compute the portion of instantaneous utility that is due to application preference and store the results in a one-dimensional array.

OptInstQoS(SA, RS): for each supplier assignment, SA, and each resource scenario, RS, compute the optimal resource allocation among the suppliers in SA when the current level of resources is given by RS. Also determine the QoS set-points for each supplier and the resulting utility. The mrmd algorithm in [8] solves the resource allocation problem *all* resource scenarios at once, using dynamic programming. The running time of the algorithm is proportionate to the size of the resource sieve.

4.2 Algorithms For Anticipatory Configuration

The first algorithm, OptAccUtilPerfect, maximizes actual accrued utility in the case when resource predictions are known precisely. The second, OptAccUtilExpectation, explicitly deals with uncertainty in resource predictions and works by maximizing the expected accrued utility.

4.2.1 Algorithm for No-Uncertainty Prediction

In the simplest case of anticipatory configuration, we assume that the resource predictors are error-free. Under this unrealistic assumption, the predictions are exact resource paths into the future for the duration of the task and as time goes by, this proves to be true. The benefits of considering this case are two-fold: (1) we would like to find out if anticipatory configuration is ever better than reactive configuration and (2) we create a shared routine that can be invoked in hind-sight for comparison purposes.

Prediction in this case is a vector of snapshots: *RS(s)*, where $0 \leq s < T$ and each *RS(s)* is a resource scenario.

We find a sequence of configurations that maximize the accrued utility using dynamic programming. Let's define PartMaxAU(j,s) to be the maximum partial accrued utility possible if the task were to run starting from time period *s* till time period *T* and if supplier assignment with index *j* were chosen to run at time *s*. To demonstrate how the dynamic programming algorithm would work, we show the terminal condition and the recursive rule:

- PartMaxAU(j,T-1) = OptInstQoS(j,RS(T-1) + SuppPrefScore(j), because *T-1* is the last time period.
- PartMaxAU(j,s) = $\max_k$ { OptInstQoS(j, RS(s)) + SuppPrefScore(j) + Penalty(j,k) + PartMaxAU(k,s+1)}.

The first three terms in the last sum are pre-computed and together add up to the instantaneous utility possible when choosing to run supplier assignment *j* in period *s*. The fourth term is the future partial accrued utility from time period *s+1* till the end of the task if supplier assignment with index *k* is chosen next. In addition to recording the maximum utility, we also record the value of *k* for which that maximum is achieved.

The dynamic programming algorithm will start from time period *T-1* to compute PartMaxAU(j,T-1) and work backwards in time in a simple loop to compute PartMaxAU(j,s). The maximum of PartMaxAU(j,0) over all possible supplier assignments *j* will be the maximum possible accrued utility for the task. The sequence of supplier assignments is also recorded. We call this algorithm OptAccUtilPerfect.

Next we analyze the runtime complexity of the algorithm. To help in this analysis, we define the following variables:

- *nServices*, the number of services in the task,
- *nAltSupp*, the typical number of alternative suppliers for each service type,
- *nResources*, the number of resources,
- *nResPoints*, the number of different resource points for a typical resource,
- *nRSieve*, the size of the resource sieve or the number of different resource scenarios. This number is O(*nResPoints^ nResources*).
- *nSA*, the number supplier assignments. This number is O(*nAltSupp^ nServices*).
- *nQoS*, the number of maximum different possible QoS points among all suppliers,
- *T*, the duration of the task or the number of time periods.

Here are the running times of the prerequisite algorithms:

- GenSuppAssignments is O(*nSA*nServices*),
- GenResourceSieve is O(*nRSieve*),
- Penalty is O(*nSA*nSA*),
- SuppPrefScore is O(*nSA*),
- OpUtil is O(*nQoS*nRSieve*nSA*),
- OptAccUtilPerfect is O(*nSA*nSA*T*).

After adding the running times of the above algorithms, the following two terms dominate all the others:

- O(*nQoS*nRSieve*nSA*) + O(*nSA*nSA*T*).

We conclude that the running time is pseudo-polynomial with respect to the inputs of the problem. We argue that this algorithm is feasible for online computation.

```
<double, int> OptAccUtilFullSearch(int t,int s,
              Vector RPath (0..s),
              Vector Seq(-1..s-1),
              Vector RPred(s+1..T-1) ){
  <RSim[],Prob[]> = SimRScenario(s+1,
             RPath (0..s), RPred(s+1..T-1));
  for each a in SA {
    Seq(1..s+1) = Seq(1..s), SA[a];
    double instUtil = OptInstQoS(a, RPath[s]) +
      SuppPrefScore(a) + Penalty(a,Seq(s-1));
    double expUtilFuture = 0;
    if ( s < (T-1) )  // termination condition
      for each rs in RSim {
        RPath(0..s,s+1) = RPath(0..s),RSim[rs];
        <U,next> = OptAccUtilFullSearch (t,
             s+1, RPath(0..s+1),
             Seq(-1..s), RPred(s+2..T-1)) ;
        expUtilFuture += Prob[rs] * U;
      }
    // find + record max of expUtilFuture
  }
  return <maxExpAccU, bestSA>;
}
AnticipatoryDynConfig()
{
  Obtain RHistory;
  Initialize RPath = RHistory, Seq, RPred;
    for s = 0 to T-1  {
    <util, a> = OptAccUtilFullSearch (s, s,
              RPath(0..s), Seq(-1..s-1),
              RPred(s+1..T-1);
    ExecuteConfig(a, RHistory(0..s), prevSA);
    Update RHistory, RPath;
    UpdatePred(RPred, RPath[s+1]);
    prevSA = a;
  }
}
```

Figure 2: The Full Search Anticipatory Algorithm.

0-7695-2906-2/07 $25.00 © 2007 IEEE

4.2.2 Algorithm for Uncertainty in Prediction

In practice, resource predictors are noisy, and an anticipatory algorithm must handle the noise in the predictors.

Figure 2 shows a generic algorithm that maximizes the expected value of accrued utility when predictors are noisy.

The algorithm, OptAccUtilFullSearch, simulates likely paths of resources and computes the expected future accrued utility along these paths for each candidate supplier assignment. *t* is the current time, *s* is the time of simulation and is continually rolled forward, *RPath* contains actual resource availability history up to time *t* and simulated resource history up to time *s*, *Seq* contains supplier assignments that are selected to run at each time, *RPred* contains the predictor objects conditional on information up to time *s*.

The algorithm first simulates possible resource states and their probabilities for the next time period. Next it cycles through all candidate supplier assignments and calculates the expected future accrued utility in the hypothetical case when a particular supplier assignment is selected to run in the current time period. The expected future utility is calculated in the inner loop by iterating through the simulated resource states and computing the probability weighted average of future expected utility from each state. The instantaneous utility from running that supplier in the current period is added to the expected future accrued utility.

The AnticipatoryDynConfig routine is the entry point of configuration. This routine is responsible for "rolling" time forward, injecting the system with actual resource availability information, executing (starting / stopping) the necessary applications and setting their runtime state.

The algorithm computes the maximum expected accrued utility as defined in section 3.6. However, because of the liberal use of recursion, the running time of the algorithm is exponential in *T*. Indeed, the algorithm does a complete scan of all possible simulated resource paths, with a branching factor proportionate to *nSA*nRSim*, the latter being the number of simulated resource state at each recursive step. Even for small problem sizes the running time of the algorithm can quickly escalate.

We considered several possibilities to overcome this problem. By memoizing computation results and using dynamic programming, we can reduce the running time, but will need exponential storage space. We can also partially memorize computation results, rearrange the two loops, and reduce the branching factor of the recursion, but this will not reduce the running time below exponential. We also considered Monte Carlo simulation.

We discovered that reducing the depth of the recursive search does not affect the optimality of the algorithm dramatically, but reduces the running time to less than exponential. We modify the Full Search algorithm, by limiting the depth of complete simulations to a configurable parameter. For the remainder of the search, we obtain an approximation of future expected accrued utility using the OptAccUtilPerfect algorithm over the *expected* path of the resources. We call this modified algorithm OptAccUtilExpectation.

5. EXPERIMENTS

We implement the algorithms from Section 4 and the reactive model. We experimentally compare the algorithms along two metrics: (1) the actual accrued utility to the user over the duration of the task and (2) runtime efficiency.

5.1 Experimental Setup

The basis for our experiments is a task of a newspaper movie critic, who watches clips and writes reviews. This task has 2 services: *video playing* and *browsing*. The user simultaneously watches streaming clips using a video player and searches for information using a browser. Both the browser and the server support levels of data compression and the server can provide content at varying levels of fidelity (e.g., text-only, images, multi-media). There are three alternative applications for video playing and three alternative applications for browsing, generating 8 alternative supplier assignments (*nSA*).

The model requires three inputs: (1) user preferences, (2) application profiles, and (3) resource availability predictions. We profile 6 applications: 3 video players and 3 browsers. As an experimental platform, we use a relatively old IBM T30 laptop that can operate in power-saving mode and limit the available CPU level to a percentage of the maximum. For user preferences, we use synthetic data.

In this case study we consider 2 resources: CPU and bandwidth. For CPU availability predictions, we use only relative move and bounding predictors, because the user is in complete control of his hardware and there are no external demands on the CPU to require the use of a linear predictor. Variations in CPU availability come from a number of sources: (1) whether the laptop is plugged into an outlet or not, (2) planned background tasks (e.g., virus checker or backup). For bandwidth prediction, it is appropriate to use a linear predictor. We combine an AR(5) with several relative move predictors (so a bandwidth prediction very much looks like the graph in Figure 1).

We create a resource sieve of about 350 points (*nRSieve*) and consider a task of duration 25 (*T*). Based on these numbers, OptAccUtilFullSearch is not feasible to run online.

5.2 Algorithm Comparisons

5.2.1 Comparisons in Utility to User

We now address the following questions. Under what conditions is anticipatory configuration better than reactive configuration? How do we quantify the improvement?

These factors influence whether anticipatory configuration can outperform reactive configuration:

- The magnitude of switching (re-configuration) costs relative to other components of instantaneous utility,
- Similarity of the profiles of suppliers.

If there are no switching costs, or those costs are very small, then several locally optimal decisions provably add up to a globally optimal decision. In that case, reactive configuration is temporally globally optimal.

With respect to the second factor, consider the extreme case when all the suppliers providing the same service have identical application profiles, i.e. their resource requirements for each QoS level are identical. Mathematically, the problem reduces to having only one supplier assignment, and there is never a need to switch suppliers to capture better utility when resources change.

We have observed that suppliers offering the same service can have vastly different resource requirements. Applications from large commercial vendors tend to be feature-rich and resource-intensive, while open-source applications tend to be more efficient. Also, different vendors offer different runtime options in their applications, contributing to the diversity of application resource profiles. Thus, even with static user preferences, the ranking of the supplier assignments changes under different resource scenarios.

Assuming the above factors are satisfied, there are two reasons why reactive configuration might under-perform anticipatory configuration. First is thrashing and is likely to occur when switching penalties are small (but not insignificant). Oscillating resource paths will force reactive configuration to change supplier assignments and pay switching penalty frequently. The second reason is lack of amortization of switching costs over multiple time windows and is likely to occur when penalties are relatively high. Reactive configuration might not find it optimal to switch a configuration when resources change, although doing so will pay in the long term, if the resources persist at that level.

To investigate these questions, we performed experiments of 1000 trials that compared the actual accrued utility achieved by 4 different algorithms under the same resource conditions: OptAccUtilPerfect, OptAccUtilExpectation, Reactive, and Random. Random randomly selects a supplier assignment in the beginning of the task and commits to that assignment throughout the task. As resources change, Random can change the resource allocation to maximize QoS portion of IU. Obviously, Random does not incur penalties since it can't switch the suppliers.

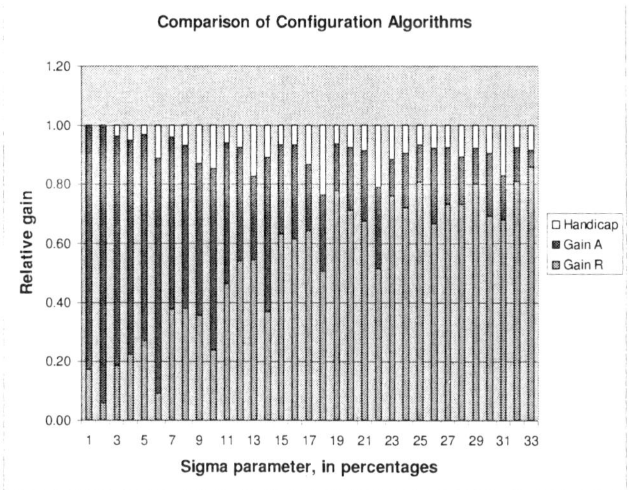

Figure 3: Comparison of the relative gain measures. The stacks, from lower to upper, are: GainReactive, GainAnticipatory, and Handicap.

We calculated the average accrued utility achieved over 1000 trials for each algorithm. Next, we computed GainReactive as the difference between the average utility of Reactive and Random. Similarly, we computed GainAnticipatory as the difference between the averages of OptAccUtilExpectation and Reactive. We computed Handicap as the difference between OptAccUtilPerfect and OptAccUtilExpectation. Since OptAccUtilPerfect is run after the resource availability is known for the entire duration, it calculates the maximum possible accrued utility for that resource path.

We varied the *sigma* parameter of the linear predictor from 1% to 33% of the mean (This parameter determines the range of the one-standard deviation band around the predicted mean). Figure 3 shows the resulting graph.

From the graph, we conclude that:

- With accurate prediction, GainAnticipatory exceeds the GainReactive by a factor of 3-4. As prediction accuracy falls, GainAnticipatory disappears,
- With accurate prediction, OptAccUtilExpectation performs very close to OptAccUtilPerfect,

We also tallied the number of beat OptAccUtilExpectation exceeded Reactive. The results are in Figure 4.

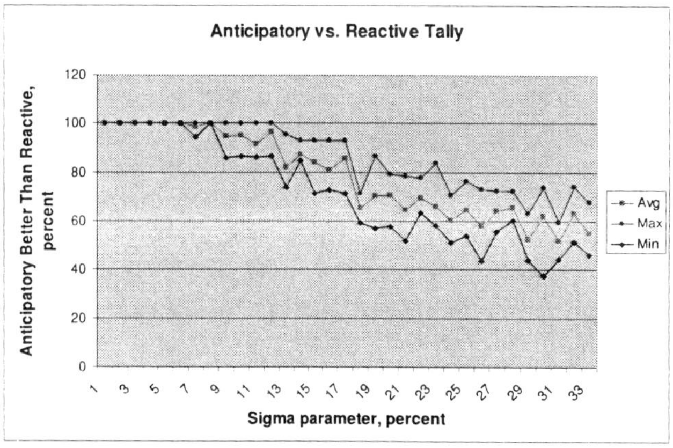

Figure 4: The tally of the percentage of times Anticipatory is better than Reactive. We show the average, maximum, and minimum of 4 experiments.

We investigated the effect that the relative magnitude of the switching penalty has on the algorithms. We confirmed that when penalties are very small, there is no substantial difference in the utility of the Anticipatory (Perfect or Expectation) and Reactive algorithms. This is consistent with the observation made in the beginning of this sub-section.

5.2.2 Runtime Efficiency

To evaluate the runtime efficiency of the anticipatory algorithms, we measure the resource (CPU) demand and latency of one configuration decision.

We measure the time it takes to make one configuration decision using the standard C clock() function. For OptAccUtilExpectation, we vary the depth of recursive simulation from 2 to 6 (experiments for section 5.2.1 used value of 3). We use two different CPU speed settings: maximum and slowest possible. The results in Table 1 show that the latency of one configuration decision is very small.

Table 1: running times of one invocation of the algorithm, OptActUtilExpectation, in milliseconds. The row labels show the simulation depth, and the column labels show CPU speed. CPU is 100 percent utilized.

	2	3	4	5	6
Max	0.50	1.95	7.65	24.20	72.50
Slow	1.71	6.15	23.30	72.00	201.50

The latencies of both OptAccUtilPerfect and Reactive algorithms are in the nanoseconds and have the same order of magnitude. For comparison, OptAccUtilExpectation with simulation depth of 2 is about 40 times slower than either of the former two. Since the configuration framework has other overheads (communication, application control), the additional time required by the anticipatory algorithm is not significant.

Anticipatory configuration requires one invocation of the algorithm during each time period. The resource demand of the algorithm depends on the size of the time window. This size depends on a number predictor and application parameters, but is on the order of dozens of seconds. Thus, we conclude that the OptAccUtilExpectation algorithm can run in near-real-time with very little CPU demand.

6. EVALUATION

We now refer to the requirements set earlier in the paper and discuss how our work has addressed those. Next, we enumerate the engineering benefits of our work.

6.1 Addressing the Requirements

R1. *Define a measure of accrued utility.* We have introduced a discrete time model and defined accrued utility as the sum of instantaneous over the duration of the task. Accrued utility represents user's satisfaction with the running state of the task over the entire duration, is backwards compatible to the reactive model of configuration and allows comparisons between algorithms, satisfying this requirement.

R2. *Express and combine prediction into the model.* We have formalized three representative predictors and defined a predictor calculus. The linear recent history predictor is grounded by resource prediction research and factors in uncertainty of predictions. The other two predictor types are motivated by other sources of available information.

R3. *Design optimal and efficient algorithms for anticipatory configuration.* We have designed and experimented with two anticipatory algorithms. OptAccUtilPerfect provides a benchmark for maximum possible accrued utility when resource predictions are exact, while OptAccUtilExpectation explicitly handles uncertainty in predictors. With reasonable accuracy of predictors, we have demonstrated that OptAccUtilExpectation nearly always performs better than Reactive and the gain in utility is substantial.

We have also demonstrated that OptAccUtilExpectation is fast and resource efficient, and can be used online on a resource constrained platform.

6.2 Engineering Benefits

We have presented the design and partial implementation of a self-adaptive system that leverages resource predictions for user preference-driven application configuration and resource allocation. We argue that our solution addresses a number of important engineering concerns: (1) combining multiple sources of predictive information, (2) optimal decision making under uncertainty, and (3) runtime efficiency.

Our approach defines three predictor types and a calculus for combining information from multiple sources into a single generalized prediction. The model allows expressing near and long term predictions about resource availability. To the best of our knowledge, previous adaptive systems have not considered multiple sources of information.

The second benefit of our approach is demonstration of improved decision making under uncertainty. Presently, many systems choose to ignore uncertainty: they operate by waiting and then reacting. We have argued that when predictors are sufficiently accurate, system decision making can be improved despite uncertainty.

Third, our approach addresses runtime efficiency, an important concern for self-adaptive systems. We have demonstrated that the anticipatory configuration system can make decisions on-line, while consuming very little resources. The result holds even for resource constrained platforms, making the approach usable in pervasive and mobile environments.

6.3 Limitations

Our approach has limitations:

- while linear recent history predictors are empirically grounded, the other two predictor types are merely plausible. There are no studies that demonstrate the statistical validity of relative move or bounding predictors,
- the results we have demonstrated are sensitive to the choice of preference functions. In particular, for anticipatory configuration to have an edge over the reactive version, the penalty term in instantaneous utility must satisfy certain bounds,
- we have not modeled resources with intertemporal substitution such as battery. This is the subject of future work.

7. CONCLUSION

We have leveraged research in resource prediction to improve the decision making of a self-adaptive system that allocates resources among concurrent fidelity-aware applications. As part of incorporating long-term predictions in a model of self-adaptation, we have formally expressed the uncertainty inherent in such predictions. We have demonstrated that the new anticipatory decision making approach improves over an earlier reactive approach, while remaining resource-efficient on a limited capability device.

Our approach presents several engineering benefits, including formal treatment of predictors and analysis of improved utility as a function of the uncertainty of the predictors. We conjecture that other self-* systems (e.g., Rainbow [5]) can potentially benefit from predictive information. We hope that our paper has provided a blue-print for integrating predictive information in other self-* systems that address adaptation, repair, and configuration.

8. ACKNOWLEDGMENTS

This work was funded in part by NSF grants CCR-0205266, CCF-0438929, CNS-0613823, by DARPA grant N66001-99-2-8918, and by the Korean ETRI Institute. Authors thank professors Anthony Brockwell and Peter Steenkiste of Carnegie Mellon, Peter Dinda of Northwestern University for their help in this work as well as the anonymous reviewers for their constructive suggestions.

9. References

[1] P. Dinda. Design, Implementation, and Performance of an Extensible Toolkit for Resource Prediction In Distributed Systems. *IEEE Transactions on Parallel and Dist Systems (TPDS)*, 17:2, February 2006.

[2] R. Bent and P. Van Hentenryck. Regrets Only! Online Stochastic Optimization under Time Constraints. *Proc 19th AAAI*, 2004.

[3] P. Dinda, D. O'Hallaron. Host Load Prediction Using Linear Models. *Cluster Computing*, 3:4, 2000.

[4] D. Garlan, et al. Project Aura: Towards Distraction-Free Pervasive Computing. *IEEE Pervasive Computing*, 21:2, April-June, 2002.

[5] D. Garlan, et al. Rainbow: Architecture-Based Self-Adaptation with Reusable Infrastructure. *IEEE Computer*, 37:10, 2004.

[6] S. Gurun, et al. NWSLite: A Light-Weight Prediction Utility for Mobile Devices. *Proc. 2nd IEEE Int'l Conf. on Mobile Systems, Applications, and Services (MobiSys), 2004.*

[7] P. Hentenryck, et al. Online Stochastic Optimization Under Time Constraints. Working paper, last accessed in February 2007 at http://www.cs.brown.edu/people/pvh/aor5.pdf.

[8] C. Lee. On Quality of Service Management. *PhD Thesis, Carnegie Mellon University Technical Report CMU-CS-99-165*, 1999.

[9] D. Narayanan, M. Satyanarayanan. Predictive Resource Management for Wearable Computing. *Proc. 1st IEEE Int'l Conf. on Mobile Systems, Applications, and Services (MobiSys), 2003.*

[10] R. Neugebauer and D. McAuley. Congestion Prices as Feedback Signals: An Approach to QoS Management. *Proc. ACM SIGOPS European Workshop*, 2000.

[11] B. Noble, et al. Agile Application-Aware Adaptation for Mobility. *Proc. ACM Symp on Operating Systems Principles (SOSP)*, 1997.

[12] V. Poladian, et al. Dynamic Configuration of Resource-Aware Services. *Proc IEEE Intl Conf on Software Engineering (ICSE)*, 2004.

[13] Y. Qiao, J. Skicewicz, P. Dinda. An Empirical Study of the Multiscale Predictability of Network Traffic. *Proc Intl Symposium on High Performance Distributed Computing (HPDC)*, 2004.

[14] A. Sang and S. Li. Predictability analysis of network traffic. *Proc. of INFOCOM*, 2000.

[15] M. Satyanarayanan. Pervasive Computing: Vision and Challenges. *IEEE Personal Communications*, August 2001.

[16] J.P. Sousa, D. Garlan. The Aura Software Architecture: an Infrastructure for Ubiquitous Computing. *Carnegie Mellon Technical Report, CMU-CS-03-183*, 2003.

[17] R. Wolski, et al. The network weather service: A distributed resource performance forecasting system. *J. of Future Generation Computing Systems*, 1999.

[18] R. Wolski, et al. Predicting the CPU availability of time-shared Unix systems. *Proc Intl Symp High Perf Dist Computing (HPDC)*, 1999.

10. APPENDIX A

Below we produce a nearly verbatim copy of the definition of instantaneous utility published in [12].

10.1.1 QoS Preferences

QoS preferences specify the utility function associated with each QoS dimension. The names of the QoS dimensions are also part of the shared vocabulary. The utility of service *svc* as a function of the quality of service is given by:

$$U_{QoS}(svc) \triangleq \prod_{d \in QoS\ \dim(svc)} F_d^{c_d}$$

where for each QoS dimension d of service svc, $F_d : dom(d) \rightarrow (0,1]$ is a function that takes a value in the domain of d, and the weight $c_d \in [0,1]$ reflects how much the user cares about QoS dimension d. As an example, *video playing* has a QoS dimension of *frame update rate*. The function $F_{frameRate}$ gives utility for various frame rates, and $c_{framerate}$ specifies the weight of frame rate.

Weighted product specifies an "AND" semantics when combining QoS dimensions. A utility value of zero in one dimension indicates that the user is not interested in the configuration even if the quality of other dimensions is high.

10.1.2 Supplier Preferences And Switching Penalty

To evaluate the assignment of specific suppliers, we employ a supplier preference function, which is a discreet function that assigns a score to a supplier, based on its type. Also, we account for the *cost of switching* from one supplier to another at run time.

Precisely, the utility of the supplier assignment for a set a of requested services is:

$$U_{Supp}(a) \triangleq \prod_{svc \in a} h_{svc}^{x_{svc}} \cdot F_{svc}^{c_{svc}}$$

where for each service svc in the set a, $F_{svc} : Supp(svc) \rightarrow (0,1]$ is a function that appraises the choice of a supplier for service svc; and the weight $c_{svc} \in [0,1]$ reflects how much the user cares about the supplier assignment for that service.

The term $h_{svc}^{x_{svc}}$ above (10.1.2) expresses a change penalty as follows: h_{svc} indicates the user's tolerance for a change in supplier assignment: a value close to 1 means that the user is fine with a change, the closer the value is to zero, the less happy the user will be. The exponent x_{svc} indicates whether the change penalty should be considered (x_{svc}=1 if the supplier for s is being exchanged by virtue of dynamic change in the environment) or not (x_{svc}=0 if the supplier is being newly added or replaced at the user's request).

10.1.3 Instantaneous Utility

Overall utility is the product of the QoS preference, supplier preference, and change penalty. Let a' be the previous assignment of suppliers and a be the current. Then the instantaneous utility is:

$$IU(a,a') = \prod_{svc \in a} h_{svc}^{x_{svc}} \cdot F_{svc}^{c_{svc}} \left(\prod_{d \in QoS\ \dim(svc)} F_d^{c_d} \right)$$

Towards Supporting Interactions between Self-Managed Cells

Alberto Schaeffer-Filho[1], Emil Lupu[1], Naranker Dulay[1], Sye Loong Keoh[1], Kevin Twidle[1], Morris Sloman[1], Steven Heeps[2], Stephen Strowes[2], Joe Sventek[2]

[1]Department of Computing, Imperial College London
{aschaeff, e.c.lupu, n.dulay, slk, kpt, m.sloman}@doc.ic.ac.uk

[2]Department of Computing Science, University of Glasgow
{heeps, sds, joe}@dcs.gla.ac.uk

Abstract

Management in pervasive systems cannot rely on human intervention or centralised decision-making functions. It must be devolved, based on local decision-making and feedback control-loops embedded in autonomous components. We have previously proposed the self-managed cell (SMC) as an architectural pattern for building ubiquitous applications, where a SMC consists of hardware and software components that form an autonomous administrative domain. SMCs may be realised at different scales, from body-area networks for health monitoring, to an entire room or larger distributed settings. However, to scale to larger systems, SMCs must collaborate with each other, and federate or compose in larger SMC structures. This paper discusses requirements for interactions between SMCs and proposes key abstractions and protocols for realising peer-to-peer and composition interactions. These enable SMCs to exchange data, react to external events and exchange policies that govern their collaboration. Dynamically customisable interfaces are used for encapsulation and interaction mediation. Although the examples used here are based on health-care scenarios, the principles and abstractions described in the paper are more generally applicable.

1 Introduction

Management in pervasive systems cannot rely on human intervention or centralised decision-making functions. The former because pervasive devices must be usable by non technically savvy users. The latter because pervasive devices are mobile and cannot refer to centralised management applications for re-configuration and adaptation directives. Systems such as body-area networks of sensors and actuators for monitoring a patient's health, unmanned vehicles or fleets of vehicles must be autonomous and continuously adapt to changes in their environment or in their usage requirements. They must therefore be *self-managing* with local decision making and feedback control to enable seamless adaptation. Whilst this structuring in autonomous entities is a necessity in pervasive environments, it has also been advocated as a means of constructing large distributed systems and networks. In essence, this is the proposition of autonomic computing [10]. To an extent, this goes against the network management tradition, which focuses on the functional integration of management components across an entire corporate system and relies on centralised network operations centres manned by human administrators.

We have previously introduced the concept of a *Self-Managed Cell (SMC)* as an architectural pattern for building ubiquitous computing applications [11]. A SMC consists of a set of hardware and software components which form an autonomous administrative domain. SMCs implement a policy-driven feedback control-loop that determines which management and re-configuration actions should be performed in response to events of interest such as device failures, context changes or changes of state in the SMC's resources. The policy approach is itself based on previous work at Imperial College [5, 16]. SMC examples include body-area networks for health monitoring, unmanned vehicles, or control of pervasive spaces such as rooms, buildings or urban environments.

Although SMCs are autonomous, they must be able to interact with each other in complex ways, federate or compose into larger structures. For example, a body-area network monitoring a patient's health may comprise "smart" sensors and complex diagnosis devices that are SMCs in their own right. In the same way, a SMC controlling a room will be aggregated under the control of a house SMC and autonomous unmanned vehicles may be aggregated into fleets with a common mission. Body-area network SMCs may interact with a number of other *peer* SMCs such as the SMC running on the PDA of a nurse, a doctor or other health-care worker, or the SMC controlling the room in which the wearer is present.

We propose here a way of realising "cross-SMC" interactions that enable complex collaborations between SMCs in either peer-to-peer or compositional settings. This permits realising scalable pervasive environments in which SMCs can aggregate into larger structures and engage in ad-hoc peer-to-peer collaborations. We focus on the basic abstractions for interactions in terms of exchanges of data, events and policies between the SMCs and discuss the main design decisions and architectural choices. Goal-driven collaborations relying on distributed planning approaches remain part of our plans for future work.

The examples used here are derived from requirements for e-Health. However, the principles and results are more generally applicable to other pervasive environments. In particular, we are currently applying them within the context of self-management for fleets of unmanned vehicles as well as management of large virtual organisations.

This paper is structured as follows: Section 2 discusses related work. Section 3 describes the SMC architectural pattern while Section 4 presents the SMC interactions framework. Section 5 details the behavioural specification of cross-SMC interactions. Our prototype and early results are described in Section 6. Concluding remarks and future work are presented in Section 7.

2 Related work

Although several studies have been devoted to designing frameworks for pervasive spaces, they tend to share two limitations: they focus on pervasive spaces of a relatively fixed size (e.g., a room) and they fail to cater for dynamic interactions between pervasive spaces. Both issues are however key points in the SMC design.

Often, research studies assume pervasive spaces of a relatively *fixed size*. For example, Gaia [13] seeks to extend the traditional operating system concept, by providing a view of a meta-operating system but focuses on room-sized environments. On the other hand, ISAM [1] aims to address resource management and application adaptation and focuses on large-scale multi-institutional environments. One.world [7], in turn, provides a less sophisticated infrastructure that enables applications to adapt to context changes but focuses on small room-like environments. iROS [8] emphasises the ability to integrate *"legacy"* applications but relies on centralised servers and limits itself to room-sized environments. Oxygen [12] is mainly concerned with how users interact with the system. It mentions the dynamic establishment of collaborative regions, which can be room-sized or even campus-wide but does not detail how this is achieved.

The second aspect relates to the federation of pervasive spaces. Whilst much of the literature focuses on the architecture of pervasive spaces and their supporting services, less attention is paid to the *interactions and collaboration* between such spaces. Gaia recognises the importance of federating Gaia spaces, but this is not part of the core view of its *active spaces* and is regarded as future research. ISAM assumes that the neighbourhood of each *execution cell* is configured by an administrator, and remains static for most of the time. iROS deliberately assumes a single pervasive space. Finally, Oxygen recognises the importance of establishing collaborative regions. However, details on how they are established are scarce. Furthermore, it is not clear whether this can be extended to collaborations between collaborative regions, where collaborative regions interact with each other.

In contrast, we consider the SMC as an architectural pattern applicable at different levels of scale, ranging from body-area networks, to large-scale virtual organisations. SMCs are expected to dynamically discover and collaborate with other SMCs, whilst most other projects focus on a single-size, single-instance perspective.

The IBM autonomic manager has some similarity to our SMC approach in that it autonomously manages a set of resource, while exposing a management interface to other autonomic managers, as though it is a managed resource. However, interactions between SMCs are considerably more sophisticated than the simple resource sensor/effector interface described in [3].

3 Self-managed cell architectural pattern

To provide autonomous management in pervasive environments, we have introduced the self-managed cell (SMC) as the basic building block of our pervasive systems [11]. A SMC consists of hardware and software components which form an administrative domain that is able to operate autonomously. Components (also referred to as managed resources), include physical sensors and actuators, devices such as PDAs, Gumstix, mobile phones and computers as well as software services and components within those devices. They are heterogeneous in nature and must be accessed by the SMC's management services through *adapter* objects that provide a uniform management interface and hide the specifics of the interactions with those components. A typical set-up we use for health-care monitoring comprises a Gumstix[1] device hosting management services that control several sensors (e.g., heart-rate, temperature, acceleration) hosted on BSNs (Body Sensor Nodes) [2] as well as other devices such as diagnostic devices hosted on PDAs

[1] http://www.gumstix.com

[2] http://vip.doc.ic.ac.uk/bsn/

or other Gumstix. Communication with BSN nodes typically occurs through IEEE 802.15.4 radio links while communication between Gumstix devices or with PDAs occurs through Bluetooth or Wi-Fi.

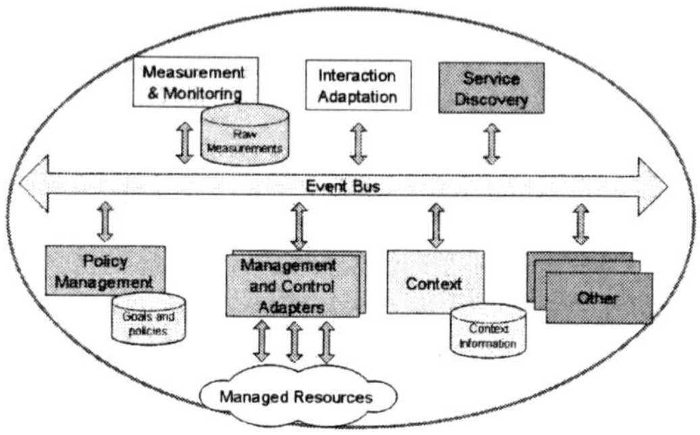

Figure 1. Self-managed cell architecture.

A SMC comprises a dynamic set of management services that are integrated through a common publish/subscribe *event bus* (Figure 1). This has the advantage of de-coupling the services, as an event publisher does not require prior knowledge of the recipients when sending a message, and permits adding new services to the SMC without disrupting the behaviour of existing ones. The *core services* of a SMC are: the *event service*, the *policy service* and the *discovery service*; however, other services such as context, authentication, accounting or application specific services may be used in different SMCs. The SMC's core services implement a policy-driven feedback control-loop (Figure 2) [15] in which changes of state in the managed resources or changes of context are published on the event bus and trigger the execution of *obligation* policies in the form of *event-condition-action* rules that determine which adaptation actions need to be performed.

The *policy service* caters for two types of policies: *obligation policies* that define the management actions that must be performed in response to events, and *authorisation policies* that specify which actions are permitted on which resources and services. Policies can be added, removed, enabled and disabled to change the behaviour of a SMC without interrupting its functioning. The managed objects to which policies apply can be internal SMC resources, adapters for external services or policies themselves. All managed objects are kept in a domain structure that implements a hierarchical namespace similar to a file system; however, domains may overlap and a managed object may belong to several domains. The SMC policy service is based on the Ponder2[3] system, which in addition to policies can interpret nested sequences of commands that identify the managed object to be used and parameters or sub-elements within the XML that are to be sent to the object.

[3]http://www.ponder2.net

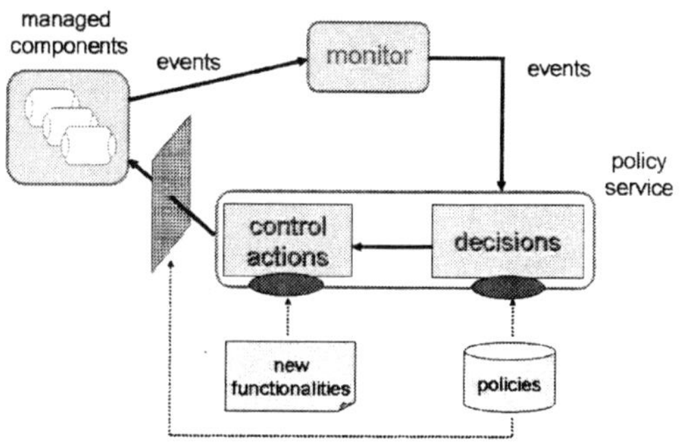

Figure 2. The feedback control-loop.

The *event bus* disseminates the events needed to trigger obligation policies. Events generated by managed resources and by the services are transmitted to all the subscribed services enabling them to react concurrently to event occurrences within the SMC. Asynchronous events are well suited to pervasive systems in which most of the applications are event driven. However, we do not require that all interactions between SMC services be event driven.

The *discovery service* is used to detect new devices which are capable of joining the SMC, such as sensors and other SMCs in the vicinity. It interrogates new devices to establish a profile describing the services they offer and generates an event describing the addition of a new device for other SMC components to use it as appropriate. The discovery service is also responsible for vetting new devices before accepting them in the SMC and managing the SMC's membership, as it is necessary to distinguish transient failures which are common in wireless communications from permanent departure from the SMC (e.g., device out of range, switched off, or failure). When a new device is discovered, policies are used to decide in which domains the device and its accessible components should be placed. Policies applying to those domains will then automatically apply to the respective components.

4 SMC interactions

Although SMCs are autonomous, they need to interact with each other and aggregate into complex structures to scale to larger systems. Such interactions must be established autonomously with little or no user intervention.

4.1 Interaction requirements

A SMC managing a patient's health needs to interact with numerous *peer* SMCs. During home visits by a nurse or other health-care practitioner it needs to permit the nurse SMC to access the data held on the patient's current physiological condition and must notify the nurse of events occur-

0-7695-2906-2/07 $25.00 © 2007 IEEE

ring within the patient SMC. The patient SMC may also need to be notified of events occurring within the nurse SMC, for example the fact that the nurse has started a specific diagnostic procedure. The nurse may need to load policies for execution by the patient, for example for defining new thresholds or alert behaviour. Similarly, the patient SMC may need to load policies onto the nurse SMC for example, to trigger re-calibration of the patient sensors if needed. Similar exchanges would be required when the patient SMC encounters a SMC controlling devices in a General Practitioner's (GP) clinic, however, a GP may have additional access to the patient's resources e.g., the ability to change dosage on drug delivery pumps. Other *peer to peer* interactions may also occur between the patient SMC and SMCs surrounding it such as environmental monitoring (e.g. pollen count, allergies), pharmacies, or other public services.

We can draw several requirements from the example above. Firstly, SMCs must detect the presence of peer SMCs and decide autonomously whether to establish an interaction. Interactions between peer SMCs require a SMC to be able to invoke operations on its peer, to receive event notifications from its peer as well as to notify its peer of selected internal events occurring within itself. More complex interactions may require exchanges of policies between the SMCs, if a SMC can request another to behave in a specific way. Secondly, the interface exposed to a peer SMC may include only a subset of the available operations and events depending on the kind of SMC and the role (e.g. doctor or nurse) it can play in the interaction. Finally, a SMC may wish to expose the resources it possesses though an external interface and may choose to mediate the interactions with those resources.

Whilst peer-to-peer interactions occur frequently as SMCs interact with neighbouring autonomous components, *composition* interactions enable grouping SMCs into larger autonomous structures and scaling SMC management to larger environments. Composition encapsulates a SMC with its own resources, as a managed resource within the containing SMC. This implies that the SMC can be programmed by the containing SMC in terms of policies that it must enforce. Moreover, the device may expose to its containing SMC a management interface for re-configuration. For example a diagnostic device may be part of a body-area network that will load new decision algorithms and new policies into it. Similarly, larger sensors may be autonomous components and thus SMCs in their own right. For example, even BSN nodes can be connected to multiple analogue sensors and support internal event-based interactions. We have also implemented a basic policy service for BSNs to cater for adaptation to changing circumstances [9].

Composition also implies that the contained SMC behaves as a managed resource within the outer SMC and ceases to advertise itself independently. Interactions between the contained SMC and external SMCs are subject to the authorisation and possibly mediation from the outer SMC which may require preventing access to them from the outside environment. A SMC cannot be contained, i.e. treated as a managed resource, by more than one containing SMC, although it may interact with other SMCs for application purposes subject to authorisation from its managing SMC. Although a contained SMC is a managed resource, it must retain control of the interfaces it exposes and the policies it accepts from its managing SMC. This is for reasons of integrity rather than security as it is important to ensure that an autonomous device cannot be compromised i.e., devices preserve their autonomy.

Note that composition interactions have similar requirements to peer-to-peer interactions in terms of permitting invocations, raising and receiving events, and exchanging policies between the contained and the containing SMC. The differences between composition and peer to-peer interactions lie in the degree of access permitted i.e., which methods and events are exposed and which policies are accepted from the containing SMC. The second important difference is that there can be only a single containing SMC and thus some of the methods and events are guaranteed to be invoked by a single entity. Finally, the third important difference is that a contained SMC ceases to advertise itself and thus its interactions with other devices are governed by its containing SMC. This allows the outer SMC to selectively hide the complexity of the composed structure, and only expose selected functionality in its external interactions (for example, the patient SMC would expose its sensors to the doctor, but hide them from other patients).

A SMC's interface may need to change dynamically as the SMC may acquire or lose functionality, for example through the addition/failure of a particular sensor or through composition with a new SMC. To achieve this we are using a variation of the *role object pattern* [4] that enables dynamically adding new functionality to a *core* object by associating it with a new capability.

4.2 Customised interfaces

As discussed above, a SMC must determine which functions it wishes to export to its peers, and do so through specific *customised interfaces*. The customised interface exposed depends on the the kind of SMC it is interacting with (e.g. doctor, nurse) and even that SMC's identity. Although it would be possible to expose all the functions on a single interface and use authorisation policies to restrict access from external entities, this would make all operations to services and resources visible externally even if they are not accessible. This could have unwanted privacy implications for example in medical applications or security implications in military applications. Therefore, an external SMC should *see* only those functions that a SMC wants to expose in a *customised interface* generated specifically for that interaction. Note that this interface could be generated from the SMC's authorisation policies.

A SMC typically *mediates* interactions between its resources and other SMCs. This mediation is implemented by a proxy object which maps the functions exposed in the customised interface to internal operations on the SMC's resources (e.g., a method named *"readTemperature"* is mapped to the *"/sensor/temp.read"* operation on an internal sensor). This approach avoids exposing the internal resources directly and permits realising more complex transformations e.g., of the parameters received or the result returned, when interacting with other SMCs. Additionally, this approach permits controlling which methods are exposed by adding or removing the respective mappings. In our prototype, the interface exposed by a SMC is implemented as a managed object that provides the functionality of the proxy object described above. For example, the interface exported by a patient to a nurse will also act as a proxy for the invocations where the nurse tries to access the internal sensors of the patient SMC.

In addition to invocations on a remote SMC, asynchronous communication through events is an important means of interaction between SMCs. Thus, an *interface* defines: *(a) events*, which can be published externally by the SMC (i.e., to which external SMCs can subscribe); *(b) notifications*, which are external events of which the SMC can be notified (i.e., that external entities publish within the SMC); and *(c) operations*, which are the methods that can be invoked on the SMC by a remote entity. Figure 3 shows the XML commands for generating an interface that a patient may export to a doctor SMC. It specifies that the doctor SMC may receive *monitoringReady* events and may raise *startMonitoring* and *stopMonitoring* events within the patient SMC. Additionally, the doctor SMC can invoke the *readECG* and *scheduleTask* operations on the patient SMC.

```
<create>
  <event name="monitoringReady"
          localEvent="ready"/>
  <notification name="startMonitoring"
          localEvent="start"/>
  <notification name="stopMonitoring"
          localEvent="stop"/>
  <operation name="readECG"
          localOp="/local/hearBeatSensor.read"/>
  <operation name="scheduleTask"
          localOp="/local/javaTimer.createTask"/>
</create>
```

Figure 3. Customised interface of a patient.

Figure 3 also shows the mappings of the events, notifications and operations to local resources within the patient SMC. These mappings would not be visible to the client SMC when it queries the specification of the interface. Note that new operations, events and notifications can be added or removed from the interface definition, to change the functions exported.

4.3 Interaction establishment

Interaction establishment is initiated as a result of a *newSMC* event being generated by the SMC's discovery service [11], as depicted in Figure 4. This event contains the name of the discovered SMC, its profile, which identifies its type (e.g. patient, doctor or sensor), and a generic interface. The *generic interface* is application independent and common to all discoverable SMCs. It defines the operations necessary for exchanging customised interfaces and establishing the interaction.

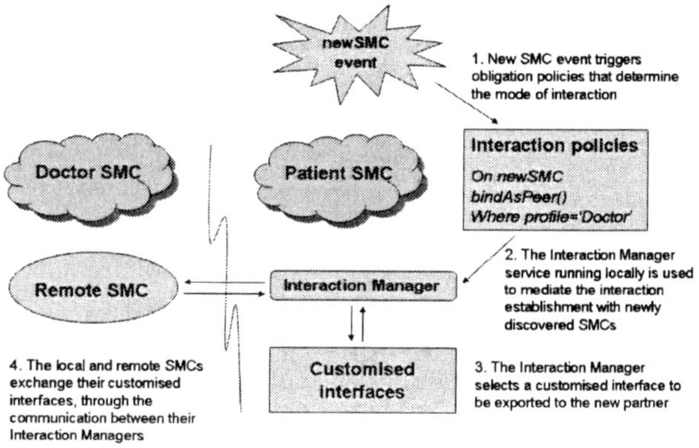

Figure 4. Interaction establishment overview.

Obligation policies triggered by the *newSMC* event determine whether to establish a peer-to-peer or composition interaction. The *interaction manager* is a service running locally in each SMC, and it is used to bootstrap interactions. For example, the policy shown in Figure 5, deployed in a *patient* SMC, specifies that a peer-to-peer interaction should be established when discovering a *doctor* SMC. It achieves this by invoking the method *bindAsPeer* in the local interaction manager. Similarly, a composition relationship can be established with a *sensor* through the *bindAsResource* method.

The interaction managers in the two SMCs then exchange their *customised interfaces*. The interaction manager from the discoverer SMC selects a customised interface based on the remote SMC's profile and sends it to the interaction manager in the remote SMC. Similarly, the remote SMC selects a customised interface and returns it to the discoverer if it accepts the interaction. Each SMC stores the received interface in its local domain structure. Note that simple BSN nodes will not initiate discovery but will only respond to being discovered.

```
<create type="obligation" event="/event/newSMC">
  <arg name="name"/>
  <arg name="genericInterface"/>
  <arg name="profile"/>
  <condition>
    <eq>!profile;<!--   -->doctor</eq>
  </condition>
  <action>
    <use name ="/SMCCore/interactionManager">
      <bindAsPeer name="!name;"
                  genericInterface="!genericInterface;"
                  profile="!profile;"/>
    </use>
  </action>
</create>
```

Figure 5. Interaction policy.

4.4 Domain structure and roles

When two SMCs interact, obligation policies specified in one SMC may define invocations to be performed on the other SMC. Furthermore, as discussed in Section 4.1, SMCs may exchange policies between them. One SMC may request that the remote SMC behave in a particular way and can achieve this by sending to the remote SMC a set of obligation policies. In both cases policies are written in terms of the events and actions of a remote SMC before that SMC comes into proximity. Therefore, a SMC must know the interface it expects an encountered SMC to have e.g., a patient will have a description of the interfaces it expects a doctor or a temperature sensor to have. Policies applicable to that SMC can then be specified in terms of this *expected interface*.

We use *roles* as placeholders within the local domain structure for SMCs discovered at run-time. Roles are associated with an *expected interface*, that defines the operations, events and notifications that remote SMCs are expected to provide in order to be assigned to that role. Then, policies for that role can be defined in terms of the expected interface's events and operations as explained in the following section. When an interaction is established, the remote SMC is assigned to a role based on its profile. At this point the SMC verifies that the customised interface offered by the remote SMC provides a superset of the elements required in the expected interface. Policies already specified for that role will then apply to the remote SMC. Several SMCs might be assigned to the same role (e.g., a doctor can interact with several patients). Additionally, the role is also a suitable place to store the customised interface that can be exported to that SMC. For example, the doctor will store in the *patient* role the interface it expects patients to provide as well as the interface that it will export towards patients. Figure 6 illustrates a domain structure for a patient SMC with roles for interacting with *sensors*, *doctors* and *nurses*.

In summary, a role provides three functions to facilitate cross-SMC interactions: *(a)* it identifies the *expected interface* that remote SMCs must provide to be assigned to that role; *(b)* it identifies the interface that the SMC will export to remote SMCs of that kind (e.g., the *setTemperatureThreshold* method is to be exported to a doctor but not to a nurse); and *(c)* it defines a placeholder for the remote managed objects and SMCs for which policies are specified.

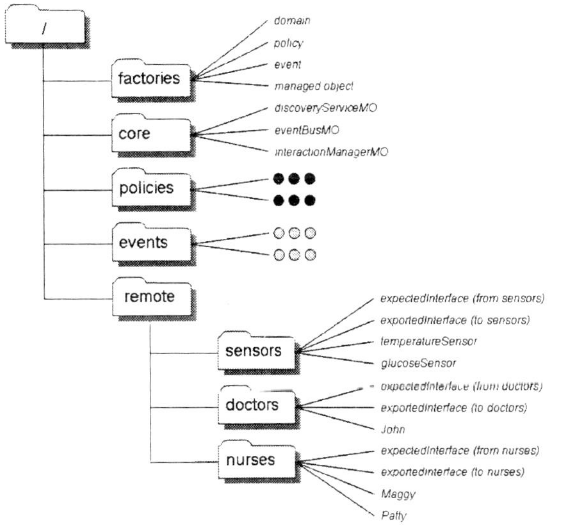

Figure 6. Domain structure and roles.

5 Missions: behavioural specifications of SMC interactions

After the initial steps for establishing an interaction have been performed, the SMCs can start their collaboration (collaborations between ubiquitous entities is also called *recombinant computing* [6]). This permits a SMC to be notified of and react to events occurring in the other SMC and thus extend its control-loop.

Complex interactions can be defined by exchanging policies between SMCs. These policies define how the SMCs should behave in the context of the interaction in terms of sending notifications to other SMCs, and reacting to both internal events and external notifications by invoking management actions locally or on remote SMCs. We introduce the concept of a *mission* as a means of grouping the duties of the remote SMC in the interaction specified in terms of the obligation policies it must enforce. Thus, a mission is a group of obligation policies specified in terms of the interfaces of two or more interacting SMCs.

A mission is normally specified before the target SMC has been discovered and is therefore defined in terms of the *expected interfaces* of the SMCs involved. As described in Section 4.4 these interfaces are associated with roles within the local SMC so we informally say that a mission is written as a function of the roles of the SMCs involved. The obligation policies i.e., event-condition-action rules grouped

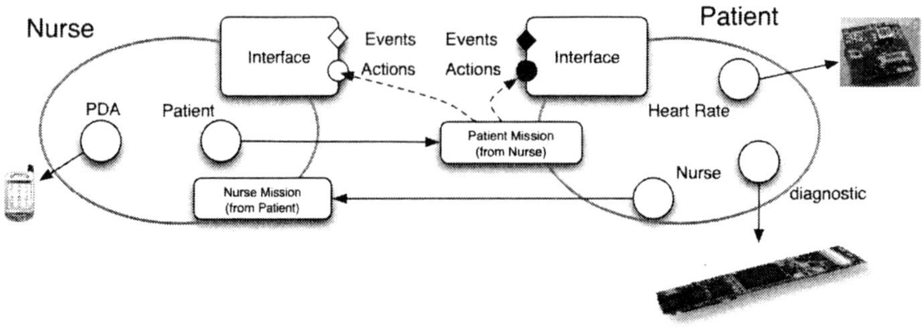

Figure 7. Missions across SMCs.

within the mission are thus written in terms of the events and actions defined in the expected interfaces associated with the roles. When a new SMC is discovered and assigned to a role, obligation policies within the current SMC determine which missions should be instantiated on it.

As shown in Figure 7, when the nurse SMC discovers a patient's body-area network SMC, it instantiates a mission on it if permitted by the latter. Similarly, the patient may instantiate at the nurse a mission defining the policies it expects the nurse to fulfil in the interaction. Note that it is not necessary that both missions be initiated.

In essence, missions are a constrained form of programming a remote SMC and are akin to a form of dynamically loaded code. Thus, before executing this code i.e., instantiating the mission and its policies, the receiving SMC must validate the received mission through a procedure detailed in Section 5.2. This is necessary in order to avoid that the received mission compromises the integrity of the SMC either accidentally or maliciously.

5.1 Specifying a mission

Figure 8 shows an example of a mission for *ECG monitoring* downloaded from a nurse to a patient. This specification is a template taking as arguments the roles (and implicitly their interfaces) to which it relates as well as two additional arguments (*time* and *frequency*) that will be specified at run-time when the mission is instantiated. Conceptually, the mission specifies the obligations that patients must enforce in order to enable a nurse to perform an ECG. The argument values refer to the specific nurse and patient that are to interact and are given upon instantiation.

This mission comprises an obligation policy triggered by a *startMonitoring* event received from the nurse, which requests the patient to schedule two tasks: one reads the patient's ECG for a specified time and at a specific frequency, and the other notifies the nurse when the monitoring has finished. Thus, this mission relies on the methods *scheduleTask* and *readECG* that are expected to be present in the patient's interface, and on events that must be either generated or received by the SMC. The method *generate* used in this example is a generic method through which an entity can publish an event to an external SMC. Its argument must be one of the notifications defined in the receiving SMC's interface. The method *load*, not shown in the example, is used to load a mission and is also generic to all SMCs.

```
<create>
  <arg name="nurse" type="interface/nurse"/>
  <arg name="patient" type="interface/patient"/>
  <arg name="time" type="integer"/>
  <arg name="freq" type="integer"/>
  <policy name="ECGMon" event="!nurse;.startMonitoring">
    <action>
      <use name="!patient;">
        <scheduleTask freq="!freq;" time="!time;">
          <use name="!patient;">
            <readECG />
          </use>
        </scheduleTask>
        <scheduleTask delay="!time;">
          <use name="!nurse;">
            <generate event="!patient;.monitoringReady"/>
          </use>
        </scheduleTask>
      </use>
    </action>
  </policy>
</create>
```

Figure 8. Patient monitoring mission (from nurse).

When a mission is specified, a first verification of the mission is performed, to ensure that it complies with the *expected interfaces* of the roles involved. This is achieved by parsing the different policies and building a dependency table that includes all the events and actions which policies refer to as well as the role interface to which they are expected to belong. This table is then checked against the expected interfaces associated with those roles. The mission is considered valid if all the dependencies are satisfied.

5.2 Loading a mission

When a mission is instantiated at a remote SMC, that SMC receives the mission specification and the parameters and must instantiate the obligation policies contained in the mission within its own scope. However, before doing this it must check that the mission is well-formed, that all the mission's dependencies can be satisfied within its local environment and that the policies received do not conflict either with its own policies or with policies originated from other missions. We discuss here how the first two requirements are addressed. Although we have, in the past, developed several algorithms for policy conflict analysis [2] their implementation has not yet been integrated in the SMC framework.

5.2.1 Step 1: Check that the mission is well-formed

A source SMC may maliciously or accidentally embed additional code in the mission and attempt to load it in the target SMC. Therefore, the first step in validating the mission is to check that it is well-formed; namely, that it contains only arguments and obligation policies and that it is syntactically correct. This includes inspecting the policies in the mission and verifying that they use solely operations and events pertaining to the role interfaces given as arguments. A policy attempting to invoke operations on other objects will generate an error and abort the instantiation of the mission. This ensures that the mission is self-contained and prevents malicious SMCs from "guessing" operations available in the target SMC.

5.2.2 Step 2: Check mission parameters

When a mission is instantiated by one SMC on another e.g., the doctor instantiates a mission on a patient, the argument values sent to the patient are the generic interfaces of the SMCs involved. This is because in missions involving more than two SMCs each SMC has a different view of the capabilities of the SMCs with which it interacts. For example, in Figure 9, where the dashed lines represent interface exchanges and the solid lines represent mission instantiation, the doctor's interface to a nurse SMC (*NS*) may be different from the interface that the patient has to the same nurse SMC (*NS'*). Thus, if the doctor wants to instantiate in the patient SMC a mission that involves interactions with the nurse SMC it will pass as argument to the mission the generic interface of the nurse SMC. It will be up to the patient SMC to contact the nurse SMC and obtain an interface to that SMC if it does not have one already.

Thus, when receiving a mission, the recipient SMC must establish the interactions and obtain a customised interface from all the SMCs given as mission parameters.

5.2.3 Step 3: Check mission dependencies

A SMC that has received a mission must check the policy dependencies (i.e., events, notifications and operations used

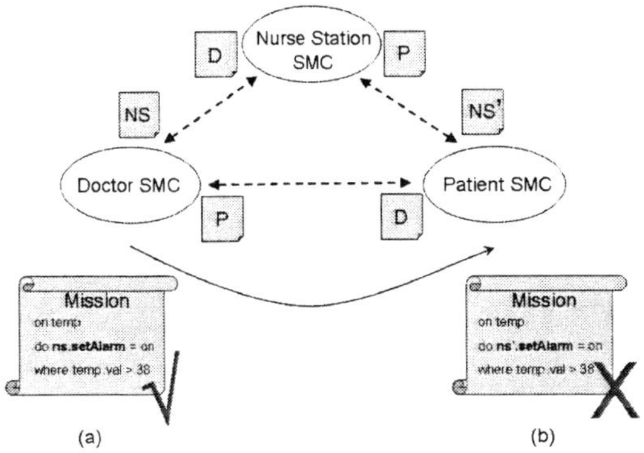

Figure 9. Mission requirements satisfied by the interfaces known to the doctor (a) but not by those known to the patient (b).

in the mission's policies) against the interfaces that it has for the SMCs given as mission parameters. This can be achieved by computing the policy dependencies and checking them against either: *(a)* expected interfaces it knows for those SMCs or *(b)* the customised interfaces it has obtained from the remote SMCs once it has established an interaction with them. The former is sufficient because an interaction will subsequently be established with a SMC only if the customised interface received from that SMC is more specific (i.e., supports a superset of events, notifications and operations) than the expected interface for that SMC. This approach enables delaying binding to the remote SMC until the binding is actually required, but is more restrictive since it requires the SMC to have an expected interface for the remote SMC and the customised interface may offer additional operations that are not present in the expected interface. The second approach is more permissive as it allows the mission to contain policies that use operations not present in the expected interface but requires establishing an interaction with the remote SMCs when the mission is received. In terms of our previous example (Figure 9) the doctor instantiates a mission on the patient which requires the patient to interact with a nurse. The patient will verify this mission against the expected interface it has for nurses or may obtain a customised interface from the nurse given as parameter and check the policy dependencies of the mission against this interface. In our implementation, we have chosen the latter option as it enables the doctor to deploy a mission to the patient that takes advantage of operations provided by the specific nurse the patient will be interacting with (e.g., the nurse in that specific GP clinic or ward).

5.2.4 Step 4: Instantiate mission

If all the above steps succeed, the receiving SMC instantiates the obligation policies contained in the mission, using the argument values provided by the source SMC. Arguments that are basic types require a trivial variable substitution, and the interfaces are substituted with the appropriate adapter object for the remote SMC. These policies can now trigger internal actions within the patient based on events occurring in either the doctor or the nurse SMC or trigger remote invocations on the doctor and nurse SMCs in response to events occurring within the patient SMC. It is thus possible to encode complex collaborations between the SMCs and both the patient and the nurse SMCs can deploy missions to each other in a similar fashion.

For a SMC to deploy a mission to another it must be authorised to do so by authorisation policies in the recipient SMC. Furthermore, the actions specified in the mission's policies also need appropriate authorisations in the receiving SMC. The access control framework for the SMC is presented in detail in [14].

6 Implementation and discussion

Our current implementation caters for most of the concepts described in this paper, including the implementation of the obligation policies in the Ponder2 interpreter, the selection and exchange of interfaces between interaction managers, the deployment of missions, the verification of missions by the recipient SMC, and their instantiation. The current implementation of the *interaction framework* is in Java and is integrated with the newest version of the Ponder2 policy interpreter. However, porting the interaction framework to the Gumstix, where initial versions of the core services are running already, remains to be done. Integration with the lightweight implementation of the SMC core services [9] for constrained BSN sensors also remains to be addressed.

When instantiated, the SMC starts the policy service, which in turn creates a local instance of the interaction manager and of the other core services. All managed objects, including missions, interfaces and roles are created through factory objects that can be loaded on-demand and can be invoked at run-time using XML based commands to create new instances. This also enables us to cater for scenarios in which interactions occur spontaneously and the role descriptions need to be loaded dynamically.

In order to build the scenario described in this paper, we have pre-deployed in the SMCs: (a) the policies that determine which type of interactions need to be created (Figure 5), (b) the role definitions for doctors, patients and sensors, and (c) the mission specification illustrated in Figure 8. Customised interfaces are at present specified rather than generated from authorisation policies as the access control framework has only recently been implemented.

The discovery service discovers new devices over IEEE 802.15.4, Wi-Fi or Bluetooth. If the new device is a SMC (as indicated by its profile) a *newSMC* event is generated that will trigger the policies that decide if an interaction should be established, and whether it is a peer-to-peer or a composition one. The interaction managers in the two SMCs then exchange customised interfaces, assign the interface received from the remote SMC to the appropriate role and generate a local *newSMCBinded* event at each SMC. This triggers policies that determine which missions should be loaded on the partner SMC. The verification procedure described in Section 5.2 is then carried out before the policies included in the mission are instantiated.

We have tested our implementation in a small-scale setup consisting of three SMCs: *ECG sensor*, *patient* and *doctor*. The ECG sensor and the patient establish a composition interaction while the patient and the doctor establish a peer-to-peer interaction. The doctor is then given access to the ECG sensor but the access is mediated by the patient SMC. Missions have been loaded from the patient SMC to the ECG sensor, and from the doctor to the patient SMC. We were able to test the functionality of our implementation running on workstations, but not on Gumstix devices yet. Therefore, we have not included performance results, as the measurements obtained in workstations would not reflect a realistic situation. We have used XML for both the policy specification and for operation invocation on objects. Although this adds some performance overhead, it increases implementation flexibility as we can have different types of policy interpreters and managed objects implemented in various programming languages. It can also be mapped on to many different communication mechanisms. We are working on a more intuitive higher-level policy specification notation which can be transformed into XML. Overall, our evaluation indicated that the SMC framework is suitable for realising self-management but may not be suitable for real-time application data such as high-frequency sensor measurements.

For body-area networks for health monitoring we have implemented our own discovery service and event bus. Although a number of applications offering similar functionality exist, we needed implementations that could scale down to small devices and could be used in conjunction with policy decisions. However, when using the SMC pattern in larger scale environments, more efficient implementations (e.g., such as SIENA for the event bus) can be used.

7 Concluding remarks and future work

Using the SMC as an architectural pattern, basic SMCs can be dynamically assembled into larger and more complex structures. This allows SMCs to scale-down to individual devices, and scale-up to cater for larger pervasive applications. Policies provide not only a means of adapting to events corresponding to changes of state in the managed resources (e.g. failures or performance degradation) but also to define how SMCs should behave when they encounter new autonomous entities and in particular new SMCs. Through the concept of *missions*, obligation policies in the form of event-condition-action rules can be used to enact a rich spectrum of collaborations between SMCs.

Although we started by considering peer-to-peer relations as intrinsically different from composition relations, their requirements proved to be quite similar in terms of the need to cater for cross-SMC invocations and exchanges of events and policies. What varies substantially are the invocations that are permitted, events that can be exchanged and policies that can be accepted. The other substantial difference lies in the ability of a composite SMC to hide its underlying complexity. The use of customised interfaces and mediated interactions have proved useful in terms of both reducing complexity and handling interactions with heterogeneous components. Mediated interactions are essentially for management activities and do not preclude establishing direct interactions with resources for application purposes.

The SMC pattern, which is based on a dynamic set of services integrated around a publish/subscribe event bus and uses policy-based adaptation, has proved applicable to a wide spectrum of environments. Although this paper has focused on health monitoring, we have worked on similar applications for fleets of unmanned autonomous vehicles (the term *mission* originates from there) and in large distributed settings such as virtual organisations.

Finally, the abstractions and protocols defined here provide a basis on which SMC collaborations can be defined. However, further work remains to be done towards: *(a)* integrating in the current framework procedures for checking policy analysis, conflict detection and resolution, *(b)* integrating the current implementation with the access control framework and *(c)* extending the mission concept to both cascaded configurations and higher-level abstractions for SMC interactions. In respect to the latter we are currently working on the appropriate infrastructure for defining missions that can encapsulate other mission specifications e.g., the doctor would deploy a mission to the nurse SMC that itself contains the instructions for the nurse to load specific (sub-)missions to any of the patient SMCs that it encounters. Higher-level abstractions may include collaboration definitions whose enforcement is itself distributed and collaborations based on exchanges of high-level goals which require planning procedures and algorithms to be scaled down to embedded devices.

Acknowledgments

The authors wish to thank the UK Engineering and Physical Sciences Research Council for their support of this research through grants GR/S68040/01, GR/S68033/01 and EP/C547586/1. The work reported in this paper was partly funded by the Systems Engineering for Autonomous Systems (SEAS) Defence Technology Centre established by the UK Ministry of Defence.

References

[1] I. Augustin et al. ISAM - a software architecture for adaptive and distributed mobile applications. In *7th IEEE Symp. on Computers and Communications*, pages 333–338, Taormina, Italy, July 2002. IEEE-CS.

[2] A. Bandara, E. C. Lupu, and A. Russo. Using event calculus to formalise policy sepcification and analysis. In *IEEE 4th Int. Workshop on Policies for Distributed Systems and Networks (Policy 2003)*, Como, Italy, June 2003. IEEE.

[3] D. F. Bantz et al. Autonomic personal computing. *IBM Systems Journal*, 42(1):165–176, 2003.

[4] D. Bäumer et al. The role object pattern. In *Proc. Int. Conf. on Pattern Languages of Programs (PLoP 1997)*, Washington University, 1997. Technical Report WUCS-97-34.

[5] N. Damianou et al. The Ponder policy specification language. In *Proc. IEEE Workshop on Policies for Distributed Systems and Networks*, pages 18–39, Bristol, U.K., Jan 2001. IEEE-CS.

[6] W. K. Edwards et al. Challenge: recombinant computing and the speakeasy approach. In *Proc. 8th ACM Int. Conf. on Mobile computing and Networking*, pages 279–286, New York, NY, USA, 2002. ACM Press.

[7] R. Grimm. One.world: experiences with a pervasive computing architecture. *IEEE Pervasive Computing*, 3(3):22–30, Jul.-Sep. 2004.

[8] B. Johanson, A. Fox, and T. Winograd. The interactive workspaces project: experiences with ubiquitous computing rooms. *IEEE Pervasive Computing*, 1(2):67 – 74, April-June 2002.

[9] S. L. Keoh et al. Policy-based management for body-sensor networks. In *Proc. 4th Int. Workshop on Wearable and Implantable Body Sensor Networks (BSN)*, LNCS, pages 92 – 98, Aachen, Germany, Mar. 2007. Springer.

[10] J. O. Kephart and D. M. Chess. The vision of autonomic computing. *IEEE Computer*, 36(1):41–50, Jan 2003.

[11] E. Lupu et al. AMUSE: autonomic management of ubiquitous systems for e-health. *J. Concurrency and Computation: Practice and Experience, John Wiley (to appear)*, 2007.

[12] Oxygen website, 2006. Available at: <http://www.oxygen.lcs.mit.edu/>.

[13] M. Roman et al. A middleware infrastructure for active spaces. *IEEE Pervasive Computing*, 1(4):74–83, Oct.-Dec. 2002.

[14] G. Russello, C. Dong, and N. Dulay. Authorisation and conflict resolution for hierarchical domains. In *Proc. IEEE Int. Workshop on Policies for Distributed Systems and Networks*, Bologna, Italy, Jun. 2007. IEEE CS-Press.

[15] M. Sloman. *Network and Distributed Systems Management*, chapter Monitoring Distributed Systems, pages 303 – 347. Addison-Wesley, 1994.

[16] M. Sloman and E. Lupu. Security and management policy specification. *IEEE Network*, 16(2):10–19, Mar.-Apr. 2002.

Research Track, Session 8: Security

Identifying Malicious Peers Before It's Too Late: A Decentralized Secure Peer Sampling Service*

Gian Paolo Jesi, David Hales
Dept. of Computer Science,
University of Bologna (Italy)
E-mail: {jesi , hales}@cs.unibo.it

Maarten van Steen
Dept. of Computer Science,
Vrije Universiteit Amsterdam (The Netherlands)
E-mail: steen@cs.vu.nl

Abstract

Many unstructured peer to peer (P2P) systems rely on a Peer Sampling Service (PSS) that returns randomly sampled nodes from the population comprising the system. PSS protocols are often implemented using "gossiping" approaches in which connected nodes exchange their links in a randomized way. However, such services can be defeated easily by malicious nodes executing "hub attacks" which distort the PSS such that all nodes in the network, ultimately, only gain access to malicious nodes. From this leading status - i.e. being a "hub" - the malicious nodes can affect the overlay in several ways, ranging from total network disruption to obtaining an application dependent advantage. We present a completely distributed defense against such attacks and give results from simulation experiments. The approach is generic as it is independent of the adopted PSS *implementation.*

***Keywords**: P2P, overlay, security, gossiping.*

1 Introduction

P2P systems, without central servers, need to provide some method of initiating and maintaining connections between the nodes that comprise them such that all nodes form a single component. A partitioned network reduces the efficiency of the system, for many tasks, because nodes in different components cannot communicate. This can be a significant problem in unstructured systems which operate under highly dynamic environments with nodes constantly entering and leaving the system.

One general approach to this problem is to implement a protocol that maintains a connected overlay network between nodes which approximates a random topology. An overlay network topology consists of each node maintaining logical links to other nodes. A logical link consists of a node identifier that is sufficient to establish communication using some underlying network infrastructure (e.g. and IP address and port number over the Internet).

It is well known that a random network topology can maintain a fully connected network that is highly robust to benign node and link failure. Additionally, a random network offers short paths between any two nodes in the network which is valuable for many kinds of P2P tasks (e.g. broadcasting or routing messages between nodes).

A specific method for maintaining robust overlays with random-like topologies is through gossiping. Gossiping protocols rely on the randomized spreading of information between neighbors in a network. Typically, nodes maintain a set of neighbor links (a so-called cache or view) which indicates their currently neighbors. Periodically, each node selects some random neighbor from its view and communicates some information – i.e. gossips – which the receiving node may store and later forward to its own neighbors. The approach is loosely analogous to individuals in a social network gossiping between themselves or the spread of an epidemic in a population.

Gossip approaches are attractive because they spread information quickly and robustly over networks yet require only simple protocol implementations. A number of gossip-based protocols exist to maintain random overlay networks in unstructured P2P systems [4, 13]. Although implementations vary, the basic mechanism involves nodes gossiping their current neighbor links. In this way, using suitable update functions in the nodes, the cache (or view) can be kept up-to-date and maintain a random-like connected topology under conditions of high dynamism – where nodes constantly join and leave the network.

Ironically, however, the power of the gossip approach to spread information quickly over the entire network can become an achilles' heel if it is exploited by malicious nodes who wish to defeat the system by spreading false information to partition the network. Because information

*Partial support for this work was provided by the European Union within the 6th Framework Programme under contract 001907 (DELIS).

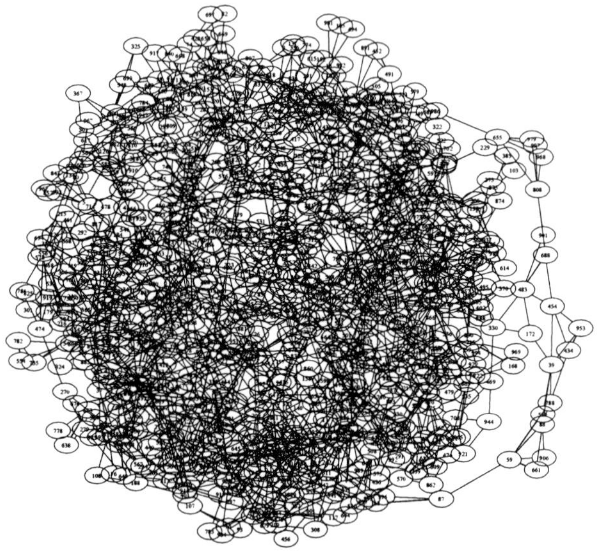

(a) A healthy random graph topology

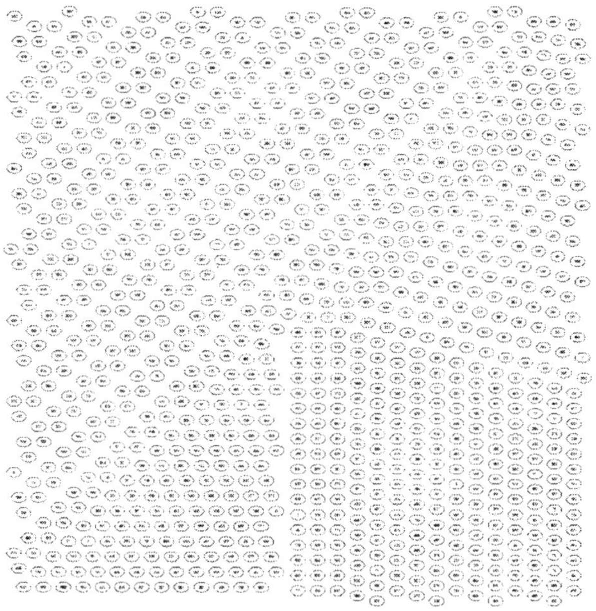

(b) The graph after malicious attack

Figure 1. Overlay topology before and after a simple attack: the random graph depicted in (a) becomes fully disconnected in (b). The graph out-degree (constant) is set to 20, but only 3 links per node are displayed for clarity. Less than 20 gossiping cycles are required to disrupt the graph. Network size is 1000 nodes.

spreads so quickly in gossip networks the problem for non-malicious nodes is that *by the time they identify other nodes as malicious it is too late for them to take action* since they are already disconnected from the network - i.e. their view is completely polluted by the malicious nodes.

We show that by maintaining multiple views over the network (multiple neighbor lists) nodes can identify malicious nodes before it is too late such that they can take appropriate action by placing them on an individually maintained black-list. The approach is adaptive, allowing formally blacklisted nodes to be white-listed if their behavior changes and vice versa. In addition no reputation information must be shared between nodes because blacklists and white-lists are only individually maintained. In other words, we present a fully decenralized Secure Peer Sampling Service (SPSS).

Previously, we proposed a centralized SPSS approach and obtained good results [6]. However such an approach requires one or more central trusted servers which present a single point of failure and/or add administrative overhead. We found that our distributed approach produces comparable results without producing such overhead.

The remainder of this paper is organised as follows: we describe a "hub attack" scenario in which several colluding malicious nodes are sufficient to completely partition a network using a gossip based protocol. We describe our gossip network model, followed by a brief description of the PSS implementation adopted. Then, we outline our previous centralised approach to tackle the problem and then the distributed protocol. We perform simulations that test the effectiveness of the distributed approach and compare it with the centralised approach. Finally, we briefly survey related work and conclude with a summary, open issues and possible future work.

2 Hub attack scenario

Here we describe an example of an attack scenario applicable to a gossiping topology maintenance approach. This attack is a form of the so-called "hub attack" (see [6]) and its effect is summarized in Figure 1. In a hub attack malicious nodes attempt to get other nodes to connect exclusively to them. If this is achieved, then the malicious nodes can exit the network leaving their former neighbors without any valid neighbors and hence partitioning them from the network. To illustrate the problem, consider a gossiping network in which each node maintains a list of c neighbors ($c = 20$, see Section 3), called its *cache* or *view*. When the network is performing correctly the peers are wired in a random graph topology with out-degree c and the graph is continuously rewired over time. The elements of these caches are continuously updated and exchanged between nodes during gossiping interactions.

At some point, k nodes in the system (e.g., $k = c$ in the example) start colluding and behaving maliciously exchanging forged caches; then, after a short amount of time spent in their malicious activities, they leave the network. The forged caches exchanged by the attacker nodes hold the identifiers of the other malicious nodes; this exact malicious content of the cache is always replayed at every gossip exchange.

Figure 1(a) shows the overlay in normal conditions; Figure 1(b) shows the same graph after the malicious nodes exit: within a very short time the original overlay is completely disrupted. The infection rate proceeds quickly, as can be expected from a gossiping protocol. In fact, every well-behaving node will accept the attacker's cache with high probability (see Section 5); this means that in just one exchange a node will have all its cache polluted by malicious identifiers if it is directly connected to a malicious node. In other words, all its neighbors are now malicious nodes and it can no longer *initiate* a gossip exchange with a non-malcious node.

Only a nondefeated, nonmalicious, node B can help a defeated one, say A, provided B has As identifier in its local cache. However, when B contacts A, we can expect that after the exchange half of the local caches of A and B, respectively, will be polluted with identifiers of malicious nodes. As a consequence, both nodes will have 50% of their cache polluted; therefore, even contacting a nonmalicious node will generally also spread the pollution and increase the chance that a nondefeated node contacts a malicious one.

There is no way for a nonmalicious node to identify a malicious one as they seem to play fairly; however, as the attackers always pass on the same cache (or a very similar one), it is easy for any node to keep track of the last cache provided by a neighbor in order to detect them. Sadly, when a non-malicious node detects the bogus cache replayed by the same neighbor, *it is too late to react* since the node cache is completely filled with malicious identifiers. When each node's cache is completely polluted, the malicious nodes may decide to leave the network, leaving it in a completely disrupted state without any hope of recovery, as shown in Figure 1 (b).

This example refers to a small, 1000 nodes network, but as we have shown in previous work [6], no matter what the size of the network, a successful attack can be carried out swiftly. In this section we have introduced the general idea of a hub attack as applied to a gossip based topology manager service. In the next section we specify in a little more detail the generic gossip protocol approach and the specific protocol variant we used for the purposes of our simulations.

3 Gossip and attack model

We consider a network consisting of a large collection of nodes that can join or leave at any time. Leaving the network can be voluntary or due to a crash. We assume the presence of an underlying routed network (e.g., the Internet) in which any node can, in principle, contact any other party. Any node in the network must be addressable by a unique node identifier (ID), such as an $\langle$IP-address, port$\rangle$ pair. We do not address the presence of firewalls and NAT routing among peers.

Due to scalability constraints, a node knows about only a small subset of other participants. This subset, which may change, is stored in a *local cache*, while the node IDs it holds are called *neighbors*. This set provides the connectivity for a node in the overlay; the relation "who knows whom" induced by the neighborhood set defines the overlay *topology*. The absence of items in the cache or the presence of incorrect or bogus IDs leads to an unrecoverable situation. In this case, a new initialization or *bootstrap* is required. In general, P2P applications provide a set of well-known, highly available nodes in order to provide a bootstrap facility and hence the initial neighborhood set.

In general, a *timestamp* is associated with each distinct node ID stored in the cache in order to eventually purge "old" ID references according to an aging policy.

The notion of time in our model is not strict because our gossip protocols need not be synchronized. We measure time in generic *time units* or *cycles* during which each node has the possibility to initiate a gossip exchange with another randomly selected node from its local cache.

In our attack model, we consider a practical scenario in which a small set of colluding malicious nodes or attackers play in the system. The size k of this set is equal to the cache size ($k = c$) in the worst case. *The goal an attacker is to subvert the network in order to become a hub.* The attack method involves the spreading of fabricated data through the messages gossiped among the participants which affects the logical links of the overlay. We suppose the attackers are "clever", in the sense that they operate in a beyond suspicious manner, in order to avoid being easily discovered.

A malicious node runs the actual PSS implementation as any other well-behaving node, but the content of its messages is fabricated with a specific (malicious) intent. At every gossip exchange it always replays a message containing the forged IDs of other malicious nodes in the system. This behavior is perfectly valid from a PSS point of view, as the only mandatory constraint is that cache entries are distinct. This intrinsic weak integrity constraint complies to reality; in real-world P2P file-sharing systems (see [8,11,12]), when a peer receives an advertisement for an item.

Other lower level details of the attack model have been extensively discussed in [6]. We use the following terminol-

```
while(TRUE) do
wait(Δt);
neighbour = SELECTPEER();
SENDSTATE(neighbour);
n_state = RECEIVESTATE();
my_state.UPDATE(n_state);
```

(a) Active Thread

```
while(TRUE) do
n_state = RECEIVESTATE();
SENDSTATE(n_state.sender);
my_state.UPDATE(n_state);
```

(b) Passive Thread

Figure 2. The epidemic or gossip scheme.

ogy: the *pollution* is the presence of IDs of malicious nodes in a peer's cache. A *node is defeated* if all the entries in its cache refer to malicious nodes (i.e., 100% polluted) and an *overlay is defeated* or *destroyed* if it is completely partitioned (e.g., each peer has no more neighbors as depicted in Figure 1(b)).

In this work, we adopted a specific implementation of the PSS called NEWSCAST. However, our approach is generic and can be applied to any PSS implementation. Before introducing our SPSS approach in detail, we provide a brief background of NEWSCAST.

Newscast protocol: NEWSCAST is a gossip-based protocol heavily inspired by the prototypal gossip scheme depicted in Figure 2. It is a *topology manager* protocol that builds and maintains a continuously changing random graph (or *overlay*). The generated topology is very stable and provides robust connectivity. This protocol has been a successful building block for implementing several P2P protocols [3,5,7].

In NEWSCAST, each node maintains a cache containing c IDs extended with a logical timestamp (ts) representing its creation time. The protocol behavior follows strictly the gossip scheme; periodically, a node A does the following: (i) it selects a random peer B from its local cache; (ii) then updates its local timestamp; and (iii) performs a *cache exchange* with B. The exchange involves sending A's cache along with its own ID and receiving B's cache and ID.

After the exchange, each party merges the received cache with its current one and keeps the c "freshest" IDs as measured by the timestamp associated with each ID. The only requirement imposed to a cache is that no multiple copies of the same ID are allowed.

This exchange mechanism has three effects:

1. caches are continuously shuffled, creating a topology with a low diameter that is close to a random graph with out-degree c. Experimental results (see [4]) proved that a small 20 elements local cache is already sufficient for a very stable and robust connectivity.
2. the resulting topology is strongly connected.
3. the overlay is self-repairing, since crashed nodes cannot inject new descriptors any more, so their information quickly disappears from the system due to the timestamp aging policy.

NEWSCAST is also cheap in terms of network communication (see [4]). Essentially, the number of exchanges per cycle can be modeled by the random variable $1+\phi$, where ϕ has a Poisson distribution with parameter 1. Thus, on average, we expect two exchanges per cycle. Practically, this involves the exchange of at most a few hundred bytes per cycle for each peer.

4 Centralized SPSS

In our previous work on preventing the hub attack [6], we designed the SPSS as an extension to the ordinary PSS. We summarize here the basic concepts of our previous work in order to introduce our new SPSS approach.

The system requires the presence of a central *Certification Authority* (CA). The CA is not involved in the protocol itself; it is just needed to acquire the credentials and to join the overlay. We cryptographically secure each ID structure using $[ID_A, ts_{creation}, ts_{expiration}, PK_A, \sigma]$, where ID_A is A's node identifier (see Section 3), the ts are timestamps, PK_A is A's public key and σ is the digital signature on the message.

The key idea relies in the introduction of a new primitive, `checkids()`, to verify whether the exchanged states (caches) are valid for further processing, such as merging with other caches. Essentially, the checking process has a stochastic nature and it is based on the fact that the *attackers always replay the same cache or at least the same subset of malicious nodes*. The probablity to raise a suspicion is proportional to the fraction of the common IDs found: (#common IDs) / c. When the check fails, a suspicion about the potential malicious neighbor is raised and delivered to a TRUSTED PROMPT node; it is similar to a proxy of the Certification Authority and provides peer credential management and access control.

The TRUSTED PROMPT collects the requests sent by any well-behaving node P and builds a table by logging (or updating) an entry $\#(P)$ in a *frequency table* indicating how many times P has been reported as suspect. Finally, the TRUSTED PROMPT builds a new cache of size c for the querying peer. To build the new cache, the TRUSTED PROMPT picks nodes randomly from the network. A node Q is selected for inclusion in a cache proportional to $1 - \#(Q)/N$, where N is the (estimated) size of the network. A lower value in the frequency table corresponds to a higher chance to be present in the cache (and to be a nonmalicious node).

When considering the scalability of our approach, one may come to think that a single TRUSTED PROMPT is going to be a source of problems, but we have shown (see [6]) that, in order to improve the resilience of our distributed system, we can use multiple TRUSTED PROMPT nodes without introducing any modification to our basic algorithm. In addition, we have shown that the message traffic generated by the queries in a large network can be sustained by just a single TRUSTED PROMPT. However, the trade-off between the

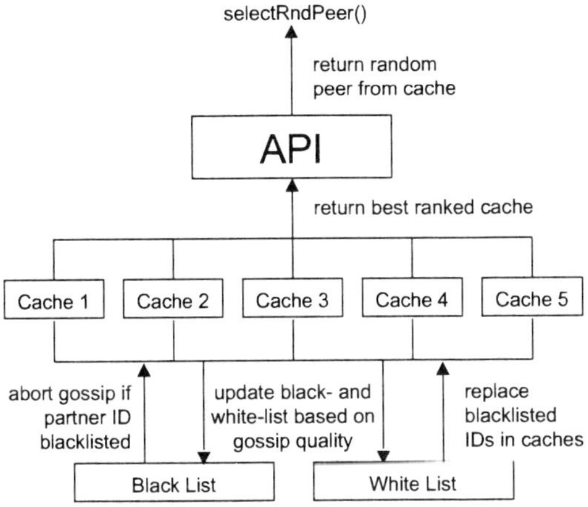

Figure 3. Schematic of the decentralized SPSS; it maintains multiple caches to support multiple random overlays. Black and white-lists screen incoming gossip requests and refresh malicious cache entries.

robustness and the extra effort spent in deploying, configuring and maintaining many TRUSTED PROMPT nodes must be evaluated by the overlay designers.

5 Decentralized SPSS

We believe that the main shortcoming of our centralized SPSS solution is that the deployment of trusted nodes over the Internet, in order to sustain our secure gossip system, is a viable approach only for organizations or companies with trusted administrative control.

In other words, the TRUSTED PROMPT approach requires some extra trusted infrastructure that complicates the system deployment and maintenance. Using the simplest setup, i.e., using a single TRUSTED PROMPT, we minimize the deployment issue, but produce a single point of failure. If the single TRUSTED PROMPT is hacked or crashes then the whole network is vulnerable to attack.

A fully decentralized solution would be preferred as it would lower the burden to design and to deploy secure gossip systems and would not require trust external to the system (other than the CA which is external to the protocol), but is this possible to achieve? And what kind of trade-offs do we need to consider? Our aim is to refactor our previous approach in order to obtain a fully decentralized solution, in which each node has the chance to detect the malicious nodes using its own resources.

Multiple overlays: As we have seen the main obstacle to prevent and detect the hub attack is represented by its *high spreading speed*. Such a high speed leaves no time to the peers to make any successful guess about the identity of the attackers. This is why in our previous SPSS solution we rely on the TRUSTED PROMPT assistance.

The basic idea for the fully distributed SPSS is based on using multiple, concurrent instances of the PSS. Therefore, each node participates in multiple overlay graphs, and the neighborhood at every instance will be distinct with very high probability because the overlays have independently random-like topologies. Essentially, the multiple caches over the same node population, which every node adopts, give each peer a snapshot of what is going on in distinct (random) neighborhood of the overlay. We call *extra caches* the set of caches belonging to each peer; every cache in the set is a random snapshot of a distinct PSS overlay

We assume the same attack model as before: a set of k colluding attackers, but running multiple PSS instances as well, will pollute all the available instances. This hypothesis makes our scenario more challenging.

Each node can monitor the pollution ratio by looking at its extra caches. Since the network population of all the PSS instances is the same, all the extra caches will become polluted by the same k malicious node IDs, if no checking action is performed. However, an attacker can pollute at most only a single node's cache at a time per overlay. In addition, due to the random nature of the available overlays, it is very unlikely that an attacker could defeat all caches of the same victim peer in a short time window. Essentially, the multiple caches are useful in order to perceive how malicious node are spreading the infection from distinct directions over distinct overlays. Due to the spreading infection, we expect that common node ID patterns will emerge in all (or in the majority) of the caches.

Quality rating: Each peer can build a set of statistics in order to guess or detect who are the malicious nodes from the emerging patterns. This knowledge base is stored as private, local black- and white-lists that it is never exchanged among neighbors (see [11]). This obviates the second-order issue of malicious nodes spreading incorrect reputation information.

During a gossip exchange, both parties *rate the quality of the exchange*. The quality rate is given by the number of items lying in the intersection of the exchanged caches among node A and B: $r = |\{cache_A \cap cache_B\}|$. This quality rate influences the probability to conclude the gossip exchange with this current neighbor. Essentially, when two caches are similar (or identical) it is likely that the current neighbor is a malicious node and with high probability it should not be accepted. The probability to abort the exchange is proportional to the fraction of the common IDs found among the two caches: r/c, where c is the usual cache size.

The rank results are collected in the node's *knowledge base*. The information collected in this structure is refreshed according to an aging policy to avoid that any wrong guess would have unbounded consequences over time.

Any attempt to exchange with a neighbor (black-) listed as a high frequency and low quality rated node is declined. In addition, when a node suspects one of its caches is polluted, it tries to refresh the cache randomness by substituting the currently blacklisted node IDs with high quality rated node IDs collected during the previous exchanges (if any).

During the protocols execution, one or more cache can be defeated by the attackers. However this is not critical, as the cache will be restored as soon as the node has collected a suitable knowledge base. It is very unlikely that all node's caches become polluted in a short amount of time; in this unlucky condition and if the knowledge base is not ready or not correct, the only chance for a node is to be contacted by a well behaving node in order to partially restore at least one of its caches. This is the exact situation we have in the previous SPSS version. Figure 3 shows a schematic of the main components maintained by the protocol within each node.

The algorithm: Our distributed approach is focused on the knowledge base each node has to build. Essentially, the knowledge base is represented by two list structures: BLACKLIST and WHITELIST; the former holds high frequency and low quality rated node IDs, while the latter holds high quality rated node IDs. We do not set any explicit size limit for these structures and, as a consequence, their size may grow to the actual network size. However, due to presence of an aging policy, their actual size is much less than the theoretical maximum. The SPSS algorithm pseudo-code executed by a node A is the following:

1. Select a random neighbor $B \notin$ BLACKLIST, if any
2. Compute the rank value r with B; proportionally to r/c decline and blacklist B, otherwise accept the gossip exchange, and:
   (a) whitelist B
   (b) perform the standard PSS exchange with B

These steps are performed in each cycle for every available cache. Two additional actions are performed concurrently by two threads at the end of each cycle. The first action is to purge the BLACKLIST and WHITELIST according to an aging policy; the second action instead, is to repopulate the caches suspected of being polluted (if any): each node ID in the cache listed in the BLACKLIST is substituted by a random node ID picked from the WHITELIST.

Another issue is to clarify how node IDs can be inserted and swapped from the BLACKLIST to the WHITELIST and vice-versa. When a node ID has to be inserted in the BLACKLIST for the first time, a standard TTL value (2 cycles) is bound to the stored ID; if the ID is already present instead, its TTL value is reinforced (i.e., dubling the current TTL value). This reinforcement process is needed in order to keep in the BLACKLIST the most frequent node IDs (with a poor rate).

About swapping the IDs among the two structures, suppose node B's ID is already in node A's WHITELIST, but now node A had to insert B's ID into its BLACKLIST. B's ID is removed from A's WHITELIST and it is inserted in the BLACKLIST. In other words, the BLACKLIST has more authority than the WHITELIST. Likewise, if node A has to whitelist node B's ID, but it is already in A's BLACKLIST, the swap between the two list is not allowed until B's ID is purged from the BLACKLIST. This rule is designed to avoid that a node's PSS instance exchanging with a malicious node for the first time, would not overwrite a possible correct suspicion made by a more experienced instance.

Why it works: It is important to note that having multiple caches belonging to distinct PSS instances is very different from having a single PSS with a possibly huge cache. Multiple caches add extra randomness to the node's state and avoid to be defeated in just one exchange; in addition, in extreme conditions (i.e., when the set of attackers is larger than the cache size, see section 6) they stil give the chance to identify the attackers.

The value added by multiple PSS overlays is that the infection proceeds from distinct multiple paths. These dynamics gives each peer more time to detect the most frequent node IDs that appear in their caches.

A higher-level protocol working on top of this fully distributed SPSS can see just a single cache, in order to maintain a seamlessly integration with the standard PSS API. A smart implementation of the fully distributed SPSS can dynamically export the *current best cache* according to concentration of suspected malicious nodes currently listed in the knowledge base (see Figure 3).

Evolutionary link: The multiple caching concept originates from previous socially inspired evolutionary models of "group selection" [1, 2]. In these models anti-social behavior between nodes was avoided by allowing nodes to form and move between different clusters or groups in the population based on utility value comparisons. Essentially, nodes evaluated the quality of their neighbors by measuring the effectiveness of interaction with them over time – involving some application level task – and represented this as a utility value. By comparing utilities with other randomly selected nodes and copying the neighborhoods (caches) of those with higher utility, nodes could avoid interaction with anti-social free-riding nodes. In this approach nodes maintained a single overlay and made intra-overlay movements to find better (higher utility) neighborhoods.

For the distributed SPSS we implemented a similar scheme by allowing each node to store multiple caches and only selecting the best cache based on a measure of utility expressed as cache quality. From the point of view of what is passed to the API, nodes are constantly shifting between

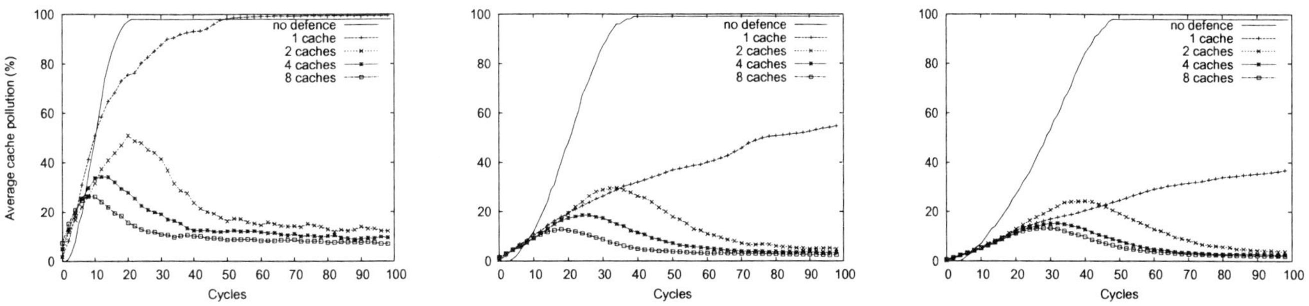

(a) 1,000 nodes (b) 5,000 nodes (c) 10,000 nodes

Figure 4. Fully decentralized SPSS algorithm. The average pollution level in the caches is shown over time; multiple distinct caches per node are compared (i.e., 1, 2, 4 and 8 caches) for each network size (i.e., 1,000, 5000 and 10,000 nodes). 20 malicious nodes are involved in the attack.

different views of the network since each cache represents a different set of neighbors. Furthermore, when the quality for a particular cache becomes low due to possible identification of malicious information, it is wiped and reinitialized from the white-list, hence low quality caches are dropped.

Hence in SPSS nodes do not move between distinct groups or clusters in a single overlay but maintain and effectively move between distinct overlays (inter-overlay movement) comprising the same population of nodes but in different topological configurations. Hence what is being selected here by each node is the overlay which produces the best cache quality at each given point in time. Since all nodes actually stay in all overlays at all times (by maintaining a fixed number of multiple caches) this approach is less a form of evolution and more a form of redundancy with dynamic selection.

6 Experimental results

In order to evaluate our new approach, we investigate the following main issues: (a) how much time is required to achieve a tolerable[1] amount of pollution in the node's caches, (b) how many extra caches are required to prevent the attack, (c) how the performance scales according to the number of the extra caches adopted, (d) the performance of our approach in terms of communication cost; finally, we are also interested in (e) the performance when the hub attack is played by a larger number of k malicious nodes ($k > c$).

If not stated explicitly, in the following evaluation, we have considered the usual scenario for a hub attack: when the number of malicious nodes k is equal to the (*single*) cache size ($k = c = 20$). All the results are averaged over 10 experiments.

[1]We consider the pollution in a *tolerable range* if the graph does not split into clusters when the malicious nodes leave.

Static environment: Figure 4 shows the average pollution level in the node's caches for each considered network size (1,000, 5,000 and 10,000 nodes respectively). In this scenario, we consider a static network in which both malicious and well-behaving nodes are not subject to crashes; also network links are considered perfect and without message loss. Each plot shows a SPSS setup using a distinct number of concurrent caches per node; we have shown the results for 1, 2, 4 and 8 caches setups. As a reference, we also plotted what happens when no attack countermeasures are taken (see the solid topmost line in each chart). Of course, when nothing prevents the malicious node's activities, the cache pollution level quickly reaches 100%. When the distributed SPSS is run with just one cache, the pollution level monotonically increases; the smaller network becomes defeated in about 50 cycles because a degree of 20 is quite high compared to its size. However, this setup cannot be considered a full countermeasure since we still use only a single cache. Essentially, the blacklist mechanism is not sufficient per se in order to recover the network. By using two or more concurrent caches per node, the situation changes dramatically. Two caches are already sufficient to recover the network, regardless the network size. In all cases, the pollution level is never dangerous. Here, by dangerous, we refer to a level over which the network would suffer from partitioning if the malicious nodes leave the network; in general, this happens when the cache pollution is $\geq 75\%$ (see [6]). By increasing the number of caches, we further lower the pollution, however, especially in the bigger network, the advantage in the adoption of 8 instead of 4 concurrent caches is almost negligible. In addition, a pollution level below 20% does not pose any threat of partitioning the network. For this reason, according to our experiments, we consider the 4 extra caches setup a good tradeoff between complexity and effectiveness.

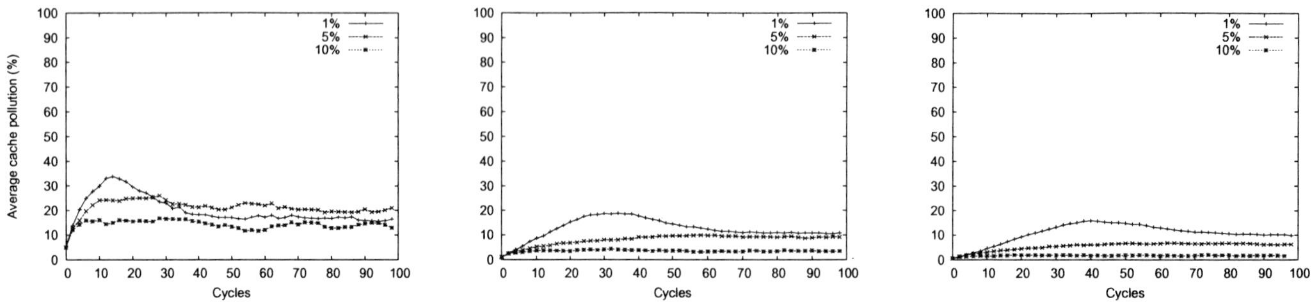

(a) 1,000 nodes (b) 5,000 nodes (c) 10,000 nodes

Figure 5. Fully decentralized SPSS under churn conditions. The average pollution level in the caches is shown over time according to three churn set sizes (1%, 5% and 10% of the network population) and for each network size (i.e., 1,000, 5000 and 10,000 nodes). 4 concurrent caches are adopted by each participant. 20 malicious nodes are involved in the attack.

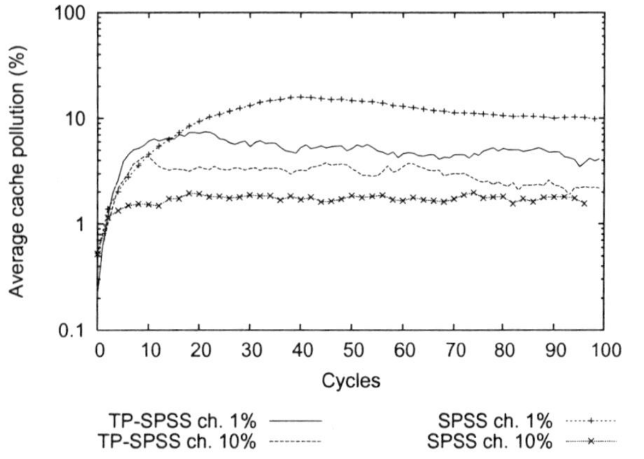

Figure 6. Comparison among our previous TRUSTED PROMPT based SPSS and the current decentralized one (4 extra caches). Two distinct churn scenarios are shown for each one. Network size is 10,000.

Churn: Figure 5 shows the performance of the SPSS under churn. We measured the average pollution level in the node's caches for each distinct network size (1,000, 5,000 and 10,000 nodes). We allowed three distinct churn set sizes: 1%, 5% and 10%, respectively; this amount of nodes leaves the network at every cycle and it is substituted by an equal number of new participants. The malicious nodes, however, stay in place and attempt to pollute caches for the whole duration of the experiment. Note that these values are actually quite high [9], but will allow to demonstrate the feasibility of our solution. Each node has a 4 extra caches setup.

It is surprising to see that the dynamism of the network helps the SPSS to keep the pollution level low. In fact, the level is lower than in the static scenario, for all the considered network sizes. In addition, a higher level of dynamism corresponds to a lower level of pollution. The reason lies in the fact that there is a higher proportion of fresh nodes injected in the system with a very low probability of having a malicious ID in cache; the well-behaving nodes that work in system for a longer time, will hardly diffuse the malicious IDs as they have already blacklisted them with high probability. Therefore, it becomes harder and harder for the malicious nodes to diffuse their bogus caches.

Essentially, on average no well-behaving node will play in the system enough time to detect successfully all malicious nodes, but this total knowledge is not required at all. The knowledge of who are the malicious nodes is distributed over the system as a whole; in other words, it is sufficient that every attacker is known by *some* healthy node.

In Figure 6, we show a comparison between our previous centralized TRUSTED PROMPT based SPSS and the new decentralized one in the dynamic environment. The setup of the decentralized SPSS consist of 4 extra caches. We adopted two churn set sizes: 1% and 10% of the network population. The lines marked with the symbols $+$, $\times$ and $*$ depicts the decentralized SPSS, while the standard lines depict the TRUSTED PROMPT version. The cache pollution levels achieved are quite similar. The new version has a small disadvantage when the churn rate is low (e.g., 1%). However, in the worst case the pollution reaches a stable 10% and it is far from a critical range. In other words, we do not run the risk to have the network partitioned if the malicious nodes leave. In general, the decentralized SPSS achieves a more stable pollution level than the centralized version.

Message overhead: The main advantage of the decentralized version over the TRUSTED PROMPT based one, is the minimal message traffic cost. In fact, we avoid the traffic generated by the queries sent to the TRUSTED PROMPT (e.g., about 1,000 of queries per cycle in a 10,000 nodes network).

Using NEWSCAST as implementation, the cost is n times the cost of each PSS instance; as the average number of exchanges per node can be modeled by the random variable 1+ϕ (see [4]), where ϕ has a Poisson distribution with parameter 1; the overall node cost per cycle is: $\sum_{i=1}^{n} PSS_i = \sum_{i=1}^{n} 1 + \phi_i = 2 \cdot n$.

Extreme conditions: We are interested in verifying the tolerance limit of our approach in terms of number of colluding attackers and to make a comparison with the centralised approach. In the previous section we have seen that the decentralised SPSS can recover the overlay when $k = c$ malicious nodes and $n \geq 2$ caches are involved. This performance is given by the redundancy of the node's state. The experiments shown in Figure 7 depict the performance of the (decentralised) SPSS when $k > c$ malicious nodes are involved in a 10,000 nodes network.

Figure 7(a) shows what happens in the extreme case in which $k = c \cdot n$ attackers are injected in the network. Essentially, we consider to pollute all the extended state of the node. As before, we consider $c = 20$ the size of a single cache and n the number of caches adopted; we considered 2, 4 and 8 caches, corresponding to 40, 80 and 160 malicious nodes respectively. The effect of the presence of $c \cdot n$ attackers grows much faster than the benefit given by the multiple caches.

We may come to think that having $k = c \cdot n$ attackers is the same as the single cache case ($k = c \cdot 1$, see Figure 4), but, instead, the multiple cache presence allows the decentralised SPSS to slowly recover the network. However, the recovering process can be very slow and, more important, the pollution level grows over the dangerous level, depicted by the thick horizontal line, with any number of caches; if the attackers leave, the network will be severely partitioned. Basically, when the whole state can be polluted by a sufficiently large set of malicious nodes, the performance is bad (i.e., the network can be partitioned), but the decentralised SPSS is not paralysed as it is still capable of detecting the attackers.

In Figure 7(b), we check how many malicious nodes can be tolerated by a SPSS using 2 caches. We are interested to know the maximum number of attacker we can successfully tolerate, according to the actual redundancy (caches), without exceeding the threshold represented by the horizontal line. With this set-up, the system can tolerate $k = c \cdot 1.5 = 30$ malicious nodes. However, as can be argued by the situation depicted in Figure 7(a), an increment of the state redundancy (the number of the caches) has a less than linear increment in the number of tolerable attackers. When considering $k = c \cdot n$ attackers, the centralised version is successful as the TRUSTED PROMPT handles the node states; therefore, the node states can always benefit from an extra state help.

7. Related work

In our previous work [6], we surveyed the literature about attacks in overlay networks. Here, we just remind the attacks that are closely related with the hub attack.

The *index poisoning* attack [8] focuses on lowering the quality of the indexes that map hash keys to current file locations in file-sharing applications. A poisoned index, for example, may contain hash keys that refer to nonexisting or nonaccessible files. works because many P2P systems do not check the integrity of their indexes. Index poisoning can be applied to structured as well as unstructured overlays. However, in contrast to a hub attack, index poisoning affects only the overall QoS, but otherwise allows applications to continue functioning correctly. A typical countermeasure is to authenticate or rate the sources that insert keys. In [10] the authors combine the previous index poisoning attack with poisoning routing tables in DHT file-sharing systems. This combination leads to an effective denial-of-service (DoS) attack. In this case, a selected victim host is referenced by many other (poisoned) overlay participants, effectively signficantly increasing the probability that a message will be routed to the victim. As in our attack, poisoning routing tables disrupts the topology. The main difference is that in the hub attack, a malicious node will first need to obtain a leader position before the attack can be carried out successfully.

8 Conclusion

We have presented a decentralised secure peer sampling service (SPSS) which maintains the underlying random overlay in the presence of malicious nodes playing the hub attack. We compared our results with those obtained from a previously developed centralized method and obtained similar results.

On one hand, the decentralised approach gives up the presence of the TRUSTED PROMPT, while on the other hand allows each node to store a redundant state (multiple caches). This achieves our goal to build a fully decentralised and lightweight solution in terms of communication cost. avoid the extra infrastructure requirement and the costs associated with flux of queries delivered to the TRUSTED PROMPT. We have seen that by allowing nodes to maintain a number of independent overlays they can halt the spread of malicious information by identifying the malicious source nodes before it is too late to take action. We found that this resulted in a situation in which no healthy node knows about *every* malicious node but every malicious node is known by *some* healthy nodes. This is sufficient to stop the attack from being successful. This insight may

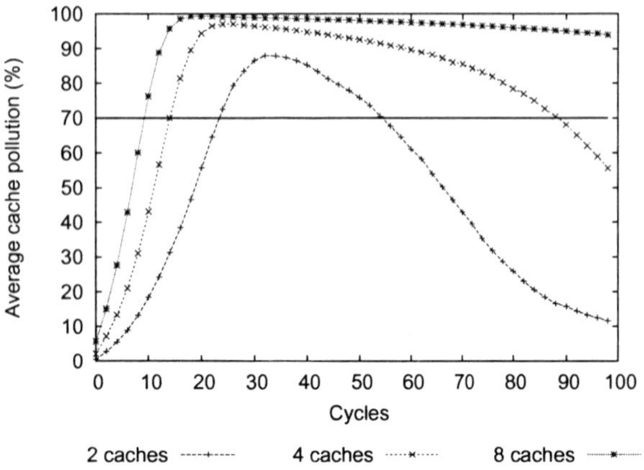

(a) $k = c \cdot n$ m. nodes

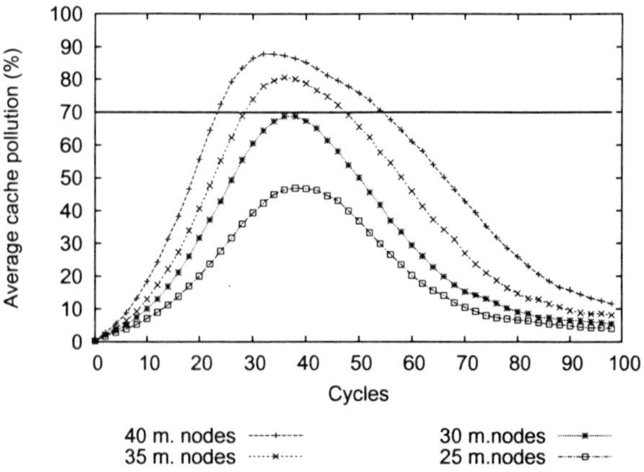

(b) 2 caches, $k > c$ m. nodes

Figure 7. Pollution levels in extreme conditions. In (a), $k = c \cdot n$ attackers are involved; 2, 4 and 8 caches are considered. In (b), the maximum tolerable number of attackers, using 2 caches, is shown.

have implications for counteracting other kinds of infection spreading over networks and this is possible future work. The centralised SPSS achieves better results - i.e., is successful - when the entire node state is polluted ($k = c \cdot n$ attackers, with $n = 1$ in the centralised case). However, the TRUSTED PROMPT manages the node states and we can say it is part of the node state in some sense. Essentially, until the TRUSTED PROMPT is up and running the node's state it is not really completely polluted. In the decentralised approach instead, if the full state - i.e., all the caches - becomes polluted ($k = c \cdot n$ attackers, with $n > 1$ caches) the network is exposed to partitioning if the malicious nodes leave the network; nevertheless, the system does not becomes paralysed, but it can still slowly recover. We have shown an example in which we identify the maximum number of malicious nodes that can be tolerated for a particular n cache set-up.

In essence, these two approaches are two distinct philosophies that privileges distinct aspects. We do not claim that our SPSS is secure against other attack scenarios such as "Sybil attack" variants or more complex collusive attacks. Rather we propose a relatively generic and lightweight solution for plugging the obvious vulnerability of gossip based protocols to simple hub attacks. SPSS therefore has applications for augmenting several proposed protocols that currently rely on unsecured gossip based PSS such as [1, 3, 5, 7].

References

[1] D. Hales and S. Arteconi. Slacer: A self-organizing protocol for coordination in p2p networks. *IEEE Intelligent Systems*, 21(2):29–35, March / April 2006.

[2] D. Hales and B. Edmonds. Applying a socially-inspired technique (tags) to improve cooperation in p2p networks. *IEEE Transactions in Systems, Man and Cybernetics - Part A: Systems and Humans*, 35(3):385–395, 2005.

[3] M. Jelasity and O. Babaoglu. T-Man: Gossip-based Overlay Topology Management. In *ESOA*, volume 3910 of *Lecture Notes in Computer Science*, pages 1–15. Springer, July 2005.

[4] M. Jelasity, W. Kowalczyk, and M. van Steen. Newscast computing. Technical Report IR-CS-006, Vrije Universiteit, Amsterdam, The Netherlands, Nov 2003.

[5] M. Jelasity, A. Montresor, and O. Babaoglu. Gossip-based aggregation in large dynamic networks. *ACM Trans. Comput. Syst.*, 23(1):219–252, 2005.

[6] G. P. Jesi, D. Gavidia, C. Gamage, and M. van Steen. A Secure Peer Sampling Service. UBLCS 2006-17, University of Bologna, Dept. of Computer Science, May 2006.

[7] G. P. Jesi, A. Montresor, and O. Babaoglu. Proximity-aware Superpeer Overlay Topologies. In *SelfMan'06*, volume 3996 of *Lecture Notes in Computer Science*, pages 43–57, Dublin, Ireland, June 2006. Springer.

[8] J. Liang, N. Naoumov, and K. Ross. The Index Poisoning Attack in P2P File Sharing Systems. In *INFOCOM*, Barcelona, Spain, Apr. 2006.

[9] R. Mahajan, M. Castro, and A. Rowstron. Controlling the Cost of Reliability in Peer-to-peer Overlays. In *IPTPS*, volume 2735 of *Lecture Notes in Computer Science*, pages 21–32. Springer, Feb. 2003.

[10] N. Naoumov and K. Ross. Exploiting P2P Systems for DDoS Attacks. In *InfoScale*, page 47, New York, NY, 2006. ACM Press.

[11] S. J. Nielson, S. Crosby, and D. S. Wallach. A Taxonomy of Rational Attacks. In *IPTPS*, volume 3640 of *Lecture Notes in Computer Science*, pages 36–46. Springer, 2005.

[12] A. Rowstron and P. Druschel. Pastry: Scalable, Distributed Object Location and Routing for Large-Scale Peer-to-Peer Systems. In *Middleware*, Nov. 2001.

[13] S. Voulgaris, D. Gavidia, and M. van Steen. CYCLON: Inexpensive Membership Management for Unstructured P2P Overlays. *J. Network Syst. Manage.*, 13(2), 2005.

STORM: A Secure Overlay for P2P Reputation Management

Aina Ravoaja
IRISA
Campus Universitaire de Beaulieu
Rennes, France
aravoaja@irisa.fr

Emmanuelle Anceaume
IRISA
Campus Universitaire de Beaulieu
Rennes France
anceaume@irisa.fr

Abstract

A fundamental problem that confronts decentralized reputation systems is the design of efficient, secure and incentive-compatible mechanisms to gather trust information despite malicious peers, and particularly collusion. This paper presents STORM (for Secure sTructured Overlay for Reputation Management*), a P2P protocol which addresses this issue. STORM provides support for gathering peers reputation information safely by self-organizing peers into clusters of peers of common interests. To mitigate the effect of malicious peers, STORM relies on a randomized decision algorithm aiming at securing the routing table maintenance, and on constrained redundant routing focusing on securing information lookup. We show STORM efficiency and robustness through a formal analysis. Specifically, we prove a lower bound on the number of malicious peers that can be inserted in routing tables and we show that our solution is very close to optimal. Finally, we show that our constrained redundant routing approach succeeds at countering collusive behavior.*

1 Introduction

Enabling e-commerce in decentralized peer-to-peer systems relies on the consumer confidence in online service providers. Reputation systems have been proven effective at encouraging trust among peers that usually do not know each other [14]. They enable consumers to decide whether a future interaction with a target entity is conceivable or not by collecting, aggregating and ranking opinions about the past behavior of that target peer. Establishing trust in decentralized P2P systems is a fundamental problem, essentially because peers are autonomous, rational, and can be strategic. Peers are rational because they wish to maximize their utility (either by taking advantage of the efficiency of the reputation mechanism, or by maximizing their own reputation, or by reducing their contribution in the reputation estimation effort to save their resource). Peers can be strategic because they can devise complex strategies to subvert the system (e.g. they can manipulate the routing tables or intercept requests to subvert the system). This impact can be greatly increased when groups of malicious peers coordinate their actions to achieve a common goal. Collusion of malicious peers may cause severe damages on the whole system online market. By sending unfair opinions about target peers behaviour, they can abusively inflate the reputation of that peers, and push users to be involved in fraudulent transactions. On the other hand, harming competitors' reputation may discourage further interactions with that competitors leading to unfair market. Thus reputation mechanisms must be robust to a variety of severe attacks, coordinated or not.

Motivations. In a prior work [2], we proposed a solution to the robust reputation problem. Essentially this problem aims at evaluating peers reputation despite free-riding and dishonest behaviours. In that work, robustness to attack is accomplished through an aggregation technique in which collected first-hand feedback is weighted by a credibility factor locally computed by the requesting peer, while incentive for participation is implemented through a fair differential service mechanism relying on peers' level of participation and peers' credibility. We showed within modest churn the presence of a high fraction of malicious peers does not prevent a correct peer from accurately evaluating the reputation value of a target peer. However, this is achieved at the expense of a non negligible number of messages mainly due to the way feedback are collected. Indeed, to face malicious peers, feedback is gathered from peers randomly selected within the system which clearly makes the efficiency of this crawling technique highly reliant on the way the graph of witnesses is constructed. Finding the right set of witnesses in an efficient way is a challenging issue since the reputation value depends on the feedback provided by these peers.

Contributions. In the present work, we present a cost effective solution to this problem by relying on two schemes: first, to increase the likelihood of collecting a large amount of feedback from the right set of witnesses, secure gathering techniques are identified. Briefly, these techniques aim at guaranteeing that feedback is collected only from a cluster of peers sharing a similar interest for the target service provider, and that bribes and collusion do not interfere by constraining the gathering scheme. STORM is designed to gather information on the reputation of a peer in $O(\log N)$ steps, with N the number of peers. Complementary to this scheme, secure routing tables maintenance and secure routing techniques are provided. These techniques ensure first that routing tables cannot be attacked by malicious peers by keeping the distribution of malicious peers uniform. This is achieved by a *randomised decision* algorithm, which prevents malicious peers from strategizing to get inserted in routing tables. We show that this algorithm eventually minimises the expected number of malicious peers in routing tables. Second, to prevent malicious peers from dropping or delivering a feedback request to their collusion group instead of a legitimate peer, STORM uses *constrained redundant routing*. This scheme guarantees that each request is successful with high probability if the fraction of colluders in a cluster does not exceed $1 - \left(\frac{1}{2(1-c')^{(\log_2 N)/2}}\right)^{\frac{2}{\log_2 N'}}$, with N the size of the system, N' the size of the cluster, and c', the expected number of malicious peers in routing tables. To summarise, the contribution of this paper is a scalable protocol for efficient and secure information gathering in a system with high churn and presence of colluding peers.

Roadmap. The paper is organised as follows: Section 2 presents related work, Section 3 presents the model and problem definition, Section 4 presents the basic protocol, Section 5 addresses the security issues, and finally, Section 6 concludes. For space reasons pseudo-codes of some procedures and involved proofs of correctness are presented in the full version of the paper [13].

2 Related Work

This section analyses previous work on storage reputation information trustworthily despite collusion and on secure routing. Aberer and Despotovic [1] propose a reputation mechanism in which trust information, actually complaint information, is stored in P-Grid, a distributed hash table-based overlay distributed over the system. Their mechanism is made robust by guaranteeing that trust information is replicated at different peers, and thus can be accessed despite malicious entities. The efficiency of their approach relies on peers propensity to fully cooperate by storing trust information locally and by forwarding requests to feed the P-Grid overlay. Additionally, as for most of the DHT-based approaches, peers have to store data they are not concerned with, and thus for different reasons may discard them. This is to prevent such issue that in STORM, trust information are stored at peers sharing similar interest with such information. Simulations based on P-Grid have shown that even sophisticated metric trust are vulnerable to collusion and worse may render the system less efficient than without these metrics [18]. More generally, Zhang et al. [19] have shown that eigenvector-based reputation systems such as PageRank [11] and HITS [10] are very sensitive to collusion essentially because they rely on the notion of transitive trust which can be easily manipulated. To face this issue, presence of pre-trusted peers [9], hash-function applied on long-lived peers [8], and reciprocative-based incentive techniques [7] are proposed. While these approaches show heir effectiveness against different undesirable scenarios, the former one requires the presence of trusted peers known by all the peers in the system, while the two last one can only tolerate modest churn.

Regarding the secure routing problem, Castro et al. [3] are among the first ones to focus on secure routing. They propose the *redundant routing* approach. Essentially, their technique consists in for each request, to send multiple copies of that request over independent routes so that at least one copy almost surely reaches a legitimate recipient. We extend their approach to cope with colluders by constraining the result of a query, which guarantees to reach the legitimate receipeient with high probability. Sit and Morris [16] take advantage of the fact that distance between the sender and the legitimate destination should decrease at each step of the lookup. By making the sender observe his query progress, he can detect re-routing toward malicious destinations, however their implementation doubles the optimal cost of a lookup.

3 Model and Problem Definition

We adopt the model proposed in [2]. We consider a peer-to-peer system populated with at most N peers. Some peers called *service providers* repeatedly offer the same service to interested peers. The effort exerted by a service provider determines its Quality of Service (QoS). We assume that a server 's effort is the same for all the peers that solicit him and takes its value within the [0,1]. After each interaction with server s, each peer has an imperfect observation of the effort exerted by s. Peers may have different tastes about s QoS, but basically, these observations are closely distributed around s's effort. Estimation of the expected behaviour of a server s is based on its recent past behaviour, that is, its recent interactions with the peers of the system. Every time a peer desires to interact with a service provider s, it asks

0-7695-2906-2/07 $25.00 © 2007 IEEE

for feedback from peers that have recently interacted with s. In the following, a *witness* denotes a peer having interacted with a given service provider.

Some peers try to manipulate the system by exhibiting undesirable behaviours. Such peers are called *malicious*. Malicious peers can drop messages, forward requests to illegitimate peers, send dishonest feedback or no feedback at all. Note that malicious peers are rational, that is, they try to maximise their utility within the system. Thus they follow STORM protocol when it is in their interest to do so. However, they can be strategic, that is, they can elaborate strategies to subvert the system. Malicious peers may act independently or may be part of a *collusion group*. A member of a collusion group is called *colluder*. A peer which always follows STORM protocol is said to be *correct*. We assume that there exists at most a fraction $f(0 \leq f < 1)$ of malicious peers in the whole system. The set of malicious peers is partitioned into independent disjoint collusion groups with size bounded by $cN(1/N \leq c \leq f)$. When $c = f$, all malicious peers collude with each other to cause the most damage to the system [3]. In this work, we do not consider sybil attacks [6], that is peers that pollute the system by creating numerous fake identifiers. We suppose that STORM uses some external technique to counter this problem and leave this issue for future work. We use cryptographic techniques to prevent a malicious peer from observing or modifying a message physically sent between any two correct peers. However a malicious peer has complete control over messages it receives, i.e., it can drop them or forward them to illegitimate peers. Finally, we assume that every peer in the P2P overlay has static IP address at which it can be contacted. Note that P2P overlays can be extended to address dynamic IP addresses [5].

Specification of the Secure Gathering Problem. A reputation mechanism collects, aggregates and rates feedback. Collecting honest feedback in a dynamic environment in which a non null fraction of malicious peers can collectively collude to subvert the system is the problem we address in this work. A solution to this problem should satisfy the following property:

Property 1 (Secure feedback collect). *If a peer p requests w opinions regarding the service provided by s, then p receives w such opinions with high probability, and each one is sent by a correct witness with probability* $1 - f'$. [1]

4 STORM Protocol

STORM is a scalable protocol for efficiently gathering numerous and honest feedback to evaluate the reputation of service providers. The principles that led to STORM are the following ones: first, to increase the likelihood of locating sufficiently enough feedback, all the peers having interacted with a target server (witnesses) should dynamically self-organise into clusters with respect to that target server. In the following, $cluster_s$ denotes the group of peers having interacted with service provider s. Second, to efficiently retrieve these opinions in a large scale system, each such cluster should be reachable in a logarithmic number of hops. Finally, to prevent collusive peers from subverting the gathering scheme (either by re-routing, by dropping feedback, or by flooding the system with dishonest feedback), collusion formation should be prevented. All these tenets have been integrated in STORM and are now presented.

This section describes the STORM protocol, namely, location of service providers and witnesses, insertion of new peers and departures of existing ones. Prior to this description, we recall some background on DHT-based protocols, by focusing on Chord. Indeed, we take advantage of the attractive features of Chord (i.e., its scalable key location and dynamic join and leave operations) to adapt them to the secure gathering problem. Note that other DHT-based protocols such as Pastry [15] or CAN [12] could have been adapted too, however, the choice of Chord was motivated by security considerations as discussed in Section 5.

4.1 Background

4.1.1 DHT-based Protocols

DHT-based protocols [17, 15, 12] provide substrates for the construction of large-scale, decentralised applications. They allow applications to locate an object in a probabilistic bounded small number of hops while requiring per-peer routing tables with only a small number of entries. These protocols are scalable, fault-tolerant and provide effective load balancing. In a structured overlay, peers are assigned unique random identifiers, *nodeIds*, from a large *id space*. Application-specific objects are assigned unique identifiers, called *keys*, selected from the same id space. Each key is mapped by the overlay to a unique peer, called the key's *root*. The routing protocol routes messages with a given key to its associate key's root. To route messages efficiently, each peer maintains a *routing table* with nodeIds of other peers and their associated IP address.

4.1.2 Chord Protocol

In Chord, peers are uniformly assigned nodeIds from a circular m-bits id space through a consistent hashing function, with $m = \log_2 N$, and N the size of the system. Each Chord peer maintains a routing table, called *finger table*, consisting of up to m pointers to other peers. The ith pointer of

[1] f' is explicited in Section 5.

peer (of nodeId) n refers to the peer with the smallest nodeId clockwise from $n + 2^{i-1}$. Each Chord key is mapped to the peer with the closest preceding nodeId to the key. To find a particular key, a request is forwarded in clockwise direction to the peer in the routing table with the closest preceding nodeId to the key. Thus, the expected number of routing hops in Chord is $(\log_2 N)/2$. A newly joining peer p initialises its fingers, and notifies existing peers, which in turn updates their fingers to reflect p's arrival. Chord handles abrupt peers departure through a periodic invocation of a stabilisation protocol which exchanges messages among a small number of peers. A complete description of Chord is presented in [3].

4.2 STORM Overview

As previously said, STORM adapts Chord to gather opinions regarding the service provided by servers. Briefly, the very notions of keys and peers are at the roots of the adaptation we propose. As previously mentioned, Chord assigns keys to peers. That is application resources are physically assigned to peers. In STORM, the notion of cluster of witnesses acts as a substitute for the notion of application resource, while the notion of (physical) peer is replaced by the one of (logical) label or key. Specifically, each cluster $cluster_s$ is assigned as a whole to a *key* which is obtained by hashing the IP address of the service provider s. Keys are ordered on a *key circle* modulo 2^m. Note that m must be large enough to make the probability of two service providers IP addresses hashing to the same key negligible. In the rest of the paper, key circle will refer to the *backbone ring*, and the term "service provider" will refer to both the service provider and its key under the consistent hash function. Let us now focus on clusters structure. A consistent hash function assigns witnesses of a given cluster *identifiers* ordered on a *identifier circle* modulo 2^n.[2] The identifier circle is referred in the following as the *witnesses ring*. Note that a peer may belong to x witnesses rings if it has interacted with x service providers. Figure 1) illustrates the backbone ring on which five witnesses rings W_1, W_2, W_3, W_5, W_6 sit, with W_s the witnesses ring including witnesses having interacted with server s. For clarity purpose, we focus on witnesses ring W_1, W_2, and W_3, and consider only peer p_1's tables. Each witness $p \in W_s$ maintains two tables: a *routing table*, denoted $Routing_p^s$, to maintain the inter-ring connectivity, and a *witnesses table*, denoted $Witnesses_p^s$, to maintain the inner-ring connectivity (both tables are described hereafter). Beyond such tables, each witness stores the opinion it has about the experiences it has had with the given service provider. Note that game theoretic results and empirical studies on eBay show that only recent ratings are meaningful [4]. Thus a witness stores only its latest observations.

Note that in most of the reputation systems based on DHT overlays [9, 1] the opinions of peers are located at remote peers. Specifically, the feedback that peer p has on some target server s is not locally stored at p but rather is owned by some remote peer p' whose location is given by some consistent hash function, for instance by hashing s's Id to a key. Generally, p' has no reason to be interested in the feedback related to s, while the cost incurred by storing such information is not negligible. As a consequence, it may be a clear disincentive to actively and honestly participate to the reputation process. This is the reason why the alternative approach has been adopted in STORM.

4.2.1 Witnesses Table

As aforementioned, witnesses tables ensure the inner connectivity of a witness ring. For scalability reasons, we do not require each witness to know about every other witness in the witnesses ring. Rather, a witness points to only a small number of other witnesses. Thus, similarly to Chord's *finger table*, p's witnesses table contains at most m entries, such that the ith entry points to the first witness p' that succeeds p by 2^{i-1} on the ring (that is p' is the first peer that succeeds $(p + 2^{i-1}) \bmod 2^m$, with $1 \leq i \leq m$). Entry i includes both p''s *identifier* and p''s IP address. Witness p' is indifferently called the ith witness of p, or the ith *succeeding witness* of p. By symmetry, p is a *preceding witness* of p'. From Chord properties, each witness maintains information about only $O(\log N)$ other witnesses, and with high probability the number of witnesses that must be contacted to find a particular witness in a witnesses ring is $O(\log N)$ (Theorem IV.2 of [17]).

4.2.2 Routing Table.

Routing tables ensure the connectivity between the different witnesses rings. As for witnesses rings, only a small amount of routing information can be maintained by each witness. Thus p's routing table contains at most m entries, such that the ith entry refers to the first witnesses ring $\mathcal{W}_{s'}$ that succeeds $\mathcal{W}_s$ by at least 2^{i-1} on the backbone ring. In the sequel $\mathcal{W}_{s'}$ is called the ith successor ring of W_s, or simply a *successor* of W_s. By symmetry, $\mathcal{W}_s$ is a *predecessor* of $\mathcal{W}_{s'}$. From here on, we denote by $E_p[i]$ the ith entry of the routing table of p. Each entry $E_p[i]$ contains a set of witnesses' identifiers associated to their IP address, such that each of those witnesses belongs to $\mathcal{W}_{s'}$. We have $|E_p[i]| \leq d$ for all i, with d an application parameter. Referring to Figure 1, the routing table $Routing_1^2$ of peer p_1 contains 3 entries $E_1[1]$, $E_1[2]$, and $E_1[3]$ referring respectively to W_3, W_5, and W_6. The first entry $E_1[1]$ of $Routing_1^2$ refers to the witnesses ring W_3, and points to

[2] In practice $m = n$ since each witness may potentially be a service provider.

witnesses p_2 and p_5. As will be described in Section 5, this set is introduced first for security reasons (it aims at preventing collusion formation), and second for fault-tolerance considerations. Assuming that each peer fails independently with probability p_f, the probability that all d witnesses fail simultaneously is only p_f^d. Note that d is independent of the size of the system N, and thus the amount of information maintained by a peer in its routing table is in $O(\log N)$. Putting things together, the amount of information needed to maintain both tables is $O(\log N)$.

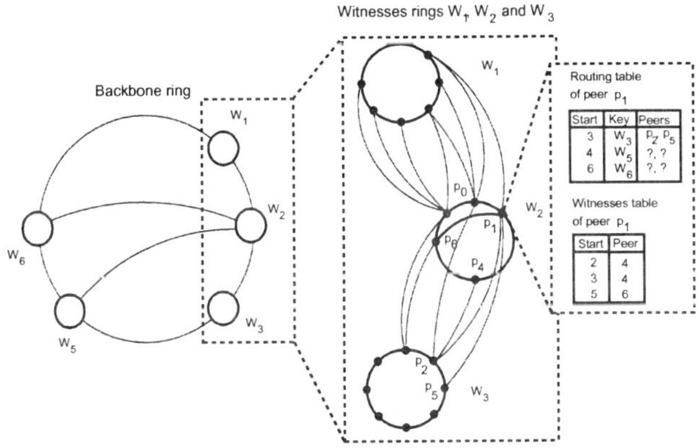

Figure 1. A STORM architecture with $m = 3$ and $d = 2$

4.3 Routing Procedure

We now describe how a witnesses ring is located in S-TORM. Basically, the routing procedure of STORM follows the lines of Chord but applied to witnesses rings. The first difference lies in the fact that unlike in Chord where a finger table entry contains the identifier of a single peer, in STORM a routing table contains a *set* of peers. Then at each hop of a STORM message routing procedure, the next peer is chosen from the relevant routing table entry at random. This random choice is motivated by load balancing and, more importantly, by security considerations (see Section 5.2). The second difference is that a STORM message keeps track of the first encountered peer *pred* that refers to the target witnesses ring. Finding such a peer is useful for the update procedure (Section 4.4), for the secure insertion procedure (Section 5.1), and for the secure routing procedure (Section 5.2).

When a peer p sends a request for the witnesses ring $\mathcal{W}_s$ of service provider s, p executes the `find_witness()` procedure. This procedure returns a tuple (*pred,target*), with *pred* a peer that refers to $\mathcal{W}_s$, and *target* a peer in $\mathcal{W}_s$. `find_witness()` consists of the following steps. If the routing table of p contains a non empty entry $E_p[i]$ (that refers to $\mathcal{W}_s$) then `find_witness()` ends and returns (p, p'), with p' a peer chosen at random from $E_p[i]$. Otherwise, p searches in its routing table for the entry $E_p[i]$ that refers to the witnesses ring $\mathcal{W}_{s'}$ whose key s' most immediately precedes s. Then p picks a random peer p' from $E_p[i]$, which in turn invokes `find_witness()`. Note that if key s of $\mathcal{W}_s$ falls between key s' of $W_{s'}$ and key s'' of the witnesses ring $\mathcal{W}_{s''}$ that immediately succeeds $\mathcal{W}_{s'}$, then it means that $\mathcal{W}_s$ does not exist and `find_witness()` returns (p', *null*).

Locating a witness within the witnesses ring is done exactly as previously, with the difference that witnesses tables contain only one pointer per entry.

As the backbone ring is placed on a Chord-like ring, searching for a witnesses ring costs $O(\log N)$ hops.

```
/* peer p wishes to find W_s                                   */
p.find_witness(s) {
    E_p = entry of p that refers to the closest ring W_s' to W_s;
    p' = choose a random peer from E_p;
    q = p;
    while( s ∉ ]s'; s''] ){
        q = p';
        E_q = entry of p that refers to the closest ring W_s'' to W_s';
        p' = choose a random peer from E_q;
    }
    if( s = s' ){
        result.pred = q;
        result.target = p';
    }else{
        result.pred = p';
        result.target = null;
    }
    return result;
}
```

Algorithm 1: Routing procedure

4.4 Handling Witnesses Arrivals and Removals

This section presents how new witnesses are inserted on the STORM rings, and how departures (voluntary or not) of existing witnesses are handled.

4.4.1 Insertion Operation

When an interaction between service provider s and peer p is completed, peer p may want to join STORM as witness to actively participate to the estimation of server s's reputation. In the sequel, we assume that p knows at least one peer already inserted in STORM. A bootstrap peer can be obtained using for example a set of dedicated servers. Peer p issues an insertion request to the bootstrap peer in order to be inserted in $\mathcal{W}_s$ (invocation of a "join" procedure). The "join" procedure first locates the witnesses ring $\mathcal{W}_s$ on the backbone ring using the `find_witness()` procedure described hereabove. As previously explained, this procedure returns a tuple (*pred*, *target*), with *pred* a member of a witnesses ring $\mathcal{W}_{s'}$ that points to $target$, with $target \in \mathcal{W}_s$. Two cases have to be considered:

case a) $target = null$, **i.e.,** $\mathcal{W}_s$ **does not exist**. In that case, $\mathcal{W}_s$ has to be created and this creation has to be reflected in all the witnesses rings that precede $\mathcal{W}_s$ on the backbone ring. Creation of $\mathcal{W}_s$ is done by initialising p's routing table (by successively contacting the successors of *preds*). p's witness table is not initialised at this stage since p is the only member of $\mathcal{W}_s$.

Creation of $\mathcal{W}_s$ is reflected in the other routing tables by invoking a procedure which updates the routing tables of peers concerned in p's arrival. Briefly, this procedure consists in contacting all the witnesses belonging to all the witnesses rings $\mathcal{W}_{s'}$ that precede $\mathcal{W}_s$. Each witness p' in $\mathcal{W}_{s'}$ inserts $\mathcal{W}_s$ as a new entry i in its routing table, and makes this entry point to p, i.e., $E_{p'}[i] = p$. Note that this costly procedure is applied only at the creation of a witnesses ring. Once a witnesses ring exists, the insertion of a new witness in that ring is reflected in at most one routing table entry (see below). Note also that once a witness has been inserted in a witnesses ring, his next interactions with the same service provider are transparent for STORM: feedback is locally updated if necessary, but no insertion operation has to be invoked as long as he does not leave that witnesses ring. Malicious peers may try to be inserted several times in the same witnesses ring to subvert the system, however the insertion procedure guarantees that once a peer exists in the ring it cannot be inserted a second time.

case b) $target \neq null$, **i.e.,** $\mathcal{W}_s$ **exists**. In that case, p's insertion in $\mathcal{W}_s$ needs to be reflected at some of the members of $\mathcal{W}_s$ and to be possibly incorporated in *pred*'s routing table. Specifically, p's insertion is achieved by first locating his position on $\mathcal{W}_s$, and then by asking p's preceding witnesses to update their witnesses tables to incorporate p as witness (recall that witness p' precedes p if it exists i such that p is the first peer that succeeds $(p' + 2^{i-1}) \bmod 2^m$, with $1 \leq i \leq m$). Then p initialises his own witnesses table by successively contacting its succeeding witnesses. This procedure follows the lines of the "join" procedure of Chord.

On the other hand, and contrary to case a) only one routing table is susceptible to incorporate p's identifier. This routing table is *pred*'s one, and p's incorporation is conditioned by the sequence of insertion requests previously received by *pred*. Indeed, by constraining peers' insertion in routing tables, we prevent malicious peers from devising strategies (collective or not) to infect routing tables entries. Consequently we decrease the likelihood that such peers get control over both the witnesses ring they point to (and thus the danger that they illegitimately reply to requests addressed to other members of those witnesses rings), and the backbone ring (and thus the risk that they intercept requests they should forward). The *randomised decision* algorithm responsible for that insertion is presented in Section 5.

4.4.2 Departure and Failure Operation

By construction STORM does not impose any constraints on feedback availability. Indeed, since witnesses are responsible for their own feedback, feedback of failed left witnesses does not have to be kept by other peers. Thus, the only property that needs to be maintained by STORM is to guarantee that peers' departure (volunteer or not) does not compromise connectivity on the backbone and within witnesses rings. Regarding connectivity among the witnesses rings, each peer periodically sends alive messages to each of his successors of his routing table. If a peer notices that one of his successors has left then it removes him from his routing table. Recall that each routing table entry contains up to d witnesses pointing to a same witnesses ring, and thus up to d concurrent failures have to occur to damage witnesses rings inter-connectivity, and this case happens only with probability p_f^d. Regarding connectivity within witnesses rings, we adopt the solution proposed in Chord. Their solution consists in maintaining at each witness p a successor list containing p's b immediate successor. If a p's immediate successor does not respond, p can substitute the second entry in its successor list. As for routing tables entries, up to b concurrent failures have to occur to damage connectivity within witnesses rings, which happens with only a probability p_f^b.

5 Security Issues

In this section we focus on the security aspects of STORM. We argue that DHT-based overlay for reputation systems should satisfy the following two properties:

- Routing tables should be insensitive to collusion. That is, if before a table update procedure the probability that a link points to a malicious peer is f', then after the update this probability should not exceed f'.
- Routing should be efficient. That is, a request should reach a legitimate destination (i.e. should neither be dropped, nor derouted) with high probability.

Probability f' corresponds to the maximal fraction of malicious peers that can be inserted in a witnesses ring that is $f\frac{N}{|\mathcal{W}_s|} < f'$ for all service providers s.

In the sequel we propose strategies that enjoy both properties, and show that their combination allow to build a secure feedback gathering procedure.

Before describing our contribution regarding secure routing table maintenance and secure routing, we present arguments which guarantee that peers cannot choose their own identifiers or identifiers of other peers. These arguments are very similar to Castro et al's ones [3]. First, by safely assigning keys and identifiers through a trusted Certification Authority (CA) (central or installed as part of the peer software itself), peers cannot practically forge a key or an identifier. Second, from the consistent hash function property, keys and identifiers are distributed uniformly at random over the backbone ring and over each witnesses ring. Moreover, as keys and identifiers are assigned through a cryptographic hash function, malicious peers can arduously know which IP address has generated a particular key or identifier. Thus, they cannot target a particular point on the key or identifier space. Finally, from Chord properties, strong constraints on the keys and identifiers positions on the rings are imposed, i.e., a peer has to be the closest to some fixed point on the ring. Thus a peer cannot manipulate the system to be inserted close to a target peer, this target being either another malicious peer to form a collusion, or a correct peer harmed by the manipulating peer.

5.1 Secure Insertion in Routing Tables

The aforementioned arguments are sufficient to prevent malicious peers from choosing their position in witnesses rings. However they cannot prevent them from choosing the witnesses ring in which they will be inserted. Indeed, the only condition required to be inserted in a witnesses ring $\mathcal{W}_s$ is to claim a recent interaction with service provider s. On the other hand, additional mechanisms can be designed to prevent malicious peers from devising strategies (collective or not) to infect routing tables entries. We address this issue by randomising the insertion process. Intuitively, colluders can more easily draw a successful adversarial strategy from a deterministic algorithm than from a randomised one. For example, colluders may easily subvert a First-In-First-Out (FIFO) insertion algorithm by executing periodic rapid-fire insertion requests. In contrast, a colluder can hardly make up a successful strategy if the inserted peers are chosen randomly among the requesting peers. We show that regardless of the adversarial strategy colluders employ, the randomised decision algorithm we propose guarantees that the expected number of colluders in each routing table is eventually minimal.

Specifically, suppose that among a sequence of t insertion requests, colluders can send at most x requests, with $x < t$, and that colluders can strategize on the order of these requests. For instance, they can send all the x insertion requests at the beginning of the sequence, or they can spread the x requests over the whole sequence. Note that $x/t \leq f'$. Our algorithm guarantess that the expected number of malicious peers inserted in a routing table entry is at most $(x/t)d$. For $t = 30$, $x = 10$, and $d = 10$, if a FIFO insertion policy were used, colluders would be able to infect 100% of the peers in the routing table entry by sending rapid-fire insertion requests. Using our randomized algorithm, only 33% of these peers would be malicious. Note that to prevent a malicious peer p already inserted in a witnesses ring $\mathcal{W}_s$ to send new insertion requests in order to infect the routing table of a peer *pred* that refers to $\mathcal{W}_s$, *pred* checks whether p is not already in $\mathcal{W}_s$ before executing the randomized insertion algorithm.

In the following, an insertion request originating from a colluder is called a *malicious insertion request*. Now, let p be a peer issuing a insertion request to be in $\mathcal{W}_s$. Let *pred* be the peer belonging to $\mathcal{W}_{s'}$ such that $\mathcal{W}_{s'}$ precedes $\mathcal{W}_s$, and such that the ith routing table entry of *pred*, $E_{pred}[i]$, contains up to d witnesses belonging to $\mathcal{W}_s$. Finally, let *transit*$_i$ be a list containing the identifiers of the t last peers that have solicited *pred* to be inserted in $\mathcal{W}_s$. Upon receipt of p's insertion request, *pred* runs the *randomised decision* algorithm which consists of the following five steps:

1. if *transit*$_i$ is full, remove the oldest peer from it,
2. insert p in *transit*$_i$,
3. pick at random a peer p' from *transit*$_i$,
4. if $E_{pred}[i]$ is full then drop a random a peer from $E_{pred}[i]$,
5. insert peer p' in $E_{pred}[i]$.

Recall that this algorithm is executed only if $\mathcal{W}_s$ exists (see Section 4.4). Before showing that this algorithm guarantees that the expected number of malicious peers is eventually equal to $(x/t)d$, we first show that the algorithm is vulnerable to malicious peers during the STORM creation. By construction, the first i, with $i < t$, peers issuing an insertion request are inserted in $E_{pred}[i]$ with probability $1/i$. After that, the probability of insertion of a peer in $E_{pred}[i]$ is always equal to $1/t$. Clearly, as colluders generally try to maximize the probability of being inserted in a routing table entry, the t first insertions constitute the most vulnerable phase of the randomized decision algorithm. Note that a possible alternative would be to wait for the t first insertion requests before inserting the first peer in $E_{pred}[i]$. The drawback of this strategy would be to prevent requesting peers from getting any feedback for service provider s during this initial period of time. While this vulnerability exists, the routing table entry is eventually "cleaned up" by our randomized algorithm as now demonstrated.

Analysis. In the following we show first that the expected number of malicious peers in each routing table is eventually at most equal to $(x/t)d$ (Theorem 1), and second that for any randomized algorithm, there exists adversarial strategies for which the expected number of malicious peers is equal to $(x/t)d$ (Theorem 2).

Theorem 1. *Using the randomized decision algorithm, the expected number of malicious peers in a routing table entry is eventually at most equal to* $(x/t)d$.

Theorem 2. *For any randomized algorithm, there exists a sequence of* t *insertions such that the expected number of malicious peers in a routing table entry is at least* $(x/t)d$.

The randomized decision algorithm eventually bounds the expected number of malicious peers in each routing table entry to $(x/t)d$, which is the best result that can be achieved. Note however that this mechanism cannot be used to minimize the number of malicious peers in witnesses tables. Indeed, by excluding some peers from witnesses tables, their potential feedback would not be available, which would degrade the efficiency of the reputation estimation.

5.2 Secure Routing

The previously described randomized decision algorithm prevents the formation of collusion. Even if this schema limits the likelihood of requests being dropped or being routed toward undesirable peers, current structured p2p overlays provide best-effort routing. The probability of reaching a legitimate recipient is small for the simple reason that only one malicious peer on the path is sufficient to prevent a request from being delivered to its destination. To illustrate this problem, consider a system of N peers and a target witnesses ring $\mathcal{W}_s$ of size $N' \leq N$. By assumption the fraction of malicious peer in $\mathcal{W}_s$ and thus in each witnesses table is at most f'. We have shown (see Theorem 2) that regardless of the adverserial strategy, the expected number of malicious peers in each entry of each routing table is equal to $(x/t)d$ which is the best result that can be achieved. From the routing procedure (Section 4.3), the peer at which a request received by peer q is forwarded is chosen at random from the appropriate entry of q's routing table. Thus the probability of choosing a malicious peer at each hop is equal to $c' = x/t$. Moreover, the expected number of hops needed to reach $\mathcal{W}_s$ is equal to $(\log_2 N)/2$ and the maximum expected number of hops needed to reach a target peer in $\mathcal{W}_s$ is equal to $(\log_2 N')/2$. Therefore from above, the probability that a request reaches a legitimate destination is given by the following equation:

$$(1-c')^{(\log_2 N)/2}(1-f')^{(\log_2 N')/2}.$$

Note that this legitimate destination is correct with probability $1-f'$. Figure 2 illustrates this result by plotting the probability of a successful request for different ratio of malicious peers with $N = 100,000$ and $c' = 0.01$. For example, for $N' = 1,000$ we see that 0.08% of malicious peers (that is 80 malicious peers) in $\mathcal{W}_s$ makes the probability of success of a request for $\mathcal{W}_s$ drop to 60%.

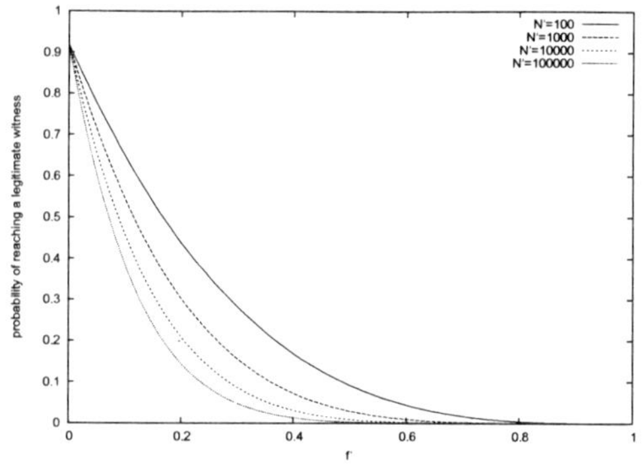

Figure 2. Probability of success of a request with respect to the fraction of malicious peers in $\mathcal{W}_s$ for $N = 1,000,000$ and $c' = 0.01$.

To improve the probability of reaching a legitimate destination, Castro et al. [3] propose the *redundant routing* approach. Essentially, for each request, multiple copies of that request are sent over independent routes so that at least one copy almost surely reaches a legitimate recipient. To cope with colluders in $\mathcal{W}_s$ and malicious peers in routing tables, we extend their approach to *constrained redundant routing*. Our approach consists in constraining the result of a request. In our case the constraint concerns the identifier of a witness. Specifically, consider a peer p that wishes to find w witness identifiers in $\mathcal{W}_s$. Then p executes the *constrained redundant routing* algorithm which consists of the following four steps:

1. generate w random numbers n_k, $k = 1 \ldots w$ from 0 to $2^m - 1$;
2. send r copies of the feedback request for $\mathcal{W}_s$ over r independent routes;
3. when a peer *pred* having an entry $E_{pred}[i]$ referring to $\mathcal{W}_s$ receives a feedback request copy, he asks all the d witnesses in $E_{pred}[i]$ to find the closest witness to each n_k, $k = 1 \ldots w$;
4. p waits until timer expires;
5. the final result of the feedback request is the w identifiers of the witnesses that have been returned the most often.

The constraint is expressed by Step 3 of the algorithm. With such a constraint, a requester can evaluate the validity of the result and can choose the appropriate one (Step 5). Such an evaluation would be impossible if peers could return arbitrary witnesses identifiers in $\mathcal{W}_s$.

Note that generating w random keys from 0 to $2^m - 1$ and asking for the closest peers to these keys can be interpreted as choosing w peers in the witnesses ring (approximately) randomly. Thus the probability that the closest peer w_k to n_k is correct is $1 - f'$.

By independent routes, we mean that routes are independently *chosen*. Thus sending multiple copies of a request over independent routes can be viewed as making multiple random walks on the set of possible paths starting from the requester to the destination. Recall that a routing table entry may contain up to d identifiers, and that at each hop of a request the subsequent peer is chosen from the appropriate routing table entry at random (see Section 4.3). Thus sending r copies of a request over independent routes simply consists in sending r request messages simultaneously.

Sending each copy of a request to the d peers in each routing table entry that refers to $\mathcal{W}_s$ is motivated by the fact that colluders are more likely to be present in $\mathcal{W}_s$ than in routing tables ($c' \leq f'$). It can be interpreted as checking many possible routes to the w target witnesses to increase the chance to reach them.

Analysis. We now show that if the fraction of malicious peers $f' < 1 - \left(\frac{1}{2(1-c')^{(\log_2 N)/2}}\right)^{\frac{2}{\log_2 N'}}$ in $\mathcal{W}_s$, then for each key n_k, the most often returned witness w_k is the legitimate destination. Such a request is called a *successful* request. To show this result, we consider that all malicious peers in $\mathcal{W}_s$ collude altogether by claiming that for each key n_k, w'_k is the legitimate destination with $w'_k \neq w_k$.

Theorem 3. *If* $f' < 1 - \left(\frac{1}{2(1-c')^{(\log_2 N)/2}}\right)^{\frac{2}{\log_2 N'}}$, *then by setting r and d to large enough values, with high probability a request is successful.*

Table 1 gives some numerical values of the maximum number of colluders that the constrained redundant routing algorithm can handle with respect to the size of $\mathcal{W}_s$ and for $N = 1,000,000$ and $c' = 0.01$.

Size of $\mathcal{W}_s$	Maximum size of a collusion group
100	16
1,000	115
10,000	876
1,000,000	7078

Table 1. Maximum tolerated size of a collusion group

Now, for more practical considerations, we seek to determine the probability that a request is satisfied with respect to r and d. From the previous analysis, we observe that the number of copies of a request that reaches a legitimate destination follows a binomial law of parameters p_s and r, with $p_s = (1 - c')^{(\log_2 N)/2}(1 - f')^{(\log_2 N')/2}$. Then, the probability of success of a request is given by the following equation:

$$\sum_{k>r/2}^{r} \binom{r}{k} p_s^k (1 - p_s)^{r-k}.$$

As illustrated by Figure 3, for $N = 100,000$, $N' = 1,000$, and $c' = 0.01$, with 0.08% of colluders (80 colluders), and for $r = 5$ and $d = 10$, the probability of success of a request increases to 94%.

The expected total number of messages for a constrained redundant routing is $r\,((\log_2 N + wd\log_2 N')/2)$. Since $N' \leq N$ and r, d, and w are fixed, the complexity of the constrained redundant routing algorithm is still $O(\log N)$.

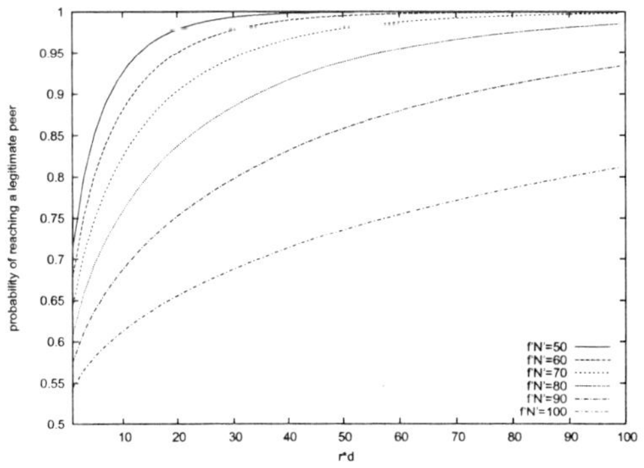

Figure 3. Probability of success of a request with respect to the number r of copies for each request.

5.3 Gathering Feedback

We can finally describe how opinions are gathered from a set of witnesses. When a peer p wishes to get w opinions regarding service provider say s, p invokes a "query" function to locate $\mathcal{W}_s$. In case no witness have ever interacted with s, this procedure returns a null pointer. Otherwise, p gets back w opinions about s. The approach simply consists in executing the secure routing procedure described in Section 5.2 to get w identifiers of witnesses. Then, p directly contacts each witness and requests their recent feedback about s.

Since this procedure returns w witnesses of s with high probability (Section 5.2), and since w are chosen at random from $\mathcal{W}_s$ (Section 5.2) and thus is correct with probability $1 - f'$ by assumption, Property 1 of the Secure Feedback Collect is satisfied.

6 Conclusions

We have presented STORM, a scalable protocol for efficient and secure information gathering in a system which high churn and collusive peers. Efficiency comes from two ingredients: The first one is self-organization. By making peers to be adjacent to other peers sharing the same interest, we increase the likelihood of finding relevant information within a small number of number of steps. The second one is Distributed Hash Tables (DHT)-based overlay. By taking advantage of the attractive features of these systems semantic clusters are located in a logarithmic number of hops and high churn is faced through simple and fast leave and join operations. Secure information gathering techniques are proposed. These techniques guarantee that feedback is collected from the legitimate cluster, and bribes and collusion do not interfere the gathering, without having to discover who the undesirable peers are.

7 Acknowledgments

We thank the anonymous reviewers for their useful comments that helped improve the paper. This work is partially supported by a grant from brittany region convention # 1306, and the ANR RIAM-011 03 "Solipsis".

References

[1] K. Aberer and Z. Despotovic. Managing trust in a peer-to-peer information system. In *Proceedings of the 10th International ACM Conference on Information and Knowledge Management (CIKM)*, 2001.

[2] E. Anceaume and A. Ravoaja. Incentive-based robust reputation mechanism for p2p services. In *Proceedings of the 10th International Conference On Principles Of Distributed Systems*. LNCS 4305, 2006.

[3] M. Castro, P. Druschel, A. Ganesh, A. Rowstron, and D. S. Wallach. Secure routing for structured peer-to-peer overlay networks. In *Proceedings of the 5th Symposium on Operating Systems Design and Implementation*, 2002.

[4] C. Dellarocas. How often should reputation mechanisms update a trader's reputation profile. *Information Systems Research*, 2006.

[5] P. Dewan and P. Dasgupta. Pride: Peer-to-peer reputation infrastructure for decentralized environments. In *Proceedings of the 13th international World Wide Web conference on Alternate track papers and posters*, 2004.

[6] J. Douceur. The sybil attack. In *Proceedings of the 1st International Workshop on Peer-to-Peer Systems (IPTPS)*, 2002.

[7] M. Feldman, K. Lai, I. Stoica, and J. Chuang. Robust incentive techniques for peer-tto-peer networks. In *Proceedings of the ACM Conference on Electronic Commerce (EC)*, 2004.

[8] D. Grolimund, L. Meisser, S. Schmid, and R. Wattenhofer. Havelaar: A robust and efficient reputation system for active peer-to-peer systems. In *Proceedings of the First Workshop on the Economics of Networked Systems (NetEcon)*, 2006.

[9] S. Kamvar, M. Schlosser, and H. Garcia-Molina. The eigentrust algorithm for reputation management in p2p networks. In *Proceedings of the 12th International Conference on World Wide Web (WWW)*, 2003.

[10] J. Kleinberg. Authoritative sources in a hyperlinked environment. In *Proceedings of the 9th Annual ACM-SIAM Symposium on Discrete Algorithms*, 1999.

[11] L. Page, S. Brin, R. Motwani, and T. Winograd. The pagerank citation ranking: Bringing order to the web. Technical report, Stanford Digital Library Technologies Project, 1998.

[12] S. Ratnasamy, P. Francis, M. Handley, R. Karp, and S. Shenker. A scalable content-addressable network. In *Proceedinds of the Conference on Applications, Technologies, Architectures, and Protocols for Computer Communications*, 2001.

[13] A. Ravoaja and E. Anceaume. Storm: A secure overlay for p2p reputation management. Technical Report 1844, IRISA, 2007.

[14] P. Resnick, R. Zeckhauser, J. Swanson, and K. Lockwood. The value of reputation on ebay: A controlled experiment. *Experimental Economics*, 2006.

[15] A. Rowstron and P. Druschel. Pastry: Scalable, distributed object location and routing for large-scale peer-to-peer systems. In *Proceeding of the International Conference on Distributed Systems Platforms (Middleware)*, 2001.

[16] E. Sit and R. Morris. Security considerations for peer-to-peer distributed hash tables. In *Proceedings of the First Int'l Workshop on Peer-to-Peer Systems (IPTPS)*, 2002.

[17] I. Stoica, D. Liben-Nowell, R. Morris, D. Karger, F. Dabek, M. F. Kaashoek, and H. Balakrishnan. Chord: A scalable peer-to-peer lookup service for internet applications. 11(1), 2003.

[18] L. Xiong and L. Liu. Peertrust: Supporting reputation-based trust in peer-to-peer communities. *IEEE Transactions on Knowledge and Data Engineering (TKDE)*, 2004.

[19] H. Zhang, A. Goel, R. Govindan, K. Mason, B. V. Roy, and L. Stefano. Making eigenvector-based reputation systems robust to collusion. *Lecture notes in computer science*, 2004.

e-SAFE: An Extensible, Secure and Fault Tolerant Storage System

Sandip Agarwala, Arnab Paul[†], Umakishore Ramachandran, Karsten Schwan
College of Computing, Georgia Tech, Atlanta, GA, {sandip, rama, schwan}@cc.gatech.edu
[†] Intel Corporation, Portland, OR, Arnab.Paul@intel.com

Abstract

This paper describes e-SAFE , a scalable utility-driven distributed storage system that offers very high availability at an archival scale and reduces management overhead such as periodic repairs. e-SAFE is designed to provide a storage utility for environments such as large-scale data centers in enterprise networks where the servers experience temporary unavailability (possibly high load, temporary downtimes due to repair or software/hardware upgrades). e-SAFE is based on a simple principle: efficiently sprinkle data all over a distributed storage and robustly reconstruct even when many of them are unavailable. e-SAFE also provides strong guarantee on data-integrity.

The use of Fountain codes for replicating file data blocks, an efficient algorithm for fast parallel encoding and decoding over multiple file segments, a utility module for service differentiation and auto-adjustments of design parameters, and a background replication mechanism hiding the cost of replication and dissemination from the user, provide a fast, durable and autonomous storage solution.

1 Introduction

In the context of a large scale distributed storage, we ask the question - *How to design a storage architecture that is robust, scalable, extensible, highly available and that delivers high performance*? The main motivation behind our query is storage technology's perceivable shift from centrally managed data servers to distributed units. Consider an organization such as a corporate house or a university that has a large set of machines; the collected capacity of their local disk-spaces far exceeds those of the typical file servers dedicated to host data for them. The key problems encountered in building a massively distributed storage are the following. (*i*) Increasing management overhead: it is increasingly becoming evident that the cost of management will strictly dominate that of the hardware. Thus the new paradigm is geared toward reducing cost of ownership of data [11].

(*ii*) Difficulty of extending the storage network: Terabyte and petabyte storage units are becoming common; but the existing applications can benefit a lot if newer storage modules can be seamlessly integrated with the existing modules. However, it is not a simple exercise always, especially for fault tolerant storage where data is striped across multiple units [5].

(*iii*) Performance cost: Robustness comes with increased latency overhead for accessing and processing redundant information. Moreover, typically in many complicated applications, servers are often loaded to serve too many requests thereby adding extra latency to the information access.

In this paper, we describe *e*-SAFE , a robust storage system that is tailored to the address the above issues. We focus on a very large scale storage system that is quite common in large organizations. Such hardware infrastructures typically grow very fast in size, are bound to work under very high loads and are required to provide high availability to the data that is stored within. The intent behind *e*-SAFE 's design is to build a more distributed and less-managed system that still provides equal service guarantees. Consequently our design goals differ substantially from a P2P like file sharing system.

e-SAFE achieves the above goals with the help of the following key design-ingredients: (*i*) Use of a special class of erasure codes called the *Fountain codes* that help us efficiently adjust *on-the-fly* the striping and distribution of data. Their encoding and decoding is very fast and they facilitate seamless extensibility. Fountain codes help in efficiently replicating and sprinkling data blocks all over a distributed storage. We don't need to care about failing units and response delays. The scheme provides high availability and load resilience. Additionally, management overhead is reduced because system administrators do not need to worry about missing data or overload conditions. (*ii*) Task parallelization over multiple file segments that can take advantage of parallel processing hardwares, (*iii*) A *background* dissemination mechanism that exploits lazy intervals between I/O bursts to disburse replicated information, hiding the cost of replication and dissemination from the user. (*iv*) To safeguard against potential corruption of data (due to

0-7695-2906-2/07 $25.00 © 2007 IEEE

partial hardware or software failures), *e*-SAFE uses a data structure called Merkle Tree for assurance of data integrity.

Several systems in the space of distributed fault tolerant storage have been reported in the literature. However, the prior art either belongs to the domain of Peer-to-Peer systems (where nodes join and leave in a regular basis) or to the design of distributed yet dedicated storage servers. In the advent of technologies such as the grid or the Internet based SAN, there is a need to focus on solutions that can enable (non-transient) desktops or clusters to participate in providing a large scale data store. We take this latter approach in the design of *e*-SAFE . The contributions of this paper are the following. First, we make the connection between availability and load resilience (detailed in section 3) that leads us to build a high-performance storage system out of commonly available desktops or cluster machines instead of dedicated data servers. Several practical obstacles arise in the implementation-path; *e*-SAFE overcomes those through the use of theoretical tools such as the fountain codes and Merkle tree and some systems optimizations such as parallel processing and background data dissemination.

The rest of the paper is organized as follows. In section 2, we present the motivation behind our work and the challenges we face. The next section presents the overview of *e*-SAFE and the rationale behind its design. In section 4 we describe the main architectural components of *e*-SAFE followed by a short discussion on its implementation in section 5. Section 6 presents the evaluation of *e*-SAFE . We discuss the related work in section 7 and also compare *e*-SAFE with similar systems solutions. Finally we conclude in section 8.

2 Motivation and Challenges

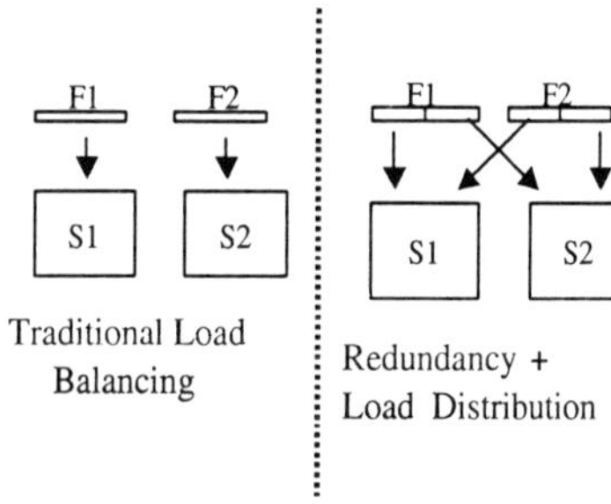

Figure 1: Load balancing vs. Distribution: S1 and S2 are *set* of servers. When most servers in S1 go down, file 1 becomes completely unavailable. However, if both files are split across S1 and S2, absence of no single set can make the files unavailable.

Load, Availability and Distribution

Large scale data servers typically serve hundreds of clients simultaneously; thus, although such systems enjoy abundance of disk-space, the units have to serve under very heavy work-loads at recurring intervals, which calls for revisiting availability of data under high load conditions. The higher the load on a server, longer is the response time. For a client issuing a `read` request therefore, data becomes practically unavailable if it is not retrieved within a threshold latency period. Thus, a high work-load condition, which is often the case in data intensive application domains, resembles a *low availability* scenario. Standard load balancing strategies, when applied to data storage would skew the data distribution in an unfavorable way. Figure 1 shows how load balancing can skew the data distribution. Hence intuitively stretching the files across servers seem to be a better alternative. If the degree of distribution is high with a high stretch factor [1], then even at the face of a very high workload that renders most of the servers *unavailable*, a client can read data with a reasonably low latency. In section 3, we shall discuss quantitatively the effect of redundancy on the load balancing.

Hazards of Fragmentation

It is well understood that fragmenting data over multiple servers provides higher availability [25, 6, 8, 1]. Under a given error rate, it can be shown that the lifetime of data (the time after which retrieval becomes *almost impossible* due to errors creeping in the storage systems) increases rapidly with the number of encoded fragments. However, higher the fragmentation, bigger is the potential for data corruption (security threats from agents that not only cause fail-stop behavior, but can maliciously alter the information which may go undetected unless otherwise safeguarded.) Corruption can also be caused by software faults; for example when the hardware or operating systems are upgraded in massively distributed systems, small patches of invisible incompatibility factors (such as a deprecated driver) may introduce wrong reads or writes, resulting in *malicious like* faults. Such experiences have been reported in recent literature such as the Google File System [13].

A standard way to safeguard against such malicious failures is to attach a fingerprint vector [20, 15, 14]. Alon *et al.* observed how such schemes can result into prohibitive space blow up under a very high failure rate [3]. Intuitively, as the fragmentation increases, for a given file, the fragments become shorter while the fingerprint-vector grows larger, and thus verification information starts dominating over the actual information.

For example, if a file of size 100 KB is split across 100 servers designed to tolerate $t = 50$ faults using some standard optimal erasure handling techniques such as Reed-Solomon codes, one can derive that for every 2 KB of original information, there will be 2KB of additional verification

[1] stretch factor s is defined as the factor of redundancy, *i.e.*, , a file of size f, after adding redundancy bytes $s.f$ bytes long.

information [3]. These numbers get unfavorably biased towards this overhead as n grows larger.

The designer of a large scale storage system thus confronts the following tension: On one hand, the continuous growth of hardware infrastructures, the understanding of the probability of *availability* and the possibility of parallelizing data processing and dissemination, all hint at fragmenting data over as many servers. On the other hand, the associated performance cost of reaching out for too many pieces and the resulting growth in verification information hint at limiting the number of encoded pieces. *e*-SAFE is designed to strike a balance; while *e*-SAFE can *efficiently* take advantage of as many storage units as possible in a seamless manner by the use of modern rate-less erasure codes, at the same time, the overhead of verification information is limited to a logarithmic blow-up factor by novel use of a data-structure known as the Merkle-Tree.

3 System Overview

3.1 Design Overview

To the user, *e*-SAFE offers a file system interface just like NFS. Underneath is a distributed storage system. Figure 2 depicts the broad design of *e*-SAFE . A small set of machines (denoted as the Directory Server) serve as the meta-data server for the documents. We assume that this set is highly secure and reliable and data stored in there is modifiable only by authorized access. Since this is a very small set, we believe these assumptions are not very restrictive from security management point of view. Underneath the directory server, a host of machines constitute the distributed block store. These machines can be distributed, from the span of a single building to the scale of geographically scattered locations. They are potentially fault prone. While locating a file, a file-system user locates the path of the file from the directory server, which provides with the file-metadata (*viz.*, inode) that contains information about the distribution of the actual data blocks over the block-store.

Documents are encoded using a class of rate-less erasure codes (called the Fountain codes). The output of the encoding, a sequence of small blocks, is sprinkled across multiple storage units. We discuss in section 3.2 why it is important for us to have a large and flexible stretch factor. The idea is that even if some of the pieces are corrupted, there is no need to spend any maintenance effort for recovery purposes.

We assume that the meta-data information for every document (such as an *inode*) is stored in a machine that is highly secure, *i.e.*, unauthorized modifications are not possible. We kept document encryption and key management outside *e*-SAFE . However, any traditional encryption mechanism can be integrated within the structure of *e*-SAFE without any compatibility issue. While we decided to keep the confidentiality issue outside our design goal, checks for data integrity are quite stringent.

3.2 Design Rationale

We investigate the question: *What does availability mean in the context of a distributed set of servers?* In a P2P setting, availability may simply mean the percentage of time a server is up. However, in a non-transient context, this definition is not appropriate. A good way to express the availability of a server is through the load. The availability index can be expressed as:

$$Availability\ Index = \frac{optimal\ response\ time}{real\ response\ time}$$

Once the above index is less than a threshold Av_{min} the system may be considered *unavailable* from a client's point view. Thus the availability (ϕ) can also be expressed as the probability :

$$\phi = Prob(Availability\ Index > Av_{min})$$

e-SAFE is targeted for very large files for which redundancy using replication becomes very expensive. As already discussed in section 1, we used Fountain codes. The unique property that such codes offer is a complete flexibility of how much a file can be stretched. Suppose a file segment is coded in the $n : k$ ratio, i.e., k blocks are encoded into n blocks, then, ideally one could reconstruct the original segment from any k blocks. Thus, given an average availability ϕ for each block, the net probability that the segment can be retrieved is equal to the probability that any k or more blocks be available. Thus the expression is straightforward:

$$P(av) = \sum_{j=k+1}^{n} \Big)\!\binom{n}{j}\Big)\phi^{j}(1 \geq \phi)^{(n* j)}$$

Simplifying the above equation, Bhagwan *et al.* [7] derived a direct expression for the stretch factor $c = \frac{n}{k}$,

$$c = \left(\frac{\phi\sqrt{\frac{\mu(1*\mu)}{k}} + \sqrt{\frac{\mu^2\mu(1*\mu)}{k}} + 4\phi}{2\phi} \right)^2$$

Figure 3 shows how the required stretch factor varies as a function of k, the number of pre-encoding blocks, keeping the availability (ϕ) constant. We show two cases for $\phi = 0.1$ and $\phi = 0.2$. It turns out that there is a sharp decrease in required c, as k goes beyond a particular threshold. And after the sharp fall, the curves flatten out, as if increasing pre-encoding fragments does not entail further stretching.

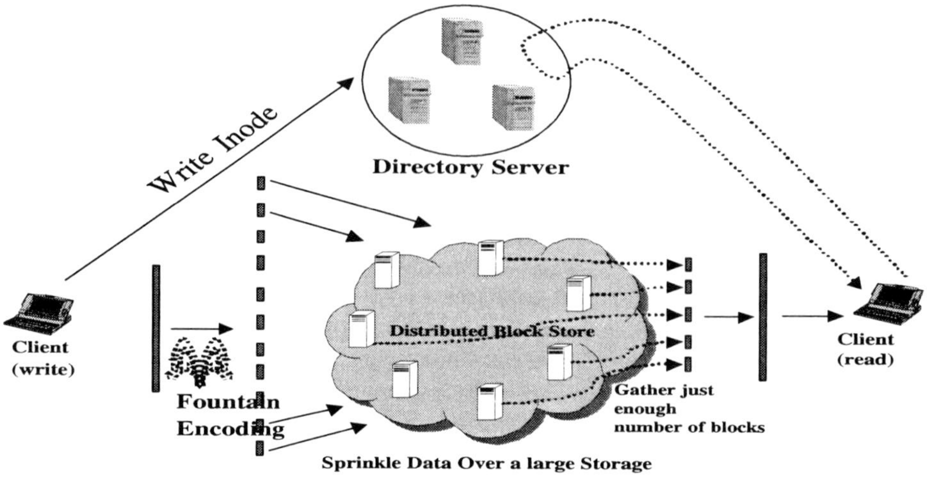

Figure 2: Overview of *e*-SAFE

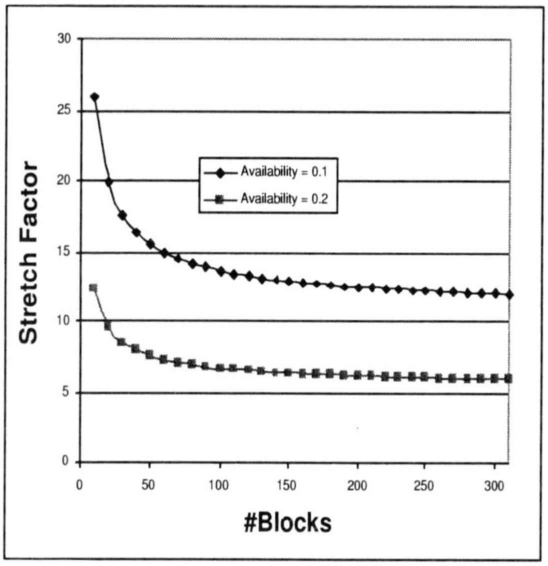

Figure 3: Stretch Factor as a function of number of initial blocks (k)

So we have two points to explore in the design space. First, use a high k and use a smaller stretch factor. The advantage is space-efficiency, while the drawback is high fragmentation with additional meta data overhead. Second, use a smaller number of pre-encoding blocks (k) and stretch further so as to cover low-availability cases. This approach is less space-efficient, but has the following advantages: (*i*) since during a read operation data must be constructed from at least k fragments, it is usually more efficient to keep this number low and (*ii*) the system can handle write operations in a more time-distributed fashion; first it writes a small number of blocks just enough to reconstruct data, and then when the write burst gets over, lazily disseminate other redundancy blocks onto the persistent storage. Thus the user programs do not see high write-latency.

Keeping in mind the two factors, we designed *e*-SAFE to automatically decide the most suitable strategy within a set of constraints. Three key variables play critical roles in the choice of parameters: Length of a segment (L_s), the number of post-encoding blocks (n_b) and the size of meta-data (L_{meta_data}) that needs to be appended to each data block. *e*-SAFE tries to find the best parameters within a given set of constraints, such as the maximum number of servers allowed, maximum meta-data overhead allowed and so on. For a single segment that is disseminated with a stretch factor c (resulting size $c.L_s$) and over n_b blocks, *e*-SAFE chooses the variable parameters so the meta-data overhead is less than a given threshold $f_{overhead}$: $\frac{n_b.L_{meta\_data}}{c.L_s} \geq f_{overhead}$, subject to the constraints: (*i*) $N_{max} \geq n_b \geq N_{min}$ and (*ii*) $c \geq c_{max}$.

4 Architecture

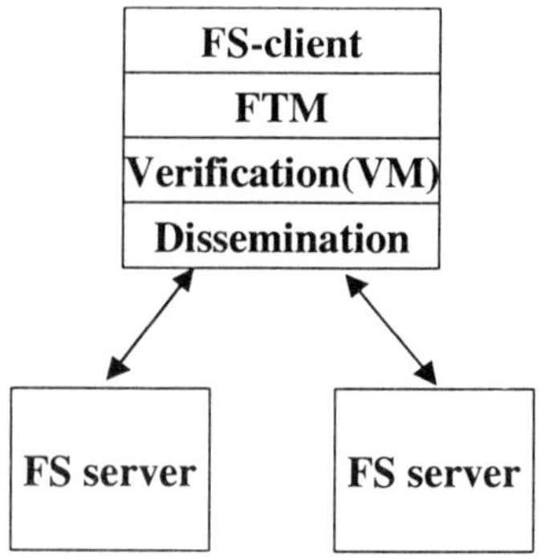

Figure 4: Broad Architecture of *e*-SAFE

Figure 4 gives a high level view of *e*-SAFE architecture. The top layer is a *file-system client* that provides `read`, write interfaces to the user. The next layer, FTM (Fault Tolerance Module) gathers/sends data stream to and from the FS-Client. FTM performs erasure encoding and decoding operation on the data streams. The key idea that FTM uses is that of a *Fountain Code*. We describe it shortly in section 4.1. The output of FTM is a series of data blocks. The next stage, *viz.*, the Verification layer, prepares fingerprint information for the data blocks that it receives as input. The fingerprint is generated by one way cryptographic hash function such as SHA-1. To survive malicious faults, *i.e.*, alteration of data, or forging of identity of storage units, fingerprint of individual blocks are also then linked together into a data structure called the Merkle Tree. This is described in section 4.2. Finally, once the data blocks are appended with appropriate fingerprint information, they are handed down to the data dissemination/aggregation layer. This stage of the software decides where to locate the server (or the storage unit) for storing or retrieving data. The FS server is a simpler structure. On the one hand it implements an RPC-based messaging protocol with the dissemination layer in the client. On the other hand this layer maintains a database of blocks indexed by their hash-values. Thus it can store or retrieve a block for the client as requested.

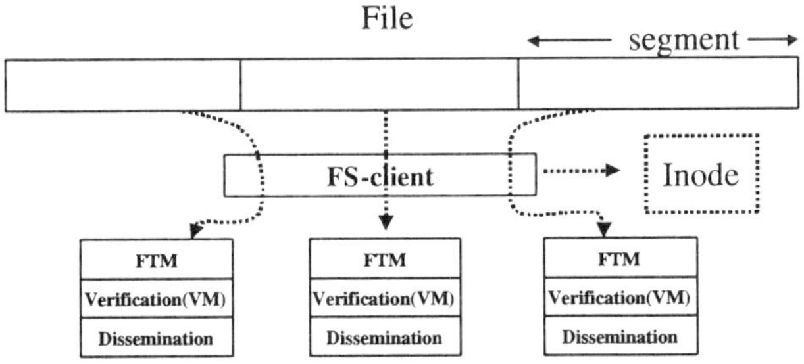

Figure 5: Parallel processing of File-Segment in *e*-SAFE

Figure 5 shows the optimization gear inherent in *e*-SAFE architecture. A large file is divided into multiple segments. Each segment is passed asynchronously to the FS-client. FS-client in turn calls the subsequent modules. The process is parallelized over different segments. Concurrent invocation of modules overlaps computation/communication of multiple blocks.

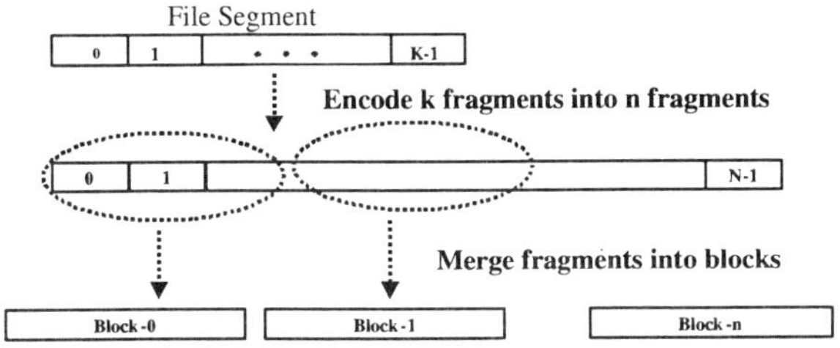

Figure 6: Preparing blocks for a File Segment *e*-SAFE

Figure 6 shows the flow of events in processing a file segment. The file segment is divided into K blocks and then expanded into N blocks using erasure codes. The ratio N/K is the stretch factor of this code. Usually it is more efficient (and guarantees higher accuracy for probabilistic codes) to choose large K and N. Out of the N small fragments, we coalesce N/n of fragments together to obtain n new blocks that are independently handed down to the block-stores underneath. Note that coalescing does not change the fault tolerance limits of the system, *i.e.*, if the encoding can tolerate $f.N$ failures out of N ($f < 1$), then after coalescing, at most $f.n$ can get faulty out of n blocks. The scaling property inherent in the erasure codes helps us adjust the scale of the system quite easily.

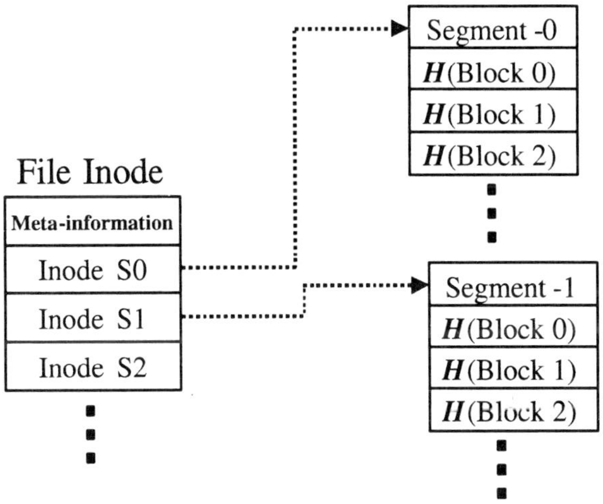

Figure 7: Structure of Inode for a multi-segment file in *e*-SAFE

To support such parallel dissemination of segments, we have to maintain separate meta-data structures for each segment. Figure 7 shows how this is organized. Each file has one master Inode. The master maintains pointers to the indirect Inodes corresponding to each file segment. A segment Inode contains the content-address (typically the hash) of the various blocks within this segment, and other information such as number of blocks, the encoding parameters and so on. Retrieval of data blocks is simple - the content hash is obtained from the Inode and then the main block is restored from the block-store underneath. However, when the block-store underneath is not content-addressable, an explicit mapping needs to be maintained.

When the number of blocks (n) is large, it becomes inefficient to keep the user waiting in a blocking mode until all the blocks are stored. Thus the control returns to the user only after a subset of blocks are stored (a subset just large enough to reconstruct the segment). The write occurs in burst. Thus, the client maintains a queue of blocks in the machine's `\temp` directory and in the gap between write operations, unobtrusively and asynchronously disseminates rest of the blocks. This way one can provision for very high stretch factors and thus for very high load factors.

4.1 Erasure Coding

An erasure code works in the following way: A document is partitioned into k blocks. These are called the *message blocks*. Next n new blocks ($n > k$) are generated from them by adding some redundancy mechanism, such as addition of extra parity bits and so on. The new blocks are called *encoded blocks*. Later on, the original document can be constructed from any k out of n encoded blocks. There are many ways erasure codes can be generated. A very standard way is the use of the Reed-Solomon codes [19]. However, these codes are inflexible in the sense that the parameters n and k are static and cannot be changed on the fly. The decoding time for such codes are $\mathcal{O}(n^2)$, which means for large n they become impractically slow. Moreover, these codes operate over mathematical structures called the finite fields. Once a field size (q) is chosen, it is not possible to change it later. The maximum length of one symbol that can be considered as one unit of encoding is limited to $\log q$, placing a limit on the width of the stripes necessary to distribute data blocks amongst multiple storage units.

To overcome all of the above problems we used a modern class of erasure code called the *Fountain Codes* [10]. The specific version that we used is known as the LT (Luby Transform) codes [17]. LT codes are rate-less, in the sense that the stretch factor n/k can be varied on-the-fly. Plus there is no limit on the symbol size - thus no restriction is imposed on the striping. And finally, these codes are inexpensive to implement and very fast in encoding (linear) and decoding times ($\mathcal{O}(n \log n)$).

4.2 Verification

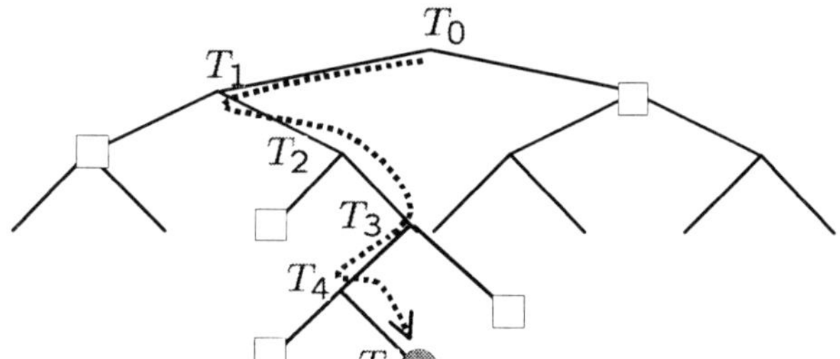

Figure 8: Construction of Verification Information from Merkle Tree: Each server is located at a leaf node. Consider server S_i, $T_0, T_1 \ldots$ represent the nodes on the path from the root to the i-th server. At any internal node of the tree the hash value V is prepared as $V(j) = Hash(V(left\_child).V(right\_child))$. The final verification information sent to S_i is the collection of hash values stored at the siblings of the vertices on this path.

We mentioned in the introduction that as data gets fragmented over more and more servers there is an impractical space overhead incurred by the verification information; especially in the face of high failure rate. To overcome this problem we took help of a data structure called the *Merkle Tree* (MT). An MT is simply a tree (assume binary tree for the time being) where each node j contains a hash value $V(j)$. The value is obtained from the child nodes; suppose L_j and R_j are the left and right children of the node j, then $V(j) = H(L_j.R_j)$, where $H()$ stands for a one-way cryptographic hash such as SHA-1 and the *dot* denotes concatenation operation.

We use the MT structure in our system in the following way. Suppose a file (or one segment of a file) is being disseminated amongst n storage units. Let's assume that $n = 2^l$ for some integer l. Now consider an MT of depth $\log n$ and n leaf nodes such that each server can be mapped to one leaf node. The hash value associated with a leaf node is the hash of the data block being sent to the corresponding server. Once the leaf hash-values are directly obtained from the corresponding data blocks, the intermediate levels of hashes are easily computed all the way up to the root. Figure 8 depicts this MT. Now, consider the i-th server (alternatively, the i-th leaf node), and the unique path from the root to this node. The vertices on this path are T_0, T_1 and so on. We collect the hash values associated with the vertices *that are siblings* of $T_1 \ldots T_5$. Since T_0 has no sibling, we keep the hash value at T_0 separately as the Root-Hash. In the figure, all the siblings are marked by a 'square'; their values are collected and packed into the verification information sent to the i-th server. While retrieving a block, one needs to re-compute the hash and then successively recompute the hashes up its path to the root (with the help of the sibling hash-values stored) and then finally verify if it is matching with the root-hash. If this test is passed, the data block's integrity can be considered intact with very high probability.

5 Implementation

e-SAFE has been implemented as a user level library written in C++ and has been tested to run on Linux. We used SHA-1 for hashing purposes, for verifying data blocks as well as creating block identifiers. There are two implementation of the data dissemination layer. The first one uses DHash, a Distributed Hash Table (DHT) based peer to peer system called Chord [22]. In our DHash based implementation of *e*-SAFE , each inode maintains a list of its block identifiers. During a store or fetch operation, lookup is initiated into the Chord network. Once a machine with appropriate nodeID is obtained, the data block is directly exchanged with it. The Inode server does not need to exclusively maintain the mapping between the blocks of a file and the servers they are stored in; that is left to DHash. Although Chord was designed to cater to P2P like systems, it has been later used to build wider area file system. Moreover, DHash performance has been enhanced (by a factor of two) by the use of a new transport scheme called the Striped Transport Protocol(STP). Thus we chose to use the STP based DHash implementation for our purpose.

We also implemented another version of the block store that does not depend on DHash. In this implementation, the Inode server maintains the mapping between blocks and the servers they are stored in. We will refer to this implementation as the Simple Block Store (SBS).

The end-to-end performance of this implementation is better than DHash, because the chord-based lookups are replaced by a direct client-server contact. SBS has two versions, synchronous and asynchronous. The former is based completely upon the synchronous RPC implementation available in Linux. The latter is an extension to it. In the asynchronous version, the RPC client maintains an extra thread receiving any incoming packets from the server asynchronously. Similarly, on the server side, an asynchronous service thread is maintained, along with a request queue. The standard RPC request handler enqueues requests that are asynchronously serviced by the service thread.

6 Evaluation

We evaluated *e*-SAFE both both with a series of micro benchmarks experiments and application workloads. All our experiments were performed on a set of 14 dual processor SMP machines, 2.8 GHz Intel Xeon processor, with 2 GB SDRAM and 512 KB L2 cache. The machines are partitioned into two physical sets - servers, hosting the block-store (acting as *e*-SAFE FS-server in Figure 4), and the clients that are outside the ring of servers, and only generate store and fetch operation for the servers. The client machines do not store anything. This division was effected partly because we wanted to separate the performance interferences of clients and servers and also to mimic the structure of a separate storage subsystem catering to its clients.

6.1 Microbenchmarks

We primarily study the latency of *e*-SAFE for storing and fetching files of different sizes. The latency increases as we split files across more and more servers, *i.e.,* split files into more and more blocks. *e*-SAFE is limited in performance by the bandwidth offered by the block-store underneath. Thus we examined *e*-SAFE under two different implementations of the block-store that we described in section 5.

Figure 9 presents the latencies for write operations for different block sizes. We observe that SBS writes are much faster compared to DHT based *e*-SAFE . As we already pointed out, SBS does not need any lookup to find an appropriate server, since the block-to-server mapping is readily available in the Inode server. The performance of the SBS version is much better than the DHT based implementation of *e*-SAFE ; with reference to figure 10(d), a file of size of 10MB is written in roughly 2 seconds, yielding a bandwidth of 5MB/s (blocksize = 1024) compared to the few hundred kilobytes of bandwidth obtained using the DHT implementation.

Figure 10 shows the performance of `read` operation. Here we see extremely fast reads happening in this setting. While the performance cost of the DHT-based implementation keeps increasing with the number of blocks, the general trend of the SBS graph is horizontal. For example, for a data size of 10KB, and split amongst 128 blocks, the DHT implementation takes around 550 ms, while the the latency of the SBS implementation is only 100 ms. Such a result is in accordance with the expectation. While true P2P systems will benefit from the DHT based systems, our results indicate that for applications running over systems of the size of not more than few hundred machines, SBS implementation is more suitable.

6.2 Performance under Workload

In order to test the performance of *e*-SAFE under real workloads, we carried out the following experiments with the workloads generated by a trace generation model called the *bmodel* [24], which has been shown to accurately approximate disk I/O behaviors of various enterprise systems. Synthetic I/O traces are generated for both reads and writes for a given time interval. Next we initiate a client to write/read by following those traces. Figure 11 presents a scenario of this workload for write operation. A total of 100 MB of data was distributed to be written over a period of 200 seconds. The distribution (into different chunk sizes as produced by the *bmodel*), is spaced evenly over the 200 sec interval. The x-axis denotes the workload index(*i.e.,* the indices of write requests of various data sizes), and on the Y axis, we measure the latency each write request takes to finish. Since the requests arrive in that order in time, the X-axis can be also be treated as a virtual time axis (for arrival of write requests). *Bmodel* generates approximately 130 different requests of various sizes within this interval(X-axis is marked from 0 to 140). We record latencies for two different modes of storing; background dissemination on and off. The lower line (write completion with background transfer) represents the former, while the upper line represents the latter. The shape of the curves show the bursty nature of the generated workload with the peaks corresponding to writes of larger blocks. Clearly, the user experiences a lower latency with the background transfer on, because much of the data dissemination happens in the background after the write-call returns. The stretch factor in these experiments is kept at 2.0. As the I/O burst continues, the write requests queue up building a backlog. The system cleans up this backlog during the lean phases of

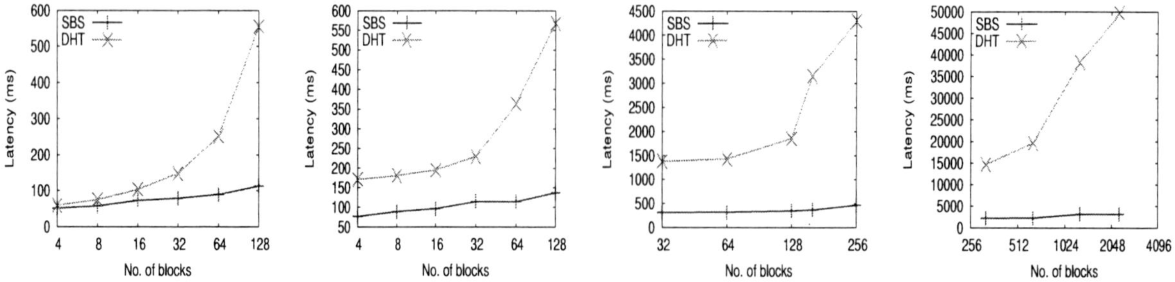

(a) file size 10KB (b) file size 100KB (c) file size 1MB (d) file size 10MB

Figure 9: Write latencies of DHT and SBS implementations of *e*-SAFE

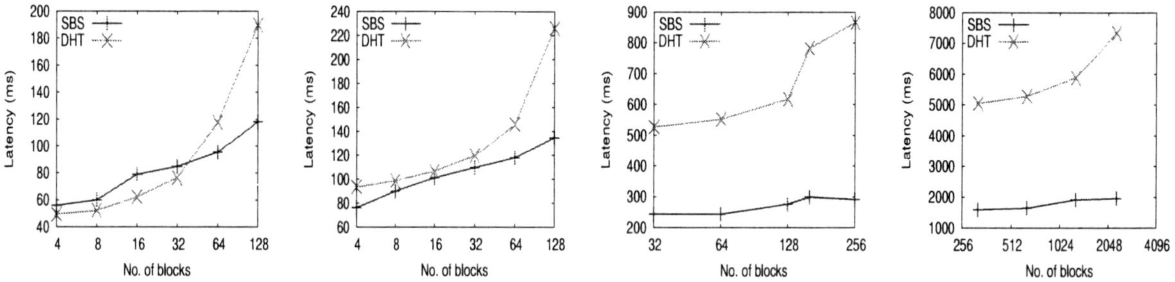

(a) file size 10KB (b) file size 100KB (c) file size 1MB (d) file size 10MB

Figure 10: Read latencies of DHT and SBS implementations of *e*-SAFE

I/O, that come immediately following the bursts.

Finally, we demonstrate the effect of higher stretch factors that we outlined in section 3. For this experiment, we use the asynchronous version of the SBS. For the experiments reported here, we use a file of size 240 KB. We store this file using stretch factor 2 and 4. In the former case, we split the file into 16 blocks, and in the latter 64 blocks of the same size as in the former case. Now we perform `fetch` operation on the file assuming the servers are highly loaded. We simulate a loaded server in the following way; for returning every block a random delay is inserted between 0 and ϕ time units. A higher value of ϕ would emulate higher load on the servers. The two results are plotted in Figure 12. ϕ was varied from 10ms to 10 seconds. As we have reasoned before, the response for the case of stretch factor 4 is much better than the case of stretch factor 2; it is literally ten to hundred times better. Such a result indicates the great benefit that a flexible stretching scheme can provide, *viz.*, the ability to attain high availability in a decentralized storage where most of the units run under heavy load. By adapting the stretch factor, an application can easily achieve the utility requirements of the data it needs to store. This result also underscores the importance of using Fountain codes that offer the flexibility of dynamically increasing the stretch factor of files as the system size scales up.

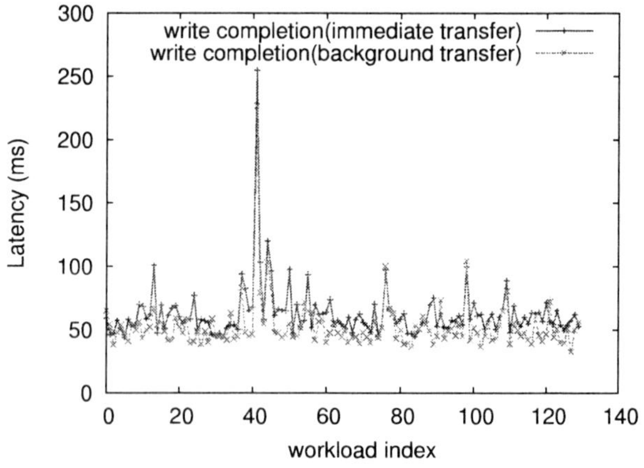

Figure 11: Write latency distribution for workload

7 Related Work

Distributed Storage is an age-old concept that has received wide attention in multiple contexts. Thus, a long list of related literature predates our work.

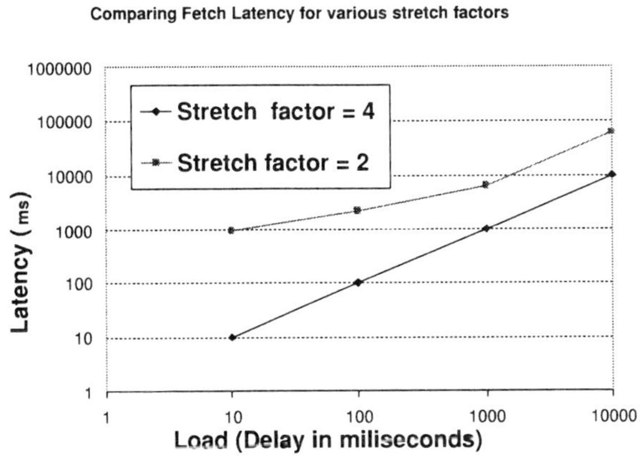

Figure 12: Effect of stretch-factors on the read latency

Distributed Storage Systems

Close to our work is the area of distributed file systems. A few recent examples are xFS [4], Frangipani (on top of Petal) [23], and so on. With the growth of the Internet, the focus is shifting to realizing file systems over wider areas. Security is one of the most critical issues. SFS is a file system based on separation of key management from file system so that it can span the Internet with heterogeneous key management policies [18]. The key idea in SFS is the use of self-certifying path name. FARSITE system [2] enables a peer to peer like environment of mutually distrusting desktops to provide a highly available and secure file system; it takes care of making copies of replicas and metadata when some of the nodes decide not to participate in the storage anymore. Security involves two aspects, *viz.*, confidentiality and integrity. While, confidentiality is not a big problem in systems that are centrally maintained (regardless of being distributed), data integrity is critical, because faults, both in the form of fail-stop and data corruption creeps in for various reasons. Wide area file systems, such as CFS [12], make sure that integrity and availability are maintained with effective replication caching. The Google file system(GFS) deploys a distributed file system spanning literally thousands of servers that deliver high bandwidth and availability [13]. GFS provides availability by splitting files into blocks and then replicating each block along with additional checksums, very much along the line of CFS.

Unlike SFS or FarSite, for *e*-SAFE confidentiality is kept out of its design. However, there are similarities in the way all these systems manage their metadata. *e*-SAFE focuses on data integrity in a space optimal way. *e*-SAFE is similar to GFS and CFS in the sense that they all fragment files and store them onto multiple units. The SBS implementation of *e*-SAFE functions like the *master server* (a dedicated server holding all the mapping between blocks and destination servers) based implementation of GFS. The DHT based implementation functions very much like the CFS. However, *e*-SAFE differs from both CFS and GFS, FARSITE and other similar file systems in the way redundancy is added. While others rely on pure replication, *e*-SAFE uses Fountain erasure codes as its redundancy mechanism. Erasure codes are known to provide more space optimal schemes than pure replication and hence *e*-SAFE provides higher storage optimality for a similar level of fault-tolerance (compared to CFS and GFS).

P2P File systems and look-ups

In recent years research in peer-to-peer systems has received very wide attention. While the span for P2P systems is the Internet, the scale is also overwhelmingly large, *i.e.,* literally millions of servers and their dynamics need to be considered. P2P systems open up a plethora of new possibilities, of which file sharing became popular even at a commercial level. Oceanstore [16, 21] system first attempted to harness the astronomically high amount of storage that might be reached through the Internet to create an archival level persistent storage that provides very high availability and durability. One of the key ingredients in its design is the use of erasure codes. Erasure codes have been shown to provide higher durability guarantees than naive replication at a much lower space cost [25]. Very recently, Bhagwan *et al.* reported TotalRecall (TR), a file system that is designed to handle the dynamic behavior of P2P systems. TR is based on the observation that in a P2P system, nodes join and disappear in a diurnal pattern over a short run, and in the long run many of the nodes leave the system permanently. To handle such scale of dynamics, TR deploys an availability monitoring unit, that checks for the availability of files on a periodic basis and repairs a file back to the desired availability whenever this factor falls below a threshold. Understanding the dynamics of P2P systems has been an important ingredient of the understanding of the availability [6, 7, 9]. It has been sometimes argued that in a P2P like environment, only a very small fraction of the nodes cooperate meaningfully and on a permanent basis, while the rest disappear mostly after a short period. However, we do not assume an environment such as P2P. We target a domain that resembles a server farm that is built out of many inexpensive local disks available individually. In our design we have decided to use a high stretch factor to replace periodic repairs. However, simple stretching will not work in a P2P context, because irrespective of the stretch factor, data, will be permanently lost in the face of constant decay [7]. For a storage system that is built out of a non-transient server-farm (*e.g.,* a corporate environment, or grid based data storage facility), constant decay of data is not a concern. As we have discussed earlier, the presence of high workloads may create the illusion of unavailability of the data. Prior Studies and experiences with the P2P systems have inspired some of our the design decisions. For example, a high workload condition in *e*-SAFE is similar to short term unavailability in a P2P setting; this similarity help us derive the conditions for the required redundancy factors.

8 Conclusions on *e*-SAFE

This paper discussed the design of *e*-SAFE , a distributed storage service targeted for very large scale decentralized systems. In the design of *e*-SAFE we have made a quantitative observation, that of equating high load with low availability. At the heart of *e*-SAFE 's design, is a special class of code, called the Fountain codes, that makes *e*-SAFE seamlessly adaptable to unlimited stretching and thus to hardware extensions of any degree. By virtue of the same codes, *e*-SAFE can sprinkle data around to any stretch factor, and achieve the utility requirements of different enterprise applications.

References

[1] M. Abd-El-Malek, W. V. C. II, C. Cranor, G. R. Ganger, J. Hendricks, A. J. Klosterman, M. Mesnier, M. Prasad, B. Salmon, R. R. Sambasivan, S. Sinnamohideen, J. D. Strunk, E. Thereska, M. Wachs, and J. Y. Wylie. Ursa Minor: versatile cluster-based storage. In *Proceedings of the FAST '05 Conference on File and Storage Technologies, San Francisco, California, USA.*, December 2005.

[2] A. Adya and et al. Farsite: Federated, available, and reliable storage for an incompletely trusted environment. In *Proceedings of 5th Symposium on Operating Systems Design and Implementation(OSDI)*, 2002.

[3] N. Alon, H. Kaplan, M. Krivelevich, D. Malkhi, and J. P. Stern. Scalable secure storage when half the system is faulty. In *Automata, Languages and Programming*, pages 576–587, 2000.

[4] T. Anderson, M. Dahlin, J. Neefe, D. Pat-terson, D. Roselli, and R. Wang. Serverless network file systems. In *In Proceedings of the 15th Symposium on Operating System Principles. ACM*, pages 109–126, Copper Mountain Resort, Colorado, December 1995.

[5] T. Barclay and J. Gray. Terraserver cluster and san experience. *Microsoft Research Technical Report*, MSR-TR(2004-67), 2004.

[6] R. Bhagwan, S. Savage, and G. Voelker. Understanding availability. In *Proceedings of 2nd International Workshop on Peer-to-Peer Systems (IPTPS '03)*, 2003.

[7] R. Bhagwan, S. Savage, and G. M. Voelker. Replication strategies for highly available peer-to-peer storage systems. Technical Report CS2002-0726, University of California, San Diego, 2002.

[8] R. Bhagwan, K. Tati, Y. Cheng, S. Savage, and G. Voelker. Total recall: System support for automated availability management. In *Proceedings of the First ACM/Usenix Symposium on Networked Systems Design and Implementation (NSDI)*, 2004.

[9] C. Blake and R. Rodrigues. High availability, scalable storage, dynamic peer networks: Pick two. In *Hot Topics in Operating Systems(HotOS)*, 2003.

[10] J. W. Byers, M. Luby, M. Mitzenmacher, and A. Rege. A digital fountain approach to reliable distribution of bulk data. In *Proceedings of ACM SIGCOMM*, pages 56–67, 1998.

[11] A. Chien. Computing elements. In I. Foster and C. Kesselman, editors, *The Grid: Blueprint for a New Computing Infrastructure*, pages 567–592. Morgan Kaufmann, 2004.

[12] F. Dabek, M. F. Kaashoek, D. Karger, R. Morris, and I. Stoica. Wide-area cooperative storage with CFS. In *Proceedings of the 18th ACM Symposium on Operating Systems Principles (SOSP '01)*, Chateau Lake Louise, Banff, Canada, Oct. 2001.

[13] S. Ghemawat, H. Gobioff, and S.-T. leung. The google file system. In *Proceedings of SOSP*, October 2004.

[14] H. Krawczyk. Distributed fingerprints and secure information dispersal. In *Proc. 13th ACM Symp. on Principles of Distributed Computating*, pages 207–218, 1993.

[15] H. Krawczyk. Secret sharing made short. *Advances in Cryptology (CRYPTO)*, 773:136–146, 1994.

[16] J. Kubiatowicz, D. Bindel, Y. Chen, P. Eaton, D. Geels, R. Gummadi, S. Rhea, H. Weatherspoon, W. Weimer, C. Wells, and B. Zhao. Oceanstore: An architecture for global-scale persistent storage. In *Proceedings of ACM ASPLOS*. ACM, November 2000.

[17] M. Luby. Lt codes. In *Proceedings of 43rd Annual IEEE Symposium on Foundations of Computer Science (FOCS)*, 2002.

[18] D. Mazieres, M. Kaminsky, M. F. Kaashoek, and E. Witchel. Separating key management from file system security. In *In Proceedings of the 17th ACM Symposium on Operating Systems Principles (SOSP)*, 1999.

[19] O. Pretzel. *Error Correcting Codes and Finite Fields.* Clarendon Press, Oxford, 1992.

[20] M. Rabin. The efficient dispersal of information for security, load balancing, and fault tolerance. *JACM*, 36(5):335–348, April 1989.

[21] S. Rhea, P. Eaton, D. Geels, H. Weatherspoon, B. Zhao, and J. Kubiatowicz. Pond: The oceanstore prototype. In *Proceedings of the Conference on File and Storage Technologies*. USENIX, 2003.

[22] I. Stoica, R. Morris, D. Karger, F. Kaashoek, and H. Balakrishnan. Chord: A scalable Peer-To-Peer lookup service for internet applications. In *Proceedings ACM SIGCOMM*, Aug 2001.

[23] C. A. Thekkath, T. Mann, and E. K. Lee. Frangipani: A scalable distributed file system. In *Symposium on Operating Systems Principles*, pages 224–237, 1997.

[24] M. Wang, T. M. Madhyastha, N. H. Chan, S. Papadimitriou, and C. Faloutsos. Data mining meets performance evaluation: Fast algorithms for modeling bursty traffic. In *ICDE*, 2002.

[25] H. Weatherspoon and J. Kubiatowicz. Erasure coding vs. replication: A quantitative comparison. In *Peer-to-Peer Systems: First International Workshop (IPTPS)*, 2002.

0-7695-2906-2/07 $25.00 © 2007 IEEE

Applications Track

Emergence of Smooth Pursuit using Chaos

Boris Duran, Giorgio Metta, Giulio Sandini
Italian Institute of Technology - University of Genova, Italy
boris@unige.it, giorgio.metta@iit.it, giulio.sandini@iit.it

Abstract

The task of tracking an object has been fully studied and many solutions presented before. However, it is a perfect test bed for the study of a novel model using Coupled Chaos Systems. Once an object appears in front of a camera, we demonstrate that the visual input is enough for the self-organization of the torques applied to each of the axes controlling the motion of a simulated eye. No learning or specific coding of the task is needed beforehand, which results in a very fast adaptation to perturbations.

1. Introduction

The research in modern humanoid robotics dates back approximately 30 years when the Bio-engineering group of Waseda University started the WABOT project. Some years later, Honda initiated their research, the result of which is one of the state-of-the-art humanoids of our time, ASIMO. Most of today's humanoid platforms follow a 50-year-old tradition of control theory that started with Industrial Automation at the beginning of the 1960s. Control theory gives us different tools for designing and evaluating the algorithms that will realize a desired motion or force application [2]. It is at this point where the problems start for the humanoids of the future.

In an industrial environment we are able to specify within centimeters, distances, area of motion, speed and acceleration of different links, force and torques, etc. But what happens when we want to move beyond this fixed framework? A more adaptive and flexible theory is needed when thinking of 'controlling' a device that is supposed to move within an ever-changing environment.

The study of nonlinear dynamics and chaos also has a long history; however, real applications that make direct use of chaos theory have not been fully developed. The purpose of this research is to demonstrate the feasibility of using coupled chaotic systems in a more realistic application by taking the model of behavior emergence introduced by Kuniyoshi et al. [8] within the area of humanoid robotics.

The task of smooth pursuit has been solved in many different and more accurate ways than the one presented here. However, this task presents a very simple and attractive challenge to use as test bed for coupled chaotic systems. Another interesting point to be considered is the notion of emergence and self-organization that characterize these systems. In fact, it is exactly at this point where a link between chaos and biological systems can be found. It would not be strange to think that this reactive-emergent kind of behavior generated by coupled chaos has its counterpart in the biological nervous system.

Walter Freeman and colleagues have done an extensive research on the dynamics found in EEG waves from the mammalian olfactory system [3]. He has demonstrated the existence of chaotic dynamics during perception at a mesoscopic level, which refers to the level in between the analysis of single neurons (microscopic) and the activity of whole brain areas (macroscopic). Since it has been shown that nature uses chaos to self-organize the information coming from our senses, we may assume that chaos is also used to organize our muscular responses. With this in mind a simple experiment of self-organizing behavior is studied in this project by using coupled chaotic systems.

The next section describes the basics of coupled chaotic systems together with the model of behavior emergence proposed in [8]. Next, a description of the setup used for smooth pursuit is presented together with the quantitative analysis of the experiment; and, finally, we present the conclusions and guidelines for future work.

2. Coupled Chaotic Systems

A network of elements whose activation is defined by a chaotic map receives the name of Coupled Chaotic

0-7695-2906-2/07 $25.00 © 2007 IEEE

Systems. Depending on the level of interaction among their elements, it is possible to classify them in systems of local or global interaction.

2.1 Coupled Map Lattices (CML)

CML were introduced by Kaneko in the middle of the 1980's as an alternative to the study of spatiotemporal chaos [7]. In short, this kind of dynamical systems uses discrete partial difference equations to study the evolution of a process described by discrete steps in space and time but with continuous states. Eq. (1) describes the dynamics of CML, whereas Eq. (2) represents the logistic map used in this work.

$$x_n^i = (1-\epsilon)f(x_{n-1}^i) + \frac{\epsilon}{2}\{f(x_{n-1}^{i+1}) + f(x_{n-1}^{i-1})\} \quad (1)$$

$$f(x) = 1 - \alpha x^2 \quad (2)$$

Where x_n^i is a variable at discrete time step n and a lattice point i. x represents a set of field variables which could be temperature, position measurements, velocities, etc. There are two parameters: α controlling the level of chaoticity of the system and ϵ controlling the coupling level among neighboring elements.

2.2 Globally Coupled Maps (GCM)

These kinds of maps were also introduced by Kaneko and represent a network of chaotic elements with interactions among all of them. While CML interact with specific points within the lattice, each of the nodes in a Globally Coupled Map (GCM) interact with all the others, Eq (3). Due to the chaotic nature of the system, specified by α, it is possible to see one of the main properties of chaotic systems: two slightly different initial conditions amplify its difference through time. On the other hand, ϵ tries to synchronize the activations of all these chaotic elements by coupling them. In between these two states of complete chaos and complete synchronization, interesting states emerge like the formation of clusters oscillating in different phases and amplitudes.

$$x_n^i = (1-\epsilon)f(x_{n-1}^i) + \frac{\epsilon}{N}\sum_{j=1}^{N} f(x_{n-1}^j) \quad (3)$$

Both of these categories have been thoroughly studied during the last two decades with researchers trying to describe them both qualitatively and quantitatively. The effects of varying both chaoticity and the coupling factor in stand-alone CML and GCM systems were studied meticulously by Kaneko's group in the late 90's [6, 5]. Approximate phase diagrams were sketched covering the entire spectrum of synchronization among the interacting chaotic elements of a network.

2.3 Coupled Chaotic Fields

The model used in this project is based on the approach followed by Kuniyoshi and Suzuki [8]. The main idea behind this model is to make use of all those interesting states mentioned before that emerge when coupling chaotic elements and, in this case, the sensory information modified by the environment. This model uses both, the local interaction (CML) and the global interaction (GCM). The system is depicted in Fig. 1.

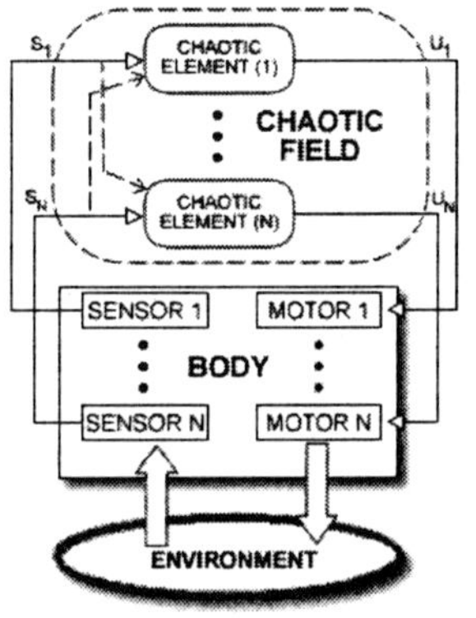

Figure 1. Body-environment interaction through coupled chaotic fields

Each one of the blocks containing "chaotic" elements and their relationship constitutes the core of the system and it is defined by Eq. (4) and (5). The function f represents the logistic map , Eq. (2).

$$u_n^i = f\left\{ s_{n-1}^i + \epsilon_1(\bar{s}_{n-1} - s_{n-1}^i) + \epsilon_2\left(\frac{s_{n-1}^{i+1} + s_{n-1}^{i-1}}{2} - s_{n-1}^i\right)\right\} \quad (4)$$

$$\begin{aligned} m_n^i &= G_u(u_n^i + O_u) \\ s_n^i &= G_s(r_n^i + O_s) \end{aligned} \quad (5)$$

Where m is the torque applied to each joint, s and u are inputs and outputs respectively of the chaotic field block, and r is the raw value coming from the plant. Finally, G_u, G_s, O_u, and O_s are gains and offsets of the sensors and motors in the body of the plant; these values are applied in the same magnitude to all the elements of the system.

3 A virtual eye

The virtual eye was created using two rotational joints, one perpendicular to the other in order to simulate the "pan" and "tilt" motions of a real eye, Fig. 2. Each joint is also modeled by a spring and a damper, trying to replicate the physical characteristics of real muscles. These two motors are actuating the virtual eye as the motion created by the main four muscles in biological eyes.

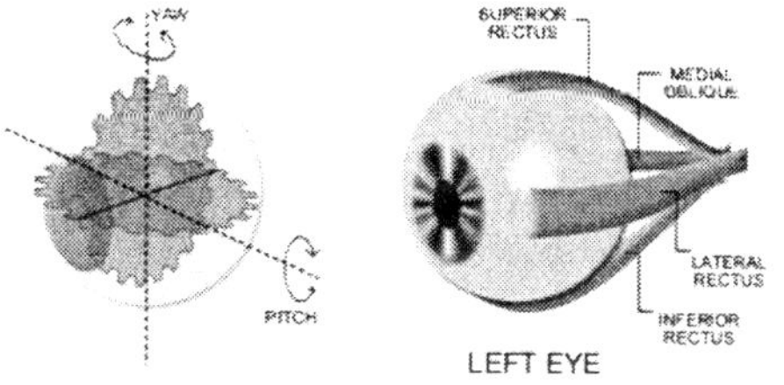

Figure 2. Biological eye and its virtual counterpart for the experiment

A virtual camera mounted in front of the eye gives the visual input needed for modulating the chaotic field. The width and height were fixed to 32 x 32 pixels with a field of view of 0.5 radians. It is assumed that values of saliency are obtained from other visual components. One of these values to be tracked was simulated by a black circular shape moving on a white screen, Fig. 3. Even though the trajectory followed by the object is circular all the time, it accelerates and decelerates several times to provide a basic test for the robustness of the system.

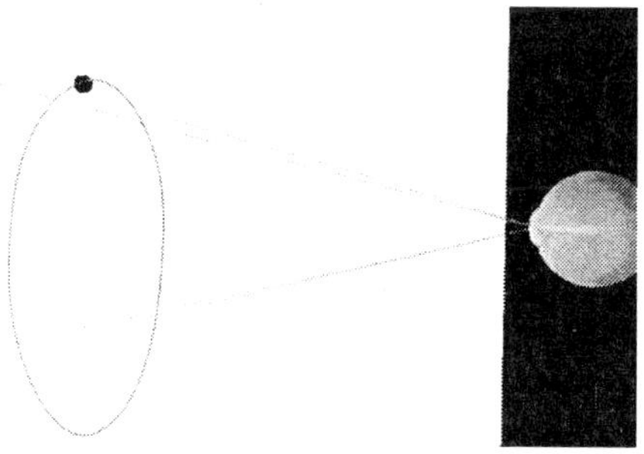

Figure 3. Screenshot of the virtual setup

The time step for the simulations was fixed to 32 milliseconds and the experiments were done without the influence of gravity and with a minimum value of friction. The offsets and gains were fixed to G_u=1.5, G_s=1.0, O_u=-0.92, and O_s=-0.2. The input to the system is given by the difference between the center of the observed object within the field of view and the position of the center of the eye, for both the vertical and horizontal motions, Fig. 4. The outputs from the chaotic field are fed to the motors after applying the respective offset and gain.

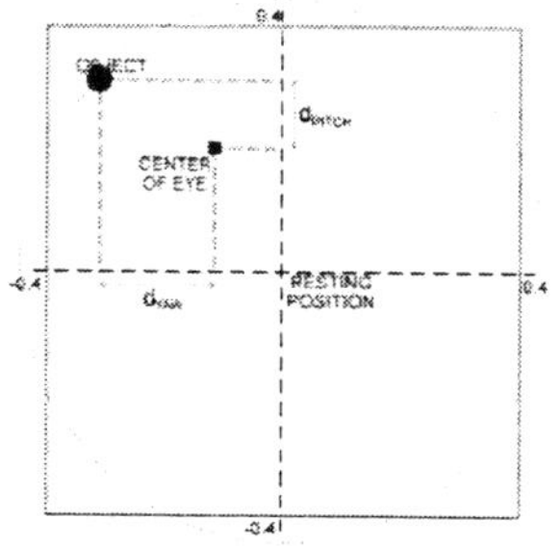

Figure 4. Geometric description for inputs to the chaotic system

The trajectory followed by our virtual eye can be observed in Fig. 5. The first reaction, once the object has entered into the eyes's field of view, is to move toward the object. As we can see, the adaptation to the path of motion is immediate, there are no overshooting oscillations like the ones normally encountered in a PID controller.

Fig. 6 shows the orientation of the motors through time. Even though both motors are trying to follow the object as smoothly as possible, a small trembling was observed specially at the maximum angle allowed in each direction. This trembling seems to be directly influenced by the physical characteristic of the hardware. Note that the synchronization of both motors remains also during those moments when the object slows down and change direction (aprox. 4 seconds). Another important information from this plot is the short time elapsed until it reaches this "steady" state.

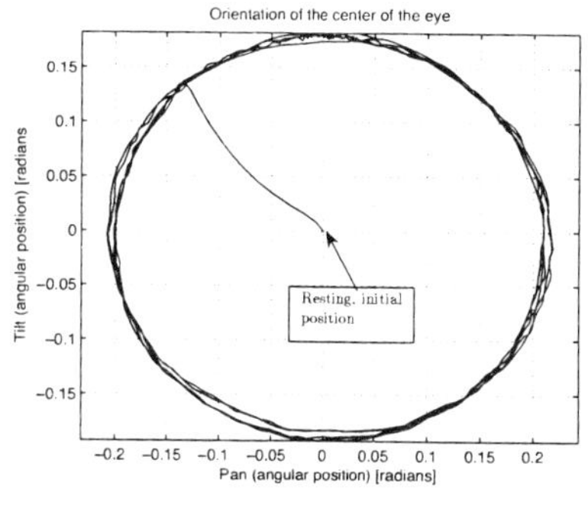

Figure 5. Trajectory of the center of the eye (α=1.95, ϵ=0.1)

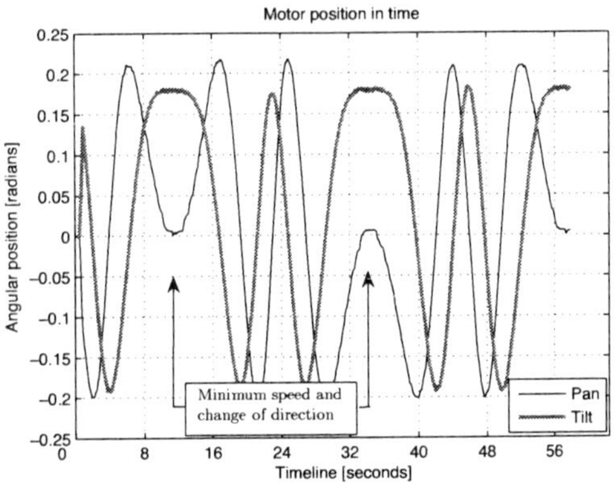

Figure 6. Motor orientation in time

In less than one second, the system adapts to the recent change in the environment.

The "smooth pursuit"-kind of motion was tested using different values of α (chaoticity factor) and ϵ (coupling factor). However when either α was lower than 1.0 or ϵ greater than 0.3 the system performs inconsistent movements, sometimes trying to follow the object and sometimes trying to escape from it. Fig. 7 shows the behavior of the 'eye' for $\alpha = 0.1$ and $\epsilon = 0.2$. A more in-depth study on the effects of varying these two parameters, α and ϵ, would be very difficult because of the local and global interaction of elements at the same time; moreover, every observation would change from time to time due to the ever changing influence of the environment.

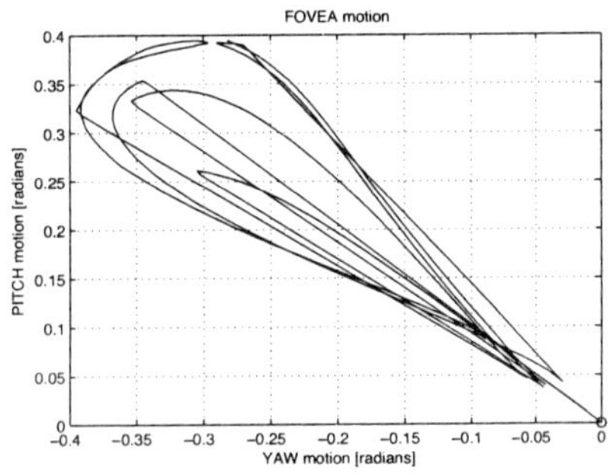

Figure 7. Trajectory of the center of the eye (α=0.1, ϵ=0.2)

4 Conclusions and Future work

A very simple experiment for demonstrating the feasibility of applying coupled chaos systems in humanoid robotics has been introduced in this project. Tracking an object moving in front of a camera has previously been solved in several different ways, from using very simple trigonometric solutions to advanced control algorithms. However, this task was simple enough to use it in the emergence of a reactive behavior that could have a better understanding in Neural Sciences.

According to neurosciences, all behavior is mediated by the central nervous system (brain and spinal cord) which is separate but functionally interconnected with the peripheral nervous system (continuous stream of sensory information about the environment). Simply put, the major difference between voluntary and reflexive movements is the intervention or not of the central nervous system [4]. In practice, it is not possible to separate the modulation signals coming from the brain into the muscles of our eyes. But according to the results of this experiment, we could speculate that visual tracking is just a reactive behavior given a saliency in our visual field. These saliencies are the necessary modulations given by our central nervous system and its areas of emotions, experiences, needs, etc.

Future work involves the coordination of motion with two eyes and finally the emergence of coordinated motion between eyes and head. The simulation environment saves a substantial amount of time and resources for these types of experiments; however, a notable amount of that saved time is dedicated only to tuning the physical parameters in these simulated environments. Most of the software for robotics simulation still creates instabilities influencing the way the algorithms are supposed to work. Therefore, an iCub head from the RobotCub project is being developed to test this and future experiments in a real environment [1].

References

[1] Robotcub project. *http://www.robotcub.org.*

[2] J. Craig. *Introduction to Robotics: Mechanics and Control.* Pearson Education, 2004.

[3] W. Freeman. *Mass Action in the Nervous System.* Academic Press Inc., New York, 2004.

[4] E. Kandel, J. Schwatrz, and T. Jesell. *Principles of Neural Sciences.* McGraw-Hill, 2000.

[5] K. Kaneko. Clustering, coding, switching, hierarchical ordering and control in a network of chaotic elements. *Physica D41*, pages 137–172, 1990.

[6] K. Kaneko. Pattern dynamics in spatiotemporal chaos. *Physica D34*, pages 137–172, 1990.

[7] K. Kaneko and I. Tsuda. *Complex Systems: Chaos and Beyond.* Springer-Verlag, 2001.

[8] Y. Kuniyoshi and S. Suzuki. Dynamic emergence and adaptation of behavior through embodiment as a coupled chaotic field. *International Conference on Intelligent Robots and Systems*, pages 2042–2049, 2004.

Distributing Genome Sequence Databases with a Publish/Subscribe Middleware

Chen Wang, Bing Bing Zhou, Fabian Brites, Bin Liu, and Albert Y. Zomaya
School of Information Technologies
University of Sydney, NSW 2006, Australia
{cwang, bbz, zomaya}@it.usyd.edu.au

Abstract

The paper presents a publish/subscribe middleware that intends to address the scalability issue of application servers hosting genome sequence similarity detection services. We give an effective annotation mechanism for distributed data and a scheduling algorithm to balance the data replication and query processing performance.

1. Introduction

The advance in genome sequencing technology produces huge amount sequence data. Supporting sequence search and analysis is an important task for computer systems to serve the bioinformatics community [2]. There are a variety of methods for sequence similarity detection and analysis. Accommodating them in a unified computer system has obvious benefits for biologists in terms of sharing data among the community and including new biological evidences into sequence analyses. However, there are two major challenges for the existing computer systems to support this.

Firstly, sequence analyses often involve heterogeneous data from a variety of sources. Central repositories such as Gene Bank, collect huge amount of sequences produced by institutions world wide, but they do not host all the methods that analyze these sequences, neither the data produced by these methods. Managing heterogeneous data for the use of different type of methods is a challenging task.

Secondly, sequence similarity detection and analysis algorithms are diverse and dynamic in nature. The *beowulf* clusters, used in most of bioinformatics centers including NCBI do not provide enough scalability for serving increasing search requests, or queries, e.g., the NCBI BLAST service face scalability issue as the size of genome sequence database increase and the incoming query rate increases [1]. Keeping adding nodes to a cluster potentially increases the number of processes that share a data file located in a shared NAS (Network Attached Storage) or SAN (Storage Area Network). The lock waiting and bandwidth competition limit the scalability of the system.

An alternative is to build a cluster with loosely coupled computers and use MapReduce programming model to improve the scalability, as Google cluster [3] does. However, the applications running on a bioinformatics cluster constructed this way will be much more diverse and compute-intensive. It is hard to fit them into one a generic programming model. In this paper, we propose a middleware for constructing scalable bioinformatics application servers on top of distributed resources. In a loosely coupled distributed environment, data can be seen as the states of computing jobs. Jobs running on different computing nodes can add, delete or modify data autonomously. Using a central server to register all the data requires that these data have relatively stable metadata structures, which is not realistic to applications in this field. On the other hand, a centralized server creates single point of failure and does not scale well. The proposed middleware uses decentralized methods to organize data and computing resources. It provides scheduling services for different applications to use data efficiently.

The paper made following contributions: (1) a decentralized model for heterogeneous data management; (2) a data centric scheduling algorithm that can efficiently match queries to distributed data and compute resources, and manage data replicas.

2. System Description

2.1. Publish/subscribe system architecture

Fig.1 illustrates a simple system organized with the proposed middleware. The system consists of a query scheduler, a number of subscribers and data nodes. They are linked together as an overlay network. A scheduler is specific to a certain type of applications and is used by a service provider to harness distributed computing and data resources. Clients submit search requests to a scheduler through a service provider. The scheduler then transforms these requests into tasks. A scheduler has a number of computing nodes subscribing to it. A subscriber may specify filters to select tasks for execution. A filter defines the maximum memory usage, running time or disk usage that a task can

0-7695-2906-2/07 $25.00 © 2007 IEEE

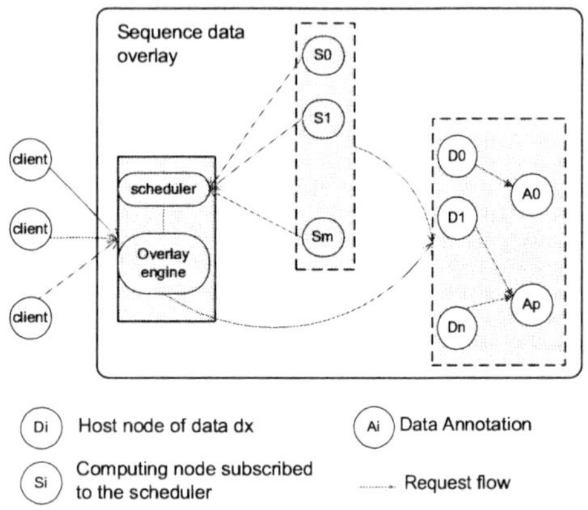

Fig. 1. A simple system architecture

use. A task is defined as a group of necessary data files and parameters.

Once a task is retrieved, a subscriber has to resolve the needed data files if they are not available locally or the local copies are out of date. The data acquisition is an overlay lookup process. Each data file is identified by its ID in the overlay. Note that a subscriber is also a data node. Once a data file is retrieved and stored locally, the subscriber announces its existence in the overlay.

The sizes of genome databases are unevenly distributed. Due to that sequence search program has big memory footprint, searching large databases normally takes much longer time than searching small ones does. Our middleware supports partitioning of large databases into small data fragments; therefore with a good scheduling strategy, running queries simultaneously on these fragments with multiple subscribers can speedup query processing.

2.2. Data annotation and publish model

There is no central data registry in the system. Each data node is responsible for making its own data files accessible by other nodes. By doing this, individual data nodes can flexibly annotate the data they store, which is suitable for data with rich and changing semantics. We give a hierarchical annotation model for genome databases. Fig.2

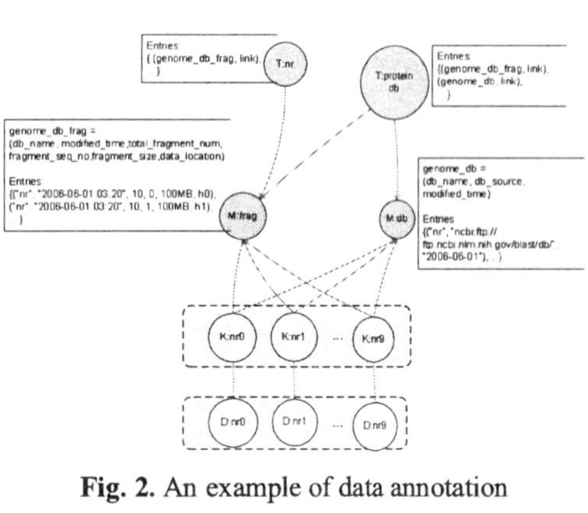

Fig. 2. An example of data annotation

shows an example about how the data fragments of the NCBI protein database *nr* are annotated. The *nr* database is partitioned into 10 fragments in this example. There are four types of information, shown as four types of *annotation nodes*, associated with each data fragment:

- *d-node*: the actual files of the data fragment. They are stored in the owners' storage;
- *k-node*: the unique ID associated with a data file. A unique ID of a file is either a URI or a hash key generated from the file. We use the hash key to identify a file in the proposed middleware;
- *m-node*: the schema (e.g., genome_db_frag and gnome_db) that describes the data fragments. An entry in an m-node refers to a data file by pointing to the file's k-node. An m-node accepts subscriptions for the data it stores. Whenever the data entries change in an m-node, affected nodes are notified the changes, e.g., when a genome database is updated, its modified time will be changed in an m-node and the change will propagate to nodes that subscribe to the m-node;
- *t-node*: data can be annotated using tags. A tag is an attribute of the data or a category that the data is classified into. In fig.2., "nr" and "protein database" are two tags for describing the *nr* database fragments. A tag links to *m-node*s that contain the detailed description of the data.

A data fragment can be located when one of its *k-node*, *m-node* or *t-node* is known, e.g., a user in search for "protein database" will be lead to the metadata repositories where all published protein database or database fragment entries are likely to be found. Some of these entries are linked to the *k-nodes* of the nr database fragment nr0 – nr9 in the example.

Computer nodes and data annotation nodes are mapped into a single Pastry [4] ID space in the middleware. The *k-node* is stored in the computer with ID closest to it. Note that multiple *d-nodes* could share the same *k-node* if they are copies from the same data file. In this case, the computer node that is responsible for the *k-node* contains multiple entries that point to these *d-nodes*. When the requests to a *d-node* arrive, the k-node responds to the requestor with a *d-node* selected from the multiple entries in round-robin manner.

An *m-node* is identified by its URI and its address is determined by the hash ID of the URI. The *t-node* is addressable through a generated ID from the tag itself.

3. Scheduling and Data Placement

A scheduler transforms sequence search requests into tasks and publishes these tasks for subscribers to execute. A query task is defined as a query runs on a database or a fragment of a database. A task consists of a number of data files and each of them is associated with a *k-node*. A few *m-nodes* link to these k-nodes.

In the initial stage, the scheduler gathers a list of *k-nodes* that link to genome database fragments in the overlay. This is done through subscribing to related *m-nodes*. The *k-node* list is regularly updated whenever one of the following occurs: 1. a new database is published; 2. an existing database is updated.

A common genome sequence similarity search tool such as BLAST is both compute- and data intensive. The response time of a search request relies on the locality of the requested data and the performance of the subscriber that runs the query. Obviously, dispatching a search task to a subscriber that has a local copy of the requested data can reduce the data retrieval time, but it may also increase the response time when the processing requirements of incoming queries to the database is above the capacity of the subscriber. On the other hand, increasing the number of replicas can reduce task queuing delay, but will inevitably increase the data replication and management cost.

We present a data centric scheduling algorithm (Q_DCSA) to improve the performance of query processing and optimize the sequence data placement. Q_DCSA can be modeled as shown in Fig. 3. Fig. 3(a) shows incoming queries are dispatched to multiple subscriber task queues based on the data placement. When a subscriber is assigned a task requesting data it does not store locally, it will fetch the data from one of the nodes that store the data. The way the data is fetched is modeled in fig. 3(b).

A subscriber that hosts multiple datasets is treated as multiple *virtual subscribers* in this model. A virtual subscriber is defined as a pair *(s, d)*, in which *s* is the subscriber and *d* is one of the dataset it stores locally. Each virtual subscriber is responsible for one dataset. As the number of datasets stored by a subscriber increases, the performance of each virtual subscribers hosted by the subscriber is likely to deteriorate.

The *maximum (task) queue size* controls the performance of each virtual subscriber. When the *maximum queue size* is reached, a new virtual subscriber is added to process data *d*, the arriving task will wait in the new subscriber task queue till the data replica is created. If a new subscriber can not be found, the task will have to wait in the query buffer till either there is room in the subscriber queue or a new subscriber can be successfully created. If nothing occurs and the query buffer is full, incoming queries will be dropped as the existing resources in the system are not enough for processing these queries.

Data request scheduling model When a task is dispatched to a subscriber that does not have the required dataset (missing or expired), the subscriber fetches the dataset in a process modeled as a M/G/k queue, as shown in fig.3(b). Under this circumstance, the subscriber first looks up the location of the data from a *k-node* that is responsible for the ID of the dataset. The *k-node* then selects a *d-node* entry to answer the lookup message. The selection is done in a round-robin manner. Therefore the data-fetch requests are evenly distributed to nodes that have the requested datasets. Assume the query incoming rate to a group of subscribers that are responsible for dataset *d* is λ_d and the probability that the data need to be fetched from a remote node is *p*. With a round-robin data-fetch request dispatching mechanism, the M/G/k model can be simplified to M/G/1 for each individual node with a query incoming rate $p\lambda_d / k$, in which *k* is the number of published entries in the *k-node* of the data fragment. As a result, the average waiting time for a data-fetch request is given using Pollaczek-Khintchine formula as the following:

$$W_{Qk}^{d} = \frac{(p\lambda_d / k)E[x_d^2]}{2(1-(p\lambda_d / k)E[x_d]}\ ,$$

in which x_d is the service distribution of the node that provide the dataset *d*. From this formula, we can see that the waiting time is reduced as the number of entries published to the *k-node* increases, meaning the data-fetch process scales up as the number of nodes that own the data increases.

Parallel Scheduling As a search request to a large database is partitioned into a group of tasks running on the data fragments of the database, its slowdown is determined by the slowest task in the group. We give a parallel scheduling mechanism to tackle the problem. The parallel tasks created from a search request are scheduled together in a pre-assignment phase introduced before the scheduler puts tasks into subscriber task queues. In the pre-assignment phase, the scheduler uses Q_DCSA to calculate the positions of parallel tasks in their target queues, e.g, tasks $\{t_0, t_1, t_2\}$ might be assigned to their corresponding queues at position 1, 5, and 3. The parallel scheduling module evaluates these positions. If the difference between the queue position of a task and the smallest queue position in the group of tasks is greater than a threshold, the task will be assigned to a subscriber

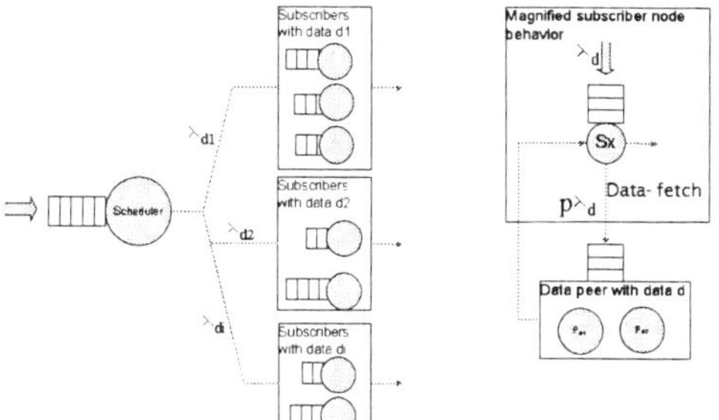

(a) (b)

Fig. 3. Data Centric Scheduling Model

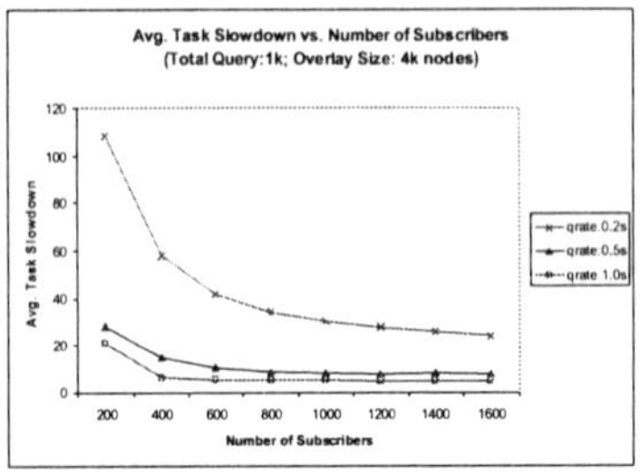

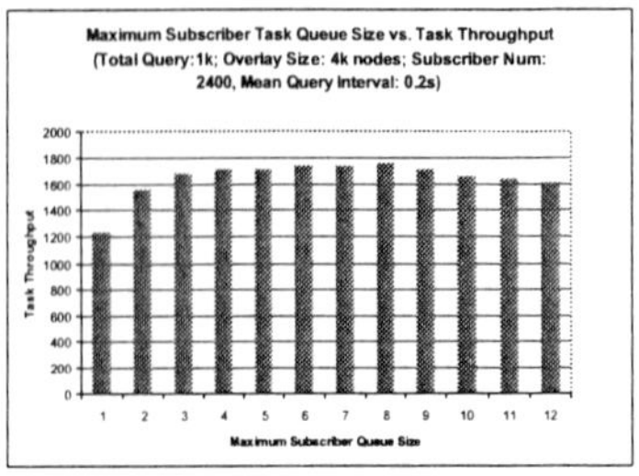

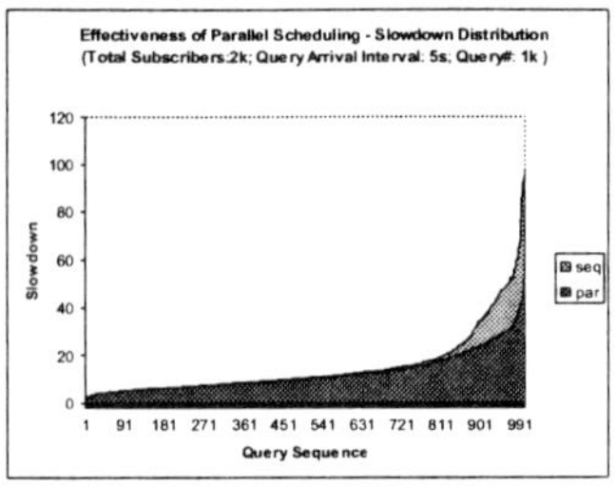

Fig. 4. Avg. task slowdown: max task queue size – 3.

Fig. 5. Max. subscriber task queue size vs. task throughput.

Fig. 6. Slowdown distribution (mean query interval – 0.2s).

with a global shortest queue. Assume the threshold is 3 in this example, t_1 will be assigned to a subscriber with shorter queue and a new replica of data requested by t_1 will be created in that subscriber. The threshold is calculated based on the average time of data retrieving cost.

4. Experiment Results

We evaluate the system model through simulation. The simulator uses Pastry for overlay construction. Initially, genome databases are stored in nodes randomly selected from the overlay. Databases are partitioned into fragments with sizes in 50-100MB range. The number of fragments belonging to databases follows *zipf* distribution with $\alpha = 1.5$ and the maximum fragments for a database is 100. These nodes then publish annotations of these fragments to the overlay. The scheduler is located in one randomly selected node in the overlay. Queries arrive in the scheduler in a Poisson process. Queries select databases using *zipf* distribution with $\alpha = 1.0$. Subscribers join the scheduler in a Poisson process with mean 1 second. The time for a subscriber to run a task follows *Bounded Pareto* distribution with $\alpha = 1.0$, lower bound 12 second and upper bound 30 seconds, a typical time range for query a 50MB protein database. The average cost for database annotation retrieval is set to 1 second and the transmission time for a data fragment is estimated based on the cost of transferring a 50MB file over 10Mbps links.

Scalability The scalability of the system is measured by average task slowdown and replica number for a data fragment. The slowdown of a query q is defined as below:

$$slowdown_q = \frac{finished\_time_q - queued\_time_q}{execution\_time_q}$$

In the experiment, we feed the system with 1000 queries and investigate the throughput change with the number of subscribers under low, medium and high query incoming rate. The result is shown in fig. 4. The average slowdown decreases as the increase of the number of the subscribers. On the other hand, the average task slowdown increases along with the increase of query incoming rate because that a subscriber task queue is more likely to become full when the query incoming rate is high and many tasks suffer longer queuing delay. Another reason is that the data distribution cost increases as more replicas need to be created in order to keep the subscriber queue sizes below the maximum value. Many tasks have to wait to be assigned before a new replica is created.

Impact of subscriber queue size When the system is heavily loaded, the average replica number is also affected by the maximum subscriber task queue size. In fig. 5., as the increase of the maximum queue size, the number of replicas per data fragment drops as a task is more likely to be queued in a subscriber that has the requested data locally. This reduces the data retrieval cost. However when the queuing delay becomes more significant than replica creation cost, the throughput drops and in this case, creating new replicas makes the system more efficient.

Effectiveness of Parallel Scheduling As Fig. 6 shows, the parallel scheduling works well under medium query incoming rates. However, when the whole system is lightly loaded or overloaded (results not included in the paper), the parallel scheduling is not as effective: when lightly loaded, the slowdown difference is not significant for parallel tasks; when overloaded, it is difficult to find queues to optimize the parallel task assignment.

References

[1] S. McGinnis and T. L. Madden: BLAST: at the core of a powerful and diverse set of sequence analysis tools, *Nucleic Acids Res.* 2004 July 1; 32(Web Server issue): W20–W25.

[2] D. L. Wheeler et. al., Database resources of the National Center for Biotechnology Information: update. *Nucleic Acids Res*, 32:D35–D40, 2004.

[3] J. Dean and S. Ghemawat, MapReduce: Simplified Data Processing on Large Clusters, *OSDI'04*, Dec. 2004.

[4] A. Rowstron and P. Druschel, Pastry: Scalable, distributed object location and routing for large-scale peer-to-peer systems. *IFIP/ACM Intl. Conf. on Distributed Systems Platforms (Middleware)*, November, 2001.

Self-Organizing Information Matching in InformANTS

Rainer Hilscher, Sven Brueckner, Theodore C. Belding, H. Van Dyke Parunak
New Vectors LLC, 3520 Green Court, Suite 250, Ann Arbor, MI 48105
{rainer.hilscher, sven.brueckner, ted.belding, van.parunak}@newvectors.net

Abstract

In current information systems, information is passive. People act upon it, either sending it to known destinations or pulling it from known sources. InformANTS makes information active, enabling it to move actively from one user to another. This paper introduces the InformANTS vision and describes one of its major system components, the Information Matching System. Particular emphasis is placed on the distinctive self-organizing processes from which emerge the information exploration and exploitation capabilities of InformANTS.

1 Introduction

InformANTS (Information Agents for Networked Teaming Support) is a *research prototype* system currently developed under funding by the Disruptive Technology Office (DTO), for deployment in the US Intelligence Community (IC). It supports groups of analysts who are independently performing intelligence gathering and dissemination tasks by identifying collaboration opportunities based on overlapping interest and by actively routing relevant information to and between analysts.

The basic notion of InformANTS is a self-organizing information ecology where active information not only organizes into semantic neighborhoods but also drives collaboration by communicating these neighborhoods to appropriate target users.

To realize the above notion InformANTS operates with a very broad definition of a user. Users may be anything from intelligence analysts to databases. InformANTS thus removes one distinction that traditionally hampers information transfer: the distinction between sources and recipients of information.

This paper is organized as follows. Section 2 provides a general overview of the InformANTS architecture. The Information Matching System (IMS) is discussed in detail in section 3. Section 4 introduces ActiveWiki as a testbed for InformANTS and section 5 highlights short and long term challenges for this project.

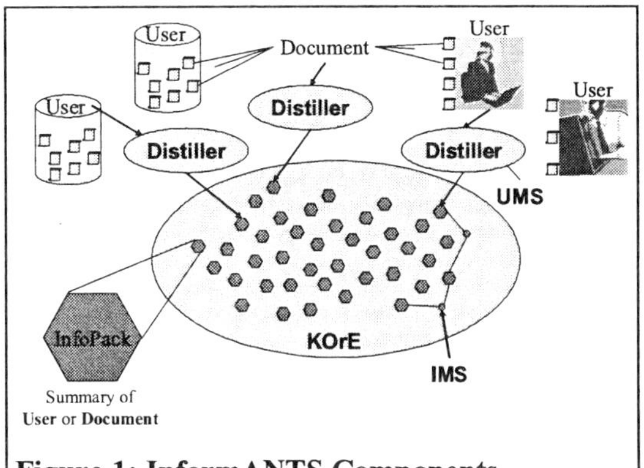

Figure 1: InformANTS Components

2 Architecture Overview

Three main components make up InformANTS (see Figure 1): a Knowledge Organizing Environment (KOrE), a User Modeling System (UMS) and an Information Matching System (IMS). This paper focuses on the IMS with its various self-organizing processes.

Documents and users are represented in the KOrE as Information Packages, or InfoPacks. A series of Distillers is responsible for extracting InfoPacks from user actions and document contents.

InformANTS' User Modeling System (UMS) is an example of a Distiller, and constructs InfoPacks representing human users by observing the interactions of those users with contents already present in the KOrE.

InfoPacks comprise three data containers. The "Head" functions as the anchor to the external source and holds the basic identifying information about an InfoPack (time of origin, type of user represented by this InfoPack). It is also the target and origin

0-7695-2906-2/07 $25.00 © 2007 IEEE

for links to/from other InfoPacks. The "Body" houses the "raw" content of an InfoPack, concepts and relations in the form of specialized concept maps. The "Chest" is the location of metadata such as summaries, tags, keywords.

We distill incoming user information or document contents into Specialized Concept Maps. These maps comprise specific types of concepts (currently "Place", "Person", "Action", and "Thing") and a (small) set of relations among these concept types. In a previous project we used generic concept maps [6] to represent the contents of documents or analyst interest and queries, but without the specialization and restriction of concepts and relations, our reasoning tasks would quickly explode in complexity. Here we essentially restrict ourselves to represent geographic networks, social networks, hierarchical task networks, object ontologies, and events that link specific instances across these topologies.

3 Information Matching System (IMS)

The primary function of the Information Matching System (IMS) is to continuously maintain, for each user and each document represented by an InfoPack in the dynamically changing KOrE, a set of pointers to other relevant InfoPacks. Thus, the IMS links users to users (*Virtual Interest Group identification*), users to documents (*information pull*), documents to users (*information push*), and documents to documents (*Topic Group identification*).

The IMS achieves this functionality through a layered set of self-organizing processes that are linked through positive and negative feedback loops, exchanging information in a shared environment. We group these processes into two major classes. The Information Exploration processes maintain a task-independent organization of the (components of the) InfoPacks in the KOrE, while the Information Exploitation processes use this organization to establish the relevance relationships between specific InfoPacks. In other words, the function of the Information Exploitation processes is to make significant relevance relations between InfoPacks explicit for possible presentation to human users.

These two classes of processes are symbiotic. Without the Information Exploration processes, Information Exploitation would have a very low performance since it would operate essentially in a random information space, and without Information Exploitation, Information Exploration would get no performance feedback.

Our design of the Information Exploration and Exploitation processes follows our approach to engineering swarming systems [4] that we have successfully applied in domains as diverse as battlefield prediction, control of autonomous robotic vehicles, or problem-pattern matching for decision support in automotive design. In our approach, we design self-organizing populations of simple individual agents that act and interact only locally in a shared dynamical environment and the desired complex system-level functionalities are then an emergent property of these swarming agent systems.

In the following, we discuss our design for the Information Exploration and Exploitation processes that we are currently implementing for the Information Matching System.

3.1 Information Exploration

InfoPacks are still very complex constructs and thus inappropriate to serve as the atomic building blocks in the self-organizing processes that seek to create an organized information landscape which can be exploited efficiently. Therefore, we base our lowest layer of self-organization on the concepts and relations contained in the "Body" of InfoPacks.

It is our goal in the IMS to find InfoPacks that are closely related to each other, and thus we need to organize them in a common space in which relevance is expressed by distance, using the information contained in the InfoPack's Body. The Information Exploitation processes will then search the InfoPack Proximity Space (IPS) to establish the desired explicit links.

The mapping of an InfoPack from the unorganized (and dynamically changing) set of InfoPacks in the KOrE to the IPS is performed by three processes (concept-to-CPS mapping, CPS adjustment, CPS-to-IPS mapping) that execute in parallel and draw on the three sources of information available in the Body of an InfoPack – concept characteristics, concept relations, and overall map composition. For simplicity of exposition, we consider these processes as though they are three steps in a sequence (Figure 2).

0-7695-2906-2/07 $25.00 © 2007 IEEE

In the first step, we map individual concepts by concept class into their respective Concept Proximity Space (CPS). In the second step, we adjust a concept's location in its CPS by the relations it has to other concepts in the InfoPack. Finally, in the third step, we combine the adjusted locations of all concepts in the Body of the InfoPack in their respective CPS into a unique location of the InfoPack itself in the IPS.

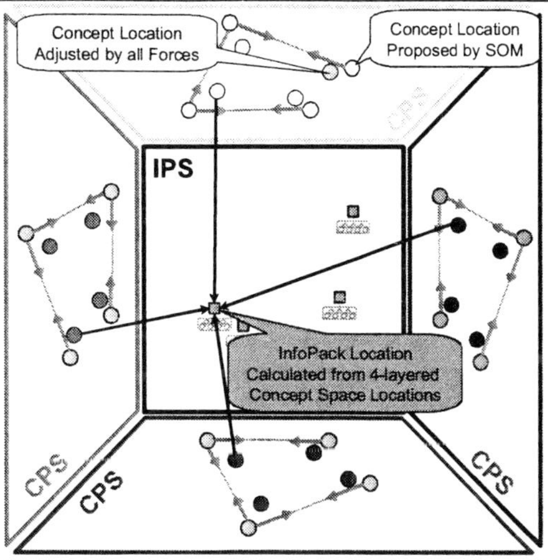

Figure 2: Derived InfoPack Location in IPS

Concepts in the specialized concept maps point to specific locations or regions in a high-dimensional abstract space that is generally non-metric and non-normalized. Consider, for instance, the "Person" concept that points into a space spanned by attributes, such as gender, age, nationality, name(s), or ethnicity. Though it may be possible to construct a similarity measure between such concepts using a subset of these attributes, typically it is very hard to usefully explore this space with sub-symbolic means, and it is computationally prohibitive to explore this space with symbolic means at the scale of our application. Thus, we need a mapping from the space of concepts of a single class as they currently occur in the InfoPacks to a low-dimensional, metric, and normalized space.

We selected Self-Organizing Maps (SOMs) [2], embedded in a 2-dimensional 1-unit-by-1-unit box and trained against the current set of concepts of one class, as our vehicle for the initial concept-to-CPS mapping. With a well-trained SOM, we are able to preserve the relative distance of concepts along the principal components of the high-dimensional space while, at the same time, embedding the concepts into a low-dimensional space that is most suitable for further swarming adjustment.

This SOM mapping, while it preserves the relative distance of concepts according to their specific characteristics (attribute settings), does not take into account the rich network of relationships that may exist between concepts. Therefore, we need to adjust the arrangements of concepts in each of the four CPSs to reflect these relationships.

The second step of the Information Exploration's mapping process uses Force-Based Clustering (FBC) [1] as a generic sub-symbolic method for the dynamic integration of guidance coming from different reasoners. In FBC, a population of particles arranges itself in an "energy-minimizing" configuration under the influence of attractive or repulsive forces of different kinds that are computed between particles. The particles find an "energy-minimizing" configuration in an iterative process where they move at finite speed along the force vector that is the sum of all component forces. In the IMS, particles are individual concepts located in the low-dimensional CPS. We initially consider two kinds of forces that affect the concepts' locations. The "home" force pulls a concept back to the location suggested by its SOM mapping, while the "relation" force attracts concepts to the current location of other concepts if they are linked in the InfoPack.

3.2 Information Exploitation

The Information Exploration processes dynamically form rich landscapes that can be searched efficiently and adjusted by performance feedback from the Information Exploitation processes. These landscapes are the Concept and InfoPack Proximity Spaces (several CPS and one IPS).

In our current system concept for the IMS we are drawing on our Polyagent construct (a single "complex" agent called an Avatar that uses "simple" probabilistic agents called Ghosts to explore complex spaces) [3] to establish useful links among InfoPacks.

The Avatar of an InfoPack's Polyagent continuously sends out Ghosts to explore the various information landscapes the InfoPack is embedded in. Some Ghosts explore the IPS, looking directly for nearby InfoPacks. Other Ghosts select specific concepts in the Body of the InfoPack and look for concepts of other (potentially related) InfoPacks in the concept's CPS. The Avatar collects and dynamically ranks the InfoPacks that have been identified by its Ghosts and thus maintains the desired list of relevant InfoPacks. As users assess this list, the Avatar may receive performance feedback, which it will communicate to the Information Exploration processes that provided the current ordering of InfoPacks.

4 Testbed: ActiveWiki

As a testbed for InformANTS, we intend to apply it to a Wiki, forming an "ActiveWiki". We are exploring an in-house Wikipedia server that will be augmented with the developing InformANTS system. The Wiki will initially be seeded with a full copy of the English version of Wikipedia.

In the ActiveWiki, the UMS observes users operating the Wiki interface and creates adaptive user model InfoPacks. These user models are stored in the KOrE, where the IMS enables the information to organize itself using swarming algorithms and dynamically identifies highly-relevant InfoPacks. The UMS processes these clusters to generate personalized virtual interest groups and data recommendations that the Wiki interface presents to the user.

5 Challenges

This paper has laid out a vision and a research agenda; there are many short- and long-term challenges that will have to be addressed to implement this vision.

5.1 Short Term

In the context of information exploration we must identify a function that will compute a meaningful location for an InfoPack in the IPS from the locations of each of its constituent concepts in their CPSs. Another short-term challenge is to fine-tune the relative strengths of the SOM and FBC in computing the location of a concept. Finally, we must develop meaningful non-numerical metric spaces for such concepts as "role".

5.2 Long Term

In the first stage of InformANTS implementation we concentrate on clustering InfoPacks according to the content of their bodies. Information exploration based on "Chest" content (meta-information) of InfoPacks is planned for the second stage. Self-Organizing Data and Search (SODAS) is a technology for dynamic, decentralized, any-time hierarchical clustering of objects, based on a defined set of object features [5]. We plan to integrate SODAS with InformANTS in order to produce multiple hierarchical cluster trees of InfoPacks, based on the features or tags contained in the InfoPacks' chests. Each cluster tree would provide a different "view" of the InfoPacks, clustered according to different criteria; these trees constitute a third type of space in addition to the CPSs and the InfoPack space.

6 Conclusion

In this paper we have presented our initial design for the IMS as a main component of the InformANTS architecture. The IMS comprises a synergistically linked set of self-organizing processes which dynamically maintain relevance relations between InfoPacks, representing information about users or documents outside the InformANTS system. Specifically, we distinguish between Information Exploration processes that produce an organized information landscape and Information Exploitation processes that search this landscape and link InfoPacks that are relevant to each other.

ACKNOWLEDGMENTS

This research was sponsored by the Air Force Research Laboratory, Air Force Materiel Command, USAF, under Contract number FA8750-06-C-0193. The views and conclusions contained herein are those of the authors and should not be interpreted as necessarily representing the official policies or endorsements, either expressed or implied, of AFRL or the U.S. Government.

7 References

[1] P. Eades. "A heuristic for graph drawing." *Congresses Numerantium*, 42:149-160, 1984.

[2] T. Kohonen. *Self-Organizing Maps*. Heidelberg, Springer-Verlag, 1995.

[3] H. V. D. Parunak and S. Brueckner. "Modeling Uncertain Domains with Polyagents." In *Proceedings of International Joint Conference on Autonomous Agents and Multi-Agent Systems (AAMAS'06)*, Hakodate, Japan, ACM, 2006.

[4] H. V. D. Parunak and S. A. Brueckner. "Engineering Swarming Systems." In F. Bergenti, M.-P. Gleizes, and F. Zambonelli, Editors, *Methodologies and Software Engineering for Agent Systems*, pages 341-376. Kluwer, 2004.

[5] H. V. D. Parunak, R. Rohwer, T. C. Belding, and S. Brueckner. "Dynamic Decentralized Any-Time Hierarchical Clustering." In *Proceedings of Proceedings of the Fourth International Workshop on Engineering Self-Organizing Systems (ESOA'06)*, Hakodate, Japan, Springer, 2006.

[6] P. Weinstein, H. V. D. Parunak, P. Chiusano, and S. Brueckner. "Agents Swarming in Semantic Spaces to Corroborate Hypotheses." In *Proceedings of AAMAS 2004*, New York, NY, pages 1488-1489, ACM, 2004.

DynCNET: A Protocol for Dynamic Task Assignment in Multiagent Systems

Danny Weyns, Nelis Boucké, Tom Holvoet, Bart Demarsin
Katholieke Universiteit Leuven, Celestijnenlaan 200A, Belgium
{Danny.Weyns, Nelis.Boucke, Tom.Holvoet}@cs.kuleuven.be

Abstract

Task assignment in multiagent systems is a complex coordination problem, in particular in systems that are subject to dynamic and changing operating conditions. To enable agents to manage dynamism and change, adaptive task assignment approaches are needed. In this paper, we introduce DynCNET, a protocol for dynamic task assignment that extends standard contract net (CNET). DynCNET allows the agents involved in the protocol to switch the assignment of tasks dynamically. We use an industrial automated transportation system as illustration and present results obtained from a real-world test setting that compare DynCNET with standard CNET and a field-based approach for task assignment.

1 Introduction

Two important factors for the growing complexity of today software systems are: the highly dynamic operating conditions under which systems have to operate such as altering workloads and variations in availability of resources, and the inherent distribution of resources which makes central control practically infeasible. In our research, we study situated multiagent systems (situated MAS) for engineering such systems. A situated MAS structures the software into a number of interacting autonomous entities (agents) that are situated in an environment. Control in situated MAS is decentralized, the system functionality results from the cooperation of the agents via the mediating environment.

One particularly challenging coordination problem in situated MAS is task assignment. Tasks in situated MAS are often characterized by delayed commencement, i.e. the execution of a task requires a preceding effort of an agent before the task can actually be executed. During delayed commencement, the conditions in the environment may change. Agents should be able to take into account these changes and dynamically adapt the assignment of tasks. A characteristic example application is a transportation system that uses multiple automatic guided vehicles (AGVs) to transport loads in an industrial environment. The stream of tasks that enter the system is typically irregular and unpredictable. Tasks in an AGV transportation system are characterized by delayed commencement, i.e., an AGV first has to drive to a load before it can pick the load and transport it to the destination. While driving toward the load all kinds of changes in the system may occur. New tasks may enter the system that are more suitable for the AGV to execute, new AGVs may become available that are more suitable to perform the task, etc. Such a problem setting requires a flexible task assignment approach that is able to cope with dynamics in the system. In this paper, we introduce a protocol called DynCNET. DynCNET is an extention of the well-know contract net protocol (CNET [8]), with "Dyn" referring to support for dynamic task assignment.

Overview. In the next section, we explain the DynCNET protocol. In section 3, we discuss test results obtained from applying DynCNET in an AGV transportation system and we compare DynCNET with CNET and a field-based approach for task assignment. Section 4 discusses related work. Finally, in section 5 we draw conclusions.

2 DynCNET Protocol

We start by explaining a number of general properties of the DynCNET protocol. Then we give an overview of the default sequence of the protocol. Next we explain how the agents involved in a protocol can switch the assignment of tasks. We will use the AGV transportation scenario depicted in Fig. 2 to illustrate the steps of the protocol. In the AGV application two types of agents are used: AGV agents and transport agents. Each AGV is controlled by an AGV agent. Transports are represented by transport agents that reside at a transport base system, i.e. a stationary computer located in the warehouse.

General Properties. DynCNET is an $m \times n$ protocol. An initiator that offers a task can interact with m participants, i.e. the candidate agents that can execute the task. On the other hand, each participant can interact with n initiators that offer tasks. As an example, consider the scenario shown in Fig. 2. In the AGV transportation system, an initiator corresponds with a transport agent that represents a task in the system and the participant corresponds with an AGV agent that can execute tasks. We denote the area where an initiator

0-7695-2906-2/07 $25.00 © 2007 IEEE

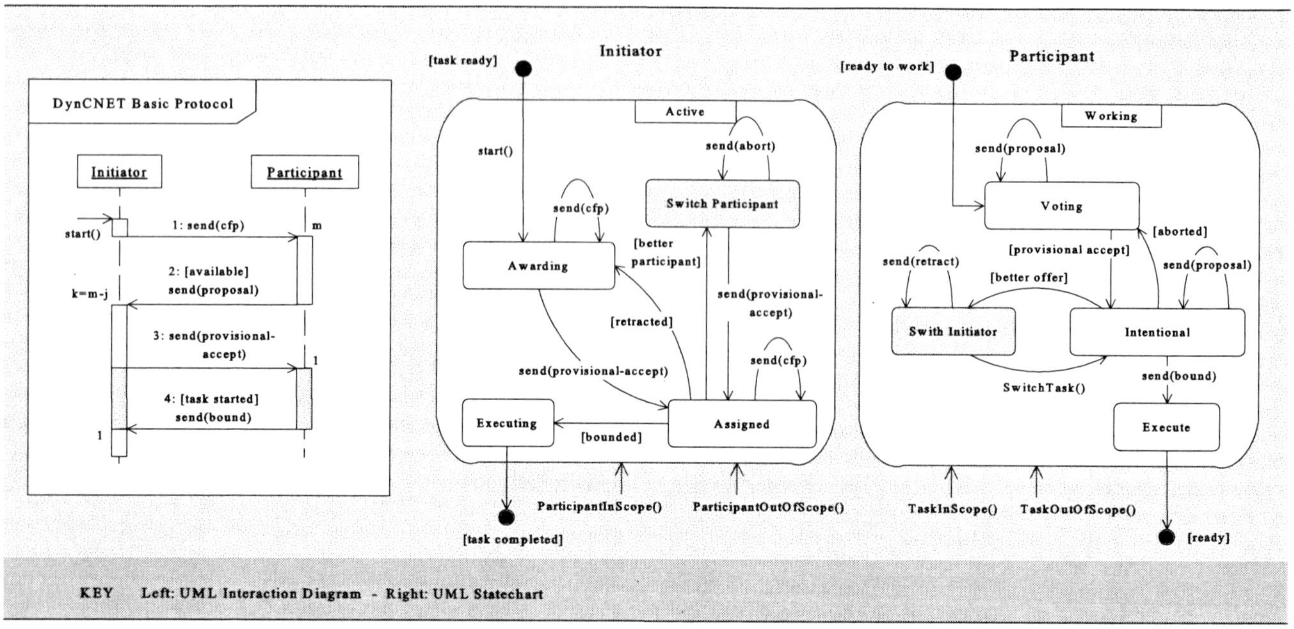

Figure 1. High-level diagrams of DynCNET. Left: interaction diagram; right: state diagram

(or participant) searches for participants (or initiators) the area of interest of the initiator (or participant). The dotted circles in Fig.2 show the current areas of interest of AGV A (top) and task x (bottom). For task x, there are currently two candidate AGVs to execute the task: F and G (AGV E is delivering a load). For AGV A on the other hand, there are three possible tasks to execute: u, v, and w. Due to the dynamics in the system, the set of candidate tasks (initiators) and agents that can execute a task (participants) can change over time. E.g., when AGV E drops its load at location s, it becomes a candidate to execute task x.

Default Sequence. The AUML interaction diagram of Fig. 1 shows the default message sequence of DynCNET. The default protocol consists of four steps: (1) the initiator sends a call for proposals; (2) the participants respond with proposals; (3) the initiator notifies the provisional winner; and finally, (4) the selected participant informs the initiator that the task is started. These four steps are basically the same as in the standard CNET protocol. The flexibility of DynCNET is based on the possible revision of the provisional task assignment between the third and fourth step of the protocol, i.e. the shades zones in Fig. 1.

Switching Initiators and Participants. To explain how agents can switch tasks when the conditions in the environment change, we use the UML state diagram in Fig. 1 that shows a compact representation of the behavior of the agents in the protocol. First we look at the protocol from the perspective of the participant, then we look from the point of view of the initiator.

Switching Initiators. Consider the situation in Fig. 2 where AGV A has a provisional agreement to execute task w.

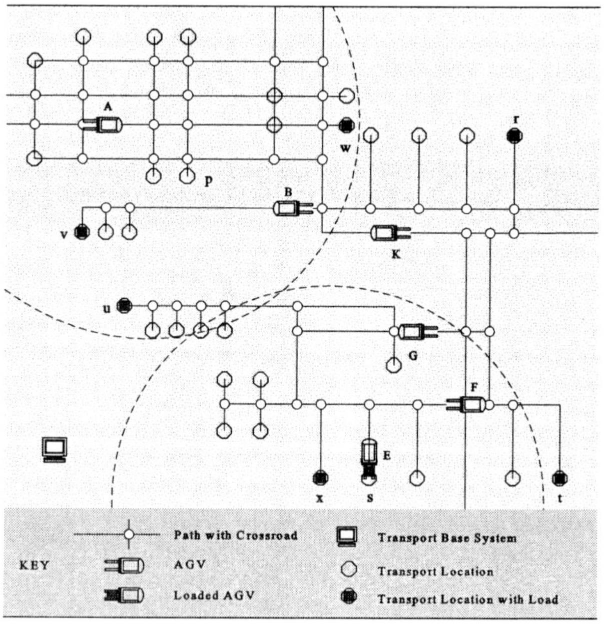

Figure 2. Scenario to illustrate DynCNET

While AGV A drives toward the pick location of task w, a new task may enter at the transport location p. This new task is an opportunity for AGV A. DynCNET enables participants to switch initiators and exploit such opportunities. When a participant is ready to execute a task, it enters the `Voting` state where it answers `cfp`'s with `proposals`. When the participant receives a `provisional-accept` message (step 3 in the interaction diagram of Fig. 1), it enters the `Intentional` state. As soon as the participant starts the task, it sends a `bound` message to inform the initiator. The participant is then committed to execute the task. However, if a new opportunity occurs before the task is started, i.e. the participant receives a `better offer`, the participant changes to the `Switch Initiator` state. In this state the participant `retracts` from the provisional task assignment and switches to the more suitable task (`SwitchTask()`).

Switching Participants. Consider the situation in Fig. 2 where the task x has a provisional agreement with AGV G. While AGV G drives toward the pick location of task x, AGV E may drop its load at transport location s and becomes available. This new AGV is an opportunity for transport x. DynCNET enables initiators to switch participants and exploit such opportunities. When an initiator has sent a `cfp` and received the `proposals` from the participants, it sends a `provisional-accept` message (step 3 in interaction diagram of Fig. 1) and enters the `Assigned` state. As soon as the initiator receives a `bound` message from the selected participant it enters the state `Executing` in which the task is effectively started. However, if a new opportunity occurs before the task is started, i.e. the initiator receives a `better offer`, the initiator changes to the `Switch Participant` state. In this state the initiator sends an `abort` to the provisionally assigned participant and switches to the more suitable participant.

`TaskInScope()` and `TaskOutScope()` are functions that notify the participant when new tasks enter and leave its area of interest. Such functionality can be provided by the perception module [11] of the participant that monitors the area of interest of the agent in the environment. Similarly, the functions `ParticipantInScope()` and `ParticipantOutOfScope()` notify the initiator when new participants enter and leave its area of interest.

Convergence. A potential risk of DynCNET is that the assignment of tasks oscillates between participants and no tasks are executed. In the AGV application, oscillations were avoided by: (1) limiting the areas of interest of the agents, and (2) choosing different areas of interest for initiators (task agents) and participants (AGV agents). In particular, the area of interests of AGV agents covered up to 1/10th of the total area of the map and the area of transport agents was 4 times smaller as that of AGV agents.

Synchronization messages. To handle synchronization, confirmation messages are used. For example, when an initiator switches participants it first sends an abort to the participant that has provisionally accepted, see state diagram in Fig. 1. This latter then sends a message to confirm the abort. However, if this participant has already started the task (transition `Intentional to Execute`) but the initiator has not yet received the bound message, it refuses the abort. The switch will then canceled. Due to space limitations, we have made abstraction of these synchronization messages in our explanation. For details, see [10].

3 DynCNET Applied in Practice

In this section, we give a number of test results obtained from applying DynCNET in a simulated AGV transportation system. These tests where performed in the context of a joint R&D project between AgentWise and Egemin (http://emc2.egemin.com). The tests are performed on the map of an transportation system with 14 AGVs that is implemented by Egemin at EuroBaltic. We used a standard transport test profile that generates 140 transports with a random pick location and a random drop location per hour real time. Every simulation was run for 200.000 timesteps, corresponding to approximately 4 hours real time. Displayed test results are average values over 30 simulation runs. Error bars in the figures show the 95 % confidence interval for the test results.

We compare DynCNET with standard CNET and a field-based approach for task assignment (FiTA [9]). In FiTA, AGV agents are guided towards pick locations of transports by following the gradient of a field that combines attractive fields emitted by transport agents and repulsing fields emitted by other AGV agents.

Test Results. We discuss the test results of communication load and reaction time. To compare the communication load, we have measured the average number of messages sent per finished transport. The left part of Fig. 3 shows the results of the test. DynCNET requires (as FiTA) about twice the bandwidth of standard CNET. Average waiting time is expressed as the number of timesteps a transport has to wait before an AGV picks up the load. The right part of Fig. 3 shows the test results for average waiting time for transports. After four hours in real-time, this resulted in CNET having handled 380 transports, DynCNET having handled 467 transports, and FiTA 515 transports. For the 467 executed transports of DynCNET, we measured an average of 414 switches of transport assignments performed by transport agents and AGV agents.

Discussion. DynCNET has similar performance characteristics as FiTA and both outperform CNET, the cost is a doubling of required bandwidth. DynCNET allows to specify and reason about the behavior of the agents by means of common engineering diagrams such as interaction and state diagrams, such common engineering approaches are currently not available for FiTA. On the other hand, DynCNET requires explicit support to deal with message loss. In FiTA, the freshness of the received fields is taken into account toe determine the attraction an repulsion of fields giving older field values less importance.

4 Related Work

CNET was originally proposed by Smith and Davis [8] and is included in a FIPA-standard [2]. [3] describes a protocol that allows a bidder to place bids for multiple tasks.

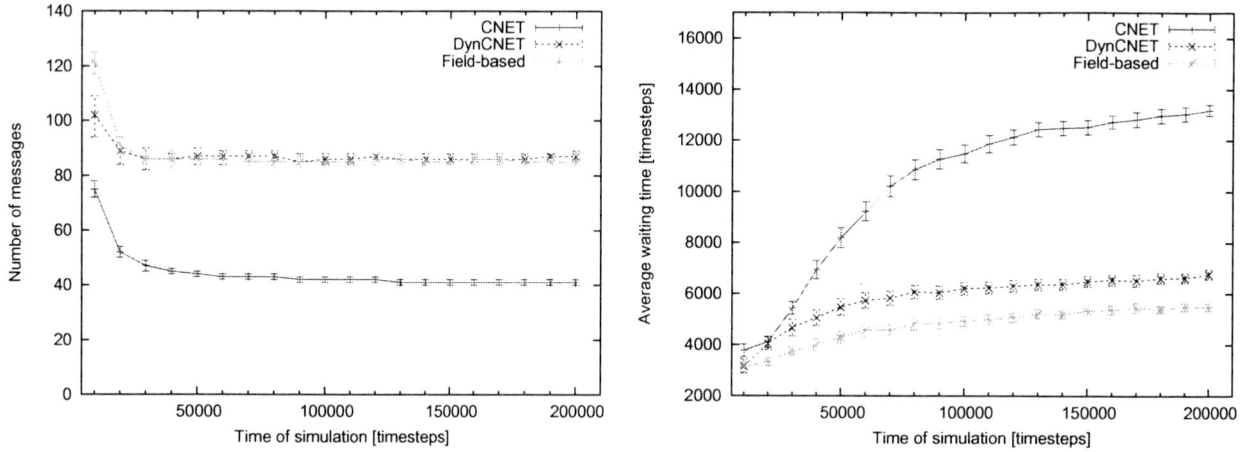

Figure 3. Left: amount of messages being sent per finished transport. Right: average waiting time

This protocol does not supports changes at both sides or delayed commencement.

The protocol introduced in [1] introduces two levels of bidding, i.e. a pre-bidding phase in which the participants can still change their commitment and a definitive bidding phase in which the task is effectively assigned to a single participant.

The FIPA Iterated CNET protocol allows multi-round iterative bidding [2]. Related are leveled-commitment contracts [6]. The idea of a leveled-commitment contract is that any of the agents in a contract can de-commit by paying an agreed penalty to the other agent(s) in the contract. Leveled-commitment contracts are typically intended for negotiation protocols between self-interesting agents.

Finally, several researchers combine CNET with other strategies to provide support for dynamism. [7, 4, 5] are examples that use a mediator pattern for dynamic scheduling and CNET to produce a schedule. These mechanisms allow for some flexibility, but task rescheduling is time consuming making the approaches more suitable for systems with limited dynamics.

5 Conclusions

In this paper, we presented DynCNET, a protocol for dynamic task assignment in situated MAS and we showed test results from a real-world test setting that compare the approach with standard CNET and a field based approach. DynCNET allows agents to switch the assignment of tasks dynamically. Our experiences show that DynCNET outperforms standard CNET, while it has similar performance characteristics as FiTA. There is an important difference between DynCNET and FiTA with respect to engineering support. DynCNET allows to use common engineering diagrams for design and reasoning, wheras no common engineering support is currently available for FiTA. On the other hand, DynCNET requires explicit support to deal with message loss while this is naturally supported in FiTA.

References

[1] S. Aknine, S. Pinson, and M. F. Shakun. An Extended Multi-Agent Negotiation Protocol. *Journal on Autonomous Agents and Multi-Agent Systems*, 8(4), 2004.

[2] FIPA TC Communication. FIPA Contract Net Protocol and Iterated Contract Net Protocol Specification, Doc. SC00029, Doc. SC00030, 2002.

[3] T. Knabe, M. Schillo, and K. Fischer. Improvements to the fipa contract net protocol for performance increase and cascading applications. In *Multiagent Interoperability*, 2002.

[4] F. Maturana, W. Shen, and D. Norrie. Metamorph: An adaptive agent-based architecture for intelligent manufacturing. *Journal of Production Research*, 37(10), 1999.

[5] D. Ouelhadj, P. Cowling, and S. Petrovic. Intelligent systems design and applications. Springer-Verlag, 2003.

[6] T. Sandholm and V. Lesser. Levelled-commitment contracting: A backtracking instrument for multiagent systems. *AI Magazine*, 23(3):89100, 2002.

[7] W. Shen and D. Norrie. An agent-based approach for dynamic manufacturing scheduling. In *Agent-Based Manufacturing, Minneapolis*, 1998.

[8] R. Smith. The contract net protocol: High level communication and control in a distributed problem solver. In *IEEE Transactions on Computers, C-29(12)*, 1980.

[9] D. Weyns, N. Boucké, and T. Holvoet. Gradient Field Based Transport Assignment in AGV Systems. In *5th International Joint Conference on Autonomous Agents and Multi-Agent Systems, AAMAS, Hakodate, Japan*, 2006.

[10] D. Weyns, N. Boucké, T. Holvoet, and B. Demarsin. *DynCNET: A Protocol for Flexible Transport Assignment in AGV Transportation Systems*. Technical Report CW 478, Katholieke Universiteit Leuven, Belgium, 2007. http://www.cs.kuleuven.ac.be/publicaties/rapporten/CW/2007/.

[11] D. Weyns, E. Steegmans, and T. Holvoet. Towards Active Perception in Situated Multi-Agent Systems. *Applied Artificial Intelligence*, 18(9-10):867–883, 2004.

Improving ICE Service Selection in a P2P System using the Gradient Topology

Jim Dowling[1] Jan Sacha[2] Seif Haridi[1]

[1]Swedish Institute of Computer Science, Kista, Sweden
[2]Distributed Systems Group, Trinity College Dublin
{jdowling,seif}@sics.se, jsacha@cs.tcd.ie

Abstract

Internet Connectivity Establishment (ICE) is becoming increasingly important for P2P systems on the open Internet, as it enables NAT-bound peers to provide accessible services. A problem for P2P systems that provide ICE services is how peers discover good quality ICE servers for NAT traversal, that is, the TURN and STUN servers that provide relaying and hole-punching services, respectively. Skype provides a P2P-based solution to this problem, where super-peers provide ICE services. However, experimental analysis of Skype indicates that peers perform a random walk of super-peers to find one with an acceptable round-trip latency. In this paper, we discuss a self-organizing approach to discovering good quality ICE servers in a P2P system based the walk Topology. The walk Topology uses information about each peer's ability to provide ICE services (open IP address, available bandwidth and expected session times) to construct a topology where the "better" peers for providing ICE services cluster in the center of the topology; this adaptation of the super-peer search space reduces the problem of finding a good quality ICE server from a random walk to a gradient ascent search.

1. Introduction (ICE and Relay Peer Selection)

Recently, large-scale distributed and peer-to-peer (P2P) systems, such as Googletalk and Skype, respectively, have enabled nodes behind Network Address Translation (NAT) gateways and firewalls, that we call NAT'd nodes, to provide services, such as Voice over IP (VoIP) telephony and file transfer. In these systems, peers cannot establish direct IP connections with NAT'd nodes without the use of a 3rd party server to either help the connecting node hole-punch through any intermediary NATs or to help establish an indirect connection via a relay (or rendezvous) node, which relays traffic to the NAT'd node. Two commonly used protocols for NAT traversal are Simple Traversal of UDP over NAT (STUN) [13] for hole-punching to set up a direct UDP connection through a NAT, and an extension to STUN called Traversal using Relay NAT (TURN) [12], that provides relaying services to nodes behind NATs by routing UDP and TCP traffic to and from them. Peers in both Skype and Googletalk attempt to use STUN to establish connections, and if this fails they fall back to using a relay (TURN) node. Guha estimates that 9.6% of Skype's traffic travels over relay nodes [4], which corresponds closely to Google's estimate that 8% of the GoogleTalk traffic is routed using relay nodes [3].

Internet Connectivity Establishment (ICE) is a draft IETF specification [2] that defines how to establish sessions (primarily aimed at Session Initiation Protocol sessions) that can traverse NATs and firewalls. ICE specifies how both STUN and TURN protocols are used to enable nodes provide each other a set of candidate transport addresses for communication. The problem of how nodes find a host providing these ICE services (i.e., the STUN and TURN servers) is outside the scope of the specification. However, two different approaches have become popular: deploy ICE services on well-known names in a centralized server farm, as in relay.l.google.com and stun.l.google.com for Google Talk [3], or provide a decentralized solution, such as Skype, where peers with an open IP address and sufficient available bandwidth are upgraded to super-peers that provide STUN and TURN-like services to ordinary peers [10, 4, 1].

In Skype super-peers are connected over their own P2P topology, and ordinary peers connect to super-peers to both discover Skype users and use ICE services to establish VoIP sessions with NAT'd peers [5, 1, 10]. NAT traversal covers four cases in Skype: Initiator NAT'd, Recipient NAT'd, Both NAT'd (behind well-behaved NATs) and Both NAT'd (behind broken NATs) [10]. Only in the final case, do peers use relay nodes for VoIP traffic. Ren et al. observed that peers select several super-peers to act as a relay nodes, apparently at random, and measure the round-trip time (RTT) to the relay nodes [10]. If the RTT is below an acceptable level, the VoIP session stabilizes routing over those relay nodes, otherwise super-peers continue to be selected and probed until a few of them are discovered with a low-

0-7695-2906-2/07 $25.00 © 2007 IEEE

enough RTT. They concluded from their experiments that peer selection of relay nodes is both slow, with a worst case in their experiments of 329 seconds taken for traffic to stabilize over selected relay nodes, and suboptimal in use of system resources, with most sessions probing over 20 super-peers before stabilizing on relay nodes [10]. We suggest that this poor performance is due to Skype performing a random walk of the super-peer topology, where no use is made of domain knowledge to improve search efficiency, see Figure 1 (a).

In the rest of this paper, we show how the the Gradient Topology [15, 14] enables the construction of an efficient, self-organizing system for providing ICE services, where ICE services are deployed on high-quality peers and efficiently discovered by clients using gradient ascent search. We show that the cost of finding high quality super-peers on the Gradient Topology using a general search algorithm, random walk, is substantially higher than gradient ascent search.

2. ICE Services on the Gradient Topology

The Gradient Topology is a self-organizing P2P topology where peers use a local utility level to adapt their connections to other peers, such that and peers with highest utility levels are clustered in the center of the topology while peers with decreasing utility are found at increasing distance (or "orbits") from the center [15, 14]. Gradient search to and from the center of the topology follows the peers' utility gradient. As an application of the Gradient Topology, we are developing a P2P middleware that provides ICE services. In this system, there are two types of peers: NAT'd peers that cannot provide ICE services, and super-peers that have an open IP address, and, hence, can potentially provide ICE services. Only a sub-set of the super-peers are suitable for providing relay services: those peers with high available bandwidth and session times that are long relative to application usage scenarios. For different applications that use ICE services, such as VoIP systems, web servers or video streaming, typical application usage may produce different requirements on how long a super-peer's session time should be to provide a reliable relaying service. In the Gradient Topology we can design super-peers, so that only those super-peers with high enough expected session times are upgraded to provide relay services, see Figure 1 (b). For context, in Skype, the median super-peer session time has been measured at 5.5 hours - easily long enough to provide relay services for VoIP conversations that have a median length measured at 2 minutes 50 seconds [4].

In our system, peers connect to the Gradient Topology and determine whether they have an open IP address or are NAT'd using a pool of well-known bootstrap servers. Peers with open IP addresses become super-peers and are connected using the Gradient Topology, while the NAT'd peers are edge nodes that can have redundant connections to super-peers. In effect, the NAT'd peers are clients of the Gradient Topology, while the super-peers are servers that provide ICE services or routing to ICE services.

In order to construct the Gradient Topology, super-peers have a utility function that captures good properties for ICE services, and relay services in particular. The utility function can be customized to consider different host and application attributes, but our current utility function is based on available bandwidth at peers and their expected session time:

$$Utility\left(n_i\right) = \left(AvailBandwidth_i * E\left(SessionTime_i\right)\right)$$

where $AvailableBandwidth_i$ has a value greater than zero if it exceeds a minimum threshold value and the expected session time, $E\left(SessionTime_i\right)$, is calculated using a probabilistic model based on observations of the peer's recent session times. Peers use the output of the utility function to adapt their connections to preferentially connect to other peers with similar utility levels. This causes peers with higher utility to migrate towards the center of the topology and peers with lower utility to migrate to the edge of the topology. Peers also maintain connections to random peers, which provide negative feedback on the excessive clustering induced by peers connecting to other peers with similar utility values. For more details on the algorithm, see [15, 14].

Search on the Gradient Topology can be done efficiently using gradient ascent search [14], see Figure 1 (b), where the search query includes a utility threshold that the super-peer providing the ICE service must exceed for the search to succeed. NAT'd peers can determine an appropriate utility threshold by estimating the distribution of utility levels of super-peers using an aggregation algorithm, such as the one described in [15]. Similarly, super-peers can use the estimated distribution of utility levels to determine if they should provide an ICE service or not. These utility thresholds can be customized for different applications.

Figure 2 shows the results of experiments performed on simulations of the Gradient Topology comparing random walk with gradient ascent. In the first experiment, the simulated P2P network is under constant churn, and new peers are assigned a session-time according to the Pareto distribution with an exponent of 1.5; this roughly corresponds to the power-law distribution of super-peer session times observed by Guha et al. for Skype [4]. Peers search for any super-peer with a utility above a given threshold, i.e., the super-peers that provide the ICE services. As can be seen in Figure 2 (a), the gradient ascent algorithm requires significantly fewer hops to find a high utility super-peer than random walk. This is because gradient ascent can exploit knowledge of peers' utilities captured in the gradient topology, whereas the random walk algorithm is blind to peer

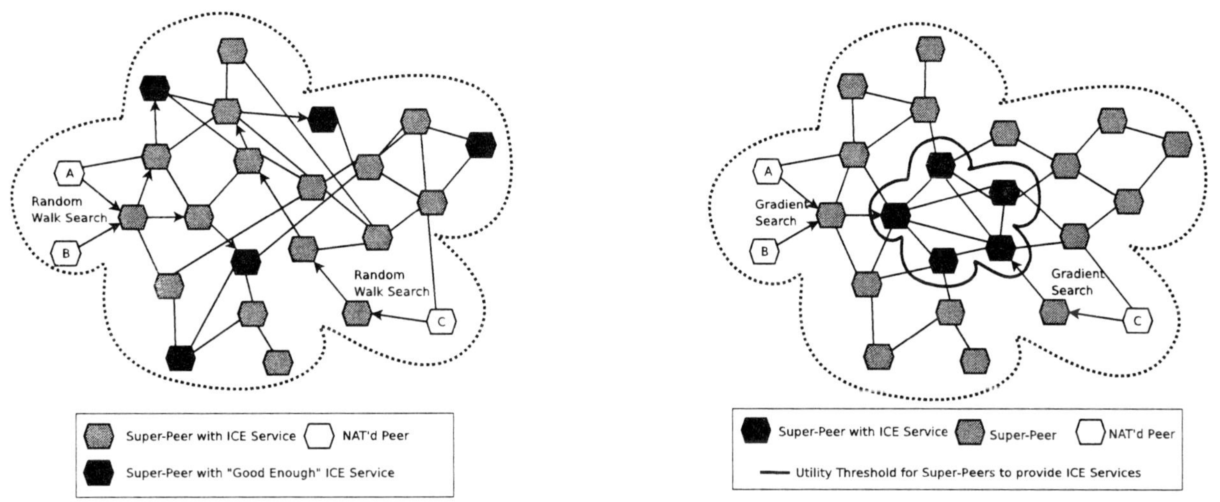

(a) Skype searches for better quality relay nodes using a random walk of its Super-Peer Topology

(b) Gradient Descent Searching for ICE Services on the Gradient Topology

Figure 1. Searching on P2P Topologies for ICE Services

utilities. In the second experiment, the performance of random walk and gradient ascent are evaluated when the system is under churn. The network contains 10,000 peers, and even under extremely heavy churn (with 10% of the peers replaced at every discrete time step), gradient ascent search continues to have a low failure rate for searches, see Figure 2 (b).

Status of our P2P ICE Middleware Currently, work is in progress on an implementation of the Gradient Topology, and we are leveraging implementations of STUN and relay servers in the Berkeley-licensed libjingle library [16, 3] to provide ICE services.

3. Related Work

The ASAP protocol addresses the problem of improving the selection of relay nodes by making the protocol aware of the nodes' Internet Autonomous System (AS) [10]. For NAT traversal, there have been recent attempts to extend ICE to cover TCP-based media, including the ability to offer a mix of TCP and UDP-based candidates [11]. There is also ongoing research on hole-punching for TCP, with systems such as STUNT, NATBlaster and P2PNAT demonstrating some success [5].

SG2 addresses the problem of developing a super-peer topology where clients connect to a single super-peer with a low round-trip time (RTT) [7]. In SG2, peers are connected in a random topology using Newscast, while super-peers connect to one another if their latency is below a threshold level. Jelasity and Kermarrec have simulated a gossiping model, also based on Newscast, that partitions peers into "slices", where the protocol takes into account specific attributes of the nodes [6]. This system addresses the problem of the partitioning a P2P topology, but the authors have not yet proposed search algorithms for their topology.

Semantic overlay networks (SONs) address a similar problem to the gradient topology, namely, how to structure a P2P topology to improve the search performance for resources in a system. They aim to exploit semantic structure in resources or in successive search queries, generally by constructing a topology that organizes resources in accordance with the semantic space of resources, such as documents or multimedia. Often resources are mapped on to a semantic space, for example, mapping feature vectors to a euclidean space, and the distance between resources represents their semantic closeness. This is similar to our notion of mapping node utility to the gradient topology, except that utility is defined on a per node, rather than per resource, basis. Examples of SONs include [17], a small world semantic overlay topology [8], and a semantic overlay clustering for super-peer networks [9], where peer-to-super-peer connections are adapted to improve search performance.

4. Conclusions

In this paper, we showed how a P2P topology can be adapted to build more efficient search algorithms to find ICE services deployed on super-peers. We described how the Gradient Topology can be used to build a P2P middleware that provides ICE services for NAT-traversal, and how it can be constructed so that the ICE services are deployed on peers with higher utility. We showed how gradient as-

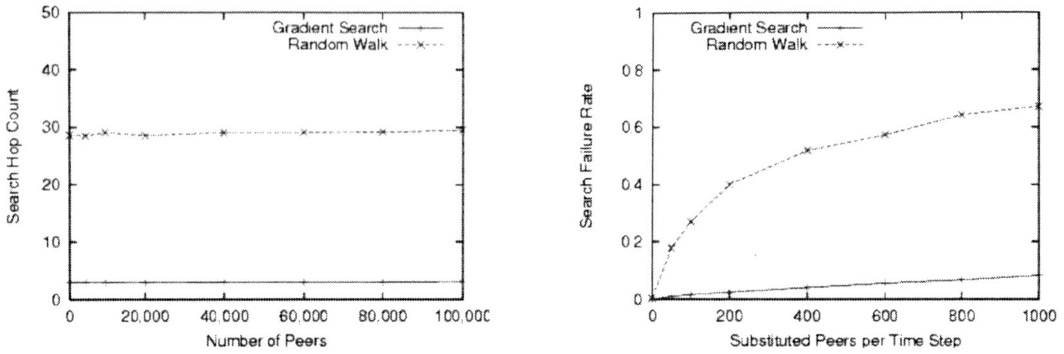

(a) Average Search Hop Count

(b) Average Search Failure Rate.

Figure 2. Comparison of Random Walk and Gradient Ascent Search on the Gradient Topology when searching for peers above the utility threshold.

cent search algorithm is significantly more efficient than random walk when searching for ICE services on the Gradient Topology, and how gradient ascent search functions continues to work under high churn levels where random walk breaks down. This approach should not only improve the time required to find a good quality of ICE server, but also help optimize the global utilization of resources in the P2P system. Future work will involve a real-world implementation of the middleware and evaluation using applications built on the ICE services.

Acknowledgements This research was supported by a Marie Curie Intra-European Fellowship within the 6th European Community Framework Programme. The authors thank Ray Cunningham for comments on an earlier version of the paper.

References

[1] S. Baset and H. Schulzrinne. An analysis of the skype peer-to-peer internel telephony protocol. In *IEEE Infocom*, 2006.

[2] Cisco. Interactive connectivity establishment (ice). In *IETF Draft*, Jan 2007.

[3] Google. Google talk, Accessed, Feb 22, 2007. http://code.google.com/apis/talk/libjingle.

[4] S. Guha, N. Daswani, and R. Jain. An Experimental Study of the Skype Peer-to-Peer VoIP System. In *Proceedings of The 5th International Workshop on Peer-to-Peer Systems*, pages 1–6, 2006.

[5] S. Guha and P. Francis. Characterization and measurement of tcp traversal through nats and firewalls. In *Internet Measurement Conference*, pages 199–211, 2005.

[6] M. Jelasity and A.-M. Kermarrec. Ordered slicing of very large-scale overlay networks. In *Proceedings of the Sixth IEEE International Conference on Peer-to-Peer Computing*, pages 117–124. IEEE Computer Society, 2006.

[7] G. Jesi, A. Montresor, and O. Babaoglu. Proximity-aware superpeer overlay topologies. In *Proceedings of the 2nd IEEE International Workshop on SelfMan*, volume 3996 of *LNCS*, pages 43–57. Springer-Verlag, june 2006.

[8] M. Li, W.-C. Lee, and A. Sivasubramaniam. Semantic small world: An overlay network for peer-to-peer search. In *ICNP '04: Proceedings of the Network Protocols, 12th IEEE International Conference on (ICNP'04)*, pages 228–238, Washington, DC, USA, 2004. IEEE Computer Society.

[9] A. Loser, F. Naumann, W. Siberski, W. Nejdl, and U. Thaden. Semantic overlay clusters within super-peer networks. In *DBISP2P*, pages 33–47, 2003.

[10] S. Ren, L. Guo, and X. Zhang. Asap: an as-aware peer-relay protocol for high quality voip. In *Proceedings of the 26th IEEE International Conference on Distributed Computing Systems*, pages 70–79, 2006.

[11] J. Rosenburg. Tcp candidates with interactive connectivity establishment. In *IETF Draft*, October 2006.

[12] J. Rosenburg and a. C. H. R. Mahy. Turn - traversal using relay nat. In *IETF Draft*, October 2006.

[13] J. Rosenburg, J. Weinberger, C. Huitema, and R. Mahy. Stun - simple traversal of user datagram protocol through network address translators. In *RFC 3489*, March 2003.

[14] J. Sacha, J. Dowling, R. Cunningham, and R. Meier. Discovery of stable peers in a self-organising peer-to-peer gradient topology. In *Proceedings of DAIS*, volume 4025 of *LNCS*, pages 70–83. Springer-Verlag, 2006.

[15] J. Sacha, J. Dowling, R. Cunningham, and R. Meier. Using aggregation for adaptive super-peer discovery on the gradient topology. In *Proceedings of the 2nd IEEE International Workshop on SelfMan*, volume 3996 of *LNCS*, pages 77–90. Springer-Verlag, 2006.

[16] P. Saint-Andre, J. Beda, S. Ludwig, J. Hildebrand, and S. Egan. Jingle ice transport. In *XMPP Draft*. XMPP Standards Foundation, Dec 2006.

[17] S. Voulgaris, A.-M. Kermarrec, and L. Massoulie. Exploiting semantic proximity in peer-to-peer content searching. In *Proceedings of the 10th IEEE International Workshop on Future Trends of Distributed Computing Systems*, pages 238–243. IEEE Computer Society, 2004.

Adaptive SSL: Design, Implementation and Overhead Analysis

C. J. Lamprecht and Aad P. A. van Moorsel
University of Newcastle upon Tyne, School of Computing Science
Newcastle upon Tyne, NE1 7RU, United Kingdom
{c.j.lamprecht, aad.vanmoorsel}@ncl.ac.uk

Abstract

Adaptive security is based on the observation that the security requirements of a system or service heavily depend on the environment in which they operate and should therefore be dynamically adjusted to best operate within that environment as the environment changes. In this paper we are concerned with adapting the choice of cryptographic algorithms applied to client-server interactions. To that end, we design and implement an adaptation controller for SSL (Secure Socket Layer), called Adaptive SSL.

1 Introduction

Applications for adaptive security have been proposed in a number of diverse areas. Examples include mobile ad-hoc networks where current network conditions play a role in choosing relevant security protocols at runtime [2]. Media streaming research proposes the use of additional contextual information, in the form of an intelligent routing infrastructure, to allow for flexible security levels [4]. There have also been proposals to provide adaptive system security through system event monitoring [6]. The inspiration for this paper however comes from web sites or e-commerce applications. Managing the security of such applications are non-trivial and requires a plethora of technologies. These include firewalls, encryption technologies, intrusion detection systems and single sign-on techniques. In this paper, we consider adaptation of the protocol used to secure the communication channel between an application or web server and the client. In particular, we consider adaptation of the Secure Socket Layer (SSL) protocol [3].

Adaptive SSL (ASSL) aims to provide appropriate security mechanisms for SSL sessions at any particular moment in time as the environment changes. Attributing environmental factors could include the threat level, server load or transaction type. Client attributes such as processing power, bandwidth or type of client can also be considered. These factors are monitored by specialized third party applications that inform ASSL of affected clients and appropriate security measures.

In this paper we present the design and implementation of Adaptive SSL and study the overhead of the approach. Although this paper reports on a considerable amount of work, it should be considered work-in-progress towards a (self-)adaptive security solution in which SSL can be flexibly manipulated in order to change security levels automatically at runtime.

2 Design of Adaptive SSL

2.1 SSL

SSL is a solution for confidentiality, integrity and non-repudiation of messages at the Transport Layer, which has been standardized through the Transport Layer Security effort [3]. An SSL secure transport layer connection is established through a handshake mechanism where algorithms are selected, based on those available to both the client and the server, for the aforementioned three security properties. This process is commonly known as SSL *negotiation* and the resulting connection is called a *session*. Once established, the session can conduct a *renegotiation*, but how and when this should be done is not specified in the standard. Hence, it is left to the SSL implementation to determine the extent to which to facilitate such renegotiation. In this paper we suggest a generic design for controlling the renegotiation within SSL. We call the resulting system 'Adaptive SSL'.

Web servers typically provide their own SSL implementation that extends SSL with rule-based decision making to initiate the renegotiation process. Renegotiation decisions in web servers are normally based on the location (such as the directory in which the requested data is stored) and the type of the data requested. The decision rules are usually determined prior to starting the web server.

Fig. 1 depicts a standard web server request-response processing cycle during an SSL secured session. The numbers in the figures indicate the event order and the labels the interaction type. Events with the same number indicate a decision point and only one of the events take place. Fig. 1 shows the client sending an encrypted request to the server in step 1. The request is initially passed to SSL which then

0-7695-2906-2/07 $25.00

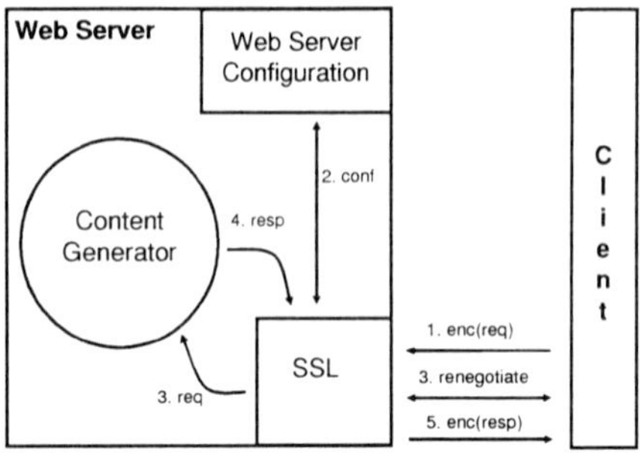

Figure 1. SSL (enc = encrypted; req = request; resp = response; conf = configuration)

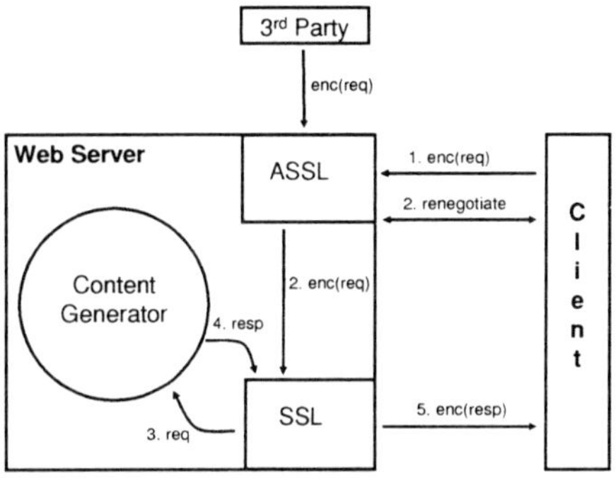

Figure 2. Adaptive SSL

queries the web server's configuration file (where the renegotiation decision rules are typically stored) and decides either to process the request or renegotiate the session.

The disadvantage of the basic SSL approach is that security needs to be preconfigured and only predefined static information, namely the data and its location, can be utilized when making renegotiation decisions.

2.2 Adaptive SSL

We propose a more flexible approach to session management where renegotiation logic is decoupled from the main SSL implementation and web server configuration. Separating these concerns enables us to build a more powerful adaptive security model since the renegotiation rules can be determined and deployed independently and parallel to the web server and its components.

The ASSL module effectively intercepts requests between the client and SSL module and, based on a set of conditions, may decide to renegotiate the session security. The set of conditions are specified and altered at runtime by 'third parties', that is, other programs such as firewalls, system performance monitors, network monitors, server administrators, etc. Note that the proposed solution requires no changes to the client code and supports traditional SSL interactions as well.

Fig. 3 is a magnified version of the ASSL module in Fig. 2. It shows how ASSL adapts the session security, during the request-response cycle in Fig. 2, based on conditions specified in the Request Filter.

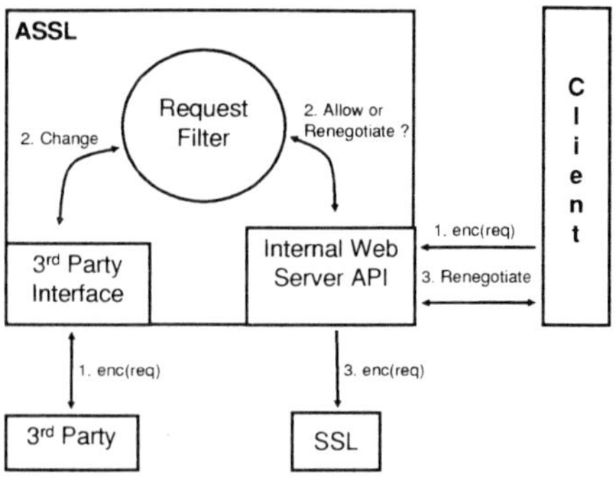

Figure 3. ASSL Session Security

3 Implementation

3.1 SSL in Apache

Apache [7] is built on a modular design where nearly all of its functionality is provided through modules. Modules may register an interest to manipulate a client's request at various points during the request-response processing cycle. Apache provides various hooks to facilitate this. Apache is configured using *directives* which are read from a file at startup (*httpd.conf*) or at runtime through *.htaccess* files which are stored in the particular directories accessed during a client request. Modules may also have their own directives which can be included in these files.

SSL is one such module which integrates the OpenSSL toolkit [8] into Apache. SSL session security is configured through the *SSLCipherSuite* directive. This directive specifies a subset of security algorithms that can be used to establish a secure session with the client.

SSLCipherSuite directives may also be included in .htaccess files by web space owners and thus allow the session security to be changed at runtime. Apart from the fact that checking and parsing .htaccess files introduces certain overhead, we decided against using these files in Adaptive SSL because renegotiation directives can only be specified using the available predefined static information, such as the directory accessed and filetype, thus limiting it's use in dynamic environments where we may wish to adapt security based on connection- or client information.

3.2 Adaptive SSL Module

Adaptive SSL is also implemented as an Apache module and can be installed on existing Apache installations as it requires no additional Apache source code changes. The significant parts are detailed below:

Hooks: ASSL registers a number of hooks with Apache in such a way that they are interleaved with existing SSL hooks, in essence forming a wrapper around SSL session renegotiation and so taking control of the SSL renegotiation functionality without altering the existing SSL implementation.

Request Filter: The request filter is a sequence of [condition, SSLCipherSuite] pairs on which the security of a session with the client will be renegotiated if one of the conditions match the client request and the current session security is not a subset of the newly selected SSLCipherSuite. Each condition in the list is checked in turn and the first that matches is selected, much in the same way as firewall filters. Conditions are formulated using the powerful SSLRequire directive. Each condition is an arbitrarily complex boolean expression which can make use of standard CGI, Apache and SSL related variables. Section 4 provides a sample expression.

The SSLRequire directives are expressed using an extensive subset of contextual information at the right level of abstraction. It uses only contextual information relating to the end-to-end client server connection (which is the primary concern of SSL), nothing higher (application context) and nothing lower (data context).

Handler: ASSL also registers a content generator, or handler (see Fig. 3), which handles all third Party requests to Apache to insert condition pairs in the Request Filter. This provides a platform independent and secure means (allowing third party verification) by which the security can be changed as all third Party requests are made over HTTPS.

4 Overhead Analysis

The following section details a performance evaluation of our Adaptive SSL module to ascertain its suitability for runtime SSL session management. In each experiment we compare Apache's SSL implementation to a 'best' and 'worst' case performance scenario for Adaptive SSL. In the best case the Request Filter list is empty and in the worst case the Request Filter list is full, containing twenty of the following complicated boolean expressions.

```
%{SSL_CIPHER} =~ m/^(EXP|NULL)/
and %{SSL_CIPHER} =~ m/AES256/
and %{SSL_CIPHER_USEKEYSIZE} < 52
and %{REMOTE_ADDR} =~ m/^192.76.162.[0-9]+$/
and %{REQUEST_FILENAME} =~ m/secure/
and %{REMOTE_URI} =~ m/.mov/
and %{HTTP_USER_AGENT} =~ m/^Mozilla/
```

When evaluating a client request, each expression evaluates to false and so every expression in the Request Filter is evaluated for each client request. ASSL+ represents ASSL with a full Request Filter (the worst case scenario).

We first consider the security overhead for a single client request in experiment 1 to gain insight in the absolute time spent in the ASSL module. Experiment 2 evaluates the effect of this overhead on the server by stressing the server to determine the maximum number of requests it can process at any one time.

Experimental environment. All experiments were conducted on a 2.80GHz Intel Pentium 4 with 2GB RAM, running Apache 2.2.3 on Linux Fedora Core 5 (Kernel 2.6.17.11). SSL negotiations were performed with a 1024 bit RSA key and the RSA-DES-SHA1 cipher suite was utilized. OpenSSL 0.9.8d toolkit was used by Apache's SSL- and our module. The SSL enabled Apache server was benchmarked using workload generated by Httperf [5]. Autobench [1] was used to simulate a request flow from multiple clients located on a number of machines. All requests were for a 44 byte index.html file.

Stage	Protocol		
	SSL	*ASSL*	*ASSL+*
Negotiation	115	*	*
Renegotiation	2	61	423
Wait for client	71768	*	*
Decryption	354	*	*

Table 1. Average processing times, in microseconds.

4.1 Experiment 1

Table 1 shows the average time the server takes to process various stages of the client request before content for the response can be generated. Stages include the server processing time consumed during negotiation, renegotiation and request decryption. "Wait for client" indicates server idle time during the negotiation between client and server. An * indicates that the values are the same as for SSL.

The table shows that in the best case scenario ASSL introduces about 60 microseconds overhead in the renegotiation phase compared to SSL. This increases to up to close to half a millisecond (423 microseconds) when the Request Filter demands more processing. To put this into perspective, the table shows that these amounts are easily outweighed by the time SSL spends in waiting for the client for instance. The overhead of ASSL in absolute numbers thus seems very minor. Note also that although SSL's use of .htaccess files for runtime security changes does not show up in SSL renegotiation time, it does increase Apache's request processing time depending on the size of the file. This overhead is avoided by ASSL.

4.2 Experiment 2

The maximum number of requests the server can process at any one time depends greatly on client usage patterns. We therefore conduct two experiments, one where the clients establish few new SSL sessions and the other where the clients establish a new SSL session per request. In realistic situations the client behavior will be a mixture of these two extremes. We evaluate the overall effect of using ASSL in these extreme scenarios.

Scenario 1. In this experiment we evaluate ASSL's performance for the case where clients create minimal new SSL sessions. To that end, 1000 requests are made per session and SSL sessions are reused. In this scenario the server spends proportionately more time checking for rene-

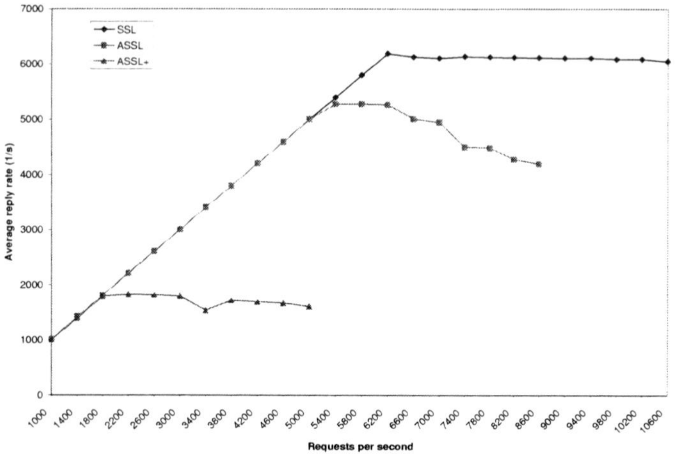

Figure 4. Performance Graph showing a 1000 requests per session

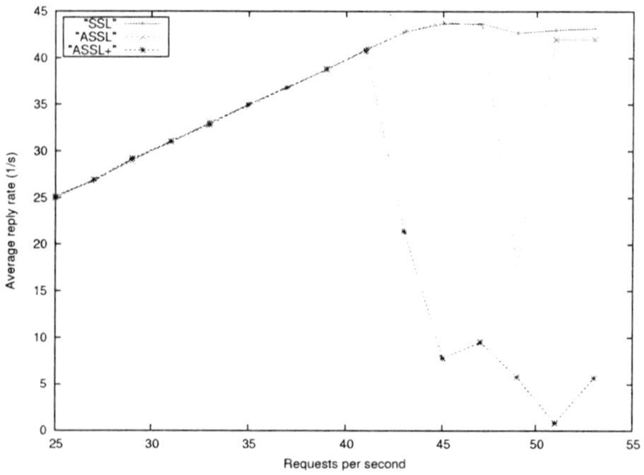

Figure 5. Performance Graph for one request per SSL session

gotiations than negotiating new connections, which should penalize ASSL's performance.

Figure 4 shows that when using ASSL, Apache experiences peak load between 30% and 85% of the maximum number of requests that SSL can support, depending on the Request Filter length and complexity. So, we indeed see that checking if renegotiation is in order can be costly and will reduce the amount of clients that can be supported by a server. Note again that this client behavior represents an extreme case.

Scenario 2. In this experiment we evaluate ASSL's performance when clients create the maximum number of new sessions, namely one session per request. In this scenario SSL does more work and so ASSL has minimal effect on server performance.

Figure 5 shows that even when using a full Request Filter the server incurs negligible additional overhead when using ASSL under normal client workloads. However, the performance breaks down when the server reaches peak load. We think this is because we hit another bottleneck. We observed that the number of child processes created by Apache rapidly increases for ASSL and ASSL+ under peak load. This likely due to requests waiting for a lock on the Request Filter which results in Apache not releasing resources allocated to that request. Apache was configured with a theoretical limit of 40000 child processes and so we believe that the drop in performance is likely due to the number of connections that can be supported by the system itself. A bespoke locking and threading solution could remedy the observed behavior but this is beyond the scope of our work.

Summarizing, we conclude from Experiment 1 that the amount of overhead introduced by ASSL is small (about 60 microseconds) but that the overhead is sensitive to the contents of the Request Filter (moving up to the order of milliseconds). When stressing the server (Experiment 2) much depends on the client behavior, which determines what proportion of processing time is spent executing the Request Filter. In general terms, the added functionality of being able to adapt the security level comes at a cost that only becomes prohibitive when the Request Filter is complex and executed in vain too often.

5 Future work

The presented research is preparatory work to create a self-adaptive security solution based on flexible use of renegotiation in SSL. Our work shows that the overhead associated with the proposed Adaptive SSL design and implementation is small in absolute numbers (per request) but that one should guard against unnecessary processing. These results encourage us now to further research the deployment of Adaptive SSL in a realistic scenario and establish strategies that optimize the trade-off between security and performance (overhead as well as server performance) when renegotiating security levels.

References

[1] Autobench, `http://www.xenoclast.org/autobench/`.

[2] C. Chigan, L. Li and Y. Ye, "Resource-aware Self-adaptive Security Provisioning in Mobile Ad Hoc Networks", *Proc. IEEE Wireless Communications and Networking Conference*, pp.2118–2124, 2005.

[3] T. Dierks and C. Allen, *RFC 2246 - The TLS Protocol Version 1.0*, Jan. 1999.

[4] C. Gentry, A. Hevia, R. Jain, T. Kawahara and Z. Ramzan, "End-to-end security in the presence of intelligent data adapting proxies: the case of authenticating transcoded streaming media", *IEEE Selected Areas in Communications*, Vol. 23, No. 2, pp.464–473, 2005.

[5] Hewlett Packard's webserver benchmarking tool, `http://www.hpl.hp.com/research/linux/httperf/`.

[6] H. Hinton, C. Cowan, L. Delcambre and S. Bowers, "SAM: Security Adaptation Manager", *Computer Security Applications Conference*, pp.361–370, 1999.

[7] B. Laurie and P. Laurie, *Apache: The Definitive Guide, Third edition*, O'Reilly, 2003.

[8] OpenSSL Toolkit, `http://www.openssl.org/`.

Work-in-Progress Track, Session 1: Software Engineering and Multiagent Systems

Designing Self-Organising Emergent Systems based on Information Flows and Feedback-loops

Tom De Wolf and Tom Holvoet, {Tom.DeWolf,Tom.Holvoet}@cs.kuleuven.be
Dep. of Computer Science, KULeuven, Celestijnenlaan 200A, B-3001 Leuven, Belgium

Abstract

For self-organising emergent solutions, there is no support to explicitly design system-wide information flows and feedback loops in those flows. This is problematic because the problem-solving power mainly resides in coordination between agents which needs information exchange. The flows of inherently decentralised information are essential for emergence. Feedback loops are a prerequisite for self-organisation. The design should explicitly focus on information flows. Otherwise, engineers are overwhelmed by details of decentralised coordination mechanisms such as gradient fields without first looking at the bigger coordination picture. We introduce "Information Flow" as abstraction to design a solution independently of the coordination mechanism details by explicitly identifying information flows and designing feedback-loops. UML 2 activity diagrams are the notation. An automated guided vehicle transportation system shows the usefulness and feasibility.

Introduction. Self-organising emergent solutions are a promising approach for inherently decentralised and highly dynamic problem domains. A system exhibits emergence when there are coherent macroscopic or system-wide properties, behaviours, structures, etc, that arise solely from the microscopic or local interactions between agents which know nothing of the desired macroscopic property [2]. Self-organisation is a dynamical and adaptive process where systems acquire and maintain structure without external control [2]. A combination of both promises a decentralised, flexible, and robust solution. Typically, decentralised coordination mechanisms such as gradient fields are used [3]. Designers are overwhelmed by the details of these mechanisms (e.g. large set of parameters, which mechanism?, how to use it?, etc.). The bigger coordination picture needs to be considered beforehand.

The main problem-solving power of emergence resides in coordination between agents instead of in intelligent reasoning of individual agents. Agents need local access to information located elsewhere in the system to coordinate their next actions. Emergence requires information flows towards agents. Explicitly modelling macroscopic information flows and relating them to microscopic actions allows to design at an abstraction level closer to the macro-level and independent of microscopic details of decentralised coordination mechanisms that enable information flows. Feedback-loops in information flows are a prerequisite for self-organisation [8]: *Think Flows rather than Transitions.* "Our training [.. conceives ...] processes in terms of discrete state transitions, but the role of autocatalysis in [..] self-organization urges us to pay attention to the flows of information among them, and to ensure that these flows include closed loops." Autocatalysis comes from chemistry and indicates that a product of a reaction serves as a catalyst for that same reaction. Agent actions need to stimulate other actions and eventually re-stimulate the first actions. The interplay between information flows and actions of agents has to form closed feedback loops. Modelling information flows allows to design loops explicitly and focus the creative effort on the enabler of self-organisation.

We introduced "Information Flow" as design abstraction in [4] to explicitly identify information flows. This paper additionally identifies the need for feedback-loops, and applies the approach to a new and complex case study on automated guided vehicles. UML 2 activity diagrams [1] are the notation because they serve the need to indicate which actions need which information flow(s). An extended version of this paper in which UML 2 diagrams are motivated extensively, in which a second case is worked out in detail, and with more related work can be found in [5].

Case Study: Automated Guided Vechicles. An Automated Guided Vehicle (AGV) warehouse transportation system uses multiple computer guided vehicles, called AGVs. AGVs move loads (e.g. packets, materials) in a warehouse. Each AGV can only do a limited set of local actions such as move, pick load, and drop load. The goal is to efficiently transport incoming loads to their destination. Figure 1 shows a simple factory lay-out: locations where loads must be picked up at the left, destinations at the right, and a network in-between of stations and segments on which AGVs move. The AGV problem is dynamic: many lay-outs, loads arrive at any moment, AGVs

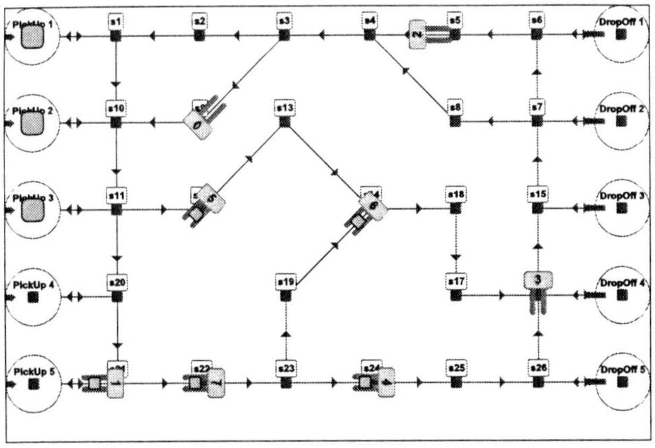

Figure 1. AGV case: example factory lay-out.

move constantly and fail, obstacles and congestion appear, etc. Information on this is scattered through the system, but needed by AGVs to decide on their next move. AGV movement should result in feedback to each other.

Information Flow Design. To take information into account it must be available to the agent locally. An AGV needs to know the available loads to pick up, but this information is located with the loads elsewhere in the system. To make the notion of 'local' more concrete we define 'Locality'. 'Locality' w.r.t. a system entity (e.g. an agent, loads, stations, etc.) is defined as that limited part of the system for which the information located there is directly accessible to the entity, i.e. no need to communicate with other entities. A locality is designed for each system entity, and differs in each application. A locality can be limited in distance, time, number of network hops, etc. To achieve global coordination in a decentralised way, information scattered through the system flows or propagates between localities of entities needing and/or providing the information:

An information flow is a stream of information from source localities towards destination localities and this stream is maintained and regularly updated to reflect changes in the system. Between sources and destinations, a flow can pass other localities where new information can be aggregated and combined into the information flow.

Experience in building self-organising emergent solutions indicates that it is impossible to analytically derive the microscopic actions and information flows for achieving a given macroscopic behaviour. This remains a creative step. Information flows at least explicitly support designers to first focus on the system-wide flows, and less on overwhelming details of coordination mechanisms [3]. What follows outlines the information flows and feedback loops for the AGV case. There is a small notational difference in this paper compared with UML 2 [1]. Data flow edges are dashed lines instead of solid lines to emphasise them as information flows. Tick gray arrows annotate feedback-loops.

Identifying Information Flows. The steps to identify information flows shown below are are not necessarily performed sequentially. An iterative process typically provides feedback to revise decisions if needed.

Step 1: architecture and locality. Before the design of information flows, the main structure or architecture is designed. This includes identification of agents, other entities, and the "locality" of each entity. There is no step-by-step procedure for this and needs to be done creatively. Each AGV is controlled by an agent. The locality of an AGV is its view range, i.e. the current station on which it is located and its outgoing segments. For a load this is its current location (AGV or station), and a station is its own locality.

Step 2: microscopic actions. A macroscopic requirement is achieved by microscopic actions that contribute to that requirement. Decomposing macroscopic behaviour in a set of actions is an important step. There are two main macroscopic requirements. First, incoming loads have to be dispatched to AGVs. Second, AGVs have to be routed in a factory. For dispatching the action is `assign load`. Routing AGVs implies `move` actions towards goal stations (i.e. pick-up or drop-off station). Also `pick-up` and `drop-off` actions are needed.

Step 3: information needed. The information needed in the localities of agents deciding on the actions is identified. AGVs can only locally decide where to move if they know which directions lead to the goal and how fast (e.g. distance). Also information on which directions lead to congestions and/or obstacles is important. This information is located with the destination and intermediate stations. To assign a load information is needed on the available loads which is located with the loads.

Step 4: information flows. Once the designer knows which information is needed and where it originates, the information flows can be established. The diagram in figure 2 is constructed as follows. Each locality (e.g. AGV view range, load location, station) has its own partition in which the actions (e.g. `Move Towards`) are executed by the entity of the locality (e.g. `AGV x`). Information flows are shown as data flow edges with the type of information as the data type (e.g. `Load Info`). Some localities have parameters x and i indicating that it exists for multiple AGVs and loads. Information flows to all AGVs or loads, unless indicated by a condition on the flow (e.g. `[AGV within distance Y]`). We discuss the different information flows for dispatching and routing. These flows should form feedback loops (see later).

Dispatching. We only assign a load permanently to an AGV when the load is picked-up. Until then, other AGVs that are better suited can take over (upper-left of figure 2). An AGV chooses the best load d (`Choose Best Load d`) and intends to pick it up by `Moving Towards Load d`.

0-7695-2906-2/07 $25.00 © 2007 IEEE

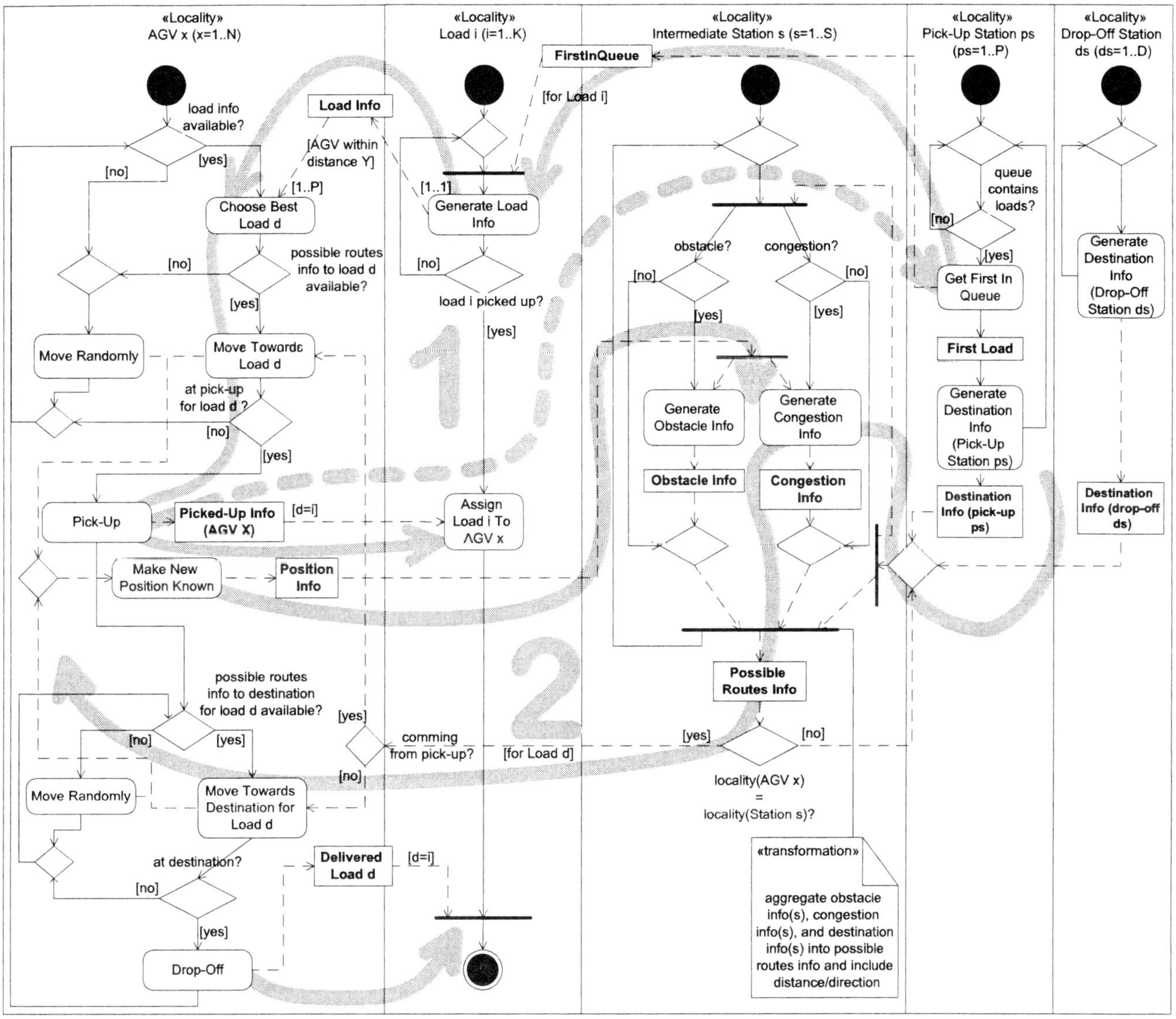

Figure 2. Information flows in AGV application.

This is repeated until `Pick-Up` is executed. Then `Assign Load i To AGV x` is executed. We use these flows:

- *FirstInQueue and Load Info:* To choose a load an AGV needs information on available loads, i.e. `Load Info` flow from the load locality. This flow only starts for the first load in the pick-up station queues. A `FirstInQueue` flow from the pick-up station locality towards the load locality triggers this.
- *Picked-Up Info:* After a pick-up, the load is assigned to the AGV (`Assign Load i To AGV x`). Information is needed on when the load is picked-up, i.e. `Pick-Up Info` flow to load d only ($[d = i]$).
- *Delivered Load Info:* This is feedback on a drop-off.
- *Possible Routes Info:* To move to load d, information is needed on the possible routes (see below).

Routing. The following information flows are needed for `Move Towards` actions (bottom-right of figure 2):

- *Possible Routes Info:* AGVs move towards pick-up stations (`Move Towards Load`) to `Pick-Up` loads, then move towards drop-off stations (`Move Towards Destination for Load`) to `Drop-Off` loads. Each AGV needs information on `Possible Routes` towards a destination, taking into account distance, obstacles, and congestions. A more complex information flow is required that aggregates and calculates the information while flowing through the system. Information on pick-up and drop-off stations (`Destination Info`) flows towards AGVs. The information passes through stations and segments on the route between the AGV and the destination (i.e. `Intermediate Station`). Information on obstacles and congestion is incorporated in the flow when it passes (`Obstacle Info`, `Congestion Info`). The flow can pass multiple `Intermediate Stations` before reaching the AGV locality. A transformation represents the combination of obstacle/congestion info collected at multiple stations with info arriving from the pick-up or drop-off stations into `Possible Routes Info`. The transformation also calculates the distances. Eventually this flow arrives with AGVs looking for or holding the load (*[for load d]* conditions).

- *Position Info:* The `Possible Routes Info` flow needs info on AGV locations to generate congestion and/or obstacle info. `Position Info` flows from AGV localities towards intermediate station localities when AGVs move.

Step 5: coordination mechanisms. Information flows still need to be achieved by decentralised coordination mechanisms. Examples are digital pheromones, gradient fields, market-based coordination, etc. [3]. Each flow imposes requirements on the mechanism, and each mechanism has characteristics to consider when deciding on its suitability. The `Possible Routes Info` flow requires a mechanism that enables aggregation and calculation (i.e. distances) of extra information while flowing through intermediate stations. Gradient fields allow this and are a good choice [3]. Information flows are data flows in activity diagrams which allow to design a solution independently from the details of decentralised coordination mechanisms (e.g. direct messages or gradient fields).

Feedback-loops. The feedback-loops in the AGV case:

AGVs - Dispatching - Loop 1. A first loop is established for dispatching loads (tick gray arrows and number 1 in figure 2). From the pick-up station the `FirstInQueue` flow triggers the `Load Info` flow in the load locality. This triggers the `Choose Best Load`, `Move Towards Load`, and `Pick-Up` actions. At that moment the AGV locality equals the pick-up station locality and a new load becomes first in the queue. This restarts the loop (dashed tick arrow).

AGVs - Routing - Loop 2. A second loop is established for routing AGVs (tick gray arrows and number 2 in figure 2). AGVs move based on `Possible Routes Info`. This movement generates the `Position Info` flow towards where `Obstacle Info` and `Congestion Info` are added to the `Possible Routes Info` flow. As such AGVs give feedback to each other while routing.

Reflection. To design self-organising feedback loops, the interplay between information flows AND actions on control flows needs to be considered. Thus diagrams only showing information flows such as UML 2 information flow diagrams [7] serve as a clear but limited view. Activity diagrams are more expressive to establish a good solution.

Discussion. The information flow diagram in figure 2 is rather complex. It includes both control and information flows. Separating these concerns could simplify the diagrams but makes it harder to get an overview on how control and information flows interact. This makes designing feedback loops harder because loops result from the interplay between control and information flows. It is a trade-off between separation of concerns, complexity, and having a complete picture. Data Flow Diagrams (DFDs) [6] are a similar notation which only shows data flows. This makes it impossible to discover all self-organising loops. DFDs have no formal specification like UML 2 activity diagrams. DFDs are less expressive: no control nodes, partitions, or multiplicities. DFDs are well-known but exist next to the more widely used UML notation which is therefore preferred. Also our approach needs a more rigorous formal specification, for example, to automatically check for loops.

Conclusion. The information flow based modelling approach allows to design a solution independently of coordination mechanism details. The approach addresses emergence by explicitly identifying flows of inherently decentralised information through the system. Self-organisation is addressed by explicitly designing feedback-loops. An engineer designs at an abstraction level relating system-wide information flows with individual agent actions, which is where the creative effort is needed for self-organising emergent solutions.

References

[1] C. Bock. UML 2 Activity and Action Models (Part 1-6). *Journal of Object Technology*, 2003-2004-2005. Vol. 2 (no.4 pp. 43-54, no. 5 pp. 41-56, no.6 pp. 7-23) and Vol. 3 (no. 1 pp. 27-41, no. 7 pp. 37-56) and Vol. 4 (no. 4 pp. 43-66).

[2] T. De Wolf and T. Holvoet. Emergence Versus Self-Organisation: Different Concepts but Promising When Combined. In *Engineering Self Organising Systems: Methodologies and Applications*, volume 3464 of *LNCS*. 2005.

[3] T. De Wolf and T. Holvoet. A Catalogue of Decentralised Coordination Mechanisms for Designing Self-Organising Emergent Applications. CW 458, Dep. of Computer Science, K.U.Leuven, Leuven, Belgium, 2006.

[4] T. De Wolf and T. Holvoet. Information Flows for Designing Self-Organising Emergent Systems. In *Proc. of the 1st Engineering Emergence for Autonomic Systems (EEAS) Workshop*, pages 22–29, Dublin, Ireland, 2006.

[5] T. De Wolf and T. Holvoet. Using uml 2 activity diagrams to design information flows and feedback-loops in self-organising emergent systems. In *Proc. of the 2nd Int. Workshop on Engineering Emergence for Decentralised Autonomic Systems (EEDAS)*. Greenwhich Univ Press, June 2007.

[6] C. P. Gane and T. Sarson. *Structured Systems Analysis: Tools and Techniques*. Prentice Hall, 1979.

[7] OMG. Unified Modeling Language (UML) specifications, v2.0. (online at *www.uml.org*), August 2005.

[8] H. Parunak and S. Brueckner. Engineering Swarming Systems. In *Methodologies and Software Engineering for Agent Systems*, pages 341–376. Kluwer, 2004.

Toward Requirements Engineering for Self–Organizing Multi–Agent Systems

Jan Sudeikat[1] and Wolfgang Renz
Multimedia Systems Laboratory (MMLab),
Faculty of Engineering and Computer Science,
Hamburg University of Applied Sciences,
Berliner Tor 7, 20099 Hamburg, Germany
{wr|sudeikat}@informatik.haw-hamburg.de

Abstract

Since Multi-Agent Systems (MAS) are composed of sets of (inter–)acting autonomous and pro-active agents, they provide suitable concepts to the construction of self–organizing processes, promising robust and adaptive system behaviors. An examination of current software–engineering approaches to self-organizing MAS identified a lack of requirement engineering approaches, established in general-purpose engineering methodologies. As self–organizing dynamics are typically utilized to enforce continuous MAS adjustment we discuss how expectations on MAS adaptivity can be expressed and validated, considering both the intended system configurations as well as the system dynamics that steer system (re–)configuration. We argue that self–organizing MAS development typically intends recurring pattern of system dynamics and exemplify their specification and validation, transferring requirements engineering practices to self–organizing MAS development.[1]

1. Introduction

Agent–Oriented Software Engineering (AOSE) proposes the decomposition of distributed systems into sets of interacting agents, situated in an environment. As the actual applications result from agent interplay, MAS are prominent tools for the construction of self–organizing systems [12].

Development efforts typically rely on field–tested and well–understood *coordination mechanisms* [12] that help to anticipate resulting system behaviors. Design heuristics [2] guide the mapping of mechanism components to application domains and simulation–based processes [4, 19] guide adjustment of system as well as agent parameters. Purposeful *redesign* of these mappings is a research issue [15].

Established software–engineering methodologies (e.g. [8]) structure development procedures in *iterations*, composed of sequences of activities (so–called *workflows* or *disciplines*) that development teams are to complete successively. These activities commonly comprise *requirements* engineering, *analysis*, *design*, *implementation* and *testing*. A recent review of established best practices to the development of self–organizing MAS [16] revealed that design approaches mature, while testing and requirements analysis found yet minor attention (results outlined in section 2).

In order to enhance and stimulate current engineering practices, we outline how intended system dynamics can be modeled, therefore providing an approach to requirements engineering for self–organizing MAS. Development teams typically utilize self–organizing dynamics to enable system adaptivity [22], i.e. system reconfigurations according to external forces. Specifying sets of intended MAS configurations and the macroscopic observable dynamics that steer MAS reconfiguration, allows developers to define intended MAS behaviors. In addition, it provides means for a pattern language, as the self–organizing MAS typically intended recurrent types of dynamics (cf. section 3).

Requirement models provide qualitative descriptions of the intended dynamics and can be refined – in agreement with system stakeholders – to comprise macroscopic parameter ranges. During analysis stages developers can revise MAS abstractions, i.e. simulation models, to ensure that the intended dynamics are exhibited in proposed MAS designs (qualitative evaluation). In later development stages MAS will be simulated to ensure compliance to intended macroscopic parameter ranges (quantitative evaluation).

This paper is structured as follows. In the following section established best practices to the development of self–organizing MAS are summarized. In section 3 a framework for the specification of requirements for self–organizing systems is presented and their validation is exemplified. Finally, we conclude and give prospects for future work.

[1] Jan Sudeikat is doctoral candidate at the Distributed Systems and Information Systems (VSIS) group, Computer Science Department, University of Hamburg, Vogt–Kölln–Str. 30, 22527 Hamburg, Germany

0-7695-2906-2/07 $25.00 © 2007 IEEE

2 Engineering Self–Organizing Dynamics

In [16], techniques for the development of self–organizing MAS are discussed. Here, we summarize the obtained results, focusing on established coordination mechanisms, development procedures and formal tools.

2.1 Coordination Mechanisms

Utilization of specific – typically nature inspired – coordination mechanisms facilitates self–organizing MAS development [12]. These mechanisms provide field–tested and well–understood template MAS designs, guiding the coordination of collective agent behavior adjustment, that steers the rise of self–organizing phenomena. Mechanisms have been cataloged according to (1) underlying computational techniques [3, 12], (2) the properties of resulting phenomena [21] and (3) their sources of inspiration [10].

Self–organizing dynamics in MAS require the presence of positive and negative feedback loops, steering individual behavior adjustment [2]. In [16] we have examined the reported mechanisms according to their support for underlying feedback mechanisms. The presence of feedback loops in MAS requires both the perception of MAS state information as well as interpretation of perceptions leading to agent behavior adjustment. Therefore, mechanisms can be distinguished between *interdependency*–level and *behavior adaption*–level mechanisms [16].

2.2 Methodologies

In [4] it has been argued that the non-linear dynamics of self–organizing processes impair top–down design. Experimental methods have been proposed that understand development as sequences of experiments (e.g. [4, 19]).

In [20] the notion of *design pattern* has been transferred to self-organizing systems to catalog established distributed coordination mechanisms (cf. section 2.1). Pattern selection is based on macroscopic properties of intended self–organizing effects(see [21]). The rationale is that these properties map directly to the above described coordination mechanisms (named *best practices* in [19]), leading to look–up tables [21]. This selection is the initial stage for the application of an adjusted *Unified Process* [7] that supports macroscopic MAS simulations [19].

Solely the ADELFE methodology [1] approaches the top–down construction of adaptive behaviors. An adjustment of the *Rational Unified Process* [8] facilitates the design of MAS composed of *cooperative* agents. ADELFE particularly stresses the identification of cooperation failures (so–called non-cooperative situations) and agent procedures to recover from these.

2.3 Formal Models of Complex MAS Dynamics

The applied development processes rely on empiric approaches, i.e. macroscopic system simulations. Therefore, the utilization formal tools has been proposed to speed up simulation cycles [5, 9]. These tools provide succinct ways to describe MAS [11] and have been used to either *analyse* MAS implementations or to examine abstract MAS designs providing *proof–of–concept* validations that foreseen system designs enable the intended dynamics.

The usage of *stochastic transition systems* for the analysis of self–organizing MAS has been reviewed in [17]. Differential equations are established tools to describe self–organizing system dynamics (e.g. [6]) and have been proposed [9] to describe macroscopic MAS behaviors. When agents exhibit a fixed number of behaviors, i.e. states or roles, differential equations can represent the rate of role/behavior changes in terms of mean occupation numbers of individual agent states. These equations can be used to resemble MAS when underlying time–continuous Markov process can be assumed, as argued and exemplified in [14].

Process algebra allows modeling and validation of concurrent and reactive systems as sets of independently executing *processes*, communicating information via synchronous *channels*. Stochastic extensions to these algebra are established to model biological and chemical processes and have also been applied to self–organizing MAS [5, 17], to examine macroscopic system behaviors via simulation.

Recently, *temporal logic* has been applied to formally model and verify self–organizing MAS. These logics have been proved useful for the specification of dynamic systems and powerful tools are available to perform *model checking*, i.e. prove that specifications are supported by the non–deterministic branching evolution of a Finite State Automaton that represent system execution. E.g. in [18] simplified robotic systems have been modeled and self–organizing properties been verified. I.e. it has been shown that the specified MAS abstraction gives rise to properties that continue to hold or reestablish in future states.

2.4 Development Life-Cycle Support

In [16] it has been examined how the current usage of the previously described techniques supports these development activities. From this comparison we conclude that requirements engineering and testing approaches found yet minor attention. This lack can be traced back to the fundamental difficulty to anticipate and validate the non–linear interactions that give rise to self–organizing dynamics [15]. In the following, we outline a requirements modeling approach to support empiric MAS development procedures.

3 Towards Requirements Engineering for Self–Organizing MAS

Requirements engineering activities lead to specifications of the functionality the system to be should provide. By considering the future usage, stakeholders and developers are to agree on the intended functionalities. Common tools are sets of *use cases* [7], that specify how users and third parties interact with the future system.

Self–organizing dynamics are applied when system configurations are intended to be maintained and adjusted, enabling system *adaptivity* [22] due to the decentralized (re–) configuration of agents. Self–organizing phenomena typically result from well–understood types of non-linear dynamics (cf. section 3.1) that are examined in interdisciplinary research activities [6, 13]. Their examination and classification in MAS development is expected to provide a future *pattern language* for the intended dynamics.

Listing identified reconfigurations represent the expected macroscopic system dynamics. As each requirement describes transitions between MAS configurations and can be regarded as *use cases for self–organizing systems*. Lists of these intended system adaptions, allows developers to design simulation settings to validate each requirement for (prototype) MAS implementations.

3.1 Requirements Specification

To define the intended MAS adaptivity, specifications of *adaptation requirements* are listed, each composed of a system *configuration space* and an *adaption dynamic*. Configuration spaces comprise sets of possible system states in terms of role occupation numbers or group member counts. The adaption models define how the system is expected to perform transitions between the macroscopic states.

Interdisciplinary system examinations have lead to sets of recurrent models of non-linear dynamics [13]. These pattern arise from non–linear entity interactions and are universally found. We expect future reviews of self–organizing MAS behaviors to reveal similar sets of typically intended dynamics. Established description formats for complex system dynamics are available. Differential equations are typically utilized to describe rates of changes [6] and *system dynamics* research [13] utilizes *Causal Loop Diagrams* (CLD) to model causal relations between system entities.

Figure 1 exemplifies a prominent non-linear dynamic. *Logistic growth*, also known as *Verhulst* model or *S–shaped growth*, is found in numerous natural systems, where entity populations (x) are amplified (k), while consuming limited system resources, i.e. approaching carrying capacities (ax) following: $\frac{dx}{dt} = x(k - ax)$. In CLD (figure 1), denote arrows positive ($+$) and negative ($-$) contributions, leading to *balancing* (b) or *reinforcing* (r) feedback.

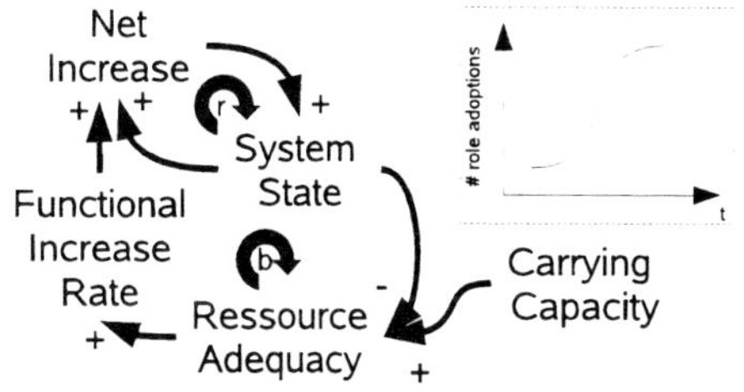

Figure 1. Causal Loop Diagram (from [13]).

3.2 Requirements Validation

Adaptation requirements guide simulation settings to validate (prototype) implementations. In early iterations, *qualitative* validations will show that intended dynamics are present. In later stages, MAS developers examine *quantitatively* the behavioral regimes of implementations, by comparing simulations to macroscopic parameters in requirement models.

For the sake of brevity, we exemplify here solely the validation of an adaptation requirement, steered by logistic grows, in an immune system inspired *Intrusion detection systems* (IDS). The system needs to be capable to remove *epidemics*, i.e. large numbers of malicious *intruder* agents at once. Therefore, *searcher* agents are equipped with specific detection algorithms. Via stigmergy [2], these trigger the removal of intruders by *remover* agents. The requirement concerns the transition between a MAS configuration that comprises an amount of undetected intruders to configurations where all intruders have been removed by activation of all available removers. The decay of intruders should happen quickly and is therefore expected to be *exponential*.

These adaption requirements guide simulation settings to their validation. In figure 2 simulation results[2] of a prototype MAS implementation[3] are plotted. Due to a quick activation rate of remover agents, the number of intruders decreases exponentially. Exponential decay is fitted on a logarithmic scale according to $f(x) = Ae^{-x/x_0}$.

A requirements analysis procedure that extends current engineering approaches (cf. section 2.2), a detailed analysis of the outlined dynamics and the validation of further adaption dynamics will be published elsewhere.

4 Conclusions

Inspired by requirements engineering activities in software engineering practices, it has been discussed how macroscopic models of MAS behaviors can be used to express intended adaptivity [22] in self–organizing MAS.

[2] where 60 intruder agents are removed by 40 searchers and 15 removers

[3] using the NetLogo System http://ccl.northwestern.edu/netlogo/

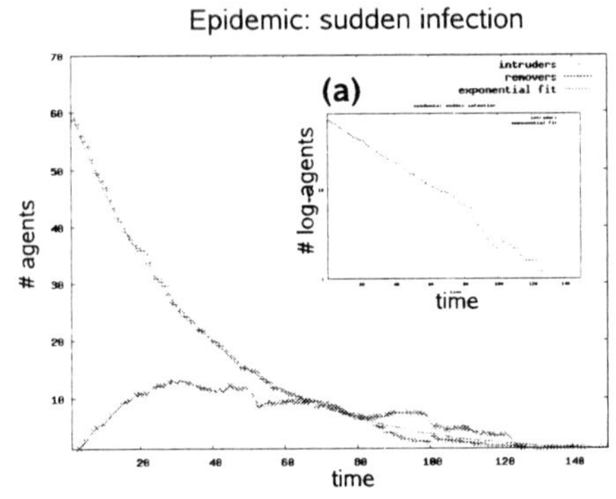

Figure 2. Exponential decay of epidemics.

The adaptation requirements proposed here allow the specification and validation of the dynamics that are typically exhibited by established distributed coordination mechanisms [3, 10, 12, 16]. Future work will examine how to move beyond these simple dynamics.

The identified *adaptation dynamics* resemble common pattern, resulting from non–linear agent interactions, and their usage promises a pattern language for self–organizing MAS. As we exemplified how the intended requirements can be validated for (prototype) implementation behaviors, will future work examine how these models can be used to automate black-box tests according to [22]. Furthermore, the impact of *mesoscopic* modeling [16] will be examined.

Acknowledgments

One of us (J.S.) would like to thank the *Distributed Systems and Information Systems* (VSIS) group at Hamburg University, particularly Winfried Lamersdorf, Lars Braubach and Alexander Pokahr for inspiring discussion, smart suggestions and encouragement.

References

[1] C. Bernon, M.-P. Gleizes, S. Peyruqueou, and G. Picard. Adelfe: A methodology for adaptive multi-agent systems engineering. In *LNCS*, volume 2577, pages 156 – 169, 2003.

[2] S. Brueckner and H. Czap. Organization, self-organization, autonomy and emergence: Status and challenges. *Int. Trans. on Systems Science and Applications*, 2(1):1–9, 2006.

[3] T. DeWolf and T. Holvoet. A catalogue of decentralised coordination mechanisms for designing self-organising emergent applications. Technical Report Report CW 458, Department of Computer Science, K.U. Leuven, August 2006.

[4] B. Edmonds. Using the experimental method to produce reliable self-organised systems. In *Engineering Self Organising Sytems: Methodologies and Applications*, number 3464 in LNAI, pages 84–99, 2004.

[5] L. Gardelli, M. Viroli, and A. Omicini. On the role of simulations in engineering self-organising mas: The case of an intrusion detection system in tucson. In *Engineering Self-Organising Systems*, volume 3910 of *LNAI*, pages 153 – 166. Springer, 2006.

[6] H. Haken. *SYNERGETICS. Introduction and Advanced Topics*. Springer, 2004.

[7] I. Jacobson, G. Booch, and J. Rumbaugh. *The unified software development process*. Addison Wesley, 1999.

[8] P. Kruchten. *The Rational Unified Process: An Introduction*. Addison Wesley Professional, 2003.

[9] K. Lerman and A. Galstyan. Automatically modeling group behavior of simple agents. In *Agent Modeling Workshop, AAMAS-04*, New York, NY, 2004.

[10] M. Mamei, R. Menezes, R. Tolksdorf, and F. Zambonelli. Case studies for self-organization in computer science. *J. Syst. Archit.*, 52(8):443–460, 2006.

[11] C. A. Rouff, M. G. Hinchey, W. F. Truszkowski, and J. L. Rash. Experiences applying formal approaches in the development of swarm-based space exploration systems. *Int. J. Softw. Tools Technol. Transf.*, 8(6):587–603, 2006.

[12] G. D. M. Serugendo, M. P. Gleizes, and A. Karageorgos. Self–organisation and emergence in mas: An overview. In *Informatica*, volume 30, pages 45–54, 2006.

[13] J. D. Sterman. *Business Dynamics - Systems Thinking an Modeling for a Complex World*. McGraw–Hill, 2000.

[14] J. Sudeikat and W. Renz. Monitoring group behavior in goal–directed agents using co–efficient plan observation. In *Proc. of the 7th Inernational Workshop on Agent Oriented Software Engineering (AOSE'06).*, 2006.

[15] J. Sudeikat and W. Renz. On the redesign of self–organizing multi–agent systems. *International Transactions on Systems Science and Applications*, 2(1):81–89, 2006.

[16] J. Sudeikat and W. Renz. *Intelligent Complex Adaptive Systems*, chapter Building Complex Adaptive Systems: On Engineering Self–Organizing Multi–Agent Systems. IDEA, 2007. to be published.

[17] J. Sudeikat and W. Renz. On simulations in mas development. In *Kommunikation in Verteilten Systemen (KIVS 2007)*, pages 279–290. VDE–Verlag, 2007.

[18] F. T. Winfield, J. Sa, M.-C. Fernandez-Gago, C. Dixon, and M. Fisher. On formal specification of emergent behaviours in swarm robotic systems. *International Journal of Advanced Robotic Systems*, 2(4):363–370, 2005.

[19] T. D. Wolf and T. Holvoet. Towards a methodolgy for engineering self-organising emergent systems. In *Proceedings of the International Conference on Self-Organization and Adaptation of Multi-agent and Grid Systems*, 2005.

[20] T. D. Wolf and T. Holvoet. Decentralised coordination mechanisms as design patterns for self-organising emergent applications. In *Proceedings of the Fourth International Workshop on Engineering Self-Organising Applications*, pages 40–61, 2006.

[21] T. D. Wolf and T. Holvoet. A taxonomy for self-* properties in decentralised autonomic computing. In *Chapter in 'Autonomic Computing: Concepts, Infrastructure, and Applications'*, 2006.

[22] L. A. Zadeh. On the definition of adaptivity. *Proceedings of the IEEE*, 51(3):469 – 470, 1963.

On the Problem of Over-clustering in Tuple-based Coordination Systems

Matteo Casadei
Università di Bologna
DEIS
Cesena (FC), Italy
m.casadei@unibo.it

Ronaldo Menezes
Florida Tech
Computer Sciences
Melbourne, Florida, USA
rmenezes@cs.fit.edu

Robert Tolksdorf
Freie Universität Berlin
Institut für Informatik
Berlin, Germany
tolk@inf.fu-berlin.de

Mirko Viroli
Università di Bologna
DEIS
Cesena (FC), Italy
mirko.viroli@unibo.it

Abstract

When it comes to communication performance, open distributed tuple-space systems depend heavily on the proximity of tuples to processes. Researchers have proposed many approaches for storing tuples in a way that processes benefit from the organization of tuples. Although some progress has been made, most of the proposed solutions fail to address the reverse problem: if most tuples are kept close to processes, the system's robustness is affected—the over-clustering of tuples in particular nodes creates a dependence on that particular node. Hence, we have a dichotomy where it is important to organize tuples in clusters close to processes, but it is equally important to avoid over-clustering. This paper presents a self-organized solution to the tuple distribution problem, in which the possibility of over-clustering is considered.

1 Introduction

LINDA is a coordination language in which shared spaces of tuples are manipulated by a minimal set of operations [4]. Its advantage lies on the extent of uncoupling the coordinated entities—they interact only asynchronously and anonymously. The use of self-organized approaches in LINDA systems is not new; approaches such as the one introduced by Mamei *et al.* [5] and by Menezes and Tolksdorf [6] have started a trend in which solutions based on self-organization are used to ameliorate problems such as scalability and fault tolerance. The characteristics of self-organization such as local communications and lightness of agents, make it an ideal choice in the implementation of large scale systems.

In the specific case of tuple-space systems, the tuple distribution in a network of tuple spaces is likely to be the most important single task affecting the scalability of a system. This problem has been addressed in several implementations of LINDA. For instance, Lime [7] features processes endowed with local tuple spaces where all the storing takes place. This is contrasted with standard approaches, which base tuple organization on the use of hashing of tuples to locations (tuple spaces). Even though the use of hashing yields very efficient solutions, it is inappropriate to large distributed applications, because adaptation to dynamic scenarios is difficult. While solutions such as Lime's does improve on the standard case, it does not consider that the mobility of data is independent from the mobility of processes. Menezes and Tolksdorf [6] proposed a new direction for solving this problem. They argued that approaches inspired from Swarm Intelligence can be used to improve tuple organization and tuple retrieval in LINDA systems. Their approach is called SwarmLinda and argues that the placement of a tuple should be stochastically decided according to a similarity between the tuple to be stored and the others already stored in the tuple spaces.

Independently of the solution used, it is quite easy to disregard a problem resulting from tuple organization: *over-clustering*. While trying to organize tuples according to certain criteria, one can easily forget that the over-clustering of these tuples in a single location may also be undesired. We characterize a situation as over-clustering when the tuple organization strategy forces all or most of the tuples (of a particular template) to be located in a single tuple space. For this reason, over-clustering can be a threat to system integrity in open distributed tuple-space systems: if a node aggregating tuples with the same template fails, the whole system operation may be compromised.

The tuple-hashing approach normally causes over-clustering since all tuples of a template are placed in the same location. However, even self-organized solutions such as the ones proposed in SwarmLinda may yield over-clustering (as we discuss later in this paper). To overcome this problem we propose a mechanism where tuple organization takes into consideration the possibility of over-clustering. In essence, when tuples of the same template start to form a large cluster, the cluster itself stops being an attractor and it becomes a detractor.

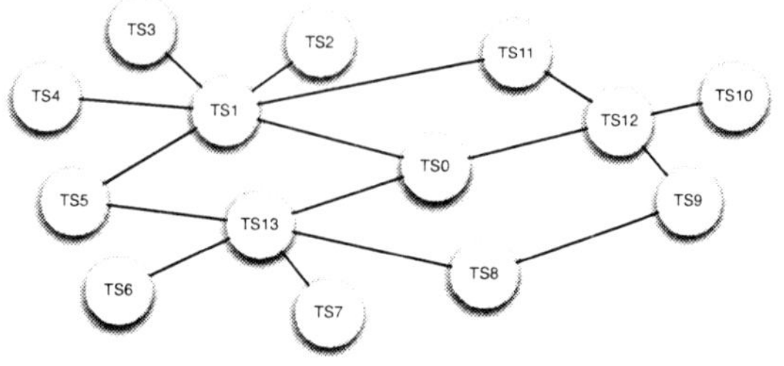

Figure 1. Topology used in all experiments.

2 Tuple Organization in SwarmLinda

The tuple organization process is one of the most important tasks to optimize coordination systems. It relates to the `out` primitive, since this is LINDA's way of allowing processes to store information. In SwarmLinda, the goal is to have similar tuples being placed closer to each other, forming a cluster on the basis of their template. However, SwarmLinda aims at achieving this organization using an emergent process resulting from simple decisions taken by the `out`-ants. The `out`-ants are processes inspired from Swarm Intelligence that roam on the terrain (network of tuple spaces) and decide at each hop of their roaming in the network if the tuple (food) should be stored. The decision is made stochastically, but biased by the amount of similar tuples around the ant's current location.

The tuple has to be stored eventually. This is achieved by having an aging mechanism associated with the `out`-ant. For every unsuccessful step of the `out`-ant, the probability of dropping the carried food-tuple in the next step increases and it is guaranteed to eventually reach 1.

The concept of *similarity function* is also important to be understood. Since having a monotonic scheme for the similarity of two tuples may be too restrictive, we want to have a function that says *how similar the two tuples are*. The next section describes the SwarmLinda mechanism for tuple distribution.

3 Simulation of Distribution of Tuples

The SwarmLinda distribution mechanism is designed and simulated using the stochastic simulation framework defined in [2]. Using the framework, we executed many experiments using the network of 14 tuple spaces shown in Figure 1—a *scale-free topology* [1].

We think of tuples as of the form $N(X_1, X_2, ..., X_n)$, where N represents the tuple name and $X_1, X_2, ..., X_n$ represent the tuple arguments. Then, using this definition, we consider a similarity function δ that takes two tuples and compares them, yielding a numerical value between 0 and 1. The higher this value the more similar the two tuples are, with 1 meaning the tuples are identical. The specific implementation of this similarity function is of no interest in the context of this paper—different application contexts can call for different similarity functions. A study of the appropriate similarity function for an application needs to be done considering many issues such as number of tuple templates, topology of the network, and application domain. The SwarmLinda solution to the distribution problem is composed of a *decision phase* that decides whether to store a tuple `tu` in the current tuple space, and a *movement phase* that chooses the tuple space for the next hop, if the decision taken in the previous phase was not to store `tu` in the current tuple space.

During the *decision* phase, the `out`-ant primitive decides whether to store the carried tuple `tu` (food) in the current tuple space or not. This involves the calculation of the concentration F of tuples having a template similar to `tu`, using the similarity function, and the calculation of the probability P_D to drop `tu` in the current tuple space TS. The concentration F is calculated considering the similarity of `tu` with all the other tuples t in the tuple space. F is given by:

$$F = \sum_{\forall t \in TS} \delta(tu, t) \qquad (1)$$

Note that $0 \leq F \leq Q$, where Q is the total number of tuples within the current tuple space (for all templates). According to the original brood sorting algorithm [3] used in SwarmLinda, the probability P_D to drop `tu` in the current tuple space is given by:

$$P_D = \left(\frac{F}{F+K}\right)^2 \qquad (2)$$

with $0 \leq P_D \leq 1$. Differing from the original idea in brood sorting, here the value of K is not a constant; K represents the number of steps remaining for the `out(tu)` primitive, namely, the number of tuple spaces that an `out`-ant can visit. When an `out` operation is initially requested on a tuple space, the value of K is set to *Step*, that is, the maximum number of tuple spaces each `out`-ant can visit. Each time a new tuple space is visited by an `out`-ant without storing the carried tuple `tu`, K is decreased by 1. When K reaches 0, P_D becomes 1 and `tu` is automatically stored in the current tuple space, independently of the value of F. So K implements the *aging mechanism* for an `out`-tuple.

The *movement* phase occurs when the tuple carried by an `out`-ant is not stored in the current tuple space. The goal is to choose, from the neighborhood of the current tuple space, a good neighbor for the next hop of the `out`-ant. The best possible neighbor is the tuple space with the highest concentration F of tuples similar to the carried tuple `tu`.

If we denote by n the total number of neighbors in the *neighborhood* of the current tuple space, F_j the concentra-

0-7695-2906-2/07 $25.00 © 2007 IEEE

tion of tuples similar to tu in neighbor j (obtained using Equation 1), then the probability P_j of having an out-ant move to neighbor j, is calculated using a concentration-proportional procedure:

$$P_j = \frac{F_j}{\sum_{k=1}^{n} F_k} \tag{3}$$

The higher the value of F_j for a neighbor j, the higher the probability for that neighbor to be chosen as the next hop of the out-ant. After a new tuple space is chosen, the whole process is repeated starting from the decision phase.

Using the network shown in Figure 1, we simulated the storage of tuples of four different templates: $a(X)$, $b(X)$, $c(X)$ and $d(X)$. In particular, we simulated the insertion of 210 tuples for each template. The obtained results are reported in Figure 2. Figure 2 (a) shows the tuple distribution in the network, at the end of the simulation: this distribution corresponds to a state of quasi-complete clustering, since tuples of the same template are stored in the same tuple space. Figure 2 (b) reports the trend of tuple concentration in tuple space 10 and 13: again, note that similar tuples are placed together forming clusters per tuple template.

These figures feature a situation of over-clustering, due to the tendency of similar tuples to be placed in the same tuple space: this is clearly visible referring to tuple template $a(X)$, $c(X)$ and $d(X)$ in Figure 2 (a). Therefore, even though clustering is a desirable feature, it can lead to over-clustering.

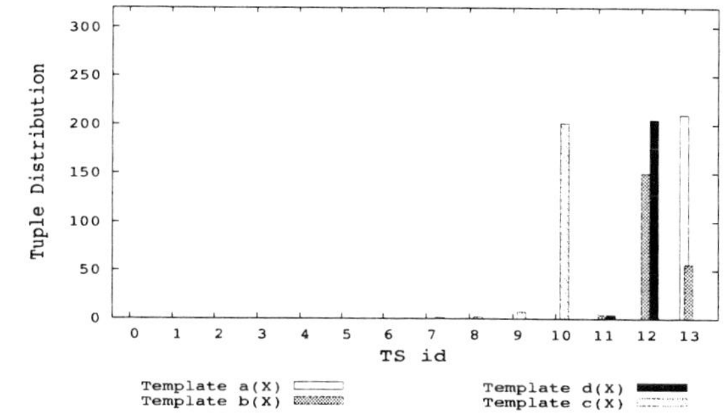

(a) Tuple-template distribution.

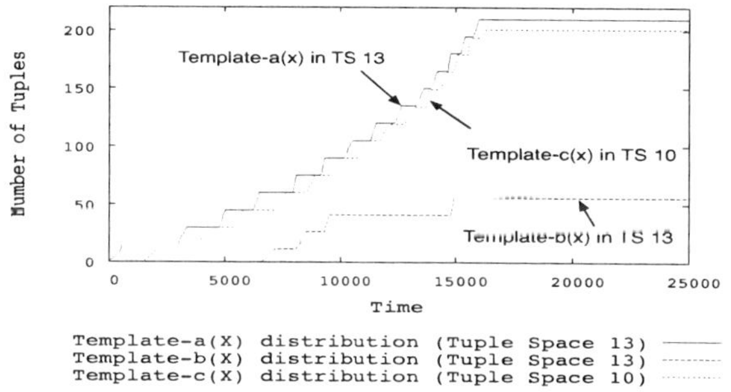

(b) Trend of tuple concentrations in tuple space 10 and 13.

Figure 2. The effects of over-clustering.

4 Avoiding Over-clustering in SwarmLinda

The results described in Section 3 clearly show that over-clustering can take place if the SwarmLinda algorithm is used without care. In order to avoid over-clustering, we introduced the parameter *Max-Size*, that represents the maximum number of tuples allowed for each cluster. Then we exploit a *generalized logistic function* (a sigmoid function), so that the probability P_D can be normalized according to a sigmoid curve. More precisely, we used an instance of the generalized logistic function, characterized by the equation:

$$P'_D = P_D - \left[0.01 + \left(\frac{P_D - 0.01}{(1 + 0.5e^{-b(X-2m)})^2}\right)\right] \tag{4}$$

where P_D is the drop probability calculated using Equation 2, b is the slope of the curve and m is the value of the X variable at which we observe the maximum value of the curve derivative. Equation 4 defines a *complemented* generalized logistic function, since we want to obtain the maximum value of P'_D when X has a small value. Indeed, the value assigned to X is the concentration F calculated considering the current tuple to be stored. The value of m depends on the total number of tuples per template expected in the network, while the slope value b depends on the values chosen for *Max-Size*: the lower the value of *Max-Size*, the higher the value of b.

According to Equation 4, as the number of tuples of a given template (the concentration F) approximates to *Max-Size*, the drop probability P'_D will degenerate towards 0 (zero). More precisely, the P_D value calculated using Equation 2 is used as the maximum value returned by our generalized logistic function when $F = 0$. Then, depending on the concentration F calculated by Equation 1 , the new value P'_D of drop probability is returned adopting our generalized logistic function—again, a simple normalization based on the current level of clustering. In our experiments *Max-Size* is set to 100: this choice was based on the number of tuples stored in the network, and on the size of the network itself. In our future work, we intend to devise a solution based on a *dynamic Max-Size* parameter. In particular, we would like *Max-Size* to be a function of the clustering status, the size of the network, or the current entropy of a tuple space (its level of organization). Adopting the anti-over-clustering mechanism, we performed the same simulations described in Section 3. The results are shown in Figure 3. Comparing these results with the ones from Figure 2, we can see that the improvement in terms of over-clustering

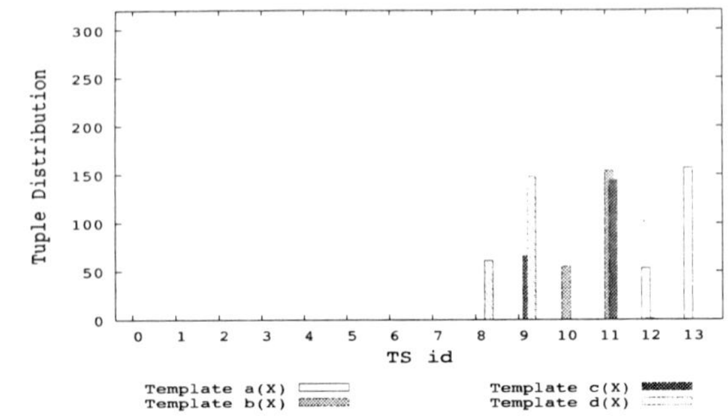

(a) Tuple-template distribution.

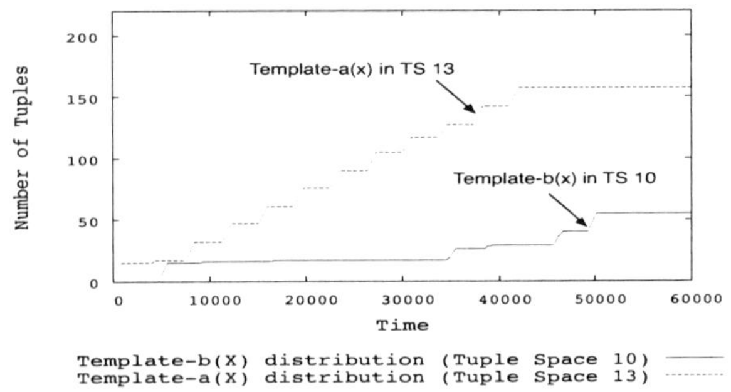

(b) Trend of tuple concentrations in tuple space 10 and 13.

Figure 3. Results obtained by applying the SwarmLinda anti-over-clustering strategy.

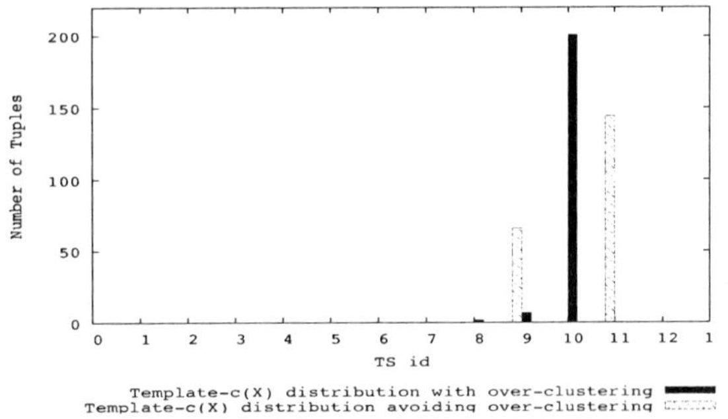

Figure 4. Distribution of tuples matching template $c(X)$ with and without over-clustering.

avoidance is significant. While the tuple distribution still shows a good performance in terms of clustering, tuples of the same template tend to aggregate in more than one tuple space, thus forming more clusters per tuple template.

Choosing template $c(X)$ as reference, Figure 4 compares the concentration of such tuples in the network in the two cases: this makes it easier to observe the effect of *Max-Size* in terms of over-clustering avoidance. While in the case without anti-over-clustering mechanism we have a heavy concentration of $c(X)$ tuples on one tuple space, now the same amount of tuples is divided on two tuple spaces. In particular, observing the distribution with anti over-clustering, the average concentration of $c(X)$ tuples in tuple space 9 and 11 is of the same order of the value chosen for *Max-Size*. Furthermore, we do not loose the clustering ability—the tuples are clustered in a group of close nodes rather than in individual nodes far from each other.

5 Conclusion

We developed a solution to the over-clustering problem and ran simulations considering the case without anti over-clustering and the case with anti over-clustering. We proved that when adopting self-organized solutions based on newer approaches, one can still get a over-clustering situation. Our approach to the problem was to consider the effect of over-clustering in the probability to store a tuple in a node.

There are improvements that need to be incorporated in this approach. The most important is to devise a truly self-organized solution that is able to *dynamically* adapt the *Max-Size* value according to the network characteristics.

References

[1] A.-L. Barabási and R. Albert. Emergence of scaling in random networks. *Science*, 286:509–512, October 1999.

[2] M. Casadei, L. Gardelli, and M. Viroli. Simulating emergent properties of coordination in Maude: the collective sorting case. In *Proceedings of the 5th International Workshop on Foundations of Coordination Languages and Software Architectures (FOCLASA'06)*, Bonn, Germany, Aug. 2006.

[3] J.-L. Deneubourg, S. Goss, N. Franks, A. Sendova-Franks, C. Detrain, and L. Chretien. The dynamic of collective sorting robot-like ants and ant-like robots. In *Proceedings of the 1st International Conference on Simulation of Adaptive Behavior: From Animals to Animats 3*, pages 356–365, Cambridge, MA, 1991. MIT Press.

[4] D. Gelernter and N. Carriero. Coordination languages and their significance. *Communications of the ACM*, 35(2):97–107, 1992.

[5] M. Mamei, F. Zambonelli, and L. Leonardi. Tuples on the air: A middleware for context-aware computing in dynamic networks. In *Proceedings of the 23rd International Conference on Distributed Computing Systems*, page 342. IEEE Computer Society, 2003.

[6] R. Menezes and R. Tolksdorf. A new approach to scalable linda-systems based on swarms. In *Proceedings of the ACM Symposium on Applied Computing*, Melbourne, FL, USA, Mar. 2003. ACM.

[7] G. P. Picco, A. L. Murphy, and G.-C. Roman. Lime: Linda meets mobility. In *Proceedings of the 21st International Conference on Software Engineering (ICSE'99)*, pages 368–377. ACM, 1999.

Task Selection in Multi-Agent Swarms using Adaptive Bid Auctions

Prithviraj Dasgupta, Matthew Hoeing
Computer Science Department
University of Nebraska, Omaha, NE 68182, USA
E-mail: {pdasgupta,mhoeing}@mail.unomaha.edu

Abstract

In the recent past, emergent computing based self-adaptive systems such as multi-agent swarms have become an attractive paradigm for designing large-scale distributed systems. In this paper, we consider a multi-agent swarm-based system for performing tasks in a domain characterized by search and execute operations. Our main focus is on the task allocation problem among the swarm units in our system. The main contribution of this paper is a multi-agent auction-based algorithm with dynamically adjustable bids that enables a swarm unit(agent) to plan its path efficiently while maintaining certain constraints on its cost and on the completion times of the tasks in the system. Experimental results of our algorithm within a simulated environment show that the auction-based algorithm performs significantly better than other heuristics-based strategies.

Keywords: Self organization, multi-agent swarms, task allocation, auction

1 Introduction

In the recent past, self-organizing systems such as swarms have been used as an attractive design paradigm to build complex, distributed systems. In this paper, we focus on the problem of coordinated task allocation among swarm units performing search and execute tasks. We combine a biologically inspired stigmergy based model that disseminates information about task priorities across agents in a swarm, with an auction-based protocol to enable coordinaton between the agents while optimizing certain performance objectives. The main contributions of our paper are two auction based task allocation algorithms for multi-agent swarms. The first algorithm builds on a market-based approach for task allocaton in multi-agent swarms[5], and includes a more complex task allocation and execution model involving collaboration of multiple agents for each task. In the second algorithm, we introduce the novel concept of dynamically adjustable bids within certain prescribed bounds. The dynamic bid auction algorithm finds a suitable task allocation among agents that reduces both task completion times and costs incurred by individual agents. Simulation results of our auction algorithms show that the auction based strategies outperform other heuristic and market based strategies by $30 - 60\%$in terms of completion times for tasks in the system while achieving significantly (90%)lower communication overhead.

2 Multi-Agent Swarming for Search and Execute Operations

We consider a search-and-execute problem domain where swarm units have to search and discover objects of interest individually but require to collaborate with each other to perform the actions on the objects of interest. In our system, each swarm unit is modeled as a mobile robot with a software agent embedded within it. The agent of each swarm unit implements the algorithms required for performing its actions and coordinating its activities with other agents(swarm units). Following are some of the important features of our multi-agent swarmed system: **1)** The environment is two-dimensional. **2)** Tasks are distributed randomly within the environment. The spatial distribution of tasks is not known *a priori* by the agents and must be discovered by the agents in real-time. In this paper, we consider stationary tasks only. **3)** A single agent is only capable of discovering and partially performing tasks but lacks the computational resources required to complete a task on its own. **4)** A task can be completed only if multiple agents share their computational resources towards executing the task. **5)** To enlist the cooperation of other agents required to complete a task, an agent that discovers a task communicates the task's information to other agents. **6)** An agent requires to move to the vicinity of a task discovered by another agent to execute it. Each agent executes the tasks independently and on completing its portion of execution on the task, communicates the progress of its execution (fraction of task still incomplete) to other agents within its communication range.

0-7695-2906-2/07 $25.00 © 2007 IEEE

To realize the swarming behavior in our system, we use the *stigmergetic* activity of social insects such as ants [1]. Stigmergy is a coordination mechanism that enables swarm units to exchange information about the environment with each other, possibly using an indirect communication technique such as depositing a chemical substance called *pheromone* on the ground. In our system, when an agent encounters a task, it deposits a certain amount of synthetic pheromone to mark the location and priority of the task. Pheromone decays over time. The set of tasks and the corresponding locations and pheromone values that each agent is aware of, is stored in a local data structure within the agent called the *pheromone landscape*, and corresponds to the agent's task list. An agent communicates its pheromone landscape to other agents within its communication range to disseminate task information across the swarm and coordinate its actions with other agents. The operations performed by an agent to manifest swarming can be divided into the following phases: deployment, search and discovery, task selection and task execution. A detailed description of our environment and the actions of each swarm unit is given in [2, 6]. In the rest of the paper, we focus on the task selection problem in our multi-agent swarmed system.

3 Auction Algorithm with Fixed and Dynamic Bids

We have used the following parameters in our model:

R	Set of robots(agents)
ρ_c	Communication range of a robot(agent)
G	Set of agent types
π_g^t	Amount of pheromone deposited at a task by an agent of type $g \in G$ at time t
π_{Thr}	Amount of pheromone required to be associated with a task, to consider it as complete
δ	Pheromone decay rate
v	Average speed of a robot(agent)
$B_{\tau,Ac}$	Set of bids received in response to auction for task τ by auctioneer Ac
$b_{a,\tau,Ac}$	Bid from bidder a in response to auction for task τ by auctioneer Ac for task τ by auctioneer $Ac \in R$
n_{bid}	Expected number of bidders required to complete a task
t_{max}	Duration of one round of an auction
r_{max}	Number of rounds after which an auction that has not received any bids is aborted

When an agent discovers a task τ that it has not encountered before and is still incomplete, it associates a certain amount of pheromone with the task. The amount of pheromone associated with the task is determined by the agent's type $g \in G$. Following [2, 3], the amount of pheromone to be associated with a task is determined from the agent's perceived values for priority(severity) of the task and its confidence in the perceived value. The agent discovering the task then gets into the role of an auctioneer agent and starts an auction for the task. The algorithm used by an auctioneer agent is given in Figure 1. All agents that receive the bid request message decide to respond to the auctioneer based on their current task commitments and previous information, if any, about the task. From the set of responding bidders, the auctioneer selects n_{bid} winners of the auction using a first(least)-price-wins auction protocol.

```
function auctionTask returns void
inputs: int n_bid, t_max, r_max;
      double π^τ;
      Coordinate τ_{x,y};
variables: int t, round, i;
      IndexedSet B_{τ,Ac}[agent_id];
      Set bdrs, winners;
      Message m;
B_{τ,Ac} ← ∅, winner ← ∅;
timer ← 0, round ← 0;
whle (round < r_max)
  m ← new Message("BidRequest",π^τ, τ_{x,y}, Ac);
  broadcastMessage(m);
  while (t < t_max)
    m ← receiveMessage();
    if ((m.getType()="TaskCompleted") ∨
       m.getType()="DuplicateAuction"))
       broadcastMessage(new Message(
             "AuctionAbort",τ_{x,y}, Ac));
       return;
    else if (m.getType()="Bid")
       bid ← getBidFromMessage(m);
       a ← getSenderFromMessage(m);
       bdrs ← bdrs ∪ a;
       B_{τ,Ac}[a] ← bid;
    t ← t + 1;
  if (| B_{τ,Ac} |= 0)
    round ← round + 1; π^τ ← π^τ × δ;
  else winners = selectWinners(B_{τ,Ac}, bdrs);
    for each a ∈ winners
       sendMessage(a, "Won",τ_{x,y}, Ac);
       for each a ∈ bdrs − winners
       sendMessage(a, "Lost",τ_{x,y}, Ac);
    return;
```

Figure 1. Algorithm used by an auctioneer agent Ac to auction a task τ

The algorithm used by a bidder agent to respond to bid requests received from an auctioneer is given in Figure 2. Winning bidder agents visit the task, update the pheromone value associated with it, and communicate the updated pheromone value to all agents within communication range which are participating in the same auction. The last winning bidder visiting the task determines if the task's pheromone level has reached the threshold level of π_{Thr}, and communicates a task-confirmed message to all agents within its communication range. On the other hand, if the pheromove level of the task is below the threshold, the last agent becomes an auctioneer and starts another auction for the task.

function auctionResponse **returns** *void*
inputs: *Message* bidRequest;
variables: *int Ac*, $agent_{id}$;
    double π^τ, bid;
    Coordinate $\tau_{x,y}$;
    Heap TaskList;
    Set CompletedTasks;
TaskList $\leftarrow$ {list of currently scheduled and bidded on tasks};
CompletedTasks $\leftarrow$ {list of completed tasks currently aware of};
Ac $\leftarrow$ getTaskAuctioneer(bidRequest);
$\tau_{x,y}$ $\leftarrow$ getTaskLocation(bidRequest);
π^τ $\leftarrow$ getTaskPheromone(bidRequest);
if($\tau_{x,y} \in$ CompletedTasks)
  sendMessage(Ac,"TaskCompleted");
else if ($\tau_{x,y} \in$ TaskList)
  sendMessage(Ac,"DuplicateAuction");
else{
  bid = dist(currentLocation, $\tau_{x,y}$);
  sendMessage(Ac,"Bid", bid, $agent_{id}$);

Figure 2. Algorithm used by an agent to respond to an auctioneer with fixed bid auctions

In the algorithm described in Figure 2, the bid for a task submitted by a bidder corresponds to the path cost it expends to reach the task from its current location. Once an auction is closed, a winning bidder is committed to the bid it made, and therefore, to the path(path cost) corresponding to the bid. This prevents the bidder from replanning and following an optimal cost path to visit multiple tasks and results in increased path costs for the bidder and reduced performance of the system. In this paper, we describe a novel approach in auction algorithms for multi-robot task allocation which allows a bidder to specify a bid as estimated lower and upper bounds $\{bid^l, bid^u\}$ of its actual bid(cost), instead of bidding with a single value. The bidder could then replan its path as long as its bids remain within its proposed bounds. The algorithm used by an auctioneer with dynamic bid auctions is given in Figure 3. The corresponding bidder algorithm is given in Figure 4.

function selectWinners **returns** *winners*
inputs: *IndexedSet* $B_{\tau,Ac}[agent_{id}]$;
    Set $bdrs$;
variables: *int* i;
  Set $winners$;
for each $a \in bdrs, b \in B_{\tau,Ac}$ | bidder(b)=a;
  $\gamma_a \leftarrow \frac{1-\exp^{(b^l-b^u)/v}}{n_bid \exp^{b^l/v}+1}$;
  $\Gamma_{\tau,Ac} \leftarrow \Gamma_{\tau,Ac} \cup \gamma_a$;
if $(1 <| B_{\tau,Ac} |< n_{bid})$
  $winners \leftarrow B_{\tau,Ac}$;
else
  for $i = 1$ to n_{bid}
    if $(i = 1)$
      $w_i = (\arg\min_{a \in bdrs} bid \mid$
        $bid \in B_{\tau,Ac}) \wedge$
      $(\arg\min_{a \in bdrs} \gamma \mid$
        $\gamma \in \Gamma_{\tau,Ac})$;
    else
      $w_i = (\arg\min_{a \in bdrs - \{\cup_{j=1}^{i-1} w_j\}} bid \mid$
      $bid \in B_{\tau,Ac} - \cup_{j=1}^{i-1} B_{\tau,Ac}[j]) \wedge$
      $(\arg\min_{a \in bdrs - \{\cup_{j=1}^{i-1} w_j\}} \gamma \mid$
      $\gamma \in \Gamma_{\tau,Ac} - \cup_{j=1}^{i-1} \Gamma_{\tau,Ac}[j])$;
    $winners \leftarrow winners \cup w_i$;
return $winners$;

Figure 3. Algorithm used by an auctioneer agent Ac to select winners given the set of bidders and corresponding bids in a dynamic bid auction

The experimental results of our algorithm using 18 robots, 20 tasks in a 50 $\times$ 50 m environment are shown in Figure 5 through 7

4 Conclusion and Future Work

In this paper, we have described auction based algorithms for task selection by agents in a multi-agent swarmed system. Experimental results within a simulated environment show that the auction based strategies perform significantly better than other heuristic-based task selection strategies. Future directions under consideration include a reward framework to incentivize bidder agents to complete tasks more rapidly, dynamically adjusting the size of the task list based on the arrival rate of tasks and incorporating mobile tasks in the environment with data fusion techniques on agents to identify, track and execute mobile tasks.

References

[1] E. Bonabeau, M. Dorigo and G. Theraulaz, "Swarm Intelligence: From Natural to Artificial Systems," Oxford University Press, 1999.

function auctionResponse **returns** *void*
inputs: *Message* bidRequest;
variables: *int Ac*, $agent_{id}$;
double π^{τ}, bid;
Coordinate $\tau_{x,y}$;
Heap TaskList;
Set CompletedTasks;
TaskList $\leftarrow$ {list of currently scheduled and bidded on tasks};
CompletedTasks $\leftarrow$ {list of completed tasks currently aware of};
$Ac \leftarrow$ getTaskAuctioneer(bidRequest);
$\tau_{x,y} \leftarrow$ getTaskLocation(bidRequest);
$\pi^{\tau} \leftarrow$ getTaskPheromone(bidRequest);
if($\tau_{x,y} \in$ CompletedTasks)
sendMessage(Ac,"TaskCompleted");
else if ($\tau_{x,y} \in$ TaskList)
sendMessage(Ac,"DuplicateAuction");
else
schedule = minimumCost$(t, \tau_{x,y})$; $\forall t \in$ TaskList,
subject to $c_t \leq bid_t^u$, and,
$min \sum_{t \in TaskList} (bid_t^u - c_t)$
bid^l = costFromSchedule($\tau_{x,y}$);
$bid^u = N(\frac{bid^l + \rho_c}{2}, 1.0)$;
sendMessage(Ac,"Bid", bid^l, bid^u, $agent_{id}$);

Figure 4. Algorithm used by an agent to respond to an auctioneer for dynamic bid auctions

[2] P. Dasgupta, S. O'Hara, P. Petrov, "A Multi-agent UAV Swarm for Automatic Target Recognition," LNCS, vol. 3890, (Proc. DAMAS), 2005, pp. 80-91.

[3] P. Dasgupta, "Distributed automatic target recognition using multi-agent UAV swarms," Proc. AAMAS 2006, pp. 479-481.

[4] B. Gerkey, "On multi-robot task allocation," Ph.D Thesis, Univ. of Southern California, 2003.

[5] N. Kalra and A. Martinoli, "A Comparative Study of Market-Based and Threshold-Based Task Allocation", Proc. DARS(Distr. Auton. Rob. Sys), 2006.

[6] D. Miller, P. Dasgupta, T. Judkins, "Distributed Task Selection in Multi-agent based Swarms using Heuristic Strategies," Lecture Notes in Computer Science, vol. 4433, (Proc. 2nd Swarm Robotics Workshop) 2006, pp. 158-172.

[7] L. Parker, Distributed Algorithms for Multi-Robot Observation of Multiple Moving Targets, Autonomous Robots, vol. 12, no. 3, 2002, pp. 231-255.

[8] R. Zlot, "Complex Task Allocation for Multi-robot Teams," Ph.D Thesis, Carnegie Mellon University, October 2006.

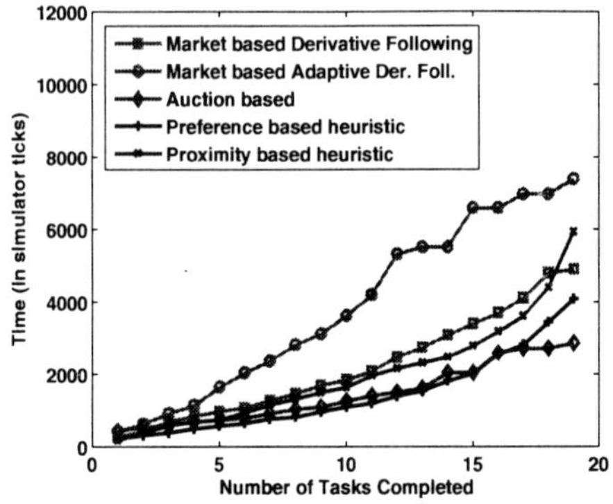

Figure 5. Time required to complete 20 tasks using different task selection strategies with 18 robots.

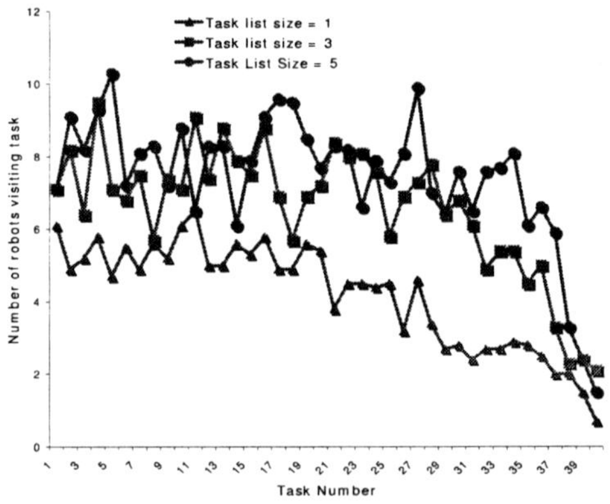

Figure 6. Effect of size of task list of each robot on the number of robots visiting each task (with 40 tasks, 18 robots).

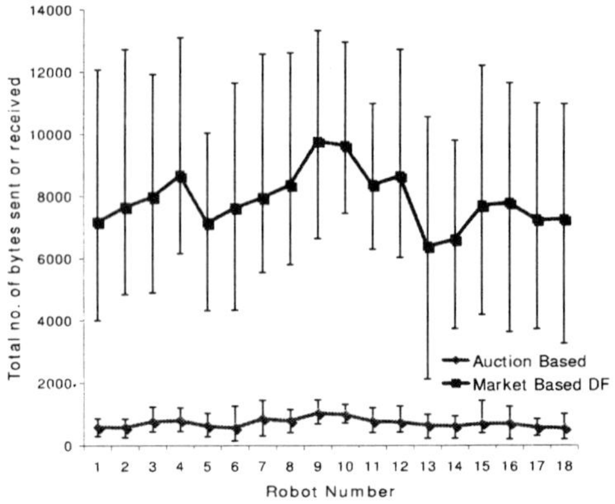

Figure 7. Comparison between the number of bytes of data sent and received by each robot using the auction and market-based algorithms for task allocation.

Self-Adapting Resource Bounded Distributed Computations

Nadeem Jamali and Xinghui Zhao
Department of Computer Science, University of Saskatchewan
176 Thorvaldson Bldg., 110 Science Place, Saskatoon, SK, Canada, S7N 5C9
n.jamali | x.zhao@agents.usask.ca

Abstract

Self-adaptation is about computations adapting to their environments. The need for adaptation may dynamically arise as a result of evolving computations or the environment. An important part of the environment is the computational resources for which computations compete.

The CyberOrgs model[1] *encapsulates distributed concurrent computations along with the computational and communication resources they require plus purchasing power for acquiring additional resources. Ownership of resources coupled with an effective control mechanism creates a predictable resource environment for computations to execute in – in a coordinated manner.*

CyberOrgs create three opportunities for self-adaptation: algorithms may be chosen using resource knowledge, additional resources may be purchased to adapt to evolving needs, and computations may coordinate use of known computational and network resources for optimal results.

The CyberOrgs model is presented and a prototype implementation is described. Our experience with using CyberOrgs' resource awareness for hierarchical coordination of distributed processor resource delivery is presented. Experimental results show that resource knowledge based reasoning leads to efficient distributed adaptation.

1. Introduction

Self-adaptation of a computation is about the computation reacting to disparities between the environment it executes in and the environment it requires for optimal execution. These disparities may result from the computation's own dynamically emerging requirements or from changes in its environment. A computation's self-adaptation may involve either altering its requirements or somehow interacting with the environment to secure what it requires.

An important aspect of an environment is the resources it affords a computation. In an open system [4], the availability of resources to a computation may be threatened by other computations competing for the bounded resources. In the context of multi-agent systems, it has been shown [2] that when there are both *logical* and *resource* dependencies between agents, resource dependencies sometimes lead to logical dependencies. Coordinating resource access by agents is hence critical to reducing uncertainty and enabling agents to make control decisions – i.e., adapt – for the best global performance [8]. Furthermore, it has been argued that computation and coordination are separate and orthogonal dimensions of all useful computing [3], necessitating coordination to be addressed explicitly.

Bounded rationality limits a computation's ability to assess the situation it may need to adapt to. However, if time-bounded resource enclaves can be created for computations to execute in, they can reason about and adapt to the enclaves' boundaries. Additionally, if there is a way for computations to negotiate the boundaries of these enclaves, a richer variety of self-adaptation becomes possible.

Our approach is to create resource encapsulation for computations to execute in. We use the CyberOrgs model, which makes explicit the relationship between a concurrent computation and the resources it requires, as well as the competition between computations for bounded resources. Cyberorgs are resource encapsulations, which support computations using the resources they own. Resources are owned by cyberorgs in time and space, and can be sold to other cyberorgs for *eCash*.

This approach offers three opportunities for self-adaptation. First, with the knowledge of owned resources within the encapsulation, given the choice, a cyberorg may choose which algorithms to execute or adjust the quality of solution sought (as in Design-to-Criteria scheduling [9]). Second, the cyberorg may purchase additional resources from other cyberorgs if required. Third, the cyberorg may strategize for optimal use of owned resources.

1 The model is *CyberOrgs*; encapsulations are *Cyberorgs*.

0-7695-2906-2/07 $25.00 © 2007 IEEE

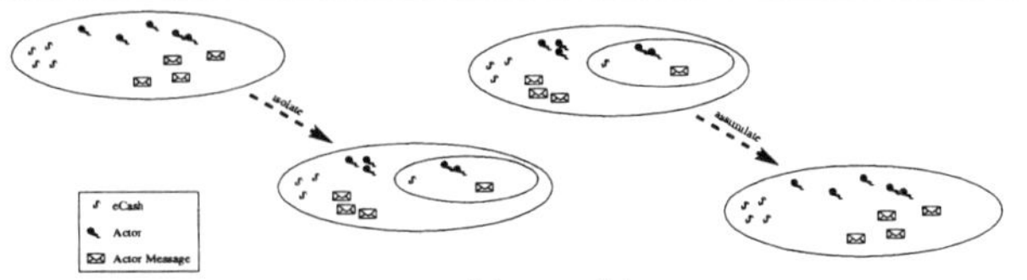

a) `isolate` b) `asmlt`

Figure 1. Creation and Absorption

2. CyberOrgs

CyberOrgs [5] is a model for resource sharing in a network of self-interested peers, where application agents may migrate in order to avail themselves of peer-owned resources. CyberOrgs organize computational and communication resources as a market, and their control as a hierarchy. Specifically, each cyberorg encapsulates one or more multi-agent distributed computations, and an amount of *eCash* in a shared currency. Cyberorgs act as principals in a market of distributed resources, where they may use their *eCash* to buy or sell resources among themselves. A cyberorg may use the resources so acquired for carrying out its computations, or it may sell them to other cyberorgs.

CyberOrgs treat computational and communication resources as being defined in time and space. In other words, a resource is not available for use at times and locations other than when and where it exists. Sale of a resource is represented by a *contract* stipulating availability of resources to the buyer for a cost. After signing a contract, a cyberorg must migrate to the prospective host cyberorg in order to avail itself of newly acquired resources. Delivery of resources to cyberorgs is determined by a hierarchy of control decisions.

Our approach in formalizing CyberOrgs [6] is to separate computational concerns from resource concerns. We represent resource requirements of each computation by a sequence of resource ticks required to complete the computation. To simplify the model, we assume that resource requirements are known in advance. As an instantiation, we assume that the computations are carried out by systems of primitive agents called *actors* [1].

Progress is represented by transitions occurring with introduction of ticks into the system. When a tick is inserted into a cyberorg, it may pass the tick on to a client cyberorg, or use it for progressing on its application or system actors. Whether a tick is passed on to a client or used locally depends on the contracts that the cyberorg has with its clients.

As illustrated in Figure 1, a new cyberorg is created by using the `isolate` primitive, which collects a set of actors, messages, and electronic cash, and creates a new cyberorg hosted locally. A cyberorg disappears by assimilating into its host cyberorg using the `asmlt` primitive, relinquishing control of its contents to its host.

A cyberorg may realize that its resource requirements have exceeded what is available by its contract with the host cyberorg. This triggers its attempt to migrate. To migrate a cyberorg searchs for potential hosts, attempts contract negotiation with them, and if successful, migrates.

3. Implementation of CyberOrgs

We have implemented CyberOrgs by extending *Actor Architecture* [7] – a Java library and run-time system for supporting agents. In this implementation, every agent requires processor time resource to carry out its computation, and the resource is received by the agent from the cyberorg containing it.

This implementation adds two key components to an AA platform: CyberOrg Manager and Scheduler Manager. CyberOrg Manager adds run-time support for a system of cyberorgs. A cyberorg has its own strategy for distributing available resources among its agents and hosted cyberorgs (according to relevant contracts). This strategy is encoded in a *facilitator* agent, which is a special agent that serves as the active part of a cyberorg. Among other tasks, a facilitator triggers primitive CyberOrgs operations which react to changes in the environment as well as its cyberorg's requirements.

Scheduler Manager has two parts: cyberorg scheduler and thread scheduler. The cyberorg scheduler keeps track of the CyberOrgs' hierarchical structure for a single platform and converts the hierarchical schedule represented by the structure into a flat schedule for agent threads. This schedule, which contains time intervals for which each agent is to be scheduled, is dynamically updated with changes in the hierarchical schedule resulting from invocation of CyberOrgs primitives and changes in the cyberorgs' local resource distribution. The thread scheduler schedules agent threads contained in a queue for the amounts of processor time they are supposed to be scheduled.

Distributing cyberorgs over multiple physical nodes presents implementation challenges. An internally distributed cyberorg has agents located on multiple nodes, representing its distributed parts. Each part has its own local facilitator which is responsible for making local decisions and receiving requests for primitive operations involving local agents. We use a simple protocol. The *master* facilitator maintains global information of the cyberorg, and it alone is responsible for enforcing global decisions of the cyberorg by coordinating its actions with those of other *(slave)* facilitators. By default, the master facilitator is the facilitator located at the node on which the cyberorg's creation is originally requested. Slave facilitators, by themselves, only possess the resource knowledge of their own parts of the cyberorg, and a slave facilitator can autonomously make local decisions involving agents in its own part of the cyberorg.

The way cyberorgs encapsulate computational and communication resources creates unique opportunities for scalable distributed coordination. Because delivery of network and processor resources to computations is controlled at a fine grain, idle resources are known precisely. As a result, communication and processing delays in carrying out fixed length system communications required for coordination become predictable. This – in turn – allows the distributed coordination components to reason about the feasibility of coordinated action based on good estimates of delays, and attempt only promising coordinated actions.

Coordination of distributed processor resource delivery can be treated as an example of a distributed coordination problem, illustrating how to estimate coordination delays. Consider a 2-node (N_1, N_2) request for a coordinated primitive operation to be carried out across the nodes hosting a cyberorg. The delay Δ in reaching agreement consists of several parts: D_1, the time delay from when the request is generated by the master facilitator on N_1 (or received from a slave) to when the request is scheduled to be processed on N_1; $P(a)$, the computational cost of analyzing the request and creating distributed tasks (where a is the total number of agents involved in the request); $C(N_1, N_2)$, the network delay in sending a message from N_1 to N_2 (assuming clocks are synchronized within some epsilon); D_2, the delay from when the request is received on N_2 to when the request is scheduled to be processed on N_2; $P(a_2)$, the computational cost of interpreting the request, and evaluating its feasibility on N_2 (where a_2 is the number of agents on node N_2 involved in the primitive); $C(N_2, N_1)$, the network delay of sending an acknowledgment back from N_2 to N_1; D_3, the delay from receipt of the acknowledgment to when the message is processed on N_1. Therefore, the coordination cost should be:

$$\Delta = D_1 + P(a) + (C(N_1, N_2) + D_2 + P(a_2) + C(N_2, N_1)) + D_3 \quad (1)$$

The delays D_1, D_2, and D_3 can be estimated from details of CPU scheduling. Communication costs $C(N_1, N_2)$ and $C(N_2, N_1)$ can be estimated from details of network resource control. If f_{N_i,N_j} is the network cost between nodes N_i and N_j, we can generalize equation 1 for n nodes where the master facilitator is located at N_1:

$$\Delta = D_1 + P(a) + max(f_{N_1,N_i} + D_i + P(a_i) + f_{N_i,N_1}) \quad (2)$$

for i between 2 and n. Although estimating $P(a)$ for a general purpose computation would be difficult, because we are dealing with special purpose computations for assessing feasibility of local actions, it is possible to obtain good estimates, so long as local resource availability is known, which it is in this case.

A global decision of a master facilitator may require modifying resources available to agents spread across multiple nodes. In order to guarantee that the corresponding actions associated with an n-node global decision will be performed successfully by time t on all involved nodes, a master facilitator must generate the decision by time t', so that $t' < t - \Delta$. However, some savings can be obtained by eliminating some communication. Particularly, if the master facilitator can calculate Δ without explicitly communicating with the slave facilitators, it can send requests to the slave facilitators to carry out their parts of the global action, with the knowledge that all actions will indeed succeed. Although this is not possible in general, if the the master facilitator receives periodic updates from the slaves about their locally available resources, along with promises to maintain those availabilities for certain time intervals, the master may be able to assess feasibility of remote actions so long as the actions can be completed before expiration of the resource availability promises received from the slaves.

If the coordinated action itself is required in the future, the master facilitator may estimate the delay required for agreement on feasibility of the coordinated action in a similar manner. In this case, instead of waiting for each slave facilitator to acknowledge agreement, the master facilitator may be optimistic. In other words, the slave facilitators no longer have to send acknowledgments; they only report back if they find the action infeasible. The master facilitator, in turn, waits for Δ time for possible infeasibility reports, rather than wait for each slave to acknowledge. The master would be able to calculate this Δ if the promises of resource availability received from the slaves do not expire before the slaves finish assessing local feasibilities. Additionally, instead of waiting to be informed by the master of global agreement, the slaves too optimistically wait long enough to give the master a chance to inform them about possible cancellation of the coordinated action. Because the master facilitator calculates Δ prior to communication with the slaves, it can advise the slaves in the initial communication to wait for a period $\Delta + T_r$, where T_r is the time the master would take to report cancellation to them after it has received an infeasibility report from some slave. As a result, in the case when global agreement is achieved, all parties are ready for coordinated action after a delay of $\Delta + T_r$, without any need for communication after the initial requests from the master facilitator. Furthermore, any cancellations too are known by all parties by $\Delta + T_r$.

4. Experimental Results

A number of experiments were carried out to assess the effectiveness and scalability of our approach. We collected results on delays in completing distributed schedule update tasks involving up to 1500 agents distributed over networks of two and three processors. Because a particular task would involve only a fraction of the total number of agents, this represents systems with 10^4 or more total number of agents. Specifically, we compared the delay in achieving group agreement on feasibility of success or failure of global updates to distributed processor schedules, when using and not using our approach of exploiting predictability of resource availability in cyberorgs.

We applied the approach to an implementation of CyberOrgs. In the first set of experiments – in the absence of resource availability information – we used the pessimistic approach of requiring a series of acknowledgments confirming that the requested updates can indeed be carried out at the required time. In the second set, we relied on knowledge of available resources to (optimistically) assume that the requests have been satisfied unless a failure message is received by a deadline. Note that this is not a fair comparison because in the resource unaware case, there is no guarantee of success of coordinated action until after the distributed actions have actually been attempted; nor is there a determination of failure, in which case a backtrack is required wherever the actions did happen to succeed. However, short of indicating that no comparison is possible, this appears to be a reasonable compromise.

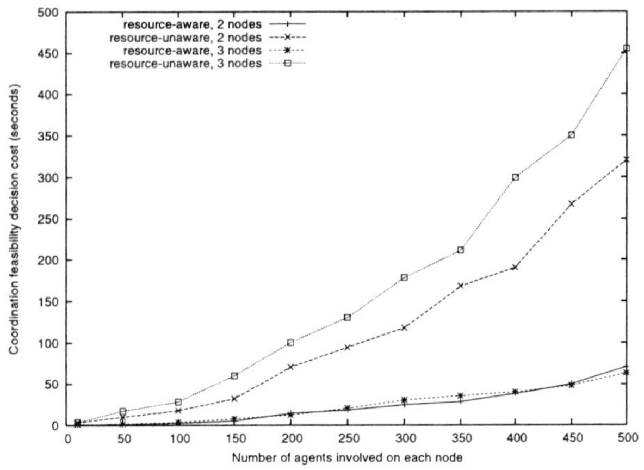

Figure 2. Delay in achieving agreement on coordinated distributed schedule update.

Figure 2 compares the delays described above for the two approaches for coordinated update of schedules for up to 1500 agents distributed across two and three physical nodes. Significant savings in the delay for global agreement on coordinated action are achieved using the CyberOrgs based resource-aware approach. These savings are in addition to the savings achieved by avoiding attempting infeasible actions, which cannot be avoided in the resource-unaware approach, even when local resource information is available. Furthermore, the penalty of increasing the number of agents linearly with the number of nodes is insignificant.

5. Conclusion

Self-adaptation is about computations staying in sync with their environments. It is difficult to reason about adapting to available resources without encapsulating computations in resource boundaries.

We described our experience with using the CyberOrgs model to address this challenge. CyberOrgs create three opportunities for self-adaptation. First, computations may use the knowledge of owned resources to choose the most suitable algorithms; second, computations may purchase additional resources to adapt to their evolving needs; third, computations may coordinate their use of known computational and network resources for optimal results.

We presented a prototype implementation which uses CyberOrgs' resource awareness for hierarchical coordination of distributed processor resource delivery. Experimental results illustrate that CyberOrgs based reasoning involving knowledge of resources aids distributed adaptation.

Although preliminary results are promising, case studies are required to obtain more authoritative results.

Acknowledgments Research funded by NSERC, Canadian Foundation for Innovation, and Saskatchewan Govt. grants.

References

[1] G. Agha. *Actors: A Model of Concurrent Computation in Distributed Systems.* MIT Press, Cambridge, Mass., 1986.

[2] L. Gasser. DAI approaches to coordination. In N. M. Avouris and L. Gasser, editors, *Distributed Artificial Intelligence: Theory and Praxis*, pages 31–51. Kluwer Academic, 1992.

[3] D. Gelernter and N. Carriero. Coordination languages and their significance. *CACM*, 35(2):97–107, Feb 1992.

[4] C. Hewitt and P. de Jong. Open systems. In J. Mylopoulos, J. W. Schmidt, and M. L. Brodie, editors, *On Conceptual Modeling*, chapter 6, pages 147–164. Springer, 1984.

[5] N. Jamali. *CyberOrgs: A Model for Resource Bounded Complex Agents.* PhD thesis, Univ. Illinois U-C, 2004.

[6] N. Jamali and X. Zhao. Scalable hierarchical coordination of multi-agent resource usage. In *Proc. of Intl. Workshop on Massively Multi-Agent Systems*, Kyoto, Dec 2004.

[7] M. Jang and G. Agha. On efficient communication and service agent discovery in multi-agent systems. In *Proc. of SELMAS '04*, pages 27–33, Edinburgh, May 2004.

[8] N. R. Jennings. Commitments and conventions: The foundation of coordination in multi-agent systems. *The Knowledge Engineering Review*, 8(3):223–250, 1993.

[9] T. Wagner, A. Garvey, and V. Lesser. Criteria directed task scheduling. *Journal for Approximate Reasoning–Special Scheduling Issue*, page 91.

Continuous Space-Time Semantics Allow Adaptive Program Execution

Jonathan Bachrach, Jacob Beal, Takeshi Fujiwara
MIT Computer Science and Artificial Intelligence Laboratory
77 Massachusetts Ave, Cambridge, MA, USA
jrb@csail.mit.edu, jakebeal@mit.edu, fujiwara@sophie.q.t.u-tokyo.ac.jp

Abstract

A spatial computer is a collection of devices filling space whose ability to interact is strongly dependent on their proximity. Previously, we have showed that programming such a computer as a continuous space can allow self-scaling across computers with different device distributions and can increase robustness against device failure. We have extended these ideas to time, allowing self-scaling across computers with different communication and execution rates. We have used a network of 24 Mica2 Motes to demonstrate that a program exploiting these ideas shows minimal difference in behavior as the time between program steps ranges from 100 ms to 300 ms and on a configuration with mixed rates.[1]

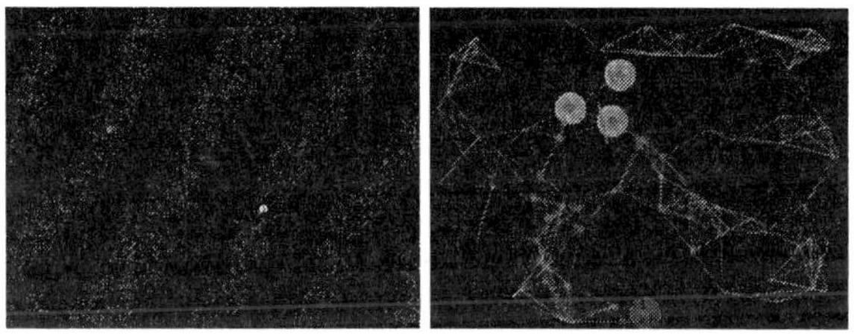

(a) Plane Wave (b) Target Tracking

Figure 1. Proto code allows compact descriptions of complicated behaviors.

1 Introduction

Spatial computers are an increasingly prevalent class of systems, in which the computer is composed of a collection of devices that fill space and whose ability to interact is strongly dependent on their proximity. Spatial computers emerge across a wide variety of domains, including swarm robotics, biofilms, sensor networks, and reconfigurable computing.

In previous work, we have advocated abstracting a spatial computer as a continuous, space-filling computational material, which we call an *amorphous medium*. Our language, Proto[5], provides geometric primitives like neighborhood, density, and distance that make it simple to write programs that self-scale to spatial computers with different distributions of devices and that handle some device failures transparently. For example, a directable plane wave (Figure 1(a)) takes 31 lines of code and target tracking (Figure 1(b)) takes 28 lines.

We now take the same approach to time, viewing a computation as a process evolving over continuous time, and define continuous time semantics for Proto. An appropriate choice of primitives then makes it possible to write programs that self-scale to execute equivalently on spatial computers with different communication and execution characteristics.

The core problem is the duality between the continuous model of space and time and its imperfect simulation using discrete chunks of execution. The advantage of the continuous model is that it will allow us to talk about aggregates. Our challenge is to give the user tools for managing and adapting to the inaccuracies of execution.

2 Related Work

The Proto language is previously described in [5] and [2] using a discrete time semantics of global rounds of execution. Proto is built on the dual foundations of the amorphous medium abstraction for programming in continuous space[4] and the Gooze lightweight stream processing language[1].

The spatial computing languages closest to Proto are *LISP[8], which operates on field values similarly but assumes a regular grid of devices, and Regiment[11], which explicitly implements geometric operations but has a base-station centered semantics. More foreign approaches include TinyDB[10], which provides a database view of the

[1]This work partially supported by NSF Grant #CCF-0621897

devices making up the computer, and Kairos[7], which operates on the computer as an abstract graph.

Continuous time evolution has been a concern in other specialized domains of computing, such as multimedia processing (see, for example [6]), and is approximated in computational models of chemical and biological computing such as the Gamma calculus[3] and P-Systems[12].

The fact that computing devices evolve continuously is a major concern throughout the fields of networking and parallel and distributed computing. In these fields, however, the primary concern is often not to embrace the continuous evolution of time, but to banish it. This is difficult and, in many cases, impossible—see, for example, the many asynchronous impossibility results in [9].

3 Space-Time Programs

The key enabling idea for continuous time programming is the *configuration path*—a function that specifies the output value at each point in the amorphous medium as a function of time. We borrow this idea from variational mechanics, particularly the approach in [13]. Pushing the analogy further, we view the program as an invariant description of the dynamics of the system. To compute a configuration path, we need only know the initial state and evolve it forward in time according to the dynamics of the system.

Configuration paths allow us to use continuous time without giving our outputs continuous values[2] This is important because many familiar programming constructs use discrete values. For example, a finite state machine changes from state to state without passing through intermediate states in the transition. Configuration paths allow us to separate the quantization of state and time.

We can combine this with our continuous space abstraction, the *amorphous medium*, in which the computer is represented as a manifold where every point is a computational device. In this combined view, a space-time program specifies the evolution of a manifold function over time. This execution can then be approximated with discrete steps on individual devices.

4 Space and Time Operations

Using the configuration path model allows us to choose a few critical space-time primitives that make it simple to approximate a global continuous program using discrete steps on individual devices. By limiting space/time interaction to a few simple mechanisms, Proto allows the programmer to write succinct global programs that compile to an efficient implementation. Due to limited space, we will not explain Proto or how these operations are actually implemented.

[2] Alternatives like derivatives and continuous-time feedback control do not allow this.

Space Restriction Conditional code needs to be thought of differently when programming an aggregate rather than a single device, since in general different devices may need to take different branches. We handle this by providing a **restrict** operation, which limits the region of space where a piece of code is being evaluated. An ordinary branch is then implemented with a pair of **restrict** operations, one for the "true" branch and one for the "false" branch.

Incremental Evolution The evolution of program state over time is expressed incrementally, using a feedback loop construction **letfed**. The programmer controls evolution with two expressions: an initial state (used at the beginning or when a branch begins to run) and an incremental configuration path that takes the current state and a time difference **dt** and returns the state evolved forward by **dt**.

Field/Summary Operations The family of field/summary operations select data across continuous regions of space-time, compute with that data, then summarize into a single value (e.g. the minimum value in the region or the integral over the region). There are two sets of field/summary operations: one for neighborhood and one for histories.

Neighborhood operations use values from the past light-cone of a point (implying message-passing in the discrete approximation) and give access to the computer's geometry through special operators. In the discrete approximation, the relationship between space and time may break down at short distances, so we provide independent **nbr-range** and **nbr-lag** operators that allow automatic compensation.

History operations are like neighborhood operations, but select values from the past of a single point rather than across a neighborhood. A history extends backward in time for as long as the value is defined; when a value becomes undefined due to the start of execution or space restriction, the history terminates. Because the past is fixed, the history operations are effectively just stereotyped feedback loops.

Evaluation Rate Although programs are specified in terms of continuous evolution, when they finally run they will be approximated with a sequence of discrete increments. If the size of each increment is too large, however, a program might get into trouble in any number of ways, from going unstable to breaking its specifications.

Consider, for example, running collision avoidance code on a swarm of robots. If the code is evaluated too infrequently, the robot may not have time enough to brake before slamming into an obstacle.

Rather than try to figure out a safe interval automatically, we give the programmer simple operations to limit increment size. The programmer can specify increment limits either in terms of frequency with **min-freq** or in terms of

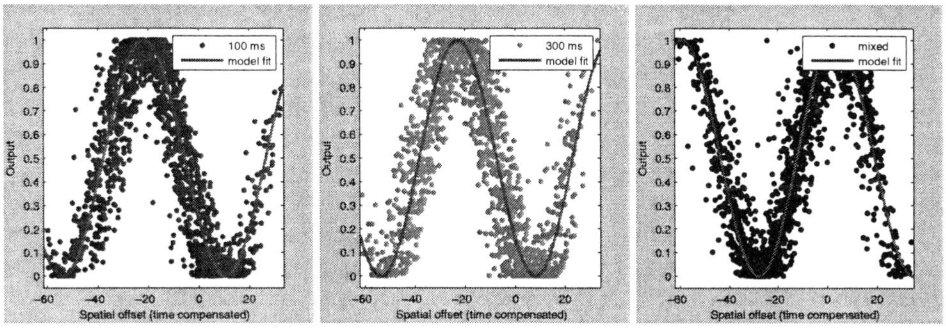

(a) 100 ms (b) 300 ms (c) 100/200/300 ms

Figure 2. Spatial frequency of a plane wave is minimally affected by differences in execution rate.

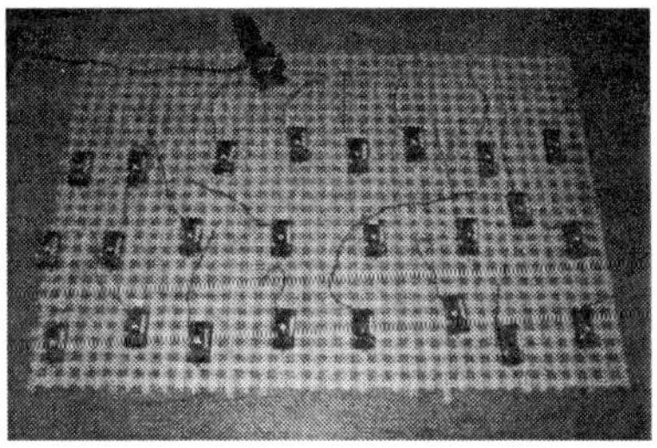

Figure 3. Experimental deployment of 24 Mica2 motes organized as three randomized rows of eight.

period with **max-period**. These point controls may then be composed to control the execution of the entire program.

5 Example and Verification

In order to verify our approach, we ran our plane wave application[5] with different processor update speeds and measured the impact on the application output. The plane wave application allows one to direct the angle of a planar wave by placing markers in the network.

We verified the code by executing it on 24 Mica2 motes arranged in three randomized rows of eight as shown in Figure 3. The leftmost mote in the middle row was set to be the destination, the rightmost in the middle set to be the source, the space period of the wave set to be 10 (20π cm) and the time period of the wave set to be 1 (2π seconds).

The motes were provided with coordinates and their radio range software limited to 9cm, allowing us to record data through a single logging device. The motes were then run with three different evolution increments: (a) all motes running at one update every 100 milliseconds, (b) all at 300 ms, and (c) a mixed population with five at 100 ms, five at 200 ms and the rest running at 300ms.

We gathered data by logging messages sent for approximately 12 wave cycles, ending up with approximately 1600 messages over approximately 80 seconds. Many messages apparently sent do not appear in the log, likely due to interference between messages. The motes nearest to the logging device are represented preferentially in the logs, with a maximum of 214 messages for a nearby mote, a minimum of 28 messages for a distant mote, and medians of 48.5 for run (a), 60 for (b) and 58.5 for (c).

Figure 4 shows that the motes synchronized to the same time frequency in all three runs. We plot time minus phase against output, which should re-align the outputs, then fit it against a sine function where phase and frequency are the free parameters. For run (a), the best fit frequency is 1.024, with RMSE 0.156, for run (b), the best fit is 1.026, with RMSE 0.161 and for run (c), the best fit is 1.024, with RMSE 0.135. This shows that the frequency of the wave is not affected by execution rate.[3]

Figure 2 shows that the motes also synchronized to the same spatial frequency in all three runs. We plot output against position (compensated for time offset using our previous fit), then fit it as before. For run (a), the best fit frequency is 0.0974, with RMSE 0.1519, for run (b), the best fit is 0.1021, with RMSE 0.1606 and for run (c), the best fit is 0.1001, with RMSE 0.1338. Although not as precise as the time fit, the space fit shows that impact from differences in execution rate is minimal.

Finally, Figure 5 shows interpolated space time plots for the first 400 samples of the three experiments. Although the interpolation is noisy due to missing data, visual inspection shows that the individual waves at least appear decently regular.

6 Conclusion

We advocate modelling computation on a spatial computer using continuous space and time. Using this abstrac-

[3]The slight speed-up comes from a naive time synchronization method.

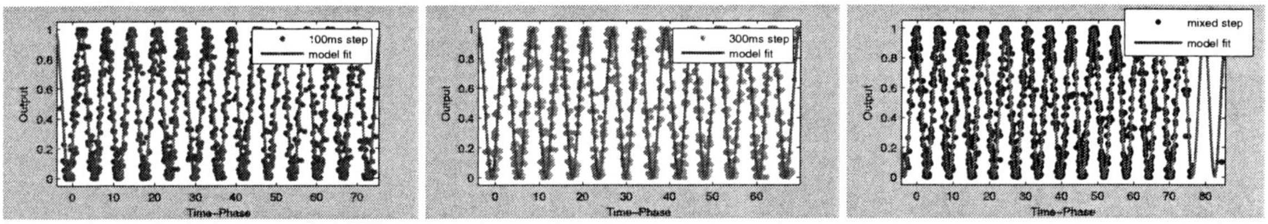

(a) 100 ms (b) 300 ms (c) 100/200/300 ms

Figure 4. The time frequency of the plane wave is not affected by differences in execution rate.

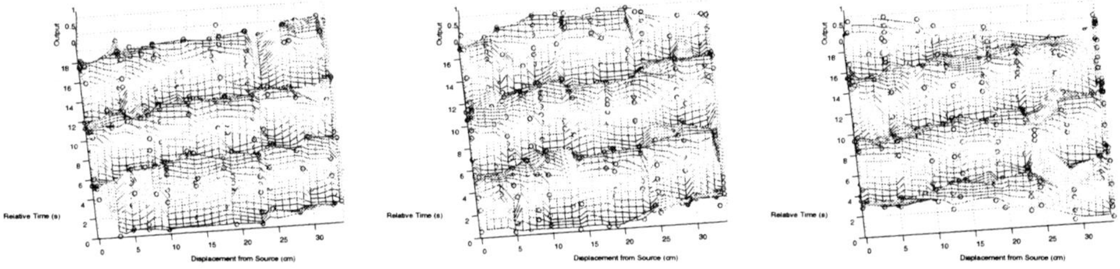

(a) 100 ms (b) 300 ms (c) 100/200/300 ms

Figure 5. Interpolated space-time waves for the first 400 samples of each experiment show that individual waves are fairly regular (though the interpolation is noisy due to missing data).

tion with an appropriate choice of primitives allows programs to scale automatically to spatial computers with different communication and execution characteristics. We have modified the Proto spatial computing language to demonstrated scaling on a network of Mica2 Motes.

The work presented in this paper represents only the beginning of investigation into continuous space/time models of computation. Changing to a continuous model of time does not resolve problems so much as it exposes them. There are many open problems at every level: how best to describe and control aggregate behavior, how best to represent discrete issues in the continuous abstraction, and how to manage trade-offs between cost, efficiency and accuracy in discrete approximation.

Finally, the problems driving this model are not unique to our approach to spatial computers, but derive from basic issues of time and communication. Perhaps other languages for controlling aggregates could benefit from incorporating ideas of continuous state evolution, either in improving their expressiveness or decreasing the cost of implementation by relaxing constraints.

References

[1] J. Bachrach. Gooze: a stream processing language. In *Lightweight Languages 2004*, November 2004.

[2] J. Bachrach and J. Beal. Programming a sensor network as an amorphous medium. In *DCOSS 2006 Posters*, June 2006.

[3] J.-P. Banatre, P. Fradet, and D. L. Metayer. Gamma and the chemical reaction model: Fifteen years after. In *WMP*, pages 17–44, 2000.

[4] J. Beal. Programming an amorphous computational medium. In *Unconventional Programming Paradigms International Workshop*, 2004.

[5] J. Beal and J. Bachrach. Infrastructure for engineered emergence in sensor/actuator networks. *IEEE Intelligent Systems*, pages 10–19, March/April 2006.

[6] C. Elliott. Functional images. In *The Fun of Programming*, "Cornerstones of Computing" series. Palgrave, Mar. 2003.

[7] R. Gummadi, O. Gnawali, and R. Govindan. Macro-programming wireless sensor networks using *airos*. In *DCOSS*, pages 126–140, 2005.

[8] C. Lasser, J. Massar, J. Miney, and L. Dayton. *Starlisp Reference Manual*. Thinking Machines Corporation, 1988.

[9] N. Lynch. *Distributed Algorithms*. Morgan Kaufman, 1996.

[10] S. R. Madden, R. Szewczyk, M. J. Franklin, and D. Culler. Supporting aggregate queries over ad-hoc wireless sensor networks. In *Workshop on Mobile Computing and Systems Applications*, 2002.

[11] R. Newton and M. Welsh. Region streams: Functional macroprogramming for sensor networks. In *First International Workshop on Data Management for Sensor Networks (DMSN)*, Aug. 2004.

[12] G. Paun. *Membrane Computing: An Introduction*. Springer-Verlag, Berlin, 2002.

[13] G. J. Sussman and J. Wisdom. *Structure and interpretation of classical mechanics*. MIT Press, Cambridge, MA, USA, 2001.

Work-in-Progress Track, Session 2: Self-Adaptation

Adaptive Self-optimization in Distributed Dynamic Environments

Wolfgang Trumler, Andreas Pietzowski, Benjamin Satzger, Theo Ungerer
Department of Computer Science
University of Augsburg
Eichleitnerstr. 30, 86159 Augsburg, Germany
{trumler, pietzowski,satzger,ungerer}@informatik.uni-augsburg.de

Abstract

Grid and ubiquitous computing systems generally consist of a large number of networked nodes with applications implemented as distributed services or processes, respectively. A crucial point is the distribution of the services to balance the load within the system during runtime.

In a former work we developed a self-optimization mechanism which shows outstanding performance in static environments where the services do not change their resource consumptions (e.g. CPU, memory, communication bandwidth). In this paper we present simulation results for the self-optimization within dynamic environments where the services change their load during runtime.

1. Introduction

Large distributed computing environments are state of the art in many areas. Grid computing uses networked servers all over the world to build massively parallel and powerful computing environments. Ubiquitous systems are rising up to be widely deployed in every day environments like smart offices and smart homes. All of these systems are comprised of a huge number of networked nodes, thus it is impossible for an administrator to manually fine tune the system for optimal performance. Furthermore, if the optimization parameters change due to application requirements the administrator would have to optimize the system again to meet the new requirements.

It is obvious that these systems should self-optimize and adapt to changing environments and application requirements at runtime. Self-optimization is one of the key features of autonomic [2] and organic computing systems [3]. Both initiatives propose systems that expose life-like features to be more robust and reliable even in unexpected situations.

The middleware system OCμ [6] was developed to offer self-configuration, self-optimization, self-healing, and self-protection capabilities. It is based on the assumption that applications are composed of services, which are distributed to the nodes of the network. The services are distributed to the nodes during the initial self-configuration phase considering the available resources and the resource requirements of the services. At runtime the services' resource consumptions are monitored. A service can be relocated or transfered to another node to balance the resource consumption (load) between the nodes.

In a former work we developed a self-optimization mechanism [7] which shows outstanding performance in static environments where the services do not change their resource consumptions (e.g. CPU, memory, communication bandwidth). In this paper we present some evaluation results of our former proposed self-optimization in dynamic environments.

The remainder of this paper is structured as follows. The next section gives a brief overview of the metrics we used for the the self-optimization. In section 3 we describe different scenarios of a dynamic environment as we expect them in a typical OCμ setup. The simulation results are presented in section 4. Section 5 gives an overview of related work and the paper closes with a conclusion and future work in section 6.

2. Transfer Strategies

The load of a distributed system based on services can be balanced by transferring services between the nodes. The metrics we use to decide wether the load between two nodes of the network should be balanced are named transfer strategies because they decide on the transfer of a service.

All the relevant information of the message exchange between the nodes and a detailed description of the employed Transfer Strategies (TS) can be found in [6, 7].

We developed four TS. The *Simple Transfer Strategy* transfers a service any time a load difference is encountered between two nodes. The *Transfer Strategy with Load Estimator* tries to estimate the average load of the network and transfers a service only if one node is beyond and the other is below the estimated load. This reduces the amount of service transfers to 40% to 50% of the former TS. The *Transfer Strategy with adaptive Barrier* employes an adaptive barrier, which is calculated out of the load difference between the nodes. This value gives a hint about the optimization potential of the load in the network. If the load difference of the nodes is high the barrier decreases and vice versa. This suppresses the transfer of services which would add only little gain to the overall optimization. In fact, the adaptive barrier further reduces the amount of service transfers about 10%. The *Hybrid Transfer Strategy* combines the advantages of the TS with Load Estimator and the TS with adaptive Barrier in one TS.

3. Dynamic Behavior of Services

It is very hard to describe the dynamic behavior of a system in terms of resource consumptions because there might be more than one influencing factor. On the other hand to gain meaningful evaluation results about the capabilities of the TS in dynamic environments it is crucial to differentiate between the possible load changes of the system.

We identified two different ways the load of a system can change. With combinations of both it should be possible to describe most of the dynamics in terms of resource consumption. The first is the periodic peak load and the second is an upswelling and decongesting load, respectively.

3.1. Periodic Peak Load

A typical dynamic behavior of a distributed system based on services or tasks which respond to incoming requests is a periodic peak load. If a request arrives at the service it begins to compute the response consuming resources like memory or CPU. After the computation, the response is sent to the requesting instance and the service waits for the next request. Figure 1 shows such a dynamic behavior of a single service.

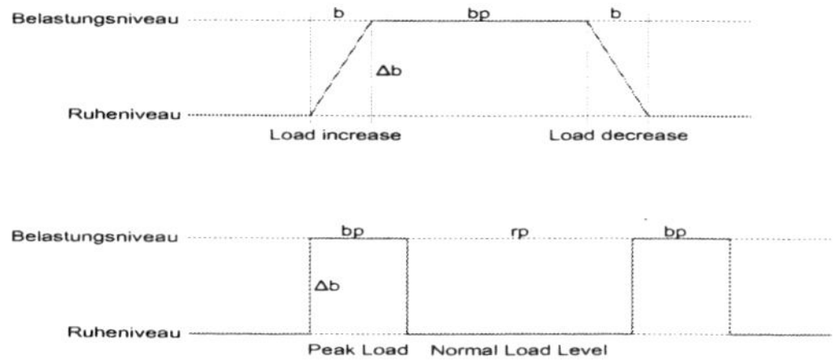

Figure 1. Parameter definition of the periodic peak load for the simulation

At the beginning the service is on a normal load level either sleeping or doing some background processing which will produce a certain base load to the system. For the simulations we assume an increase of the peak load of Δb if a request arrives. The computation requires bp simulation steps. After that time the load of the service is reduced to the normal load level. The service waits for the next request rp simulation steps which ends one duty cycle.

The load increase is proportional to the duty cycle of a periodic peak load. The cycle time is $bp+rp$ and the portion responsible for the load increase is bp. In the simulations the duty cycle time can be defined as an amount of simulation steps and bp can be defined as a percentage of the duty cycle time.

The overall load change of the system can be calculated with formula 1. where Δs is the percentage of services that behave dynamically.

$$\Delta B_{peak} = \Delta s * \Delta b * \frac{bp}{bp + rp} \qquad (1)$$

3.2. Upswelling and Decongesting Load

The second kind of a load change is an upswelling and decongesting load. A number of services or tasks increase their load during a given time, stay at the higher load level for a while, and return to the normal load level during another interval. This kind of dynamic behavior can occur if a large number of services are needed to fulfill a certain job like a batch processing at night or a data mining run at certain times. Also cron-jobs known from Unix systems can produce a similar behavior. Figure 2 shows the upswelling and decongesting load with the parameters used for the simulations.

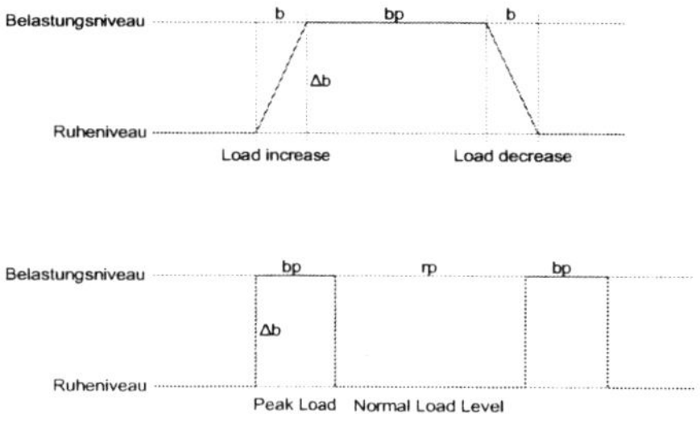

Figure 2. Parameter definition of the upswelling and decongesting load

The load of the services is increased by Δb during b simulation steps starting from their normal load level. They stay at the higher load level for bp simulation steps and return to the normal load level within b simulation steps. For the sake of simplicity we chose the interval of the upswelling load and the decongesting load to be the same. Formula 2 expresses the load increase of the overall system.

$$\Delta B = \frac{s}{S} * \Delta b \qquad (2)$$

0-7695-2906-2/07 $25.00 © 2007 IEEE

The overall load increase is defined by the additional load Δb and the portion of the services that are subject to the load increase. In this case s is defined as an absolute value of the interval $[0...S]$, while S is the total amount of services.

4. Evaluations

To evaluate the dynamic behavior of the services we extended our simulator to change the loads of the services as explained in the last section.

All simulations were done a hundred times to avoid misinterpretations due to good starting conditions. Every simulation was reinitialized with the same parameter setting but the initial service assignment of the nodes was created randomly within the given parameters.

The default simulation setup consists of 1000 nodes and about 8300 services. The initial load of the services is chosen randomly between 1% and 10% of a node's load. During the initialization every node is filled up with new services until the next generated service would exceed the node's capacity. Then the next node is initialized the same way. The overall capacity of a node is also generated randomly prior to service creation. This guarantees that there are all kinds of nodes in the network from heavy loaded to unloaded nodes. Due to the randomized initialization it is further guaranteed that every simulation run starts with a different initial setup of services.

4.1. Periodic Peak Load

The periodic peak load has three relevant simulation parameters that can be varied: (1) the load ratio $bp : rp$, (2) the load change Δb, and (3) the amount of dynamic services. The dynamic behavior of the services starts right from the beginning which means that there is no initialization time for the TS to find a good optimization.

Figure 3 shows the results of the four TS for 100% dynamic services. The left chart shows the amount of service transfers and the right chart shows the average error. The average error is a measure for the quality of the optimization. If the average error is 0 all the nodes have exactly the same load. It can be observed that the TS with dynamic Barrier and the Hybrid TS are able to adopt to the dynamic behavior of the network even with 100% of dynamic services.

4.2. Upswelling and Decongesting Load

The upswelling load has also three parameters that can be varied to evaluate the TS: (1) the height of the load increase, (2) the amount of simulation steps for b and bp, and (3) the amount dynamic processes.

The setup of the simulations is the same as for the periodic peak load. The only difference is that the simulation runs take 3000 simulation steps and that the upswell of the load starts after 1500 simulation steps. For the simulations we defined 25% of dynamic services with a load change of 100%.

Figure 4 shows the simulation results for $b = 50$, $bp = 500$. All TS try to balance the increasing load, which results in an increase of transfered services. The Hybrid TS needs the lowest amount of transfers.

As a conclusion to all the simulations we have done so far (more than 50 different settings beside those shown here) we can state that the Hybrid TS is the best in terms of the amount of service transfers. The best concerning the average error is the TS with Load Estimator.

5. Related Work

The presented self-optimization differs from state of the art load balancing mechanisms [5, 9] in two important points: first, no additional messages are used for the self-optimization except those needed for the transfer of the services and second, the load information is collected only locally. Furthermore there is no central instance that coordinates the self-optimization process. Thus, we want to compare it to systems that employ the same approach.

A very similar system, the Digital Hormone Model (DHM) [4], uses the Reaction-Diffusion-Model investigated by Alan Turing in 1952 [8]. The main idea is that the flow of information is modeled by the diffusion process of hormones. The DHM achieves interesting results with robot swarms. The main disadvantage is the high computation power needed to do the calculations of the differential equations. This would not be suitable for ubiquitous or embedded systems.

6. Conclusion and Future Work

In this paper we present the evaluation results of our self-optimization mechanism gained from simulations of dynamic environments. The metrics (Transfer Strategies) used to decide whether a service should be transfered to another node or not perform good even in large networks with 1000 nodes and more than 8000 services. The results show that the TS with adaptive barrier and the Hybrid TS are able to adapt to the average dynamics and to suppress unwanted transfers. One of the most outstanding issues about the self-optimization is that it is completely distributed without any central control and that no extra messages are used except for those needed to transfer a service to another node.

We plan to further evaluate the Hybrid TS in different real systems, especially in embedded systems. Therefore

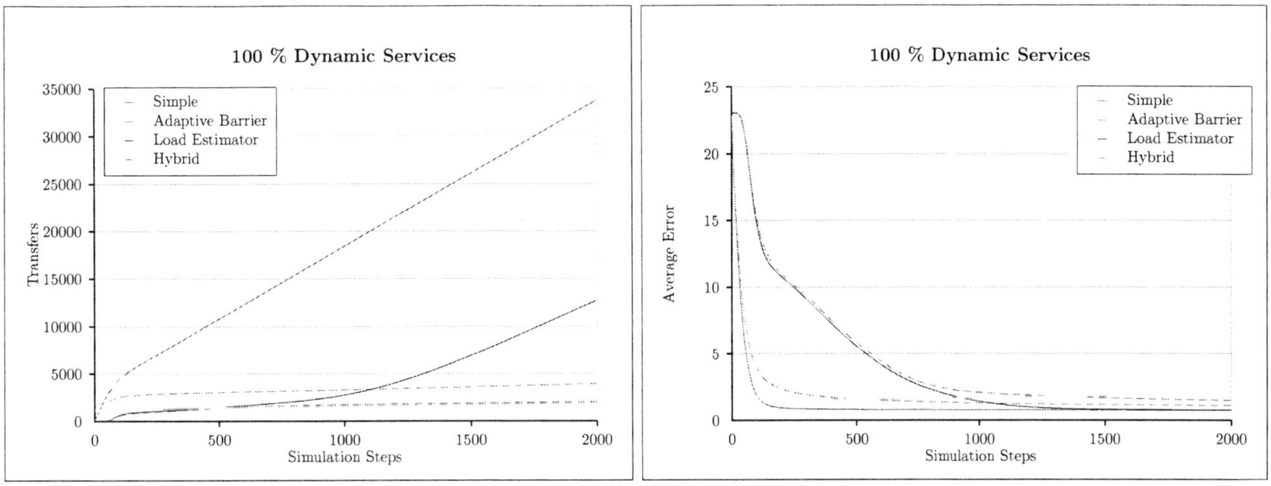

Figure 3. Simulation results for 100% dynamic processes with periodic peak loads

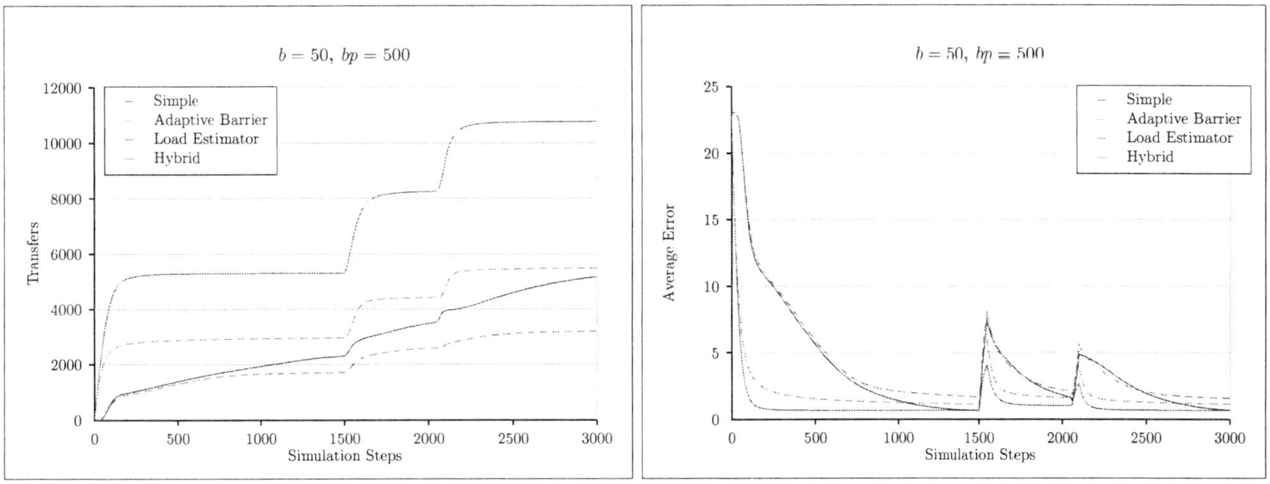

Figure 4. Simulation results for an upswelling and decongesting load

we need to improve the measurement of the resource consumption to get more accurate load values.

References

[1] F. Horn, G. Lindenmeier, and I. Moc. *Biochemie des Menschen*. Georg Thieme Verlag, Stuttgart, 2002.

[2] IBM Corporation. Autonomic Computing. *IBM Systems Journal*, 42(1), 2003.

[3] H. Schmeck. Organic computing-vision and challenge for system design. In *Proceedings of the Parallel Computing in Electrical Engineering, International Conference on (PARELEC 2004)*, pages 3–3, Washington, DC, USA, 2004. IEEE Computer Society.

[4] W.-M. Shen, P. Will, A. Galstyan, and C.-M. Chuong. Hormone-inspired self-organization and distributed control of robotic swarms. *Autonomous Robots*, 17:93–105, 2004.

[5] B. A. Shirazi, K. M. Kavi, and A. R. Hurson. *Scheduling and Load Balancing in Parallel and Distributed Systems*. Wiley-IEEE Computer Society Press, 1995.

[6] W. Trumler. *Organic Ubiquitous Middleware*. PhD thesis, Universität Augsburg, July 2006.

[7] W. Trumler, T. Thiemann, and T. Ungerer. An artificial hormone system for self-organization of networked nodes. In *IFIP Conference on Biologically Inspired Cooperative Computing*, pages 85–94, Santiago de Chile, August 2006. Springer-Verlag.

[8] A. M. Turing. The chemical basis of morphogenesis. *Philosophical Transactions of the Royal Society of London. Series B, Biological Sciences*, 237(641):37–72, August 1952.

[9] H. Zhu, M. Parashar, J. Yang, Y. Zhang, S. Rao, and S. Hariri. Self adapting, self optimizing runtime management of grid applications using pragma, 2003.

Root Cause Isolation for Self Healing in J2EE Environments

Umesh Bellur, Amar Agrawal
{umesh, amar}@it.iitb.ac.in
School of Information Technology, IIT Bombay

Abstract

The increasing complexity of distributed enterprise systems has made the task of managing these systems difficult and time consuming. The only way to simplify the management process is to automate much of the work so that minimum human effort needs to be invested. This has lead to research in autonomic systems that are self-healing, self-configuring, self-protecting and self-securing. We believe that the starting point of any autonomic system is to understand the dependencies between various components of the system and use it to perform higher order management tasks. As a proof of concept, we are trying to build self-healing capabilities into distributed enterprise applications by modeling the failure dependencies within the system. In a complex distributed environment, failures tend to propagate from one part of the system to the other. Hence, the failure symptoms may be observed at a point far removed from the actual cause of these failures. Therefore, localizing observed failures to its root cause is an important prerequisite to initiating micro-recovery procedures on a failed system. In this paper, we suggest a methodology to obtain a failure model of the application and use it to perform root-cause analysis based on observed system failures. [1]

1. Introduction

The lack of human expertise and the flood of monitoring data that complex modern enterprise systems generate has led researchers to build self-managing capabilities in these systems. The resulting self-healing, self configuring, self-protecting and self-optimizing systems - also known as autonomic systems - try to adapt themselves to changes (failures, reconfiguration, addition/deletion of components, etc.) in a way that requires minimum human intervention.

[1]This project was sponsored in part by a IBM Faculty Award for Autonomic Computing in 2006 and a generous research grant in Autonomic Computing from the IT Research council of Intel Corp

Self-healing systems are a class of autonomic systems that can actively recover from failures. The self-healing process involves the following steps:

1. Monitoring the application for failure symptoms.
2. Localizing these symptoms to root-cause faults.
3. Initiating appropriate recovery procedures.

The various software and hardware components, that make up an application, interact in complex ways to provide required functionality to the user. Dependencies naturally exist between these components, due to which a fault in one of them tends to propagate to other parts and multiple symptoms being thrown throughout the system. Localizing these symptoms to the root-cause of the failure is crucial prerequisite to initiating any recovery procedures. Accurate root-cause analysis would mean quicker and more effective recovery. The possible recovery actions are system specific and may require rebooting the failed components for transient failures, replacing or switching to a backup component or just isolating the failed parts while reducing the available functionality.

Several approaches to root-cause analysis have been proposed in literature. Expert systems[6, 7] that use past failure data to build a failure database have been traditionally used. Observed failure symptoms are mapped to known fault cases to identify current faulty components. Such approaches require huge amounts of failure data that cover the entire failure space and are usually insufficient for unknown or multiple fault scenarios. There are other approaches which use correlation-based analysis[3, 4] to find components that are most correlated with failed requests. No failure data is assumed, but results in a much bigger faulty set which is not very useful. For a detailed survey of related work, refer [2].

We believe that, by modeling the failure dependencies in the distributed system, we can do better diagnosis. The propagation of failure along the call stack can be captured using the topology of the application. The assumption here is that the failure dependencies mirror usage dependencies, i.e. faults propagates to a component only when it

0-7695-2906-2/07 $25.00 © 2007 IEEE

uses a failed component either directly or through some other mediating component. To handle the possibility of uncertainty, in terms of lost or spurious symptoms, we adopt a probabilistic methodology using Bayesian Belief Networks (BBNs). The diagnosis task is largely event driven where the stream of failure events generated are fed to the BBN model. The model outputs a ranked set of components based on a probabilistic quantification of the belief in their failure given the failure symptoms so far.

2 Our Approach

In this section, we discuss the methodology of generating the BBN model and using it for failure diagnosis. The BBN model is based on the topology of the application. The term "Topology" represents:

- Physical, logical infrastructure and their configuration.
- Dependencies that exist between the application components as well as those between application components and infrastructure (software, hardware and network).

The topology graph gives the usage dependencies between the application components as well as usage probabilities between them. This is supplemented with exception propagation analysis of the application code to generate the failure dependency graph. This graph is encoded into a BBN for easier diagnosis of observed failure symptoms. The rest of this section details these steps.

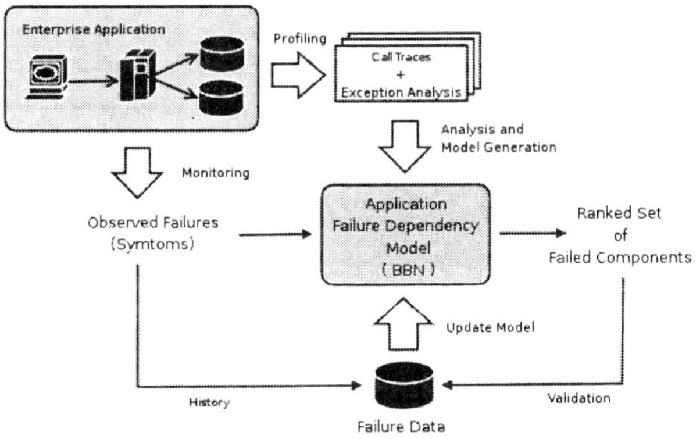

Figure 1. Failure Diagnosis Tool Architecture.

2.1 Generating Call Traces

The AutoTopology[9] tool extracts usage dependencies between the software components of any J2EE application. It uses the JVMPI interface provided by all JVM implementations and the concept of Interceptors in J2EE application servers to generate call traces for the application.

2.2 Generating the Topology Graph

The call traces generated by AutoTopology tool is then aggregated into a topology graph. The topology graph is directed graph with nodes representing the components in the application and direction of the edges indicating the usage dependency. For example, if a component A uses component B then the graph will have an edge $(A \rightarrow B)$ representing this dependency. Edge $(A \rightarrow B)$ is also annotated with a dependency strength that represents the probability of component A using component B in the application. Following call scenarios in the original call trace need to be considered while transforming them into topology graphs:

1. **Sequential path** : A sequential call-edge is mapped directly to corresponding usage edge in the topology graph with the usage probability equal to the probability of reaching the caller node.
2. **Alternate path** : When the call trace has an AlternatePath node, the execution can take any of the available alternate paths and the probability of usage splits at this node. If no additional information regarding the probability distribution of taking these alternate paths is known, a uniform distribution is assumed. If the same call-edge occurs multiple times in a call trace, then the probability of making that call needs to be accumulated to generate a single value for the usage probability.
3. **Concurrent path** : Concurrent paths are executed in parallel, but are reduced similar to the sequential path case.
4. **Loop path** : The loop path is treated as a single sequential path.

The topology of the application can be generated by computing a weighted addition across all the use-cases using the probability of executing the use-case as weights. The use-case probabilities can be obtained from historical data or in the simplistic case assumed to be uniform across all use-cases.

2.3 Exception Analysis

The failure dependency strength is a function of usage dependencies between the various components and the failure propagation probabilities between components. The usage probabilities are obtained from aggregating the usages across all call traces. Failure propagation probabilities can be obtained either through available failure data if available or using static analysis on the application code. We use JeX[10], an exception visualization tool, that helps to determine the dependencies between various exceptions that the application can throw and their associated probability values. In the context of JAVA components failure manifests as exception and we use it synonymously with failure of the component.

The probability of an exception E_1 propagating from one component A to the other component in the form of exception E_2 can be estimated statically as:

$$P(E_1\ triggers\ E_2) = P(B\ uses\ A) * P(E_1\ triggers\ E_2 | B\ uses\ A)$$

The usage probability $P(B\ \ uses\ \ A)$ is derived from the topology graph while static analysis using JeX files provides exception propagation probability $P(E_1\ triggers\ E_2|B\ uses\ A)$ in the above equation.

2.4 Generating the BBN Model

We represent every exception that a component can throw as a node in the BBN. We then connect those exceptions that have a propagation dependency between them. For example, consider a component B that uses another component A in the topology graph. Also, A can throw an exception E_1 that triggers an exception E_2 in component B. Thus, exception E_1 can propagate to component B and we add an edge from node A::E_1 to node B::E_2 in the BBN. The dependency strength for this edge represents the probability of the exception propagation which is determined as described in Section 2.3. Under the *Noisy-OR*[5] model, this dependency strength maps directly to $P(E_2|E_1)$ in the CPT(Conditional Probability Table) of node E_2. The *Noisy-OR* model also requires a leak probability which is the probability of an exception occurring given that all its causes are absent. We choose a random low value for this leak probability. The BBN also contains some 'decision' nodes which are basically known fault cases that can be mapped to one or more exceptions in the BBN. For instance, in a J2EE application scenario, a *FinderException* thrown by an entity bean is indicative that there is more than one entity with the same primary key. For this case, we can add a 'Duplicate Entity Entries' fault node in the BBN with an edge to the $FinderException$ node. The prior probability associated with all such nodes can only be determined through a failure database. We also add nodes representing various use-cases in the application. Information regarding failure of a use-case can be fed by instantiating the node with its state set to $Failed$. In case of loss of symptoms down the call stack, this provides some information regarding the possible nodes responsible for failure.

2.5 Symptom Monitoring

Once the BBN model for the application is ready, we can monitor the application for failure symptoms. We make an assumption here that various software and hardware faults in the system manifest themselves as exceptions in the application being monitored. For example, a crash of a node on which an application server is loaded, might cause $RemoteException$ in those EJBs that use components deployed on that server. In order to extract all such exception events being generated by the application, we require a monitoring module that can catch exception events.

We have written a JVMDI(Java Virtual Machine Debugging Interface) agent for Java applications, that can register for exception events being generated in the JVM. These events are filtered using class and/or method based filters to generate a stream of exceptions which are treated as failure symptoms in context of failure diagnosis.

2.6 Inferencing on Failure Evidence

The failure events generated by the monitoring unit are fed to the bayesian model as evidence. Inferencing algorithms for the Bayesian belief network are used to propagate this evidence to other nodes. The belief in the state of all nodes is updated so that each node has some posterior probability of failure given the failure evidence. A ranking of the components based on this posterior probability is produced.

In a test environment, the output of the model is evaluated against known fault cases for correctness and completeness of the diagnosis. In a production scenario, the ranking helps in locating the root-cause of failures and directing recovery efforts towards components that are believed to be the most faulty.

3 Test Setup and Experimental Results

ECPerf[8] is a standard benchmark application for J2EE application servers. We present preliminary test results in root-cause analysis using our approach for the ECPerf application. The test setup includes an ECPerf implementation deployed on two JBOSS application servers, the web tier on one machine and the business tier on the other. A MySQL server is used as backend database system and holds the business data. We use GeNIe [1], a Bayesian belief network tool for modeling and inferencing. We generate a failure BBN model for the ECPerf application using the methodology described above. We induce faults in the application and log the exceptions generated. These are then fed to the BBN and

	Single Fault		Multiple Faults
	ItemEnt Bean Undeployed	Connections in DB Pool Exhausted	ItemEnt, CartSes Undeployed
Database	0.081	0.074	0.079
ConnectionPool	0.291	**0.709**	0.158
CustomerEnt	0.137	0.141	0.139
ItemEnt	**0.326**	0.232	**0.304**
OrderEnt	<u>0.172</u>	0.419	<u>0.194</u>
OrderLineEnt	0.239	0.149	0.193
DiscountEnt	0.134	0.128	0.155
RuleEnt	0.134	0.128	0.155
OrderSes	<u>0.214</u>	<u>0.411</u>	<u>0.199</u>
CartSes	0.115	<u>0.108</u>	0.128
ProcessListBean	<u>NA</u>	<u>NA</u>	<u>NA</u>
CartBean	<u>0.091</u>	<u>0.059</u>	<u>0.088</u>
OrderSesBean	<u>0.217</u>	<u>0.144</u>	<u>0.240</u>

Table 1. Test Cases for ECPerf Application

the predicted failure ranking is evaluated for correctness and completeness.

Table 1 lists a few test cases we used for evaluating the ECPerf failure model. The failure probabilities predicted by the model for each of the components in the ECPerf application given the observed failure symptoms is summarized for both single and multiple fault test cases. The component with the highest probability of failure has been marked in **bold**, while components that threw symptoms are <u>underlined</u>.

4 Conclusion

Failures tend to propagate from one part of the system to another due to the dependencies in the system components. Hence, root-cause analysis is a crucial step for self-healing systems where the observed failure symptoms are localized to a root fault set.

We use the application topology to determine the failure dependencies within the system. These dependencies are quantified in terms of failure propagation probabilities from one component to another. We use Bayesian belief networks to encode the failure model and use it to infer the failure states of system components using the stream of failure symptoms obtained by monitoring the application as evidence. We do not require a huge failure database to construct the failure model. Instead, as more failure data becomes available, it can be fed back to improve the apriori probabilities in the BBN model. Diagnosing multiple simultaneous faults is possible, as we evaluate the state of the entire system based on observed system behavior. The system can be extended naturally to include hardware failures as well as performance and QoS failures. For further details, refer [2].

References

[1] GeNIe, The Bayesian Net Tool (http://genie.sis.pitt.edu).

[2] A. P. Agrawal. Topology-aware failure diagnosis for distributed enterprise systems. Master's thesis, Kanwal Rekhi School of Information Technology, IIT Bombay, 2006.

[3] M. Chen, A. Zheng, J. Lloyd, M. Jordan, and E. Brewer. Failure diagnosis using decision trees. *Autonomic Computing, 2004. Proceedings. International Conference on*, pages 36–43, 2004.

[4] M. Y. Chen, E. Kiciman, E. Fratkin, A. Fox, and E. Brewer. Pinpoint: Problem Determination in Large, Dynamic Internet Services. In *DSN '02: Proceedings of the 2002 International Conference on Dependable Systems and Networks*, pages 595–604, Washington, DC, USA, 2002. IEEE Computer Society.

[5] F. Diez. Parameter adjustment in bayes networks. the generalized noisy or-gate. *Proceedings of the Ninth Conference on Uncertainty in Artificial Intelligence*, pages 99–105, 1993.

[6] S. Klinger, S. Yemini, Y. Yemini, D. Ohsie, and S. Stolfo. A coding approach to event correlation. *Proceedings of the fourth international symposium on Integrated network management IV table of contents*, pages 266–277, 1995.

[7] L. Lewis. A Case-Based Reasoning Approach to the Resolution of Faults in Communication Networks. *Proceedings of the IFIP TC6/WG6. 6 Third International Symposium on Integrated Network Management*, pages 671–682, 1993.

[8] S. Microsystems. ECperf Specification, 2001.

[9] S. Reddy. Dynamic Topology Extraction for Component Based Enterprise Application Environments. Master's thesis, Kanwal Rekhi School of Information Technology, IIT Bombay, 2005.

[10] M. P. Robillard and G. C. Murphy. Analyzing exception flow in Java programs. In *Software Engineering – ESEC/FSE'99*, volume 1687 of *Lecture Notes in Computer Science*, pages 322–337. Springer-Verlag, September 1999.

0-7695-2906-2/07 $25.00 © 2007 IEEE

A Weighted Voting Mechanism for Action Selection Problem in Self-Adaptive Software

Mazeiar Salehie and Ladan Tahvildari
Software Technologies Applied Research Group
Dept. of Electrical and Computer Engineering
University of Waterloo,ON, Canada, N2L 3G1
{msalehie, ltahvild}@uwaterloo.ca

Abstract

Self-adaptive software is a closed-loop system which aims at adjusting itself in response to changes at runtime. Such a system is required to monitor domain events, detect significant changes, decide how to react, and act in order to execute the decisions. This paper focuses on the deciding process particularly for application-level adaptation actions. For this purpose, a weighted voting mechanism has been proposed which makes decisions based on a Goal-Action-Attribute Model (GAAM). The decision-making algorithm traverses GAAM, determines activated goals and feasible actions for voting, and ultimately selects an action as the social choice. The proposed mechanism and GAAM are evaluated within a simulated model of a news web site.

1. Problem Definition

The main motivation for research in self-adaptive software comes from increasing cost of the management complexity in software due to changing context and variable goals/requirements. The adaptivity aims at giving a degree of variability to software, and navigating it during applying *adaptation actions*. Generally, the *adaptation mechanism* is decomposed to monitoring, detecting (analyzing), deciding (planning), and acting (effecting) processes. Most of the existing solutions realize the adaptation processes in an external *adaptation engine*. This engine manages the adaptation for an *adaptable software*, which is implementing the application logic.

Among adaptation processes, deciding is a vital process, and its realization is still a challenge, as discussed by McKinley *et al.* [6]. Existing solutions for self-adaptive software have not addressed variant requirements for a desired deciding process [8]. The deciding process essentially needs to know about the adaptable software, objectives related to self-* properties and business goals, and articulated preferences by the system's stakeholders. These objectives can be decomposed to low-level objectives and consequently to goals determining the aspiration levels of system attributes. A set of actions is also required to satisfy the goals.

For satisfying the objectives and goals under different conditions of the attributes, it is required to select the most appropriate action(s). Without loss of generality, we can assume the set of goals and objective are one single set. The focused problem can be formally defined as: *Given a goal set* $GL = \{gl_i, i = 1..m\}$, *an adaptation action set* $AC = \{ac_i, i = 1..n\}$ *and an attribute set* $AT = \{at_i, i = 1..p\}$, *the problem is how to select the most appropriate action* a_i *to satisfy goals in different conditions of attributes.*

Central to our view, in this paper, is to propose a deciding process which is flexible/scalable, timely efficient, and multi-objective. The proposed process is based on a weighted voting mechanism.

2. Related Works

In decision-making approaches, it is convenient to build a structure to relate, goals, attributes and actions, as discussed in [4]. In software engineering, goals are mostly involved in requirements specifications. The Soft-goal Interdependency Graph (SIG) is one of the model used for this purpose in the Non-Functional Requirements framework (NFR) [2]. Subramanian *et al.* adopted the NFR Framework to build a knowledge-based system for developing adaptable software architectures based on the requirements [9]. However, to our best knowledge there is still no remarkable goal-driven approach in software engineering research which contains an explicit representation of goals involved in decision-making at runtime.

The focused problem in this paper is similar to Action Selection Problem (ASP) in autonomous agents [5] and behavior-based robotics [7]. The similarity is mainly because of dynamism and uncertainty of the environment, as well as online decision-making. However, the problem

0-7695-2906-2/07 $25.00 © 2007 IEEE

in software domain is generally more complex due to not obeying physical rules; in addition of having more control variables and disturbances.

The idea of behavior-based robotics is to use distributed specialized task-achieving modules, called behaviors, and to apply a command selection/fusion mechanism instead of sensor fusion. By this mean, there is no need to develop and maintain a monolithic model for the adaptable software and its context. Distributed Architecture for Mobile Navigation (DAMN), introduced by Rosenblatt, realizes the behavior-based control using a voting mechanism. DAMN is used for command fusion regarding the safety behaviors for turn and speed of the mobile robot [7]. The beauty of DAMN design is that the deliberative and reactive components of the architecture can operate at the same level and also it is scalable due to lack of hierarchy.

On the other hand, Maes argues that the lack of explicit goals and goal-handling capability in autonomous agents lead to significant limitations in their operation [5]. Maes proposes an activation network consisting of several actions with their own preconditions, postconditions and activation levels. The actions are connected to each other and can be activated by environment states, goals as well as successor/predecessor actions. Although this solution has the advantage of distributedness and planning without pitfalls of traditional AI-planning, there are no clear guidelines for choosing network parameters.

3. Proposed Approach

This section sets out to define the goal-action-attribute model, and to elaborate the decision-making algorithm based on this model.

3.1. Goal-Action-Attribute Model

The main purpose of the Goal-Action-Attribute Model (GAAM) is representing the key entities of the deciding problem -goals, attributes and actions- and relating them in a well-defined structure. Goals $GL = \{gl_i, i = 1..m\}$ in GAAM have the following two parameters:

Activation Level: An ACtivation Level (ACL) vector is defined as $ACL = \{acl_i, i = 1..m\}$. An acl_i can be a threshold value or a rule specifying how the gl_i will be activated. Another option for activating the goals is to have a rate by which each goal participates in the decision-making.

Preference Vector: The stakeholders' preferences order the goals, in the form of $g_i \preceq g_j \preceq ... \preceq g_m$, by designating weights or priorities relating to each goal in the vector $PV = \{pv_i, i = 1..m\}$. We also consider the constraint $\sum_{i=1}^{m} pv_i = 100$ or 1.

The system attributes $AT = \{at_i, i = 1..n\}$ are divided into two categories of controllable and non-controllable attributes. Non-controllable attributes may not be directly manageable attributes, such as the response time, or disturbances like the user traffic.

Adaptation actions $AC = \{ac_i, i = 1..p\}$ (e.g. "restart") generally have preconditions and postconditions. Before considering an action for being selected, its preconditions must be checked. These preconditions can be denoted as $PC = \{pc_i, i = 1..p\}$, in which each PC_i can be a vector of preconditions for each action. The postconditions are basically the impacts of the actions on attributes and goals. In this paper for the GAAM, the postconditions are impacts on the goals which indirectly covers the consequences on the attributes.

Moreover, we define the following relationship matrices to relate the aforementioned entities:

Impact Matrix for relationship among m goals and p actions $IM = \{im_{ij}, i = 1..m, j = 1..p\}$.

Activation Matrix for relationship among m goals and n attributes $AM = \{am_{ij}, i = 1..m, j = 1..n\}$.

Aspiration Level Matrix for specifying aspiration levels of each goal in terms of n attributes $ASL = \{asl_{ij}, i = 1..m, j = 1..n\}$.

The values of im_{ij} and am_{ij} can be a boolean, a number or a fuzzy term. The GAAM specifies a graph $G = \{V, E\}$ in which vertices are $V = \{GL \bigcup AT \bigcup AC\}$ and edges are $E = \{IM \bigcup AM \bigcup PV\}$.

3.2. Decision-Making Algorithm

Figure 1 illustrates the flow of the proposed deciding process. Before making decision, it is essential to determine which goals have been activated and which actions are feasible to take effect. The activated goals ($\hat{GL}$) are voters and the feasible actions ($\hat{AC}$) are eligible candidates. As shown in Figure 1, events are detected by the aspiration values of each goal, asl_{ij}. In GAAM, low-level goals are used which are directly related to the attributes.

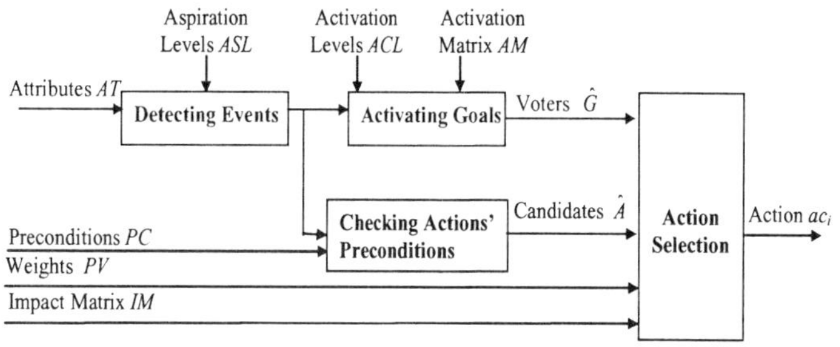

Figure 1. Action Selection Process

Generally, the decision-making algorithm traverses the GAAM graph from attributes to actions in order to select the most appropriate action. The algorithm is summarized in the following steps:

Step 1: Preparing attributes AT- Collect attributes at_i and prepare $at_i * am_{ji}, i = 1..n, j = 1..m$.

Step 2: Selecting voters- First, filter attribute values using $asl_{ij}, \forall gl_i \in GL, \forall at_j \in AT$. Then, aggregate all the processed at_j (by summation) and filter them using $acl_i, \forall g_i \in GL, i = 1..m$ to compile the activated goals in $\hat{GL} \subseteq GL$.
Step 3: Selecting candidates- Check each action's preconditions to compile the feasible set in $\hat{AC} \subseteq AC$ as the voting candidates.
Step 4: Updating preferences- Collect the preferences to update PV as weighting values for voters.
Step 5: Collecting votes- Collect votes of each goal as $gl_i * im_{ij}, i = 1..m, j = 1..p$.
Step 6: Selecting an action- Aggregate all values related to each action ac_i as $\sum_{i=1}^{n} gl_i * im_{ij}, i = 1..m, j = 1..p, \forall ac_j \in \hat{AC}$. Select an action, for instance by selecting the maximum value in the votes.

4. Proof of Concept

As a proof of concept, the action selection problem is used only for the application-level adaptation. One example of need to such an adaptation was news web sites after 9/11. For instance, according to a Los Angeles Times report, CNN.com surged to 162.4 million page views in 24 hours from a 14 million average. The website technical staff did an emergency redesign of the site just to strip out all the extraneous information and downgraded the service to give more significant news content.

The experimental model is a simplified model of a news web site implemented by Simevent toolbox in Simulink/Matlab. The model, illustrated in Figure 2, is a network of queues (or queueing network [3]) which is modeled as an open network with infinite population. The "front-end controller" interprets (preprocesses) requests and passes them to the proper components. In this example, there is only one path for requests. So, all the requests pass to the "news retrieval" component in order to retrieve the content (i.e. text, image or video). The "view-rendering" component prepares the final HTML page for the end-user.

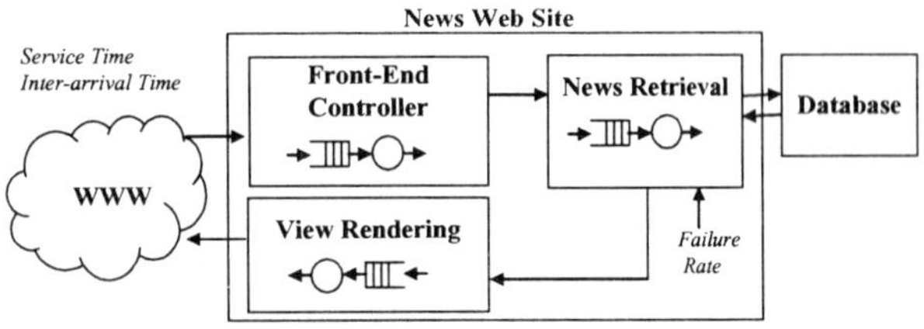

Figure 2. The Experimental Model

Each component has a priority queue based on service time of requests. The inputs are {*service time, failure duration, failure probability, restart signal, in traffic*} and outputs are {*average response time, number of requests served per second, component state, average load, out traffic*}.

For traffic generation *inter-arrival time* and *service time* have to be taken into account. Because there are different types of requests containing text, image and video, for each time interval there are different uniform probability functions for service times. In the experimental model, the service time for the "front-controller" does not depend on the type of requests. But, the randomly generated service time is used for the "news retrieval" and proportionally for the "view rendering" components. The failure rate is also generated by a uniform probability distribution function. The restart action is designed as a micro-reboot mechanism, discussed by Candea *et al.* [1]. Failure, restart and warmup processes of the component are modeled by a state-flow diagram in StateFlow toolbox of Matlab.

4.1. GAAM Specification

In this example, the system stakeholders are administrators and users which define their expectations as objectives of the system. Three objectives have been taken into account, namely: *self-optimizing*, *self-healing* and *max user satisfaction*. Self-optimizing is translated to "best performance" and then to "min end-to-end response time" and "max throughput". Self-healing is translated to "max availability" and then to "min Mean Time To Repair (MTTR)". As Candea *et al.* [1] discuss, reducing MTTR can be as effective as increasing Mean-Time-To-Failure (MTTF) in maximizing availability. Max user satisfaction is decomposed to "best news data type" and "best news data quality". The low-level goals in this goal model are the ones which are directly related to measurable attributes.

For the experimental model the controllable attributes are as follow: i) news quality: video resolution {High, Low}, and image size {Normal, Small}, and ii) news data type: {Video, Image, Text}. Non-controllable attributes are End2End Response time, User load (i.e. average number of waiting requests in a queue) and throughput (i.e. number of requests served per second). The component state is partially controllable (by restart action) and is partially a disturbance (by failure event). For the sake of simplicity of the design, we combine data type and quality in one attribute, at_1. If we denote Text as T, Normal and Small image mode as N and S, High and Low video resolutions as H and L, different feasible states for at_1 in the experiment is from the set $C = \{HNT, LNT, NT, ST, T\}$.

In this model, there are six actions containing restart and switching to each of the entities in set C (enumerated from 1-6). For each action, an action time t_{ac_i} between 200-600msec has been set. The voting module is disabled for t_{ac_i} for each action, in order to prevent the quick oscillation between actions. Preconditions of each action can be identified by the attributes, design constraints and resource limitations. For this example, only the states from set C have been considered.

We also need to designate ACL, PV, IM, AM and ASL entities. The value of asl_{ij} is the aspiration level of each goal regarding its corresponding at_i. For instance, for min end-to-end response time the asl_{ij} value for response time is 400msec. Preference vector PV is set to $\{30, 10, 15, 25, 20\}$ respectively for goals min MTTR, best news data type, best news data quality, min end-to-end response time and max throughput. The last goal, will not be activated unless the throughput is low and the load is high enough to pass the asl_{ij} values.

4.2. Obtained Results

Figures 3-a to 3-d show results in one of the experiments performed with the model in 5×10^5 steps with high load of user requests. Because the "news retrieval" component is the bottleneck of the system, the load and the service time has been shown only for it.

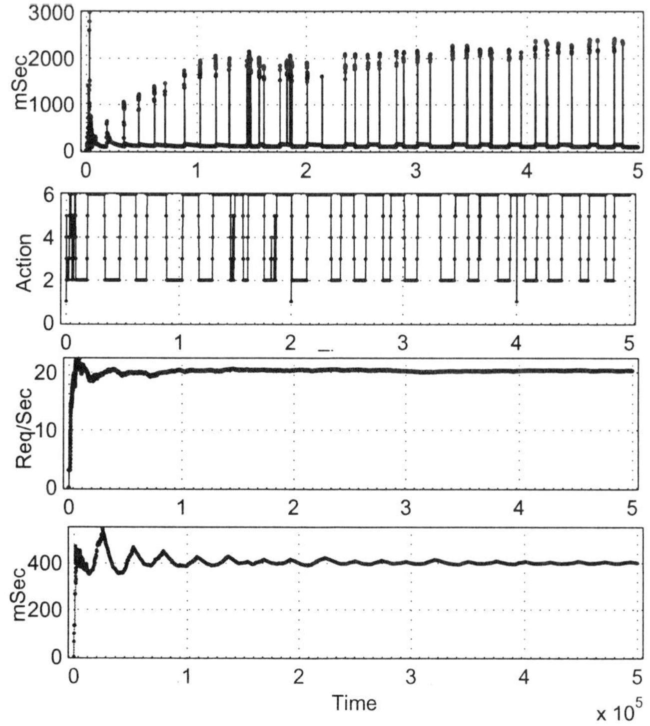

Figure 3. From top: a) Service Time of Requests, b) Selected Actions, c) Throughput (in Second), d) End-to-End Response Time

Figure 3-a depicts the inter-arrival time of web requests for the news web site. Small values of inter-arrival time are likely because of a high load in case of a high service time and remarkable number of requests in components' queues. In addition of the high load, failure can also lead to availability and performance degrade. In this specific experiment three failures occurred for the "news retrieval" component.

Figure 3-b depicts the actions selected by the deciding process. By changing the data type/quality, adaptation engine tries to satisfy both the min end-to-end response time subgoals of the max user satisfaction. Figure 3-c and 3-d show how the end-to-end response time and the throughput are changing after each action selection.

Although, there is no standard set of metrics to evaluate the quality of adaptation, we can discuss on how effective the results are. First, we calculate a utility function $\sum_{i=1}^{5} pv_i \times gl_i$, which at each step shows how much goals are satisfied. It turned out that in %36 of steps all goals are satisfied. We also calculate mean value and standard deviation for system's attributes. Type/Quality values show that on average the system gave NT (normal size image and text) to users with response time 403mSec and throughput 20 when average inter-arrival time was 200mSec.

5. Conclusion

In the proposed model, GAAM, the goal set plays a key role in navigating the deciding process. This matter results in having a better insight for action selection in comparison with the approaches based on state-action rules. The goals and actions can be realized more complex in the GAAM to address different aspects of the domain. The discussed decision-making algorithm is scalable, timely efficient, and not complex. This allows the system managers to extend the GAAM model of an adaptive system during its runtime by changing the goals, attributes or even actions.

The decision-making algorithm is sensitive to the weights (pv_i). We used the values set by stakeholders, but in fact they are required to be adjusted. Moreover, the algorithm uses a cardinal utility (im_{ij} values) for actions, while it can also utilize an ordinal utility. In this case a social choice procedure (e.g. Borda count) can be used.

References

[1] G. Candea, J. Cutler, and A. Fox. Improving availability with recursive microreboots: a soft-state system case study. *Performance Evaluation*, 56(1-4):213–248, 2004.

[2] L. Chung, B. A. Nixon, E. Yu, and J. Mylopoulos. *Non-Functional Requirements in Software Engineering*. Springer, 2000.

[3] R. Jain. *The art of computer systems performance analysis*. John Wiley and Sons, 1991.

[4] R. L. Keeney and H. Raiffa. *Decisions With Multiple Objectives*. John Wiley and Sons, 1976.

[5] P. Maes. Situated agents can have goals. *Robotics and Autonomous Systems*, 6:49–70, 1990.

[6] P. K. McKinley, M. Sadjadi, E. P. Kasten, and B. H. C. Cheng. Composing adaptive software. *IEEE Computer*, pages 56–64, 2004.

[7] J. Rosenblatt. DAMN: a distributed architecture for mobile navigation. *Journal Exp. Theory AI*, 9(2-3):339–360, 1997.

[8] M. Salehie and L. Tahvildari. Autonomic computing: emerging trends and open problems. In *Proc. of ICSE Workshop on Design and Evolution of Autonomic Application Software (DEAS)*, pages 82–88, 2005.

[9] N. Subramanian and L. Chung. Software architecture adaptability: An NFR approach. In *Proc. of Int. Workshop on Principles of Software Evolution*, pages 52–61, 2001.

Self-Adaptive Systems for Information Survivability: PMOP and AWDRAT

Howard Shrobe
MIT CSAIL
mule 32 Vassar Street
Cambridge, MA 02139

Robert Laddaga
BBN Technologies
10 Moulton Street
Cambridge, MA 02139

Bob Balzer, Neil Goldman
Dave Wile, Marcelo Tallis
Tim Hollebeek, Alexander Egyed
Teknowledge
4640 Admiralty Way, Suite 1010
Marina del Rey, CA 90292

Abstract

Information systems form the backbones of the critical infrastructures of modern societies. Unfortunately, these systems are highly vulnerable to attacks that can result in enormous damage.

This paper describes two related systems PMOP and AWDRAT[1] that were developed during the DARPA Self Regenerative Systems program. PMOP defends against insider attacks while AWDRAT is intended to detect compromises to software systems. Both rely on self-monitoring, diagnosis and self-adaptation. We describe both systems and show the results of experiments with each.[2]

1 Background and Motivation

The infrastructure of modern society is controlled by computational systems that are vulnerable to information attacks. There is an urgent need for new approaches to protect the computational infrastructure from such attacks and to enable it to continue functioning even when attacks have been successfully launched.

Our premise is that to protect this infrastructure we need to restructure its software systems as *Self Adaptive Survivable Systems*. In particular, we believe that a software system must be capable of detecting its own malfunction, it must be capable of diagnosing the cause of the problem, it must be capable of repairing itself, and it must be capable of preventing itself from doing harm, even if it is compromised.

This paper describes 2 related systems, PMOP and AWDRAT that were developed as part of the DARPA Self Regenerative Systems program. These two systems share a base of common tools and were applied to the defense of a common test system. However, PMOP's focus is detection of insider attacks, while AWDRAT's is on external threats. Both share a common philosophy that the system must monitor its own behavior, have models of itself that it can reason about and adapt itself to prevent harm from occurring.

Both PMOP and AWDRAT are model based and detect differences from expected behavior. AWDRAT detects differences from predicted behavior (what the system was contracted to do) and PMOP detects differences from benign behavior (what the larger system - comprising the user and the application - was designed to do). AWDRAT detects when the *application* has been compromised while the PMOP detects when the *user* has been compromised.

1.1 A Common Monitoring Infrastructure

The common infrastructure shared by these systems is a self-monitoring framework consisting of:

- **Wrappers** that are placed around critical parts of the system, to collect data and control whether and how application level operations are performed.
- **An Architectural System Model** that is capable of predicting how the system ought to behave in response to user-level and internal requests. It is fine-grained enough to provide an architectural level view of how the system operates, but coarse grained enough to avoid excessive overhead.

PMOP and AWDRAT employ two distinct wrapper technologies: SafeFamily[1, 2] and JavaWrap. The first of these encapsulates system DLL's, allowing AWDRAT and PMOP to monitor accesses to external resources such as files or communication ports. The second wrapper facility provides method wrappers for Java programs. These two capabilities

[1]This article describe research conducted at the Computer Science and Artificial Intelligence Laboratory of the Massachusetts Institute of Technology. Support for this research was provided by the Information Processing Technology Office of the Defense Advanced Research Projects Agency (DARPA) under AFRL Contract Numbers FA8750-04-2-0240 and FA8750-04-C-0252 The views presented are those of the author alone and do not represent the view of DARPA or AFRL.

[2]A longer version of this paper with more technical details may be found at "http://hdl.handle.net/1721.1/37151".

0-7695-2906-2/07 $25.00 © 2007 IEEE

are con all ap-
plicatic to op-
eration r of the
Java la 1.

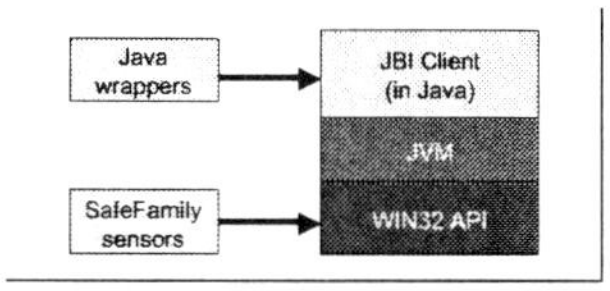

Figure 1. Two Types of Wrappers Used in PMOP and AWDRAT

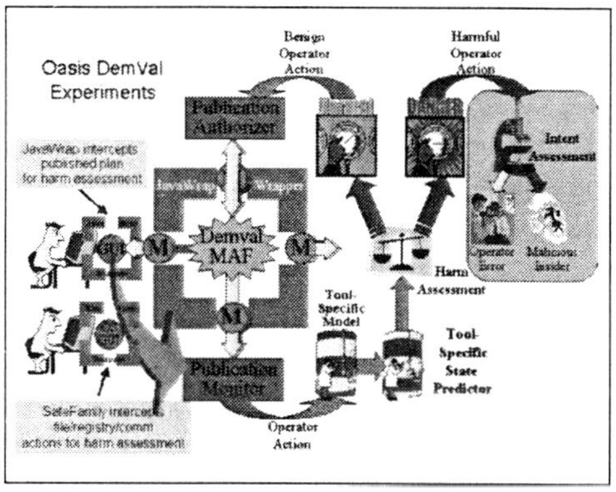

Figure 2. The PMOP Architecture

2 PMOP: Protecting Against Insider Threats

PMOP (Prevention of Misuse of Operator Privileges) is concerned with threats from insiders. Insiders are distinguished from other attackers by the fact that they have been granted access to the system being defended, have been granted privileges on that system, and know how it operates. This means that we must assume that the insider has all the access, privileges, and knowledge needed to effect an attack Therefore, the PMOP project focuses on detecting the application behavior that will cause harm in the real world.

2.1 The PMOP Architecture

The job of the PMOP architecture is to detect and prevent actions that could lead to harm. The components that comprise the overall PMOP architecture are shown in figure 2. Wrappers intercept operator requests issued to the running application and forward the stream of requests to the operational system model which makes predictions about the effects of the actions that the system is asked to perform. The predictions of the operational system model are then assessed for whether they would lead to harmful effects. If so, then a further assessment is made as to the likelihood that the harm was intended. If it appears so then the system increases its degree of suspicion of the user (and notifies human security personnel); if not, then the actions are deemed to be an operator error and feedback is provided to the user. If the user's request is deemed to be legitimate (i.e. causes no harm) then the intercepted operator request is passed to the application to be processed.

A level of suspicion is established by the relative degree to which the user's actions fit the role-based plans to the exclusion of the attack plans. This level of suspicion triggers unique effectors that contain the effects of suspected insider attacks (in a dynamic process-level virtual machine) to protect the system while additional evidence is gathered; administrators can determine whether to authorize or quarantine the contained actions.

Two unique capabilities result from detecting attacks based on model-based predicted harm (about to be) caused to a system: First, there is no need to update the defense as new insider attacks are discovered or new ways to obfuscate them are invented. Second, attacks based on corrupted operand values or the situation in which operations are invoked can be detected and blocked.

Because our attack detectors are model based, and thus harder to fool, the vast majority of insider attacks can be detected and blocked (at least to the level of sophistication of the system models and harm inference reasoning).

The assumption that the insider has all the access, privileges, and knowledge needed for an attack - which defines what it means to be an insider - means that insider attack detection and thwarting must be based on the attack behavior itself. Although detection could occur after the fact, from observation of the damage caused, thwarting requires the detection to occur before the damage has been caused so that it can be prevented.

The detection must therefore be based on pre-damage activity - namely the user's commands or directives to some software system and that software's execution of system level operations to effect those commands or directives. Neither of these phenomena is normally available, but can be made so through proper instrumentation (discussed below).

Operational System Model These additional capabilities do not come for free. They are based on the availability of an individually constructed operational system model, whose quality is determined by the fidelity of that model. In the example system studied in this project, the models were initially propositional rule bases, from which we inferred both the predicted state of the system and the likelihood of harm resulting from the change of state. In addition to modeling the system in its nominal state, one could also model the system in various states of compromise. For example, if a system has had its effective communication bandwidth reduced by a network denial of service attack, we need to infer the effect of user actions in that context, not simply the nominal context. More subtle attacks, as for example, injecting truthful but misleading information into a database, will have to wait for more refined operational system models and more powerful harm-inference reasoners. The operational model we developed for the OASIS system was used to detect corrupted data, effectively data whose use in the final air tasking order would have harmed the mission. The model itself is expressed as a set of rules that constitute the application semantics. The following sample rules are typical of those that determine whether an air tasking order produced by the MAF / CAF operators is harmful.

- Planes cannot land or takeoff in restricted-access zones.
- Refueling can only occur in designated refueling areas.
- The duration of a leg must exceed the time needed to fly that leg (i.e. the distance between its start and end locations) at the plane's maximum speed

Malicious Behavior Detector We developed a malicious behavior detector based on data received from PMOP's wrappers that analyzes the application-level user modification history relative to a role-based model of expected behavior. This model identifies both the types of behavior expected in a situation and the means for assessing the appropriateness of the particular behavior observed. The assessment uses a variety of mechanisms for determining the appropriateness of an action such as safety models, plant models, design rules, best practices, and heuristics. This analyzer detects both intentional and accidental actions that harm the system.

Intent Inference Inferring the actual intent of an operator is a very difficult task. We use Computational Vulnerability Analysis [3] to develop a library of abstract attack plans that an insider might use to render harm. Similarly we provide a library of abstract normal (or role-based) plans that are consistent with normal operator behavior. Using plan recognition techniques, we then assess how well the logged behavior matches any of these plans and then accordingly score the operator actions.

Demonstration System To demonstrate the applicability of our Misuse Prevention architecture to legacy systems, we chose a moderately large example legacy system to model and defend against insider attacks, the OASIS Dem/Val system, developed under an earlier DARPA program. In particular, we focused mainly on a single application within OASIS Dem/Val, the MAF/CAF mission planner, an interactive, Java-based, graphical editor for producing flight plans.

Harm is detected by determining whether the plan satisfies the integrity constraints illustrated above. If not, its publication is blocked to prevent that harm. An analysis is then performed on the offending action, the failed integrity check(s), and the history of operator actions that led to the offending action to determine whether there is a consistent pattern of malicious operator activity.

2.2 Validation: Red Team Experiment

In order to validate our system's ability to detect and thwart insider attacks either through the application's GUI or through the operating system GUI (the Explorer process), a Red Team experiment was conducted. Out of 14 attempts to harm the application or induce a false positive, no attacks causing harm and one false positive were induced through the application's GUI, while one attack causing harm and no false positives were induced through the operating system GUI.

3 AWDRAT: Protecting Against External Threats

AWDRAT provides immunity to compromises of the target system, making it appear self-aware and capable of actively checking that its behavior corresponds to that intended by its designers. "AWDRAT" stands for Architectural-differencing, Wrappers, Diagnosis, Recovery, Adaptivity and Trust-modeling. AWDRAT has been reported on in [4], so we will only briefly review it here.

3.1 The AWDRAT Architecture

The AWDRAT architecture is shown in Figure 3. This architecture includes a variety of models maintained by AWDRAT (the round boxes in the figure) as well as a number of major computational components (the square boxes in the figure). AWDRAT is provided with a model of the intended behavior of the target system (the System Architectural Model in the figure). The Wrapper Synthesis module in the figure is responsible for synthesizing non-bypassable wrappers (shown in the figure surrounding the target system). These wrappers instrument the target system and deliver observations of its behavior to the component labeled "Architectural Differencer". This module consults the System Architectural Model and check that the observations of the target system's behavior are consistent with the prediction of the System Architectural Model suspending the target system's execution if they are inconsistent. In the event that unanticipated behavior is detected, a description of the discrepancy between expected and actual behaviors is sent to the component labeled Diagnosis in the figure. The Diagnosis module uses Model-Based Diagnosis to determine the possible ways in which the system could have been compromised so as to produce the observed discrepancy. AWDRAT proceeds to use the results of the diagnosis to calculate the types of compromise that may have affected each computational resource of the target system. AWDRAT also calculates the likelihood of each possible compromise. These results are stored in an internal model, labeled "Trust Model" in the figure.

Next, AWDRAT attempts to help the target system recover from the failure. First it uses backup and redundant data to repair any compromised resources (the component labeled Recover and Regeneration in the figure). During (and after) recovery, the module in the figure labeled "Alternative Method Selection" helps the target system avoid using any residual compromised resources by selecting alternative methods that are capable of achieving the target system's goals and that don't require the use of the compromised resources.

Part of the reasoning involved in making these choices is guided by the Trust Model: If a resource is potentially compromised then there is a possibility that any method using it will lead to a system failure. However, some methods might be much more desirable than others because they deliver better quality of service. The method selection module, therefore, attempts to find a combination of method and resources that makes a good tradeoff, maximizing the quality of service rendered and minimizing the risk of system failure.

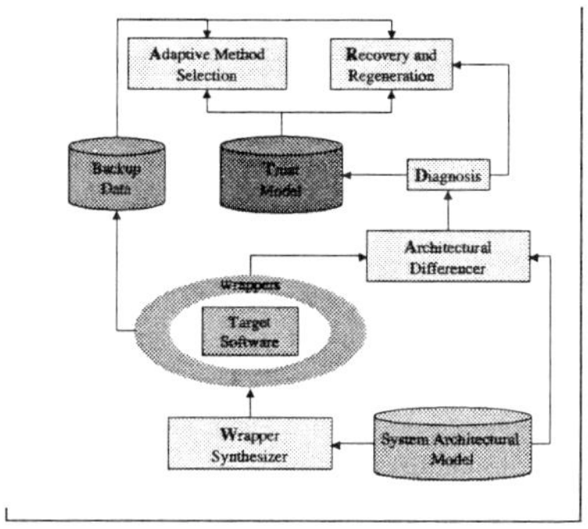

Figure 3. The AWDRAT Architecture

AWDRAT also uses the target system's System Architectural Model to recognize the critical data that must be preserved in case of failure. AWDRAT's Wrapper Synthesizer module generates wrappers that dynamically provision backup copies and redundant encodings of this critical data (labeled Backup Data in the figure).

3.2 Experimentation and Results

AWDRAT's goal is to guarantee that the target system faithfully executes the intent of the software designer. To assess AWDRAT we applied it to the defense of the same target system used in the PMOP experiments. We identified the following properties that AWDRAT should guarantee:

- The data structures maintained by the application should accurately reflect user requests.
- The application should not be able to open a port to any application other than to those JBI servers that it must communicate with (i.e. the JBOSS server).
- The application should not be able to write files except in the specified set of directories that constitute its temporary storage areas.

The results of our experiments show that 91% of all attempts to launch an application, write a file other than those sanctioned or to open an un-sanctioned port or to inappropriately modify a MAF data structure were detected and correctly diagnosed. Finally we note that there are no false positives.

4 Conclusions

AWDRAT and PMOP are frameworks to which an application system may be tethered in order to provide survivability properties such as error detection, fault diagnosis, backup and recovery. They remove the concern for these properties from the domain of the application design team, instead providing these properties as infrastructure services. They use cognitive techniques to provide the target system with the self-awareness and self-adaptivity necessary to monitor its behavior, diagnose failures, adapt and recover from both insider and external attackers. This frees application designers to concentrate on functionality instead of exception handling, and provides a framework for ensuring a high level of system survivablility, independent of the skills of the application designers.

References

[1] R. Balzer and N. Goldman. Mediating connectors: A non-bypassable process wrapping technology. In *Proceedings of the First Darpa Information Security Conference and Exhibition (DISCEX-II)*, volume II, pages 361–368, Jan 25-27 2000.

[2] T. Hollebeek and R. Waltzman. The role of suspicion in model-based intrusion detection. In *Proceedings of the 2004 workshop on New security paradigms*, 2004.

[3] H. Shrobe. Computational vulnerability analysis for information survivability. In *Innovative Applications of Artificial Intelligence*. AAAI, July 2002.

[4] H. Shrobe, R. Laddaga, B. Balzer, N. Golman, D. Wile, M. Tallis, T. Hollebeek, and A. Egyed. Awdrat: Awdrat: A cognitive middleware system for information survivability. In *Innovative Applications of Artificial Intelligence*. AAAI, July 2006.

Self-Adapting Context Definition

Neil O'Connor, Raymond Cunningham and Vinny Cahill
Distributed Systems Group
Trinity College Dublin, Ireland
{neil.oconnor, raymond.cunningham, vinny.cahill}@cs.tcd.ie

Abstract

Many approaches to context-aware computing have focused on providing means for developers to define application contexts. In these approaches, correct application behavior depends on the developer defining the right contexts. The application cannot adapt incorrectly defined contexts as they are statically defined by the developer. We propose a method by which an application can use feedback to evaluate its contexts and adapt them where necessary. This results in more accurate context definitions and should lead to improved application performance. We discuss how this is achieved using Q-learning, and present a scenario and experimental results to support our approach.

1 Introduction

The growth of context-aware computing has seen a move away from the development of "one-off" applications that use context, toward the provision of generic solutions such as middleware and toolkits that support defining and reasoning about context [6], and ontologies that can be used to describe contexts [4]. Using all these approaches relies, to varying degrees, on the developer to provide knowledge to the application.

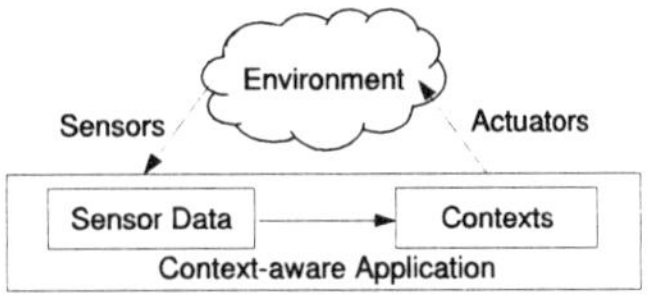

Figure 1. A context-aware application

Context information is often derived from sensor data (Fig. 1). Contexts can then be described as *abstractions* of environmental situations recognizable by sensors. By environmental situations we mean distinct states in which the environment can be. For example, office applications (e.g. ParcTab [1]) use location-sensor data to infer contexts. A context such as "in a room" is an abstraction of many distinct positions within the room. In particular, contexts should be abstracted from situations that share the same *meaning* to the application.

Typically developers are responsible for defining contexts. They use their knowledge of the operating environment, sensors and actuators to define relevant contexts. Sets of sensor readings are mapped to corresponding contexts.

For linear sensor data [12] the developer does not need to explicitly define each sensor reading relevant to a context. Instead the limits of a context can be defined, e.g. "room temperature" abstracts readings from 16-22°C. This is possible for many sensors such as distance, location, weight, velocity etc.

Machine Learning approaches reduce the dependency on the developer to define correct behavior; by allowing an application improve itself. These approaches use abstractions in order to scale to real world problems, and function approximation has been applied to learning these abstractions [13]. Function Approximation is a supervised learning technique [13] so it relies on correct examples to learn from [10]. The developer selects these examples, so similar to context approaches there is a dependency on developer knowledge when defining abstractions.

We identify two issues with developer-dependent approaches to context/abstraction definition:

Inaccurate Contexts: If the developer has incorrect or incomplete knowledge of the domain then contexts may be poorly chosen, e.g., "room temperature" = 10-15°C when it should be 16-22°C. In addition, the dynamic nature of the real world may result in accurate contexts becoming inaccurate, e.g. in the summer room temperature might be regarded as 18-25°C. Inaccurate contexts lead to incorrect behavior.

Inflexible Context Definitions: Developer-defined contexts imply fixed relationships with sensor data. The application is only aware of the implication of being in a context, rather than why the abstraction is appropriate. It cannot reason about the suitability of the abstraction, so it cannot

0-7695-2906-2/07 $25.00 © 2007 IEEE

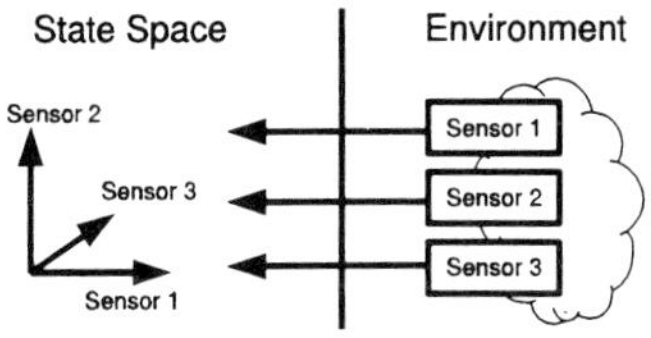

Figure 2. Application perception

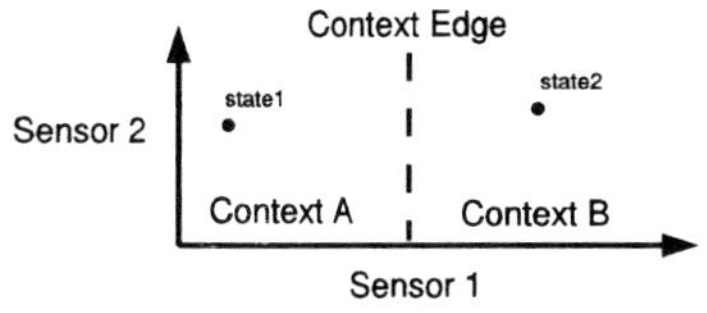

Figure 3. Contexts in the state space

adapt it to correct it or even identify that it is incorrect.

Using our approach the application adapts its context definitions to address these issues. We define a meaning for sensor data that is relevant to the application. The application uses feedback to learn this meaning and identifies contexts based on it. By defining more accurate contexts the application should perform better.

2 Application-Centric Context

There are a variety of definitions for context. They define types of information that make up context [3, 11], or how it is relevant to an application [5]. We consider context to be an abstraction of situations that have similar meaning (Section 1). In order for an application to abstract contexts it must have some notion of meaning for sensor data.

2.1 Meaning for Sensor Data

In [8] Nehaniv argues that the meaning of information is revealed in how it influences an agent. A discussion of the meaning of sensor data in [9] also suggests that the meaning of something is grounded in how it is used by the entity interpreting it.

Brown [3] states that context-aware applications change their behavior according to the context. If contexts adapt behavior and contexts are abstracted from sensor data, then it logically follows that sensor data adapts behavior. Based on this usage we define application-centric meaning as a mapping *M* from sensor data to application actions

$$M : Sd \rightarrow A$$

where *Sd* is the set of possible sensor values and *A* is the available actions. Feedback is used to identify this meaning, and the process is dependent on an underlying learning technique.

2.2 Context Definitions

The application perceives environmental situations through its sensors. We have chosen to consider sensor data as a state space in order for the application to reason about and compare situations, and abstract contexts.

The combined readings of an application's n sensors form a unique point in n-dimensional space. Figure 2 shows an application with three sensors. When combined the sensor readings form a triple (sensor1_value, sensor2_value, sensor3_value) that uniquely identifies a situation in the environment. Situations are distinguished at the highest resolution offered by the sensors. We assume that sensor data is linear [12], which allows the proximity of states within the state space to be calculated using a metric.

From the perspective of the application, a context is a group of states within the state space that share the same meaning. Due to our linear state space it is our intuition that similar states will be close to each other. In this case contexts emerge as continuous spaces within the state space.

Contexts are defined in terms of *context edges*. A context edge is the border between two contexts. Atkin [2] explores the issue of state definition in continuous search spaces, and proposes that only states at which a decision is made are needed. Our context edges are equivalent to these points, as a context change causes a change in behavior. If neighboring states within the state space have dissimilar meaning then we say that a context edge exists between them.

Figure 3 shows a two-dimensional state space. *Contexts A* and *B* are regions within the state space, separated by a context edge. All of the states in *Context A* have the same meaning as *state1*, and all of the states in *Context B* have the same meaning as *state2*. *Context A* is defined as any state to the left of the context edge, and *Context B* is defined as any state to the right. The meaning of a context is the same as that of the states it abstracts; it influences the behavior of the application in the same way as each of its states.

By defining contexts in terms of context edges we make our context definitions flexible. The application identifies context edges, and uses their locations in the state space to evaluate and update existing context definitions.

3 Implementation

There are two main phases to the implementation. Meaning is associated with sensor states, and contexts are subsequently abstracted based on the meaning. For this implementation we used Q-learning to identify meaning.

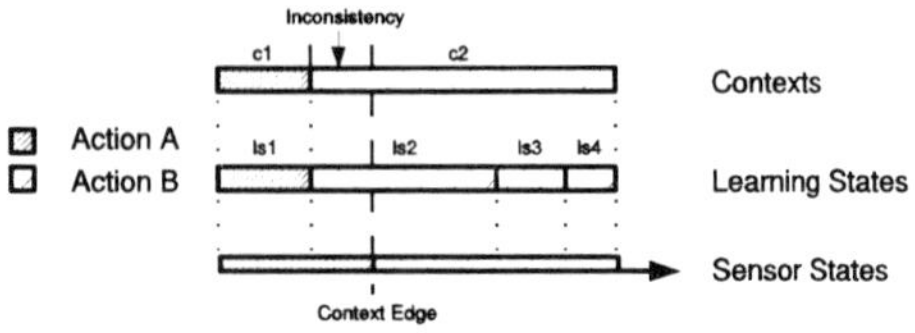

Figure 4. Inconsistent learning state

3.1 Adding Meaning to Sensor States

Q-learning [13] is a Reinforcement Learning algorithm that uses feedback to learn appropriate behavior. The aim of the learning algorithm is to find the optimal action for each of a set of states. To achieve this the algorithm receives a reward from the environment when an action is taken in a state. By exploring all combinations of states and actions the application learns the optimal action for each state- a policy for optimal behaviour.

In our implementation the policy maps states in the sensor state space to actions. This is the same as our notion of application-centric meaning (Section 2.1). The policy defines the meaning of states to the application.

Our metric for comparing states is based on this policy, e.g. if states *s1* and *s2* have different optimal actions we say they have dissimilar meaning.

3.2 Scaleable Learning

Learning becomes infeasible in large state spaces [10] so we cannot apply Q-learning to all states in the state space. We introduce another layer of abstraction between the sensor state space and contexts called *learning states,* to reduce the number of states to be learned about.

Figure 4 shows the two levels of abstraction. Contexts are expressed on learning states rather than directly on the sensor states, so the accuracy of context definitions depends on the accuracy of the learning states. A learning state accurately represents the sensor states below it if the appropriate action is consistent across the learning state.

Figure 4 illustrates a situation where the learning states are not accurate. *ls2* is an *inconsistent* learning state as it contains two distinct regions where different actions are appropriate. The size of the inconsistency is the distance between the context edge and the nearest learning-state boundary. A context edge based on these learning states is inaccurate by this amount.

Some Reinforcement Learning approaches have been extended to include state-space adaptation [7]. They adjust their states to maximise performance. We use a similar approach to evolve an accurate set of learning states.

Our focus is on identifying context edges. Therefore our algorithm focuses on increasing the accuracy of learning

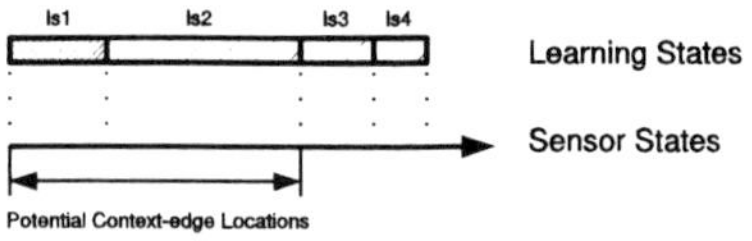

Figure 5. Locating context edges

states in areas of the state space where there is a context edge. To identify these areas neighboring learning states are compared using our similarity metric (Section 3.1). A context edge exists somewhere in the state space represented by neighboring, dissimilar learning states.

Figure 5 shows an area that contains a context edge. The states *ls1* are *ls2* are dissimilar, therefore there is a context edge somewhere in their combined state space. To refine our knowledge of the context-edge location a new learning state is introduced between the dissimilar states, increasing the resolution. Q-learning is applied again to find the meaning for the adjusted set of learning states. Increasing the resolution in the region of the context edge reduces the size of the area shared by dissimilar states, and therefore decreases the uncertainty regarding the context edge location.

This process is repeated to increase the accuracy. Ideally the learning-state boundary matches the context edge exactly, however it may be infeasible to reach this level of accuracy due to the demands of learning.

3.3 Adjusting the Context Definitions

Context edges are identified once an accurate set of learning states is discovered. Learning states are compared to their neighbors, again using our similarity metric (Section 3.1). Dissimilar neighbors have a context edge between them, while similar neighbors are in the same context. Context edge locations are compared to existing context definitions. If the bounds of existing definitions do not match the identified edges they are updated.

4 Experimental Results

To validate our initial implementation we performed experiments on a simple scenario where the environment is represented by a single-dimension state space (Fig. 6). The environmental situation at any point in time is some real value in the range 0-100. There are two actions: action A changes the environment towards 100, and action B changes it towards 0. This might equate to a real-world scenario such as a heating controller based on temperature readings.

The goal of the application is to keep the environment near a particular value. This value is the context edge between situations where Action A and Action B are appropriate. The task of the algorithm is to discover this edge so contexts can be defined.

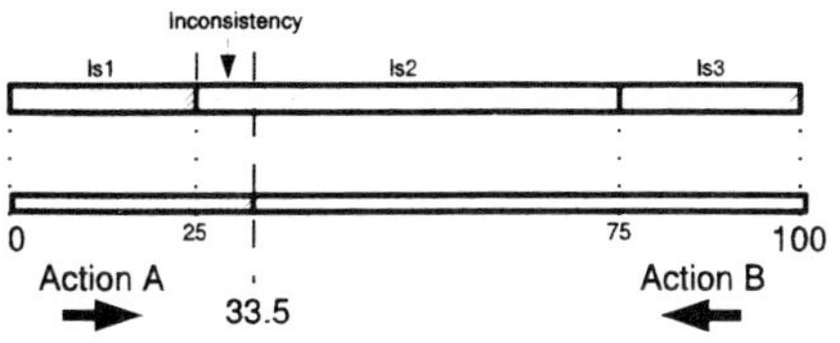

Figure 6. Initial scenario set up

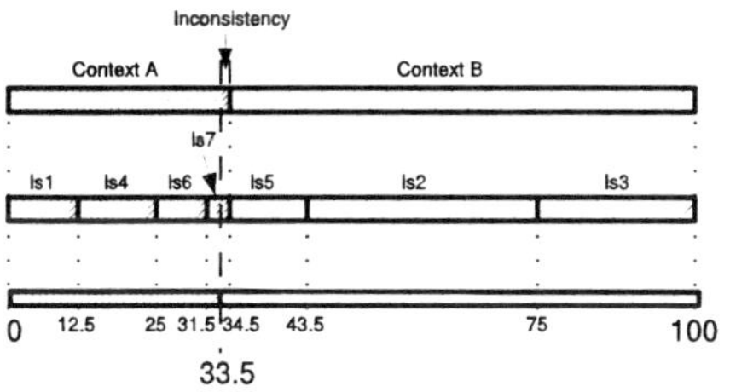

Figure 7. Context edge after four passes

To illustrate the algorithm we outline an experiment where the context edge was 33.5 units. We summarize the results of our experiments in Section 4.2.

4.1 Context-edge Identification

We applied the approach discussed in Section 3.2. Three default learning states were initially defined (Fig. 6), and the inconsistency was 8.5 units. Figure 7 shows the learning states after four passes of the algorithm. The region of state space near the context edge has been refined by new learning states, and the inconsistency is 1 unit.

A context edge was identified between *ls7* and *ls5*. Based on this edge *Context A* was defined as the region below 34.5 and *Context B* as the region above. This definition was within 1% of the actual context edge (33.5).

4.2 Inconsistency-Related Results

We performed 100 experiments on this scenario with randomly chosen context edges. Table 1 summarizes the inconsistency observed in learning states after 0, 2 and 4 iterations of the algorithm.

The average and standard deviation values demonstrate the algorithm's effectiveness. Both values fell as the number of iterations increased. By the fourth iteration a context definition based on the evolved learning states was on average within 1.03% $\pm$ 1.02 of the actual context definition.

# Iterations	Average	Standard Deviation
0	11.23	6.56
2	3.38	2.56
4	1.03	1.02

Table 1. Inconsistency-related statistics

5 Conclusion

We have presented an approach for making context definitions adaptable. It focuses on the application identifying context edges by interpreting sensor information for itself, and addresses some limitations of developer-defined contexts.

Having validated our approach using this simple scenario, we intend to apply it to a set of more complex context-aware scenarios. In the longer term, we hope to use this approach to allow the application adapt the set of sensors it uses to distinguish contexts.

References

[1] Parctab, http://sandbox.parc.com/parctab/.

[2] M. S. Atkin and P. R. Cohen. Using simulation and critical points to define states in continuous search spaces. In *Winter Simulation Conference (WSC)*, Orlando, 2000.

[3] P. J. Brown, J. D. Bovey, and X. Chen. Context-aware applications: from the laboratory to the marketplace. In *IEEE Personal Communications*, 1997.

[4] H. Chen, F. Perich, T. Finin, and A. Joshi. Soupa: Standard ontology for ubiquitous and pervasive applications. In *Mobile and Ubiquitous Systems*, 2004.

[5] A. K. Dey and G. D. Abowd. Towards a better understanding of context and context-awareness. Technical report, Georgia Institute of Technology, 1999.

[6] A. K. Dey, D. Salber, and G. D. Abowd. A conceptual framework and a toolkit for supporting the rapid prototyping of context-aware applications. *Special issue on context-aware computing in the HCI Journal*, 16, 2001.

[7] R. Munos and A. Moore. Variable resolution discretization for high-accuracy solutions of optimal control problems. In *IJCAI*, 1999.

[8] C. L. Nehaniv. Meaning for observers and agents. In *Internation symposium on Intelligent Control/Intelligent Systems and Semiotics*, Cambridge, 1999.

[9] D. Polani, T. Martinetz, and J. Kim. An information-theoretic approach for the quantification of relevance. In *European Conference on Artificial Life (ECAL)*, Prague, 2001.

[10] S. Russell and P. Norvig. *Artificial Intelligence: A Modern Approach*. Prentice-Hall, 2nd edition, 2003.

[11] B. Schilit, N. Adams, and R. Want. Context-aware computer applications. In *1st IEEE Workshop on Mobile Computing Systems and Applications*, California, 1994.

[12] R. Siegwart and I. R. Nourbakhsh. *Introduction to Autonomous Mobile Robots*. MIT Press, 2004.

[13] R. Sutton and A. Barto. *Reinforcement Learning*. MIT Press, 1998.

Self-optimizing Peer-to-Peer Networks with Selfish Processes

Amlan Bhattacharya
University of Iowa
bhattach@cs.uiowa.edu

Sukumar Ghosh
University of Iowa
ghosh@cs.uiowa.edu

Abstract

Request patterns in peer-to-peer networks are not uniform, and the cost of communication depends on the traffic flows among peers. This paper illustrates how processes in an overlay network can use the information about traffic flow pattern and spontaneously adjust the topology to minimize their communication costs. Four different self-optimization protocols are presented. The selfish *protocols allow peers to modify their routing tables to suit their individual needs, and are easy to implement, but the improvements are limited. Compared to this, the* altruistic *protocols that allow peers to adjust the routing tables based on the needs of* other *processes, promise a better performance. Since selfish peers may not comply, a penalty mechanism is proposed to discourage selfishness.*

1 Introduction

Peer-to-peer systems derive their power from the collaboration of numerous peers who contribute their resources to provide a scalable service without any central authority. For all such networks, efficient routing is a key concern. Gummadi et al [5] showed how the access patterns follow a Zipf-like distribution for web objects and how that access patterns get tempered for immutable (like KaZaA) objects. The bottomline is that the access pattern is skewed. Well-known *structured* p2p networks like Chord and Pastry have rigid topologies with no tuning parameters, and are clearly inefficient (as measured by the total routing hops needed to communicate with peers) for dealing with skewed demands. *Unstructured* networks on the other hand, have more freedom in tuning the network topology to skewed demands in traffic. Our goal is to study mechanisms using which the topology of peer-to-peer networks can adapt to the changing communication requirement of the peers. One approach is *content caching*, that has a large space overhead but a wider scope. An alternative approach with a limited goal is to tweak the network topology, and neighbor selection strategy, so that the hop count to the frequently accessed nodes becomes smaller. This is called *route caching*. Route caching addresses only communication cost reduction, and leaves the congestion unchanged. In this note, we focus on adaptation via route caching.

Some significant related work are: (1) reduction of communication cost in Gnutella due to Wang [10] (2) Shen and Xu's elastic routing tables to deal with skewed lookup in DHT-based networks [9], (3) flow-adaptivity in structured p2p networks via request profiling and identifying interest-based clusters (Ghosh and Bejan [1]). Adaptation strategies are challenged (1) *churns* and (2) *selfishness* of the peers. Fabrikant et al [4] presented a game theoretic view of network creation by selfish agents, and studied the existence of Nash equilibria under various cost models. Subsequently, many researchers (for example [3] [7]) extended this. The simple cost model did not consider skewed demands. Moscibroda, Schmid and Wattenhofer [7] showed that P2P topologies formed by selfish peers under Fabrikant's cost model may not stabilize, even if there is no churn. Extreme selfishness in neighbor selection can be detrimental, since it can cause network partition. Therefore, our base topology is a network that preserves connectivity. We assume that a set of n peers (machines) 0 through $n-1$ resides in a metric space. Each peer hosts one or more objects, and their locations are determined by a known hashing function. By definition, each peer i has a link to peer $(i+1)$ $mod\ n$. On top of the underlying unidirectional ring, each peer has k additional links to k distinct peers. The number of neighbors that a peer can support will depend on the capacity and the quality of its network connection. The set of k neighbors defines the *strategy* of the peer. The strategy will be determined by its communication requirement specified as follows:

Let the *flow* $f(i,j)$ denote the number of packets from i to j delivered per unit time, and $d(i,j)$ be the latency (as measured by the number of hops) for one such communication after each peer added its strategy edges. Define two cost functions for the peers:

Private cost. For peer i, $C_i = \sum_{j=0}^{j=n-1} f(i,j).d(i,j)$,

Total cost. $C = \sum_{i=1}^{n} C_i$.

0-7695-2906-2/07 $25.00 © 2007 IEEE

These costs should be as low as possible, and they interplay in different ways. A low value of the total cost reflects an efficient network. However, individual processes may have a selfish goal too. A peer responsible for routing packets between other peers may adopt a routing policy that minimizes its own cost, possibly at the expense of others. With a growing trend of sharing audio (e.g Skype) or video, or managing streaming RSS feeds over a P2P network, each node is faced with dual responsibilities: that of forwarding other's data vs forwarding one's own data/query. Determining priorities is a classic scheduling problem in P2P computing. Given the flows between pairs of nodes, the goal of self-optimization is to minimize the communication cost(s) by letting each peer choose an appropriate *strategy* and an appropriate *routing algorithm*.

Flows between peers change over time. We assume each peer will record the flow using an inexpensive profiling algorithm running in the background, and periodically *self-optimize* by adapting its strategy to the new flow. The problem under consideration involves a subtle interplay between cooperation and competition. Peers cooperate with one another to guarantee that eventually every packet reaches its destination, but compete to minimize their private costs at the expense of other processes. Based on Fabrikant's work, once can formulate this as a non-cooperative game – the target configuration will reflect a *Nash equilibrium*, where no user can decrease its private cost by unilaterally changing its strategy. However, this requires each peer to have knowledge of the routing tables of all other peers, which is unrealistic. As an alternative, we propose four different adaptation protocols, each protocol is defined by a strategy and a routing mechanism. The first strategy is *selfish*, where for each peer the neighbors are destinations with highest flows originating from itself. The second strategy is *altruistic*, where each peer selects neighbors that are destinations of highest flows originating from *other* peers. We demonstrate that when the top flow destinations are uniformly distributed, the altruistic policy is much more effective for lowering the communication cost than its selfish counterpart. Finally, despite a prescription of policies, some peers will cheat. To deal with cheating, we propose a penalty mechanism that will promote compliance.

The paper is organized as follows: Section 2 formalizes the model. Section 3 introduces the adaptation protocols, and analyzes the communication costs. Section 4 describes the penalty mechanism for mandating compliance. Finally, Section 5 contains some concluding remarks.

2 Preliminaries

A P2P network is an overlay network whose topology is a directed graph $G = (V, E)$, and $V = \{0, 1, \cdots, n-1\}$. Each $i \in V$ denotes a process (peer) and every directed edge $(i, j) \in E$ represents an overlay link from i and j. Each peer can choose a subset of other peers as its immediate neighbors, and this choice is called its *strategy*. The *strategy space* of a peer i is represented by $S_i = 2^{V\setminus\{i\}}$, and $s_i \in S_i$ denotes a specific strategy of peer i. A collection of the strategies of all peers $(s_0, s_1, \cdots, s_{n-1}) \in (S_0 \times S_1 \times \cdots S_{n-1})$ defines the topology G.

The strategy of each peer has a *fixed* component, and a *variable* component, The fixed component is externally mandated, whose violation may jeopardize the connectivity of G. In the present case, by definition, the fixed component of the strategy of peer i is $(i + 1)$ mod n, so the strategy space shrinks to $2^{V\setminus\{i,i+1\}}$. In the variable part, each peer can arbitrarily choose k peers to minimize its private cost. The actual value of k may vary from one peer to another. but for the purpose of analysis, we will assume that all peers use the same value of k. Structured networks have fixed strategies, and there is no variable component.

Let $f : V \times V \longrightarrow \mathbb{Z}^*$ denote the network *flow*. Given the flow, the network topology and the routing policy, one can compute the communication cost. For each peer i, model the non-uniformity of the network flow by an ordered set of h destination nodes $(h < n)$ $\{i_1, i_2 \cdots, i_h\}$. By definition, (1) $\forall j : 1 \leq j \leq h : f(i, i_j) \geq f(i, i_{j+1})$, and (2) each such flow is substantially larger than the flow towards the remaining $(n-h)$ destinations, so that the packets to the remaining destinations contribute minimally to the communication cost. It is well-known that most often each peer frequently communicates with a small number of peers based on its interests. This is also a simplistic way of modeling a Zipf-like query pattern for analytical purposes. We assume $h > k$, otherwise each peer will choose its top flow destinations as elements of its strategy set, and the costs become trivially optimal. By modifying the variable component of the topology, the communication cost of a peer-to-peer network can be optimized, and this is the essence of adaptation.

Given a flow f, a viable adaptation protocol must satisfy three requirements:

Stabilization. The strategies must stabilize, so that the routing tables converge to a final configuration, and continue in that configuration unless the system records another change of flow.

Reachability. The terminal configuration of the routing tables must guarantee that each packet sent by a node reaches its destination in a bounded number of hops.

Cost optimization. The communication cost for the given flow f must be as low as possible, certainly lower that what it was for the unoptimized network.

Lemma 2.1. *Given a flow, the problem of finding an optimal topology that minimizes the communication cost is NP-hard.*

0-7695-2906-2/07 $25.00 © 2007 IEEE

This follows from a possible reduction of this problem to the network creation game [4] known to be NP-hard.

3 Adaptation protocols

We deviate from the classic game-theoretic formulation [4] on the ground that peers do not have an easy mechanism for inspecting the residual graph when a fraction of the strategy edges have been added. We present four different protocols for flow-adaptation. Each protocol is characterized by a *strategy* and a *routing mechanism.* These are: (1) Selfish strategy with last-hop routing (2) Selfish strategy with greedy routing (3) Altruistic strategy with last-hop routing (4) Altruistic strategy with greedy routing.

3.1 Selfish protocols

The selfish protocols are based on the following strategy: $\forall i \in V : s_i = \{i_1, \cdots, i_k\}$ Using this protocol, packets directed towards k of the h top flow destinations will arrive in a single hop regardless of the routing strategy chosen, but the cost of of routing packets to the remaining $(h-k)$ destinations deserves a close look, and will depend on the routing strategy. We consider two different cases.

Case 1. Selfish strategy with last-hop routing. The routing is *last-hop*, when each packet from node i is always forwarded to the next node $(i+1)\ mod\ n$ unless there is a link to the final destination.

Theorem 3.1. *For the selfish protocol using last-hop routing, if the top flow distributions are randomly distributed, then packets from a peer i will arrive at the top k-out-of-h destinations in a single hop, and reach the remaining $(h-k)$ destinations in an expected number of $\frac{n-1}{k}$ hops.*

Since k is much less than n, the expected $O(n)$ hop count is unacceptably large. Thus this protocol performs poorly.

Case 2. Selfish strategy with greedy routing. With greedy routing, a packet towards a destination j will be forwarded by every peer i to neighbor i_t such that $\forall t : 0 \leq t \leq k : d(i_t, j)$ is the smallest.

If the top flow destinations are distributed around the ring with uniform random probability, then the diameter of the graph is approximately $\log n$. However, Kleinberg [6] showed that no efficient algorithm exists for finding such paths[1]. Routing in polylog time is possible, when the existence of an edge between nodes i and j is proportional to $\frac{1}{d(i,j)^r}$ (for a ring $r = 1$). In [8], Shah showed that with k such edges, the routing time is $O(\frac{\log^2 n}{k})$. This is a special case and is unlikely to help out the selfish strategy in general.

[1]The best decentralized algorithm has an expected routing time of $O(n^{\frac{2}{3}})$.

3.2 Altruistic protocols

In the altruistic strategy, each node i ranks the flows originating from *other* nodes $j \neq i$ (and routed through i) in the descending order, and chooses the top k of these destinations as its strategy.

Case 1. Altruistic strategy with last-hop routing. The altruistic strategy defines the routing tables of the peers. Using last-hop routing, if the destination of a packet does not belong to the strategy of a given peer, then the packet is forwarded to the next peer $(i+1)\ mod\ n$.

Theorem 3.2. *The altruistic strategy with last hop routing delivers packets to the top h destinations at an average of $O(\frac{h}{k})$ hops.*

Proof. (Hint only) Consider a global order of all flows in the network: $q.1 \geq q.2 \geq q.3 \geq \cdots$ If the routing tables stabilize, then the nodes that generate the flows $q.1 - q.k$ must have their packets delivered within at most two steps, and nodes that generate flows $q.(m-1)k+1 - q.mk$ must have the packets delivered in at most $(m+1)$ steps. As a result, all packets directed to the top $n.h$ destinations (for n nodes) will be delivered within $1 + \frac{n.h}{k}$ steps. Hence the result. □

Theorem 3.3. *Using altruistic strategy and last-hop routing, the routing tables stabilize in $O(n.k)^2$ steps.*

We conjecture that the average stabilization time for the routing tables is much lower than the worst case figure.

Case 2. Altruistic strategy with greedy routing. For the altruistic strategy with greedy routing, we first show that if there is only one peer sending out requests, then packets to the its top h destinations in an expected number of $\frac{\log h}{\log k}$ hops. To understand this, consider the k-ary tree with node i as the root. After r hops, packets to the top $(k + k^2 + \cdots + k^{r-1})$ destinations will be delivered. Thus $h = (k + k^2 + \cdots + k^{r-1})$, which leads to the result. This is a lower bound. The following theorem computes the expected hop count in the general case of multiple peers.

Theorem 3.4. *If the top flow destinations are uniformly distributed, then the altruistic strategy with greedy routing delivers packets to the top h destinations in an expected number of $\frac{h}{k}$ hops.*

Proof. A packet from a node i will be delivered to its destination by another node $j \neq i$ if the flow to that destination ranks among the top k of all flows passing through j. Since there are $n.h$ total contenders, the expected number of contenders at a single node is h and the probability of making the cut is k/h. If this packet fails to make the cut, then it is forwarded to another node. The probability of making the cut after r hops is $\frac{k}{h}.(1-\frac{k}{h})^{r-1}$ So, the expected routing time of $\frac{h}{k}$ hops. □

The selfish protocol with the strategy edges satisfying Kleinberg's distribution can outperform the altruistic protocol when $\frac{\log^2 n}{k} < \frac{h}{k}$, i.e. $h > \log^2 n$.

4 Protocol enforcement

Despite the attempt to mandate the altruistic protocol, a fraction β ($\beta < 1$) of all peers will try to derive undue advantage by switching to the selfish protocol, while expecting others to be altruistic. Restricting the game to a choice between the selfish and the altruistic protocols, the following lemma quantifies the advantage of the cheaters.

Lemma 4.1. *In a network of n peers, if a small fraction β cheat by using the selfish protocol, then the average hop count of the cheaters will be $\frac{1}{h}\left(k + (1-\beta)(h-k)\frac{h}{k}\right)$, and the average hop count of the loyal peers will $\frac{h}{k(1-\beta)}$*

The advantage of the cheaters will gradually fade away as β increases, making cheating less lucrative. However, due to the concern that the cheaters may get undue advantage, in a stable equilibrium, all peers will eventually revert to the selfish protocol. This leads to the following theorem:

Theorem 4.2. *The Nash equilibrium corresponds to all peers using the selfish protocol.*

Since the selfish strategy leads to an expected average routing cost of $O(\frac{n}{k})$, and the altruistic strategy reduces this to $O(\frac{h}{k})$ (or perhaps lower if we use the formulation from [4]), adoption of the selfish strategy raises the communication cost by a factor at least $O(\frac{n}{h})$

Mandating compliance with the altruistic protocol needs (1) a mechanism for the detection of cheating, and (2) a deterrent for penalizing the cheaters, The following lemma is the cornerstone for the detection of cheating.

Lemma 4.3. *In the altruistic protocol, no loyal peer should route its packets in a single hop, unless the destination of the packet matches with a top destination of another peer.*

This is a detectable event by the destination peer, unless there is a coalition of cheaters working to suppress such observations. The penalty for this action is the addition of an amount ζ to the hop count for packets originating from the potential offender, so that they are discouraged from cheating. In practice, ζ will translate to an additional delay. Consider the flows from a cheater i to its h top destinations. Assuming these flows to be identical, the total cost for routing (including the penalty) will be $Cost_1 = k + (h-k)(\frac{h}{k} + \zeta)$

If peer i did not cheat, then the cost for routing to the top h destinations would have been $h.\frac{h}{k} = \frac{h^2}{k}$. However, there is a small probability that some of the top destinations of i will match with a peer in its strategy set, and routing to these destinations will cause i to be unfairly penalized. Assuming uniform distribution of the top flow destinations, the probability of each such event is $O(\frac{k}{n})$. Thus the routing cost without cheating will be $Cost_2 = h(1-\frac{k}{n}).\frac{h}{k} + h.\frac{k}{n}.\zeta$

To be a deterrent, $Cost_1 > Cost_2$. Since $k << h << n, \zeta > 1$.

5 Conclusion

Our analysis disregarded churns. Intuitively, churns tend to destabilize the routing tables generated by the altruistic protocols. The ability to combat churns will depend on the speed at which the network adapts to the new flow pattern, as well as the churn rate. If the mean time between the arrival or departure of peers exceeds the mean time to stabilize the routing tables, then the protocol will fail to deliver the promised performance. One method is to first adapt the network to the reputation of the peers [2], and then run our protocol on top of this. This will prevent or minimize adversarial churns. The impact of random churns is likely to be much gentler.

References

[1] Bejan, A. Ghosh, S. Self-Optimizing DHTs using Request Profiling. *OPODIS 2004, pp. 87-95* (also in LNCS 3544, 140-153).

[2] Condie T., Kamvar, S.D., and Garcia-Molina H. Adaptive Peer-to-Peer Topologies. *Proc. 4th International Conference on Peer-to-Peer Computing (P2P'04) 2004.*

[3] Eidenbenz S, Kumar V, and Zust S. Equilibria in Topology Control Games for Ad Hoc Networks. *DIALM-POMC, 2003.*

[4] Fabrikant A, Luthra A, Maneva E, Papadimitriou C.H., and Shenker, S. On a Network Creation Game. *ACM PODC 2003*, 347-351.

[5] Gummadi P.K., Dunn R.J., Saroiu S., Gribble S.D., Levy H.M., Zahorjan J. Measurement, Modeling, and Analysis of a Peer-to-Peer File-sharing Workload. *SOSP 2003, 314-329.*

[6] Kleinberg, J. The Small-World Phenomenon: An Algorithmic Perspective. *STOC 2000.*

[7] Moscibroda T, Schmid S, Wattenhofer, R. On the Topology formed by Selfish Peers. *ACM PODC 2006.*

[8] Shah G. Distributed Data Structures for Peer-to-Peer Systems. *Ph.D. thesis, Yale University, 2003.*

[9] Shen H, Xu C-Z: Elastic Routing Table with Provable Performance for Congestion Control in DHT Networks. *ICDCS 2006.*

[10] Wang, C. Xiao, L., Lin Y., and Zheng, P. Distributed Caching and Adaptive Search in Multilayer P2P Networks. *ICDCS 2004.*

A Self-Adaptive Extensible Embedded Processor

Lars Bauer, Muhammad Shafique, Dirk Teufel and Jörg Henkel
University of Karlsruhe, Chair for Embedded Systems, Karlsruhe, Germany
{lars.bauer, shafique, henkel} @ informatik.uni-karlsruhe.de

Abstract

Extensible embedded processors allow the designer to adapt the instruction set to a certain application profile. It is either done during design time or at run time. In the latter case it is fixed when which part of the instruction set is used. The processor is then configured according to a predefined schedule. Our approach goes a step further: our extensible processor is self-adaptive. That means, during run time the processor analyzes the usage of Special Instructions and self-adapts when and how these are used and configured. We show that this kind of self-adaptation leads to a high efficiency (e.g. performance per chip area, etc.) and is superior to state-of-the-art extensible processors. In this paper we present the main techniques of our novel self-adaptive approach. We evaluate by means of an H.264 Video Encoder.

1. Introduction and Related Work

The term *ASIP* (Application Specific Instruction Set Processor) was introduced in the early 90s and denoted processors that are application specific, i.e. their instruction set performed efficient in terms of performance per chip area, etc. Since the early 2000s the term *ASIP* is far more expanded. Major vendors like Tensilica [4], ARC [1], CoWare [2], etc. offer their tool suites and processor cores and the user can now create a very specific instruction set that is tailor-made for a certain application. Typically these tool suites come with a whole set of retargetable tools, such that code can easily be generated for that specific extensible processor. As a result, extensible processors are more efficient than the first generation of *ASIPs*. However, still the designer decides during design time which part of the instruction set is invoked at which time.

Reconfigurable computing addresses this problem in terms of run-time reconfiguration. And indeed, there are approaches that aim to adapt the instruction set during run time in order to overcome this limitation [3], [12], [14]. However, the designer still has to decide when reconfiguration takes place such that the processor can run more efficiently. The designer also decides during design time the granularity of a Special Instruction (SI) and offers exactly one implementation per SI which circumvents dynamic adaptation at run time.

Investigating large real-world applications, we have found that it is hard or even impossible to exactly predict the requirements (performance, etc.) of an embedded processor during design time. As a result, an extensible processor may run non-efficient for large parts of an application. In order to overcome these shortcomings, we have designed a self-adaptive extensible processor that analyzes the SI usage during run time and self-adapts when and how a certain SI is used and configured.

Our novel contributions are as follows:

- A self-adapting scheme that decides when and which Special Instructions to deploy at certain run-time points depending upon the changing application requirements.
- A run-time monitoring technique that checks the current state of the system, collects the relevant data, and forwards it to the self-adapting scheme.

Beneath the previously mentioned commercial tool suites and processor cores there are also academic approaches like LISA [6] and many more. A general overview for the benefits and challenges of ASIPs is given in [7]. A major focus was spent in automatically generating Special Instructions (SIs) for application speedup. A library of reusable functions is used in [8], whereas in [9], [10] the authors describe methods to generate SIs from operation patterns matching.

Overviews for reconfigurable computing can be found in [11]. The Molen Processor couples a reconfigurable processor to a core processor via a dual port register file and an arbiter for shared memory [12]. The run-time reconfiguration is explicitly predetermined by additional instructions in the application. An overview for reconfigurable computing with a more fine-grained connection to the CPU is given in [13]. The OneChip98 project [14] uses a reconfigurable functional unit coupled to the host processor and obtains speedup mainly from memory streaming applications.

2. Motivational Case Study

Our extensible embedded processor provides the foundation for time-multiplexed utilization of available hardware resources with self-adaptation to the dynamic needs of an application. We explicate our concept and justify its advantages by means of an H.264 Video Encoder [5] case study.

Within the H.264 Video Encoder every frame is segmented into Macro Blocks (MBs, i.e. 16x16 pixels). Each MB is either predicted by the neighboring MBs in the same frame (I-MB) or by an MB in the previous frame (P-MB). The execution paths for encoding I- and P-MBs differ significantly and are implemented with a different set of Special Instructions (SIs). The ratio of I-to-P MB in a frame can not be predicted statically. In case of high motion scenes the *Motion Estimator* normally fails to provide a good match, i.e. an MB with small pixel-wise Sum of Absolute Differences (SAD). Then, the resulting residue (pixel-difference of current and predicted MB) is too high and for a given bit-rate this deteriorates the encoded quality. At this time the *Rate Controller* decides to insert an I-MB if it gives smaller residue. There can be two types of I-MB injections: *Random* and *Contiguous* depending upon the object size. A simple decision equation looks like following:

if (SAD_P-SAD_I > *Threshold*) **then** MB_Type := *INTRA*;
else MB_Type := *INTER*;

We have carried out a study of various video sequences with different types of motion contents. Figure 1 shows a typical distribution of smooth-to-hectic motion scene with a varying number of I-MBs per image. It is apparent from the figure that a sudden variation in the motion content of a video scene radically changes the ratio of I- to P-MBs.

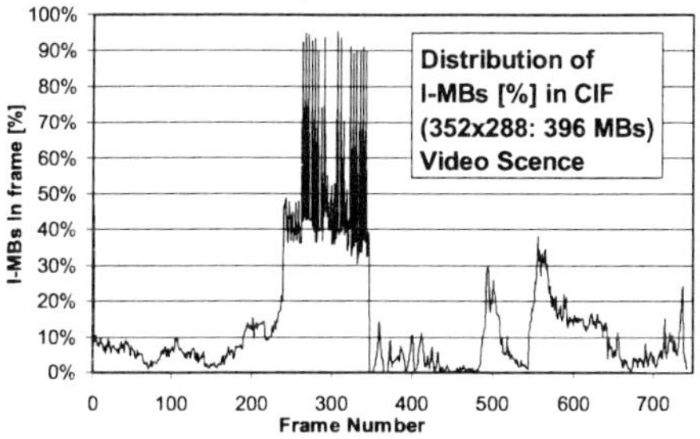

Figure 1: Distribution of I and P MBs

Analysis: Extensible Processors and static reconfiguration schemes either provide tailor-made hardware designed for a fixed average ratio of I-to-P MBs or provide full hardware for both. The first case suffers from performance degradation for different ratios while the second case requires more silicon area (which is then inefficiently utilized). **We solve this problem with our novel self-adaptive extensible embedded processor platform** (described in subsequent sections).

3. Fine-grained Instruction composition

We noticed that all discussed architectures in the related work are using mostly exactly one implementation for each Special Instruction (SI). This severely limits the potential for self-adaptation. Our architecture is based on offering the SIs in a much more fine-grained manner. Instead of implementing full SIs independently, we implement data paths as our elementary processing units in reconfigurable Hardware (therefore called *Atoms*) and then combine these *Atoms* to create an implementation (called *Molecule*) of an SI. This allows us to reuse the *Atoms* for different SIs and to increase the efficiency compared to traditional approaches. We additionally observed that an SI often needs certain *Atoms* multiple times. We exploit this property by making these SIs available in different *Molecules* that vary in their level of parallelism (temporal vs. spatial computation). The system can then automatically adapt the SI performance at run time. As a special *Molecule* we offer an execution with Base Instructions (BIs: instructions of base processor) that does not consume any dynamic hardware but therefore is typically the slowest kind of execution for a certain SI. Figure 2 shows an example of 3 SIs with their implementing *Molecules* and the composition out of the *Atoms*.

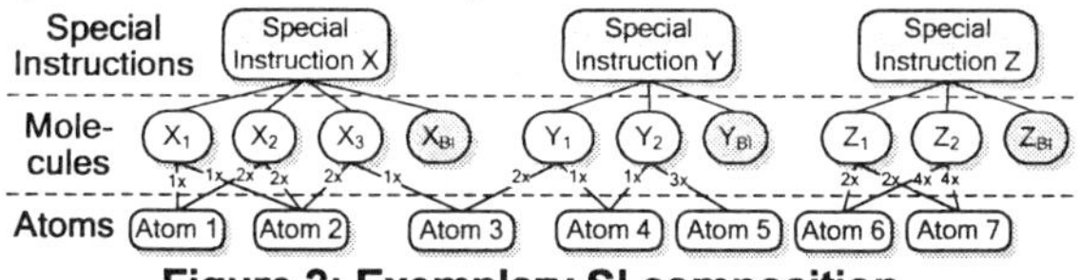

Figure 2: Exemplary SI composition

4. Self-adaptive Processor

As pronounced, our processor self-adapts during run time and we aim to execute as many decisions as necessary at run time and as many as possible during design time to reduce the run-time overhead.

4.1. Preparation at compile time

As the *Atom* re-loading is nearly 1 *ms* [15], the system needs information about upcoming SIs in order to avoid penalties (i.e. waiting). Therefore, we perform a compile-time analysis on the application control flow graph, where each node is a base block (BB). Each BB contains profiling information about its execution time, execution frequency, the invocation probability of its successors, and which SIs are needed within this BB. Out of this information a tool automatically determines BBs, where the future SI usages are forecasted. For the selected BBs, *Forecast Instructions* (FCs) are automatically embedded into the application containing information about the SIs (i.e. when, how often, and with which probability these will be executed) [15].

4.2. Run-time architectural overview

A functional overview of the run-time system is given in Figure 3. We extend a typical CPU pipeline by *Atom Containers* (ACs, i.e. *Containers* that can be dynamically reloaded with different *Atoms*) and the *Rotation Manager*, which is controlling the run-time behavior, i.e. the rotation (adaptation) of the SI implementation. The ACs are tightly connected to the execution data path of the pipeline. The main tasks of the *Rotation Manager* are:

i) Controlling the execution of SIs
ii) Observing and adapting to changing situations
iii) Determining the rotation decision

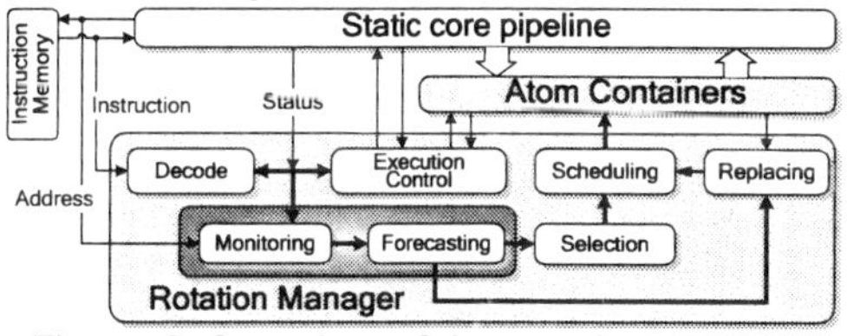

Figure 3: Overview of the run-time system

The pipeline executes the Base Instructions (BIs), provides the parameters for SIs, and writes their computed results to the register file. The *Rotation Manager* is recognizing the SIs and FCs by decoding the instructions. When an SI or FC is noticed, this information is forwarded to the *Execution Control* and the *Monitoring*. The *Execution Control* is taking care of the actual execution of the SIs (either executed with accelerating hardware when all necessary *Atoms* are available or by the base instructions triggered by a synchronous trap). The *Monitoring* records the SI usages and the *Forecasting* updates the FCs to adapt them to changing run-time situations, as we will see in section 4.3. The *Selection* uses the adapted FCs to choose a set of *Molecules* to implement the forecasted SIs. The *Scheduling* and *Replacing* finally determine the AC re-loadings to offer the *Atoms* that are needed to implement the selected *Molecules*.

4.3. Observation and Self-Adaptation

For self-adaptation the system needs to observe changing surroundings. Specifically, the knowledge of future SI usages is needed to start reconfiguration right in time in order to avoid delays. At compile time, FCs are embedded into the application. We call a set of subsequent FCs a Forecast Block FB. Figure 4 shows a sequence of FBs B_i that are executed sequentially. The *Monitoring* inside the *Rotation Manager* considers the time between the last executed FB B_t and the next executed FB B_{t+1}, as it is indicated by the sliding window. The actual usages U_{t+1} of SIs are counted between two FBs and compared against the forecast from B_t. The difference between $FC(B_t)$ and $U_{t+1} + FC(B_{t+1})$ denotes the forecast error E_t:

$$E_t = U_{t+1} + \gamma FC(B_{t+1}) - FC(B_t) \quad (1)$$

The parameter γ is used to adapt of how strong the forecast of B_{t+1} should contribute for computing the error E_t, which is then used to update $FC(B_t)$. The strength of this back propagation is adjusted with the parameter α:

$$FC(B_t) = FC(B_t) + \alpha E_t \quad (2)$$

The parameter γ in (1) makes sure, that the usage of an SI is not back propagated too far before the actual usage, whereas the parameter α in (2) makes sure, that no thrashing between two extreme values can occur. The correction term αE_t may not only be back-propagated to the directly preceding FB B_t, but potentially to all previously executed FBs. The strength of the back-propagation to the farther away FBs is diminished by the parameter λ, as shown in Figure 4.

Techniques that are using differences between distinct points in time are called Temporal-Difference (TD) methods [16]. The TD method is based on the Markov property, i.e. the conditional property to reach a specific FB and to count a specific number of SIs (between the last and reached FB) depends only on the previous FB and not on the chain of preceding FBs. This Markov property can not be guaranteed in real-life problems, but experiments suggest, that the TD scheme nevertheless achieves good results in practice [17]. This is due to the fact that the Markov property is mainly needed to derive the TD scheme and to prove its convergence, which is not relevant for our approach, as the behavior of executed applications varies and thus we are not interested in convergence, but in adaptation [18].

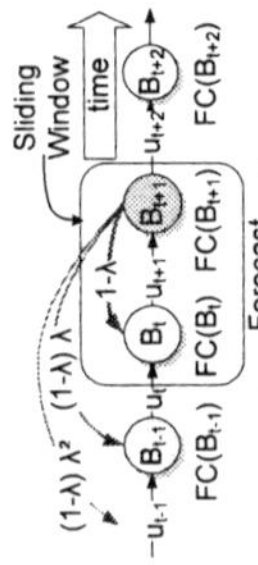

Figure 4: Temporal-Difference (TD) method

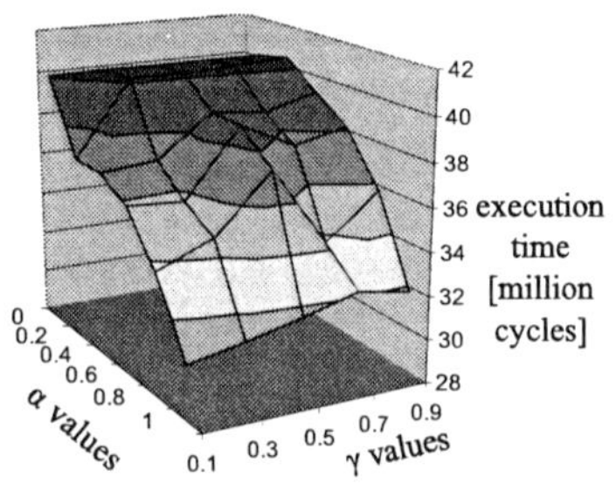

Figure 5: TD Parameter evaluation for λ=0

As for hardware implementation $\lambda>0$ accounts for a significant overhead due to its ability to update multiple previous FBs, whereas the special case $\lambda=0$ only updates the directly preceding FB. We therefore evaluated different values for λ to appraise the impact by restricting λ to 0. For $\lambda=0.6$ we noticed an average execution time improvement of 4.8% and for $\lambda=1$ (i.e. updating all previous FBs) an average performance improvement of 8.1% compared to $\lambda=0$. The peak performance improvement (44.3%) as well as the peak performance degradation (-8.6%) were found for $\lambda=1$. As an average performance improvement of 8.1% does not justify the hardware overhead of tracking potentially all previously executed FBs in their execution sequence, all further benchmarks are obtained with $\lambda=0$. As seen in Figure 5 the execution time is dominated by the parameter α for $\lambda=0$. The fastest execution can be found for $\alpha=1$, i.e. a rapid self-adaptation to varying situations. It is in average (over the γ values) 24.6% faster than $\alpha=0$, i.e. no self-adaptation.

4.4. Self-x Properties of our Architecture

At compile time certain system parameters cannot be determined, e.g. the number of *Atom Containers* (ACs) that are assigned to the application by the Operating System (OS) is unknown as it depends on task priorities and the number of available ACs. Therefore, the system has to be able to configure itself at start-up. We call this property **Self-Configuration**: the application starts with the initial assigned ACs, constraints and information which SIs will most probably be needed in the beginning of the application (i.e. before *Self-Monitoring* has gathered sufficient information to adapt the static profiling information). According to these information the system decides which *Molecules* to choose for implementing the requested SIs and rotates the instruction set accordingly.

Self-Monitoring is key to *Self-Adaptation* as it provides feedback to the system which is then used for updating the predictions for the future. **Self-Adaptation** is implemented at 2 different levels. At OS level parameters for selecting *Molecules* are modified and at control-flow level the forecasts for the SI usages are continuously adapted. OS-level *Self-Adaptation* is achieved by an Observer-Controller-Loop, where the monitor corresponds to sensors while the controller is part of the OS. When the observer is reporting a non-optimal system behavior or a miss of constraints, then the OS is modifying parameters for choosing *Molecules*. If the observer, for example, reports non-acceptable power consumption, then the parameter for the performance-per-mW trade-off is adjusted to reduce the number of *Atom* reloadings, etc. If one of the running tasks consistently misses its timing constraints, the controller can increase the number of ACs that are dedicated to this task. Control-flow level *Self-Adaptation* serves to support the changes of parameters by the OS-level *Self-Adaptation*. If for instance, the trade-off between power consumption and performance changes or the number of available ACs varies, then the system needs a good knowledge of the future SI usages to adapt its rotation policy to follow these guidelines of the OS level.

Finally, **Self-Repairing** is a natural feature of our system: as our architecture can adapt to varying number of ACs, it can easily handle a detected failure in an AC by basically avoiding it's future usage and adapting the contents of the functional ACs to an optimal support for the requested SIs. The detection of the failure can be done with conventional approaches, e.g. applying a test vector to an AC and inspecting the computed result. As every SI can be executed with the base instructions, the *Self-Repairing* reaction is fast and inherent to the system.

5. Evaluation and Results

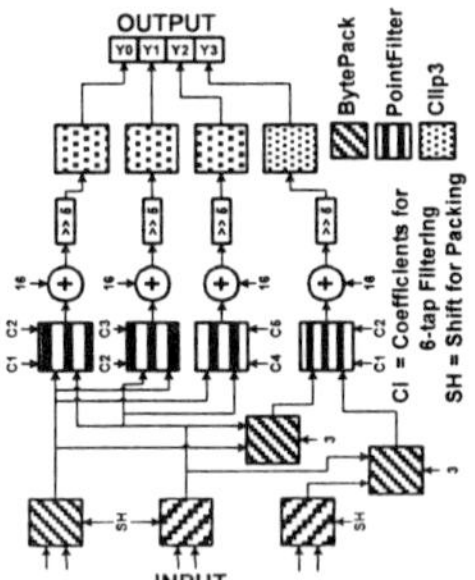

Figure 6: Block diagram for Motion Compensation, composed by different *Atoms*

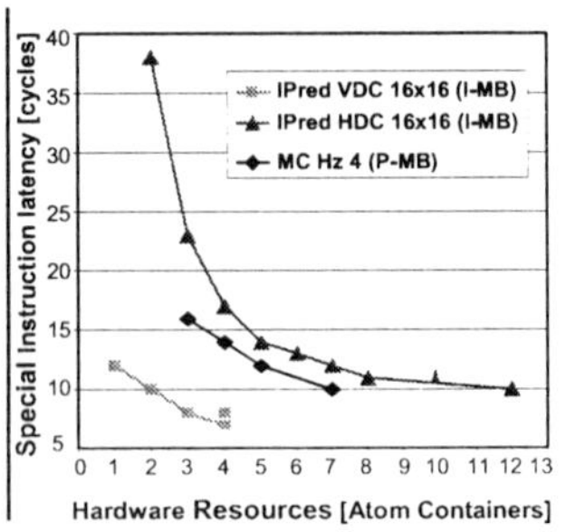

Figure 7: Performance vs. area trade-offs for different *Molecules* for SI implementation

In section 2 we have introduced and analyzed the scenario of encoding I- and P-MBs. To evaluate this scenario we have designed and implemented 3 Special Instructions (SIs) to execute the I- and P-MB computation paths in dynamic hardware. The SI for the Motion Compensation (MC) for P-MBs in Figure 6 consists of three different *Atom* types. The *BytePack* is a data alignment, the *PointFilter* is an FIR operation and the *Clip Atom* limits the output to a certain min/max value. The MC SI may be implemented by different *Molecules* having different levels of parallelism, reaching from temporal to spatial computation. The trade-offs between these extremes are shown in Figure 7 for all three SIs with the Pareto-optimal solutions that are determined at compile time (at the composition of the *Molecules*).

We have evaluated our architecture with a video sequence with the analyzed I- and P-MB ratios in Figure 1 and the three implemented SIs for encoding the MBs. We have simulated the total execution time for the SIs in this scene for varying numbers of *Atom Containers* (ACs) and compared the results of our self-adapting system with the behavior of a reference system with static reconfiguration decisions. Our forecasts are updated after a whole frame.

With only 3 ACs, our architecture already gains a performance improvement of 12.6% (compared to the static reconfiguration decisions) and in average we observed a 5.6% performance improvement. It is noteworthy that the benchmarks for the static reconfiguration decision had to be modified every time we improved the number of ACs to explicit force the static system to use the newly available hardware resources (otherwise the static system would not have used the additional ACs at all). Our self-configuring system instead automatically utilized the available ACs. Additionally the static system was highly optimized for the used video sequence. For a video sequence with a different I- to P-MB ratio, it would have been worse. Our self-optimizing system instead was always simulated with the same binary and automatically decided which *Molecules* to choose in which situation. Comparing our dynamic system with the corresponding traditional embedded processor without hardware accelerators we achieve a speedup from 10.5x (5 ACs) up to 17.5x (10 ACs).

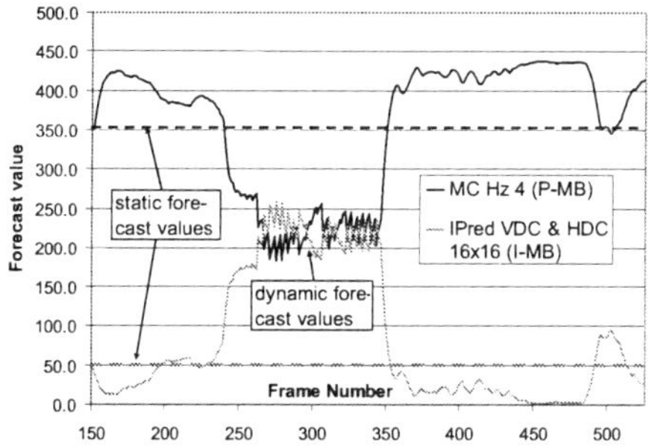

Figure 8: Dynamically updating Forecast values

To demonstrate how the updating scheme for the forecasts from section 4.3 is performing (as this is the basis for our later dynamic rotation decision), we have evaluated the dynamically updated forecast values for I- and P-MBs, as shown in Figure 8. Comparing these forecasts with the actual executed I-to-P MB ratio from Figure 1 (which is a priori unknown to the system) we see that the forecasts match the actual distribution of I- and P-MBs for the simulated frames. The major difference is that the forecasts are smoothened compared to the original ratio, which is due to the fact that we are not back propagating the full error (parameter α in section 4.3). The static system does not update the forecasts but keeps them fixed as indicated in Figure 8.

We have analyzed the run-time behavior of our self-adaptive system, i.e. which *Molecule* is chosen at which time. In Figure 9 the latencies for the chosen *Molecules* for 7 available ACs are plotted. For instance, in the *hectic scene* IPred HDC is in two steps upgraded from the *Molecule* with 2 *Atoms* to the *Molecule* with 4 *Atoms* at the cost of downgrading MC to the *Molecule* with 3 *Atoms*. After the *hectic scene* ends the system is rotating back to its original configuration that then fits best the situation. A noteworthy situation can be seen in the *smooth scene* in Figure 9, where the benefit for executing MC by rotating from the 5 *Atom Molecule* to the 7 *Atom Molecule* overcomes the penalty for executing the I-MBs with base instructions.

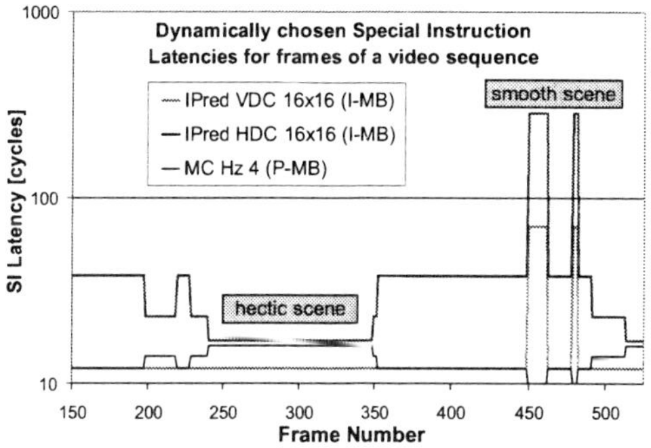

Figure 9: SI latencies at different frames

6. Conclusion

We have presented a self-adapting extensible embedded processor. It goes beyond the capabilities of state-of-the-art embedded processor approaches that fail when an application's behavior cannot be predicted at design-time. As a result of self-adaptation, our approach is more efficient. We have evaluated its functionality using an ITU-T H.264 Video Encoder and an FPGA platform. Our future work will aim at minimizing the additional overhead in order to further increase its efficiency.

7. References

[1] Arctangent processor: www.arc.com/configurablecores/
[2] CoWare Inc, LISATek: www.coware.com
[3] Stretch processor: www.stretchinc.com
[4] Xtensa processor, Tensilica Inc: www.tensilica.com
[5] ITU-T Rec. H.264 and ISO/IEC 14496-10 (E) "Advanced video coding for generic audiovisual services", 2005
[6] A Hoffmann et al. "A novel methodology for the design of application-specific instruction-set processors (ASIPs) using a machine description language", IEEE Trans. on CAD of Integr. Circuits and Systems 2001
[7] J Henkel "Closing the SoC Design Gap"; IEEE Computer Volume 36; Issue 9; September 2003
[8] N Cheung, J Henkel, S Parameswaran „Rapid Configuration & Instruction Selection for an ASIP: A Case Study", DATE 2003
[9] K Atasu, L Pozzi, P Ienne "Automatic Application-Specific Instruction-Set Extensions Under Microarchitectural Constraints", DAC 2003
[10] F Sun, A Raghunathan, S Ravi, NK Jha "A scalable application specific processor synthesis methodology", ICCAD 2003
[11] K Compton, S Hauck "Reconfigurable computing: a survey of systems and software", ACM Computing Surv. 02
[12] S Vassiliadis, et al. "The MOLEN polymorphic processor", IEEE Transaction on Computers, Issue 11, 2004
[13] F Barat, R Lauwereins „Reconfigurable Instruction Set Processors: A Survey", RSP 2000
[14] JE Carrillo, P Chow "The Effect of Reconfigurable Units in Superscalar Processors", FPGA 2001
[15] L Bauer, M Shafique, S Kramer, J Henkel "RISPP: Rotating Instruction Set Processing Platform", DAC'07
[16] RS Sutton, "Learning to Predict by the Methods of Temporal Differences" Machine Learning 3, Springer
[17] RS Sutton, AG Barto, "Reinforcement Learning: An Introduction." MIT Press, Cambr., MA, 98
[18] T Sherwood, S Sair, B Calder, "Phase Tracking and Prediction" Int'l Symp. on Computer Architecture, 2003

Work-in-Progress Track, Session 3: Self-Organization

Scalable and Efficient Sensor Network Self-Configuration in BioANS

Michael Breza, Department of Computing, Imperial College, London email: mjb04@doc.ic.ac.uk
Richard Anthony, Department of Computer Science, University of Greenwich, London
email: R.J.Anthony@gre.ac.uk

Julie McCann, Department of Computing, Imperial College, London email: jamm@doc.ic.ac.uk

Abstract

BioANS is a protocol for wireless sensor networks (WSN) whose design is inspired by organisation mechanisms observed in nature. It enables an information requester to access data from a sensor network which meets a qualitative criterion based on context in an efficient manner.

A model of BioANS is used to simulate the performance of the protocol in a variety of possible WSN deployments.

1. Introduction

Wireless Sensor Networks (WSN) is a growing area of research increasing the ability to remotely monitor an environment and collecting information that can be used as context for applications. For example a well-cited experiment in the use of WSN to obtain data from an inaccessible environment is GlacsWeb[11]. This project monitors the movement and temperature of glaciers to measure the effects of global climate change.

Constrained resources pose the greatest challenge to the use of WSN. Power availability is severely constrained due to the capacity of current battery technology. Sending and receiving wireless communication is the greatest consumer of power in WSN, and so must be limited as much as possible. The applications also impose other constraints such as: robustness, scalable deployment platforms; stability despite configuration change; and low communication latency because the applications can have a real-time aspect.

Data is requested by an application which meets a qualitative criterion. This criterion is referred to as Quality of Context (QoC)[5] and describes context information about the data requested. This can be temperature given to a certain degree of precision, data delivered at a certain rate, or a sensor sensing a certain spatial area. This means that a sensor capable of delivering this information within the constraints needs to be found as part of the protocol.

BioANS (Bio-inspired Autonomic Networked Services) is a WSN protocol which is efficient in terms of communication overhead. The design allows the dynamic selection of sensor nodes based on their ability to deliver data at a given QoC. It is also robust to sensor failure and message loss, scales well to large sensor networks, and exhibits low request latency.

As BioANS is bio-inspired and exhibits engineered emergence we describe what we mean by this in section three. BioANS's predecessor ANS and its use of quality of context (QoC) is described in section four. Section five describes the experiments carried out and their results. Related work is discussed in section six and then we conclude.

2. Sensor Network Concepts

WSN are made up of a number of sensor nodes, with one or more sensors, a low power processor, a low powered wireless transceiver, and a battery. The sensor nodes can be homogeneous or heterogeneous. There is also one or more information requester nodes who request data from the sensors.

The sensor nodes form a communication network among themselves, and more importantly with the information requester node(s). Communication (sending, receiving and listening) uses the most energy of any sensor node task. As battery power is a finite resource, communication needs to be as efficient as possible. A way to reduce power consumption is to keep the number and size of messages small.

0-7695-2906-2/07 $25.00 © 2007 IEEE

3. Engineered Emergence in WSNs

Emergence is employed in BioANS to achieve simultaneously scalable and robust negotiation in sensor network applications. Emergence describes higher-level states, patterns or other behaviours that arise in systems of numerous lower-level components that have local autonomy to interact with their neighbours. The higher-level behaviour cannot be predicted by examining the individual components or their behaviour in isolation. The science of emergence is described in [9] [6] [8].

The term 'engineered emergence' describes the purposeful design of interaction protocols so that a predictable, desired outcome is achieved at a higher level (i.e. emerges), although at lower levels the specific behaviour of individual components at any moment cannot be predicted. See for example [2]. The negotiation protocol needs to be stable and predictable in terms of its higher-level behaviour (i.e. a suitable context provider needs to be located within a reasonable time-frame), although the low-level behaviour (such as the actual interactions with and between sensor nodes, and the ordering of events such as message transmission) has elements of randomness and can thus not be precisely predicted.

Engineered emergence is a general approach to building systems that benefit from these characteristics (scale robustness and stability), but that do not require precise knowledge of lower-level activity. Sensor networks, which contain numerous sensors each having slightly different QoC characteristics (different locations, different accuracy, different levels of battery life remaining etc.), but fundamentally serving as redundant spares for one another, are a highly suitable domain in which applications can take advantage of engineered emergence.

Traditional design of distributed applications focuses on strict protocols, message acknowledgements and event ordering which imposes sequenced or synchronised behaviour which is generally deterministic. Each message and event is considered important and randomness is generally undesirable. Such a design paradigm can lead to inefficiency, for example through large numbers of transmitted messages and additional communication latency, especially when some of these messages do not directly contribute to correct application behaviour at higher levels [3].

Natural biological systems are fundamentally non-deterministic. Many examples exist of large-scale systems that are stable and robust at a global level; the most commonly cited examples are drawn from cellular systems and insect colonies [7]. BioANS requires that a small number of appropriate quality bids are elicited from sensor nodes (service providers) in potentially very large systems. In this application domain it is important to minimise the total amount of communication, the latency of service negotiation, and also to preserve the battery power at each sensor node.

4. ANS and its emergent features

Autonomic Networked Systems (ANS) is a wireless sensor network protocol that is the predecessor to BioANS [13]. The term autonomicity refers to the ability to self manage certain system attributes like configuration, healing, optimisation, and protection [10]. Autonomicity is achieved by ANS through the ability to dynamically choose the best sensor for each request.

The notion of Quality of Context (QoC) [4] is used by ANS to choose a sensor when a request is made by an information requester node. A process called 'tendering' is used to select the sensor node. The information requester node will broadcast a 'request' command containing the name of a sensing service (like PH or water flow rate) and preferences for the QoC attributes (like degree of precision). Every sensor node within range and able to fulfil the service must respond. The sensor nodes use a utility function to calculate its ability to deliver data at the requested QoC. The result from the utility function is a signed integer called 'closeness', and is used as the sensor nodes response to the information request. The sensor node with the QoC closest to that requested wins the tender, and becomes the sensor supplying its data to the information requester. Frequent 'retendering' allows the requester nodes to autonomously adapt to the best sensor available, discover new devices in the network, and recover from sensor node failure.

ANS uses broadcast communication, this is good with respect to the simplicity and efficiency of the protocol. As the system size increases however, the chances of creating congestion in the communication medium increases.

BioANS solves this problem by adding to ANS certain techniques found in biological systems. This includes the use of randomisation, and the use of low-value messages. The delayed-bid mechanism [3] is included, adding a random timing component to spread out the responses of the sensor nodes to an information request. As soon as a response with sufficient QoC is received, a stop-bids message is sent, stopping all of the sensor nodes still waiting to respond.

Low-value messages means that the protocol will still function well in the event of message loss.If a requester node receives no replies after a given time-out, the request message is considered lost, and simply retransmitted. Failure of a sensor node to receive an information request message means only that that sensor will not take part in the bidding. Loss of the stop-bids message means only that the medium may suffer congestion until all of the sensors have stopped transmitting replies. The approach to messages means that BioANS is resilient to failures and scales extremely well.

5. Simulation of BioANS

BioANS was modelled as a discrete event simulation. The input was modelled using observed performance from ANS implemented on Beastie sensor nodes [12]. The trade-off between protocol overhead and the percentage of time an information requester received its requested QoC is investigated.

The first experiment shows a comparison of the communication overhead of the original ANS protocol to that of BioANS. The next set of experiments focus on the percentage of time the QoC was received as the density of the sensors in the area being sensed decreased. Next, we fix the network density, and examine the change in QoC received as the size of the sensor population increases. The final two experiments look at how BioANS handles failures. The first compares QoC received to various sensor node failure/resumption rates, and the second watches the same as the sensors fail and are not replaced. Figure 1 shows that the ratio

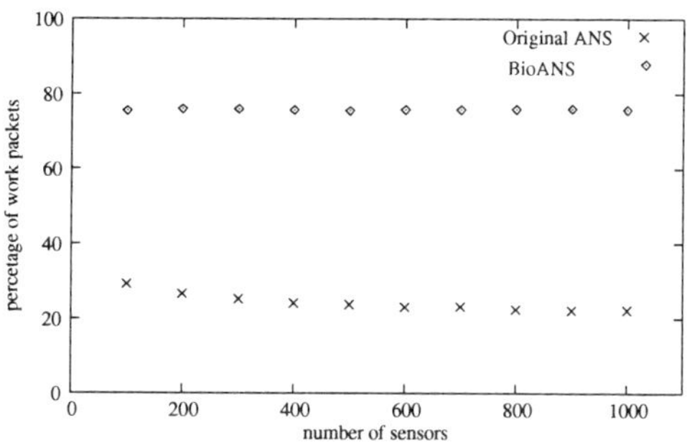

Figure 1. Communication overhead of the original ANS protocol and BioANS. Overhead is expressed in terms of the ratio of work related packets to total packets sent and received.

of work (non-protocol related packets) to overall packets sent and received was much higher with BioANS than with its predecessor ANS. This result shows how the introduction of emergent mechanisms, such as the delayed bid, improve upon the efficiency of the original ANS. The ratio measured is an inverse of protocol overhead where the focus is on protocol related packets. The average QoC received by 50 requesters in a network of 500 sensors is shown in Figure 2. The bottom axis is the density factor of the monitored region occupied by

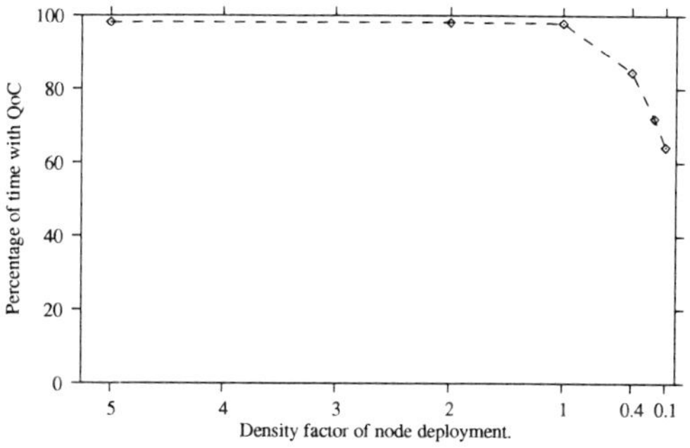

Figure 2. Relationship between average percentage of time requesters got QoC and density factor.

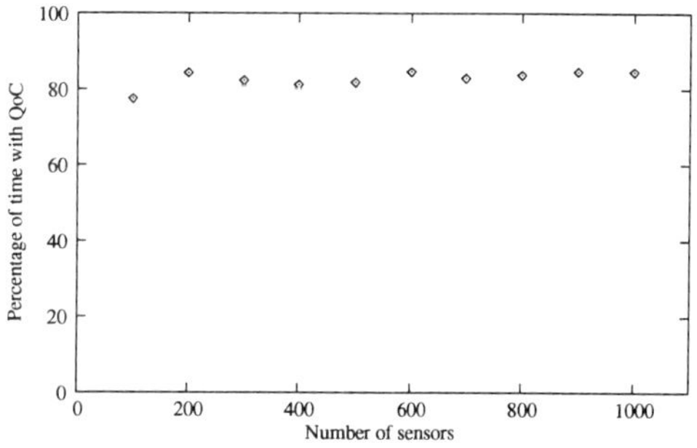

Figure 3. Average percentage of time requesters got QoC as network size increases with fixed density.

the nodes (sensors and requesters). We describe density factor as the average sensor node population per 100 grid cells used to represent area in the simulation. Sensor node communication range is limited to a radius of 20 grid cells (i.e. coverage is 400π grid cells). The density decreases as area in the monitored region occupied by the node decreases. The average QoC obtained by the requester is almost 100% until the density factor falls below 1. From that point the average QoC drops. At a density factor of 0.4 the requesters are only getting their QoC an average of 85% of the time. By density factor 0.2 that figure has dropped to 72%, and 64% by density factor 0.1. A further look at the raw data not graphically presented here shows that with a density factor of 1 a requester can hear an average of 8 sensors. A density factor of 0.4 reduced that to an average of 2 sensors. These figures are below the expected mathematical average because of sensor failure in the network.

The simulation results demonstrate that BioANS scales for networks of at least 1000 sensor nodes with 100 information requester nodes. Figure 3 further confirms scalability in that the average QoC received is insensitive to network size. The average time that information requesters had no sensor fluctuated a bit, but remained below 1% of the simulation run time.

Experiments were run where the failure and resumption rate of the sensors was varied to test the robustness of BioANS in the face of a dynamic network.

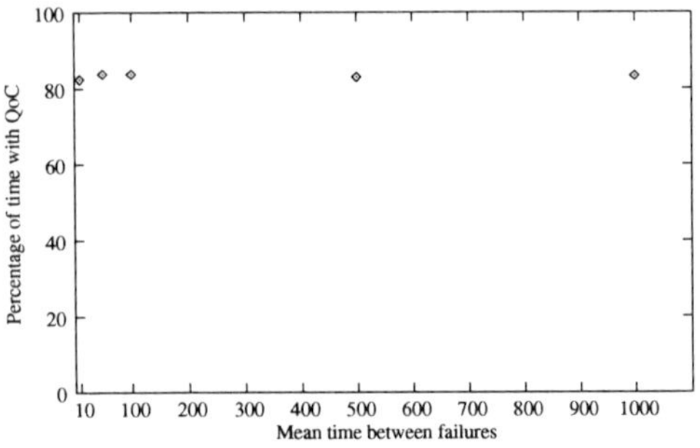

Figure 4. Average percentage of time requesters had QoC in relation to mean time between failures.

In figure 4 we see the average received QoC remaining consistent as the failure rate increases. Even when failures occur with a high frequencies of every 100, 50, and 10 time units, the received QoC is above 80%.

6. Related Work

Rajkumar et al. [14] present a resource allocation model for QoS management within a single system.

The Context Toolkit [15] is a framework aimed at facilitating the development and deployment of context-aware applications. Similar to the work presented here, it abstracts context services, e.g. a location service, from the sensors that acquire the necessary data to deliver the service.

The inspiration for BioANS is stylistically bio-inspired. In [1] an emergent leader election algorithm is given whose communication style is based on the mechanics of pheromone based communication.

7. Conclusion

BioANS uses emergence engineering concepts to satisfy the requirements of scale, robustness, low latency negotiation and efficient resource usage in large-scale applications deployed on Wireless Sensor Networks.

The experiments showed that the bio-inspired optimisations of BioANS where successful and provided a stable, highly scalable and robust protocol that has general applicability to a wide range of applications in sensor networks and similar resource constrained domains.

References

[1] R. Anthony. An autonomic election algorithm based on emergence in natural systems. *Integrated computer-aided engineering*, 13(1):3 -22, 2006.

[2] R. Anthony. Emergent graph colouring. *Engineering Emergence for Autonomic Systems (EEAS), First Annual International Workshop, at the third International Conference on Autonomic Computing (ICAC), Dublin, Ireland*, pages 4–13, June 2006.

[3] R. Anthony. Engineering emergence for cluster configuration. *Journal of Systemics, Cybernetics and Informatics*, 4(3), 2006.

[4] T. Buchholz, A. Kupper, and M. Schiffers. Quality of contex: What it is and why we need it. *10th Workshop of the HP OpenView University Association (HPOVUA03).*

[5] T. Buchholz, A. Kupper, and M. Schiffers. Quality of Context: What It Is And Why We Need It. *10th Workshop of the HP OpenView University Association (HPOVUA03).*

[6] J. Casti. *Complexification: Explaining a Paradoxical World Through the Science of Surprise.* Abacus, London, 1994.

[7] M. Gell-Mann. *The Quark and the Jaguar: Adventures in the Simple and the Complex.* Abacus, London, 1994.

[8] R. Genet. *The Chimpanzees who would be Ants: A Unified Scientific Story of Humanity.* Nova Science Publishers Inc, New York, 1997.

[9] S. Johnson. *Emergence: The connected lives of Ants, Brains, Cities and Software.* Penguin Press, London, 2001.

[10] J. Kephart and D. Chess. The vision of autonomic computing. *Computer -IEEE Computer Society*, 36(1):41–51, 2003.

[11] K. Martinez, P. Padhy, A. Elasify, G. Zhou, A. Riddoch, J. K. Hart, and H. L. R. Ong. Deploying a sensor network in an extream environment. In *Proceedings of Sensor Networks, Ubiquitous and Trustworthy Computing*, pages 186–193, 2006.

[12] J. McCann and A. Hoskins. Proof of concept adaptivity and performance benchmark results. Technical report, Imperial College London, May 2006.

[13] J. McCann, M. Huebscher, and A. Hoskins. Context as autonomic intelligence in a ubiquitous computing environment. *International Journal of Internet Protocol Technology (IJIPT) special edition on Autonomic Computing*, 2006.

[14] R. Rajkumar, J. L. C. Lee, and D. Siewiorek. A resource allocation model for qos management. In *Proceedings of the 18th IEEE Real-Time Systems Symposium (RTSS '97)*, page 298. IEEE Computer Society, 1997. ISBN 0-8186-8268-X.

[15] D. Salber, A. K. Dey, and G. D. Abowd. The context toolkit: aiding the development of context-enabled applications. In *Proceedings of the SIGCHI conference on Human factors in computing systems*, pages 434–441. ACM Press, 1999. ISBN 0-201-48559-1.

Towards Self-organizing Virtual Macro Sensors

Nicola Bicocchi, Marco Mamei, Franco Zambonelli

DISMI – Università di Modena e Reggio Emilia – Via Amendola 2 – Reggio Emilia – ITALY
{nicola.bicocchi, marco.mamei, franco.zambonelli}@unimore.it

Abstract

The future mass deployment of pervasive and dense sensor network infrastructures calls for proper mechanisms to enable extracting general-purpose data from them at limited costs and in a compact way. The approach presented in this paper relies on a simple algorithm to let a sensor network self-organize a virtual partitioning in correspondence of spatial regions characterized by similar sensed patterns, and to let distributed aggregation of sensorial data take place on a per-region basis. This makes it possible to perceive the network as if it were composed of a limited number of virtual macro sensors, a feature which promises to be very suitable for a number of incoming usage scenarios.

1. Introduction

In the next few years, we will assist to an increasing deployment of sensor network systems. Rather than being closed special-purpose systems devoted to monitor specific phenomena, as they are today, they will form the basis of truly pervasive and dense shared infrastructures, publicly available for general-purpose sensing activities.

This novel perspective of usage introduces peculiar challenging requirements [1, 3, 4, 6, 7]. First, it is expected that the sensor network, despite being intensively used in unpredictable ways, will be able to control its energy consumption. Second, it is expected that the network will be able to provide users with expressive and compact information related to the phenomena under sensing rather than raw individual sensor data. In the presence of dense sensor networks generating huge amounts of data, dealing with the transfer and the ex-post analysis of individual sensors data can be become simply unmanageable. Third, the network should quickly answer users' requests. Since users can be highly mobile a late answer to a query can either fail to reach the user or reach him at a location where the answered information could be useless.

To tackle the dynamism and scale of such a new scenario, the idea underlying our proposal is that of delegating to the sensor network the execution of distributed self-organizing algorithms that – by continuously running in the network with bounded energy costs – can enforce:

- self-partitioning of the network into spatial regions characterized by similar patterns for sensed data, via the self-organization of an overlay network.
- distributed aggregation of sensorial data on a per-region basis [5].

The result of this process is that a sensor network can be perceived by users as made up virtual of macro sensors, each associated to a well-characterized region of the physical environment (i.e., a region exhibiting a uniform pattern for some specific property such as a light, temperature, etc.). Within each region, each physical sensor has the local availability of aggregated data and can act as an access point to such data.

The approach based on virtual macro sensors makes it possible for multiple and mobile users to promptly access global information about the surrounding environment by simply querying the closest sensor. Also, it makes possible to effectively transfer aggregated data towards a centralized collection point in a more compact and efficient way, yet avoiding loss of information typical of global aggregation algorithms. Moreover this process is independent of the actual density, topology, and dynamics, of the underlying physical sensor network.

2. Virtual Macro Sensors

The virtual macro sensors approach considers: *(i)* a self-organized region formation algorithm to define the boundaries of each macro sensor; *(ii)* localized aggregation algorithms to provide macro sensors with regional sensorial capabilities; *(iii)* solutions to self-adapt to transitory and dynamic situations.

2.1. Region Formation

We consider a sensor network deployed in an environment in which the value v of some specific environmental property can be locally sensed. The value v could represent a temperature, a light level, or whatever property a sensor is able to measure about its portion of the environment (see Figures 2-a).

0-7695-2906-2/07 $25.00 © 2007 IEEE

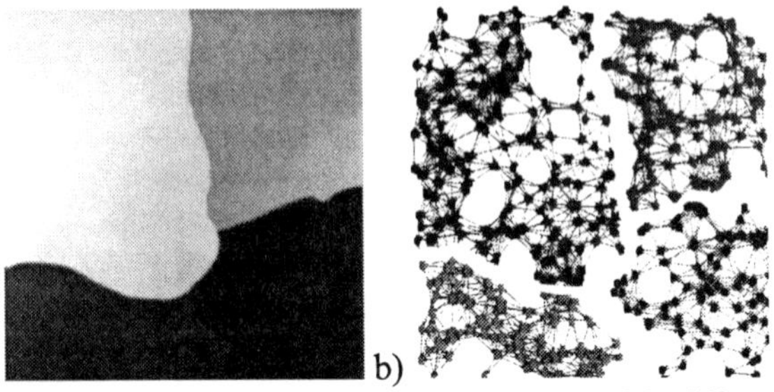
a) b)

Figure 2. a) a scalar field with 4 regions with different values of a property v; b) overlay region organization leading to a partitioning into 4 small regions.

The proposed region formation algorithm has the goal of letting sensors self-organize into disjoint sets of spatial regions each characterized by "similar" measures of the property v (see Figures 2-b). Organization in regions occurs via a process of building an overlay of weighted links between neighbor nodes, such that nodes belonging to the same region have strong links, while neighbor nodes belonging to different regions have weak links. In general, the region organization can reflect some actual property of the physical space and can lead to a "logical" organization of sensors.

More in detail, let s_i and s_j be two neighbor sensors, i.e., two sensors whose distance is smaller than their wireless radio range r. Let $v(s_i)$ and $v(s_j)$ be the values of a property sensed by s_i and s_j, respectively. Let us assume that a distance function D can be defined for couples of v values. Region formation is then based on iteratively computing the value of a logical link $l(s_i,s_j)$ for each and every node of the system (see Fig. 3).

```
Update_link:
    if ( D(v(si), v(sj)) < T )
        l(si,sj) = min(l(si,sj) + delta, 1)
    else
        l(si,sj) = max(l(si,sj) - delta, 0)
```

Figure 3. Pseudo code for the Update_link procedure.

Where: T is a threshold determining whether the measured values are close enough for $l(s_i,s_j)$ to be re-enforced or, otherwise, weakened; and *delta* is a value affecting the reactivity of the algorithm in updating link.

Based on the above algorithm, it is rather clear that if $D(v(s_i), v(s_j))$ is lower than the threshold T, $l(s_i,s_j)$ will rapidly converge to *1*. Otherwise it will converge to *0*. In the simplest case, one could consider two nodes s_i and s_j to be in the same region when $l(s_i,s_j)$ is over a threshold T. Transitively, two nodes s_h and s_k are defined in the same region if and only if there is a chain of nodes such that each pair of neighbors in the chain are in the same region. For the actual execution of the algorithm, each node stores a vector describing, for each of the neighbors, the current value of the link towards it and a flag signaling the status of the link (connected or not).

The distributed execution of the algorithm is based on a sort of diffusive gossip scheme which act as a sort of continuous background activity in the sensor network: each node periodically wakes up, randomly selects a specific number or a specific percentage of its neighbors (in the case of broadcast-based wireless channels, this implies inviting a limited number of neighbors in participating in the protocol), exchanges with them the needed data, and then executes the "*Update_link*" procedure for each selected neighbors (see Fig. 4).

```
Do_forerever:
    Wait(t);
    Foreach(neigh[]=Select_neighbor(num_neigh))
        Data = Exchange_data();
        Update_link(data);
        // aggregation part
        Global_aggregation(); // if needed
        If(connected) Local_aggregation();
Done
```

Figure 4. Main algorithm. The aggregation part will be described in Sect. 2.2.

From the above description it is clear that our algorithm tends to impose a uniform load to the system. Each node executes the same amount of operations. The interval t determines the frequency of such operations and the number of neighbors *num_neigh* selected at each round determines the communication cost of these operations. Shorter t or higher *num_neigh* tend to speed up the convergence of the algorithm, but increase the energy consumed by sensor per time unit (as quantified in the performance evaluation section). Therefore, one can select the appropriate values for such parameters on the basis of the application requirements.

Concerning T, an apparently challenging issue in our approach consists in tackling the difference between the strictly local nature of "*Update_link*" interactions and the inherently global meaning of the threshold T. How can two nodes evaluate the right threshold if they don't know anything about the rest of the network? Fortunately, in the vast majority of the cases, a domain expert can provide suitable and relevant thresholds to highlight the phenomena of interest and to drive the self-partitioning accordingly. For example, a difference of 5°C can be considered of relevance for a biologist to distinguish different types of landscape, and (s)he could rely on a region-partitioning based on such a threshold. Alternatively, fire guards may be interested in much higher thresholds (e.g., 40°C) to detect anomalies. In any case, it is worth emphasizing that our approach does not prescribe the existence of a single region partitioning: multiple partitions (i.e., overlays) could be computed across the network by considering different thresholds.

In the absence of any a priori known domain data, it is still possible to define *T* by exploiting dynamically collected global values of the property *v*. For instance, in some experiments, we defined *T* as a portion of the whole range of values seen over the network. Using scalar values, we defined *T* as:

$$T = (globalMax - globalMin) * p$$

where *p* is a real number between *0* an *1*. In this way, one can parameterize the sensibility of the algorithm by using a relative value *p* rather than some absolute value requiring a priori knowledge on the range of *v* values.

To locally acquire the *globalMax* and *globalMin* value at each node, one can execute a global diffusive aggregation algorithm over the whole network. The above aggregation algorithms requires minimal additional effort by nodes. In fact, one can piggyback such *globalMin* and *globalMax* data into the messages already exchanged by nodes.

2.2. Per-Region Aggregation

The local availability of aggregated information over the whole sensor network may be of some use independently of regions. However, globally aggregated values give very little details on the status of the network, are prone to obsolescence and high losses, and are definitely of little use for users wishing to acquire information about nearby environmental properties. For this reason, our approach mostly relies on per-region aggregation algorithms. Local aggregation algorithms enable each sensor in a region to act as an access point for aggregated data in that region, and thus realize the concept of virtual macro sensor: from the application viewpoint, one can perceive a region as including a single sensor with sensorial capabilities extended to the whole region.

When regions are already formed (transitory situations will be discussed later on), computing aggregation function in a region reduces to executing a diffusive aggregation algorithm only between those couples of neighbor nodes that are in the same region (i.e., for which the *l* is over the *T* threshold). Again, computing per-region aggregation function does not introduce significant additional burden to the network. The exchange of data between nodes can occur by piggybacking over existing messages, and the computation of local aggregation algorithms reduces to add a simple "*Local_aggregation*" function in the main body of our basic scheme (see Fig. 4).

The "*Local_aggregation*" function can include the identification of the local minimum and the local maximum of any sensed value *w* (other than the *v* property on which regions are based) within the region (computed as in the global case), as well as the calculus of the average *Avg* of any value *w*.

In our scheme, we also decided to enforce two additional peculiar aggregation functions that are of great use for facilitating the gathering of information by users.

A first aggregation function considers that each node at the border of a region (i.e., each node which has at least one virtual link *l* below the threshold) propagates within the region a "hop counter" initialized at *0*. By having such counter re-propagated by each node on per-minimum basis, the results is that each node in a region eventually becomes aware of its distance form the closest border. We also plan to experience more sophisticated aggregation function to enable nodes to locally reach a higher-level understanding of the shape and topology of the local region, possibly relying on existing work of distributed topology recognition. What is important is that these kinds of topological measures are important to asses, within regions, the sensing coverage of the macro sensors.

A second aggregation function exploits a sort of per-region minimum identification towards the election of a region leader. By having each sensors exchange its unique *ID* with its neighbor, the minimum *ID* eventually recognized by each node will define the leader (and the leader itself will recognize itself as that). This is very important to give a recognizable unique identity to each macro sensor.

2.3. Transitory and Dynamic Situations

In this section we analyze the dynamic behavior of the algorithms during region formation and region re-shaping (changes in the values of the property *v* upon which region formation relies can induce changes in the shape and dimensions of regions, as well as in the aggregated values).

In general, the initial values of the virtual links *l* between nodes are irrelevant for region formation. Therefore, let us assume an initial situation in which all nodes are disconnected from each other (i.e., each node is a region in itself). As the algorithm will start running, nodes with similar values of *v* will start connecting with each other, and sets of regions with growing dimensions will start forming and possibly merge with each other, until a stable situation will be reached.

Concurrently with the above region formation

process, the local aggregation procedure starts executing as soon as two nodes gets virtually connected in the same region, and it proceeds gradually involving more and more sensors, eventually converging when a stable region situation is reached. It can be shown that the proposed aggregation algorithms do not experience problems if executed on a growing number of nodes, as in the region formation transitory. This also applies for the identification of the region leader (when two regions merge, one of the two leaders will be eventually overtaken by the other one). Similar considerations apply to the case in which new sensors are dynamically added in the system.

The case in which some existing regions shrink, (either because a confining region has expanded or because some sensor nodes have died) is a bit more complex to handle. In fact, two problems may arise: *(i)* the values computed by the local aggregation functions may no longer be valid (e.g., the former maximum may have left the region and/or the average may have changed) and the cumulative nature of aggregation does not enable them to be properly updated; *(ii)* the region leader may have exited the region. To tackle the above two problems we are studying and evaluating both epoch-based [5] and evaporative approaches [2] to identify the best option.

3. Conclusions and Future Works

The proposed virtual macro sensor approach makes a sensor network self-organize into regions characterized by similar sensing patterns, so as to promote aggregation of data on a per-region basis, as if each region were monitored by a single macro sensor.

The most direct way of exploiting the virtual macro sensor approach is for supporting queries by multiple and mobile users. A user that wants to retrieve information about the surrounding will typically access the nearest sensor and query it about some local patterns of sensed data. For example, "give me the maximum temperature within 500 meters" or, by referring to some more logical environmental concept, "give me the average temperature in this room". At this point, in most of the cases, the queried sensor can immediately answer to the user without further burdening the network, independently of the number of mobile users.

To test the effectiveness of the approach, we have experimented it both in a simulation environment and in a small sensor network test bed. Simulations have been built over the Repast simulation framework [http://repast.sourceforge.net/]. We have conducted several experiments with sensor networks of different sizes and densities, immersed in different types of scalar fields, always obtaining similar qualitative and quantitative results. The proposed approach seems to be effective and scalable and could represent a concrete alternative to tree-based approaches. The experiments have been verified also in a real testbed of 16 Micaz Crossbow motes distributed across two confining rooms in our department. Despite the encouraging results obtained so far, we are aware of a number of limitations of our work, subjects of our current research work. These include: generalizing the approach to support multiple overlays and general-purpose queries; exploring inter-region algorithms to support more global queries; defining algorithms to promote the building of high-level knowledge about the global structure and properties of the of virtual macro sensors network; creating a framework and an API to allow users to easily access macro sensors in a convenient way.

Acknowledgments. Work supported by the project CASCADAS (IST-027807) funded by the FET Program of the European Commission.

References

[1] M. Baumgarten et al., "Self-organizing Knowledge Networks for Smart World Infrastructures", International Conference on Self-organization in Multiagent and Grid Systems, Erfurt (D), 2006.

[2] N. Biccocchi, M. Mamei, F.Zambonelli., "Self-organizing Virtual Macro Sensors", Techical Report DISMI-UNIMORE, Feb 2007.

[3] G. Castelli, A. Rosi, M. Mamei, F. Zambonelli, "A Simple Model and Infrastructure for Context-aware Browsing of the World", International Conference on Pervasive Computing and Communication, New York (NY), 2007.

[4] C. Curino, M. Giani, M. Giorgetta, A. Giusti, A. Murphy, G. Picco, "Mobile Data Collection in Sensor Networks: The TinyLime Middleware", Journal of Pervasive and Mobile Computing, (4)1:446-469, 2005.

[5] M. Jelasity, A. Montresor, O. Babaoglu, "Gossip-based Aggregation in Large Dynamic Networks", ACM Transactions on Computer Systems, 23(3):219-252, 2005.

[6] C. Lu, G. Xing, O. Chipara, C. Fok, S. Bhattacharya, "A Spatiotemporal Query Service for Mobile Users in Sensor Networks", International Conference on Distributed Computing Systems, Columbus (OH), 2005.

[7] R. Müller, G. Alonso, "Shared Queries in Sensor Networks for Multi-User Support", Technical Report 508, ETH Zürich (CH), 2005.

Biologically inspired Self-Organized Blob Structures on Amorphous Computers

Moïse Valvassori
Laboratoire d'Intelligence Artificielle de Saint-Denis (LIASD)
Université Paris 8, 2 rue de la liberté 93526 St Denis Cedex
djcdi@ai.univ-paris8.fr

Abstract

In this paper, we present a biologically inspired self-organized implementation of the Blob structures on amorphous computers. Amorphous computers rely on asynchronous and spatially distributed processor sets where each processor broadcasts to communicate only with its local neighborhood. Blob machines are abstract parallel machines designed to exploit space. Our work-in-progress implementation relies on recruitment gradients *to ensure the Blob consistency.*

1. Introduction

In this paper, we present a self-organized implementation of the Blob structural primitives on an amorphous computer. Amorphous computers [1] are large processor sets. Each processor, called *cell*, is identical, randomly located, runs the same program and communicates with its local neighborhood via broadcast messages. As cells may have limited resources, the challenge is to build programs and structures sharing the cell resources.

Coore and Nagpal have already built respectively two languages operating on amorphous computers: GPL [4] and OSL [8]. Both languages "draw" spatial structures on the amorphous medium.

Gruau et al. [7] propose a spatially distributed abstract machine named *Blob*. A Blob is a set of processing units located on a computing medium. Blobs can *move* on the medium. Blob can be *linked* to others Blobs. A Blob can be *divided* into two independent Blobs. Gruau et al. [6] also propose cellular automata implementation for their abstract machine.

Some amorphous structures have already been defined [2]. Blob machine on an amoprhous computer defines a new class of structures for amorphous programs. In a previous work, we proposed a reaction/diffusion based implementation of the Blobs primitives [11].

In this paper, we present an work-in-progress implementation based on *recruitment gradients. Recruitment gradients* are a mechanism widely by used biological systems to located resources [3].

Section 2 details the platform used to develop our algorithms. In section 3, we present two amorphous primitives, *moving* and *recruitment gradient*, used to build Blob primitives. Section 4 presents four algorithms to build Blobs. In section 5, we discuss the potential applications of the Blob primitives.

2. Amorphous Computer Platform

We simulate amorphous computers made of several thousands cells distributed uniformly on a square surface [10]. Each cell contains: a program p, n private states, n' public states called messages,a blackboard of size $v \times n'$ containing the neighborhood messages with v representing the maximum neighborhood size. This blackboard is automatically updated on message receptions. Program p is a component collection containing several aspects: message reception handling, reaction to certain cell states and general programs. Program p can read and modify the states without restriction. Messages are automatically transmitted to the cells in the neighborhood. Communications are perfect and instantaneous.

3. Amorphous primitives

In this section, we present two amorphous primitives: *moving cells* and *recruitment gradient*. These two algorithms are used to build the Blob primitives.

3.1. Moving Cells

As Blobs must move, *Moving cells* primitive is fundamental to implement: cell state can be moved to another cell in its neighborhood. Cells have a $cstate$ which can hold four states: $empty$, $active$, $copy$, $wait\_end\_copy$. Source cells start in the *active* state and the target cells must be *empty*. A public state *tid* holds the cell id.

Require: $cstate = active$
  $tid \leftarrow$ select_id (qualified empty cell)
  $cstate \leftarrow wait\_end\_copy$
  publish (tid)
  publish (state)
  wait **until**
    received (tid) = tid **and**
    received ($cstate$) = $copy$
  $cstate \leftarrow empty$
  clean (state)

Algorithm 1: Moving cell state (source cell view).

Moving cell is a three step algorithm. In the first step (see algorithm 1), the source cell selects an empty cell according to determined conditions and announces the selected target id. In the second step (see algorithm 2), the target duplicates the source state and announces to the source that the copy is finished. The last step cleans the source cell, marks it empty and activates the source cell.

This algorithm can also duplicates a cell if the source cell is not cleaned after the duplication.

Require: $cstate = empty$
  if received (tid) = id **then**
    state $\leftarrow$ received (state)
    $cstate \leftarrow copy$
    publish (received (tid))
    wait **until**
      received (tid) = id **and**
      received ($cstate$) = $empty$
    $cstate \leftarrow active$
  end if

Algorithm 2: Moving cell state (target cell view).

3.2. Recruitment Gradient

Recruitment Gradient is a variation around the classical gradient [5] used in many amorphous computing projects. Gradient are generated amorphously by propagating a value g_l incremented in each hop. When a cell received a gradient g, it keeps the minimal value between g and g_l.

Gradient are persistent until a lower value g is presented to the system. Our Blob algorithms need non persistent gradients in order to produce other gradients. *Recruitment gradients* try to mimic recruitment pheromones used in some biological systems to locate resources. Pheromones are not persistent. Once they are left on the medium then they evaporate.

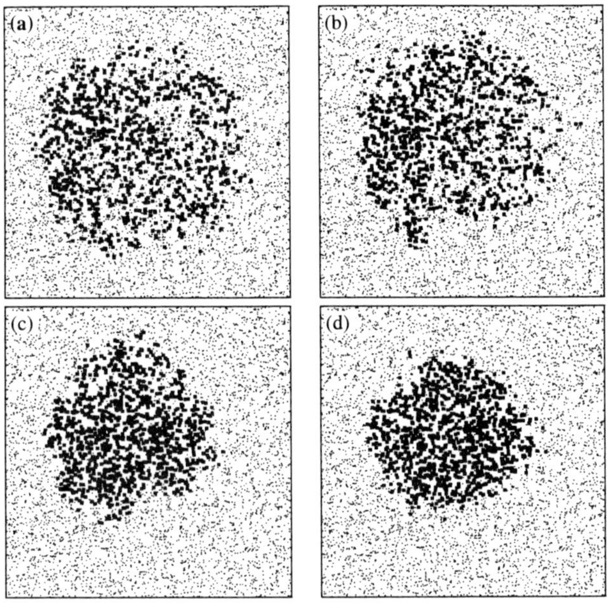

Figure 1. Cells aggregating to a Blob. (a) shows an active cell cloud represented by squares. Empty cells are represented by dots. (b) and (c) are snapshots during the aggregation. (d) shows the aggregated Blob composed by 2000 cells.

loop
  when received (g) **do** $g_l \leftarrow \min(g_l, g)$
  publish ($g_l + 1$)
  $g_l \leftarrow c_e.g_l$
  when $g_l < th$ **do** $g_l \leftarrow undefined$
end loop

Algorithm 3: Recruitment Gradient

Algorithm 3 details the *recruitment gradient.* g_l is the local value and g the values received from the neighborhood. The coefficient $c_e < 1$ is the evaporation constant. Values below threshold th reset the gradient to the $undefined$ value such as $\min(g, undefined) = g$. The reset allows us to start a new gradient.

4. Blob Primitives

In this section, we present an implementation of four Blob primitives: *aggregation*, *linking*, *dilatation* and *division.*

4.1. Aggregation

Aggregation builds a Blob from scattered cells. Blob cells should be aggregated in order to minimize intra-Blob

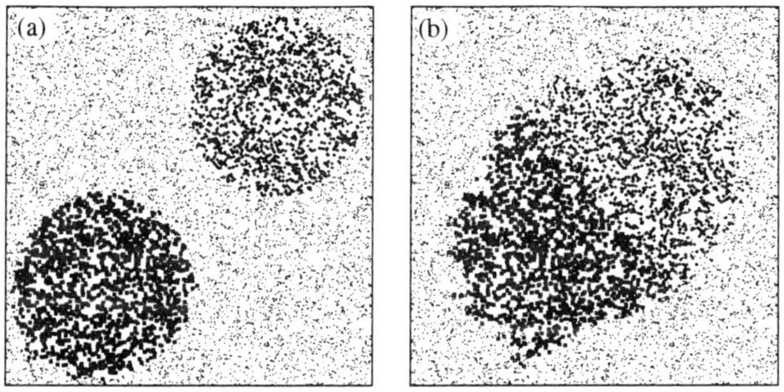

Figure 2. Linking two blobs. Figure (a) is the two Blobs before the link. Figure (b) is the linked Blobs.

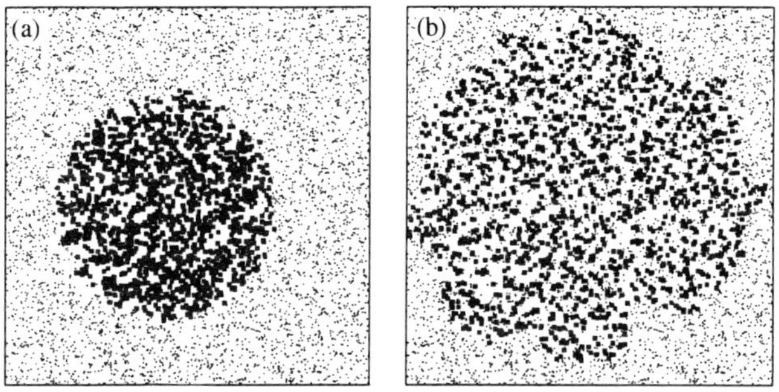

Figure 3. (a) A Blob with a density of 1. (b) The same Blob with a density of 0.5.

communications (we haven't yet implemented this primitive).

Algorithm 4 describes the two aggregation steps. First, a cell starts a *recruitment gradient* g_A with a low probability p. We usually use $p = \frac{1}{10^5}$. The second step is the *recruitment gradient* descending when it exists.

As a larger cell aggregation have a higher probability to produce a *recruitment gradient*, it attracts smaller ones as well as isolated cells. Figure 1 shows four snapshots of an aggregation process.

Require: $blob = A$
  loop
    with probability() = p **do**
      start_recruitment_gradient(g_A)
    when received (g_A) **do** move_to (min (g_A))
  end loop

Algorithm 4: Blob aggregation

4.2. Linking

Linking two Blobs A and B allows them to communicate. In order to communicate efficiently, we need to reduce the distance between the two Blobs. So Blob A attracts Blob B and reciprocally Blob B attracts Blob A.

Algorithm 5 details the *link* primitive. Blob A cells starts a *recruitment gradient* as describe in the previous section. When a cell is near Blob B, it follows the *recruitment gradient* of Blob A else it follows the *recruitment gradient* of Blob B.

Require: $blob = A$
  loop
    with probability() = p **do**
      start_recruitment_gradient (g_A)
    when received (g_B) **and** $density_B() = 0$ **do**
      move_to (min (g_B))
    when received (g_A) **and** $density_B() > 0$ **do**
      move_to (min (g_A))
  end loop

Algorithm 5: Blob linking

4.3. Dilatation

Dilatation primitive controls the Blob density. *Dilatation* isn't part of the abstract Blob machine as it isn't used in the Blob computing model. We'll use it as a part of the division primitive. *Dilatation* also uses *recruitment gradient*. Instead of descending it, cells climb the gradient when the Blob cells density is greater than the required density.

Require: $blob = A$
  with probability() = p **do**
    start_recruitment_gradient (g_A)
  when received (g_A) **and** $density_A() > density$ **do**
    move_to (max (g_A))

Algorithm 6: Blob dilatation to density $density$

Algorithm 6 exposes the *dilatation* primitive. Cell starts producing *recruitment gradient.* If its density is higher than $density$ then the cell climbs the *recruitment gradient.* Figure 3 shows the same Blob before and after a dilatation to density of 0.5.

4.4. Division

Blob *division* duplicates all cells of a Blob. After the *division*, the new Blob is independent. This primitive uses the three previous ones.

As Blob A is aggregated to a density close to 1, there are not enough empty cells to duplicate the Blob. So the first step consists of the Blob dilatation to a density of 0.5 (see algorithm 7). The next step is the duplication. The Blob name sent to the target is changed to B. Links information

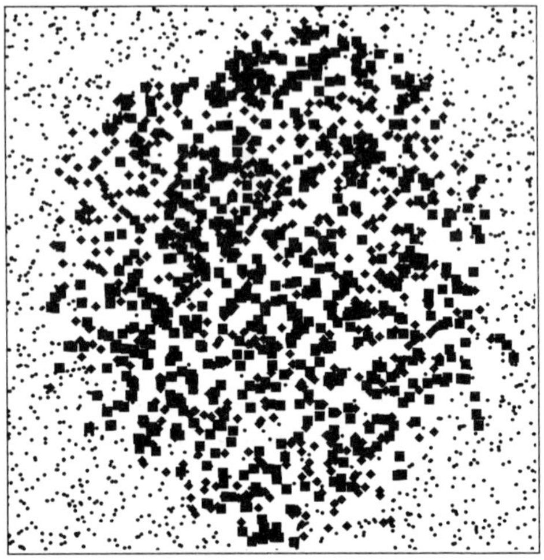

Figure 4. An incorrect blob division: Blob A (square) and Blob B (diamond) are not distinct.

can also be altered during the copy in order to create new links. In the third step, Blobs A and B aggregate to produce compact Blobs.

Require: $blob = A$
  start_dilatation (0.5)
  wait **until** $density_A <= 0.5$
  duplicate(B)
  wait **until** B = duplicated
  start_aggregation(A)
  start_aggregation(B)

Algorithm 7: Blob division

Actually, this algorithm doesn't produce the expected result and is still in development. As figure 4 shows, the two final Blobs are not distinct. Instead we obtain one entity mixing the cells of A and the cells of B.

5. Applications

Amorphous computing principles find applications in programming scalable wireless sensors networks and FPGA. Blobs primitives may be used to implement a complete Blob machine. Blob primitives may also be used in all applications that involve structured and linked groups of cells. P-Systems [9] are targets of choice for Blob primitives. Each primitive may have its own application. *Aggregation* primitive is a general spatial group formation method. These groups can contain processes or data. *Linking* primitive may be used to build topological structures such as trees and graphs. *Division* primitive may implement process forking. It may also break data sets according to defined conditions. Then it may be used to implement *divide and conquer* algorithms on amorphous computing.

6. Conclusion

We presented an implementation of the Blob structure on amorphous computers. Our implementation uses a biologically inspired structure: *recruitment gradients*. It allows a leaderless, simple and efficient implementation of the Blob primitives. The *division* primitive is still incorrect as the final step doesn't produce two distinct Blobs. As a work in progress, our implementation needs improvements: correct the *division* primitive. We will explore a finer control of the *recruitment gradient* starting cells and we will exploit *recruitment gradient* blending; Blob abstract machine provides intra and extra Blob communications which need to be implemented.

References

[1] H. Abelson, D. Allen, D. Coore, C. Hanson, G. Homsy, T. F. Knight, R. Nagpal, E. Rauch, G. J. Sussman, and R. Weiss. Amorphous computing. *CACM*, 43(5):74–82, may 2000.

[2] J. Beal and G. Sussman. Biologically-inspired robust spatial programming. AI-MEMO 2005-001, MIT, january 2005.

[3] R. Beckers, O. Holland, and J.L.Deneubourg. From local actions to global tasks: stigmergy and collective robotics. In *ALIFE IV*, 1994.

[4] D. Coore. Botanical computing: A developmental approach to generating interconnect topologies on an amorphous computer. Master's thesis, MIT Department of Electrical Engineering and Computer Science, feb 1999.

[5] D. Coore, R. Nagpal, and R. Weiss. Paradigms for structure in an amorphous computer. AI Memo 1614, MIT, 6 october 1997.

[6] F. Gruau, Y. Lhuillier, P. Reitz, and O. Temam. Blob computing. In *Computing Frontiers 2004 ACM SIGMicro.*, 2004.

[7] F. Gruau and P. Malbos. The blob: A basic topological concept for "hardware-free" distributed computation. In *Unconvational Models of Computation (UMC'02)*, pages 151–163, Kobe, Japan, 2002.

[8] R. Nagpal. *Programmable Self-Assembly: Constructing Global Shape using Biologically-inspired Local Interaction and Origami Mathematics*. PhD thesis, MIT, june 2001.

[9] G. Păun. Computing with membranes. Technical report, Institute of Mathematics of the Romanian Academy, october 2000.

[10] M. Valvassori and A. A. Cherif. Aspect and component oriented language for amorphous computers. In *UC07'*, Santa-Fe, USA, march 2007. CNLS LANL.

[11] M. Valvassori and A. A. Cherif. Defining the blob primitives on amorphous computers. In *ICMC07*, Venice, Italy, march 2007. ECLT.

Robot Search in 3D Swarm Construction

Justin Werfel
Harvard University
Cambridge, MA 02138
jkwerfel@eecs.harvard.edu

Abstract

Robots in a swarm construction system need to be able to find their way to all potential places to add material to a structure. In two dimensions, a (trivial) procedure exists for a stateless robot moving along the outside of a structure, that will let it start at any point, take it to all potential attachment sites exactly once, and return it to its starting point, regardless of what part of the structure has already been built. Here we show that for three-dimensional structures made from cubic building blocks, where each exposed face of a block is a potential attachment site, no such procedure exists. Any robot search scheme must then necessarily involve excess movement and/or increased component complexity (e.g., memory or communication).

1. Introduction

A swarm construction system is one in which a large, unspecified number of autonomous robots collectively build a structure according to some set of user specifications. This framework belongs to the class of self-organizing systems, engineered in such a way that the independent actions of many simple interacting components produce a desired high-level result. In this paper we prove a geometric result about structures made from cubic building units, which implies for three-dimensional systems that efficiency and simplicity are not simultaneously attainable.

Swarm systems might one day be used for construction in settings difficult or dangerous for humans, e.g., building habitats in extraterrestrial or underwater environments to await human travelers, or shoring up partially collapsed structures in disaster areas. Other applications might include highly flexible fabrication of smaller-scale artifacts, as in a complementary approach to current rapid prototyping methods. The swarm approach can potentially provide many advantages over centralized systems, including parallelism, scalability, and robustness.

The robots' task in such a system can be broken into two independent parts:

1. Find all sites where material might potentially be added (the *search problem*).
2. Determine, for any such site, whether adding material there is consistent with eventually achieving the structure desired. This issue comprises both whether material should ultimately appear at a site, and whether adding it there now, given the current state of the partial structure, will later prevent robots from reaching other sites where material is desired.

In previous work [6–9] we have focused on the second part of the problem, which depends heavily on such features of the system as movement constraints of robots and building material. Here we consider only the first part, the search problem of finding sites for potential attachment.

We discuss the case where the building material consists of square or cubic blocks, and robots are able to maneuver along the surface of the structure [1–9]. To avoid unnecessary movement (and associated waste of time and energy), it is desirable for robots to minimize the number of times they repeatedly visit sites that they previously visited and rejected. The ideal path would take a robot to visit each potential attachment site exactly once, starting from any point on the structure surface. Such a sequence would be a Hamiltonian path on a graph where nodes correspond to potential attachment sites, and edges connect physically adjacent sites. If the path is static and robots may start anywhere, the path should be a cycle to ensure that all sites are visited.

For two-dimensional structures, there exists a trivial procedure robots can follow to take such a path: following the perimeter of the structure in a given direction, say clockwise, will take a robot to each site once and return it to its starting point (Figure 1). Whether such a procedure exists for three-dimensional structures is less clear. The "hairy ball theorem", which states that there is no vector field tangent to the surface of a sphere which is nonzero everywhere, suggests that no such cycle exists in a domain where sites are continuous: a robot following any path will eventually

0-7695-2906-2/07 $25.00 © 2007 IEEE

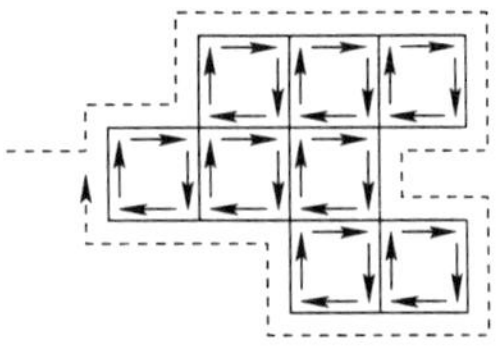

Figure 1. No matter where a robot starts along the perimeter of a 2-D structure, it will visit each potential attachment site exactly once and return to its starting point (dotted line) if it moves clockwise at every step (or, equivalently, follows clockwise-pointing arrows drawn on every block).

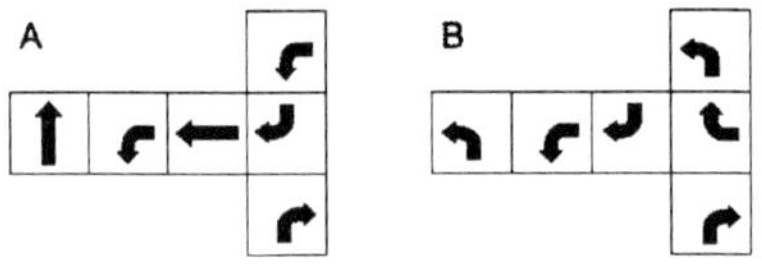

Figure 2. The two possible Hamiltonian cycles on the surface of a cube (unfolded). A robot following such a cycle will repeatedly go through the sequence of moves (A) {left, right, straight} or (B) {left, right}. (A third possibility is a reflection of the first: {right, left, straight}.)

reach a point where it must stop (or else return to a previously visited location) before returning to its origin. However, when sites are discrete, the theorem does not apply. For instance, multiple Hamiltonian cycles exist to visit all the faces of a cube (Figure 2).

Even if such a path exists, the problem remains of a robot finding it. Some approaches might require very significant capabilities from the robot in terms of perception, memory, and/or computation, and may not scale well with structure size. Other approaches may make use of complex building material, e.g., blocks with embedded processors and the ability to communicate [3, 9]. For greatest simplicity and lowest cost, it would be best if a stateless robot could determine how to follow the path at any point based only on very limited local information.

Information left in the environment—the "stigmergy" often used in swarm systems and inspired by social insects—can be of great use to simple robots. In particular, a path could in effect be drawn on the surface of the structure, telling a robot crawling along the surface which way to go next. If cues of this sort are static, then adding any new block to the structure needs to result in an appropriate path without requiring an update to any of the rest of the existing path.

The question of interest, then, is whether a fixed scheme exists for coding and assembling a set of blocks such that (1) a Hamiltonian cycle exists for any structure at any stage of completion, and (2) attaching another block at any site still gives a Hamiltonian cycle.

For two-dimensional structures of square blocks, such a scheme is to draw a clockwise-pointing arrow on each face of each block (Figure 1). A robot whose movement is determined by following these arrows will take a Hamiltonian path around the perimeter of the structure no matter where it starts. Attaching a block to the structure at any site in any orientation (assuming blocks cannot be rotated through the third dimension, making the arrows point counterclockwise) will yield a structure with a Hamiltonian cycle.

In the next section, we will show that no such scheme exists for three-dimensional structures of identical cubic blocks. As a result, any sufficient approach to the search problem necessarily must involve repeated visits to potential attachment sites (as with a random walk), potentially complex robots (as with a systematic search that maintains a history of visited sites), and/or communication between blocks (as with following a dynamic gradient maintained by the blocks of the structure). Previous work [9] explores three such approaches and the tradeoffs between them.

2. Three-dimensional analysis

A structure is built starting from a single block. Thus whatever path is drawn on the surfaces of all blocks must constitute a Hamiltonian cycle for each block in isolation. It is easy to show by exhaustion that there are only two such cycles on a cube, shown in Figure 2.

When connecting a block to a face of an existing structure, the new block needs to be oriented in such a way that the arrows on the block are consistent with the arrows on the structure. The head of every arrow on the structure that points the way onto the block should point to the tail of an arrow on the block, and vice versa (Figure 3), in order for the paths represented by arrows to be continuous everywhere. Otherwise, a path will be broken; two arrows will point to the same face, and some face will have no arrows pointing to it, inconsistent with a Hamiltonian cycle.

The unique way to ensure matching up two blocks and their arrows in this way is to have identical arrows on the faces that are brought into contact, and orient them head-to-tail. With this rule, the arrow that led into the joined face on one block will lead into the arrow that led out of the joined face on the other block.

In section 2.1 we show that for path A in Figure 2, this rule cannot in general be followed to allow a new block to be attached to a structure consistent with all arrows already

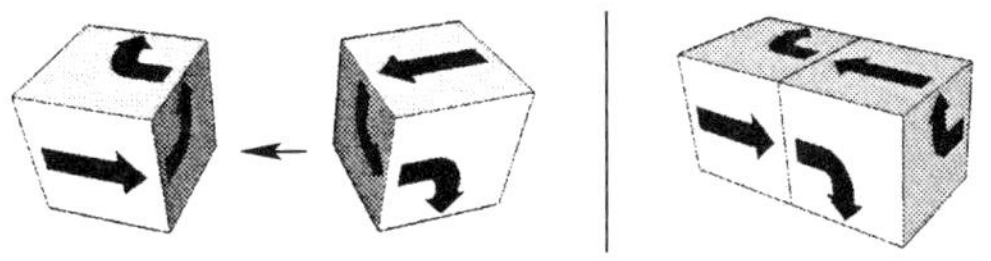

Figure 3. An example of attaching two blocks such that their arrows are consistent. The faces brought into contact each have left arrows, in opposite orientations. The resulting structure has a single Hamiltonian cycle drawn on its surface.

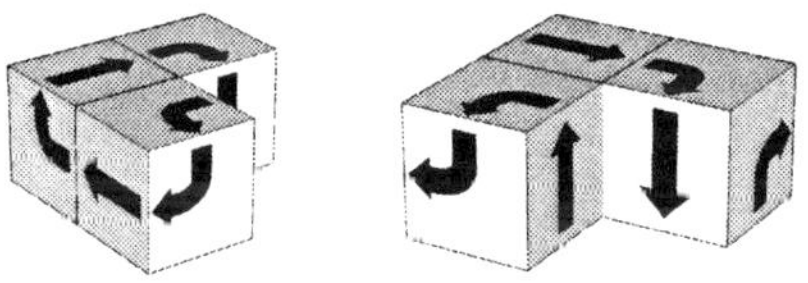

Figure 4. Two views of an example structure built of cubes encoded with path A, where there is no way to attach a fourth cube at the corner site consistent with both of its neighbors.

present. In section 2.2 we show that for path B, a new block can always be added in this way, but the result is not always a single Hamiltonian cycle. Therefore there is no way to encode static cubes such that they can be used to build a structure where, at every stage of completion, a stateless robot moving along the surface can always follow a path visiting every exposed face exactly once.

2.1. Path A

Figure 4 shows an example demonstrating that path A of Figure 2 can lead to situations where no cube can be attached at a site so as to be consistent with all its neighbors. Three blocks have been connected according to the attachment rule and consistent with their neighbors, and the arrows on the surface form a Hamiltonian cycle. However, no block can be attached at the empty site with two neighbors: the two neighboring faces both have straight arrows, inconsistent with path A. (In fact, there is no way to draw arrows on a cube such that, if it were attached at that site, the four-block structure would have a Hamiltonian cycle on its surface.) Path A, then, cannot in general be used to build a structure such that a Hamiltonian cycle is present at every step of construction.

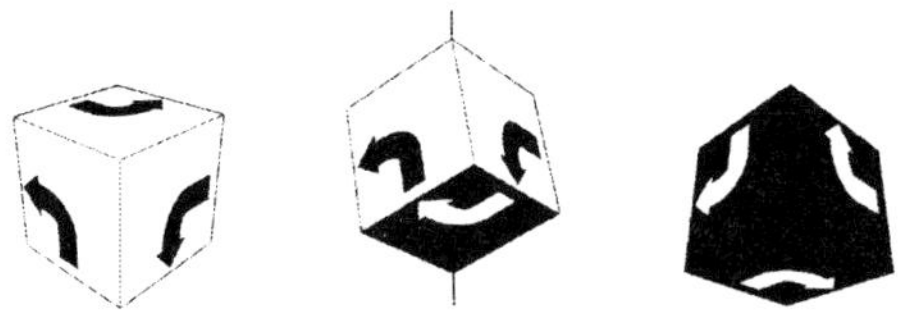

Figure 5. Three views of a cube patterned with path B. The cube has threefold rotational symmetry about the axis shown (middle).

2.2. Path B

Coloring left-arrow faces white and right-arrow faces black, as in Figures 5, 7, and 8, makes several properties of this path clearer. The three white faces border one vertex of the cube, with arrows directed outward; the three black faces border the diagonally opposite vertex, again with arrows directed outward (Figure 5). The block has threefold rotational symmetry about the axis that passes through these two vertices. Thus a block in a cubic lattice has exactly eight possible distinct orientations; the "white" vertex can be in any of the eight corners.

Because of the attachment rule about matching up arrows, the orientation of one block determines the orientation of its neighbors, which determine the orientation of their neighbors, and so on. It is easy to show that all of these orientations are mutually consistent: it will always be possible to attach a block to a structure so that there are no broken paths, and the head of every arrow on every face will point to the tail of an arrow on a neighboring face.

All of space can then be consistently tiled with blocks marked with path B; the orientation of each is uniquely determined by that of the first. Figure 6 shows how these orientations fit together. An interesting property is that no matter how the structure is built, any exposed faces in the same plane will always be the same color (Figure 7).

While it is always possible, using path B, to attach blocks anywhere so as to be consistent with the existing structure, the resulting paths are not always Hamiltonian. Adding a block may end up splitting an existing cycle into separate cycles (Fig. 8). A robot following such a path would return to its starting point before visiting all potential attachment sites. As a result, path B is also unsuitable for building a structure so as to provide a Hamiltonian cycle at every stage.

3. Conclusion

We have shown that no way of drawing a static path on identical cubic blocks will let them be assembled into a structure such that a Hamiltonian cycle, visiting all exposed faces exactly once, will necessarily exist at every step. Thus

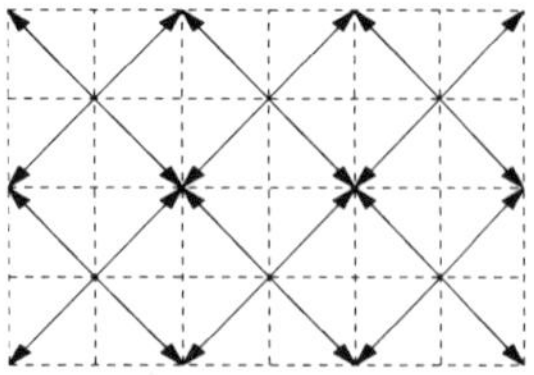

Figure 6. Tiling pattern of consistent block orientations, projected into any of the three orthogonal planes. Dashed lines show block boundaries; arrows show orientation, pointing from "black" vertex to "white" vertex (Figure 5). In three dimensions, arrows have a component pointing into or out of the plane, so that eight "black" vertices or eight "white" vertices come together at a single point.

Figure 7. An example structure showing that, using path B, exposed faces in the same plane will all be the same color. (Arrows are omitted.)

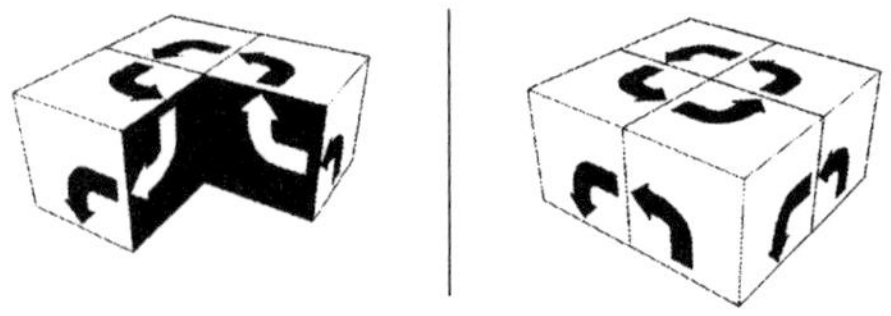

Figure 8. (Left) A three-block structure built of cubes encoded with path B, with a Hamiltonian cycle. (Right) Adding a fourth block gives a structure with two continuous but separate closed paths, one visible on top, the other winding around the sides and bottom.

it is in general impossible for stateless robots, acting on the basis of limited local information, to reliably find all potential attachment sites on a partially completed structure they build of passive cubic blocks, without revisiting sites.

A swarm construction system using cubic blocks thus requires greater complexity from its components, greater expenditure of time and energy, or both. Previous work [9] discussed three possible search schemes and explored the tradeoffs between them. One scheme is a random walk: robots simply move at each step to a random neighboring face. This approach in general results in a very great deal of unnecessary movement, more so for structures with greater surface area. A second possibility is a systematic search, where robots keep track of visited sites and choose their movement in a principled way to visit unexplored areas. While this approach can eliminate considerable revisiting of sites, some repeated movement remains; it also has robot memory requirements that increase with the size of the desired structure, and depending on the details of the search, may restrict the class of structures that can be built. A third scheme is to embed processors in the building blocks, let them communicate with physically attached neighbors, and have them direct robots straight to the nearest available attachment site. This approach requires substantially more complex blocks, and can call for a very great deal of communication among them, with associated energy costs.

It would be ideal if all these complexities could be avoided and stateless robots could find their way to all potential attachment sites without repeated movement or communication. However, some such increased complexity is necessary for any such 3D swarm construction system—regardless of the nature of the rules dictating where material may legitimately be attached.

References

[1] D. Arbuckle and A. Requicha. Active self-assembly. In *Proc. ICRA 2004*, pp. 896–901, 2004.

[2] C. Jones and M. Matarić. Automatic synthesis of communication-based coordinated multi-robot systems. In *Proc. IROS 2004*, pp. 381–387, 2004.

[3] K. Støy and R. Nagpal. Self-repair through scale independent self-reconfiguration. In *Proc. IROS 2004*, pp. 2062–7, 2004.

[4] Y. Terada and S. Murata. Automatic assembly system for a large-scale modular structure: hardware design of module and assembler robot. In *Proc. IROS 2004*, pp. 2349–2355, 2004.

[5] J. Wawerla, G. Sukhatme, and M. Matarić. Collective construction with multiple robots. In *Proc. IROS 2002*, 2002.

[6] J. Werfel, Y. Bar-Yam, and R. Nagpal. Building patterned structures with robot swarms. In *Proc. IJCAI-05*, 2005.

[7] J. Werfel, Y. Bar-Yam, D. Rus, and R. Nagpal. Distributed construction by mobile robots with enhanced building blocks. In *Proc. ICRA 2006*, pp. 2787–2794, 2006.

[8] J. Werfel and R. Nagpal. Extended stigmergy in collective construction. *IEEE Intelligent Systems*, 21(2):20–28, 2006.

[9] J. Werfel and R. Nagpal. Three-dimensional construction with mobile robots and modular blocks. In review, 2007.

Towards Cooperative, Self-Organised Replica Management*

David Hales, Andrea Marcozzi
University of Bologna
Dept. of Computer Science
Bologna, Italy
{hales, marcozzi}@cs.unibo.it

Giovanni Cortese
University of Rome
Laboratori di Radiocoms. (RadioLabs)
Roma, Italy
g.cortese@computer.org

Abstract

Nodes in a network often store and serve content to other nodes. However, each has a finite capacity and if requests for content exceed the capacity then queries fail. It is generally not possible for a priori predictions of load demand because at given times some content may suddenly become popular and at others hardly requested at all. Hence over a given time period a population of nodes has a certain total capacity to serve requests (the sum of all individual node capacities) and some demand load (queries going to the nodes). Assuming nodes can replicate content and redirect queries we present a simple node level protocol that self-organises nodes into cooperative clusters leading to efficient outcomes in some simple scenarios. The approach is scalable, robust and self-organising but there are several open issues. We present this as work-in-progress.

1. Introduction

As demand for information increases, centralized servers become a bottleneck. Content providers, system administrators or end users cope with the problem by distributing replicas of content to machines scattered throughout the network. Replica Management refers to the problem of deciding how many replicas of each file to distribute, and where to place them. Enough replicas should exist to handle the cumulative demand but with too few replicas, servers become overloaded, and clients see reduced performance. Conversely, extra replicas waste bandwidth and storage.

Our approach uses a simple protocol that dynamically self-organises clusters of servers that mutually replicate content and redirect queries in order to share load. We have adapted a protocol from a previous abstract model which tested behavior using a simple interaction game (the Prisoner's Dilemma) to capture the contradiction between individual and social goals [1]. We present initial simulation work and discuss what needs to be done to refine the model towards a plausible implementation.

*This work is partially supported by the EU within the 6th Framework Programme under contract 001907 (DELIS).

2 The CacheWorld Scenario

We assume a population of N server nodes which form a peer to peer (P2P) overlay network. In addition to being part of the overlay, each node functions as a server responding to requests (queries) from clients outside of the overlay. An example could be that each node is a web server with the overlay linking the servers and clients being web browsers on user machines. Servers store a copy of their own content item (e.g. a website) and have additional storage for k replicated items from other servers. The overlay links servers bidirectionally if they mutually replicate content. In our website example this would mean two linked servers hold a copy of the others' site. We also assume servers have access to three services: a replication service that copies items between servers; a peer sampling service that supplies a random server from the overlay; a content server that serves or redirects queries as required. Figure 1 shows a schematic diagram.

2.1 Query handling

Over a given time period nodes receive queries (load) from clients to serve their content item. Each node has a capacity, C, specifying the total queries it can serve in the given time period. If the load exceeds capacity then the nodes is said to be "overloaded". Overloaded nodes redirect queries to randomly selected neighbors. If a neighbor is not itself overloaded it will serve the query from its local content replica, otherwise it will ignore the query. The essential idea therefore is that overloaded nodes will have neighbors that are not overloaded and can serve queries.

0-7695-2906-2/07 $25.00 © 2007 IEEE

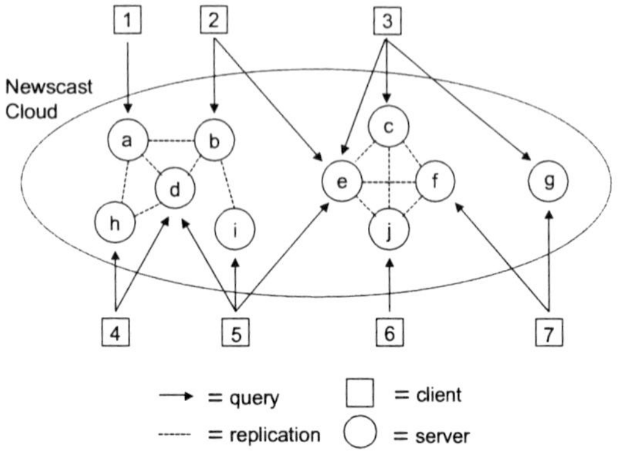

Figure 1. CacheWorld scenario. Server nodes service queries from clients. All server nodes are within a Newscast cloud and may link to other nodes in a P2P overlay. Neighbors mutually replicate content. Overloaded nodes redirect queries neighbors.

```
Passive thread
on receiving a query q, node i:
    if not overloaded, service q directly
    else if neighbors > 0 and q is not
    already a redirected query
        j ← selectRandomNeighbor()
        redirect q to j
    end if
```

```
Active thread
periodically each node i:
    if not satisfied
        drop all neighbor links
        j ← selectRandomPeer()
        if j is receptive then link to j
    end if
```

Figure 2. Outline pseudocode for the CacheWorld protocol. The passive thread is activated when a node receives a query, the active thread is activated periodically - once per load cycle.

2.2 Satisfaction and movement

Each node maintains an estimate of the proportion of queries for its own content that are actually served (ps). A node is said to be satisfied when $ps \geq t$, where t is some threshold value. Periodically nodes attempt to change their neighbors (move) in the overlay network if they are not satisfied. When a node i moves, it drops all its current links and selects a random node, j, from the population. i then attempts to link to j. The link is accepted if j is in a *receptive* state. A node is defined as receptive if it is currently not satisfied or if it has spare capacity which is unused. This captures the notion that a node only wants new connections if it is either not satisfied or if it has spare capacity to offer. If a receptive node accepts an incoming link but already has the maximum k links then it drops a randomly selected old link to make space for the new link. Figure 2 gives outline pseudocode for the protocol.

As stated previously, when two nodes link they mutually replicate each others content. Hence movement implies a cost due to the replication process. Currently we do not model this cost in terms of reduction of node capacities. However we do measure the amount of movement that occurs (see later).

3 Simulation Specifics

A simulation model was implemented within the *Peersim*[1] system, an open source P2P systems simulator platform. Our initial experiments have been performed with a small number of nodes $N = 50$. However, we found our results to be broadly scalable. We ran tests up to $N = 10^4$. For our initial experiments we chose two very simple node loading and capacity scenarios (described in section 3 below). First we explain the structure of the simulation model.

Peersim divides time into cycles (we call these *Peersim Cycles*). Some number of Peersim cycles constitutes what we term a *Load Cycle*. In each Peersim cycle each node i is fired, in random order, and may receive a client query. If a query is received, it will be answered directly if the node is not currently overloaded. If the node is overloaded it will redirect the query to a randomly selected neighbor node if it has one. The neighbor node will then answer the query or, if it is also overloaded, will ignore it.

The number of queries (load) given to each node $1..N$ in one Load Cycle constitutes what we call the *Load Profile* L. For a node i, Li specifies the load for that node. If L specifies the same value for each node then all receive the same number of queries and their load is equal. Variation in loads between nodes indicates that some nodes receive more queries than others. Each node also stores an individual capacity value, Ci, that specifies the total number of queries it can serve over a Load Cycle. The set of all Ci capacity values for all nodes $1..N$ constitutes what we call the *Capacity Profile* C. Hence the sum of all Ci values constitutes the total system capacity, TC, which is the maximum number of queries the system as a whole can serve in one Load Cycle.

At the end of a Load Cycle each unsatisfied node con-

[1] http://peersim.sourceforge.net

siders moving in the overlay with probability $mp = 0.1$. A node is not satisfied if the proportion of queries, it directly received from clients, that were eventually served, ps, is below threshold t. Here we set $t = 1$ for all nodes, so a node is only satisfied if *all of its queries are served.* We currently do not model how nodes calculate the proportion of answered queries but assume some service or method exists to approximate it. Movement follows the scheme previously described.

We simulated two very simple query load scenarios on the nodes. In each case the node capacities were evenly distributed but the query loads were not. This means some nodes were overloaded and some under-loaded. In bother cases the Capacity and Load Profiles stay constant.

In the first scenario we set the Capacity Profile such that all nodes had capacity $C = 10$ queries and the Load Profile such that half the nodes had a load of 15 and the other half 5 queries. This means half the nodes are under loaded by 5 and half are overloaded by 5. We set $k = 1$ for this scenario meaning that nodes only maintain a single link and therefore form pairings rather than complex network topologies.

In the second scenario we set the Capacity Profile such that all nodes had $C = 20$ and the Load Profile such that 10% of nodes had zero load, 10% of nodes had load 40, 40% of nodes had load 15 and the remaining 40% of nodes had load 25. This means that, like the first scenario, half the nodes are overloaded and half are under-loaded. But here nodes are over- or under-loaded by different amounts. This makes coordination a little more tricky than in the first scenario. We set $k = 4$ meaning that nodes maintain a maximum of four links to other nodes.

In all cases experimental results were produced by collecting results from 10 independent simulation runs that ran for 1000 load cycles each. To asses performance we recorded three measures, Q, S and M. Q gives the proportion of queries actually served as proportion of all submitted; S gives the proportion of nodes satisfied and M the amount of node movement as a proportion of the node population per load cycle. Q and S were calculated as averages over all runs for the last 500 cycles indicating performance after some level of stability is reached. M was calculated as an average over the entire 1000 load cycles indicating how much node movement (and hence replication effort) was required to reach and maintain the given performance.

4 Results

We present results from three different experiments (isolated, random and dynamic) for each of the two load scenarios. The *Isolated* experiments gives a performance baseline by running the simulation with all CacheWorld services turned-off: no links between nodes, no query redirection and no movement. This captures the situation where nodes simply answer their own queries and do not know about other nodes. The *Random* experiments give a secondary baseline. Here the overlay is initialized to a random topology (degree k) that is fixed - i.e. no node movement is possible. However, nodes my redirect their queries to neighbors if they become overloaded. In the *Dynamic* experiments the CacheWorld protocol is fully enabled allowing for dynamic node movement based on satisfaction, as previously described. By comparing *Random* and *Dynamic* experiments we can determine how much extra performance dynamic movement produces over just a fixed random overlay. By comparing *Isolated* and *Dynamic* experiments we can determine the overall increase in performance obtained by using CacheWorld over letting servers deal with all their own queries individually.

Results for scenario one are shown in figure 3. For the *Isolated* experiments we found, Q = 0.75, S = 0.5 with negligible variances. This is what we expected given the Load and Capacity Profiles. For the *Random* experiments we initialized the overlay network to a random topology with $k = 1$. This gives a further baseline showing how well a purely random approach performs. As might be expected there was some improvement because nodes have the chance to share load. We found $Q = 0.79$, $S = 0.58$. Finally in the *Dynamic* experiments the full CacheWorld protocol is used allowing movement by unsatisfied nodes. Again the initial topology of the overlay is randomly generated as before but nodes can change the topology over time by movement. We found improved performance with only 1% of queries not answered. We found $Q = 0.99$, $S = 0.98$, again variances were negligible. This improvement in performance comes at the cost of node movement (nodes making and breaking links to other nodes in the overlay). More movement occurs in the early Load Cycles and then the network settles to a more stable state. We found $M = 7.2 \times 10^{-4}$ which equates to a total of 36 node movements over 1000 cycles. This indicates that that a relatively small amount of movement suffices to improve performance. The main result here is that turning on the CacheWorld protocol improves total queries served, Q, by 24%, keeping 98% of nodes satisfied and resulting in only a small amount of node movement and hence replication effort. However, this is a very simple loading scenario in which load and capacities are constant and optimal pairs of nodes are easy to find so we would expect good results and indeed the scenario was selected as a minimal test.

For the second load scenario we conducted the same set of experiments. The results are shown in figure 3. Notice that for both the *Isolated* and *Random* experiments we gain comparable values for the number of satisfied nodes S but higher values for queries answered Q. This is due to the unbalanced nature of the load distributed and capacities which gives higher loads and capacities to some nodes. For

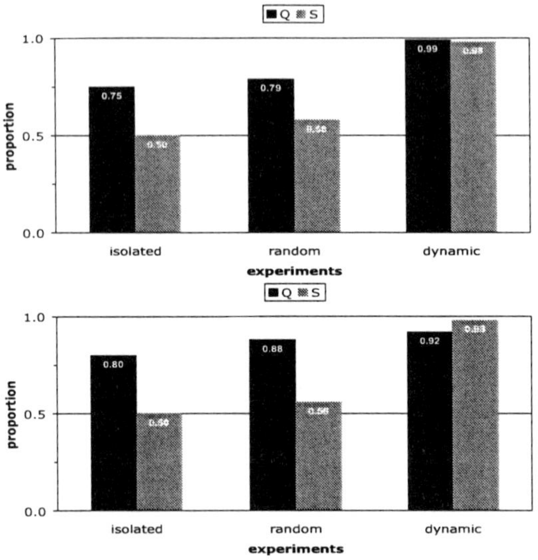

Figure 3. Results from three experiments for load scenario one (upper chart)) and two (lower chart). The scenarios are described in section 3 and experiments are described in section 4. Q = proportion of queries answered, S = proportion of nodes satisfied.

the *Dynamic* case we found $Q = 92$ and $S = 98$. However, more movement occurs compared to scenario one. We found $M = 9.5 \times 10^{-3}$ which equates to a total of 475 node movements over the 1000 cycles. This indicates that an order of magnitude more movement is required to obtain the performance increase in this more tricky, yet still relatively simple, scenario.

5 Discussion and future work

The idea behind CacheWorld is that the movement of nodes in the overlay network leads to the formation of clusters of servers that replicate each others content and deal with redirected queries. Elsewhere we have called similar formations *tribes* [1]. A stable tribe is one that satisfies all of its members otherwise they will move away and over time the tribe will dissolve. Stable tribes comprise nodes with complementary loads (i.e. loads that tend to be negatively correlated). This may be plausible when demand for content follows daily patterns. Peers then would effectively supplement capacity for daytime load peaks in one time zone with spare overnight capacity from another.

In these initial experiments we have considered loads where an equal number of nodes are either under- or overloaded consistently so stable clusters can easily emerge. The results then, show, that at least in these simple scenarios our simple node movement heuristic is sufficient to produce stable clusters giving high performance. Although the scenarios are simple, we placed a 100% load on the system and set all node satisfaction thresholds to 100%. This means that the system only fully stabilizes when 100% of capacity is utilized.

A number of open issues need to be addressed. We have not tested the system under realistic query load (highly dynamic and skewed) and we have only modeled nodes holding a single monolithic content item (rather than many small items). We have not extensively tested the system with free-rider nodes that do not replicate, or serve queries, from others. However, initial experiments (not shown here) indicate that the system punishes free-riders because they need to move more often (twice as often as non-freeriders) because they tend to become isolated[2].

Several Replica Management systems already exist and are in use. However existing systems (e.g. Squirrel [3], Globule [4]), which manage replication, do not have specific mechanisms for adjusting the cooperation among nodes. For example, for balancing global policies (i.e. the goals of the community) against local (i.e. that of individual nodes / agents) policies. The policies in such systems are fixed by design. We aim to examine the applicability of augmenting these existing systems with our simple protocol to improve adaptability.

Our aim is to produce a distributed, scalable, robust and self-organising protocol. Our approach is not to guarantee optimality or absolute security but rather to produce very simple protocols utilising, where possible, existing technologies that perform reasonably well over a range of conditions.

References

[1] D. Hales and S. Arteconi. SLACER: A self-organizing protocol for coordination in peer-to- peer networks. *IEEE Intelligent Systems*, 21(2):29-35, Mar/Apr 2006.

[2] M. Jelasity, M. van Steen. Large-Scale Newscast Computing on the Internet. *Report IR-503, Vrije Universiteit Amsterdam, Dept. of Comp. Sci.*, Amsterdam, 2002.

[3] S. Iyer, A. Rowstron, and P. Druschel. Squirrel: A decentralized peer-to-peer web cache. In *Proc. 21st ACM SIGACT-SIGOPS Symposium on Principles of Distributed Computing (PODC)*, 2002.

[4] Guillaume Pierre and Maarten van Steen. Globule: a Collaborative Content Delivery Network *IEEE Communications Magazine* 44(8), pp. 127-133, August 2006.

[2]Free-riders were modeled as nodes that never answered other's queries and always redirected their queries, even when they had capacity.

In Search of Simplicity: A Self-Organizing Group Communication Overlay

Matei Ripeanu
University of British Columbia
matei@ece.ubc.ca

Adriana Iamnitchi
University of Florida
anda@cse.usf.edu

Ian Foster Anne Rogers
The University of Chicago
{foster, amr}@uchicago.edu

Abstract

Group communication primitives have broad utility as building blocks for distributed applications. The challenge is to create and maintain the distributed structures that support these primitives while accounting for volatile end-nodes and variable network characteristics. Most solutions proposed to date rely on complex algorithms or global information, thus limiting the scale of deployments and acceptance outside the academic realm.

This article introduces a low-complexity, self-organizing solution for maintaining multicast trees, that we refer to as UMM (Unstructured Multi-source Multicast). UMM uses traditional distributed systems techniques: layering, soft-state, and passive data collection to adapt to the dynamics of the physical network and maintain data dissemination trees. The result is a simple, adaptive system with lower overheads than more complex alternatives. We have implemented UMM and evaluated it on up to 1024-node emulated ModelNet networks and on the PlanetLab testbed.. Extensive experimental evaluations and quantitative comparisons with alternative solutions demonstrate UMM's low overhead, efficient network usage, and ability to quickly adapt to network changes and to recover from failures.

1. Introduction

Collaborative applications such as conferencing, shared virtual workspaces, or multi-player games rely on multi-source multicast functionality. Recently, this functionality has been used in contexts such as peer-to-peer resource discovery or resource monitoring [2]. Limited native multicast support in the Internet [3] and application-specific requirements (e.g., reliability, message stream semantics) make application overlays an attractive alternative to IP-layer multicast. Application overlays [4] employ participating end-systems to implement functionality not provided by the underlying communication layer or to improve the characteristics of services provided by lower network layers. When providing multicast functionality, overlays serve as support for extracting dissemination trees used to send data from each source to all destinations.

Two broad classes of overlays have emerged, differentiated by the existence of global rules (or the lack of thereof) that restrict their geometry. *Unstructured overlays* allow unrestricted interaction patterns between participating nodes, while *structured overlays* impose global, regular structures. Intuitively, unstructured overlays are less expensive to create and maintain and are more flexible to map on inherently heterogeneous sets of end-nodes linked by diverse physical network topologies [5]. However, existing solutions for multi-source multicast based on unstructured overlays have limited scalability or incur large overheads [6]. On the other side, the scalability advantage offered by structured overlays is offset by less efficient usage of underlying network resources and high protocol complexity [7].

The structured vs. unstructured overlay debate is particularly relevant in a data-distribution context because of the tension between scalability and efficient network usage. To inform this debate, we address the problem of multisource multicast and propose a simple self-organizing solution based on unstructured overlays and we extensively evaluate it against the best alternatives proposed so far. Although novel as a whole solution, the multi-source multicast infrastructure we propose builds on traditional, building blocks. We have reached this design in our quest for *simplicity*. We use recently proposed heuristics to build and optimize an unstructured base overlay. On top of it, we use flood-and-prune techniques to select efficient, source-specific data distribution trees: we use the implicit information contained in the duplicate messages filter out redundant overlay paths. The result is a self-adaptive, self-organizing system that performs better than alternative solutions along different performance metrics. In the following, we refer to the resulting Unstructured Multi-source Multicast solution as UMM. This solution:

- has <u>*low complexity*</u>: it relies on soft-state and passive data collection to extract multicast dissemination trees and adapt to physical network dynamics.

- is *self-organizing*: independent decisions made at each node based on partial, local information result in desired global system behavior.
- is *scalable* with the number of sources and independent of the number of participants.
- *recovers* quickly from significant failures and *adapts* to changes in underlying network topology with minimal disruption to the service offered.
- is *independent of the topology of the base overlay* and of the mechanisms used to build it which makes it reusable in a wide array of situations.

This work makes multiple contributions. First, we combine a number of traditional, distributed systems techniques to build a simple, efficient data dissemination solution presented in Section 2. Second, and more importantly, we show, via extensive experimental evaluations presented in Section 3 that although UMM uses a low-complexity protocol and nodes maintain little state, it is more efficient than alternative solutions. Third, we identify optimal overlay layouts and use them to quantify the overheads introduced by UMM and alternative solutions. This offers an upper bound for potential gains achievable through better overlay mapping algorithms. Fourth, we present an empirical method for choosing the parameters that drive the tradeoff between agility to adapt and stability, a tradeoff faced by all adaptive systems.

2. Architecture and Protocols

This section presents challenges and success metrics associated with building a self-organizing multicast overlay and briefly presents UMM design. a complete description of UMM techniques is presented in [8].

2.1. Challenges and Success Metrics

The key challenges and the corresponding performance metrics are:

i.) Efficient usage of underlying network resources. Since application-level multicast overlays are implemented on top of IP, their efficiency should be compared with that of IP-multicast. An efficient dissemination tree minimizes: (1) *relative delay penalty* (RDP), defined as the ratio between the message propagation delay in the overlay and in the underlying network; and (2) *network stress*, which is the number of duplicate messages generated due to mapping multiple overlay tunnels over the same physical link. These metrics are defined with respect to a common IP-layer multicast base and have been traditionally used to evaluate multicast solutions.

ii.) Scalability is obtained by minimizing the overheads to maintain efficient distributed structures. Two main types of overheads can be identified: overheads for estimating the conditions of the underlying network (e.g., latency, bandwidth) and state maintenance overheads (e.g., routing table and connectivity maintenance, partition detection).

iii.) Resilience. When not bandwidth-constrained, a multicast infrastructure should deliver each message to all destinations in spite of node failures or adaptation events. To quantify resilience, we estimate *delivery rates* under various failure scenarios.

iv.) Adaptation. The infrastructure should build and maintain efficient delivery trees in spite of end-host failures and changes in the topology and state of the underlying network. Moreover, the overlay should adapt quickly to changes in the properties of participating resources and routing failures.

2.2. Solution Overview

We design UMM as a *best effort service,* with minimal dependence on centralized components, minimal state at each participating host, and targeting *medium scale* groups with thousands rather than millions of sources. UMM builds two layers: the *base overlay* and the *source-specific multicast distribution trees.*

i.) The Base Overlay. UMM uses relatively simple heuristics to build and maintain the base overlay: the aim is simply to include efficient distribution trees that can be later selected by the upper layer. While the base overlay is initially random, nodes optimize it incrementally, an approach common to other systems. In keeping with our decentralization and self-organization design principles, nodes decide independently based only on local information what overlay tunnels to add or delete. As in Shen et al. [9], nodes maintain a fixed proportion P_{short} (defaulting at 50%) of their tunnels *short*, i.e., to nearby nodes, and the other tunnels *long,* to distant nodes. We use a latency threshold D_{short} to discriminate between short and long tunnels. At fixed time intervals, a node runs an optimizer task that randomly selects a small subset of participating nodes, evaluates new tunnels, and replaces its worst tunnel with a new one, if better. We limit changes to one tunnel replacement per iteration.

Short tunnels are optimized for latency: that is, a node replaces its worst short tunnel if a new shorter tunnel is found. Long tunnels are optimized for bandwidth: that is, a node replaces its worst long tunnel if it finds a new tunnel with better bandwidth. To avoid oscillations due to measurement errors or variations in network conditions, a threshold is used when deciding whether to replace an existing tunnel.

ii.) Extracting Efficient Dissemination Trees. UMM

extracts efficient, source-specific dissemination trees using the implicit information from duplicate messages resulting from flooding. The key idea is that an initial flooding stage allows each node to infer the properties of the base overlay just by detecting duplicate messages: duplicates arrive on paths with worse properties than those taken by the first message. Once duplicates are detected, this information can be used to filter out redundant paths for efficient message dissemination.

3. Experimental Evaluation

This section presents experiments that evaluate UMM techniques described above and the effectiveness of our UMM implementation: We have performed extensive controlled experiments in an emulated network environment (ModelNet [10]) that allow us to compare UMM with IP-layer multicast and with alternative solutions using relative delay penalty and network stress metrics. These experiments have three goals: First, we compare the quality of the dissemination trees produced by UMM with that of trees built by alternative approaches. Second, we estimate the cost of self-organization: we benefit from having full information on the network topology and we compare UMM-generated dissemination trees with optimal trees generated by heuristics using global topological knowledge. Finally, we test UMM ability to operate and adapt when the set of participating nodes is dynamic. The rest of this paper presents the results on the first experiment. Our technical report [8] presents in detail all these experiments as well as experiments on PlanetLab, a live testbed.

i.) Experimental Setup. We use ModelNet' suite of tools to generate physical network topologies: Modelnet classifies network links as Client-Stub, Stub-Stub, Transit-Stub, and Transit-Transit depending on their location in the network. Bandwidth for each link is assigned depending on its type: Client-Stub links have bandwidth randomly assigned in the 2 - 8Mbps range, Stub-Stub links: 4 - 10Mbps, Stub-Transit links: 5 - 10Mbps, and Transit-Transit in the 10 - 20Mbps.

End-hosts are attached randomly to stub level routers. Overlay nodes then are picked randomly from these hosts. In the experiments presented in this section, for each overlay size we ran ten simulations on ten different physical network topologies. Each topology has 4,040 backbone routers. Simulated overlay size varies from 64 to 1,024 nodes.

ii.) *Evaluating Relative Delay Penalty and Network Stress.* To compare the quality of the dissemination trees produced by UMM with that of trees built by alternative approaches, we use two sets of comparisons: First, we perform a head-to-head comparison of UMM with Macedon-generated implementations of alternative approaches running on the same emulation platform. Second, we compare UMM performance with that of alternative approaches as reported in a previous simulation-based study by Jain et. al [1]. In this latter comparison, we use ModelNet and attempt to reproduce the physical topologies used in [1] in order to offer a meaningful comparison base. Due to limited space and qualitatively similar results we present here only the results of this latter set of experiments. .

Jain considered three unstructured overlays (Narada [11], Nice [12], and a power-law overlay that is mapped randomly on the physical topology) and structured overlays employing various mapping

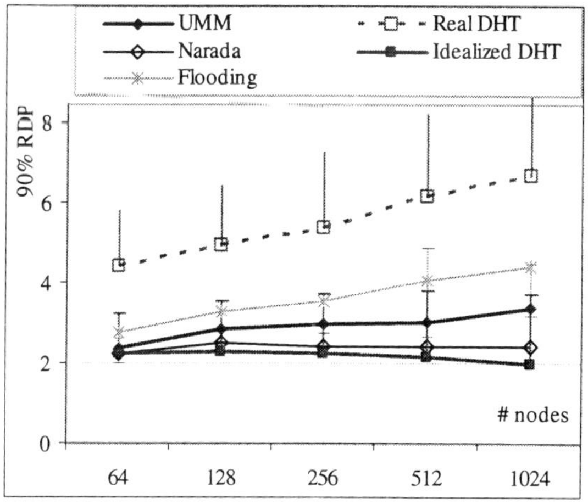

Figure 1: 90%-tile RDP for UMM and alternative solutions for overlay size varying from 64 to 1024 nodes. For UMM, Narada, and flooding, each point presents, average values from at least 9 runs (20 for UMM), while error bars present minimum and maximum values. Structured overlay results (labeled as DHT in the plot) present the average RDP for the best of three heuristics considered by Jain while the performance of alternative heuristics is presented in the error bars. Non-UMM results are extracted from Jain et al. [1].

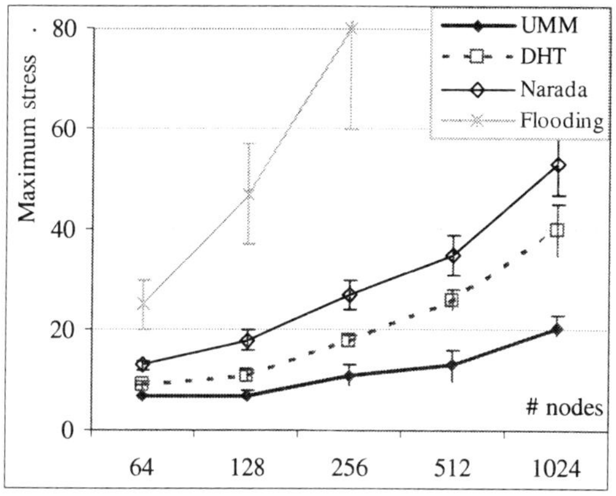

Figure 2: Maximum link stress for UMM and alternative solutions. Each point presents average values from at least 9 runs (20 for UMM), while the error bars present minimum and maximum values.

heuristics. Figures 1 and 2 summarize the results of this comparison for overlays varying from 64 to 1024 nodes. These results show that UMM generally performs at least as well as other alternatives: The 90%-tile RDP offered by UMM is better than that obtained using *realistic* structured overlays (i.e., structured overlays that do not assume a global view when mapping on the physical network). Compared to solutions that assume global view for optimization (such as Narada and the *idealized* structured overlays), the *90%-tile RDP* offered by UMM is slightly higher, thus worse (Figure 1). In all experiments UMM offers lower (thus better) *maximum link stress* than Narada, structured overlays, and naïve flooding on power-law random graphs (Figure 2).

In summary, these experiments support two conclusions: First, we show that it is possible for passive data collection and local decisions to extract *efficient* multicast data dissemination from unstructured overlays. Second, we demonstrate that although UMM uses significantly simpler heuristics than those used by alternative solutions, the data dissemination trees extracted have better or comparable performance.

4. Conclusions

UMM, the self-organizing, adaptive multi-source multicast system we propose, is based on a simple approach to extracting source-specific multicast trees from an unstructured overlay. This solution offers two important properties: first, it decouples the overlay construction and maintenance mechanism from the tree-extraction mechanism, allowing for separate component optimization. Second, it relies on soft-state and passive data collection to adapt to the dynamics of the physical network, resulting in low protocol complexity and low overheads.

Experimental and analytical evaluations demonstrate low communication overhead, efficient network usage compared to alternative solutions, and ability to adapt quickly to network changes and recover from node failures. Direct experimental comparisons with alternative solutions implemented by other researchers and deployed on ModelNet along with comparisons with previously published results support our claim that the dissemination trees produced by UMM have better characteristics (better RDP for similar stress) than those built by alternative approaches. Additionally, the performance degradation brought by the simple UMM heuristics based on *local* information is small when compared with heuristics that employ *global* topology information to extract optimized dissemination trees. Finally, we demonstrated the ability of UMM to operate in dynamic environments and adapt when the set of participating nodes is dynamic.

Most importantly, we show that a low-complexity design can lead to a self-organizing, scalable, and adaptive overlay with performance generally better than that offered by more sophisticated solutions and, additionally, with low overheads compared to idealized solutions based on global resource views. Reduced complexity is a highly desirable property of distributed, large-scale systems. When two mechanisms offer similar efficiency for comparable costs, the discriminating factor is complexity. Additionally, in production environments an increasing premium is placed on deployable, manageable, in other words *simple* systems.

5. References

[1] S. Jain, R. Mahajan, and D. Wetherall, "A Study of the Performance Potential of DHT-based Overlays," 4th USENIX Symposium on Internet Technologies and Systems, Seattle, WA, 2003.

[2] M. L. Massie, B. N. Chun, and D. E. Culler, "The Ganglia Distributed Monitoring System: Design, Implementation, and Experience," *Parallel Computing*, vol. 30, 2004.

[3] C. Diot, B. N. Levine, B. Lyles, et al., "Deployment Issues for the IP Multicast Service and Architecture," *IEEE Network*, 2000.

[4] J. D. Touch, "Overlay Networks," *Computer Networks*, vol. 36, pp. 115-116, 2001.

[5] M. Faloutsos, P. Faloutsos, and C. Faloutsos, "On Power-Law Relationships of the Internet Topology," SIGCOMM, 1999.

[6] M. Ripeanu, I. Foster, and A. Iamnitchi, "Mapping the Gnutella Network: Properties of Large-Scale Peer-to-Peer Systems and Implications for System Design," *Internet Computing Journal*, vol. 6, 2002.

[7] A. R. Bharambe, S. G. Rao, V. N. Padmanabhan, et al., "The Impact of Heterogeneous Bandwidth Constraints on DHT-Based Multicast Protocols," IPTPS, 2005.

[8] M. Ripeanu, A. Iamnitchi, I. Foster, et al., "In Search of Simplicity: A Self-Organizing Group Communication Overlay," University of British Columbia TR-2007-05, 2007.

[9] K. Shen, "Structure Management for Scalable Overlay Service Construction," First USENIX/ACM Symposium on Networked Systems Design and Implementation (NSDI'04), San Francisco, CA, 2004.

[10] A. Vahdat, K. Yocum, K. Walsh, et al., "Scalability and Accuracy in a Large-Scale Network Emulator," OSDI, 2002.

[11] Y.-h. Chu, S. G. Rao, S. Seshan, et al., "A Case for End System Multicast," *IEEE Journal on Selected Areas in Communication (JSAC), Special Issue on Networking Support for Multicast*, vol. 20, 2002.

[12] S. Banerjee, S. Lee, B. Bhattacharjee, et al., "Resilient Multicast using Overlays," ACM Sigmetrics 2003, San Diego, CA, 2003.

Meta-Regression: A Framework for Robust Reactive Optimization

Daniel W. McClary and Violet R. Syrotiuk
Department of Computer Science & Engineering
Arizona State University
{Daniel.McClary,Syrotiuk}@asu.edu

Murat Kulahci
Department of Industrial Engineering
Arizona State University
Murat.Kulahci@asu.edu

Abstract

Maintaining optimal performance as the conditions of a system change is a challenging problem. To solve this problem, we present meta-regression, *a general methodology for alleviating traditional difficulties in nonlinear regression modelling. Meta-regression allows for* reactive optimization, *in which system components self-organize to changing conditions in a manner that is* robust, *or affected minimally by other sources of variability. Meta-regression extends profiling, providing a methodology for model-building when there is incomplete knowledge of the mechanisms and interactions of a nonlinear system.*

1 Introduction

Solving optimization problems in a complex system is often challenging. Typically a model is formulated, and an objective function is identified that is to be optimized subject to some constraints. Optimum solutions may be fragile with respect to changes in the modelling assumptions or the environment of the real system. A great many modelling techniques exist for specific conditions, regression analysis among them. Ideally, individual components in a system should be able to self-organize to changing conditions to maintain optimum performance. When self-organization of individual members of a system is a goal, the models employed in optimization must both capture the behaviour of the system and allow for practical use. By providing simple mathematical models of system performance, regression analysis meets both of these requirements.

Regression analysis is a collection of mathematical and statistical techniques used to model and analyze problems in which a *response* (or output variable) is influenced by several *factors* (or input variables). Regression analysis often proves useful in systems with a great many factors, or in which the system dynamics are not perfectly understood. In these cases only approximate models and optimizations may be possible. Regression models can take many forms, but process optimization studies often focus on functions that accurately approximate system behaviour with a low-order polynomial. If linear models of a system are possible, *response surface optimiztion* (RSM) provides a methodology for finding approximate optimums for linear regressions. The *response surface* formed by the regression model, captures how a response varies with respect to significant factors and allows for adjustment of factor levels to reach optimum response values. One of the chief benefits of RSM studies is that they are not black-box processes. The experimenter learns about the dynamics of the system at all stages of the process.

When dealing with nonlinear systems, *nonlinear regression analysis* is a preferred approach. In a nonlinear regression, there are two critical issues which must be addressed before a regression can be performed. Specifically, both the model form and the initial coefficients must be identified *a priori*. Nonlinear model fitting requires a great deal of caution, as convergence is not guaranteed if errors are made in either of these choices. Often examination of system dynamics or visual inspection of data provides the basis for model form and coefficient choices. However, as the number of factors increase, choosing an initial model can become difficult.

In this paper, we introduce *meta-regression*, a general methodology to alleviate difficulty in both choice of a functional form and initial coefficient estimates. Meta-regression provides models of both changes in factor relationship and the system itself. These models, along with the overall regression model, allow for *reactive optimization*. In a reactive optimization, system components self-organize smoothly to changing conditions in a manner that is *robust*, or affected minimally by other

0-7695-2906-2/07 $25.00

sources of variability. Rather than finding the exact optimum for specific conditions, our goal is to provide an improved response over a wide range of conditions.

At a high level of abstraction, meta-regression consists of two steps. First, profiling is employed to characterize the effect of each factor on the response as well as their interactions with one another. Second a *meta-model* is constructed. This is a surface derived from the set of profiles fitted to one another. It allows interpolation and extrapolation of factor levels in order to maximize the response as conditions change. The first step of meta-regression is run offline, while the meta-model is used online for on-the-fly optimization.

The rest of this paper is organized as follows. Meta-regression is described in detail in §2. In §3 we provide an overview of the statistical foundations of meta-regression. While our work on meta-regression is in its infancy, it suggests many promising research directions. We summarize and describe some of these in §4.

2 Meta-regression

The core of meta-regression is inspired by the method of profiling [1]. The contribution of meta-regression is that it is a complete modelling methodology. Here we present the general methodology and a small example.

Profiling is often used to deduce information about factor behaviour in a nonlinear system when the number of factors is high or the function is unknown. Several values of one factor are plotted against the response or a chosen statistical measurement, while all other factors are kept fixed. By repeating this process at different levels of the fixed factors, the behaviour of the factor being profiled can be monitored over various conditions. Creating profiles for each factor in the system builds a sizable body of data from which the experimenter can draw conclusions about the behaviour of the system.

For a system with k independent variables, the dependent variable $y = f(x_1, x_2, \ldots, x_k) + \epsilon$ is any function f that relates the x_i to y. ϵ represents noise; this includes the effects of all extraneous factors that are not included in the model. For highly nonlinear systems, we propose the following modelling strategy:

1. Profile the system through experiments.

2. Starting with one x_i, a model is fit to each profile with the other independent variables at fixed levels.

3. When the last set of parameters is modelled in the last independent variable, an overall model is obtained in terms of all independent variables.

4. "Spot checks" are used to validate the model.

The experiments in step 1 are designed so that a profile of the response y is obtained for each x_i when the other $x_j \neq x_i$ are at fixed levels. Thus, two-dimensional plots of these profiles are generated for the y against each x_i. Step 2 provides several estimates of the model parameters which in turn can be modelled in terms of the remaining independent variables using the same strategy. The model obtained at the end of step 3 can be used as the starting model in the nonlinear model fitting effort, with the parameter estimates used as starting values. An overall model is fit using nonlinear estimation techniques. Once a final model has been fit, the spot checks in step 4 evaluate accuracy at randomly selected values of the independent variables and the value fit is compared to the actual response. These spot checks are performed within the experimental region or outside of the original ranges of the independent variables.

In some systems, the number of factors may be very large. In such situations it may be undesirable to conduct the number of experiments necessary to construct profiles for each factor. A *partitioned* approach can be employed to reduce the number of experiments; a full discussion is beyond the scope of this work.

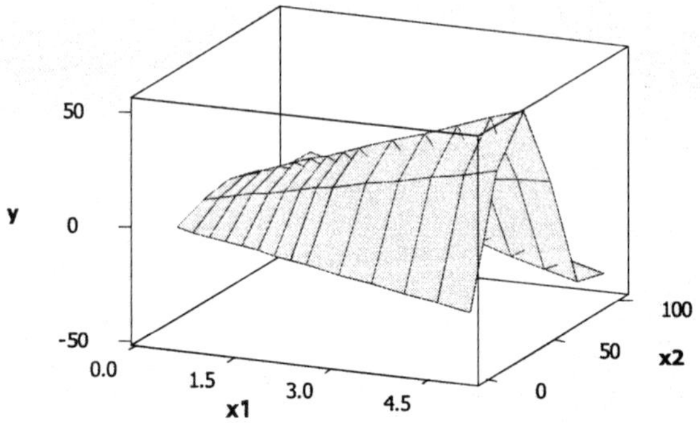

Figure 1. Example response surface.

As an example, consider a system with two independent variables and assume that a set of designed experiments results in the apparently nonlinear response surface in Figure 1. It is difficult to come up with a candidate model to estimate. To apply our proposed approach we obtain the profiles for each independent variable; these are given in Figure 2 and 3 respectively.

A simple linear trend model is used to model the profile in Figure 2. x_1 is selected to model the response using $\hat{y} = b_0 + b_1 x_1$ for each level of x_2. These models result in various estimates of b_0 and b_1 as given in Table 1. We write b_0 and b_1 in terms of x_2 and modify

0-7695-2906-2/07 $25.00

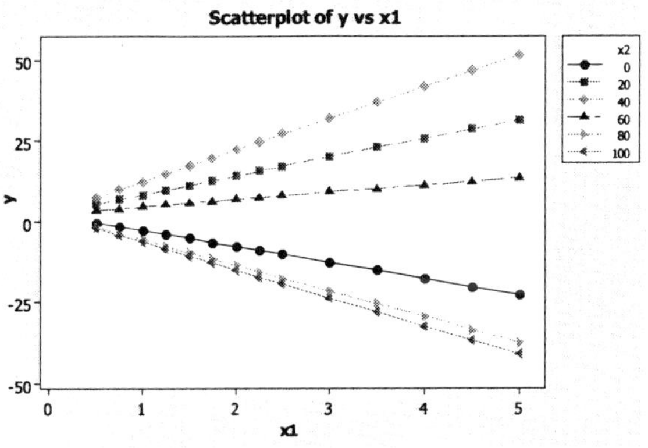

Figure 2. Profile for x_1.

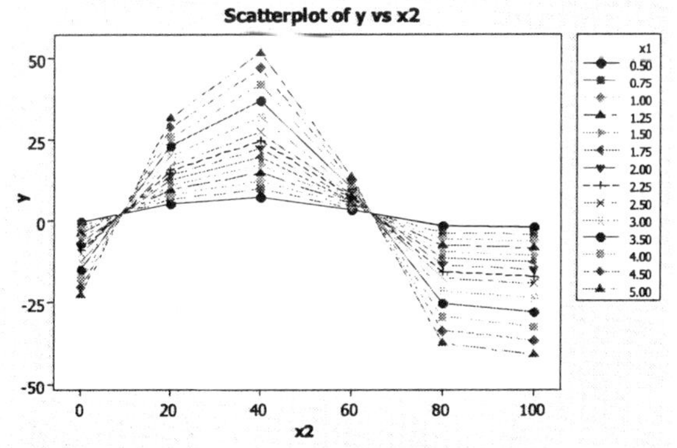

Figure 3. Profile for x_2.

the equation as $\hat{y} = b_0(x_2) + b_1(x_2)x_1$. Figure 4 reveals that b_0 is more or less constant for various values of x_2 (note the y axis scale). Figure 5 suggests to model b_1 by a third order polynomial in x_2: $b_1 = b_{10} + b_{11}x_2 + b_{12}{x_2}^2 + b_{13}{x_2}^3$. The final model (with 95% confidence) is: $\hat{y} = b_0 + (b_{10} + b_{11}x_2 + b_{12}{x_2}^2 + b_{13}{x_2}^3)x_1$ where $b_0 = 2.3050$, $b_{10} = -5.6691$, $b_{11} = 1.1067$, $b_{12} = -0.024$, and $b_{13} = 0.0001$. This model is a polynomial because at each stage only polynomials are employed. A nonlinear model is obtained if nonlinear models are employed at any one of the modelling stages.

Table 1. Estimates of b_0 and b_1

x_2	b_0	b_1
0	2.3013	-5.0258
20	2.2981	5,852
40	2.3161	9.8383
60	2.3053	2.2242
80	2.2971	-7.9751
100	2.3124	-8.7001

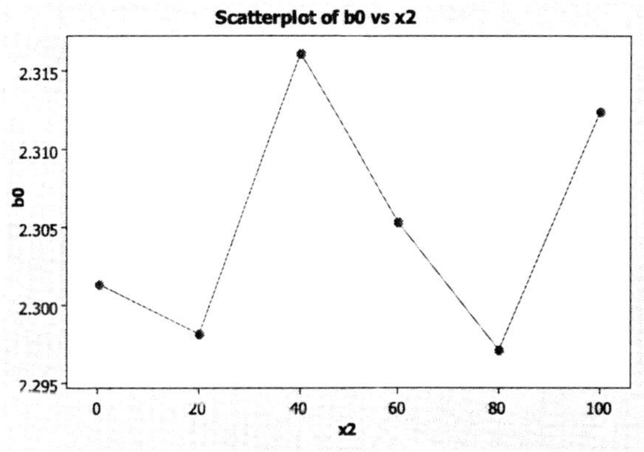

Figure 4. Scatterplot of b_0 vs x_2.

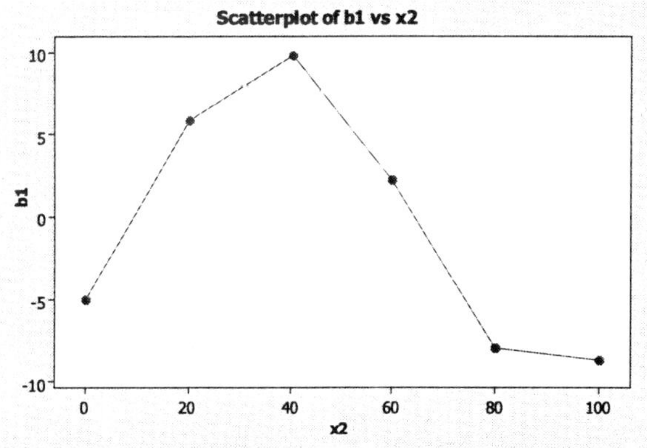

Figure 5. Scatterplot of b_1 vs x_2.

The fitted value and the residuals are given in Figure 6 and 7 respectively. There might be some "signal" left in the residuals; this can be remedied by applying the same modelling methodology to the residuals.

2.1 Applicability of meta-regression

Meta-regression can be successfully applied to any highly nonlinear system in which the functional form is unknown or coefficient estimates are needed. Partitioning of linear and nonlinear factors can significantly reduce the number of necessary experiments and intermediate models. Dividing the input set allows the number of experiments necessary for the linear factors to be substantially reduced. Yet, even when partitioning is employed, if the total number of factors, or of nonlinear factors, is very high, the sheer number of experiments may be impractical when real-world measurements are required. In these cases, meta-regression can still be successfully applied to simulation studies, since many simulation trials can reused.

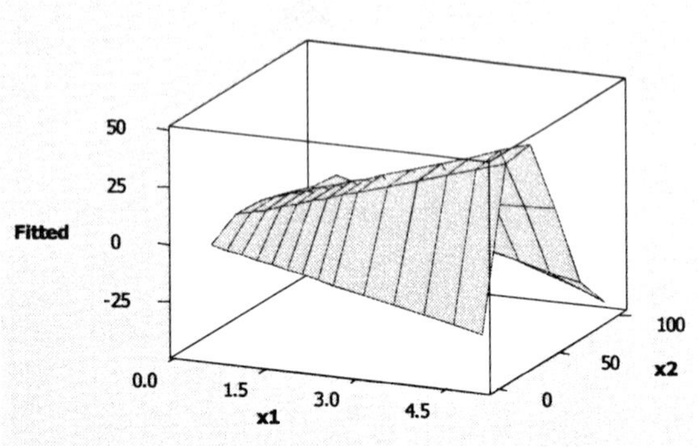

Figure 6. Surface plot of the fitted model vs. x_1 and x_2.

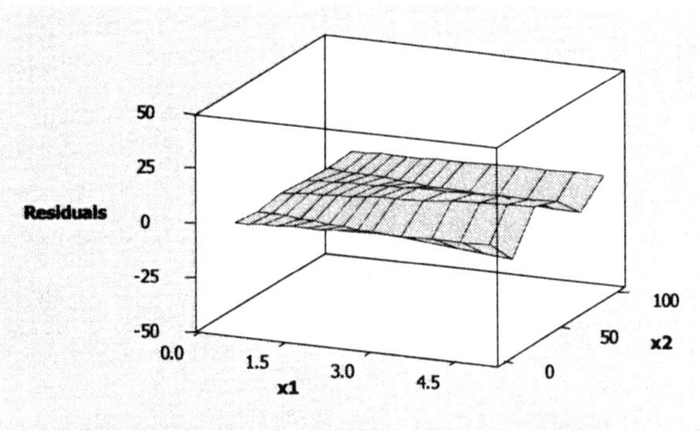

Figure 7. Surface plot of the model residuals vs. x_1 and x_2.

3 Related work

The root of our meta-regression is the investigation into the factors that significantly affect our chosen responses. To identify these significant factors and model their effects, we employ *design of experiments* (DOE) and *response surface methodology* (RSM) [3, 4].

While DOE and RSM provide a time-tested means of finding optimizations for systems that exhibit linear behaviour, nonlinear systems present a significantly larger challenge. Systems exhibiting nonlinear behaviour in one or more dimensions cannot be effectively modelled using the least-squares method key to *analysis of variance* (ANOVA). As such the field of *nonlinear regression analysis* has grown in importance; see the classic text by Bates and Watts [1].

However, when the nonlinear aspects of a system are not immediately identified as known function families considerable difficulty emerges in both choosing initial modelling parameters and the direction in which analysis should proceed. In 1962, Box and Hunter [2] introduced a model-building technique for dealing with systems for which basic theoretical models exist. Their method provides experimenters a way to determine the best way to "force" a model to fit a system using preexisting domain knowledge. This contributed to the development of *profiling* [1]. Profiling allows an experimenter to construct several restricted plots of the functions in a system so as to better understand their nonlinearity and interactions. Meta-regression further extends profiling, providing a methodology for classifying and approximating nonlinearity when only incomplete knowledge about a system's mechanisms and interactions is known.

4 Summary and future work

This paper introduced *meta-regression*, a general methodology for *reactive optimization* that alleviates traditional problems in modelling nonlinear systems. Meta-regression allows system components to self-organize to changing conditions in a manner that is *robust*, or affected minimally by other sources of variability. This is achieved via a new profile-based nonlinear modelling methodology that uses a stepwise process to provide parameter scaling equations to yield an approximate model of the nonlinear system, that can be used as the starting point for more traditional nonlinear regression techniques. The technique is applicable to complex dynamic systems in which one or more factors inhibit linear modelling techniques.

Acknowledgments

Supported, in part, by NSF grant ANI-0240524.

References

[1] D. Bates and D. Watts. *Nonlinear Regression Analysis and Its Applications*. John Wiley and Sons, Inc., 1988.

[2] G. E. P. Box and W. Hunter. A useful method for model building. *Technometrics*, 4:301– 318, 1962.

[3] D. C. Montgomery. *Design and Analysis of Experiments*. John Wiley and Sons, Inc., 6 edition, 2005.

[4] R. H. Myers and D. C. Montgomery. *Response Surface Methodology: Process and Product Optimization Using Designed Experiments*. John Wiley and Sons, Inc., 2 edition, 2002.

Author Index

Notes